DATE			

FILM THEORY AND CRITICISM

FILM THEORY
AND
CRITICISM

Introductory Readings

Second Edition

Gerald Mast
Marshall Cohen

New York   Oxford
OXFORD UNIVERSITY PRESS
1979

Copyright © 1974, 1979 by Oxford University Press, Inc.

Library of Congress Cataloging in Publication Data

Mast, Gerald, 1940-   comp.
  Film theory and criticism.

  Bibliography: p.
  1. Moving-pictures—Addresses, essays, lectures.
I. Cohen, Marshall.   II.   Title.
PN1994.M364   1979   791.43'01   78-14333
ISBN 0-19-502503-2
ISBN 0-19-502498-2 pbk.

Selections from works by the following authors were made possible by the kind permission of these publishers, representatives, and authors:

Joe Adamson: "Suspended Animation" was originally published in the first edition of this volume by arrangement with the author. Copyright © 1974 by Joe Adamson.

Charles Affron: "Uncensored Garbo" is here published for the first time by arrangement with the author. Copyright © 1979 by Charles Affron.

James Agee: *Agee on Film: Volume I.* Copyright © 1958 by The James Agee Trust. Reprinted by permission of Grosset & Dunlap, Inc., and Peter Owen Ltd., Publishers.

Rudolf Arnheim: *Film as Art.* Copyright © 1957 by The Regents of the University of California. Reprinted by permission of the University of California Press.

Printed in the United States of America

PREFACE
TO THE SECOND EDITION

The Preface to the original edition of this collection closed with the following wish: "It is our hope that this anthology will contribute to the growing interest in film theory and to the practice of a more rigorous criticism than that which prevails at the present time." It is difficult to say whether the appearance of this anthology in 1974 should be taken as a prophecy, or merely as another symptom of what has become clear five years later: that the last decade has been an extremely fertile and fervent period of theorizing about film, perhaps the richest period of film theorizing in quantity, quality, and diversity since the invention of cinema itself. This recent theory is fully conscious of the context of theoretical debate, within which each new question or solution must be placed, in a way that was not true of previous generations of film theorists.

The second edition of *Film Theory and Criticism* attempts to give the reader a sense of these developments. To do so we have devoted more space to certain issues, especially to the discussion of film *genres,* and have payed greater attention to certain theoretical trends, particularly to the semiotic and structuralist approaches to film theory and criticism. Several traditional approaches to film theory continue to be employed by the most recent theory—approaches which borrow the methodologies and terminology of such related humanistic disciplines as literary criticism, art history, and aesthetics. But the newer semiotic and structuralist approaches, often influenced by the methodologies and even the conclusions of related disciplines in the social sciences—of Marxist economic historical analysis and Freudian psychoanalysis—have become increasingly important to film theory (and a subject of controversy within it) during the last decade. Writers in this tradition have offered new perspectives on such "classical" issues of film theory as the relation of film to reality or the precise characteristics of film as a "language." The sections of the anthology devoted to these questions have, therefore, been revised to give a fuller account of these approaches.

The semiotic school, particularly in its Marxist manifestations, has also been particularly concerned with the ways that films reveal the underlying social attitudes and "ideologies" of the cultures that produce them, the ways films manipulate audience beliefs, and the ways they exploit and satisfy audience desires. Although the importance of these issues is reflected throughout the anthology, we have given them a sharper focus by reconceiving and retitling the final section "Film and Society" to reflect the concern with treating a film not as a self-contained work of art, as much "classical" film theory does, but as a social-economic product and a cultural manifestation. To accommodate these additions, we have found it necessary to eliminate the discussion of Shakespeare and Film, a topic which other anthologies, devoted exclusively to it, have treated more fully.

We would like to thank all those who sent us suggestions for additions, eliminations, and emendations: Kent R. Brown; Robert E. Golden; Bruce Kawin; Barbara Leaming; Charles J. Maland; Joan Mellen; James Monaco; and William Siska. Our final decision to eliminate an essay (certainly the most difficult decision we had to make) was based both on general opinion of its usefulness as well as our opinion of its relevance to an important theoretical issue. We can only apologize if we have eliminated some of the essays readers considered most useful and interesting. We would also like to express our special thanks to Jean Shapiro, who aided us so patiently and so diligently in assembling the final manuscript.

PREFACE
TO THE FIRST EDITION

This collection of readings gathers together under one cover the most significant theories and theorists of film. Given the youth of the film art, the variety of its possibilities, and the fact that it incorporates so many other arts, it is not surprising that the general pattern of film theory is one of disagreement and diversity. Theorists have responded in many different ways to the fact that film has been both silent and with sound, in color and black-and-white, short and long, plotted and plotless, realistic and fantastic, logical and irrational, two- and three-dimensional, in wide and narrow screen, fictional and factual, live and animated, entertaining and educational.

In order to give some shape to this complexity, the book organizes its selections around seven topics which have emerged as the basic subjects of film theory. In the first section, Film and Reality, the collection examines the relationship between the motion picture and the reality which it photographs. In the second, Film Image and Film Language, the theorists examine the syntax and structure of the film itself. They ask how it generates "meaning." The third section, The Film Medium, considers the term "cinematic" and asks what qualities, if any, make the film art unique. The fourth section, Film, Theater, and Literature, continues this line of questioning and asks, in particular, how the film is related to those literary arts with which it has so much in common and from which it yet differs so greatly. The fifth section, Kinds of Film, analyzes some of the main genres of film and discusses the difficulties that arise in attempting to categorize films in these ways. The sixth section, The Film Artist, investigates the question of who, if anyone, ought to be called the artist in the collaborative endeavor of filmmaking. The seventh section, The Film Audience, asks what kind of experience film provides for its audience and what kind of experience it ought to provide.

Film theory is of importance not only for its own sake but also for the contribution it can make to film criticism. Each section therefore includes, in addition to the more theoretical articles, critical essays which show how the more general issues arise in connection with specific films and filmmakers. It is our hope that this anthology will contribute to the growing interest in film theory and to the practice of a more rigorous criticism than that which prevails at the present time.

We wish to thank Dudley Andrew, Hannah Arendt, Richard Balkin, Stanley Kauffmann, Harriet Serenkin, and John Wright for their helpful advice and comments.

CONTENTS

xiii

CONTENTS

III

THE FILM MEDIUM

237

CONTENTS

IV

FILM, THEATER, AND LITERATURE
345

V

KINDS OF FILM
435

CONTENTS

VI

THE FILM ARTIST

637

CONTENTS

VII
FILM AND SOCIETY
741

I

Film and Reality

The main tradition of Western aesthetics, deriving from Aristotle's *Poetics*, adopts the view that art "imitates" nature or, in Hamlet's phrase, holds "the mirror up to nature." Painting, from the early Renaissance to the late nineteenth century, from Giotto to Manet and the impressionists, pursued this ideal with ever-increasing success. Later the novels of Balzac and Tolstoy achieved a more accurate representation of nature and society than anything literature had previously known, and the plays of Ibsen and Chekhov seemed to carry Hamlet's ideal of the theater to its limit. All these achievements were eclipsed, however, by the invention of photography. For the camera, and especially the motion picture camera, was unique in its ability to represent nature. If the ideal of art is to create an illusion of reality, the motion picture made it possible to achieve this ideal in an unprecedented way.

But is the aim of art to imitate nature at all? And if it is, what role remains for the other arts when film achieves it so simply and perfectly? An anti-realist tradition therefore denies that the goal of art is the imitation of nature. It has argued that to create a work of art is not simply to copy the world but to add another, and very special, object to the world. This object may be valuable because it offers an interpretation or idealization of the world, or even because it creates another, wholly autonomous, world. Others in this anti-realist tradition argue that the value of such an object may be that it expresses the feelings and emotions of its creator, or that the artist manages to impose a beautiful or a significant form on the

1

materials with which he works. The artist's feelings may be expressed abstractly, and the resulting form may be purely imaginative. The work of art may not allude to nature at all.

For example, theorists of modern painting have argued that painting should not even attempt to provide a three-dimensional representation of reality but acknowledge, instead, that it is essentially the application of pigments to a two-dimensional surface. This modernist view assumes that painting cannot and should not compete with film in attempting to mirror reality. Painting must renounce that task altogether. Others have argued, however, that film cannot reproduce reality either. And, even if it could, it ought not to try. According to this anti-realist view, film, like any other art form, must offer an interpretation of the world or, by the manipulation of the camera, create an alternative world. Just as painting must acknowledge that it is not really a mirror but pigments on canvas, cinema must acknowledge that it is simply projected images on a screen. To claim that these images ought to be images of physical reality—as opposed to any other kinds of images—is pure dogma. Why should these images not liberate the imagination from the tedium of reality, introducing us to the world of abstractions or of dreams instead?

Siegfried Kracauer, the German-born film historian and aesthetician, is a leading exponent of the realist view of cinema. In his book, *Theory of Film*, Kracauer argues that because film literally photographs reality it alone is capable of holding the mirror up to nature. Film actually reproduces the raw material of the physical world within the work of art. This makes it impossible for a film to be a "pure" expression of the artist's formative intentions or an abstract, imaginative expression of his emotions. Kracauer insists that it is the clear obligation and the special privilege of film (a descendant of still photography) to record and reveal, and thereby redeem, physical reality.

Kracauer's attitude is a response to the common complaint that the abstractions and categorizations of modern science and technology make it impossible for us to appreciate the concrete world in which we live—what John Crowe Ransom called "the world's body." The distinct function of art (especially of poetic imagery) might well be to help us possess the concrete world once more. Kracauer believes that the film art actually does this; it "literally redeems this world from its dormant state, its state of virtual non-existence, by endeavoring to experience it through the camera." For Kracauer film delivers us from technology by technology.

In his earlier work, *From Caligari to Hitler*, a study of the German cinema from 1919 to 1933, Kracauer traces the decline of German political culture as reflected in the history of its cinema. His view is that the German film's concern for artistic design and its dedication to purely formal values actually prepared the way for Hitler's rise by subtly diverting the audience from a serious appraisal of social realities. This era of German film, usually considered one of the great periods in the history of cinema, is for Kracauer an example of all that cinema must avoid. By ignoring the claims of camera reality the German cinema achieved the damnation, not the redemption, of German life.

André Bazin, who also insists on the unique realism of cinema, does so, however, from a markedly different viewpoint. Bazin, a French critic who founded the influential journal, *Cahiers du Cinéma*, in the late 1940s and whose practicing disciples include Jean-Luc Godard, François Truffaut, and Claude Chabrol, is perhaps the most important theorist of the "second" film generation, a generation for whom the experience of the silent film was no longer decisive. Unlike Kracauer, Bazin views the film's realism as an expression of the mythic, not of the scientific, spirit and believes that its function is not to redeem physical reality but to exempt us from our physical destiny. This magical aim finds expression in the "myth of total cinema," the ideal of a complete recreation of the world in its own image. Bazin welcomes the sound film as a necessary step toward this ideal. For similar reasons, he believes that *mise-en-scène* (arranging the elements of the scene and the camera's relationship to them so as to preserve their physical reality) is a more natural technique than *montage*.

But Bazin's conception of total cinema also leads to interesting questions—particularly in view of the most recent decade (the "third" generation) of film technology and film style. Would he have welcomed the widespread use of color and the advent of holography and of three-dimensional cinema, as his principles seem to indicate? And what would his attitude have been to the self-consciousness and self-referential tendencies of the film in the last decade? Devices such as slow motion, the freeze frame, the split screen, and color tinting call attention to the screen itself, rather than treating it as a simple window on the world. Although Bazin put his trust in the mechanical representation of uninterpreted reality, many of his followers have insisted on the artifice of the cinematic image.

Rudolph Arnheim, the psychologist and film aesthetician, is a leading "first generation" exponent of the anti-realist tradition in film theory. For Arnheim, if cinema were the mere mechanical reproduction of real life it could not be an art at all. Arnheim acknowledges the existence of a primitive desire to get material objects into one's power by creating them afresh, but he believes that this primitive impulse must be distinguished from the impulse to create art. The "wax museum" ideal may satisfy our primitive impulse, but it fails to satisfy the true artistic urge—not simply to copy, but to originate, to interpret, and to mold. The very properties that keep photography from reproducing reality perfectly must be exploited by the film artist, for they alone provide the possibilities for a film art. Bazin's myth of "total" cinema is nothing more than Arnheim's fallacy of the "complete" film. The pursuit of an ever more complete realism through the use of sound, color, and stereoscopic vision is simply a prescription for undermining the achievement of film art, which must respect, even welcome, the inherent limitations of the art.

For William Earle, a contemporary philosopher in the existentialist and phenomenological tradition, film art is not anti-realist by definition, but the medium is peculiarly apt for expressing an anti-realist sensibility. By severing the connection between sensations and perceptions, by divorcing things from their scientific connotations, and by calling attention to the film image itself, the anti-realist tradition expresses its attitude toward an all too "boring" reality. For anti-realists the attempt of realists to record and reveal physical reality is not only naïve; it is an inauthentic attempt to allay man's anxiety about the reality of physical existence. For Earle, the realist ideal is simply an invitation to spiritual death.

V.F. Perkins, the English film critic and theorist, attempts to incorporate the insights of both the realist and the anti-realist traditions. For him the film medium is capable of both documentation and fantasy, of copying and creation. But the central achievement of film is to be found in fictional narration, and this type of movie achieves a synthesis of films' two tendencies. Cinema obscures the distinction between authentic and staged events, making us feel like eye-witnesses at what are in fact fictional events. The credibility which photography and movement confer on films' images encourages us to place an inaccurate construction on an accurate series of images. Film thereby achieves its unique blend of photographic realism and dramatic illusion.

Jurij Lotman, the Russian semiologist, also insists on film's ability to synthesize the real and the illusionary. He acknowledges that the film audience must at least in part believe that it is observing real life, and he grants that its purely technical features do endow cinema with a realistic texture greater than that enjoyed by any other art. But the aim of art, he thinks, is not simply to reproduce objects. It is, rather, to make them into conveyors of information, to transform them into signs which convey meaning. Film images can only become carriers of meaning if they are placed in contexts and governed by conventions which allow the artist to choose between significant alternatives. The choice between employing black-and-white and colored images presents the artist with one such alternative. Paradoxically, certain film conventions established by the history of film (for example, newsreels and documentaries have always used black and white) lead us to accept the black-and-white image rather than the colored one, as the more natural and realistic. Similarly, the Italian neorealists' attempt to achieve greater verisimilitude by refusing to employ stars or even professional actors to play stereotyped heroes, like their refusal to use fully prepared scripts or conventional montage, could only be effective against a remembered background of cinema art of a contrasting type. Indeed, so great is Lotman's emphasis on the conventional relationship between the "likeness" of the film image and the reality it represents that, along with many other semiologists, he has difficulty offering a convincing explanation of the realism that audiences assign, and that he himself grants, to the film image.

SIEGFRIED KRACAUER
FROM THEORY OF FILM

BASIC CONCEPTS

Like the embryo in the womb, photographic film developed from distinctly separate components. Its birth came about from a combination of instantaneous photography, as used by Muybridge and Marey, with the older devices of the magic lantern and the phenakistoscope. Added to this later were the contributions of other nonphotographic elements, such as editing and sound. Nevertheless photography, especially instantaneous photography, has a legitimate claim to top priority among these elements, for it undeniably is and remains the decisive factor in establishing film content. The nature of photography survives in that of film.

Originally, film was expected to bring the evolution of photography to an end—satisfying at last the age-old desire to picture things moving. This desire already accounted for major developments within the photographic medium itself. As far back as 1839, when the first daguerreotypes and talbotypes appeared, admiration mingled with disappointment about their deserted streets and blurred landscapes. And in the 'fifties, long before the innovation of the hand camera, successful attempts were made to photograph subjects in motion. The very impulses which thus led from time exposure to snapshot engendered dreams of a further extension of photography in the same direction—dreams, that is, of film. About 1860, Cook and Bonnelli, who had developed a device called a photobioscope, predicted a "complete revolution of photographic art. . . . We will see . . . landscapes," they announced, "in which the trees bow to the whims of the wind, the leaves ripple and glitter in the rays of the sun."

Along with the familiar photographic leitmotif of the leaves, such kindred subjects as undulating waves, moving clouds, and changing facial expressions ranked high in early prophecies. All of them conveyed the longing for an instrument which would capture the slightest incidents of the world about us—scenes that often would involve crowds, whose incalculable movements resemble, somehow, those of waves or leaves. In a memorable statement published before the emergence of instantaneous photography, Sir John Herschel not only predicted the basic features of the film camera but assigned to it a task which it has never since disowned: "the vivid and lifelike reproduction and handing down to the latest posterity of any transaction in real life—a battle, a debate, a public solemnity, a pugilistic conflict." Ducos du Hauron and other forerunners also looked forward to what we have come to label newsreels and documentaries—films devoted to the rendering of real-life events. This insistence on recording went hand in hand with the expectation that motion pictures could acquaint us with normally imperceptible or otherwise induplicable movements—flashlike transformations of matter, the slow growth of plants, etc. All in all, it was taken for granted that film would continue along the lines of photography. . . .

PROPERTIES OF THE MEDIUM

The properties of film can be divided into basic and technical properties.

The basic properties are identical with the properties of photography. Film, in other words, is uniquely equipped to record and reveal physical reality and, hence, gravitates toward it.

Now there are different visible worlds. Take a stage performance or a painting: they too are real and can be perceived. But the only reality we are concerned with is actually existing physical reality— the transitory world we live in. (Physical reality will also be called "material reality," or "physical existence," or "actuality," or loosely just "nature." Another fitting term might be "camera-reality.") . . . The other visible worlds reach into this world without, however, really forming a part of it. A theatrical play, for instance, suggests a universe of its own which would immediately crumble were it related to its real-life environment.

As a reproductive medium, film is of course justified in reproducing memorable ballets, operas, and the like. Yet even assuming that such reproductions try to do justice to the specific requirements of the screen, they basically amount to little more than "canning," and are of no interest to us here. Preservation of performances which lie outside physical reality proper is at best a sideline of a medium so particularly suited to explore that reality. This is not to deny that reproductions, say, of stage production numbers may be put to good cinematic use in certain feature films and film genres.

Of all the technical properties of film the most general and indispensable is editing. It serves to establish a meaningful continuity of shots and is therefore unthinkable in photography. (Photomontage is a graphic art rather than a specifically photographic genre.) Among the more special cinematic techniques are some which have been taken over from photography—e.g. the close-up, soft-focus pictures, the use of negatives, double or multiple exposure, etc. Others, such as the lap-dissolve, slow and quick motion, the reversal of time, certain "special effects," and so forth, are for obvious reasons exclusively peculiar to film.

These scanty hints will suffice. It is not necessary to elaborate on technical matters which have been dealt with in most previous theoretical writings on film. Unlike these, which invariably devote a great deal of space to editing devices, modes of lighting, various effects of the close-up, etc., the present book concerns itself with cinematic techniques only to the extent to which they bear on the nature of film, as defined by its basic properties and their various implications. The interest lies not with editing in itself, regardless of the purposes it serves, but with editing as a means of implementing—or defying, which amounts to the same—such potentialities of the medium as are in accordance with its substantive characteristics. In other words, the task is not to survey all possible methods of editing for their own sake; rather, it is to determine the contributions which editing may make to cinematically significant achievements. Problems of film technique will not be neglected; however, they will be discussed only if issues going beyond technical considerations call for their investigation.

This remark on procedures implies what is fairly obvious anyway: that the basic and technical properties differ substantially from each other. As a rule the former take precedence over the latter in the sense that they are responsible for the cinematic quality of a film. Imagine a film which, in keeping with the basic properties, records interesting aspects of physical reality but does so in a technically imperfect manner; perhaps the lighting is awkward or the editing uninspired. Nevertheless such a film is more specifically a film than one which utilizes brilliantly all the cinematic devices and tricks to produce a statement disregarding camera-reality. Yet this should not lead one to underestimate the influence of the technical properties. It will be seen that in certain cases the knowing use of a variety of techniques may endow otherwise nonrealistic films with a cinematic flavor.

THE TWO MAIN TENDENCIES

If film grows out of photography, the realistic and formative tendencies must be operative in it also. Is it by sheer accident that the two tendencies manifested themselves side by side immediately after the rise of the medium? As if to encompass the whole range of cinematic endeavors at the outset, each went the limit in exhausting its own possibilities. Their prototypes were Lumière, a strict realist, and Méliès, who gave free rein to his artistic imagination. The films they made embody, so to speak, thesis and antithesis in a Hegelian sense.

Lumière and Méliès

Lumière's films contained a true innovation, as compared with the repertoire of the zootropes or Edison's peep boxes: they pictured everyday life after the manner of photographs. Some of his early pictures, such as *Baby's Breakfast (Le Déjeuner de bébé)* or *The Card Players (La Partie d'écarté)*, testify to the amateur photographers's delight in family idyls and genre scenes. And there was *Teasing the Gardener (L'Arroseur arrosé)*, which enjoyed immense popularity because it elicited from the flow of everyday life a proper story with a funny climax to boot. A gardener is watering flowers and, as he unsuspectingly proceeds, an impish boy steps on the hose, releasing it at the very moment when his perplexed victim examines the dried-up nozzle. Water squirts out and hits the gardener smack in the face. The denouement is true to style, with the gardener chasing and spanking the boy. This film, the germ cell and archetype of all film comedies to come, represented an imaginative attempt on the part of Lumière to develop photography into a means of story telling. Yet the story was just a real-life incident. And it was precisely its photographic veracity which made Maxim Gorki undergo a shock-like experience. "You think," he wrote about *Teasing the Gardener*, "the spray is going to hit you too, and instinctively shrink back."

On the whole, Lumière seems to have realized that story telling was none of his business; it involved problems with which he apparently did not care to cope. Whatever story-telling films he, or his company, made—some more comedies in the vein of his first one, tiny historical scenes, etc.—are not characteristic of his production. The bulk of his films recorded the world about us for no other purpose than to present it. This is in any case what Mesguich, one of Lumière's "ace" cameramen, felt to be their message. At a time when the talkies were already in full swing he epitomized the work of the master as follows: "As I see it, the Lumière Brothers had established the true domain of the cinema in the right manner. The novel, the theater, suffice for the study of the human heart. The cinema is the dynamism of life, of nature and its manifestations, of the crowd and its eddies. All that asserts itself through movement depends on it. Its lens opens on the world."

Lumière's lens did open on the world in this sense. Take his immortal first reels *Lunch Hour at the Lumière Factory (Sortie des usines Lumière)*, *Arrival of a Train (L'Arrivée d'un train)*, *La Place des Cordeliers à Lyon:* their themes were public places, with throngs of people moving in diverse directions. The crowded streets captured by the stereographic photographs of the late 'fifties thus reappeared on the primitive screen. It was life at its least controllable and most unconscious moments, a jumble of transient, forever dissolving patterns accessible only to the camera. The much-imitated shot of the railway station, with its emphasis on the confusion of arrival and departure, effectively illustrated the fortuity of these patterns; and their fragmentary character was exemplified by the clouds of smoke which leisurely drifted upward. Significantly, Lumière used the motif of smoke on several occasions. And he seemed anxious to avoid any personal interference with the given data. Detached records, his shots resembled the imaginary shot of the grandmother which Proust contrasts with the memory image of her.

Contemporaries praised these films for the very qualities which the prophets and forerunners had singled out in their visions of the medium. It is inevitable that, in the comments on Lumière, "the ripple of leaves stirred by the wind" should be referred to enthusiastically. The Paris journalist Henri de Parville, who used the image of the trembling leaves, also identified Lumière's over-all theme as "nature caught in the act." Others pointed to the benefits which science would derive from Lumière's invention. In America his camera-realism defeated Edison's kinetoscope with its staged subjects.

Lumière's hold on the masses was ephemeral. In 1897, not more than two years after he had begun to make films, his popularity subsided. The sensation had worn off; the heyday was over. Lack of interest caused Lumière to reduce his production.

Georges Méliès took over where Lumière left off, renewing and intensifying the medium's waning appeal. This is not to say that he did not occasionally follow the latter's example. In his beginnings he too treated the audience to sightseeing tours; or he dramatized, in the fashion of the period, realistically staged topical events. But his main contribution to the cinema lay in substituting staged illusion for unstaged reality, and contrived plots for everyday incidents.

The two pioneers were aware of the radical differences in their approach. Lumière told Méliès that he considered film nothing more than a "scientific curiosity," thereby implying that his cinematograph could not possibly serve artistic purposes. In 1897, Méliès on his part published a prospectus which took issue with Lumière: "Messrs. Méliès and Reulos specialize mainly in fantastic or artistic scenes, reproductions of theatrical scenes, etc. . . . thus creating a special genre which differs entirely from the customary views supplied by the cinematograph—street scenes or scenes of everyday life."

Méliès's tremendous success would seem to indicate that he

The Two Tendencies: Lumière's *Workers Leaving the Lumière Factory* (1895) and Méliès' *The Witch* (1900). "Lumière's lens did open on the world . . . Méliès ignored the workings of nature out of the artist's delight in sheer fantasy" (KRACAUER, pages 11, 14).

catered to demands left unsatisfied by Lumière's photographic realism. Lumière appealed to the sense of observation, the curiosity about "nature caught in the act"; Méliès ignored the workings of nature out of the artist's delight in sheer fantasy. The train in *Arrival of a Train* is the real thing, whereas its counterpart in Méliès's *An Impossible Voyage (Voyage à travers l'impossible)* is a toy train as unreal as the scenery through which it is moving. Instead of picturing the random movements of phenomena, Méliès freely interlinked imagined events according to the requirements of his charming fairy-tale plots. Had not media very close to film offered similar gratifications? The artist-photographers preferred what they considered aesthetically attractive compositions to searching explorations of nature. And immediately before the arrival of the motion picture camera, magic lantern performances indulged in the projection of religious themes, Walter Scott novels, and Shakespearean dramas.

Yet even though Méliès did not take advantage of the camera's ability to record and reveal the physical world, he increasingly created his illusions with the aid of techniques peculiar to the medium. Some he found by accident. When taking shots of the Paris Place de l'Opéra, he had to discontinue the shooting because the celluloid strip did not move as it should; the surprising result was a film in which, for no reason at all, a bus abruptly transformed itself into a hearse. True, Lumière also was not disinclined to have a sequence of events unfold in reverse, but Méliès was the first to exploit cinematic devices systematically. Drawing on both photography and the stage, he innovated many techniques which were to play an enormous role in the future—among them the use of masks, multiple exposure, superimposition as a means of summoning ghosts, the lap-dissolve, etc. And through his ingenuity in using these techniques he added a touch of cinema to his playful narratives and magic tricks. Stage traps ceased to be indispensable; sleights-of-hand yielded to incredible metamorphoses which film alone was able to accomplish. Illusion produced in this climate depended on another kind of craftsmanship than the magician's. It was cinematic illusion, and as such went far beyond theatrical make-believe. Méliès's *The Haunted Castle (Le Manoir du diable)* "is conceivable only in the cinema and due to the cinema," says

14

Henri Langlois, one of the best connoisseurs of the primitive era.

Notwithstanding his film sense, however, Méliès still remained the theater director he had been. He used photography in a pre-photographic spirit—for the reproduction of a papier-maché universe inspired by stage traditions. In one of his greatest films, *A Trip to the Moon (Le Voyage dans la lune)*, the moon harbors a grimacing man in the moon and the stars are bull's-eyes studded with the pretty faces of music hall girls. By the same token, his actors bowed to the audience, as if they performed on the stage. Much as his films differed from the theater on a technical plane, they failed to transcend its scope by incorporating genuinely cinematic subjects. This also explains why Méliès, for all his inventiveness, never thought of moving his camera; the stationary camera perpetuated the spectator's relation to the stage. His ideal spectator was the traditional theatergoer, child or adult. There seems to be some truth in the observation that, as people grow older, they instinctively withdraw to the positions from which they set out to struggle and conquer. In his later years Méliès more and more turned from theatrical film to filmed theater, producing *féeries* which recalled the Paris Châtelet pageants.

The Realistic Tendency

In following the realistic tendency, films go beyond photography in two respects. First, they picture movement itself, not only one or another of its phases. But what kinds of movements do they picture? In the primitive era when the camera was fixed to the ground, it was natural for film makers to concentrate on moving material phenomena; life on the screen was life only if it manifested itself through external, or "objective," motion. As cinematic techniques developed, films increasingly drew on camera mobility and editing devices to deliver their messages. Although their strength still lay in the rendering of movements inaccessible to other media, these movements were no longer necessarily objective. In the technically mature film "subjective" movements—movements, that is, which the spectator is invited to execute—constantly compete with objective ones. The spectator may have to identify himself with a tilting, panning, or traveling camera which insists on bringing motionless as well as moving objects to his attention. Or an appropriate arrangement of shots may rush the audience through vast expanses of time and/or space so as to make it witness, almost simultaneously, events in different periods and places.

Nevertheless the emphasis is now as before on objective movement; the medium seems to be partial to it. As René Clair puts it: "If there is an aesthetics of the cinema . . . it can be summarized in one word: 'movement.' The external movement of the objects perceived by the eye, to which we are today adding the inner movement of the action." The fact that he assigns a dominant role to external movement reflects, on a theoretical plane, a marked feature of his own earlier films—the ballet-like evolutions of their characters.

Second, films may seize upon physical reality with all its manifold movements by means of an intermediary procedure which would seem to be less indispensable in photography—staging. In order to narrate an intrigue, the film maker is often obliged to stage not only the action but the surroundings as well. Now this recourse to staging is most certainly legitimate if the staged world is made to appear as a faithful reproduction of the real one. The important thing is that studio-built settings convey the impression of actuality, so that the spectator feels he is watching events which might have occurred in real life and have been photographed on the spot.

Falling prey to an interesting misconception, Emile Vuillermoz champions, for the sake of "realism," settings which represent reality as seen by a perceptive painter. To his mind they are more real than real-life shots because they impart the essence of what such shots are showing. Yet from the cinematic point of view these allegedly realistic settings are no less stagy than would be, say, a cubist or abstract composition. Instead of staging the given raw material itself, they offer, so to speak, the gist of it. In other words, they suppress the very camera-reality which film aims at incorporating. For this reason, the sensitive moviegoer will feel disturbed by them. (The problems posed by films of fantasy which, as such, show little concern for physical reality will be considered later on.)

Strangely enough, it is entirely possible that a staged real-life event evokes a stronger illusion of reality on the screen than would the original event if it had been captured directly by the camera.

The late Ernö Metzner who devised the settings for the studio-made mining disaster in Pabst's *Kameradschaft*—an episode with the ring of stark authenticity—insisted that candid shots of a real mining disaster would hardly have produced the same convincing effect.

One may ask, on the other hand, whether reality can be staged so accurately that the camera-eye will not detect any difference between the original and the copy. Blaise Cendrars touches on this issue in a neat hypothetical experiment. He imagines two film scenes which are completely identical except for the fact that one has been shot on the Mont Blanc (the highest mountain of Europe) while the other was staged in the studio. His contention is that the former has a quality not found in the latter. There are on the mountain, says he, certain "emanations, luminous or otherwise, which have worked on the film and given it a soul." Presumably large parts of our environment, natural or man-made, resist duplication.

The Formative Tendency

The film maker's formative faculties are offered opportunities far exceeding those offered the photographer. The reason is that film extends into dimensions which photography does not cover. These differ from each other according to area and composition. With respect to areas, film makers have never confined themselves to exploring only physical reality in front of the camera but, from the outset, persistently tried to penetrate the realms of history and fantasy. Remember Méliès. Even the realistic-minded Lumière yielded to the popular demand for historical scenes. As for composition, the two most general types are the story film and the non-story film. The latter can be broken down into the experimental film and the film of fact, which on its part comprises, partially or totally, such subgenres as the film on art, the newsreel, and the documentary proper.

It is easy to see that some of these dimensions are more likely than others to prompt the film maker to express his formative aspirations at the expense of the realistic tendency. As for areas, consider that of fantasy: movie directors have at all times rendered dreams or visions with the aid of settings which are anything but realistic. Thus in *Red Shoes* Moira Shearer dances, in a somnambulistic trance, through fantastic worlds avowedly intended to project her unconscious mind—agglomerates of landscape-like forms, near-abstract shapes, and luscious color schemes which have all the traits of stage imagery. Disengaged creativity thus drifts away from the basic concerns of the medium. Several dimensions of composition favor the same preferences. Most experimental films are not even designed to focus on physical existence; and practically all films following the lines of a theatrical story evolve narratives whose significance overshadows that of the raw material of nature used for their implementation. For the rest, the film maker's formative endeavors may also impinge on his realistic loyalties in dimensions which, because of their emphasis on physical reality, do not normally invite such encroachments; there are enough documentaries with real-life shots which merely serve to illustrate some self-contained oral commentary.

Clashes Between the Two Tendencies

Films which combine two or more dimensions are very frequent; for instance, many a movie featuring an everyday-life incident includes a dream sequence or a documentary passage. Some such combinations may lead to overt clashes between the realistic and formative tendencies. This happens whenever a film maker bent on creating an imaginary universe from freely staged material also feels under an obligation to draw on camera-reality. In his *Hamlet* Laurence Olivier has the cast move about in a studio-built, conspicuously stagy Elsinore, whose labyrinthine architecture seems calculated to reflect Hamlet's unfathomable being. Shut off from our real-life environment, this bizarre structure would spread over the whole of the film were it not for a small, otherwise insignificant scene in which the real ocean outside that dream orbit is shown. But no sooner does the photographed ocean appear than the spectator experiences something like a shock. He cannot help recognizing that this little scene is an outright intrusion; that it abruptly introduces an element incompatible with the rest of the imagery. How he then reacts to it depends upon his sensibilities. Those indifferent to the peculiarities of the medium, and therefore unquestioningly accepting the staged Elsinore, are likely to resent the unexpected emergence of crude nature as a letdown, while those more sensitive to the properties of film will in a flash realize the make-believe character of the castle's mythical splendor. Another case in point is Renato Castellani's *Romeo and Juliet*. This attempt to stage Shakespeare in natural surroundings obviously rests upon the belief that camera-reality and the poetic reality of Shakespeare verse can be made to fuse into each other. Yet the dialogue as well as the intrigue establish a universe so remote from the chance world of real Verona streets and ramparts that all the scenes in which the two disparate worlds are seen merging tend to affect one as an unnatural alliance between conflicting forces.

Actually collisions of this kind are by no means the rule. Rather, there is ample evidence to suggest that the two tendencies which sway the medium may be interrelated in various other ways. Since some of these relationships between realistic and formative efforts can be assumed to be aesthetically more gratifying than the rest, the next step is to try to define them.

THE CINEMATIC APPROACH

It follows from what has been said . . . that films may claim aesthetic validity if they build from their basic properties; like photographs, that is, they must record and reveal physical reality. . . . One might argue that too exclusive an emphasis on the medium's primary relation to physical reality tends to put film in a strait jacket. This objection finds support in the many existing films which are completely unconcerned about the representation of nature. There is the abstract experimental film. There is an unending succession of "photoplays" or theatrical films which do not picture real-life material for its own sake but use it to build up action after the manner of the stage. And there are the many films of fantasy which neglect the external world in freely composed dreams or visions. The old German expressionist films went far in this direction; one of their champions, the German art critic Herman G. Scheffauer, even eulogizes expressionism on the screen for its remoteness from photographic life.

Why, then, should these genres be called less "cinematic" than films concentrating on physical existence? The answer is of course that it is the latter alone which afford insight and enjoyment other-

19

wise unattainable. True, in view of all the genres which do not cultivate outer reality and yet are here to stay, this answer sounds somewhat dogmatic. But perhaps it will be found more justifiable in the
light of the following two considerations.

First, favorable response to a genre need not depend upon its ade-
quacy to the medium from which it issues. As a matter of fact,
many a genre has a hold on the audience because it caters to widespread social and cultural demands; it is and remains popular for
reasons which do not involve questions of aesthetic legitimacy.
Thus the photoplay has succeeded in perpetuating itself even
though most responsible critics are agreed that it goes against the
grain of film. Yet the public which feels attracted, for instance, by
the screen version of *Death of a Salesman*, likes this version for the
very virtues which made the Broadway play a hit and does not in
the least care whether or not it has any specifically cinematic
merits.

Second, let us for the sake of argument assume that my definition of aesthetic validity is actually one-sided; that it results from a
bias for one particular, if important, type of cinematic activities and
hence is unlikely to take into account, say, the possibility of hybrid
genres or the influence of the medium's nonphotographic components. But this does not necessarily speak against the propriety of
that definition. In a strategic interest it is often more advisable to
loosen up initial one-sidedness—provided it is well founded—than
to start from all too catholic premises and then try to make them
specific. The latter alternative runs the risk of blurring differences
between the media because it rarely leads far enough away from the
generalities postulated at the outset; its danger is that it tends to entail a confusion of the arts. When Eisenstein, the theoretician, began
to stress the similarities between the cinema and the traditional
art media, identifying film as their ultimate fulfillment, Eisenstein,
the artist, increasingly trespassed the boundaries that separate
film from elaborate theatrical spectacles: think of his *Alexander
Nevsky* and the operatic aspects of his *Ivan the Terrible*.

In strict analogy to the term "photographic approach" the film
maker's approach is called "cinematic" if it acknowledges the basic
aesthetic principle. It is evident that the cinematic approach materializes in all films which follow the realistic tendency. This implies
that even films almost devoid of creative aspirations, such as news-

reels, scientific or educational films, artless documentaries, etc., are tenable propositions from an aesthetic point of view—presumably more so than films which for all their artistry pay little attention to the given outer world. But as with photographic reportage, newsreels and the like meet only the minimum requirement.

What is of the essence in film no less than photography is the intervention of the film maker's formative energies in all the dimensions which the medium has come to cover. He may feature his impressions of this or that segment of physical existence in documentary fashion, transfer hallucinations and mental images to the screen, indulge in the rendering of rhythmical patterns, narrate a human-interest story, etc. All these creative efforts are in keeping with the cinematic approach as long as they benefit, in some way or other, the medium's substantive concern with our visible world. As in photography, everything depends on the "right" balance between the realistic tendency and the formative tendency; and the two tendencies are well balanced if the latter does not try to overwhelm the former but eventually follows its lead.

THE ISSUE OF ART

When calling the cinema an art medium, people usually think of films which resemble the traditional works of art in that they are free creations rather than explorations of nature. These films organize the raw material to which they resort into some self-sufficient composition instead of accepting it as an element in its own right. In other words, their underlying formative impulses are so strong that they defeat the cinematic approach with its concern for camera-reality. Among the film types customarily considered art are, for instance, the above-mentioned German expressionist films of the years after World War I; conceived in a painterly spirit, they seem to implement the formula of Hermann Warm, one of the designers of *The Cabinet of Dr. Caligari* settings, who claimed that "films must be drawings brought to life." Here also belongs many an experimental film; all in all, films of this type are not only intended as autonomous wholes but frequently ignore physical reality or exploit it for purposes alien to photographic veracity. By the same token, there is an inclination to classify as works of art feature films which combine forceful artistic composition with devotion to significant subjects and values. This would apply to a number of adaptations of great stage plays and other literary works.

Yet such a usage of the term "art" in the traditional sense is misleading. It lends support to the belief that artistic qualities must be attributed precisely to films which neglect the medium's recording obligations in an attempt to rival achievements in the fields of the fine arts, the theater, or literature. In consequence, this usage tends to obscure the aesthetic value of films which are really true to the medium. If the term "art" is reserved for productions like *Hamlet* or *Death of a Salesman*, one will find it difficult indeed to appreciate properly the large amount of creativity that goes into many a documentary capturing material phenomena for their own sake. Take Ivens's *Rain* or Flaherty's *Nanook*, documentaries saturated with formative intentions: like any selective photographer, their creators have all the traits of the imaginative reader and curious explorer; and their readings and discoveries result from full absorption in the given material and significant choices. Add to this that some of the crafts needed in the cinematic process—especially editing—represent tasks with which the photographer is not confronted. And they too lay claim to the film maker's creative powers.

This leads straight to a terminological dilemma. Due to its fixed meaning, the concept of art does not, and cannot, cover truly "cinematic" films—films, that is, which incorporate aspects of physical reality with a view to making us experience them. And yet it is they, not the films reminiscent of traditional art works, which are valid aesthetically. If film is an art at all, it certainly should not be confused with the established arts. There may be some justification in loosely applying this fragile concept to such films as *Nanook*, or *Paisan*, or *Potemkin* which are deeply steeped in camera-life. But in defining them as art, it must always be kept in mind that even the most creative film maker is much less independent of nature in the raw than the painter or poet; that his creativity manifests itself in letting nature in and penetrating it.

1960

ANDRÉ BAZIN
FROM WHAT IS CINEMA?

THE MYTH OF TOTAL CINEMA

Paradoxically enough, the impression left on the reader by Georges Sadoul's admirable book on the origins of the cinema is of a reversal, in spite of the author's Marxist views, of the relations between an economic and technical evolution and the imagination of those carrying on the search. The way things happened seems to call for a reversal of the historical order of causality, which goes from the economic infrastructure to the ideological superstructure, and for us to consider the basic technical discoveries as fortunate accidents but essentially second in importance to the preconceived ideas of the inventors. The cinema is an idealistic phenomenon. The concept men had of it existed so to speak fully armed in their minds, as if in some platonic heaven, and what strikes us most of all is the obstinate resistance of matter to ideas rather than of any help offered by techniques to the imagination of the researchers.

Furthermore, the cinema owes virtually nothing to the scientific spirit. Its begetters are in no sense savants, except for Marey, but it is significant that he was only interested in analyzing movement and not in reconstructing it. Even Edison is basically only a do-it-yourself man of genius, a giant of the *concours Lépine*. Niepce, Muybridge, Leroy, Joly, Demeny, even Louis Lumière himself, are all monomaniacs, men driven by an impulse, do-it-yourself men or at best ingenious industrialists. As for the wonderful, the sublime E. Reynaud, who can deny that his animated drawings are the result of an unremitting pursuit of an *idée fixe*? Any account of the cinema that was drawn merely from the technical inventions that made it possible would be a poor one indeed. On the contrary, an approximate and complicated visualization of an idea invariably precedes the industrial discovery which alone can open the way to its practical use. Thus if it is evident to us today that the cinema even at its most elementary stage needed a transparent, flexible, and resistant base and a dry sensitive emulsion capable of receiving an image instantly—everything else being a matter of setting in order a mechanism far less complicated than an eighteenth-century clock—it is clear that all the definitive stages of the invention of the cinema had been reached before the requisite conditions had been fulfilled. In 1877 and 1880, Muybridge, thanks to the imaginative generosity of a horse-lover, managed to construct a large complex device which enabled him to make from the image of a galloping horse the first series of cinematographic pictures. However to get this result he had to be satisfied with wet collodion on a glass plate, that is to say, with just one of the three necessary elements—namely instantaneity, dry emulsion, flexible base. After the discovery of gelatino-bromide of silver but before the appearance on the market of the first celluloid reels, Marey had made a genuine camera which used glass plates. Even after the appearance of celluloid strips Lumière tried to use paper film.

Once more let us consider here only the final and complete form of the photographic cinema. The synthesis of simple movements studied scientifically by Plateau had no need to wait upon the industrial and economic developments of the nineteenth century. As Sadoul correctly points out, nothing had stood in the way, from antiquity, of the manufacture of a phenakistoscope or a zootrope. It is true that here the labors of that genuine savant Plateau were at the origin of the many inventions that made the popular use of his discovery possible. But while, with the photographic cinema, we have cause for some astonishment that the discovery somehow precedes the technical conditions necessary to its existence, we must here explain, on the other hand, how it was that the invention took so long to emerge, since all the prerequisites had been assembled and the persistence of the image on the retina had been known for a long time. It might be of some use to point out that although the two were not necessarily connected scientifically, the efforts of Plateau are pretty well con-

24

temporary with those of Nicéphore Niepce, as if the attention of researchers had waited to concern itself with synthesizing movement until chemistry quite independently of optics had become concerned, on its part, with the automatic fixing of the image.

I emphasize the fact that this historical coincidence can apparently in no way be explained on grounds of scientific, economic, or industrial evolution. The photographic cinema could just as well have grafted itself onto a phenakistoscope foreseen as long ago as the sixteenth century. The delay in the invention of the latter is as disturbing a phenomenon as the existence of the precursors of the former.

But if we examine their work more closely, the direction of their research is manifest in the instruments themselves, and, even more undeniably, in their writings and commentaries we see that these precursors were indeed more like prophets. Hurrying past the various stopping places, the very first of which materially speaking should have halted them, it was at the very height and summit that most of them were aiming. In their imaginations they saw the cinema as a total and complete representation of reality; they saw in a trice the reconstruction of a perfect illusion of the outside world in sound, color, and relief.

As for the latter, the film historian P. Potoniée has even felt justified in maintaining that it was not the discovery of photography but of stereoscopy, which came onto the market just slightly before the first attempts at animated photography in 1851, that opened the eyes of the researchers. Seeing people immobile in space, the photographers realized that what they needed was movement if their photographs were to become a picture of life and a faithful copy of nature. In any case, there was not a single inventor who did not try to combine sound and relief with animation of the image—whether it be Edison with his kinetoscope made to be attached to a phonograph, or Demenay and his talking portraits, or even Nadar who shortly before producing the first photographic interview, on Chevreul, had written, "My dream is to see the photograph register the bodily movements and the facial expressions of a speaker while the phonograph is recording his speech" (February, 1887). If color had not yet appeared it was because the first experiments with the three-color process were slower in coming. But E. Reynaud had been painting his little figurines for some time and the first films of Méliès are colored by stencilling. There are numberless writings, all of them more or less wildly enthusiastic, in which inventors conjure up nothing less than a total cinema that is to provide that complete illusion of life which is still a long way away. Many are familiar with that passage from *L'Éve Future* in which Villiers de l'Isle-Adam, two years before Edison had begun his researches on animated photography, puts into the inventor's mouth the following description of a fantastic achievement: ". . . the vision, its transparent flesh miraculously photographed in color and wearing a spangled costume, danced a kind of popular Mexican dance. Her movements had the flow of life itself, thanks to the process of successive photography which can retain six minutes of movement on microscopic glass, which is subsequently reflected by means of a powerful lampascope. Suddenly was heard a flat and unnatural voice, dull-sounding and harsh. The dancer was singing the *alza* and the *olé* that went with her *fandango*."

The guiding myth, then, inspiring the invention of cinema, is the accomplishment of that which dominated in a more or less vague fashion all the techniques of the mechanical reproduction of reality in the nineteenth century, from photography to the phonograph, namely an integral realism, a recreation of the world in its own image, an image unburdened by the freedom of interpretation of the artist or the irreversibility of time. If cinema in its cradle lacked all the attributes of the cinema to come, it was with reluctance and because its fairy guardians were unable to provide them however much they would have liked to.

If the origins of an art reveal something of its nature, then one may legitimately consider the silent and the sound film as stages of a technical development that little by little made a reality out of the original "myth." It is understandable from this point of view that it would be absurd to take the silent film as a state of primal perfection which has gradually been forsaken by the realism of sound and color. The primacy of the image is both historically and technically accidental. The nostalgia that some still feel for the silent screen does not go far enough back into the childhood of the seventh art. The real primitives of the cinema, existing only in the imaginations of a few men of the nineteenth century, are in complete imitation of nature. Every new development added to

26

the cinema must, paradoxically, take it nearer and nearer to its origins. In short, cinema has not yet been invented!

It would be a reversal then of the concrete order of causality, at least psychologically, to place the scientific discoveries or the industrial techniques that have loomed so large in its development at the source of the cinema's invention. Those who had the least confidence in the future of the cinema were precisely the two industrialists Edison and Lumière. Edison was satisfied with just his kinetoscope and if Lumière judiciously refused to sell his patent to Méliès it was undoubtedly because he hoped to make a large profit out of it for himself, but only as a plaything of which the public would soon tire. As for the real savants such as Marey, they were only of indirect assistance to the cinema. They had a specific purpose in mind and were satisfied when they had accomplished it. The fanatics, the madmen, the disinterested pioneers, capable, as was Berard Palissy, of burning their furniture for a few seconds of shaky images, are neither industrialists nor savants, just men obsessed by their own imaginings. The cinema was born from the converging of these various obsessions, that is to say, out of a myth, the myth of total cinema. This likewise adequately explains the delay of Plateau in applying the optical principle of the persistence of the image on the retina, as also the continuous progress of the syntheses of movement as compared with the state of photographic techniques. The fact is that each alike was dominated by the imagination of the century. Undoubtedly there are other examples in the history of techniques and inventions of the convergence of research, but one must distinguish between those which come as a result precisely of scientific evolution and industrial or military requirements and those which quite clearly precede them. Thus, the myth of Icarus had to wait on the internal combustion engine before descending from the platonic heavens. But it had dwelt in the soul of everyman since he first thought about birds. To some extent, one could say the same thing about the myth of cinema, but its forerunners prior to the nineteenth century have only a remote connection with the myth which we share today and which has prompted the appearance of the mechanical arts that characterize today's world.

1946

27

RUDOLPH ARNHEIM
FROM FILM AS ART

THE COMPLETE FILM

The technical development of the motion picture will soon carry the mechanical imitation of nature to an extreme. The addition of sound was the first obvious step in this direction. The introduction of sound film must be considered as the imposition of a technical novelty that did not lie on the path the best film artists were pursuing. They were engaged in working out an explicit and pure style of silent film, using its restrictions to transform the peep show into an art. The introduction of sound film smashed many of the forms that the film artists were using in favor of the inartistic demand for the greatest possible "naturalness" (in the most superficial sense of the word). By sheer good luck, sound film is not only destructive but also offers artistic potentialities of its own. Owing to this accident alone the majority of art-lovers still do not realize the pitfalls in the road pursued by the movie producers. They do not see that the film is on its way to the victory of wax museum ideals over creative art.

The development of the silent film was arrested possibly forever when it had hardly begun to produce good results; but it has left us with a few splendidly mature films. In the future, no doubt, "progress" will be faster. We shall have color films and stereoscopic films, and the artistic potentialities of the sound film will be crushed at an even earlier stage of their development.

What will the color film have to offer when it reaches technical perfection? We know what we shall lose artistically by abandoning the black-and-white film. Will color ever allow us to achieve a similar compositional precision, a similar independence of "reality"?

The masterpieces of painting prove that color provides wider possibilities than black-and-white and at the same time permits of a very exact and genuine style. But can painting and color photography be compared? Whereas the painter has a perfectly free hand with color and form in presenting nature, photography is obliged to record mechanically the light values of physical reality. In achromatic photography the reduction of everything to the gray scale resulted in an art medium that was sufficiently independent and divergent from nature. There is not much likelihood of any such transpositon of reality into a qualitatively different range of colors in color film. To be sure, one can eliminate individual colors—one may, for example, cut out all blues, or, vice versa, one may cut out everything except the blues. Probably it is possible also to change one or more color tones qualitatively—for example, give all reds a cast of orange or make all the yellows greenish—or let colors change places with one another—turn all blues to red and all reds to blue—but all this would be, so to.speak, only transposition of reality, mechanical shifts, whose usefulness as a formative medium may be doubted. Hence there remains only the possibility of controlling the color by clever choice of what is to be photographed. All kinds of fine procedures are conceivable, especially in the montage of colored pictures, but it must not be overlooked that in this way the subjective formative virtues of the camera, which are so distinctive a characteristic of film, will be more and more restricted, and the artistic part of the work will be more and more focused upon what is set up and enacted *before* the camera. The camera is thereby increasingly relegated to the position of a mere mechanical recording machine.

Above all, it is hardly realistic to speculate on the artistic possibilities of the color film without keeping in mind that at the same time we are likely to be presented with the three-dimensional film and the wide screen. Efforts in these directions are in progress. The illusion of reality will thereby have been increased to such a degree that the spectator will not be able to appreciate certain artistic color effects even if they should be feasible technically. It is quite conceivable that by a careful choice and arrangement of objects it might be possible to use the color on the projection surface artistically and harmoniously. But if the film image becomes stereoscopic there is no longer a plane surface within the confines of the screen, and therefore there can be no composition of that surface; what remains will be effects that are also possible on the stage. The increased size of the screen will render any two-dimensional or three-dimensional composition less compelling; and formative devices such as montage and changing camera angles will become unusable if the illusion of reality is so enormously strengthened. Obviously, montage will seem an intolerable accumulation of heterogeneous settings if the illusion of reality is very strong. Obviously also a change in the position of the camera will now be felt as an actual displacement within the space of the picture. The camera will have to become an immobile recording machine, every cut in the film strip will be mutilation. Scenes will have to be taken in their entire length and with a stationary camera, and they will have to be shown as they are. The artistic potentialities of this form of film will be exactly those of the stage. Film will no longer be able in any sense to be considered as a separate art. It will be thrown back to before its first beginnings—for it was with a fixed camera and an uncut strip that film started. The only difference will be that instead of having all before it film will have nothing to look forward to.

This curious development signifies to some extent the climax of that striving after likeness to nature which has hitherto permeated the whole history of the visual arts. Among the strivings that make human beings create faithful images is the primitive desire to get material objects into one's power by creating them afresh. Imitation also permits people to cope with significant experiences; it provides release, and makes for a kind of reciprocity between the self and the world. At the same time a reproduction that is true to nature provides the thrill that by the hand of man an image has been created which is astoundingly like some natural object. Nevertheless, various countertendencies—some of them purely perceptual—have prevented mechanically faithful imitation from being achieved hundreds of years ago. Apart from rare exceptions, only our modern age has succeeded in approaching this dangerous goal. In practice, there has always been the artistic urge not simply to copy but to originate, to interpret, to mold. We may, however, say that aesthetic theory has rarely sanctioned such activities.

Even for artists like Leonardo da Vinci the demand for being as true to nature as possible was a matter of course when he talked theory, and Plato's attack on artists, in which he charged them with achieving nothing but reproductions of physical objects, is far from the general attitude.

To this very day some artists cherish this doctrine, and the general public does so to an even greater extent. In painting and sculpture it is only in recent decades that works have been appearing which show that their creators have broken with this principle intellectually and not merely practically. If a man considers that the artist should imitate nature, he may possibly paint like Van Gogh, but certainly not like Paul Klee. We know that the very powerful and widespread rejection of modern art is almost entirely supported by the argument that it is not true to nature. The development of film shows clearly how all-powerful this ideal still is.

Photography and its offspring, film, are art media so near to nature that the general public looks upon them as superior to such old-fashioned and imperfect imitative techniques as drawing and painting. Since on economic grounds film is much more dependent on the general public than any other form of art, the "artistic" preferences of the public sweep everything before them. Some work of good quality can be smuggled in but it does not compensate for the more fundamental defeats of film art. The complete film is the fulfillment of the age-old striving for the complete illusion. The attempt to make the two-dimensional picture as nearly as possible like its solid model succeeds; original and copy become practically indistinguishable. Thereby all formative potentialities which were based on the differences between model and copy are eliminated and only what is inherent in the original in the way of significant form remains to art.

H. Baer in a remarkable little essay in the *Kunstblatt* has pointed out that color film represents the accomplishment of tendencies which have long been present in graphic art.

"Graphic art (he says) — of which photography is one branch — has always striven after color. The oldest woodcuts, the blockbooks, were finished off by being handpainted. Later, a second, colored, plate was added to the black-and-white — as in Dürer's portrait of 'Ulrich Varnbühler.' A magnificent picture of a knight

31

in armor in black, silver, and gold, exists by Burgmair. In the eighteenth century multicolored etchings were produced. In the nineteenth the lithographs of Daumier and Gavarni are colored in mass production. . . . Color invaded the graphic arts as an increased attraction for the eye. Uncivilized man is not as a rule satisfied with black-and-white. Children, peasants and primitive peoples demand the highest degree of bright coloring. It is the primitives of the great cities who congregate before the film screen. Therefore film calls in the aid of bright colors. It is a fresh stimulus."

In itself, the perfection of the "complete" film need not be a catastrophe—if silent film, sound film, and colored sound film were allowed to exist alongside it. There is no objection to the "complete" film as an alternative to the stage—it might help to take into remote places fine performances of good works, as also of operas, musical comedies, ballets, the dance. Moreover, by its very existence it would probably have an excellent influence on the other—the real—film forms, by forcing them to advance along their own lines. Silent film, for example, would no longer provide dialogue in its titles, because then the absence of the spoken word would be felt as artificial and disturbing. In sound film, too, any vague intermediate form between it and the stage would be avoided. Just as the stage will feel itself obliged by the very existence of film to emphasize its own characteristic—the predominance of dramatic speech—so the "complete" film could relegate the true film forms to their own sphere.

The fact is, however, that whereas aesthetically these categories of film could and should exist along with mechanically complete reproduction, they are inferior to it in the capacity to imitate nature. Therefore the "complete" film is certain to be considered an advance upon the preceding film forms, and will supplant them all.

1933

WILLIAM EARLE
REVOLT AGAINST REALISM
IN THE FILMS

Let us call *realist* a certain sensibility which feels most at home
living among familiar things in their familiar places, or among
persons with recognizable characters acting or suffering in comprehensible ways. I shall presently return to these adjectives, *familiar*,
recognizable, and *comprehensible*, to define reality. Meanwhile,
unquestionably there is some such sensibility; unquestionably its
pleasures are genuine and widespread—why, otherwise, would
most commercial films address themselves to it?—but equally
unquestionably, there is another sensibility which finds any such
reality the very home of the boring and a serious invitation to
spiritual death. For its life consists not so much in revisiting the
familiar, recognizing what had been seen before, or comprehending
the familiar under generalizable concepts, as in encountering something never seen before, in the primary cognition of novel singu-
larities which can not be comprehended under the universal, in
short, in a primordial disclosure of what can only be called, in our
present terms, *unreal*. For pleasure let each sensibility look at the
films of its choice; but philosophically the two sensibilities and
their respective arts are not exactly on such an equal footing. The
realist satisfaction in seeing variations on what had already been
seen and in the reconfirmation of its conviction in an eternal,
known moral order by seeing things "come out right" is clearly of
a *derived* order. Nothing can become familiar unless previously
encountered originally; and a moral order can not be reconfirmed

33

unless it has been threatened. Existentially, the satisfactions of realist art almost seem to be created precisely in order to extinguish the lurking anxiety that the real world is nothing in the first place but a delusive fiction. Any such contention must be supported by plausible evidence; so I will now turn to the general question, what is realism? in order to show its range and pervasiveness, and then consider three alternatives to it, sensory, surrealist, and ironic art. In this discussion, we shall try to keep our eyes on what might be pertinent to movies.

I. REALISM

If *realism* is taken simply as one aesthetic manner in painting, literature, and movies, an option, among others, like naturalism, expressionism, symbolism, etc., open to the artist's taste and defining a school, perhaps we shall be dealing only with certain ambiguous by-products which, whatever their use, hardly enable us to get at origins. In the case of realism, the simple truth is that it is hardly a peculiar aesthetic style at all. Every human being is already and forever *realist;* he has other potentialities but those other potentialities are necessarily rooted in a basic realism: *perception itself* is inherently realist, and *reality* is inherently defined in terms of possible perception. The simplest definition of a reality is obviously, "that which we can perceive," a definition not meant as a philosophical contention opposed, let us say, to Plato, Plotinus, Spinoza, or Hegel, who define an ultimate reality otherwise. It is a simple stipulation of meaning, and one which will, I hope, be useful to a consideration of realism as pertinent to movies. In a word, in everyday life we count something as a reality if we can perceive it; otherwise it has a dubious mode of being, best left to the philosophers. And *perception*, what does it mean? For the moment, it is enough if we consider it any continuing act of the senses, or better, all of them cooperatively, which grasps something individual. Hence the real world is composed of those things we can see, hear, touch, feel, bump into. Let us call all of this *perception;* and since movies are primarily seen and heard, the *real* for movies then will be what can be seen and heard. To this somewhat sterile beginning, I will add a few pages from the phenomenology of perception to define a little more clearly what any such perceptible reality must be. A definition is necessary since it is far from obvious what these ordinary perceptible realities are; by defining them, perhaps, we can see eventually what some radically different alternatives are to that realism which inherently adheres to perception. In short, by systematically altering every feature of perception, we can at the same time make sense of some of the origins of alternative sensibilities in contemporary cinema.

What then are some central features of perception and the real world? I will discuss them under three titles: A. The *referential* character of perception; B. its *public* character; C. the *meanings* of real things.

A. The Referential Character of Perception

Sensation, first of all, must be distinguished from *perception;* or, in the whole perceptual act, that aspect of it which is purely private to me, which is a literal part of my own flowing perceptual consciousness I call *sensation*, but insofar as these same sensations are taken by me as *referring* to something beyond myself, they are *perceptions* of that thing. Only I *sense* the ache of my tooth; yet, if I take that ache as issuing from my tooth, as "perceptive" of the tooth, then the sensation refers to a tooth which my dentist can also see. Or, as the phenomenologists say, perception "intends" a perceptual *object* which lies in a world open to all perceivers. It refers to identities beyond the sheer privacy of my own sensation.

Precisely how a stream of sensation can refer to or intend these identities beyond itself is a subtle and delicate problem, but for our purposes we can summarize some central features. The question is pertinent to movies since the realities which constitute the home of the realist sensibility are none other than these perceptual identities, things and people. And briefly, sensations will be interpreted by the perceiver as perceptions of an identity when in fact they exhibit a certain order or when they are bound together by a systematic repeatability. And so, if indeed I am perceiving a chair, then my sensations of it will change as I move nearer or farther away, but change systematically, following what we later call the *laws of perspective* but which operate informally in the very act of perception itself. Thus, if I should move closer to the chair, and my sensation of it got progressively smaller, or abruptly and nonsystematically changed at every instant, I should not then take my sensations as the perceptions of anything but rather as mere sensations, a dizziness in me. Or if every time I blinked my eye, what I saw absolutely changed in every one of its sensed qualities, I would not take my sensations as referential at all; and no real identities would be constituted in the process. A perceptual reality, therefore, can change very rapidly indeed; but every appearance of it can not be *wholly* disconnected from my previous perceptions or no reality would appear at all. My sensations would not refer to any identity and would therefore collapse into nonreferential and purely subjective sensings. In a word, real identities must be constituted through repeatability and familiarity; they are automatically built-up through recognition. If I perceive a man walking out of the door, an inherent part of that perception is the belief that *that same man could* walk back through, whether in fact he does or does not. And if he does not, then indeed he must be somewhere else, and not simply nowhere by virtue of his disappearance from my sensation.

A second aspect of perception and its world of realities is, namely, that these real identities are always taken by perception to be *in a world*. And, for perception, this world is not so much a sum total of things nor an infinite container, as it is a horizon which itself can never be perceived but which expresses the sense in perception that its realities are always somewhere even when not seen by me; that there could be other perceivers besides myself who could see the same things; and that things and persons themselves have perceptible properties even when those properties are not being actually perceived.

A reality then for perception is a recognizable identity with its own place in a world of similar identities.

B. Public Availability of Perceptual Realities

Closely connected with the above, a reality for my perception has the inherent meaning of something there *for other senses and other perceivers too*. Therefore, if I *see* something, I should in general be able to touch it, too; if these and the other senses do not yield coherent sensations, I doubt the *reality* of the thing; but also,

36

if only *I* can perceive the thing, and no one else in my place could see it, I begin to doubt the reality of my perception. It was only a subjective sensation or perhaps a mere illusion. All the properties which I ascribe as "real properties" to the real thing must similarly be publicly available. If the public sees it as red and I see it as grey, its real property is red and I am color-blind.

C. The Meanings of Things

Finally, our whole description is hopelessly oversimplified. No one *merely* perceives things and persons. Philosophers as otherwise diverse as Dewey and Heidegger have shown the vacuity of mere perception if not its theoretical impossibility. Nietzsche called it "immaculate perception." All realities we encounter have a meaning for us, a significance which is not in the least reducible to mere perception. Automobiles, pencils, buildings, streets, and above all persons, are hardly to be understood as compositions of colors, shapes, sounds, etc. They are rather things and persons we are already living with, whose very essence is *what they are for us:* what we can do with them, what they can do to us, how we feel about them, in short, their role in our complete active emotional and not merely perceptual *life*. They are structured with values, if you like; their meaning for us is not experienced as something superadded to bare perception but inherent in that perception from the start. Some aestheticians like to think of this aspect as though it were a literary association; but there is nothing literary about it, nor is it necessarily an association brought to mere things from without; the identities in the first place are invariably things and persons for us, with that meaning already there. And that meaning implicates again a public world, where such things are already in their places. And their places in the world are their already familiar relations to other things and people, where those meanings emerge. The hammer is for hammering and its place is its proximity to the hand and the hammerable, or else it is displaced. A hammer flying from tree to tree loses its sense of hammer. Or it becomes a bird-hammer.

In summary then, perception is inherently realist; it constitutes its real things out of its own order, things which are in a world, related to their proper places, and in such a way that this real world of real things is there in more or less the same way for everyone. It is *necessarily* familiar, recognizable, comprehensible. A revolt in the cinema against realism would take each of these features and by its radical removal be in a position to exhibit what can never be realistically perceived, the unreal. From our present point of view, there would be two directions. One would proceed to remove system from sensation so that it *could* not constitute real identities: this I shall call sub-realist, sensory, or, following Marcel Duchamp, "retinal art." A second, moving in the opposite direction, would retain identities, but by *dislocation*, or removing them from their proper places, constitute an unreal world, no longer comprehensible in any realist sense, and, as André Breton said, would disclose the marvellous.

II. SENSORY OR RETINAL ART

Movies are in an excellent position to accomplish the first destruction of realism; for obviously, since the realities in question are given only through a medium in the form of images, by removing the imagistic character of the medium, we can easily in the same blow remove any possibility of perceiving real identities through them. Nothing need be done except reverse every excellence in the realist camera: if lens makers have finally designed optics with virtually no sensible distortion at all, we will use cracked lenses, lenses out of focus, smeared with vaseline, or covered with filters and screens; or if a zoom lens is best used for exact framing, by moving too close, or looking at the object from an odd angle, all trace of recognizability can be removed; or if the film transport of camera and projector are designed for perfect synchronization, we can easily run them so far out of synch that motions can be arrested or wholly altered, and so on through the usual bag of camera tricks. Triple and quadruple exposure can quickly reverse any world or obliterate foreground and background relationships. Editing can be so abrupt and quick that no recognizability, familiarity, or comprehensibility can occur. Briefly, what for the realist perception was an *image*, now loses that function and what is left approximates *sensation without perception;* we suffer perhaps for the first time a continuing experience of what some philosophers used to call "sense-data." LSD films move in

38

this direction and, compared with them, dreams and hallucinations are hopelessly organized and significant of a world.

The senses, by themselves, of course quickly tire; they come alive only in change to such an extent that some animals can see nothing at all unless it moves. Sensation dies when stopped; it is perfectly natural that having deprived perception of the conditions of its operation, the sensation remaining must go faster and faster. Twenty-four absolutely diverse and unrelated frames per second seems far too slow for some; a number of projectors can, therefore, be brought to bear on the same or different screens. And if the senses left to themselves love speed, they also have an obvious longing for the *violent;* gentle changes of intensity will pass unnoticed, until the violence of light and sound approaches an assault on their very physiological limits. A friend of mine who makes films in this vein recently remarked that his ideal was a film that would "punch the audience squarely in the eyes"; oddly enough he felt that this was the best way to "teach people how to see," forgetting in his enthusiasm that no one either can or needs to be *taught* how to see: at very least, would we not have first to see the teacher who was to teach us how to see? What *can* be taught or induced by filmic conditions is *how not to see in order to sense;* and this surely is what the films presently under discussion aim at through the systematic defeat of every built-in expectation of perception.

Many of the same considerations must apply *mutatis mutandi* to the sound of sensory movies. There is a marked preference for electronic and aleatoric sound, and for *musique concrète.* For just as in realist perception, colors and shapes are the appearances of *something*, and sounds are the sounds and voices *of* things and persons, disclosing their qualities and character. Even in performance, the sounds are always the sounds of a violin, piano, singer, a real something or other giving out these sounds. If now the thing sounding or person speaking is suppressed or becomes unrecognizable, then something like a sounding which is not taken to be the sound *of anything* emerges, an aural sense-datum. Further, if all comprehensible pattern is removed, as in chance sound, then the result at last means nothing, announces nothing, expresses no one personality; we now have the perfect sound track for a sensory film.

39

III. SURREALISM

The revolt against realism can take an opposite direction, that of surrealism, and that surrealism and retinal or sensory art are indeed opposite directions was clear even in the twenties; surrealism was never friendly to purely abstract or non-representational painting. That the familiar and prefabricated perceptual reality is not the final horizon in which men must live can be shown best not by removing the conditions for all genuine perception, and thereby plunging the spirit into pure sensation, but rather by offering it what Breton repeatedly called the "marvellous." And, for Breton, the marvellous was never regarded as simply a new aesthetic style or excitement, but rather as a necessary means of liberating the spirit from any final engrossment in what passes for the real, what offers itself to perception and to comprehension. Against that world it offers another, the surreal, within which the real world is seen as but one minor variation, a variation moreover constructed by and correlative to our least admirable desires, the desire not to be oneself but rather a member of the public, the very public which defines reality.

Surrealism then is primarily an effort to effect a spiritual reorientation; its theater of operations was never exclusively in works of art but rather in that very public reality which it wished to undermine: hence the necessity for its jokes, outrages, scandals, manifestoes, demonstrations, its temporary flirtation with revolutionary communism, and its love for gratuitous scandals such as Benjamin Peret's penchant for spitting at priests. Overflowing from this particular sentiment was its aesthetic, a sensibility directed to the irrational and magical.

The surreal world, unlike that of sensory art, is indeed a world and is populated by identities; its world is composed of things drawn from the real world but now de- or sur-realized; they are set free from their public or scientific connections and places in order to live a life of their own. Perhaps the most general name for such a freeing is dislocation; for if the very meanings of the things and persons we encounter derive from their relations to their proper places, a dislocation will show that object in a new light. The bringing together of distant realities can then strike off new sparks; the surrealists never tired of repeating from Lautréamont the "beauty of the chance encounter of a sewing machine and an umbrella on a dissecting table." The displacement of things and persons from their own space and own time, from their own relative dimensions and public values is designed to offer the spirit a world closer to its own desire. Its own desire was from the beginning understood in Freudian terms; it was the subconscious, where contraries were identified, which knew nothing of the world as redefined by science, which was at home in the magical, and whose desires must be liberated from the expected, the public, the predictable, the morality of public safety.

The techniques are well-known: automatic writing and free association to eliminate reflection; collective works, where many worked on a single object, no one knowing what the other was doing, the so-called "exquisite corpse"; random trips around Paris; coincidences through chance street encounters; found objects, collage, frottage, the primitive, the insane, the erotic, the criminal, the violent; each form of subjectivity disclosed its own domain of the surreal, a world not accessible to ordinary action, perception, or reason, and appearing to those faculties as marvellous and magical.

To return to films, it is almost as though they were predestined to be an excellent surrealist medium. For if we are already accustomed to the liberties which language and painting can take with reality, moving pictures almost automatically make us expect some sort of true camera reality; films remain a form of photography, and while everyone *knows* the camera can lie, we do not look initially at photographs as though they were lies. And so the force of movies to wrench us out of our habitual realism is particularly great. Further, the conditions of viewing a movie, in a darkened room, are particularly conducive to a form of dreamy participation where the marvellous would not appear simply as wrong, silly, or outrageous. Similarly the liberties which can be taken in editing and arranging, and the very same camera tricks which are used for a wholly different effect by sensory art, can now serve surrealist purposes admirably.

If the one real world and its reflection in movies provide us with the satisfactions of recognizability and comprehension, the worlds of surrealism are inherently private, plural, organizable into no whole, and invariably either strange, marvellous, or funny. If

41

May Ray's *Étoile de Mer* (1928) and the slitting of the eyeball from Dali-Buñuel's *Un Chien Andalou* (1929). "In some of Man Ray's films, the bringing together of distant realities constructs a world closer to the hidden desires of the heart than the public reality could provide. . . ." Surrealism wishes to undermine the public reality, "hence the necessity for its jokes, outrages, scandals, manifestoes, demonstrations . . . and its love for gratuitous scandals . . ." (EARLE, pages 43, 40).

reality is not so much funny as serious, the systematic *disruption* of the expectations generated by familiarity could be, if not serious in their damage, hilarious, for example, in René Clair's *Entr'acte*. And the surrealists always regarded humor, particularly black humor, as especially liberating. Or, when serious, as in the early Buñuel films, evocative of the revolutionary sentiment of indignation, as Buñuel says, in the "conviction that this is NOT the best of all possible worlds"; or magical, as in some of Man Ray's films, where the bringing together of distant realities constructs a world closer to the hidden desires of the heart than the public reality could provide. These sentiments, obviously, are modifications of the sentiments appropriate to perceptual public reality; nothing can be strange unless measured against the familiar, or have the unexpectedness of a joke unless there were expectations to be defeated. And yet the final intent of these surrealist worlds is not to be a mere derivation of the real public world so much as the disclosure of the domain of the possible, in the middle of which the real, public world is finally seen to be just as mysterious and arbitrary as any other possibility. The real perceptual world then could be finally experienced as a surrealist poem imagined by the *public in each of us*. At this point, realism and surrealism join hands in a poetic realism; but that particular meeting is only possible after the detour into the imaginary of surrealism and not before. It is here that the late Siegfried Kracauer's view of film as the "redemption of physical reality" might find its place.

IV. IRONIC FILMS

There remains from our present perspective one more alternative to realism in the film. Realist films of course do not offer us realities themselves, but rather *images of them*. If sensory art destroys images in their function of presenting us something else of which they are images, and if surrealism retains that function of presenting something else, but profoundly alters the character of the something else presented, a remaining alternative would be to develop films which *called attention* to the image, while still employing it as an image. Here, our experience would be an ironic one, doubly aware both of the scene passing before our eyes and of our seeing it through images. In a purely realist film, every effort is devoted to making the audience unaware of the camera, unaware that they are seeing only a reflected reality. The camera moves rarely, the sequences of what is shown agree with the order of showing it; everything is shown as we would see it if we were there in person. On the other hand, in ironic films we have the double awareness of seeing some action as it is refracted through an artificial medium. Now the camera will be hand held, so its jiggle will remind the audience that they are indeed looking at a movie; sometimes processing perforations are shown, and the trailers and leaders of film as they come back from the developer; sometimes the actors ham it up so we are aware they are acting. Or, as in the case of Jean-Luc Godard, the film will make references to other films, reminding the audience that this is a film, making a commentary on or spoofing other films. Sometimes the film or film-making itself becomes the subject of the action, as in *8½*, *Muriel*, or *Blow-Up*. Insofar as there is any suggestion in these ironic films that there is no public, stable reality at all, but only imaginary or *filmic versions* of it, they fall within the general revolt against any acquiescence to the real. Alain Resnais' films also proceed to dissolve any assurance in a public reality by demonstrating the ambiguity of the meaning of the present through its dependence on the past, a past moreover which is itself ambiguous through its significance for the present. Memory here becomes the artist whose materials are always on the verge of losing any independent reality whatsoever. But this carries us into other problems.

Finally, it should be understood that realism, sensory, surrealist, and ironic are only ideal types. No film perfectly exemplifies them, or could exemplify them. Not that this is the fault of the films or of the types; in any closer consideration, we should certainly find that each film most closely exemplified nothing but its own type, that is, no type at all. Each is what it is and asks not so much to be typed as simply seen.

1968

V. F. PERKINS
FROM FILM AS FILM

FORM AND DISCIPLINE

I do not believe that the film (or any other medium) has an essence which we can usefully invoke to justify our criteria. We do not deduce the standards relevant to Rembrandt from the essence of paint; nor does the nature of words impose a method of judging ballads and novels. Standards of judgement cannot be appropriate to a medium as such but only to particular ways of exploiting its opportunities. That is why the concept of the cinematic, presented in terms of demands, has stunted the useful growth of film theory. Helpful criteria are more likely to be based on positive statements of value than on prohibitions. To regard criticism positively, as a search for the most satisfactory definitions of function and value, allows an escape from academic systems of rules and requirements. Criteria then relate to claims which the critic can sustain rather than to demands which he must make. The clarification of standards should help to develop the disciplines of criticism without seeking to lay obligations on the film-maker. Criticism and its theory are concerned with the interplay of available resources and desirable functions. They attempt to establish what the medium is good for. They cannot determine what is good for the medium, because the question is senseless. The search for appropriate criteria leads us to observe limitations; it does not allow us to prescribe them. Anything possible is also permissible, but we still have to establish its value. We cannot assess worth without indicating function.

Hence we can evolve useful criteria only for specific types of film, not for the cinema. Our standards of judgement will have to follow from definitions of types in terms of both their possibilities and their limitations. We have to discover what values we can claim for, what functions it makes sense to assign to, particular applications of the moving picture's resources. Our major concern will be with the different opportunities which can be realized within the various forms of cinema. A theory of film which claims universal validity must provide either an exhaustive catalogue of film forms or a description of the medium in such general terms as to offer minimal guidance to the appreciation of any movie. The problem arises from the embarrassing richness of the cinema's aptitudes.

The movie offers two forms of magic, since its conquest of the visible world extends in two opposite directions. The first, on which the realist theory concentrates, gives it the power to "possess" the real world by capturing its appearance. The second, focus of the traditional aesthetic, permits the presentation of an ideal image, ordered by the film-maker's will and imagination. Since the cinema's mechanism incorporates both these tendencies, neither of them can be condemned on rational, technical or aesthetic grounds. A useful film theory must acknowledge the range and diversity of the film-maker's achievements. At one end of the scale we find the most rigorous forms of documentary, which aim to present the truth about an event with the minimum of human intervention between the real object and its film image; at the other end lies the abstract, cartoon or fantasy film which presents a totally controlled vision. This diversity of methods might be attributed to the movies' mixed parentage, the "objective," factual elements being derived from the camera and the "subjective," magical ones from the Phenakistascope and its relations.

Within the first few years of the cinema's existence the polarities were firmly established. The Lumière brothers' first movie-show presented short "actualities"—a train entering a station, baby eating breakfast and so on. In the earliest days the fact that a machine could present real situations in recognizable form was sufficient sensation to draw enthusiastic audiences throughout Europe and the United States. As soon as that magic lost its appeal, Georges Méliès was ready to step in with the other kind. A professional magician, Méliès took up film-making in 1896 and devoted himself to exploiting the cinema as a medium for fantasy. Using every form of camera trickery he could invent, he told a series of amusing and amazing stories. His two most famous pictures, *A Trip to the Moon* (1902) and *The Impossible Voyage* (1904), presented fantastic situations in fantastic settings. They are packed with magical appearances, disappearances and transformations. The arrival of Méliès and the subsequent development of the narrative film revived the public's waning interest in motion pictures.

Lumière's actualities represent one extreme of the cinema and Méliès's fantasies are quite near to the other. But few films confine themselves to either a purely reproductive or a purely imaginative technique. The cinema extends across the whole of the area between the two extremes. The photographic narrative film occupies a compromise position where a fictional "reality" is *created* in order to be *recorded*. Here the relationship between reality and illusion, object and image, becomes extremely complex; any attempt to isolate either in a "pure" state becomes correspondingly inept.

The fiction movie exploits the possibilities of synthesis between photographic realism and dramatic illusion. That synthesis, its value and implications, will be the major subject of this study. Unless a wider relevance is explicitly claimed, the reader should assume that arguments are meant to apply only to the cinema of photographic fiction. I hope to present criteria which will aid discussion of various kinds and degrees of excellence within this form. I shall offer no case about the usefulness of other forms, nor will my remarks be relevant to the qualities of works outside the range of my definitions. The chosen field to some extent reflects the limits of my familiarity and enthusiasm, but that is all. It would clearly be possible and useful to argue claims and criteria for cartoon, documentary, instructional and many other kinds of film which lie beyond the scope of this study. Nonetheless the fiction movie presents the most urgent claim to attention for two reasons: by almost any reasonable method of calculation, it must be granted the central role in the cinema's development; but it is also precisely the fictional element which existing film theories have most difficulty in accommodating.

A necessary consequence of adopting positive criteria is that we are better equipped to praise than to condemn. Discriminations will be possible within the type, in so far as we see one film as a more complete or skilful realization of its opportunities than another. But the claims we can make for a comedy by Howard Hawks will not yield ammunition for use against an Ingmar Bergman allegory, because they belong to types almost as distinct as cartoon and documentary. Even within the field of cine-fiction the range of possibilities remains enormous. The critical problem is to arrive at descriptions which are both specific and comprehensive enough to be useful. The critic cannot require a movie to fit his definitions; it's his task to find the description which best fits the movie. The most he can "demand" from a film is coherence: a structure which points consistently towards the performance of comprehensible functions. Without that, judgement becomes impossible. From this viewpoint the most significant limitations are those of the form rather than of the medium, the disciplines which the film-maker obeys in order to pursue a particular range of opportunities. For if there are no rules by which every movie can be bound, there are forms which, once adopted by the film-maker, impose their own logic both on him and on the intelligent spectator, since the opportunities of the form may be realized only at the expense of other, attractive but incompatible, possibilities. Yet the central issue remains: not what the film-maker may not do, but the value we can find in what he has done.

In a hybrid form the quest for purity is much less important than the achievement of an ideal compromise, a meaningful resolution of inherent conflict. The fictional film exploits, where purer forms attempt to negate, the conflict between reality and illusion. Instead of trying exclusively either to create or to record, the story film attempts a synthesis: it both records what has been created and creates by its manner of recording. At its most powerful it achieves a credibility which consummates the cinema's blend of actuality and fantasy.

The credibility of the movies comes, I believe, from our

habit of placing more trust in the evidence of our eyes than in any other form of sense data: a film makes us feel like eye-witnesses of the events which it portrays. Moreover, our belief extends even to the least realistic forms of movie because movement so strongly connotes life. The source meaning of the term "animation" indicates that we regard a moving picture, even a cartoon, as a picture *brought to life*. In the early days of the movies words like cinematograph and kinetoscope, which meant *moving* picture, were interchangeable with words meaning *living* picture (vitascope, biograph, bioscope, etc.). The powerful combination of picture and movement tempts us to disregard the involvement of our imaginations in what we see. . . .

The most "realistic" films are the ones which convey the most complete illusion. The most obviously imaginative films, the "pure works of man"—cartoons and fantasies—lean heavily upon the cinema's realistic resources in order to make us see the impossible and believe the incredible. When the cartoon cat walks confidently off the edge of a skyscraper and stands paralysed for a couple of fearful seconds before falling, it is precisely our habit of believing our eyes that makes a piece of anti-Newtonian nonsense amusing.

Some abstract films make no use of the cinema's realism (the spectator's credulity). They do not pretend to show real objects but are an extension of non-representational painting. Yet even films in this genre—like Norman McLaren's "caprice in colour," *Begone, Dull Care*—seem to rely on our anthropomorphic tendencies. Whenever the opportunity arises movement becomes action (a round blob "bumps into" a vertical line: accident or aggression?) and shape becomes object (a coloured circle: a ball, a wheel, the sun?). Ernest Pintoff's cartoon *The Critic* comments joyfully on the abstract film's tendency to shed its abstract quality. The screen is filled with coloured shapes which apparently defy interpretation. After a few seconds we hear a Bronx-accented voice demanding "what the hell is this?" The question is momentarily resolved: "Must be a cartoon." Pause. Small blob emerges from "inside" larger blob and the interpretation begins: "Must be Birth." The shapes are rearranged and the spectator becomes confused again: "This is cute. This is cute. This is nice. What the hell *is* it?" Two black shapes converge from opposite sides of the screen: "Two Things! . . . They like each other." (Rhythmic movement of black shapes.) "Could this be the sex life of two Things?" As the commentary progresses (spiky black oval: "Uh-uh! It's a cockroach") it becomes increasingly contemptuous of the movie's imagined content ("Dirt! Dirt and filth!") until, after four minutes of "pure" abstraction the critic reaches his conclusion: "I don't know much about psychoanalysis, but I'd say this is a dirty picture." Pintoff's movie is funny because it is accurate. With any luck actual spectators can be heard commenting and interpreting before "the critic" starts to speak; the two sets of remarks are often very similar.

If abstract shapes in movement attract "realistic" interpretation as objects and actions, it is hardly surprising that the moving photograph carries such conviction. Photographic subjects, says Newhall, "can be misrepresented, distorted, faked . . . and [we] even delight in it occasionally, but the knowledge still cannot shake our implicit faith in the truth of a photographic record."[1]

In 1895 the Lumières' audience believed completely in the reality of a soundless, colourless, two-dimensional and rigidly enclosed image: the spectators feared for their lives when shown an oncoming train. Sixty years later, engulfed in Cinerama's huge screen and surrounded by a battery of realistic sound effects, people reacted to film taken from the front of a roller-coaster just as they would react to a ride on a real switchback. They gripped the arms of their seats, screamed and even felt the authentic stomach-tumbling effect. Still, we can hardly claim that *This Is Cinerama* offered a perfect illusion. Its picture, while not exactly flat, was less than three-dimensional. The joins between its three images were clearly visible. We were subject to none of the physical effects essential to a total illusion: no wind disturbed the spectator's hair as he rode the switchback, no smell reached his nostrils as he was conducted along the canals of Venice.

But although Cinerama provided only a partial illusion, it

---

[1]Newhall, *The History of Photography from 1839 to the Present Day*, p. 91.

imposed the only sort of belief which we can regard as truly complete: the audience was made to react to the image as it would to the event. The trick here is just the same as it was with the Lumières' presentation and with the 3-D films whose audiences dived for cover under a barrage of arrows, axes and ping-pong balls: not to provide a perfect illusion, that is an integral reproduction of reality, but to offer enough of reality to make the spectator disregard what is missing.

This kind and degree of belief is inevitably short-lived since "enough" means "more than ever before." Audiences rapidly adjust to an extension of the cinema's realism. The primitive magic which creates belief in the real presence of the object shown soon loses its power. "Illusion wears off once . . . expectation is stepped up; we take it for granted and want more."[2] After less than ten minutes of *This Is Cinerama* the sense of being transported around the world began to be replaced by a more conscious appreciation of the techniques by which the world was so convincingly brought into the cinema. The illusory environment of the roller-coaster or the Venetian canal is too inconsistent with what we know about our actual situation for a lasting deception.

But even if we do not believe in the actual presence of the things we see, a film remains credible so long as we are not led to question the *reality* of the objects and events presented. Verbal statements and propositions are seen as either true or false: if we believe them, we believe them; if not, not. Sights, sounds and, particularly, stories—the things which we believe *in*—present a much more complex problem. Belief here can occur in so many ways and at so many levels.

Films are often described as existing in the present tense. Like most direct linguistic analogies this one promotes confusion rather than enlightenment. It implies that we see a film as a series of events taking place for the first time. Usually we are well aware that this is not the case, just as we know that the conjurer has not magically transformed the queen of hearts into the king of spades. If films were really seen in the present tense cinema managers would have always to protect their

---

[2]E. H. Gombrich, *Art and Illusion*, Phaidon Press, 1962, pp. 52–4.

screens against assault by gallant spectators rushing to the aid of embattled heroines. If we can describe the movie as existing in any tense at all then the nearest equivalent is probably the historic present which evokes the vividness of memory or fantasy: "There I am walking along the street, and there's this old man standing on the corner. And then he steps out into the road just as this lorry comes around . . ."

Our reaction to the cinema, when we are not caught unawares by some new development like Cinerama or 3-D, is conditioned by our awareness that the camera is a recording instrument and the project film a method of reproduction. Just as we can talk of hearing Bessie Smith on a gramophone record despite our knowledge that the singer is long dead, so we can watch events taking place on the screen *now* while remaining aware that they actually occurred some time ago. In both cases we accept the accuracy of the illusion.

Ideally the sounds coming from the gramophone's loudspeaker are indistinguishable from the sounds which first went into the microphone. Even when a recorded performance falls spectacularly short of this ideal we have great difficulty in disentangling the sounds made by the artist from the noises made by the recording: it is impossible to be certain how much our concept of what Bessie Smith sounded like is derived from tones which should be attributed to primitive recording mechanisms, not to the singer. Our belief in the recording is not shaken by our knowledge that the "Bessie Smith sound" may not be a very faithful reproduction of the voice of Bessie Smith. It is hard not to feel, against reason, that the recording renders accurately the sounds made by the jazz-singer and her accompanists: if I ask myself to describe Bessie Smith's vocal quality, "scratchy" is one of the words which most immediately comes to mind.

Similarly I find it hard to form a mental picture of life in the first decade of this century which does not include people walking faster and more jauntily than they do nowadays. The image offered by accelerated projection of early films takes mental precedence over the recognized unlikelihood of an evolution towards slower walking.

It is the belief in the actual (if past) existence of the objects on the screen which enables us to discuss movies in terms of credibility. Clearly, one cannot record something which has never existed. Everything that happens on the screen in a live-action picture has happened in front of the camera. The particular magic of the narrative film is to make us put an inaccurate construction on an accurate series of images. The camera neither lies nor tells the truth, because the camera does not make statements. It is we who convert images into assertions. The cinema shows us a man holding a pistol at his head, squeezing the trigger and falling to the floor. This is precisely what happened. But we fictionalize this documentary image when we claim to have seen a man committing suicide. . . .

The camera does not discriminate between real events (which would have taken place even if it had not been on the spot to record them) and action created specifically in order to be recorded. In this respect, the movie simply extends the ambiguity present in any credible image; so long as it looks correct we have no way of telling whether a picture portrays an actual or an imagined subject. The blurred distinction between authentic and staged events helps to make the cinema a peculiarly vivid medium. It is absurd to claim that movies are like life; but it is certain that they can impress us as being more lifelike than any other form of narrative.

The moving image lends its immediacy and conviction, its concreteness of credible detail, to the fictional world. But at this point the film-maker confronts the limitation that accompanies opportunity. If he chooses to exploit the credibility of the recording, he thereby sacrifices some of the freedom to invent and arrange which is offered by the celluloid strip. The discipline is inherent in the attempt to create from a succession of images an apparently solid world which exists in its own right.

In the fiction movie, reality becomes malleable but remains (or continues to seem) solid. The world is shaped by the film-maker to reveal an order beyond chronology, in a system of time and space which is both natural and synthetic. The movie offers its reality in a sequence of privileged moments during which actions achieve a clarity and intensity seldom found in everyday life. Motive and gesture, action and reaction, cause

53

and effect, are brought into a more immediate, dynamic and revealing relationship. The filmmaker fashions a world more concentrated and more shaped than that of our usual experience.

Movies are not distinguished from other forms of narrative by the fact that they isolate and mould aspects of experience in order to intensify our perception. But films are peculiar in performing this work primarily in the sphere of action and appearance rather than of reflection or debate.

The story-teller's freedom to create is inhibited by his two first requirements: clarity and credibility. In movies, the most direct and concrete method of narration, these aims impose a greater restraint than on any other medium. The audience has to know what is happening, of course, but it must also be convinced by what it sees. The organization of image and sound must usually defer to these interests. The narrative picture, in most of its forms, submits to the twin criteria of order and credibility. The movie itself creates these criteria whenever it proposes to be at the same time significant and convincing. The impurity of the medium is consummated by a decision to project a world which is both reproduced and imagined, a creation and a copy. Committed to this impurity, the film-maker is also committed to maintaining a balance between its elements. His aim is to organize the world to the point where it becomes most meaningful but to resist ordering it out of all resemblance to the real world which it attempts to evoke. . . .

1972

JURIJ LOTMAN
FROM
SEMIOTICS OF CINEMA

THE ILLUSION OF REALITY

Every art is concerned, to some extent, that a feeling of reality be conveyed to its audience. The cinema is foremost in this respect. Later on we will consider the role played by the fantastic, starting with the films of Méliès, in transforming cinematography into art. But the "feeling of reality" now under discussion consists in something else: no matter how fantastic an event taking place on the screen might be, the audience is a witness to it and, in a sense, a participant in it. Therefore, although the audience is conscious of the irreal nature of the event, it reacts emotionally as it would to a genuine event.[1] As we shall see later, there are specific difficulties connected with the transmission by cinematographic means of the past and future tenses, as well as the subjunctive and other irreal moods in cinematic narration. The cinema, because of the nature of its material, knows only the present tense just as, we might add, do other arts employing depictive signs. This point was discussed relative to the theater by D. S. Lixačev.

The emotional faith of the audience in the genuineness of the material being shown on the screen involves cinematography with one of the most important problems in the history of culture.

All technical improvements are a two-edged sword: called

---

[1]"Reality" of the cinema in this sense has been investigated by Christian Metz in Essais sur la signification au cinéma, Paris, 1968, pp. 13–24.

upon to serve social progress and the public welfare, they have been just as successfully employed for negative purposes. One of the greatest achievements of mankind—sign communication—has not avoided this fate. Signs, although called upon to serve information, have often been used for purposes of disinformation. The "word" has often appeared in the history of culture as a symbol of wisdom, knowledge and truth (cf. the biblical statement "In the beginning was the Word"), and as a synonym for fraud or lying (Hamlet's "Words, words, words," Gogol's "The frightening kingdom of words instead of deeds"). Equating the sign with a lie, and the struggle against signs—refusing to use money, social symbols, sciences, speech itself—is met constantly in the ancient and medieval worlds, in various cultures in the East, and in recent times has become one of the leading ideas of European democracy from Rousseau to Leo Tolstoy. This process continues parallel to apologies for the sign culture and to the struggle for its development. The conflict of these two tendencies is one of the consistent dialectical contradictions of human civilization.

Against the background of this contradiction there developed a more specific but exceedingly tenacious antithesis: "a text which may be false vs. a text which can not be false." It could manifest itself as the opposition "myth vs. history" (in the period preceding the rise of historical texts, myth was counted as one of the unconditionally true texts), "poetry vs. document," etc. Since the end of the eighteenth century and the ever increasing demand for truth in art, the authority of the document has increased rapidly. Pushkin introduced genuine court documents of the 1830's into *Dubrovskij* as a part of that artistic work. In the second half of the century the place of the reliable document—the antithesis of the poet's imagination in Romanticism—was occupied by newspaper reportage. It was natural that prose writers from Dostoevsky to Zola, in their search for veracity, turned to reportage, or that poets from Nekrasov to Blok oriented their works toward it.

Within the climate of rapid development of European bourgeois civilization in the nineteenth century, newspaper reporting reached its high point of cultural importance, and then declined rapidly. The expression "He lies like a journalist" testified to the fact that this genre had also departed from the ranks of texts which could only be true, and had joined the opposition. Its place was taken by photography, which possessed all the credentials of being unconditionally documentary and true, and was perceived as something opposite to culture, ideology, poetry, tendentiousness of any kind—as life itself in its reality and genuineness. It firmly took over the position of a text having the greatest documentary quality and reliability within the overall system of texts in the culture around the beginning of the twentieth century. It was acknowledged by one and all, from criminologists to historians and journalists.

Cinematography as a technical invention which had not yet become a form of art was, first and foremost a moving photograph. The ability to register motion added to the trust in the documentary reliability of films. Psychological data indicate that the transfer from motionless photography to the moving film is seen as an introduction of greater capacity in depiction. Precision in the reproduction of life, it was thought, could go no farther.

We should emphasize, though, that it was not so much a matter of the unconditionally reliable reproduction of an object, as it was the emotional confidence of the audience. We all know how distorting and unconvincing photographs can be. The better we know a person, the less resemblance we find in photographs of him. For each person whose face is truly familiar to us we prefer a portrait by a competent artist to a photograph of equal artistry. We find more resemblance in the painting. But if we are shown a portrait and a photograph of a person whom we do not know, and are asked to select the one most clearly resembling him, we pick the photograph without hesitation—such is the "documentary" charm of this type of text.

It would appear that we are being forced to conclude that the documentary and reliable aspects of cinematography give it such great initial advantages that, merely on the strength of the technical features of this form of art, we grant to it a realistic quality much greater than that enjoyed by other sorts of artistic creation. Unfortunately, the matter is not quite so sim-

57

ple. The cinema slowly and painfully developed into an art form, and those properties which we have just mentioned both helped and hindered it along the way.

In the realm of ideology, "authenticity," on the one hand, made the cinema an exceedingly informative art and guaranteed it a mass audience. But, on the other hand, it was just this feeling of the genuineness of the pictures that activated in the first cinema audience those unquestionably base emotions which are typical of the passive observer of genuine catastrophes, auto accidents, and which appeased the quasi-aesthetic and quasi-sporting emotions of audiences at Roman circuses—not unlike the reactions of present-day fans of Western automobile racing. This base emphasis on the spectacular, fed by the viewers' knowledge that the blood which he sees is real, and that the disasters are genuine, is exploited for commercial purposes by contemporary Western television which arranges reports from the theater of military activities, and the showing of sensational, bloody real-life dramas.

The transformation of cinematographic authenticity into a means for *cognition* was a long and difficult procedure.

Attempts at aesthetic assimilation of cinematic authenticity gave rise to equally complex difficulties. As strange as it may seem, the photographic accuracy of the film shots hindered rather than helped the birth of the cinema as an art.

This situation, familiar to historians of the cinema, is clearly substantiated in the general postulates of information theory. Not every message, by any means, can have meaning, i.e., be the carrier of some specific information. If we have a series of letters—A-B-C—and we know beforehand that after A only B can occur, and after B, C, the entire sequence is totally predictable from the first letter ("entirely redundant"). Statements of the type "The Volga flows into the Caspian Sea," for a person who already knows that fact, carry no information. Information is the removal of some uncertainty, the destruction of ignorance and its replacement by knowledge. Where there is no ignorance there is no information. Neither "The Volga flows into the Caspian Sea" nor "A stone falls downward" carries any information, since they are the only ones possible, and within the limits of our experience and common sense we can-

58

not construct any alternatives. Neils Bohr noted that a non-trivial statement is one such that an assertion of its opposite is not obvious nonsense. But let us assume that we have the series

where, after event B, either C or D could ensue (assume the probabilities are equal). Then the message: "There occurred A → B → C or A → B → D" would contain a certain minimal bit of information.

Thus the quantity of potential information depends on the presence of alternative possibilities. Information is the opposite of automatism: where an event automatically has another as a consequence, no information arises. In this sense the transition from drawing to photography, although it greatly increased the accuracy of reproduction, sharply lowered the informativeness. The object was automatically reflected in the depiction with the inevitability of a mechanical reproduction. An artist has an infinite (rather, a very great) number of possibilities in choosing *how* to render an object, while non-artistic photography enforces a single, automatic dependency. Art does not simply render the world with a lifeless automatism of a mirror. In transforming images of the world into signs, it saturates the world with meanings. Signs are unable not to have meaning or not to carry information. Therefore those properties of an object which result from their automatic ties with the material world become, in art, the result of free artistic choice and thus acquire the value of information. In the non-artistic world, in the world of the object, the message "The earth was located below and the sky above" (provided that we are describing the impressions of an observer on earth, and not of an airplane pilot) is trivial and carries no information since it has no non-absurd alternative. But in the film by Chukhrai, "Ballad of a Soldier," at the moment when the German tank is pursuing Alyosha who is out of breath from running, the picture on the screen is inverted. The shot turns upside down and the tank crawls with its tread uppermost along the top of the screen, and with its turret hanging down into the sky. When the shot returns to its normal position, with the sky again above and the earth below, this message is far from trivial (the audience heaves a sigh of relief). Now we know that the normal position of earth and sky is not an automatic reflection of the photographed object, but the result of a free choice by the artist. For just this reason the message "The sky above, the earth below," which in a non-artistic context *does not mean anything.* turns out in our situation to be capable of carrying unusually important information: the hero is saved, a turning point has been reached in his duel with the tank. The transition to the next shot—a burning tank—is entirely justified.

The aim of art is not simply to render some object or other, but to make it a carrier of meaning. No one of us, looking at a stone or a pine tree in a natural landscape, would ask: "What does it mean, what did they intend to say?" (as long as we do not take the view according to which a natural landscape is the result of a deliberate act of creation). But as soon as such a landscape is portrayed in a painting this question becomes not only possible, but entirely natural.

It is now clear to us that both still and moving photography, being superb *materials* of art, were at the same time materials which had to be overcome, whose very advantages caused enormous difficulties. Photography fettered the work of art, subjecting huge areas of text to the automatism of the laws of technical representation. Those areas had to be rescued from automatic representation and subjected to the laws of creation. It is significant that each new technological improvement, before it becomes a fact of art, must be freed from technological automatism. While color was determined by the technological possibilities of film and lay outside artistic *choice*, it was not a fact of art, and at first it narrowed rather than broadened the range of possibilities out of which a director made his selection. Only when color became autonomous (cp. the literary image of the "black sun"), being subordinated at all times to the intention and selection of the director, was it introduced into the sphere of art. Let us explain our point with an example from literature. In "The Lay of Igor's Campaign" there is an exceptionally poetic image. In a dream filled with dire prophecies, *blue wine* is poured for the prince. But there is reason to assume that in the language of the twelfth century "sinee" (blue) could have meant "dark red" and that in the text we have, not a poetic image, but simply an indication of a color. Clearly this place in the work has become artistically more significant than it was for readers of the twelfth century. This is so because the semantics of color had shifted and "blue wine" became a combination of two words whose conjunction is possible only in poetry.

No less significant are the difficulties posed to cinematography by the invention of the sound track. We know that such masters as Chaplin strongly disapproved of sound in the cinema. In an attempt to "conquer" sound, Chaplin, in "City Lights," delivered a speech by an orator, during the unveiling of a statue of "Prosperity," with unnatural speed, subordinating the timbre of his speech not to the automatism of the reproduced object, but to his own artistic intent (his speech turns into chirping). In "Modern Times" he performed a song in an invented "nonesuch" language. It was a mixture of words from English, German, French, Italian and Yiddish. As early as 1928 the Soviet directors Eisenstein, Alexandrov and Pudovkin put forth an even more basic program. They pro pounded the thesis that the combination of visual and auditory images must be, not automatic, but artistically motivated, and that the motivation is revealed by the use of *displacement.* The method indicated by the Soviet directors turned out to be the most acceptable one, both in correlation of depiction and sound, and of photography and the word. When Wajda, in "Ashes and Diamonds" transmits to the audience the words of a banquet orator, the camera has already left the hall where the celebration is taking place, and we see on the screen a public toilet where an old female custodian is awaiting the arrival of the first drunks. In "Hiroshima Mon Amour" the French heroine tells her Japanese lover about her long days of solitude in a cellar where her parents had once hidden her from the rage of their fellow citizens who were persecuting her for loving a German soldier. Her only visitor in the cellar is a cat. When the cat is discussed it does not appear on the screen. Its eyes will glow in the dark later on, when the girl's story has gone far beyond the incident. Technology made possible the strict synchronization of sound and depiction and gave art the choice of observing or violating this synchrony, i.e., made synchronization a *carrier of information*. Thus we are not discussing the mandatory deformation of natural forms of an object (focus on constant deformation usually reflects the immaturity of an artistic device), but rather the *possibility* of deformation, and hence of the conscious choice of artistic solution in the event of its absence.

Actually, the entire history of the cinema as an art is a sequence of discoveries whose aim has been to drive out automatism from every element which can be subjected to artistic scrutiny. The cinema conquered motion photography, making it an active means of knowing reality. The world which it presents is simultaneously the object itself and a model of the object.

The remainder of this work will be primarily devoted to a description of the means used by cinematography in its struggle with "raw" naturalness in the name of artistic truth.

We must once again emphasize, however, that in its struggles against the natural similarity of cinematography and real life, shattering the naive faith of an audience which is prepared to equate emotions caused by a film with emotions experienced while viewing real events (including the vulgar lust for strong emotional shocks from genuinely tragic sights), the cinema at the same time endeavors to preserve a naive (perhaps too naive, at times) faith in its genuineness. The inexperienced viewer who does not know the difference between an artistic film and a documentary is far from being an ideal audience, but he is a "film audience" to a greater degree than the critic who focuses only on "devices" and never for a moment forgets about the "kitchen" of the film industry.

The greater the victory of art over photography, the more necessary it is that the audience believe, with a portion of its consciousness, that it is seeing only a photograph, only real life not set up by a director, but merely observed. Encouragement of this belief has been the aim of the same directors who simultaneously constructed a cinematic world on the basis of complex ideological models—from Dziga Vertov and Eisenstein to the Italian neorealists, the French "New Wave" and Ingmar Bergman.

This aim is also furthered by the inclusion, in artistic films, of segments of genuine documentaries from the war years. In Bergman's "Persona" the heroine is watching a television set which shows the self-immolation of a demonstrator. At first we are shown only reflections from the screen on the heroine's face and her expression of horror—we are in the world of acting in cinema. But then the television screen occupies the entire movie screen. We know that the television takes us out of the world of actors, and we become witnesses to a real tragedy which goes on for a painfully long time. By juxtaposing real life and cinema life Bergman underscored the artistic conventionality of the world he depicts and—art is able to do so—at the same time made us forget about the conventionality. The world of the film heroine and the world of the television set are one world, a genuine, interrelated world. The authors of "Paisan" achieved the same effect when they filmed a genuine corpse in an episode about the liberation of Italy.

Strangely enough, the struggle to inspire confidence in the screen involves numerous plots concerning the creation of a film, of cinema within cinema. Enhancing the feeling of conventionality (a "sense of cinema" in the audience), works of this type appear to concentrate cinematic conventionality in episodes depicting a screen on a screen: we are forced to perceive the remainder as genuine life.

This dual relationship to reality creates that semantic tension in whose field the cinema as art holds forth. Pushkin defined the formula of aesthetic experience with the words: "I shed tears over an imaginary event."

Here, with the precision of genius, we are shown the dual nature of the viewer's or reader's relation to the artistic text. He "sheds tears," i.e., he believes in the genuineness, the actuality of the text. The sight arouses in him the same emotions as life itself. But at the same time he remembers that it is an "imaginary event." Crying over a fancy is a blatant contradiction since, it would appear, we need only know that an event is fictitious for the desire to experience an emotion to vanish entirely. If the audience did not forget that a stage or screen was before it, if it continuously thought about actors wearing makeup and about directors' intentions, it is natural that it would not be moved to tears or experience other emotions connected with real-life situations. But if the viewer did not distinguish stage and screen from real life and, weeping copiously, forgot that before him was an invention, he would not be experiencing genuinely artistic emotions. Art requires a *two-fold* experience—simultaneously forgetting that you are confronted by an imaginary event and not forgetting it. Only in art can we both be horrified by the evil of an event and appreciate the mastery of the actor.

The duality of perception of a work of art[2] leads to the fact that the greater the similarity or direct resemblance of art and life, the more strongly, at the same time, must the audience feel the conventionality. *Almost* forgetting that he is experiencing a work of art, the viewer or reader must never forget it *completely*. Art is a living phenomenon and dialectically contradictory. And this requires equal effectiveness and equal value of the opposing tendencies which comprise it. The history of cinematography provides numerous examples of this principle.

At the dawn of cinematography moving images on the screen aroused a physiological feeling of horror in the audience (shots of an onrushing train) or physical nausea (shots taken from a great height or with a swaying camera). The audience did not distinguish, emotionally, between the image and reality. But cinematic depiction became an art only when the combined exposures of Méliès made it possible to augment extreme verisimilitude with extreme fantasy on the plot level, and montage made it possible to demonstrate the artificiality of shot groupings. (The actual invention of montage is at-

---

[2]For a more detailed account cf.: Ju. M. Totman, Tezisy k probleme "Iskusstvo v rjadu modelirujuščix sistem" /On the problem of "Art as a Modelling System"/. *Trudy po znakovym sistemam* III. Učenye zapiski Tartuskogo gosudarstvennogo universiteta, vyp. 198, Tartu, 1967, str. 130–145.

tributed by scholars to the Brighton school or to Griffith, but its theoretical significance was only discovered through the experiments and investigations of L. Kulesöv, S. Eisenstein, Ju Tynjanov, V. Šklovskij and a number of other Soviet cinematographers and scholars in the 1920's.)

Moreover, the very concept of "likeness" which seems so immediate and axiomatic to the audience is, in actuality, a fact of culture derived from previous artistic experience and from certain types of artistic codes employed at a particular time in history. Thus, for example, the real world which surrounds us is made up of many colors. Therefore its depiction in black and white is a convention. Only a knowledge of this convention and an acceptance of the rules for decoding a text employing it make it possible, when looking at the sky in a shot, to accept it without any difficulty as cloudless and blue. In a shot of a sunny summer day we perceive various shades of gray as signs of the colors blue and green, and correctly establish their equivalence to particular color referents (designated objects).

When color film was introduced the audience began, automatically, to associate color shots not only with multicolored reality, but also with the tradition of "naturalness" in cinematography. Actually, the more conventional black and white film, for certain traditional reasons, is perceived as the original, natural form. Ivor Montagu recalls a striking fact: "When Peter Ustinov was asked on television why he made 'Billy Budd' in black and white and not in colour he replied that he did so because he wanted it to seem real." Montagu's comment is also interesting: "This was a strange reply, but stranger still was it that nobody seemed to find anything strange in it."[3] As we see, the latter fact is not strange, but entirely fitting.

It is instructive that in contemporary films employing a montage of colored and black and white segments, the former, as a rule, are connected with plot narration, i.e., "art," and the latter refer to a reality beyond the screen. Typical in this respect is the deliberate complication of such a correlation in Wajda's film "Everything for Sale." The film is based on the

---

[3] Ivor Montagu: *Film World*, Baltimore, 1964, p. 113.

continual confusion of levels. The same shot may refer to reality outside the screen and to the plot of an artistic film about this reality. The audience is not permitted to know in advance just what it is seeing: a portion of reality accidentally captured by the camera lens, or a segment of film about this reality— considered and constructed according to the laws of art. The displacement of one and the same shot from the level of object to a metalevel (shot about a shot) creates a complex semiotic situation whose meaning lies in the attempt to confuse the viewer and force him to experience with maximum intensity the "falseness" of everything, to long for simple and genuine things and simple and genuine relationships and values which are not signs of anything. And then, into this unstable world, where even death is made ambiguous, there bursts simple, "unrehearsed" life—the funeral of an actor. This segment, in contrast to colored shots of both levels—events in life as well as their filmic depiction—is shown in two-color tones. This is real life, not reproduced by the director, but witnessed by the camera, a genuine piece in which everyone is taken aback and is therefore sincere. But here, too, the interrelationships grow complicated. The camera retreats, and what we thought was a slice of life turns out to be cinematography within cinematography. The edges of the screen are revealed and we see a room and in it are the same people who were on the screen, and they are discussing how to transform the events into an artistic film. The opposition seems to have vanished. Everything has turned out to be a game, and the opposition "color film— black and white film" has lost its meaning. But this is not true. Even when introduced as cinema within cinema, the two tone film is a documentary and not an acted film. Against the background of intermingled acting and life-acting, it serves the function of plain reality. Important, too, is the fact that in just this segment a person outside the cinema-world, a viewer, mentions that the dead artist was a legend, a myth during his lifetime, and how could such a person have existed? Precisely this statement (together with the speaker's face) becomes that extra-textual reality to which the entire complex cinematic text is equivalent, i.e., the *meaning* of the film. Without it the film would remain somewhere between a

66

laboratory experiment on cinema semiotics and a sensational exposé of the secrets and personal life of movie stars in the manner of "Private Life" by Louis Malle.

In this respect it is of some interest to consider the treatment found in "Andrej Rublev" by A. Tarkovskij. He presents us with an original artistic construct which we perceive as simultaneously unexpected and natural. The sphere of "life" is shown in black and white, which we assume to be a neutral cinematographic approach. And then at the end the audience is suddenly shown some frescoes which are done in a marvelous wealth of colors. This not only forces us to experience the ending very intensely, but also returns us to the rest of the film, providing an alternative to the black and white treatment and thereby emphasizing its significance.

Thus the attempts of cinematography to merge completely with life, and the desire to manifest its cinematographic specifics, the conventionality of its language, to assert the sovereignty of art within its own sphere—these are enemies which are constantly in need of each other. Like the north and south poles of a magnet, they do not exist without each other and form that field of structural tension in which the real history of cinematography operates. The disagreements between Dziga Vertov and Sergej Eisenstein, the argument over "prosaic" and "poetic" cinema in Soviet cinematography of the 1920's and 1930's, the polemics surrounding Italian neorealism, the articles by A. Bazin on the conflict between montage and "faith in reality" which formed the basis of the French "new wave," again and again reaffirm the regularity of the sinusoidal movement of real cinematic art within the field of structural tension created by these two poles. In this context it is interesting to note the manner in which Italian neorealism, in its struggles against theoretical pomposity, arrived at the total equation of art and extrartistic reality. Its active elements were always "refusals": refusal to use a stereotyped hero or typical film scenes, refusal to use professional actors, denial of the "star" system, refusal to employ montage and an "ironclad" scenario, refusal to use a "prepared" dialog or musical accompaniment. Such a poetics of "refusals" can only be effective against a remembered background of cinema art of the opposite type. Without

cinematography of historical epics, film operas, westerns or
Hollywood "stars" it loses a good deal of its artistic meaning.
The non-artistic role of a "scream of truth," of truth at any
cost, truth as a condition of life and not a means for attaining
some transitory goals, all this could be accomplished by
neorealism only to the extent that its language was perceived
by the audience as merciless and uncompromising. It is thus
all the more significant that, having reached the apogee of "refusals" and having asserted its conquest, neorealism made an
abrupt turnabout in the direction of restoration of shattered
conventionality. Fellini's attempts at a "metafilm," a film
about a film, analyzing the very conception of truth ("8½"),
Germi's attempt to merge the language of film acting and the
national tradition of the *commedia dell' arte*, both are profoundly instructive. Particularly interesting is the progress of
Luchino Visconti, just because in his work the theoretician has
always dominated the artist. In 1948 Visconti created the film
"La Terra Trema"—one of the most consistent realizations of
the poetics of neorealism. In this film we have everything:
from Sicilian dialect, incomprehensible even to the Italian audience but demonstratively used by the director without translation (better incomprehensible but evoking the absolute reliability of documentary authenticity, than a film which is
comprehensible but suspected of "artiness") to the choice of
types, plot, structure of cinema narration—in short, a protest
against the "artificiality of art." But by 1953 he made the film
"Senso": not entirely acceptable in its resolutions, but exceedingly interesting in its intentions. The action is set in 1866, in
the time of the uprising in Venice and the Italo-Prussian war.
The film opens with the music of Verdi. The camera focuses on
the stage of a theater in which the opera "Il Trovatore" is in
progress. The nationalistic, heroic aura of Verdi's music is bla-
tantly used as a system within which the plot and personalities of the heroes are encoded. Taken out of context the film
strikes us by its theatricality, its openly operatic dramatics
(love, jealousy, betrayal and death come one after the other),
by the frank primitivism of the stage effects and the archaic
nature of the director's approach. But in the context of the
overall movement of art, paired with "La Terra Trema," it

acquires a different meaning. The art of naked truth, trying to rid itself of all existing kinds of artistic conventionality, requires an immense culture in order to be perceived as such. Being democratic in its ideals, it becomes too intellectual in its language. The untrained audience becomes bored. The struggle against boredom leads to the reestablishment of the rights of language which is consciously primitive and traditional, but close to the audience. In Italy the *commedia dell' arte* and the opera are art forms whose traditional system of conventions is comprehensible and close to the mass audience. And cinematography which had approached the brink of naturalness had to revert to the conventional primitivism of those artistic languages which had been familiar to the audience since childhood.

The films of Germi ("Seduced and Abandoned" and especially "Divorce Italian Style") shock the audience with their merciless "cynicism." But we need only recall the language of the puppet theaters and the *commedia dell' arte* in which death can be a comic episode, murder—a buffonade, suffering—a parody. The unpitying nature of Italian (and not only Italian) folk theater is organically connected with its conventionality. The audience remembers that these are puppets or maskers on the stage and perceives their death or suffering, beatings or misfortunes, not as the death or suffering of real people, but in a spirit of carnival and ritual. Germi's films would be unbearably cynical if he invited us to see real people in his characters. But, by translating content which is normal in the social protest and humanism of neorealistic cinema into the language of buffonade, he suggests that we see the heroes as carnival clowns and puppets. The plebeian, coarse, country-fair language of his films contains just as many possibilities for social criticism as does the style, more familiar to the intellectual audience, of the humanized actor and humanized stage which dates back to European ideas of the Enlightenment. If Leoncavallo in "I Pagliacci" translated country-fair buffoonery into the language of humanistic ideas, Germi did the opposite; using the language of the folk theater he talks about serious problems of the present.

Visconti chose the direction of another national, democratic tradition—the opera. Only with respect to this tradition and to the artistic language of "La Terra Trema" can the intent of the author of "Senso" be comprehended.

Thus the feeling of actuality, the sense of resemblance to life without which there can be no art of the cinema, is not something elementary, provided by direct sense perception. Being a component part of a complex, artistic whole, it is facilitated by numerous ties with the artistic and cultural experience of society.

1973

II
Film Image and Film Language

The art of music did not arise as soon as man learned how to create pleasing sounds. It was necessary to arrange those sounds into scales, to organize them into harmonic systems, and to devise appropriate musical forms for them. Similarly, the art of poetry required more than the mere existence of a list of words. These words had to be arranged according to rules of grammar and organized into intelligible literary structures. When the poet writes an epic, his words must be capable of telling a story, and when he writes a sonnet, they must fall into specific rhyme schemes and structural patterns.

The great Soviet filmmakers, Sergei Eisenstein and Vsevolod Pudovkin, thought about the art of the cinema in a similar way. This art required more than the mere ability to make moving pictures of reality, and, therefore, it required more than the discovery of photography. But what more? What is it that transformed a new technical ability into a great new art? The answer was montage, the art of combining pieces of film or shots (film's "sounds" or "words") into larger units—first, the scene, then, the sequence, and, finally, the complete film. D. W. Griffith, the great American director of *The Birth of a Nation* and *Intolerance,* to whom the Soviet directors acknowledged a great debt, was not important because he took better pictures than anybody else. He was important for having discovered montage, the fluid integration of the camera's total range of shots, from extreme close-up to distant panorama, so as to produce the most coherent narrative sequence, the most systematic meaning, and most effective rhythmic pattern. In doing so, Griffith had, they thought, contributed to the development of a cinematic language and invented the distinctive art of the film.

The career of Sergei M. Eisenstein, the most brilliant figure in Soviet cinema, began as a stage director. The youthful Eisenstein then made four films in five years: *Strike* (1924), *Potemkin* (1925), *October* (1927), and *Old and New* (1928). In the 1930s and 1940s (until his death in 1948) Eisenstein worked primarily as a theorist and teacher, completing only *Alexander Nevsky* and *Ivan the Terrible, Parts I and II*. Eisenstein's conversion from an artist to a theorist is to be explained in part by political realities, for his emphasis on cinematic "form" was uncongenial to his government's official aesthetics. But it is equally true that his conception of montage did not easily accommodate itself to the use of synchronized dialogue and, therefore, to the kind of film which prevailed in the 1930s.

Eisenstein viewed montage as a kind of collision or conflict, especially between a shot and its successor. He sees each shot as having a kind of potential energy—in purely visual terms of its direction of movement, its volumes of shapes, its intensity of light, and so forth. This potential energy becomes kinetic when the first shot collides with the succeeding one. The two shots can produce a conflict in their emotional content (happy versus sad), in their use of light (dark versus light), in their rhythms (slow versus fast), in their objects (large versus small), in their directions of movement (right versus left), in their distances (close-up versus far shot) or in any combination thereof. In his films, this conflict produced the tense, violent rhythms that became an Eisenstein trademark. Conflict was also important to Eisenstein because he took it to be an expression, in the realm of images, of the Marxist's dialectical principle. Indeed, Eisenstein maintained that just as the meaning of a sentence arises from the interaction of its individual words, cinematic meaning is the result of the dialectical interplay of shots. His emphasis on the conflict of shots, as distinct from a mere linking of shots, distinguishes his conception from that of his colleague, Pudovkin. Pudovkin's view of montage as a method of building, of adding one thing to another, is not merely of theoretical interest. His theory pro-

72

duced his more realistic narratives (*Mother, Storm over Asia*), with their more deliberate, calmer pace.

Eisenstein, like most of the "first" generation theorists, was uncomfortable with the addition of synchronized dialogue. Because "silent" films had always used asynchronous sound effects and music, Eisenstein believed that the sound film could use these tools with even greater precision and complexity. But he positively rejected dialogue as being incompatible with the proper use of montage. By contrast André Bazin, a theorist of the "second" generation, while assenting to the incompatibility of dialogue and montage, regards synchronized speech as a necessary and proper development. For Bazin, dialogue returns film to the rightful path from which montage and silence diverted it. According to him, the film image ought to reveal nature whole, not present reality by cutting it into tiny bits. The cinematic methods Bazin endorses, which combines composing with the camera and staging an action in front of it, has, like montage, come to be known by a French term, mise-en-scène.

In Bazin's view the montage theorists did not in fact speak for all of the silent film, and he discerns in the work of von Stroheim, Murnau, and Flaherty an alternative, mise-en-scène tradition. Bazin sees this tradition as emphasizing not the ordering, but the content of images. The film's effect and meaning is not the product of a juxtaposition of images, but is inherent in the visual images themselves. For Bazin, the montage theorists' emphasis on the analogy between word and shot is false, and he rejects it along with their reluctance to employ sound as a source of cinematic meaning. Bazin argues that the mise-en-scène tradition within silent film actually looked toward the incorporation of synchronous sound as a fulfillment, not as a violation, of the film's destiny.

In the 1930s and 1940s Bazin sees German expressionism and Russian symbolism as having been superseded by a form of editing more appropriate to the dialogue film. This "analytic" editing, which characteristically manifests itself in the dramatic technique of shot and reverse-shot, was an important innovation. Still more important, however, was the development of the shot-in-depth by Orson Welles and William Wyler in the early 1940s (anticipated in the 1930s by Jean Renoir), which made even the use of "analytic" montage unnecessary. Entire scenes could now be covered in one take, the camera remaining motionless. For Bazin, the shot-in-depth, like the use of synchronous sound, constituted a crucial advance toward total cinema.

Charles Barr, a contemporary English critic sympathetic to Bazin's ideas, defends the development of CinemaScope against those who reject it as a desecration of cinematic art. He notes the similarity of the attacks on the wide screen to those earlier attacks on synchronized sound, and he believes that both attacks are corollaries of the assumptions of the montage theorists. Barr therefore expands Bazin's attacks on montage theory, questioning even more vigorously the alleged analogy between word and shot. He also disputes Eisenstein's claim that associative montage gives a viewer the freedom to participate actively in the aesthetic experience. Barr finds it no accident that the rhetorical and coercive montage of Einstein, admittedly designed to serve propagandistic purposes, can now most frequently be found in television commercials. Barr in effect brings Bazin into the 1960s by viewing the wide screen as a refinement of the shot-in-depth method that Bazin endorsed and an advance in the representation of "nature whole" that "total" cinema seeks.

A very important new direction in contemporary film theory has arisen from this parallel concern with the way an image is understood and the way a sequence of such images might constitute a kind of "language." Christian Metz, a contemporary French theorist who was also influenced by André Bazin, believes that cinema is indeed a kind of language, although its signifying processes must be carefully distinguished from those of verbal languages. Using the linguistic science as a model, Metz's goal is to discover and establish the semiotics of the cinema—a theory of cinema as a system of signs. Many contemporary film theorists wish to put film theory and criticism on a firmer scientific basis. To consider film as a semiological system would permit film study—which suffers (in the opinion of many besides semiologists) from impressionism, subjectivity, and vagueness—to attain a scientific precision and rigor.

Metz believes that the concept of a "code," of encoded signs

74

whose meanings we have learned to translate, is central to the development of a theory of film language. In the beginning, film was purely iconic—it signified exclusively by means of the resemblance of its imagery to objects in the visible world. But the development of narrative techniques required the development of various codes to denote the narrative progression. These rules and conventions, which were more or less complete by the time of D. W. Griffith, constitute the essence of film language and permit us to explain the procedures by which cinema denotes such narrative phenomena as successivity, priority, temporal breaks, and spatial continuity. As he shows in his analysis of what he calls the alternating *syntagma*, the order in which the signifying images occur may or may not be the same as that in which the realities they signify occur. The student of the language of cinema must therefore account for the processes and mechanisms which make it possible for the viewer to interpret them correctly. For Metz, the film does not simply reveal reality; it describes it in a language whose features we are only beginning to understand.

In his explication and critique of Metz, Alfred Guzzetti, an American critic, theorist, and filmmaker, explains Metz's central distinctions—between *langue* and language, code and message, syntagm and paradigm. At the same time, Guzzetti questions the alleged scientific neutrality of Metz's reliance on narrative film—and a particular type of narrative film—to develop his theory: Metz's dependence on the "classical Hollywood mode" of film narration. Guzzetti shows that such a model (derived from Bazin's notions of film realism) not only guarantees certain kinds of questions (and, therefore, answers) but also fails to describe any of the modernist experiments with film narrative of the last twenty years.

More generally, Guzzetti criticizes Metz's theory for arbitrarily differentiating between cinematic codes (those signifying processes which are unique to cinema) and filmic codes (those signs which function in cinema but also exist elsewhere in a culture or in nature). For Guzzetti, all signs in a film have been "cinematified," have acquired unique cinematic meaning; our relation to a sign in cinema is not the same as it would be to the same object outside the theater, for our response to it (and, therefore, perception of it) has been determined by both its precise cinematic context and the general fact that we have no responsibility in responding to such a sign except as viewers of cinema.

The kind of problems raised by Metz also lead Umberto Eco, the influential Italian semiologist and critic, to the Peircian theory of signs, rather than Saussure's linguistics, for his model in developing a contrasting theory of semiotics. According to the Peircian system, a sign can relate to what it signifies in three ways: as an icon (the sign resembles the signified, as a picture of a dog resembles a dog), as an index (the significance of the sign depends on a real connection between the sign and what it signifies, as when the footprint of a dog signifies a dog), or as a symbol (the sign bears a purely arbitrary or conventional relationship to the signified, as the sign "dog" does to the animal it signifies). Like Guzzetti, and unlike Metz, Eco insists that iconic resemblances of the film image to real objects cannot be exempt from further analysis. Iconic signs are governed by codes and conventions; the semiologist must analyze these if he wishes to understand how film communicates and if he wants to further the Marxist project of demonstrating that there is no such thing as a "spontaneous" or "natural" reproduction of reality. Eco believes that all representation can be shown to reveal "plots of culture." For this reason, Eco would not be content with Metz's decision to examine only the denotative signifying processes of cinema; to eliminate the semiotic study of connotation would both impoverish the potential richness of the semiotic undertaking and would leave the most complex methods of film manipulation unexamined.

The American philosopher and linguist, Gilbert Harman, in his essay on Metz and Peter Wollen, as well as in his brief reply to Eco, raises many questions about the entire semiotic approach to film study. He questions the widespread assumption that signs are necessarily used for communication, and he demonstrates the ambiguities and equivocations in the use of the central term, "code," upon which the semiotic claim to systematic rigor exists. Harman suggests, in the end, that semiotics as we know it is not a science and has very little to contribute to the practice of film criticism.

VSEVOLOD PUDOVKIN
FROM FILM TECHNIQUE

[ON EDITING]

METHODS OF TREATMENT OF THE MATERIAL
(Structural Editing)

A cinematograph film, and consequently also a scenario, is always divided into a great number of separate pieces (more correctly, it is built out of these pieces). The sum of the shooting-script is divided into sequences, each sequence into scenes, and, finally, the scenes themselves are constructed from a whole series of pieces (script-scenes) shot from various angles. An actual scenario, ready for use in shooting, must take into account this basic property of the film. The scenarist must be able to write his material on paper exactly as it will appear upon the screen, thus giving exactly the content of each shot as well as its position in sequence. The construction of a scene from pieces, a sequence from scenes, and reel from sequences, and so forth, is called *editing*. Editing is one of the most significant instruments of effect possessed by the film technician and, therefore, by the scenarist also. Let us now become acquainted with its methods one by one.

Editing of the Scene

Everyone familiar with a film is familiar with the expression "close-up." The alternating representation of the faces of the characters during a dialogue; the representation of hands, or feet, filling the whole screen—all this is familiar to everyone. But in order to know how properly to use the close-up, one must understand its significance, which is as follows: the close-up directs the attention of the spectator to that detail which is, at the moment, important to the course of the action. For instance, three persons are taking part in a scene. Suppose the significance of this scene consist in the *general* course of the action (if, for example, all three are lifting some heavy object), then they are taken simultaneously in a *general* view, the so-called long-shot. But suppose any one of them change to an independent action having significance in the scenario (for example, separating himself from the others, he draws a revolver cautiously from his pocket), then the camera is directed on him alone. His action is recorded separately.

What is said above applies not only to persons, but also to separate parts of a person, and objects. Let us suppose a man is to be taken apparently listening calmly to the conversation of someone else, but actually restraining his anger with difficulty. The man crushes the cigarette he holds in his hand, a gesture unnoticed by the other. This hand will always be shown on the screen separately, in close-up, otherwise the spectator will not notice it and a characteristic detail will be missed. The view formerly obtained (and is still held by some) that the close-up is an "interruption" of the long-shot. This idea is entirely false. It is no sort of interruption. It represents a proper form of construction.

In order to make clear to oneself the nature of the process of editing a scene, one may draw the following analogy. Imagine yourself observing a scene unfolded in front of you, thus: a man stands near the wall of a house and turns his head to the left; there appears another man slinking cautiously through the gate. The two are fairly widely distant from one another—they stop. The first takes some object and shows it to the other, mocking him. The latter clenches his fists in a rage and throws himself at the former. At this moment a woman looks out of a window on the third floor and calls, "Police!" The antagonists run off in opposite directions. Now, how would this have been observed?

1. The observer looks at the first man. He turns his head.

2. What is he looking at? The observer turns his glance in the same direction and sees the man entering the gate. The latter stops.

3. How does the first react to the appearance on the scene of the second? A new turn by the observer; the first takes out an object and mocks the second.

4. How does the second react? Another turn; he clenches his fists and throws himself on his opponent.

5. The observer draws aside to watch how both opponents roll about fighting.

6. A shout from above. The observer raises his head and sees the woman shouting at the window.

7. The observer lowers his head and sees the result of her warning—the antagonists running off in opposite directions.

The observer happened to be standing near and saw every detail, saw it clearly, but to do so he had to turn his head, first left, then right, then upwards, whithersoever his attention was attracted by the interest of observation and the sequence of the developing scene. Suppose he had been standing farther away from the action, taking in the two persons and the window on the third floor simultaneously, he would have received only a general impression, without being able to look separately at the first, the second, or the woman. Here we have approached closely the basic significance of editing. Its object is the showing of the development of the scene in relief, as it were, by guiding the attention of the spectator now to one, now to the other separate 'element. The lens of the camera replaces the eye of the observer, and the changes of angle of the camera—directed now on one person, now on another, now on one detail, now on another—must be subject to the same conditions as those of the eyes of the observer. The film technician, in order to secure the greatest clarity, emphasis, and vividness, shoots the scene in separate pieces and, joining them and showing them, directs the attention of the spectator to the separate elements, compelling him to see as the attentive observer saw. From the above is clear the manner in which editing can even work upon the emotions. Imagine to yourself the excited observer of some rapidly developing scene. His agitated glance is thrown rapidly from one spot to another. If we imitate this glance with the camera we get a series of pictures, rapidly alternating pieces, creating a *stirring scenario editing-construction*. The reverse would be long pieces changing by mixes, conditioning a calm and slow editing-construction (as one may shoot, for example, a herd of cattle wandering along a road, taken from the viewpoint of a pedestrian on the same road).

We have established, by these instances, the basic significance of the constructive editing of scenes. It builds the scenes from separate pieces, of which each concentrates the attention of the spectator only on that element important to the action. The sequence of these pieces must not be uncontrolled, but must correspond to the natural transference of attention of an imaginary observer (who, in the end, is represented by the spectator). In this sequence must be expressed a special logic that will be apparent only if each shot contain an impulse towards transference of the attention to the next. For example (1) A man turns his head and looks; (2) What he looks at is shown.

Editing of the Sequence

The guidance of the attention of the spectator to different elements of the developing action in succession is, in general, characteristic of the film. It is its basic method. We have seen that the separate scene, and often even the movement of one man, is built up upon the screen from separate pieces. Now, the film is not simply a collection of different scenes. Just as the pieces are built up into scenes endowed, as it were, with a connected action, so the separate scenes are assembled into groups forming whole sequences. The sequence is constructed (edited) from scenes. Let us suppose ourselves faced with the task of constructing the following sequence: two spies are creeping forward to blow up a powder magazine; on the way one of them loses a letter with instructions. Someone else finds the letter and warns the guard, who appears in time to arrest the spies and save the magazine. Here the scenarist has to deal with simultaneity of various actions in several different places. While the spies are crawling towards the magazine, someone else finds the letter and hastens to warn the guard. The spies have nearly reached their objective; the guards are warned and rushing towards the magazine. The spies have completed their preparations; the guard arrives in time. If we pursue the previous analogy between the camera and an observer, we now not only have to turn it from side to side, but also to move it from place to place. The observer (the camera) is now on the road shadowing the spies, now in the guardroom recording the confusion, now back at the magazine showing the spies at work, and so forth. But, in combination of the separate scenes (editing), the former law of sequence succession remains in force. A consecutive sequence will appear upon the screen only if the attention of the spectator be transferred correctly from scene to scene. And this correctness is conditioned as follows: the spectator sees the creeping spies, the loss of the letter, and finally the person who finds the letter. The person with the letter rushes for help. The spectator is seized with inevitable excitement—Will the man who found the letter be able to forestall the explosion? The scenarist immediately answers by showing the spies nearing the magazine—his answer has the effect of a warning "Time is short." The excitement of the spectator—Will they be in time?—continues; the scenarist shows the guard turning out. Time is very short—the spies are shown beginning their work. Thus, transferring attention now to the rescuers, now to the spies, the scenarist answers with actual impulses to increase of the spectator's interest, and the construction (editing) of the sequence is correctly achieved.

There is a law in psychology that lays it down that if an emotion give birth to a certain movement, by imitation of this movement the corresponding emotion can be called forth. If the scenarist can effect in even rhythm the transference of interest of the intent spectator, if he can so construct the elements of increasing interest that the question, "What is happening at the other place?" arises and at the same moment the spectator is transferred whither he wishes to go, then the editing thus created can really excite the spectator. One must learn to understand that editing is in actual fact a compulsory and deliberate guidance of the thoughts and associations of the spectator. If the editing be merely an uncontrolled combination of the various pieces, the spectator will understand (apprehend) nothing from it; but if it be co-ordinated according to a definitely selected course of events or conceptual line, either agitated or calm, it will either excite or soothe the spectator.

Editing of the Scenario

The film is divided into reels. The reels are usually equal in length, on an average from 900 to 1,200 feet long. The combination of the reels forms the picture. The usual length of a picture should not be more than from 6,500 to 7,500 feet. This length, as yet, involves no unnecessary exhaustion of the spectator. The film is usually divided into from six to eight reels. It should be noted here, as a practical hint, that the average length of a piece (remember the editing of scenes) is from 6 to 10 feet, and consequently from

100 to 150 pieces go to a reel. By orientating himself on these figures, the scenarist can visualise how much material can be fitted into the scenario. The scenario is composed of a series of sequences. In discussing the construction (editing) of the scenario from sequences, we introduce a new element into the scenarist's work—the element of so-called dramatic continuity of action that was discussed at the beginning of this sketch. The continuity of the separate sequences when joined together depends not merely upon the simple transference of attention from one place to another, but is conditioned by the development of the action forming the foundation of the scenario. It is important, however, to remind the scenarist of the following point: a scenario has always in its development a moment of greatest tension, found nearly always at the end of the film. To prepare the spectator, or, more correctly, preserve him, for this final tension, it is especially important to see that he is not affected by unnecessary exhaustion during the course of the film. A method . . . that the scenarist can employ to this end is the careful distribution of the titles (which always distract the spectator), securing compression of the greater quantity of them into the first reels, and leaving the last one for uninterrupted action.

Thus, first is worked out the action of the scenario, the action is then worked out into sequences, the sequences into scenes, and these constructed by editing from the pieces, each corresponding to a camera angle.

EDITING AS AN INSTRUMENT OF IMPRESSION

(Relational Editing)

We have already mentioned, in the section on editing of sequences, that editing is not merely a method of the junction of separate scenes or pieces, but is a method that controls the "psychological guidance" of the spectator. We should now acquaint ourselves with the main special editing methods having as their aim the impression of the spectator.

Contrast.—Suppose it be our task to tell of the miserable situation of a starving man; the story will impress the more vividly if associated with mention of the senseless gluttony of a well-to-do man.

On just such a simple contrast relation is based the corresponding editing method. On the screen the impression of this contrast is yet increased, for it is possible not only to relate the starving sequence to the gluttony sequence, but also to relate separate scenes and even separate shots of the scenes to one another, thus, as it were, forcing the spectator to compare the two actions all the time, one strengthening the other. The editing of contrast is one of the most effective, but also one of the commonest and most standardised, of methods, and so care should be taken not to overdo it.

Parallelism.—This method resembles contrast, but is considerably wider. Its substance can be explained more clearly by an example. In a scenario as yet unproduced a section occurs as follows: a working man, one of the leaders of a strike, is condemned to death; the execution is fixed for 5 a.m. The sequence is edited thus: a factory-owner, employer of the condemned man, is leaving a restaurant drunk, he looks at his wrist-watch: 4 o'clock. The accused is shown—he is being made ready to be led out. Again the manufacturer, he rings a door-bell to ask the time: 4.30. The prison waggon drives along the street under heavy guard. The maid who opens the door—the wife of the condemned—is subjected to a sudden senseless assault. The drunken factory-owner snores on a bed, his leg with trouser-end upturned, his hand hanging down with wrist-watch visible, the hands of the watch crawl slowly to 5 o'clock. The workman is being hanged. In this instance two thematically unconnected incidents develop in parallel by means of the watch that tells of the approaching execution. The watch on the wrist of the callous brute, as it were connects him with the chief protagonist of the approaching tragic *dénouement*, thus ever present in the consciousness of the spectator. This is undoubtedly an interesting method, capable of considerable development.

Symbolism.—In the final scenes of the film *Strike* the shooting down of workmen is punctuated by shots of the slaughter of a bull in a stockyard. The scenarist, as it were, desires to say: just as a butcher fells a bull with the swing of a pole-axe, so, cruelly and in cold blood, were shot down the workers. This method is especially interesting because, by means of editing, it introduces an abstract concept into the consciousness of the spectator without use of a title.

Simultaneity.—In American films the final section is constructed from the simultaneous rapid development of two actions, in which the outcome of one depends on the outcome of the other. The end of the present-day section of *Intolerance* . . . is thus constructed. The whole aim of this method is to create in the spectator a maximum tension of excitement by the constant forcing of a question, such as, in this case: Will they be in time?—will they be in time?

The method is a purely emotional one, and nowadays overdone almost to the point of boredom, but it cannot be denied that of all the methods of constructing the end hitherto devised it is the most effective.

Leit-motif (reiteration of theme).—Often it is interesting for the scenarist especially to emphasise the basic theme of the scenario. For this purpose exists the method of reiteration. Its nature can easily be demonstrated by an example. In an anti-religious scenario that aimed at exposing the cruelty and hypocrisy of the Church in employ of the Tsarist régime the same shot was several times repeated: a church-bell slowly ringing and, superimposed on it, the title: "The sound of bells sends into the world a message of patience and love." This piece appeared whenever the scenarist desired to emphasise the stupidity of patience, or the hypocrisy of the love thus preached.

The little that has been said above of relational editing naturally by no means exhausts the whole abundance of its methods. It has merely been important to show that constructional editing, a method specifically and peculiarly filmic, is, in the hands of the scenarist, an important instrument of impression. Careful study of its use in pictures, combined with talent, will undoubtedly lead to the discovery of new possibilities and, in conjunction with them, to the creation of new forms.

1926

SERGEI EISENSTEIN
FROM FILM FORM

THE CINEMATOGRAPHIC
PRINCIPLE AND THE IDEOGRAM

It is a weird and wonderful feat to have written a pamphlet
on something that in reality does not exist. There is, for example, no such thing as a cinema without cinematography.
And yet the author of the pamphlet preceding this essay* has
contrived to write a book about the *cinema* of a country that
has no *cinematography*. About the cinema of a country that
has, in its culture, an infinite number of cinematographic
traits, strewn everywhere with the sole exception of—its cinema.

This essay is on the cinematographic traits of Japanese culture that lie outside the Japanese cinema, and is itself as apart
from the preceding pamphlet as these traits are apart from the
Japanese cinema.

Cinema is: so many corporations, such and such turnovers
of capital, so and so many stars, such and such dramas.

Cinematography is, first and foremost, montage.

The Japanese cinema is excellently equipped with corporations, actors, and stories. But the Japanese cinema is completely unaware of montage. Nevertheless the principle of
montage can be identified as the basic element of Japanese
representational culture.

---

*Eisenstein's essay was originally published as an "afterword" to N. Kauf-
man's pamphlet, *Japanese Cinema* (Moscow, 1929).

Writing—for their writing is primarily representational.
The hieroglyph.

The naturalistic image of an object, as portrayed by the skilful Chinese hand of Ts'ang Chieh 2650 years before our era, becomes slightly formalized and, with its 539 fellows, forms the first "contingent" of hieroglyphs. Scratched out with a stylus on a slip of bamboo, the portrait of an object maintained a resemblance to its original in every respect.

But then, by the end of the third century, the brush is invented. In the first century after the "joyous event" (A.D.)—paper. And, lastly, in the year 220—India ink.

A complete upheaval. A revolution in draughtsmanship. And, after having undergone in the course of history no fewer than fourteen different styles of handwriting, the hieroglyph crystallized in its present form. The means of production (brush and India ink) determined the form.

The fourteen reforms had their way. As a result:

In the fierily cavorting hieroglyph *ma* (a horse) it is already impossible to recognize the features of the dear little horse sagging pathetically in its hindquarters, in the writing style of Ts'ang Chieh, so well-known from ancient Chinese bronzes.

But let it rest in the Lord, this dear little horse, together with the other 607 remaining *hsiang cheng* symbols—the earliest extant category of hieroglyphs.

The real interest begins with the second category of hieroglyphs—the *huei-i,* i.e., "copulative."

The point is that the copulation (perhaps we had better say, the combination) of two hieroglyphs of the simplest series is to be regarded not as their sum, but as their product, i.e., as a value of another dimension, another degree; each, separately, corresponds to an *object*, to a fact, but their combination corresponds to a *concept*. From separate hieroglyphs has been fused—the ideogram. By the combination of two "depictables" is achieved the representation of something that is graphically undepictable.

For example: the picture for water and the picture of an eye signifies "to weep"; the picture of an ear nearing the drawing of

a dog = "to listen";
a dog + a mouth = "to bark";
a mouth + a child = "to scream";
a mouth + a bird = "to sing";
a knife + a heart = "sorrow," and so on.

But this is—montage!

Yes. It is exactly what we do in the cinema, combining shots that are *depictive,* single in meaning, neutral in content—into *intellectual* contexts and series.

This is a means and method inevitable in any cinematographic exposition. And, in a condensed and purified form, the starting point for the "intellectual cinema."

For a cinema seeking a maximum laconism for the visual representation of abstract concepts.

And we hail the method of the long-lamented Ts'ang Chieh as a first step along these paths.

We have mentioned laconism. Laconism furnishes us a transition to another point. Japan possesses the most laconic form of poetry: the *haikai* (appearing at the beginning of the thirteenth century and known today as "haiku" or "hokku") and the even earlier *tanka* (mythologically assumed to have been created along with heaven and earth).

Both are little more than hieroglyphs transposed into phrases. So much so that half their quality is appraised by their calligraphy. The method of their resolution is completely analogous to the structure of the ideogram.

As the ideogram provides a means for the laconic imprint-

87

ing of an abstract concept, the same method, when transposed into literary exposition, gives rise to an identical laconism of pointed imagery.

Applied to the collision of an austere combination of symbols this method results in a dry definition of abstract concepts. The same method, expanded into the luxury of a group of already formed verbal combinations, swells into a splendor of *imagist* effect.

The concept is a bare formula; its adornment (an expansion by additional material) transforms the formula into an image—a finished form.

Exactly, though in reverse, as a primitive thought process—imagist thinking, displaced to a definite degree, becomes transformed to conceptual thinking.

But let us turn to examples.

The *haiku* is a concentrated impressionist sketch:

> A lonely crow
>   On leafless bough,
>   One autumn eve.
>
>   BASHO

> What a resplendent moon!
>   It casts the shadow of pine boughs
>   Upon the mats.
>
>   KIKAKU

> An evening breeze blows.
>   The water ripples
>   Against the blue heron's legs.
>
>   BUSON

> It is early dawn.
>   The castle is surrounded
>   By the cries of wild ducks.
>
>   KYOROKU

The earlier *tanka* is slightly longer (by two lines):

> O mountain pheasant
> long are the feathers trail'st thou
> on the wooded hill-side—
> as long the nights seem to me
> on lonely couch sleep seeking.
>
> HITOMARO[?]

From our point of view, these are montage phrases. Shot lists. The simple combination of two or three details of a material kind yields a perfectly finished representation of another kind—psychological.

And if the finely ground edges of the intellectually defined concepts formed by the combined ideograms are blurred in these poems, yet, in *emotional quality*, the concepts have blossomed forth immeasurably. We should observe that the emotion is directed towards the reader, for, as Yone Nobuchi has said, "it is the readers who make the *haiku's* imperfection a perfection of art."

It is uncertain in Japanese writing whether its predominating aspect is as a system of characters (denotative), or as an independent creation of graphics (depictive). In any case, born of the dual mating of the depictive by method, and the denotative by purpose, the ideogram continued both these lines (not consecutive historically but consecutive in principle in the minds of those developing the method).

Not only did the denotative line continue into literature, in the *tanka*, as we have shown, but exactly the same method (in its depictive aspect) operates also in the most perfect examples of Japanese pictorial art.

Sharaku—creator of the finest prints of the eighteenth century, and especially of an immortal gallery of actors' portraits. The Japanese Daumier. Despite this, almost unknown to us. The characteristic traits of his work have been analyzed only in our century. One of these critics, Julius Kurth, in discussing the question of the influence on Sharaku of sculpture, draws a parallel between his wood-cut portrait of the actor Nakayama Tomisaburō and an antique mask of the semi-religious Nō theater, the mask of a Rozo.

The faces of both the print and the mask wear an *identical expression.*
. . . Features and masses are similarly arranged although the mask
represents an old priest, and the print a young woman. This relationship is striking, yet these two works are otherwise totally dissimilar;
this in itself is a demonstration of Sharaku's originality. While the
carved mask was constructed according to fairly accurate anatomical
proportions, the proportions of the portrait print are simply impossible. The space between the eyes comprises a width that makes mock
of all good sense. The nose is almost twice as long in relation to the
eyes as any normal nose would dare to be, and the chin stands in no
sort of relation to the mouth; the brows, the mouth, and every
feature—is hopelessly misrelated. *This observation may be made in all
the large heads by Sharaku.* That the artist was unaware that all these
proportions are false is, of course, out of the question. It was with a
full awareness that he repudiated normalcy, and, while the drawing
of the separate features depends on severely concentrated naturalism,
their proportions have been subordinated to purely intellectual
considerations. *He set up the essence of the psychic expression as the
norm for the proportions of the single features.*

Is not this process that of the ideogram, combining the independent "mouth" and the dissociated symbol of "child" to
form the significance of "scream"?

Is this not exactly what we of the cinema do temporally, just
as Sharaku in simultaneity, when we cause a monstrous disproportion of the parts of a normally flowing event, and suddenly dismember the event into "close-up of clutching
hands," "medium shots of the struggle," and "extreme close-
up of bulging eyes," in making a montage disintegration of

90

the event in various planes? In making an eye twice as large as a man's full figure?! By combining these monstrous incongruities we newly collect the disintegrated event into one whole, but in *our* aspect. According to the treatment of our relation to the event.

The disproportionate depiction of an event is organically natural to us from the beginning. Professor Luriya, of the Psychological Institute in Moscow, has shown me a drawing by a child of "lighting a stove." Everything is represented in passably accurate relationship and with great care. Firewood. Stove. Chimney. But what are those zigzags in that huge central rectangle? They turn out to be—matches. Taking into account the crucial importance of these matches for the depicted process, the child provides a proper scale for them.*

The representation of objects in the actual (absolute) proportions proper to them is, of course, merely a tribute to orthodox formal logic. A subordination to an inviolable order of things.

Both in painting and sculpture there is a periodic and invariable return to periods of the establishment of absolutism. Displacing the expressiveness of archaic disproportion for regulated "stone tables" of officially decreed harmony.

Absolute realism is by no means the correct form of perception. It is simply the function of a certain form of social structure. Following a state monarchy, a state uniformity of thought

---

*It is possible to trace this particular tendency from its ancient, almost prehistorical source (". . . in all ideational art, objects are given size according to their importance, the king being twice as large as his subjects, or a tree half the size of a man when it merely informs us that the scene is out-of-doors. Something of this principle of size according to significance persisted in the Chinese tradition. The favorite disciple of Confucius looked like a little boy beside him and the most important figure in any group was usually the largest." [George Rowley, *Principles of Chinese Painting.* Princeton University Press, 1947, p. 56.]) through the highest development of Chinese art, parent of Japanese graphic arts: ". . . natural scale always had to bow to pictorial scale . . . size according to distance never followed the laws of geometric perspective but the needs of the design. Foreground features might be diminished to avoid obstruction and overemphasis, and far distant objects, which were too minute to count pictorially, might be enlarged to act as a counterpoint to the middle distance or foreground." [Rowley, p. 66.]

is implanted. Ideological uniformity of a sort that can be developed pictorially in the ranks of colors and designs of the Guards regiments . . .

Thus we have seen how the principle of the hieroglyph—"denotation by depiction"—split in two: along the line of its purpose (the principle of "denotation"), into the principles of creating literary imagery; along the line of its method of realizing this purpose (the principle of "depiction"), into the striking methods of expressiveness used by Sharaku.*

And, just as the two outspreading wings of a hyperbola meet, as we say, at infinity (though no one has visited so distant a region!), so the principle of hieroglyphics, infinitely splitting into two parts (in accordance with the function of symbols), unexpectedly unites again from this dual estrangement, in yet a fourth sphere—in the theater.

Estranged for so long, they are once again—in the cradle period of the drama—present in a *parallel* form, in a curious dualism.

The *significance* (denotation) of the action is effected by the reciting of the *Jōruri* by a voice behind the stage—the *representation* (depiction) of the action is effected by silent marionettes on the stage. Along with a specific manner of movement this archaism migrated into the early Kabuki theater, as well. To this day it is preserved, as a partial method, in the classical repertory (where certain parts of the action are narrated from behind the stage while the actor mimes).

But this is not the point. The most important fact is that into the technique of acting itself the ideographic (montage) method has been wedged in the most interesting ways.

However, before discussing this, let us be allowed the luxury of a digression—on the matter of the shot, to settle the debated question of its nature, once and for all.

A shot. A single piece of celluloid. A tiny rectangular frame in which there is, organized in some way, a piece of an event.

---

*It has been left to James Joyce to develop in *literature* the depictive line of the Japanese hieroglyph. Every word of Kurth's analysis of Sharaku may be applied, neatly and easily, to Joyce.

"Cemented together, these shots form montage. When this is done in an appropriate rhythm, *of course!*"

This, roughly, is what is taught by the old, old school of film-making, that sang:

> "Screw by screw,
> Brick by brick . . ."

Kuleshov, for example, even writes with a brick:

If you have an idea-phrase, a particle of the story, a link in the whole dramatic chain, then that idea is to be expressed and accumulated from shot-ciphers, just like bricks.

"The shot is an element of montage. Montage is an assembly of these elements." This is a most pernicious make-shift analysis.

Here the understanding of the process as a whole (connection, shot-montage) derives only from the external indications of its flow (a piece cemented to another piece). Thus it would be possible, for instance, to arrive at the well-known conclusion that street-cars exist in order to be laid across streets. An entirely logical deduction, if one limits oneself to the external indications of the functions they performed during the street-fighting of February 1917, here in Russia. But the materialist conception of history interprets it otherwise.

The worst of it is that an approach of this kind does actually lie, like an insurmountable street-car, across the potentialities of formal development. Such an approach overrules dialectical development, and dooms one to mere evolutionary "perfecting," in so far as it gives no bite into the dialectical substance of events.

In the long run, such evolutionizing leads either through refinement to decadence or, on the other hand, to a simple withering away due to stagnation of the blood.

Strange as it may seem, a melodious witness to both these distressing eventualities, simultaneously, is Kuleshov's latest film, *The Gay Canary* [1929].

The shot is by no means an *element* of montage.
The shot is a montage *cell*.

93

Just as cells in their division form a phenomenon of another order, the organism or embryo, so, on the other side of the dialectical leap from the shot, there is montage.

By what, then, is montage characterized and, consequently, its cell—the shot?

By collision. By the conflict of two pieces in opposition to each other. By conflict. By collision.

In front of me lies a crumpled yellowed sheet of paper. On it is a mysterious note:

"Linkage—P" and "Collision—E."

This is a substantial trace of a heated bout on the subject of montage between P (Pudovkin) and E (myself).

This has become a habit. At regular intervals he visits me late at night and behind closed doors we wrangle over matters of principle. A graduate of the Kuleshov school, he loudly defends an understanding of montage as a *linkage* of pieces. Into a chain. Again, "bricks." Bricks, arranged in series to *expound* an idea.

I confronted him with my viewpoint on montage as a *collision*. A view that from the collision of two given factors *arises* a concept.

From my point of view, linkage is merely a possible *special* case.

Recall what an infinite number of combinations is known in physics to be capable of arising from the impact (collision) of spheres. Depending on whether the spheres be resilient, nonresilient, or mingled. Amongst all these combinations there is one in which the impact is so weak that the collision is degraded to an even movement of both in the same direction.

This is the one combination which would correspond with Pudovkin's view.

Not long ago we had another talk. Today he agrees with my point of view. True, during the interval he took the opportunity to acquaint himself with the series of lectures I gave during that period at the State Cinema Institute. . . .

So, montage is conflict.

As the basis of every art is conflict (an "imagist" transformation of the dialectical principle). The shot appears as the *cell* of montage. Therefore it also must be considered from the viewpoint of *conflict*.

Conflict within the shot is potential montage, in the development of its intensity shattering the quadrilateral cage of the shot and exploding its conflict into montage impulses *between* the montage pieces. As, in a zigzag of mimicry, the *mise-en-scène* splashes out into a spatial zigzag with the *same* shattering. As the slogan, "All obstacles are vain before Russians," bursts out in the multitude of incident of *War and Peace*.

If montage is to be compared with something, then a phalanx of montage pieces, of shots, should be compared to the series of explosions of an internal combustion engine, driving forward its automobile or tractor: for, similarly, the dynamics of montage serve as impulses driving forward the total film.

Conflict within the frame. This can be very varied in character: it even can be a conflict in—the story. As in that "prehistoric" period in films (although there are plenty of instances in the present, as well), when entire scenes would be photographed in a single, uncut shot. This, however, is outside the strict jurisdiction of the film-form.

These are the "cinematographic" conflicts within the frame:
Conflict of graphic directions.

> *(Lines—either static or dynamic)*

Conflict of scales.
Conflict of volumes.
Conflict of masses.

> *(Volumes filled with various intensities of light)*

Conflict of depths.

And the following conflicts, requiring only one further impulse of intensification before flying into antagonistic pairs of pieces:
Close shots and long shots.
Pieces of graphically varied directions. Pieces resolved in volume, with pieces resolved in area.
Pieces of darkness and pieces of lightness.

And, lastly, there are such unexpected conflicts as:
Conflicts between an object and its dimension—and conflicts between an event and its duration.

These may sound strange, but both are familiar to us. The

first is accomplished by an optically distorted lens, and the second by stop-motion or slow-motion.

The compression of all cinematographic factors and properties within a single dialectical formula of conflict is no empty rhetorical diversion.

We are now seeking a unified system for methods of cinematographic expressiveness that shall hold good for all its elements. The assembly of these into series of common indications will solve the task as a whole.

Experience in the separate elements of the cinema cannot be absolutely measured.

Whereas we know a good deal about montage, in the theory of the shot we are still floundering about amidst the most academic attitudes, some vague tentatives, and the sort of harsh radicalism that sets one's teeth on edge.

To regard the frame as a particular, as it were, molecular case of montage makes possible the direct application of montage practice to the theory of the shot.

And similarly with the theory of lighting. To sense this as a collision between a stream of light and an obstacle, like the impact of a stream from a fire-hose striking a concrete object, or of the wind buffeting a human figure, must result in a usage of light entirely different in comprehension from that employed in playing with various combinations of "gauzes" and "spots."

Thus far we have one such significant principle of conflict: *the principle of optical counterpoint.*

And let us not now forget that soon we shall face another and less simple problem in counterpoint: *the conflict in the sound film of acoustics and optics.*

Let us return to one of the most fascinating of optical conflicts: the conflict between the frame of the shot and the object!

The camera position, as a materialization of the conflict between organizing logic of the director and the inert logic of the object, in collision, reflects the dialectic of the camera-angle.

In this matter we are still impressionistic and lacking in principle to a sickening degree. Nevertheless, a sharpness of principle can be had in the technique of this, too. The dry

quadrilateral, plunging into the hazards of nature's diffuseness . . .

And once again we are in Japan! For the cinematographic
method is used in teaching drawing in Japanese schools.

What is our method of teaching drawing? Take any piece of
white paper with four corners to it. Then cram onto it, usually
even without using the edges (mostly greasy from the long
drudgery!), some bored caryatid, some conceited Corinthian
capital, or a plaster Dante (not the magician performing at the
Moscow Hermitage, but the other one—Alighieri, the comedy
writer).

The Japanese approach this from a quite different direction:
Here's the branch of a cherry-tree. And the pupils cuts out
from this whole, with a square, and a circle, and a rectangle—
compositional units:

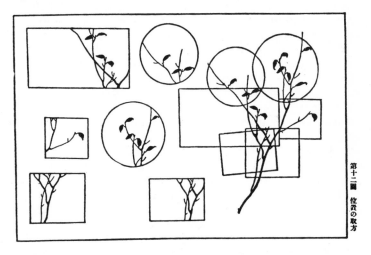

He frames a shot!

These two ways of teaching drawing can characterize the
two basic tendencies struggling within the cinema of today.
One—the expiring method of artificial spatial organization of
an event in front of the lens. From the "direction" of a
sequence, to the erection of a Tower of Babel in front of the

lens. The other—a "picking-out" by the camera: organization by means of the camera. Hewing out a piece of actuality with the ax of the lens.

However, at the present moment, when the center of attention is finally beginning, in the intellectual cinema, to be transferred from the materials of cinema, as such, to "deductions and conclusions," to "slogans" based on the material, both schools of thought are losing distinction in their differences and can quickly blend into a synthesis.

Several pages back we lost, like an overshoe in a street-car, the question of the theater. Let us turn back to the question of methods of montage in the Japanese theater, particularly in acting.

The first and most striking example, of course, is the purely cinemetographic method of "acting without transitions." Along with mimic transitions carried to a limit of refinement, the Japanese actor uses an exactly contrary method as well. At a certain moment of his performance he halts; the black-shrouded *kurogo* obligingly conceals him from the spectators. And lo!—he is resurrected in a new make-up. And in a new wig. Now characterizing another stage (degree) of his emotional state.

Thus, for example, in the Kabuki play *Narukami,* the actor Sadanji must change from drunkenness to madness. This transition is solved by a mechanical cut. And a change in the arsenal of grease-paint colors on his face, emphasizing those streaks whose duty it is to fulfill the expression of a higher intensity than those used in his previous make-up.

This method is organic to the film. The forced introduction into the film, by European acting traditions, of pieces of "emotional transitions" is yet another influence forcing the cinema to mark time. Whereas the method of "cut" acting makes possible the construction of entirely new methods. Replacing one changing face with a whole scale of facial types of varying moods affords a far more acutely expressive result than does the changing surface, too receptive and devoid of organic resistance, of any single professional actor's face.

In our new film [*Old and New*] I have eliminated the intervals between the sharply contrasting polar stages of a face's expression. Thus is achieved a greater sharpness in the "play of doubts" around the new cream separator. Will the milk thicken or no? Trickery? Wealth? Here the psychological process of mingled faith and doubt is broken up into its two extreme states of joy (confidence) and gloom (disillusionment). Furthermore, this is sharply emphasized by light—illumination in no wise conforming to actual light conditions. This brings a distinct strengthening of the tension.

Another remarkable characteristic of the Kabuki theater is the principle of "disintegrated" acting. Shocho, who played the leading female rôles in the Kabuki theater that visited Moscow, in depicting the dying daughter in *Yashaō* (*The Mask-Maker*), performed his rôle in pieces of acting completely detached from each other: Acting with only the right arm. Acting with one leg. Acting with the neck and head only. (The whole process of the death agony was disintegrated into solo performances of each member playing its own rôle: the rôle of the leg, the rôle of the arms, the rôle of the head.) A breaking-up into shots. With a gradual shortening of these separate, successive pieces of acting as the tragic end approached.

Freed from the yoke of primitive naturalism, the actor is enabled by this method to fully grip the spectator by "rhythms," making not only acceptable, but definitely attractive, a stage built on the most consecutive and detailed flesh and blood of naturalism.

Since we no longer distinguish in principle between questions of shot-content and montage, we may here cite a third example:

The Japanese theater makes use of a slow tempo to a degree unknown to our stage. The famous scene of hara-kiri in *Chushingura* is based on an unprecedented slowing down of all movement—beyond any point we have ever seen. Whereas, in the previous example, we observed a disintegration of the transitions between movements, here we see disintegration of the process of movement, viz., slow-motion. I have heard of only one example of a thorough application of this method, using the technical possibility of the film with a compositionally reasoned plan. It is usually employed with some purely pictorial aim, such as the "submarine kingdom" in *The Thief of Bagdad*, or to represent a dream, as in *Zvenigora*. Or, more often, it is used simply for formalist jackstraws and un-motivated camera mischief as in Vertov's *Man with the Movie-Camera*. The more commendable example appears to be in Jean Epstein's *La chute de la Maison Usher*—at least according to the press reports. In this film, normally acted emotions filmed with a speeded-up camera are said to give unusual emotional pressure by their unrealistic slowness on the screen. If it be borne in mind that the effect of an actor's performance on the audience is based on its identification by each spectator, it will be easy to relate both examples (the Kabuki play and the Ep-stein film) to an identical causal explanation. The intensity of perception increases as the didactic process of identification proceeds more easily along a disintegrated action.

Even instruction in handling a rifle can be hammered into the tightest motor-mentality among a group of raw recruits if the instructor uses a "break-down" method.

The most interesting link of the Japanese theater is, of course, its link with the sound film, which can and must learn its fundamentals from the Japanese—the reduction of visual and aural sensations to a common physiological denominator.

So, it has been possible to establish (cursorily) the perme-ation of the most varied branches of Japanese culture by a pure cinematographic element—its basic nerve, montage.

And it is only the Japanese cinema that falls into the same error as the "leftward drifting" Kabuki. Instead of learning how to extract the principles and technique of their remark-able acting from the traditional feudal forms of their materials, the most progressive leaders of the Japanese theater throw their energies into an adaptation of the spongy shapelessness of our own "inner" naturalism. The results are tearful and sad-dening. In its cinema Japan similarly pursues imitations of the most revolting examples of American and European entries in the international commercial film race.

To understand and apply her cultural peculiarities to the cinema, this is the task of Japan! Colleagues of Japan, are you really going to leave this for us to do?

1929

A DIALECTIC APPROACH
TO FILM FORM

*In nature we never see anything isolated, but everything in con-
nection with something else which is before it, beside it, under it,
and over it.*

GOETHE

*According to Marx and Engels the dialectic system is only the
conscious reproduction of the dialectic course (substance) of the external events of the world.*

Thus:
> The projection of the dialectic system of things
> into the brain
> *into creating abstractly*
> *into the process of thinking*
> yields: dialectic methods of thinking;
> dialectic materialism—   PHILOSOPHY.

And also:
> The projection of the same system of things
> *while creating concretely*
> *while giving form*
> yields: ART.

The foundation for this philosophy is a *dynamic* concept of
things:

Being—as a constant evolution from the interaction of two
contradictory opposites.

Synthesis—arising from the opposition between thesis and
antithesis.

A dynamic comprehension of things is also basic to the
same degree, for a correct understanding of art and of all art-
forms. In the realm of art this dialectic principle of dynamics is
embodied in

CONFLICT

as the fundamental principle for the existence of every art-
work and every art-form.

101

For art is always conflict:
(1) according to its social mission,
(2) according to its nature,
(3) according to its methodology.

According to its social mission *because:* It is art's task to make manifest the contradictions of Being. To form equitable views by stirring up contradictions within the spectator's mind, and to forge accurate intellectual concepts from the dynamic clash of opposing passions.

According to its nature *because:* Its nature is a conflict between natural existence and creative tendency. Between organic inertia and purposeful initiative. Hypertrophy of the purposive initiative—the principles of rational logic—ossifies art into mathematical technicalism. (A painted landscape becomes a topographical map, a painted Saint Sebastian becomes an anatomical chart.) Hypertrophy of organic naturalness—of organic logic—dilutes art into formlessness. (A Malevich becomes a Kaulbach, an Archipenko becomes a waxworks side-show.)

Because the limit of organic form (the passive principle of being) is *Nature*. The limit of rational form (the active principle of production) is *Industry*. At the intersection of Nature and Industry stands *Art*.

The logic of organic form *vs.* the logic of rational form yields, in collision,

the dialectic of the art-form.

The interaction of the two produces and determines Dynamism. (Not only in the sense of a space-time continuum, but also in the field of absolute thinking. I also regard the inception of new concepts and viewpoints in the conflict between customary conception and particular representation as dynamic—as a dynamization of the inertia of perception—as a dynamization of the "traditional view" into a new one.)

The quantity of interval determines the pressure of the tension. (See in music, for example, the concept of intervals. There can be cases where the distance of separation is so wide that it leads to a break—to a collapse of the homogeneous concept of art. For instance, the "inaudibility" of certain intervals.)

The spatial form of this dynamism is expression.
The phrases of its tension: rhythm.

This is true for every art-form, and, indeed, for every kind of expression.

Similarly, human expression is a conflict between conditioned and unconditioned reflexes. (In this I cannot agree with Klages, who, *a*) does not consider human expression dynamically as a process, but statically as a result, and who, *b*) attributes everything in motion to the field of the "soul," and only the hindering element to "reason." ["Reason" and "Soul" of the idealistic concept here correspond remotely with the ideas of conditioned and unconditioned reflexes.])

This is true in every field that can be understood as an art. For example, logical thought, considered as an art, shows the same dynamic mechanism:

> . . . the intellectual lives of Plato or Dante or Spinoza or Newton were largely guided and sustained by their delight in the sheer beauty of the rhythmic relation between law and instance, species and individual, or cause and effect.

This holds in other fields, as well, e.g., in speech, where all its sap, vitality, and dynamism arise from the irregularity of the part in relation to the laws of the system as a whole.

In contrast we can observe the sterility of expression in such artificial, totally regulated languages as Esperanto.

It is from this principle that the whole charm of poetry derives. Its rhythm arises as a conflict between the metric measure employed and the distribution of accents, over-riding this measure.

The concept of a formally static phenomenon as a dynamic function is dialectically imaged in the wise words of Goethe:

> *Die Baukunst ist eine ertarrte Musik.*
> (Architecture is frozen music.)

Just as in the case of a homogeneous ideology (a monistic viewpoint), the whole, as well as the least detail, must be penetrated by a sole principle. So, ranged alongside the conflict of *social conditionality*, and the conflict of *existing nature*, the *methodology* of an art reveals this same principle of conflict.

As the basic principle of the rhythm to be created and the inception of the art-form.

Art is always conflict, according to its methodology.

Here we shall consider the general problem of art in the specific example of its highest form—film.

Shot and montage are the basic elements of cinema.

Montage

has been established by the Soviet film as the nerve of cinema.

To determine the nature of montage is to solve the specific problem of cinema. The earliest conscious film-makers, and our first film theoreticians, regarded montage as a means of description by placing single shots one after the other like building-blocks. The movement within these building-block shots, and the consequent length of the component pieces, was then considered as rhythm.

A completely false concept!

This would mean the defining of a given object solely in relation to the nature of its external course. The mechanical process of splicing would be made a principle. We cannot describe such a relationship of lengths as rhythm. From this comes metric rather than rhythmic relationships, as opposed to one another as the mechanical-metric system of Mensendieck is to the organic-rhythmic school of Bode in matters of body exercise.

According to this definition, shared even by Pudovkin as a theoretician, montage is the means of *unrolling* an idea with the help of single shots: the "epic" principle.

In my opinion, however, montage is an idea that arises from the collision of independent shots—shots even opposite to one another: the "dramatic" principle.*

A sophism? Certainly not. For we are seeking a definition of the whole nature, the principal style and spirit of cinema from its technical (optical) basis.

We know that the phenomenon of movement in film resides

---

*"Epic" and "dramatic" are used here in regard to methodology of form—not to *content* or *plot!*

in the fact that two motionless images of a moving body, following one another, blend into an appearance of motion by showing them sequentially at a required speed.

This popularized description of what happens as a *blending* has its share of responsibility for the popular miscomprehension of the nature of montage that we have quoted above.

Let us examine more exactly the course of the phenomenon we are discussing—how it really occurs—and draw our conclusion from this. Placed next to each other, two photographed immobile images result in the appearance of movement. Is this accurate? Pictorially—and phraseologically, yes.

But mechanically, it is not. For, in fact, each sequential element is perceived not *next* to the other, but on *top* of the other. For the idea (or sensation) of movement arises from the process of superimposing on the retained impression of the object's first position, a newly visible further position of the object. This is, by the way, the reason for the phenomenon of spatial depth, in the optical superimposition of two planes in stereoscopy. From the superimposition of two elements of the same dimension always arises a new, higher dimension. In the case of stereoscopy the superimposition of two nonidentical two-dimensionalities results in stereoscopic three-dimensionality.

In another field; a concrete word (a denotation) set beside a concrete word yields an abstract concept—as in the Chinese and Japanese languages,* where a material ideogram can indicate a transcendental (conceptual) result.

The incongruence in contour of the first picture—already impressed on the mind—with the subsequently perceived second picture engenders, in conflict, the feeling of motion. Degree of incongruence determines intensity of impression, and determines that tension which becomes the real element of authentic rhythm.

Here we have, temporally, what we see arising spatially on a graphic or painted plane.

What comprises the dynamic effect of a painting? The eye follows the direction of an element in the painting. It retains a

---

*See discussion in preceding essay.

visual impression, which then collides with the impression derived from following the direction of a second element. The conflict of these directions forms the dynamic effect in apprehending the whole.

I. It may be purely linear: Fernand Léger, or Suprematism.

II. It may be "anecdotal." The secret of the marvelous mobility of Daumier's and Lautrec's figures dwells in the fact that the various anatomical parts of a body are represented in spatial circumstances (positions) that are temporally various, disjunctive. For example, in Toulouse-Lautrec's lithograph of Miss Cissy Loftus, if one logically develops position A of the foot, one builds a body in position A corresponding to it. But the body is represented from knee up already in position A + a. The cinematic effect of joined motionless pictures is already established here! From hips to shoulders we can see A + a + a. The figure comes alive and kicking!

III. Between I and II lies primitive Italian futurism—such as in Balla's "Man with Six Legs in Six Positions"—for II obtains its effect by retaining natural unity and anatomical correctness, while I, on the other hand, does this with purely elementary elements. III, although destroying naturalness, has not yet pressed forward to abstraction.

IV. The conflict of directions may also be of an ideographic kind. It was in this way that we have gained the pregnant characterizations of a Sharaku, for example. The secret of his extremely perfected strength of expression lies in the anatomical and *spatial disproportion* of the parts—in comparison with which, our I might be termed *temporal disproportion*.

Generally termed "irregularity," this *spatial disproportion* has been a constant attraction and instrument for artists. In writing of Rodin's drawings, Camille Mauclair indicated one explanation for this search:

> The greatest artists, Michelangelo, Rembrandt, Delacroix, all, at a certain moment of the upthrusting of their genius, threw aside, as it were, the ballast of exactitude as conceived by our simplifying reason and our ordinary eyes, in order to attain the fixation of ideas, the synthesis, the *pictorial handwriting* of their dreams.

Two experimental artists of the nineteenth century—a painter and a poet—attempted esthetic formulations of this "irregularity." Renoir advanced this thesis:

> Beauty of every description finds its charm in variety. Nature abhors both vacuum and regularity. For the same reason, no work of art can really be called such if it has not been created by an artist who believes in irregularity and rejects any set form. Regularity, order, desire for perfection (which is always a false perfection) destroy art. The only possibility of maintaining taste in art is to impress on artists and the public the importance of irregularity. Irregularity is the basis of all art.

And Baudelaire wrote in his journal:

> That which is not slightly distorted lacks sensible appeal; from which it follows that irregularity—that is to say, the unexpected, surprise and astonishment, are an essential part and characteristic of beauty.

Upon closer examination of the particular beauty of irregularity as employed in painting, whether by Grünewald or by Renoir, it will be seen that it is a disproportion in the relation of a detail in one dimension to another detail in a different dimension.

The spatial development of the relative size of one detail in correspondence with another, and the consequent collision between the proportions designed by the artist for that purpose, result in a characterization—a definition of the represented matter.

Finally, color. Any shade of a color imparts to our vision a given rhythm of vibration. This is not said figuratively, but purely physiologically, for colors are distinguished from one another by their number of light vibrations.

The adjacent shade or tone of color is in another rate of vibration. The counterpoint (conflict) of the two—the retained rate of vibration against the newly perceived one—yields the dynamism of our apprehension of the interplay of color.

Hence, with only one step from visual vibrations to acoustic vibrations, we find ourselves in the field of music. From the domain of the spatial-pictorial—to the domain of the temporal-pictorial—where the same law rules. For counterpoint is to music not only a form of composition, but is altogether the basic factor for the possibility of tone perception and tone differentiation.

It may almost be said that in every case we have cited we have seen in operation the same *Principle of Comparison* that makes possible for us perception and definition in every field.

In the moving image (cinema) we have, so to speak, a synthesis of two counterpoints—the spatial counterpoint of graphic art, and the temporal counterpoint of music.

Within cinema, and characterizing it, occurs what may be described as:

visual counterpoint

In applying this concept to the film, we gain several leads to the problem of film grammar. As well as a *syntax* of film manifestations, in which visual counterpoint may determine a whole new system of forms of manifestation.

For all this, the *basic premise* is:

The shot is by no means an element of montage.
The shot is a montage cell (or molecule).

In this formulation the dualistic division of

Sub-title and shot
and
Shot and montage

leaps forward in analysis to a dialectic consideration as three different phases of one homogeneous task of expression, its homogeneous characteristics determining the homogeneity of their structural laws.

Inter-relation of the three phases:

Conflict within a thesis (an abstract idea)—*formulates* itself in the dialectics of the sub-title—*forms* itself spatially in the conflict within the shot—and *explodes* with increasing intensity in montage-conflict among the separate shots.

This is fully analogous to human, psychological expression. This is a conflict of motives, which can also be comprehended in three phases:

108

1. Purely verbal utterance. Without intonation—expression in speech.

2. Gesticulatory (mimic-intonational) expression. Projection of the conflict onto the whole expressive bodily system of man. Gesture of bodily movement and gesture of intonation.

3. Projection of the conflict into space. With an intensification of motives, the zigzag of mimic expression is propelled into the surrounding space following the same formula of distortion. A zigzag of expression arising from the spatial division caused by man moving in space. *Mise-en-scène.*

This gives us the basis for an entirely new understanding of the problem of film form.

We can list, as examples of types of conflicts within the form—characteristic for the conflict within the shot, as well as for the conflict between colliding shots, or, montage:

1. Graphic conflict.
2. Conflict of planes.
3. Conflict of volumes.
4. Spatial conflict.
5. Light conflict.
6. Tempo conflict, and so on.

Nota bene: This list is of principal features, of *dominants.* It is naturally understood that they occur chiefly as complexes.

For a transition to montage, it will be sufficient to divide any example into two independent primary pieces, as in the case of graphic conflict, although all other cases can be similarly divided:

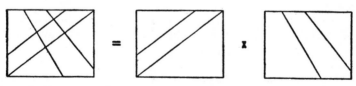

Some further examples:

7. Conflict between matter and viewpoint (achieved by spatial distortion through camera-angle).
8. Conflict between matter and its spatial nature (achieved by *optical distortion* by the lens).

9. Conflict between an event and its temporal nature (achieved by *slow-motion* and *stop-motion*)
   and finally
10. Conflict between the whole *optical* complex and a quite different sphere.

Thus does conflict between optical and acoustical experience produce:

sound-film,

which is capable of being realized as
audio-visual counterpoint.

Formulation and investigation of the phenomenon of cinema as forms of conflict yield the first possibility of devising a homogeneous system of *visual dramaturgy* for all general and particular cases of the film problem.

Of devising a *dramaturgy of the visual film-form* as regulated and precise as the existing *dramaturgy of the film-story.*

From this viewpoint on the film medium, the following forms and potentialities of style may be summed up as a film syntax, or it may be more exact to describe the following as:

a tentative film-syntax.

We shall list here a number of potentialities of dialectical development to be derived from this proposition: The concept of the moving (time-consuming) image arises from the superimposition—or counterpoint—of two differing immobile images.

I. Each *moving fragment of montage.* Each photographed piece. Technical definition of the phenomenon of movement. *No composition as yet.* (A running man. A rifle fired. A splash of water.)

II. *An artificially produced image of motion.* The basic optical element is used for deliberate compositions:

A. *Logical*

- Example 1 (from *October*): a montage rendition of a machine-gun being fired, by cross-cutting details of the firing.

110

From *Potemkin* (1925). "An illustration of instantaneous action. Woman with pince-nez. Followed immediately—without transition—by the same woman with shattered pince-nez and bleeding eye: impression of a shot hitting the eye" (EISENSTEIN, page 112).

Combination A: a brightly lit machine-gun. A different shot in a low key. Double burst: graphic burst + light burst. Closeup of machine-gunner.

Combination B: Effect almost of double exposure achieved by *clatter* montage effect. Length of montage pieces—two frames each.

Example 2 (from *Potemkin*): an illustration of instantaneous action. Woman with pince-nez. Followed immediately—without transition—by the same woman with shattered pince-nez and bleeding eye: impression of a shot hitting the eye.

B. *Illogical*

Example 3 (from *Potemkin*): the same device used for pictorial symbolism. In the thunder of the *Potemkin's* guns, a marble lion leaps up, in protest against the bloodshed on the Odessa steps. Composed of three shots of three stationary marble lions at the Alupka Palace in the Crimea: a sleeping lion, an awakening lion, a rising lion. The effect is achieved by a correct calculation of the length of the second shot. Its superimposition on the first shot produces the first action. This establishes time to impress the second position on the mind. Superimposition of the third position on the second produces the second action: the lion finally rises.

Example 4 (from *October*): Example 1 showed how the firing was manufactured symbolically from elements outside the process of firing itself. In illustrating the monarchist *putsch* attempted by General Kornilov, it occurred to me that his militarist *tendency* could be shown in a montage that would employ religious details for its material. For Kornilov had revealed his intention in the guise of a peculiar "Crusade" of Moslems (!), his Caucasian "Wild Division," together with some Christians, against the Bolsheviki. So we intercut shots of a Baroque Christ (apparently exploding in the radiant beams of his halo) with shots of an egg-shaped mask of Uzume, Goddess of Mirth, completely self-contained. The temporal conflict between the closed egg-form and the graphic star-form produced the effect of an instantaneous *burst*—of a bomb, or shrapnel. . . .

Thus far the examples have shown *primitive-physiological* cases—employing superimposition of optical motion *exclusively*.

III. *Emotional* combinations, not only with the visible elements of the shots, but chiefly with chains of psychological associations. *Association montage.* As a means for pointing up a situation emotionally.

In Example 1, we had two successive shots A and B, identical in subject. However, they were not identical in respect to the position of the subject within the frame:

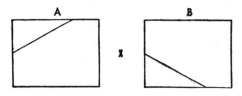

producing *dynamization in space*—an impression of spatial dynamics:

The degree of difference between the positions A and B determines the tension of the movement.

For a new case, let us suppose that the subjects of Shots A and B are not *identical*. Although the associations of the two shots are identical, that is, associatively identical.

This *dynamization of the subject,* not in the field of space but of psychology, i.e., *emotion,* thus produces:
emotional dynamization.

Example 1 (in *Strike*): the montage of the killing of the workers is actually a cross montage of this carnage with the butchering of a bull in an abattoir. Though the subjects are different, "butchering" is the associative link. This made for a powerful emotional intensification of the scene. As a matter of fact, homogeneity of gesture plays an important part in this case in achieving the effect—both the movement of the dynamic gesture within the frame, and the static gesture dividing the frame graphically.

This is a principle subsequently used by Pudovkin in *The End of St. Petersburg*, in his powerful sequence intercutting shots of stock exchange and battlefield. His previous film, *Mother*, had a similar sequence: the ice-break on the river, paralleled with the workers' demonstration.

Such a means may decay pathologically if the essential viewpoint—emotional dynamization of the subject—is lost. As soon as the film-maker loses sight of this essence the means ossifies into lifeless literary symbolism and stylistic mannerism. Two examples of such hollow use of this means occur to me:

Example 2 (in *October*): the sugary chants of compromise by the Mensheviki at the Second Congress of Soviets—during the storming of the Winter Palace—are intercut with hands playing harps. This was a purely literary parallelism that by no means dynamized the subject matter. Similarly in Otzep's *Living Corpse*, church spires (in imitation of those in *October*) and lyrical landscapes are intercut with the courtroom speeches of the prosecutor and defense lawyer. This error was the same as in the "harp" sequence.

On the other hand, a majority of *purely dynamic* effects can produce positive results:

Example 3 (in *October*): the dramatic moment of the union of the Motorcycle Battalion with the Congress of Soviets was dynamized by shots of abstractly spinning bicycle wheels, in association with the entrance of the new delegates. In this way the large-scale emotional content of the event was transformed into actual dynamics.

This same principle—giving birth to concepts, to emotions, by juxtaposing two disparate events—led to:

IV. *Liberation of the whole action from the definition of time and space.* My first attempts at this were in *October*.

Example 1: a trench crowded with soldiers appears to be crushed by an enormous gun-base that comes down inexorably. As an anti-militarist symbol seen from the viewpoint of subject alone, the effect is achieved by an apparent bringing together of an independently existing trench and an overwhelming military product, just as physically independent.

Example 2: in the scene of Kornilov's *putsch*, which puts an end to Kerensky's Bonapartist dreams. Here one of Kornilov's tanks climbs up and crushes a plaster-of-Paris Napoleon standing on Kerensky's desk in the Winter Palace, a juxtaposition of purely symbolic significance.

This method has now been used by Dovzhenko in *Arsenal* to shape whole sequences, as well as by Esther Schub in her use of library footage in *The Russia of Nikolai II and Lev Tolstoy*.

I wish to offer another example of this method, to upset the traditional ways of handling plot—although it has not yet been put into practice.

In 1924–1925 I was mulling over the idea of a filmic portrait of *actual* man. At that time, there prevailed a tendency to show actual man in films only in *long* uncut dramatic scenes. It was believed that cutting (montage) would destroy the idea of actual man. Abram Room established something of a record in this respect when he used in *The Death Ship* uncut dramatic shots as long as 40 meters or 135 feet. I considered (and still do) such a concept to be utterly unfilmic.

Very well—what would be a linguistically accurate characterization of a man?

> His raven-black hair . . .
> The waves of his hair . . .
> His eyes radiating azure beams . . .
> His steely muscles . . .

Even in a less exaggerated description, any verbal account of a person is bound to find itself employing an assortment of waterfalls, lightning-rods, landscapes, birds, etc.

Now why should the cinema follow the forms of theater and

115

painting rather than the methodology of language, which allows wholly new concepts of ideas to arise from the combination of two concrete denotations of two concrete objects? Language is much closer to film than painting is. For example, in painting the form arises from *abstract* elements of line and color, while in cinema the material *concreteness* of the image within the frame presents—as an element—the greatest difficulty in manipulation. So why not rather lean towards the system of language, which is forced to use the same mechanics in inventing words and word-complexes?

On the other hand, why is it that montage cannot be dispensed with in orthodox films?

The differentiation in montage-pieces lies in their lack of existence as single units. Each piece can evoke no more than a certain association. The accumulation of such associations can achieve the same effect as is provided for the spectator by purely physiological means in the plot of a realistically produced play.

For instance, murder on the stage has a purely physiological effect. Photographed in *one* montage-piece, it can function simply as *information*, as a sub-title. *Emotional* effect begins only with the reconstruction of the event in montage fragments, each of which will summon a certain association—the sum of which will be an all-embracing complex of emotional feeling. Traditionally:

1. A hand lifts a knife.
2. The eyes of the victim open suddenly.
3. His hands clutch the table.
4. The knife is jerked up.
5. The eyes blink involuntarily.
6. Blood gushes.
7. A mouth shrieks.
8. Something drips onto a shoe . . .

and similar film clichés. Nevertheless, in regard to the *action as a whole, each fragment-piece* is almost *abstract.* The more differentiated they are the more abstract they become, provoking no more than a certain association.

Quite logically the thought occurs: could not the same thing be accomplished more productively by not following the plot so slavishly, but by materializing the idea, the impression, of *Murder* through a free accumulation of associative matter? For the most important task is still to restablish the idea of murder—the feeling of murder, as such. The plot is no more than a device without which one isn't yet capable of telling something to the spectator! In any case, effort in this direction would certainly produce the most interesting variety of forms.

Someone should try, at least! Since this thought occurred to me, I have not had time to make this experiment. And today I am more concerned with quite different problems. But, returning to the main line of our syntax, something there may bring us closer to these tasks.

While, with I, II, and III, tension was calculated for purely physiological effect—from the purely optical to the emotional, we must mention here also the case of the same conflict-tension serving the ends of new concepts—of new attitudes, that is, of purely intellectual aims.

Example 1 (in *October*): Kerensky's rise to power and dictatorship after the July uprising of 1917. A comic effect was gained by sub-titles indicating regular ascending ranks ("*Dictator*"—"*Generalissimo*"—"*Minister of Navy*—*and of Army*"—etc.) climbing higher and higher—cut into five or six shots of Kerensky, climbing the stairs of the Winter Palace, all with exactly the *same* pace. Here a conflict between the flummery of the ascending ranks and the "hero's" trotting up the same unchanging flight of stairs yields an intellectual result: Kerensky's essential nonentity is shown satirically. We have the counterpoint of a literally expressed conventional idea with the *pictured* action of a particular person who is unequal to his swiftly increasing duties. The incongruence of these two factors results in the spectator's purely *intellectual* decision at the expense of this particular person. Intellectual dynamization.

Example 2 (in *October*): Kornilov's march on Petrograd was under the banner of "In the Name of God and Country." Here we attempted to reveal the religious significance of this episode in a rationalistic way. A number of religious images, from a magnificient Baroque Christ to an Eskimo

117

Ten shots from the montage sequence on the "Odessa Steps" from *Potemkin* (1925). "Step by step, by a process of comparing each new image with the common denotation, power is accumulated behind a process that can be formally identified with that of logical deduction" (EISENSTEIN, page 122). "The creation of a sense or meaning not proper to the images themselves but derived exclusively from their juxtaposition" (BAZIN, page 126).

idol, were cut together. The conflict in this case was between the concept and the symbolization of God. While idea and image appear to accord completely in the first statue shown, the two elements move further from each other with each successive image. Maintaining the denotation of "God," the images increasingly disagree with our concept of God, inevitably leading to individual conclusions about the true nature of all deities. In this case, too, a chain of images attempted to achieve a purely intellectual resolution, resulting from a conflict between a preconception and a *gradual discrediting of it in purposeful steps.*

Step by step, by a process of comparing each new image with the common denotation, power is accumulated behind a process that can be formally identified with that of logical deduction. The decision to release these ideas, as well as the method used, is already *intellectually* conceived.

The conventional *descriptive* form for film leads to the formal possibility of a kind of filmic reasoning. While the conventional film directs the *emotions*, this suggests an opportunity to encourage and direct the whole *thought process*, as well.

These two particular sequences of experiment were very much opposed by the majority of critics. Because they were understood as purely political. I would not attempt to deny that *this form is most suitable for the expression of ideologically pointed theses*, but it is a pity that the critics completely overlooked the purely filmic potentialities of this approach.

In these two experiments we have taken the first embryonic step towards a totally new form of film expression. Towards a purely intellectual film, freed from traditional limitations, achieving direct forms for ideas, systems, and concepts, without any need for transitions and paraphrases. We may yet have a

synthesis of art and science.

This would be the proper name for our new epoch in the field of art. This would be the final justification for Lenin's words, that "the cinema is the most important of all the arts."

1929

ANDRÉ BAZIN
FROM WHAT IS CINEMA?

THE EVOLUTION OF
THE LANGUAGE OF CINEMA

By 1928 the silent film had reached its artistic peak. The despair of its elite as they witnessed the dismantling of this ideal city, while it may not have been justified, is at least understandable. As they followed their chosen aesthetic path it seemed to them that the cinema had developed into an art most perfectly accommodated to the "exquisite embarrassment" of silence and that the realism that sound would bring could only mean a surrender to chaos.

In point of fact, now that sound has given proof that it came not to destroy but to fulfill the Old Testament of the cinema, we may most properly ask if the technical revolution created by the sound track was in any sense an aesthetic revolution. In other words, did the years from 1928 to 1930 actually witness the birth of a new cinema? Certainly, as regards editing, history does not actually show as wide a breach as might be expected between the silent and the sound film. On the contrary there is discernible evidence of a close relationship between certain directors of 1925 and 1935 and especially of the 1940's through the 1950's. Compare for example Erich von Stroheim and Jean Renoir or Orson Welles, or again Carl Theodore Dreyer and Robert Bresson. These more or less clear-cut affinities demonstrate first of all that the gap separating the 1920's and the 1930's can be bridged, and secondly that certain cinematic values actually carry over from the silent to the sound film and, above all, that it is less a matter of setting silence over against sound than of contrasting certain families of styles, certain basically different concepts of cinematographic expression.

Aware as I am that the limitations imposed on this study restrict me to a simplified and to that extent enfeebled presentation of my argument, and holding it to be less an objective statement than a working hypothesis, I will distinguish, in the cinema between 1920 and 1940, between two broad and opposing trends: those directors who put their faith in the image and those who put their faith in reality. By "image" I here mean, very broadly speaking, everything that the representation on the screen adds to the object there represented. This is a complex inheritance but it can be reduced essentially to two categories: those that relate to the plastics of the image and those that relate to the resources of montage, which after all, is simply the ordering of images in time.

Under the heading "plastics" must be included the style of the sets, of the make-up, and, up to a point, even of the performance, to which we naturally add the lighting and, finally, the framing of the shot which gives us its composition. As regards montage, derived initially as we all know from the masterpieces of Griffith, we have the statement of Malraux in his *Psychologie du cinéma* that it was montage that gave birth to film as an art, setting it apart from mere animated photography, in short, creating a language.

The use of montage can be "invisible" and this was generally the case in the prewar classics of the American screen. Scenes were broken down just for one purpose, namely, to analyze an episode according to the material or dramatic logic of the scene. It is this logic which conceals the fact of the analysis, the mind of the spectator quite naturally accepting the viewpoints of the director which are justified by the geography of the action or the shifting emphasis of dramatic interest.

But the neutral quality of this "invisible" editing fails to make use of the full potential of montage. On the other hand these potentialities are clearly evident from the three processes generally known as parallel montage, accelerated montage, montage by attraction. In creating parallel montage, Griffith succeeded in conveying a sense of the simultaneity of two actions taking place at a geographical distance by means of alternating shots from each. In *La Roue* Abel Gance created the illusion of the steadily

McTeague (Gibson Gowland) confronting Marcus Schouler (Jean Hersholt) in the wastes of Death Valley in *Greed* (1923); Nanook building his igloo in *Nanook of the North* (1922). Von Stroheim and Flaherty were two of "those who put their faith in reality" (BAZIN, page 124).

increasing speed of a locomotive without actually using any images of speed (indeed the wheel could have been turning on one spot) simply by a multiplicity of shots of ever-decreasing length.

Finally there is "montage by attraction," the creation of S. M. Eisenstein, and not so easily described as the others, but which may be roughly defined as the reenforcing of the meaning of one image by association with another image not necessarily part of the same episode—for example the fireworks display in *The General Line* following the image of the bull. In this extreme form, montage by attraction was rarely used even by its creator but one may consider as very near to it in principle the more commonly used ellipsis, comparison, or metaphor, examples of which are the throwing of stockings onto a chair at the foot of a bed, or the milk overflowing in H.G. Clouzot's *Quai des orfèvres*. There are of course a variety of possible combinations of these three processes.

Whatever these may be, one can say that they share that trait in common which constitutes the very definition of montage, namely, the creation of a sense or meaning not proper to the images themselves but derived exclusively from their juxtaposition. The well-known experiment of Kuleshov with the shot of Mozhukhin in which a smile was seen to change its significance according to the image that preceded it, sums up perfectly the properties of montage.

Montage as used by Kuleshov, Eisenstein, or Gance did not give us the event; it alluded to it. Undoubtedly they derived at least the greater part of the constituent elements from the reality they were describing but the final significance of the film was found to reside in the ordering of these elements much more than in their objective content.

The matter under recital, whatever the realism of the individual image, is born essentially from these relationships—Mozhukhin plus dead child equal pity—that is to say an abstract result, none of the concrete elements of which are to be found in the premises; maidens plus appletrees in bloom equal hope. The combinations are infinite. But the only thing they have in common is the fact that they suggest an idea by means of a metaphor or by an association of ideas. Thus between the scenario properly so-called, the ultimate object of the recital, and the image pure and simple, there is a relay station, a sort of aesthetic "transformer." The meaning is not in the image, it is in the shadow of the image projected by montage onto the field of consciousness of the spectator.

Let us sum up. Through the contents of the image and the resources of montage, the cinema has at its disposal a whole arsenal of means whereby to impose its interpretation of an event on the spectator. By the end of the silent film we can consider this arsenal to have been full. On the one side the Soviet cinema carried to its ultimate consequences the theory and practice of montage while the German school did every kind of violence to the plastics of the image by way of sets and lighting. Other cinemas count too besides the Russian and German, but whether in France or Sweden or the United States, it does not appear that the language of cinema was at a loss for ways of saying what it wanted to say.

If the art of cinema consists in everything that plastics and montage can add to a given reality, the silent film was an art on its own. Sound could only play at best a subordinate and supplementary role: a counterpoint to the visual image. But this possible enhancement—at best only a minor one—is likely not to weigh much in comparison with the additional bargain-rate reality introduced at the same time by sound.

Thus far we have put forward the view that expressionism of montage and image constitute the essence of cinema. And it is precisely on this generally accepted notion that directors from silent days, such as Erich von Stroheim, F.W. Murnau, and Robert Flaherty, have by implication cast a doubt. In their films, montage plays no part, unless it be the negative one of inevitable elimination where reality superabounds. The camera cannot see everything at once but it makes sure not to lose any part of what it chooses to see. What matters to Flaherty, confronted with Nanook hunting the seal, is the relation between Nanook and the animal; the actual length of the waiting period. Montage could suggest the time involved. Flaherty however confines himself to showing the actual waiting period; the length of the hunt is the very substance of the image, its true object. Thus in the film this episode requires one set-up. Will anyone deny that it is thereby much more moving than a montage by attraction?

Murnau is interested not so much in time as in the reality of dramatic space. Montage plays no more of a decisive part in *Nosferatu* than in *Sunrise*. One might be inclined to think that the plastics of his image are impressionistic. But this would be a superficial view. The composition of his image is in no sense pictorial. It adds nothing to the reality, it does not deform it, it forces it to reveal its structural depth, to bring out the preexisting relations which become constitutive of the drama. For example, in *Tabu*, the arrival of a ship from left screen gives an immediate sense of destiny at work so that Murnau has no need to cheat in any way on the uncompromising realism of a film whose settings are completely natural.

But it is most of all Stroheim who rejects photographic expressionism and the tricks of montage. In his films reality lays itself bare like a suspect confessing under the relentless examination of the commissioner of police. He has one simple rule for direction. Take a close look at the world, keep on doing so, and in the end it will lay bare for you all its cruelty and its ugliness. One could easily imagine as a matter of fact a film by Stroheim composed of a single shot as long-lasting and as close-up as you like. These three directors do not exhaust the possibilities. We would undoubtedly find scattered among the works of others elements of nonexpressionistic cinema in which montage plays no part—even including Griffith. But these examples suffice to reveal, at the very heart of the silent film, a cinematographic art the very opposite of that which has been identified as *"cinéma par excellence,"* a language the semantic and syntactical unit of which is in no sense the Shot; in which the image is evaluated not according to what it adds to reality but what it reveals of it. In the latter art the silence of the screen was a drawback, that is to say, it deprived reality of one of its elements. *Greed*, like Dreyer's *Jeanne d' Arc*, is already virtually a talking film. The moment that you cease to maintain that montage and the plastic composition of the image are the very essence of the language of cinema, sound is no longer the aesthetic crevasse dividing two radically different aspects of the seventh art. The cinema that is believed to have died of the soundtrack is in no sense *"the* cinema." The real dividing line is elsewhere. It was operative in the past and continues to be through thirty-five years of the history of the language of the film.

Having challenged the aesthetic unity of the silent film and divided it off into two opposing tendencies, now let us take a look at the history of the last twenty years.

THE EVOLUTION OF THE LANGUAGE OF CINEMA

From 1930 to 1940 there seems to have grown up in the world, originating largely in the United States, a common form of cinematic language. It was the triumph in Hollywood, during that time, of five or six major kinds of film that gave it its overwhelming superiority: (1) American comedy (*Mr. Smith Goes to Washington*, 1936); (2) The burlesque film (The Marx Brothers); (3) The dance and vaudeville film (Fred Astaire and Ginger Rogers and the Ziegfield Follies); (4) The crime and gangster film *(Scarface, I Am a Fugitive from a Chain Gang, The Informer);* (5) Psychological and social dramas *(Back Street, Jezebel);* (6) Horror or fantasy films *(Dr. Jekyll and Mr. Hyde, The Invisible Man, Frankenstein);* (7) The western *(Stagecoach,* 1939). During that time the French cinema undoubtedly ranked next. Its superiority was gradually manifested by way of a trend towards what might be roughly called stark somber realism, or poetic realism, in which four names stand out: Jacques Feyder, Jean Renoir, Marcel Carné, and Julien Duvivier. My intention not being to draw up a list of prize-winners, there is little use in dwelling on the Soviet, British, German, or Italian films for which these years were less significant than the ten that were to follow. In any case, American and French production sufficiently clearly indicate that the sound film, prior to World War II, had reached a well-balanced stage of maturity.

First as to content: Major varieties with clearly defined rules capable of pleasing a worldwide public, as well as a cultured elite, provided it was not inherently hostile to the cinema.

Secondly as to form: well-defined styles of photography and editing perfectly adapted to their subject matter; a complete harmony of image and sound. In seeing again today such films as *Jezebel* by William Wyler, *Stagecoach* by John Ford, or *Le Jour se lève* by Marcel Carné, one has the feeling that in them an art has found its perfect balance, its ideal form of expression, and reciprocally one admires them for dramatic and moral themes to which the cinema, while it may not have created them, has given a grandeur, an artistic effectiveness, that they would not otherwise have had. In short, here are all the characteristics of the ripeness of a classical art.

I am quite aware that one can justifiably argue that the originality of the postwar cinema as compared with that of 1938 derives from the growth of certain national schools, in particular the dazzling display of the Italian cinema and of a native English cinema freed from the influence of Hollywood. From this one might conclude that the really important phenomenon of the years 1940–1950 is the introduction of new blood, of hitherto unexplored themes. That is to say, the real revolution took place more on the level of subject matter than of style. Is not neorealism primarily a kind of humanism and only secondarily a style of film-making? Then as to the style itself, is it not essentially a form of self-effacement before reality?

Our intention is certainly not to preach the glory of form over content. Art for art's sake is just as heretical in cinema as elsewhere, probably more so. On the other hand, a new subject matter demands new form, and as good a way as any towards understanding what a film is trying to say to us is to know how it is saying it.

Thus by 1938 or 1939 the talking film, particularly in France and in the United States, had reached a level of classical perfection as a result, on the one hand, of the maturing of different kinds of drama developed in part over the past ten years and in part inherited from the silent film, and, on the other, of the stabilization of technical progress. The 1930's were the years, at once, of sound and of panchromatic film. Undoubtedly studio equipment had continued to improve but only in matters of detail, none of them opening up new, radical possibilities for direction. The only changes in this situation since 1940 have been in photography, thanks to the increased sensitivity of the film stock. Panchromatic stock turned visual values upside down, ultrasensitive emulsions have made a modification in their structure possible. Free to shoot in the studio with a much smaller aperture, the operator could, when necessary, eliminate the soft-focus background once considered essential. Still there are a number of examples of the prior use of deep focus, for example in the work of Jean Renoir. This had always been possible on exteriors, and given a measure of skill, even in the studios. Anyone could do it who really wanted to. So that it is less a question basically of a technical problem, the solution of which has admittedly been made easier, than of a search after a style—a point to which we will come back. In short, with panchromatic stock in common use, with an understanding of the potentials of the microphone, and with the crane as standard studio equipment, one can really say that since 1930 all the technical requirements for the art of cinema have been available.

Since the determining technical factors were practically eliminated, we must look elsewhere for the signs and principles of the evolution of film language, that is to say by challenging the subject matter and as a consequence the styles necessary for its expression.

By 1939 the cinema had arrived at what geographers call the equilibrium-profile of a river. By this is meant that ideal mathematical curve which results from the requisite amount of erosion. Having reached this equilibrium-profile, the river flows effortlessly from its source to its mouth without further deepening of its bed. But if any geological movement occurs which raises the erosion level and modifies the height of the source, the water sets to work again, seeps into the surrounding land, goes deeper, burrowing and digging. Sometimes when it is a chalk bed, a new pattern is dug across the plain, almost invisible but found to be complex and winding, if one follows the flow of the water.

THE EVOLUTION OF EDITING SINCE THE ADVENT OF SOUND

In 1938 there was an almost universal standard pattern of editing. If, somewhat conventionally, we call the kind of silent films based on the plastics of the image and the artifices of montage, "expressionist" or "symbolistic," we can describe the new form of storytelling "analytic" and "dramatic." Let us suppose, by way of reviewing one of the elements of the experiment of Kuleshov, that we have a table covered with food and a hungry tramp. One can imagine that in 1936 it would have been edited as follows:

(1) Full shot of the actor and the table.
(2) Camera moves forward into a close-up of a face expressing a mixture of amazement and longing.
(3) Series of close-ups of food.
(4) Back to full shot of person who starts slowly towards the camera.
(5) Camera pulls slowly back to a three-quarter shot of the actor seizing a chicken wing.

Whatever variants one could think of for this scene, they would all have certain points in common:

(1) The verisimilitude of space in which the position of the actor

is always determined, even when a close-up eliminates the decor.

(2) The purpose and the effects of the cutting are exclusively dramatic or psychological.

In other words, if the scene were played on a stage and seen from a seat in the orchestra, it would have the same meaning, the episode would continue to exist objectively. The changes of point of view provided by the camera would add nothing. They would present the reality a little more forcefully, first by allowing a better view and then by putting the emphasis where it belongs.

It is true that the stage director like the film director has at his disposal a margin within which he is free to vary the interpretation of the action but it is only a margin and allows for no modification of the inner logic of the event. Now, by way of contrast, let us take the montage of the stone lions in *The End of St. Petersburg*. By skillful juxtaposition a group of sculptured lions are made to look like a single lion getting to its feet, a symbol of the aroused masses. This clever device would be unthinkable in any film after 1932. As late as 1935 Fritz Lang, in *Fury*, followed a series of shots of women dancing the can-can with shots of clucking chickens in a farmyard. This relic of associative montage came as a shock even at the time, and today seems entirely out of keeping with the rest of the film. However decisive the art of Marcel Carné, for example, in our estimate of the respective values of *Quai des Brumes* or of *Le Jour se lève* his editing remains on the level of the reality he is analyzing. There is only one proper way of looking at it. That is why we are witnessing the almost complete disappearance of optical effects such as superimpositions, and even, especially in the United States, of the close-up, the too violent impact of which would make the audience conscious of the cutting. In the typical American comedy the director returns as often as he can to a shot of the characters from the knees up, which is said to be best suited to catch the spontaneous attention of the viewer—the natural point of balance of his mental adjustment.

Actually this use of montage originated with the silent movies. This is more or less the part it plays in Griffith's films, for example in *Broken Blossoms*, because with *Intolerance* he had already introduced that synthetic concept of montage which the Soviet cinema was to carry to its ultimate conclusion and which is to be found again, although less exclusively, at the end of the silent

132

era. It is understandable, as a matter of fact, that the sound image, far less flexible than the visual image, would carry montage in the direction of realism, increasingly eliminating both plastic impressionism and the symbolic relation between images.

Thus around 1938 films were edited, almost without exception, according to the same principle. The story was unfolded in a series of set-ups numbering as a rule about 600. The characteristic procedure was by shot-reverse-shot, that is to say, in a dialogue scene, the camera followed the order of the text, alternating the character shown with each speech.

It was this fashion of editing, so admirably suitable for the best films made between 1930 and 1939, that was challenged by the shot in depth introduced by Orson Welles and William Wyler. *Citizen Kane* can never be too highly praised. Thanks to the depth of field, whole scenes are covered in one take, the camera remaining motionless. Dramatic effects for which we had formerly relied on montage were created out of the movements of the actors within a fixed framework. Of course Welles did not invent the in-depth shot any more than Griffith invented the close-up. All the pioneers used it and for a very good reason. Soft focus only appeared with montage. It was not only a technical must consequent upon the use of images in juxtaposition, it was a logical consequence of montage, its plastic equivalent. If at a given moment in the action the director, as in the scene imagined above, goes to a close-up of a bowl of fruit, it follows naturally that he also isolates it in space through the focusing of the lens. The soft focus of the background confirms therefore the effect of montage, that is to say, while it is of the essence of the storytelling, it is only an accessory of the style of the photography. Jean Renoir had already clearly understood this, as we see from a statement of his made in 1938 just after he had made *La Bête humaine* and *La Grande illusion* and just prior to *La Règle du jeu:* "The more I learn about my trade the more I incline to direction in depth relative to the screen. The better it works, the less I use the kind of set-up that shows two actors facing the camera, like two well-behaved subjects posing for a still portrait." The truth of the matter is, that if you are looking for the precursor of Orson Welles, it is not Louis Lumière or Zecca, but rather Jean Renoir. In his films, the search after composition in depth is, in effect, a partial replacement of montage by frequent panning shots and entrances. It is based on

The shot-in-depth from *Citizen Kane* (1941). (Note the perfect focus of
the image on all three planes—the three faces extremely close to the
camera, the face in the middle distance, and the letters on the sign in
the far distance.) "Thanks to the depth of field, whole scenes are covered in one take, the camera remaining motionless. . . . Director and
cameraman have converted the screen into a dramatic checkerboard,
planned down to the last detail" (BAZIN, pages 133, 135).

a respect for the continuity of dramatic space and, of course, of its duration.

To anybody with eyes in his head, it is quite evident that the sequence of shots used by Welles in *The Magnificent Ambersons* is in no sense the purely passive recording of an action shot within the same framing. On the contrary, his refusal to break up the action, to analyze the dramatic field in time, is a positive action the results of which are far superior to anything that could be achieved by the classical "cut."

All you need to do is compare two frames shot in depth, one from 1910, the other from a film by Wyler or Welles, to understand just by looking at the image, even apart from the context of the film, how different their functions are. The framing in the 1910 film is intended, to all intents and purposes, as a substitute for the missing fourth wall of the theatrical stage, or at least in exterior shots, for the best vantage point to view the action, whereas in the second case the setting, the lighting, and the camera angles give an entirely different reading. Between them, director and cameraman have converted the screen into a dramatic checkerboard, planned down to the last detail. The clearest if not the most original examples of this are to be found in *The Little Foxes* where the *mise-en-scène* takes on the severity of a working drawing. Welles' pictures are more difficult to analyze because of his overfondness for the baroque. Objects and characters are related in such a fashion that it is impossible for the spectator to miss the significance of the scene. To get the same results by way of montage would have necessitated a detailed succession of shots.

What we are saying then is that the sequence of shots "in depth" of the contemporary director does not exclude the use of montage —how could he, without reverting to a primitive babbling?—he makes it an integral part of his "plastic." The storytelling of Welles or Wyler is no less explicit that John Ford's but theirs has the advantage over his that it does not sacrifice the specific effects that can be derived from unity of image in space and time. Whether an episode is analyzed bit by bit or presented in its physical entirety cannot surely remain a matter of indifference, at least in a work with some pretensions to style. It would obviously be absurd to deny that montage has added considerably to the progress of film language, but this has happened at the cost of other values, no less definitely cinematic.

This is why depth of field is not just a stock in trade of the cameraman like the use of a series of filters or of such-and-such a style of lighting, it is a capital gain in the field of direction—a dialectical step forward in the history of film language.

Nor is it just a formal step forward. Well used, shooting in depth is not just a more economical, a simpler, and at the same time a more subtle way of getting the most out of a scene. In addition to affecting the structure of film language, it also affects the relationships of the minds of the spectators to the image, and in consequence it influences the interpretation of the spectacle.

It would lie outside the scope of this article to analyze the psychological modalities of these relations, as also their aesthetic consequences, but it might be enough here to note, in general terms:

(1) That depth of focus brings the spectator into a relation with the image closer to that which he enjoys with reality. Therefore it is correct to say that, independently of the contents of the image, its structure is more realistic;

(2) That it implies, consequently, both a more active mental attitude on the part of the spectator and a more positive contribution on his part to the action in progress. While analytical montage only calls for him to follow his guide, to let his attention follow along smoothly with that of the director who will choose what he should see, here he is called upon to exercise at least a minimum of personal choice. It is from his attention and his will that the meaning of the image in part derives.

(3) From the two preceding propositions, which belong to the realm of psychology, there follows a third which may be described as metaphysical. In analyzing reality, montage presupposes of its very nature the unity of meaning of the dramatic event. Some other form of analysis is undoubtedly possible but then it would be another film. In short, montage by its very nature rules out ambiguity of expression. Kuleshov's experiment proves this *per absurdum* in giving on each occasion a precise meaning to the expression on a face, the ambiguity of which alone makes the three successively exclusive expressions possible.

On the other hand, depth of focus reintroduced ambiguity into the structure of the image if not of necessity—Wyler's films are never ambiguous—at least as a possibility. Hence it is no exaggeration to say that *Citizen Kane* is unthinkable shot in any other way but in depth. The uncertainty in which we find ourselves as to the spiritual key or the interpretation we should put on the film is built into the very design of the image.

It is not that Welles denies himself any recourse whatsoever to the expressionistic procedures of montage, but just that their use from time to time in between sequences of shots in depth gives them a new meaning. Formerly montage was the very stuff of cinema, the texture of the scenario. In *Citizen Kane* a series of superimpositions is contrasted with a scene presented in a single take, constituting another and deliberately abstract mode of story-telling. Accelerated montage played tricks with time and space while that of Welles, on the other hand, is not trying to deceive us; it offers us a contrast, condensing time, and hence is the equivalent for example of the French imperfect or the English frequentative tense. Like accelerated montage and montage of attractions these superimpositions, which the talking film had not used for ten years, rediscovered a possible use related to temporal realism in a film without montage.

If we have dwelt at some length on Orson Welles it is because the date of his appearance in the filmic firmament (1941) marks more or less the beginning of a new period and also because his case is the most spectacular and, by virtue of his very excesses, the most significant.

Yet *Citizen Kane* is part of a general movement, of a vast stirring of the geological bed of cinema, confirming that everywhere up to a point there had been a revolution in the language of the screen.

I could show the same to be true, although by different methods, of the Italian cinema. In Roberto Rossellini's *Paisà* and *Allemania Anno Zero* and Vittorio de Sica's *Ladri de Biciclette*, Italian neorealism contrasts with previous forms of film realism in its stripping away of all expressionism and in particular in the total absence of the effects of montage. As in the films of Welles and in spite of conflicts of style, neorealism tends to give back to the cinema a sense of the ambiguity of reality. The preoccupation of Rossellini when dealing with the face of the child in *Allemania Anno Zero* is the exact opposite of that of Kuleshov with the close-up of Mozhukhin. Rossellini is concerned to preserve its mystery. We should not be misled by the fact that the evolution of neorealism is not manifest, as in the United States, in any form of revolution in editing. They are both aiming at the same results by different methods. The means used by Rossellini and de Sica are less spectacular but they are no less determined to do away with montage and to transfer to the screen the *continuum* of reality. The dream of Zavattini is just to make a ninety-minute film of the life of a man to whom nothing ever happens. The most "aesthetic" of the neorealists, Luchino Visconti, gives just as clear a picture as Welles of the basic aim of his directorial art in *La Terra Trema*, a film almost entirely composed of one-shot sequences, thus clearly showing his concern to cover the entire action in interminable deep-focus panning shots.

However we cannot pass in review all the films that have shared in this revolution in film language since 1940. Now is the moment to attempt a synthesis of our reflections on the subject.

It seems to us that the decade from 1940 to 1950 marks a decisive step forward in the development of the language of the film. If we have appeared since 1930 to have lost sight of the trend of the silent film as illustrated particularly by Stroheim, F. W. Murnau, Robert Flaherty, and Dreyer, it is for a purpose. It is not that this trend seems to us to have been halted by the talking film. On the contrary, we believe that it represented the richest vein of the so-called silent film and, precisely because it was not aesthetically tied to montage, but was indeed the only tendency that looked to the realism of sound as a natural development. On the other hand it is a fact that the talking film between 1930 and 1940 owes it virtually nothing save for the glorious and retrospectively prophetic exception of Jean Renoir. He alone in his searchings as a director prior to *La Règle du jeu* forced himself to look back beyond the resources provided by montage and so uncovered the secret of a film form that would permit everything to be said without chopping the world up into little fragments, that would reveal the hidden meanings in people and things without disturbing the unity natural to them.

It is not a question of thereby belittling the films of 1930 to 1940, a criticism that would not stand up in the face of the number of masterpieces, it is simply an attempt to establish the notion of a dialectic progress, the highest expression of which was found in the films of the 1940's. Undoubtedly, the talkie sounded the knell of a certain aesthetic of the language of film, but only wherever it had turned its back on its vocation in the service of realism. The sound film nevertheless did preserve the essentials of montage, namely discontinuous description and the dramatic analysis of action. What it turned its back on was metaphor and symbol in exchange for the illusion of objective presentation. The expressionism of montage has virtually disappeared but the relative realism of the kind of cutting that flourished around 1937 implied a congenital limitation which escaped us so long as it was perfectly suited to its subject matter. Thus American comedy reached its peak within the framework of a form of editing in which the realism of the time played no part. Dependent on logic for its effects, like vaudeville and plays on words, entirely conventional in its moral and sociological content, American comedy had everything to gain, in strict line-by-line progression, from the rhythmic resources of classical editing.

Undoubtedly it is primarily with the Stroheim-Murnau trend— almost totally eclipsed from 1930 to 1940—that the cinema has more or less consciously linked up once more over the last ten years. But it has no intention of limiting itself simply to keeping this trend alive. It draws from it the secret of the regeneration of realism in storytelling and thus of becoming capable once more of bringing together real time, in which things exist, along with the duration of the action, for which classical editing had insidiously substituted mental and abstract time. On the other hand, so far from wiping out once and for all the conquests of montage, this reborn realism gives them a body of reference and a meaning. It is only an increased realism of the image that can support the abstraction of montage. The stylistic repertory of a director such as Hitchcock, for example, ranged from the power inherent in the basic document as such, to superimpositions, to large close-ups. But the close-ups of Hitchcock are not the same as those of C. B. de Mille in *The Cheat* [1915]. They are just one type of figure, among others, of his style. In other words, in the silent days, montage evoked what the director wanted to say; in the editing of 1938, it described it. Today we can say that at last the director writes in film. The image—its plastic composition and the way it is set in time, because it is founded on a much higher degree of realism—has at its disposal more means of manipulating reality and of modifying it from within. The film-maker is no longer the competitor of the painter and the playwright, he is, at last, the equal of the novelist.

1950—55

139

CHARLES BARR
CINEMASCOPE: BEFORE AND AFTER

CinemaScope was introduced by 20th Century-Fox in 1953. It confused a lot of people, and has continued to do so. It was assumed that its value was purely a sensational one, that it was self-evidently "inartistic," and that once the novelty wore off the companies would be forced to drop it as abruptly as they had dropped 3-D, Hollywood's previous answer to the Television Menace. A decade later, however, the CinemaScope revolution is a fait accompli. Not only are a large proportion of Hollywood films in CinemaScope or similar processes, but other countries too make Scope films in increasing numbers. Most theaters have been adapted for Scope projection without changing the old pattern of exhibition, as it had been forecast they would have to. Cinema-Scope scarcely makes an impact any longer for its own sake: most of the really big pictures today are made on 70mm film or in Cinerama. It is even possible now to be disappointed when a blockbuster *(The Guns of Navarone, The Longest Day)* is "only" in CinemaScope.

I will assume that the technical details are familiar. Since Fox holds the rights to CinemaScope itself, other companies have preferred to develop their own variants, some of which use different methods, and are arguably superior but which are similar in essentials, with an aspect ratio (height to width) of 1:2.35. All of these can be classed together, as indeed they usually are, as "CinemaScope" or just as "Scope."

CinemaScope has had a more general indirect influence: although non-Scope productions still use 35mm nonanamorphic film, very few of them are still designed for projection in the old 1:1.33 ratio. Instead, the top and bottom are masked off, and the image thrown over a wider area. This ratio is, it seems, becoming settled at 1:1.85. Thus all films, with the occasional foreign-language exception, are now widescreen films; this format will clearly share, in a minor way, some of the characteristics of CinemaScope, and normally when I talk of the effects of the "CinemaScope" ratio this can be taken to mean something like "Scope; and even more so the 70mm systems; and to a lesser extent the wide screen."

The commercial survival of Cinemascope has disconcerted critics, especially English-speaking ones. So far as I can see, all of them had condemned it from the start as a medium for anything other than the spectacular and the trivial. Its shape was apparently wrong for "serious" or "intimate" drama, for the kind of film and the kind of effects which a sensitive director aims at. Now Cinema-Scope was, obviously, a commercial innovation designed purely to save the finances of Fox, whose executives were evasive and hypocritical in their pretense that they were doing this for Art's sake. Most of the early Scope films were indeed crude. Fox was enlightened neither in choice of subjects nor of directors: among those who made the first of these films were Koster, Dunne, Johnson, Dmytryk, and Negulesco. However, since then a great number of serious and or intimate films have been made in Scope, too many to catalogue, and too many for it to be worth remarking on any longer, when each comes out. The early ones included *A Star is Born* (Cukor), *East of Eden* (Kazan), and *River of No Return* (Preminger); then, among others, all Truffaut's features; *La Dolce Vita, The Island, Trials of Oscar Wilde, Lola, Lola Montes, Rebel Without a Cause, Bitter Victory, Tarnished Angels, Man of the West, The Tall Men, Some Came Running, The Courtship of Eddie's Father* . . . not forgetting *L'Année Dernière à Marienbad* and, on 70 mm film, *Lawrence of Arabia* and *Exodus*.

The cycle of events has been very close to that which followed the introduction of sound. That too was a commercial move, designed to save Warner Brothers, and it led to a comparable, temporary chaos. Most commentators were misled into thinking that sound must be in itself inartistic, and a betrayal of "pure" cinema, but gradually it became accepted as a useful development, and one could say that Scope too is coming, tacitly, to be accepted, because there is really no alternative. . . .

The point is this: the rejection of CinemaScope was, and is, based on certain familiar, but in fact highly disputable, assumptions, the fundamental one being that the film image consists of a *frame* into which a number of things are successively *fitted*, and that a film is made by sticking such images together in a creative way. The old 1:1.33 ratio screen was compatible with this aesthetic, and the CinemaScope screen is not, but instead of considering afresh whether these preconceptions were valid the critics simply used them to make an a priori condemnation of a format which is, one admits, manifestly unsuitable for "framing" things.

One can call this the "traditional" aesthetic: it is the one which is found in books. It puts the emphasis on framing, the close-up, camera angles, and montage. Montage is only the French word for editing, and is clearly indispensable to any director; the difference is that here this stage is made into the crucial one in a process which consists of selecting details and "showing them one by one" (Pudovkin in *Film Technique*).

I believe this aesthetic was always misguided, at least in the dogmatic form in which it was applied, and that the most valuable and forward-looking films at any time have been made to some extent outside it. Ideally, Scope could have been the occasion for its ceremonial abandonment. It was no longer workable, but then it was no longer necessary. It is a hangover from the silent cinema, but people still try to muddle through using it as an implicit basis for their judgment even of Scope films: it is not surprising if they can't cope. You still get films evaluated according to whether the "set-ups" are "imaginative" or not, and a film which uses long takes and few close-ups is liable to be dismissed automatically as unfilmic or as visually dull. Any summary of the development of style is bound to be schematic, but if one bears in mind that there can be no clear-cut division between sound and silent, and between post- and pre-Scope, I think it is useful to go back and estimate how this "traditional" aesthetic was established, and became ingrained.

There were four main factors:

(1) The image was narrow and unaccompanied by sound; it was therefore difficult to make a full impact within a single shot, and

without cutting. Naturally, this objection applies less and less after the introduction of, in turn, the moving camera, sound, composition in depth, and CinemaScope.

The film was a new and bewildering medium; this aesthetic made it easy to assimilate to the pattern of other arts, notably painting and literature:

(2) It played down the film's basis in "reality," which was felt to be incompatible with art.

(3) It took the shot as a "unit," like the ideogram or the word: this made it more easily manageable and gave it the prestige of a "language" of its own.*

Finally, (4) it was formulated and applied chiefly by certain Russian directors; theirs is one kind of film, and of temperament, which it really suits.

These points merge into one another, and need to be elaborated more fully.

The first films were straightforward records of everyday reality. As such, they gave audiences a big thrill. Lumière set up his camera to take a scene in a single, static shot: workers leaving a factory, a train entering a station, a family eating out of doors, etc. The spectators' first instinct was to scramble out of the way of the approaching train, and in the background of the shot of the family eating *(Bébé Mange sa Soupe)* they noticed the detail of leaves blowing in the wind, and called out excitedly.

However, once the novelty of such shots wore off, it became apparent that the impact of a single image was limited. You do not, in fact, get a very strong sense of actuality from a narrow, silent image; it is too much of an abstraction, the picture too remote. For the same reason, there is not much scope for the integration of background detail. It was difficult to cover a scene of any complexity, as film-makers discovered when they began to extend their range and to tell stories. Few of them thought to move the camera, or to move and group people with any precision, within the frame. The usual solution would be to photograph the action in long shot, in order to get it all in, or to huddle actors and décor unrealistically

---

* "In the silent cinema, montage had a precise meaning, because it represented language. From the silent cinema we have inherited this myth of montage, though it has lost most of its meaning."

—Roberto Rossellini

close together. Then came montage, and the close-up, and this was of course a great advance. But although Griffith is associated with their development, he was already very skillful in controlling, when appropriate, all the elements of a scene within the same shot; indeed, the most striking thing today about *Birth of a Nation* is the number of scenes which are played in a remarkably modern, integral style (for instance: the scenes in the hospital; at the Camerons' home; in Lincoln's office). To judge from the few films of his that I have seen, and particularly *The Coward* (1915), Thomas Ince was working in the same way.

Meanwhile, however, pundits had decided that the film could not be art if it confined itself to recording "reality," and they extended this to mean that an uncut piece of film was nothing, that montage was all. Now "reality" is a word which has to be handled carefully. Nabokov nicely describes it as "one of the few words which mean nothing without quotes."

Both the still and the movie camera make a record of "reality" in the sense that they record, objectively, what is put in front of them. As Helmut Gernsheim (*Creative Photography*, 1960) expresses it: "The camera intercepts images, the paintbrush reconstructs them." This worried theorists from the start. No other art presented this problem, and no other art, furthermore, had ever been suddenly invented like this, rootless, instead of evolving slowly, and evolving a function as it did so. A decision had to be made. One interpretation was this: the camera records reality, but reality is not art, therefore photography cannot be art. And later: the cinema cannot be art. The second interpretation arises from this and is complementary to it: agreed, reality is not art, but we improve upon it by treating it in a creative way. In practice, this meant getting as far away as possible from objectivity, and it produced, in the first decades of photography, some quite ludicrous results, prints being posed and processed and stuck together in a form of "montage" in such a way as to be indistinguishable from painting. The "masterpieces" of this art look grotesque today, and I think warn us against dismissing as irrelevant the objective basis of the cinema. Gernsheim *(op. cit.)* puts this phase into perspective: "The mistaken ambition to compete with painting drove a minority to artificial picture-making alien to the nature of photography . . . to appreciate photography requires above all understanding of the qualities and limitations peculiar to it."

This is what André Bazin—the Gernsheim of the cinema—means when he says "Les virtualités esthétiques de la photographie résident dans la révélation du réel." In this essay* Bazin makes a far more useful analysis of the nature of film and its implications for film style, than Kracauer does in the whole of his book.

The film image is taken direct from "reality" and the spectator perceives and "recognizes" it direct; there is no intermediate process as there is when the writer "translates" his material into words which are in turn translated back by the imagination of the reader. This is a major difference which conditions the whole of the respective media, and the attempt to draw literal analogies between the two (for instance between the word and the shot) is as much of a dead end as the attempt to assimilate photography to the rules of painting.

However, to say that the camera records "reality" is not to advocate that the cinema should remain at the level of Lumière. The experience of seeing even a film like *Exodus*, which is about the furthest the cinema has gone in the direction of "reality"—70mm film, long static takes, complete surface authenticity—is not something we get each day when we go out into the street. It is *a* reality, organized by the director; and in any case a record of reality is not the same thing as reality itself. The director selects or stages his "reality," and photographs it; we perceive the image, on the screen, in the course of the film. This process *in itself* means that the experience belongs to the "imaginative" as opposed to the "actual" life to use the categories distinguished by the art critic Roger Fry (*An Essay in Aesthetics*, 1909). Fry was talking about differences in our perception of life and of paintings, but the distinction applies equally to film, and he did in fact cite the examples of the elementary newsreel-type films of his time to illustrate how even a "transparent" recording of an everyday scene was perceived in a radically different way from actuality. This distinction, which is basic to our responses to any art, is summed up thus by I. A. Richards (*Principles of Literary Criticism*): "In ordinary life a thousand considerations prohibit for most of us any complete working-out of our response; the range and complexity of the impulse-systems involved is less; the need for action, the comparative uncertainty and vagueness of the situation, the intrusion of accidental irrelevancies, in-

---

*"Ontology of the Photographic Image," *What is Cinema?*

convenient temporal spacing—the action being too slow or too fast
—all these obscure the issue and prevent the full development of
the experience. But in the "imaginative experience" these obstacles
are removed. . . . As a chemist's balance to a grocer's scales, so is
the mind in the imaginative moment to the mind engaged in ordinary intercourse or in practical affairs."

The crucial point is that in the cinema this distinction operates
before the montage stage, and independently of it.

Art does indeed involve organization, but this is just as possible
within a complex image as in a montage sequence: it can in many
ways be more subtle. I will analyze these possibilities more specifically later on. For a number of reasons, as I say, they had not been
explored very fully in the early days of the cinema. The cutting
together of separate shots is a more obviously "creative" method,
and a more straightforward one.

Even if it's true, as I think it is, that those who first imagined and
developed the cinematograph thought in terms of a *total* illusion,
with sound, color and depth† and that the restricted form it temporarily took was in this sense accidental, it is still possible to see
the history of the cinema as a nicely arranged series of advances,
each one coming when directors, and audiences, were ready for it.
First they learned to cope with the camera alone, then gradually
with more and more of the ingredients of reality: they could hardly
have controlled all of them at once, from the start, without practice or precedent, any more than primitive musicians would have
been able to cope immediately with a symphony orchestra—or
audiences to respond to it. The greater density of the sound-Scope-
color image requires a more precise control than the simple "unit"
image does. One has to ascend by stages. The idea of predetermined
advance should not be applied too rigidly, for the immediate instrument of each advance has after all been financial pressure, and
Warners' crisis, and therefore their introduction of the sound film,
could have come a few years earlier or later; similarly with Fox
and the introduction of CinemaScope. But this does not make the
whole thing fortuitous, as Macgowan seems to imply when he says
that we might easily have had Todd-AO thirty years ago, at the

---

† Cf. Bazin's essay "The Myth of Total Cinema," also published in the first volume
of *What is Cinema?*

same time as sound, only support was withheld. The cinema evolves by a form of Natural Selection: technicians and financiers provide the "mutations," and their survival depends upon whether they can be usefully assimilated at the time.

Often when "use of CinemaScope" is picked out by a critic it indicates an obtrusive style, with the director striving to "compensate" for the openness of the frame, or indulging in flashy compositional effects—as in, say, Kurosawa's *The Hidden Fortress*, or *Vera-Cruz*, the first half-hour of which Robert Aldrich makes into an absolute orgy of formalism, composing frames within frames, and blocking up the sides of the image with rocks, trees, etc. In general, what they say about the camera makes a good working rule for Scope: if you notice it, it's bad. Or, more reasonably: you don't have to notice it for it to be good. This is not to forbid the critic the phrase "use of Scope," which may be useful to avoid periphrasis, provided that it's not made into a criterion in itself, unrelated to the work as a whole.

In their book *Hitchcock*, Chabrol and Rohmer mention that in CinemaScope "the extreme edges of the screen are virtually unusable": that the edges are by no means useless, but that they will not be used for the placing of details meaningful for their own sake.

While the chief advantage of Scope is, as they maintain, its opening-up of the frame, the greater sense it gives us of a continuous space—and this is where it relates to the film they are discussing here, namely *Rope*—this is a slight over-simplification. Sometimes people can be placed at the extreme edges for perfectly legitimate effect: as in *The Tall Men* (Walsh, 1955): Jane Russell and Clark Gable play a long, intimate scene together; it ends in a fight, and they retire sulking to opposite corners of the room—and of the Scope frame, leaving a great gulf between them. A different effect: near the end of *The True Story of Jesse James* (Nicholas Ray, 1957) Jesse decides to retire: he goes out into the garden to play with his children: a green and white image, Jesse on the right: a man walks past, glimpsed on the extreme left of the frame, and calls out a greeting: the strong "horizontal" effect here reinforces the feeling of a new freedom. In *Spartacus* Kubrick uses a similar technique for the shots of Crassus and his entourage visiting the training camp; the contrast between this openness and the cooped-up images

147

showing the gladiators' existence helps express the general contrast between luxury and oppression.

But it is not only the horizontal line which is emphasized in CinemaScope (this was implied by critics who concentrated on the *shape* of the frame qua shape—as though it were the frame of a painting—and concluded that the format was suitable only for showing/framing horizontal things like crocodiles and processions). The more open the frame, the greater the impression of depth: the image is more vivid, and involves us more directly. The most striking effect in Cinerama is the roller-coaster shot, which gives us a very strong sensation of movement forward. Even though at the crucial moment we may be focussing only on the very center of the image, i.e., the area of track directly in front of the roller-coaster—an area, in fact, no larger than the standard frame—the rest of the image is not useless. We may not be conscious of what exactly is there, but we are marginally aware of the objects and the space on either side. It is this peripheral vision which orients us and makes the experience so vivid. Similar effects were tried in the early films in Todd-AO (roller-coaster; train ride) and CinemaScope (the shots from the nose of the plane in *How to Marry a Millionaire*). In Scope the involvement is less strong, but it is still considerable: so are its implications. Although the shots quoted aim at nothing more than a circus effect, *physical* sensation of this kind can be dramatically useful (elementary form-and-content). This power was there even in the 1:1.33 image, but for the most part (after Lumière's train) remained latent. But there are classic examples of movement in this plane in Renoir's *Partie de Campagne:* the long-held shot at the end, taken from the stern of the boat being rowed home; rain on the water: an overwhelming sense of nostalgia conveyed by the movement. And in Wyler's *The Best Years of Our Lives*, the shots from the nose of the plane in which the three servicemen are returning home. The movement gives us a direct insight into their sensations and through this into "what it is like" generally for them.

Scope automatically gives images like these more "weight," and it also of course enhances the effect of lateral movement.

In *Rebel Without a Cause* (Ray, 1956) a shot of extraordinary beauty comes after the first twenty minutes of the film, during which the surroundings have been uniformly cramped and de-

148

pressing, the images physically cluttered-up and dominated by blacks and browns. Now, James Dean is about to set out for school; he looks out of the window. He recognizes a girl (Natalie Wood) walking past in the distance. Cut to the first day/exterior shot, the first bright one, the first "horizontal" one. A close shot of Natalie Wood, in a light-green cardigan, against a background of green bushes. As she walks the camera moves laterally with her. This makes a direct, sensual impression which gives us an insight into Dean's experience, while at the same time remaining completely natural and unforced. On the small screen, such an image could not conceivably have had a comparable weight.

One of the climaxes of *Jesse James* is Jesse's revenge killing of a farmer. This is important to the story because it ruins Jesse's chance of an amnesty, and it is equally important to the understanding of his character in that it illustrates his pride, and his thoughtlessness. The crucial shot here has the farmer ploughing his land. Jesse rides up behind him, stops, and lifts his rifle. The man starts to run but Jesse keeps with him. The camera tracks back with them, holding this composition—the farmer in the foreground, running into the camera, Jesse inexorably behind, aiming—until finally Jesse shoots him dead. This is over in a moment but has a hypnotic, almost a slow-motion impact, which again is the result of the greater physical involvement achieved by Scope, its more vivid sense of space. The impact is direct, and there is no need to emphasize it by putting it into literal slow-motion, or making a significant "pattern."

Rudolf Arnheim, in *Film as Art*, claims that any such sensation of depth will be undesirable: compositional patterns which in the more abstract image would come across as being deliberate will, if the image is more vivid, seem natural, even accidental, so that the spectator may fail to note their symbolic force.*

From this point of view, an even more relevant Scope scene is

---

* Arnheim also wrote, and I am not making it up: "Silent laughter is often more effective than if the sound is actually heard. The gaping of the open mouth gives a vivid, highly artistic interpretation of the phenomenon 'laughter.' If, however, the sound is also heard, the opening of the mouth appears obvious and its value as a means of expression is almost entirely lost." But I don't know that this argument against sound is any more unconvincing than that against Scope—the logic is identical.

this one from *River of No Return*, analyzed by V. F. Perkins in *Movie*. I think the narrative is clear enough from his description:

"As Harry lifts Kay from the raft, she drops the bundle which contains most of her 'things' into the water. Kay's gradual loss of the physical tokens of her way of life has great symbolic significance. But Preminger is not over-impressed. The bundle simply floats away off-screen while Harry brings Kay ashore. It would be wrong to describe this as understatement. The symbolism is in the event, not in the visual pattern, so the director presents the action clearly and leaves the interpretation to the spectator."

Arnheim would no doubt regard this as a reductio ad absurdum. His attitude, which is shared, deep down, by most critics, is based on his phobia of using the camera as a "recording machine" (reality is not art). It further reflects an unwillingness to leave the spectator any freedom to interpret action or behavior, or to make connections. This concept of "freedom" has been distorted as much as that of "reality." It's taken to be absurd that a director should allow a viewer any freedom of interpretation, for he may then notice things that he isn't meant to, or fail to notice things that he should; he may get the wrong point altogether. This is in line with the idea that the test of a good film is whether it "makes statements."

Now in this scene from *River of No Return*, the spectator is "free" to notice the bundle, and, when he does so, free to interpret it as significant. But there is nothing random about the shot. The detail is placed in the background of the shot, and integrated naturally, so that we have to make a positive act of interpreting, of "reading," the shot. The act of interpreting the visual field—and through that the action—is in itself valuable. The significance of the detail is not announced, it is allowed to speak for itself. An alert spectator will notice the bundle, and "follow" it as it floats off screen.

The traditional method would be to make its significance unmistakable by cutting in close-ups. In this case we would gather that the bundle is meaningful *because* it is picked out for us. In Preminger's film, the process is reversed: we pick it out *because* it is meaningful. The emphasis arises organically out of the whole action; it is not imposed.

"The symbolism is in the event not in the visual pattern." Before Scope, it was difficult to show the "event" lucidly, with each detail given its appropriate weight. It wasn't impossible: many Renoir films, as well as Mizoguchi's *Ugetsu Monogatari*, are superlative examples of the "opening-up" of the 1:1.33 frame to achieve this kind of fluidity. But on the whole the tendency was to split up the event into its component parts, and to impose, whether deliberately or not, a "visual pattern," a pattern of montage and/or of obtrusively "composed" images. And a *visual* pattern involves a pattern of motivation, a pattern of significance, which in certain films is appropriate, but is more often damagingly crude.

At this stage one can hardly avoid talking of "participation," which is another much-abused word. Everyone agrees, in principle, that art should not so much state as reveal, and that we should not just register its meaning but understand it. Our experience of a work should involve active participation more than passive assimilation.

The Russians, in their theoretical work, appropriated this idea, and applied it in a somewhat outrageous way; but critics, even intelligent ones, have continued to accept what they said. The confusion rests on a misunderstanding of the relation between film and the other arts, notably literature. Eisenstein said that "participation" took place in the association of successive images (as in the association of juxtaposed images in poetry)—that it depended purely on montage. In *October* he had intercut shots of Kerensky with ironic titles, and then with shots of a peacock preening itself. These images in themselves are fairly neutral, but the spectator fuses them together freely, he "participates," and arrives at an "intellectual decision" at the expense of Kerensky. In *Strike* we are shown, alternately, shots of workmen being massacred and of bulls being slaughtered: again, the two sets of images are independent of each other and we have to make the imaginative link between the two. Commenting recently on passages like these, an English critic said, "Thus, Eisenstein's 'intellectual cinema' proves itself a superior means of communication by demanding the co-operation of the spectator in consideration of the conflicting ideologies that Eisenstein chose to convey."

This seems to me so much solemn nonsense. The whole is more than the sum of its parts; but then the whole is *always* more than the sum of its parts. The spectator "interprets" but there is no genuine freedom of association. A montage link of this kind re-

151

minds one of the children's puzzle which consists of a series of numbered dots: when they are joined together correctly, the outline of an animal appears. We participate in solving these, but only in a mechanical way, and there is only one correct solution. The very last thing Eisenstein really wants us to do is to evaluate for ourselves, or even experience for ourselves, what we are shown. He does not show us heroic actions—which we can recognize or judge to be heroic—he shows actions (not even that, but only *bits* of actions) and tells us that they are heroic (or alternatively brutal). Vakoulintchouk, in *Potemkin*, is "defined" by the shots which are intercut with shots of his dead body: close-ups of weeping women, sympathetic titles. Similarly we are *told* how to react to Kerensky and to the killing of the workmen—told obliquely, it is true, by a form of visual code, but still told; nothing is in any useful sense communicated. It is revealing that the whole meaning of these films can be reversed, as happened apparently in places with *Potemkin*, by merely re-arranging certain shots and titles, just as one can reverse the meaning of a slogan by replacing one name with another. (This would be inconceivable with *Birth of a Nation*.)

What is in question is not Eisenstein's artistry, within his chosen field, but rather the way his technique has been rationalized, by him and by others, and a universal validity claimed for it. The style is appropriate to what he was aiming to do, namely to make propaganda. He was not interested (in the silent films) in characterization or in shades of meaning, nor did he want to leave the spectator any freedom of response. The struggle of authority against revolution, and of Old against New, is one of Black and White. Andrew Sarris, in an excellent article on Rossellini in the *New York Film Bulletin*, contrasts this extreme montage style—"Eisenstein's conceptual editing extracts a truth from the collision of two mechanistic forces in history"—with "Rossellini's visual conception of a unified cosmos undivided by the conceptual detail of montage," and he implies one should accept each on its own terms. I think it's legitimate to say that, even if the style reflects the vision accurately, the vision is crude, and the style, although powerful, crude likewise. The words Eisenstein and his contemporaries use in describing it are significant: impact, collision, clash, the juxtaposition of "concepts"; the approach is essentially a rhetorical one. What is obvious anyway from this is that Eisenstein is a special case, that few directors see things his way, and that few subjects are amenable to this treatment. Drama is not normally reducible to concepts, clashes and collisions. (This is quite apart from the implications of the change to the sound film, after which the technique becomes still less relevant.)

People complain sometimes that Eisenstein's methods of intellectual and ideological montage have been forgotten, as have the associative techniques of Pudovkin's *Mother*, and imply that directors today must be deficient in imagination: but insofar as they reject these techniques they are more subtle. And a field where they do notably survive is that of the filmed commercial. The product may not in itself look very special (a "dead object") but it takes on associations when intercut with a smiling mother holding a smiling baby. The montage-unit style no doubt sells products, and puts over propaganda, more effectively than would a more fluid one, and there are other films too for which it is perfectly appropriate: educational work, certain documentaries, anything which aims to put over a message concisely. One would not advocate CinemaScope for these.

Jean Mitry, in his interesting book *Eisenstein* criticizes him for at times indulging in arbitrary symbolism (the slaughterhouse in *Strike*), but he accepts Eisenstein's analogies between the interpretation of film and poetic images: the film-maker juxtaposing unrelated images by montage is like the poet juxtaposing words. But the reader genuinely "participates" in the associations he makes from the words, in building them up into a fused whole: words are allusive whereas the film image is concrete. Film images follow each other in rigid sequence, which we cannot vary; the interaction of words is much more flexible. The more one goes into the differences between word and shot, and between the literary and filmic sequences of description, the more shaky do all the analogies made by the Russians seem.

There is no literary equivalent for "getting things in the same shot." This seems never to have struck them. Both Eisenstein and Pudovkin made laborious comparisons between the word or ideogram and the individual shot, and between the sentence and the montage-sequence. This seems fantastically naïve. How else can you translate "the cat sat on the mat" into film except in a single shot? Disciples tend to admit that these theories went a bit far—

153

after all, they never went quite so far in their films—but without realizing that the rest of their aesthetic, which sounds more plausible, is in fact equally shaky, and for similar reasons.

For instance: a writer has to describe details successively, even though they may exist together. In this case he will aim, by his description, to evoke a "total" simultaneous reality in the reader's mind. Because of the indirect, allusive quality of language this is not really a handicap. Thackeray, in his *Irish Sketchbook*, gives a description of a mountain scene, evoking it by a series of details and of comparisons: he adds, "Printer's ink cannot give these wonderful hues, and *the reader will make his picture at his leisure*" (my italics). But the film image is direct, it *shows* things.

In *Lolita* (the book) there is a scene which, had it been presented without comment, might have seemed a perfect vindication of the rules laid down by Pudovkin in *Film Technique*, in that it consists of a series of details, which Nabokov describes successively, and which Pudovkin would have filmed successively ("showing them one by one, just as we would describe them in separate sequence in literary work"). It is the scene of the death of Humbert's wife: "I rushed out. The far side of our steep little street presented a peculiar sight. . . . *I have to put the impact of an instantaneous vision into a sequence of words; their physical accumulation on the page impairs the actual flash, the sharp unity of impression.* Rug-heap, old-man doll, Miss O's nurse running with a rustle back to the screened porch . . ." (my italics).

It's naïve to suppose that even the most fragmented lines—"ships, towers, domes, theatres and temples lie/open unto the fields and to the sky"—can be given an exact cinematic equivalent by a montage of ships, towers, domes, and so on. Eisenstein makes much of the fragmentary narrative of Dickens; this is fair enough in that a change of scene would correspond to a cut in film, but it does not hold for the *texture* of a narrative. Thomas Hardy makes a useful reference here, and at the risk of seeming repetitive I'd like to consider some passages from his novels.

Often he will introduce a character by, as it were, discovering him within a landscape. Being a writer, he describes things one by one, but they all contribute to the creation of a broad, total environment. His protagonists emerge from this, and are in turn absorbed into it; they are never detached; we retain a mental picture of them as a part of it. The film equivalent is to *show* them as a part of it, to engulf them in it. Boetticher's *Ride Lonesome* and Ray's *The Savage Innocents* are two films which portray people dominated by, almost defined by, their natural environment, and this connection is perfectly conveyed in their first images. In *Ride Lonesome*, the camera is held on a shot of a vast plain, stretching away to mountains in the distance; then it tilts down slowly and we become aware of a rider coming toward us from deep among the rocks below. *The Savage Innocents* has a long, empty snowscape: the camera is still: a sledge enters frame left, deep within the shot, and is drawn gradually toward us. One can contrast this with the opening of *Scott of the Antarctic:* a montage of snow vistas, evocative music. We look *at* the scene instead of being involved in it, as we are in *The Savage Innocents;* and we accept, intellectually, for the purposes of the narrative, that the characters are there, instead of genuinely feeling it. Both Boetticher's and Ray's films are in Scope, and this helps enormously: it increases the involvement of the spectator and the physical integration of the characters.

It might be said that these are "landscape" films, that Scope is suitable for them but not for more confined drama. But the same principles hold; the dichotomy often expressed between interior and exterior drama is a false one.

Consider this passage from *Tess of the d'Urbervilles*. On her wedding night, Tess confesses to her husband about the child she had by Alec:

"Her narrative had ended; even its reassertions and secondary explanations were done. Tess's voice throughout had hardly risen higher than its opening tone; there had been no exculpatory phrase of any kind, and she had not wept.

"But the complexion even of external things seemed to suffer transmutation as her announcement proceeded. The fire in the grate looked impish—demoniacally funny, as if it did not care in the least about her strait. The fender grinned idly, as if it too did not care. The light from the water-bottle was merely engaged in a chromatic problem. All material objects around announced their irresponsibility with terrible iteration. And yet nothing had changed since the moments when he had been kissing her; or rather, nothing in the substance of things. But the essence of things had changed."

The Russians, again, might interpret this their own way: fragmentation, subjectivity, justifying a similar technique for film. But in film everything is concrete. Film shows the substance, it cannot *show* the essence, but it can *suggest* the essence by *showing* the substance. It suggests inner reality by showing outer reality with the greatest possible intensity. The writer has to build up a scene by description and allusion: images and metaphors, however fanciful, can help to strengthen our *objective* picture of the scene, whereas if transposed to film they would distract, and distort (imagine a close-up of the fender, grinning idly). For filming this passage from *Tess* I can't imagine a better method than to keep both of them in the frame the whole time, with the "material objects" around and between them, and to have her explanation, and then his silence, and reactions, in a single take, without any overt emphasis from the camera. Ideally, in CinemaScope, which makes the surroundings more palpable, and enables you to get close to one or both of the characters without shutting out the rest of the scene. The more precisely the camera charts the substance of things, the external movement of words, expressions, gestures, the more subtly can it express the internal movement: the essence of things.

Such a sequence would be condemned a priori by Arnheim ("immobile recording machine") and by Eisenstein, who laid down that *any* scene where a transition in feeling was observed, without a cut, was "theatrical." Need one point out that you can get a far greater control, on film, of all the elements of the scene, and of how each spectator sees them? And that the division of change into before and after can often be crudely mechanical? There could be no more eloquent illustration of this danger than the scene which Eisenstein holds up as an example of how to handle such a change in feeling: the cream-separator episode from the *The General Line*.

A great comfort to upholders of the "traditional" aesthetic has always been the Kuleshov/Pudovkin experiment (three neutral CUs of an actor, Mosjoukine, intercut with three different shots, to give the impression of three different emotions). This was felt to define the cinema for all time, and to establish that its essence was montage. If the same effect was difficult to achieve with sound, and then CinemaScope, that must prove that they were a bad thing. I do not honestly think that the effect on spectators of these sequences, presented as Pudovkin relates, can have been quite so overwhelming as he claims (is there any evidence, I wonder, that the experiment was done, and does not represent wishful thinking?), but one can accept that they do, up to a point, work: we understand what is being depicted, we complete the equations. Later experiments by psychologists have confirmed that one expression abstracted from its context looks very much like another. But this can far more reasonably be seen, I think, as an argument for not abstracting it in the first place.

The experiment illustrates that each act of perception automatically conditions succeeding ones; this is something which applies continuously, to life as well as to art, and which any intelligent artist will have taken into account in working out a style—not, however, to the extent of making it the cornerstone of his method. Pudovkin here reminds one of the bakers who first extract the nourishing parts of the flour, process it, and then put some back as "extra goodness": the result may be eatable, but it is hardly the only way to make bread, and one can criticize it for being unnecessary and "synthetic." Indeed one could extend the culinary analogy and say that the experience put over by the traditional aesthetic is essentially a *predigested* one. These two epithets have in ordinary usage a literal meaning and, by extension, a metaphorical one, applied pejoratively; the same correlation is valid here.

Writers like Manvell, Reisz, and Lindgren (all of whom base their aesthetic more or less closely on the Russians') advocate a method which gives us a *digest* of what we might see, in real life, if we were experiencing a given scene. Lindgren, in *The Art of the Film*, goes into this in most detail. He makes the usual comparisons with literary fragmentation, and then between what we see in life and in films. Sometimes we consciously see things as a whole, in their interrelationship (general shot). Sometimes we look round (pan) or walk (tracking shot). Normally we focus on one thing at a time (close-up or close-shot) and we look from one thing to another (cutting). Now it should be clear that the correspondence is by no means exact. In a film we sit facing the same direction all the time, looking at a screen which is set at a finite distance. In life we are oriented in our surroundings and our perception of them is continuous—continuous in time and space. But Lindgren claims that "in so far as the film is photographic and reproduces movement, it can give us a lifelike semblance of what we see; in so far as it employs editing, it can exactly [sic] reproduce the *manner* in which we see it."

At any time we see "central" things and "marginal" things; of the latter we may be aware, or half-aware, or they may serve merely to orient us. The traditional aesthetic separates out the central things: the marginal ones it either omits as inessential and distracting, or intercuts in close shot—in which case they are no longer marginal but central.

So an alternative method, a more strictly realistic one, which Lindgren and company pass over, is to present a complex image organized in such a way that we are induced to interpret it for ourselves. This is where genuine participation comes in, as in the sequence quoted from *River of No Return.*

Manvell *(The Film and the Public)* writes that "the comparatively narrow bounds of the normal screen shape sharpen perception by closing it in, giving the director full control of every detail which the audience should perceive." Conversely in CinemaScope "the sharpened perception of the normal film will be lost." In his aesthetic, we either see a thing or we don't. If a detail is important, the director singles it out for us; if there is a symbol or a meaningful connection to be noted, the director again does it for us, emphasizing it by close-ups. (Cf. Eisenstein's criticism of Dovshenko's *Earth,* on the grounds that he had not made the symbolism explicit enough —i.e., he had not brought the symbolic detail into close-up but had left it integrated, so that it might appear accidental.) We do not have to bother about noticing it for ourselves, or estimating whether it is significant. On the other hand when the image is complex we *have* to be alert to interpret it and the details within it. The difference between the Preminger method cited from *River of No Return* and the explicit close-up/montage style which he could have used, but didn't, corresponds to the difference between reading the meaning for ourselves and having it spelled out for us.*

"I don't think CinemaScope is a good medium. It's good only for showing great masses of movement. For other things, it's dis-

---

*Cf. also in *Citizen Kane* Welles's extremely subtle handling of the Rosebud/snow-glass paperweight imagery, which he often leaves naturally in the background of the shot for us to notice, and to make the connections. Pages could be written on this.

Composition in the wide screen. The astronaut (Gary Lockwood) receives birthday greetings from his parents in *2001: A Space Odyssey* (1968). "When the image is complex we *have* to be able to interpret it and the details within it. . . . It is much easier to put together a complex scene synthetically out of separate details . . . but you sacrifice the possibility of real conviction, of real subtlety" (BARR, pages 158, 161).

tracting, it's hard to focus attention, and it's very difficult to cut. Some people just go ahead and cut it and let people's eyes jump around and find what they want to find. It's very hard for an audience to focus—they have too much to look at—they can't see the whole thing." (Howard Hawks in an interview with Peter Bogdanovich.)

This is the danger; it was more worrying at the introduction of Scope, when audiences did apparently have to get used to "exploring" the more open image, but this I think was temporary. If a Scope image is decently organized the eyes will not just "jump around and find what they want to find," purely at random— they can be led to focus on detail, and to look from one thing to another within the frame with the emphasis which the director intends: that is, if the spectator is alert. Hawks may not like Scope (he had an apparently traumatic experience using it for *Land of the Pharaohs*, perhaps his worst film), but he approves of the 1:1.85 screen, and his style has always been one which allows the spectator freedom; in this sense he does not need Scope. One of the best of all examples of the alternative style to Lindgren's is from his *Hatari!* (wide screen). General shot of a bedroom: right of frame, in bed, waiting for her supper, Elsa Martinelli (back to camera); on the bed, John Wayne. Centre of frame, background, a tame cheetah. Left of frame, enter Red Buttons, carrying a tray; he trips over the cheetah's tail and the supper lands on Wayne, Martinelli, and the floor. Typically, Hawks takes this (exceedingly funny) scene in one static shot. It is done with a beautiful directness and lucidity, and without any of the usual look-this-is-funny comedy emphasis. The scene exists autonomously, action and reaction being integrated: Martinelli suddenly collapses with the giggles but we can only just see her at the edge of the frame. The nicest thing of all is the cheetah's reaction. He is obviously quite bewildered by the whole episode. We can see him in the background, looking up in pained manner at Red Buttons, and Hawks leaves him there, fading out the scene after a brief moment. Contrast the almost invariable procedure in other films for handling animal performers: that of extracting a certain laugh by cutting in their cute reactions in close-up. We are left "free" to interpret the scene visually, and this means we are free to respond. Our responses are not "signposted" by successive close-ups—foot tripping over tail, result, various reactions. No single reading of the scene is imposed. One could put it another way: the scene, as directed, is at once more subtle and more *authentic*. The reason why animals' reactions are normally cut in separately is not only that they thus get a surer laugh but that it's difficult to direct an animal so that it genuinely does what it is represented to be doing. It is sometimes held to be the chief glory of the cinema that you can, by montage, "create" an event like this which never happened. But the result (leaving aside certain kinds of film where the convention obviously allows this) is mechanical.*

The same applies in a less obvious way to other details of action and acting. It is much easier to put together a complex scene synthetically out of separate details—especially when you have an incompetent actor, or a child—than to organize and film the scene in its integrity. But you sacrifice the possibility of real conviction, of real subtlety.

The advantage of Scope over even the wide screen of *Hatari!* is that it enables complex scenes to be covered even more naturally: detail can be integrated, and therefore perceived, in a still more realistic way. If I had to sum up its implications I would say that it gives a greater range for *gradation of emphasis*. George Kaplan wrote in *Scene* that "there is no room for subtlety on 70mm film"; on the contrary, there is twice as much room, as is clear both from arithmetic and from *Exodus*. The 1:1.33 screen is too much of an abstraction, compared with the way we normally see things, to admit easily the detail which can only be really effective if it is perceived *qua* casual detail. There are innumerable applications of this (the whole question of significant imagery is affected by it): one quite common one is the scene where two people talk, and a third watches, or just appears in the background unobtrusively— he might be a person who is relevant to the others in some way, or who is affected by what they say, and it is useful for us to be "reminded" of his presence. The simple cutaway shot coarsens the effect by being too obvious a directorial aside (Look who's watching) and on the smaller screen it's difficult to play off foreground and background within the frame: the detail tends to look too obviously planted. The frame is so closed-in that any detail which

---

*Bazin analyzed this issue—the existence of which no one before him seems to have realized—in another definitive essay, "The Virtues and Limitations of Montage."

161

is placed there *must* be deliberate—at some level we both feel this and know it intellectually.* Greater flexibility was achieved long before Scope by certain directors using depth of focus and the moving camera (one of whose main advantages, as Dai Vaughan pointed out in *Definition* 1, is that it allows points to be made literally "in passing"). Scope as always does not create a new method, it encourages, and refines, an old one. The most beautiful example of this "gradation of emphasis" point is I think *The Courtship of Eddie's Father;* others include *The True Story of Jesse James, Ride the High Country* (all Scope)·and *Exodus* (70mm). This is not something which can be isolated from the excellence of the films as a whole, nor can it be satisfactorily documented—one just has to sit in front of the films and see how space and décor and relationships are organized, and the eye led from one point to another within the image; how connections are made, and characters introduced, not being "added on" to the rest of the context but developing *out of* it.

Few of the films like these which I'd regard as being the richest of all are liked by critics; to praise Ray, Preminger, Hawks, or Minnelli makes one liable to the charge of subscribing to a "cult," a common defense mechanism which enables critics to avoid any challenge to their preconceptions. While it's possible, of course, to reject any of these films in the last analysis, I think the disagreement is more basic than this. Mainstream critics have been conditioned to recognize only a style based on montage and the close-up, and on "signposting" of effects, as valid, and may be in effect physically unable to respond to a film which requires an active interpretation on every level. I mean by this that, as we become more sophisticated and get more familiar with ideas and concepts, we tend to interpret films in literary terms, and our visual acuteness

---

*In Antonioni's *Il Grido* there is a shot taken from inside a house: a woman goes out of the door and walks away. The door stays slightly ajar and through this very narrow aperture we continue to see her walking in a dead straight line away from the camera. This is a far too neat continued effect, and audiences groan. It is too good to be true that she should have walked along exactly the one line which would have kept her visible. On the other hand if the aperture had been wider, she would have been "free" to deviate, and even if she had in fact taken precisely the same path the shot would have been more acceptable—not in spite of but *because* of the "frame" of the door "fitting" her less well. I don't think it is fanciful to compare the door that frames her with the frame of the film image in general.

162

atrophies. Norman Fruchter, conducting a Film Appreciation course for unsophisticated teenagers, found that "the cadets' visual responses were far more acute than anyone might have given them credit for. I had to watch a film at least three times to see as much as they caught in a single viewing. They rarely missed detail. . . ." (*Sight and Sound*, Autumn, 1962). Now the traditional aesthetic allows for, and encourages, our more sophisticated tendencies by, as I described, "predigesting" a scene and serving it up in separate units, each one of which we can read like a sign. Critics who are conditioned by this will keep on (consciously or subconsciously) trying to separate out the "subject" of each shot, the "content" of each sequence, even when the film is made in a denser and more fluid style which does not admit this kind of treatment. They resent, or more commonly fail to understand, directors who give them too much work to do, and they naturally resent CinemaScope, which automatically makes for a more open, complex image.

The specific objections made to CinemaScope now, I hope, fall into place: they are really no objections at all. Sidney Lumet in an interview (*Film Quarterly*, Winter, 1960) was asked about the new screen processes and answered "I think they're ridiculous, I think they're pointless, I think they're typical Hollywood products. And typical Hollywood mentality, because the essence of any dramatic piece is people, and it is symptomatic that Hollywood finds a way of photographing people directly opposite to the way they are built. CinemaScope makes no sense until people are fatter than they are taller."

This is about as logical as to say that a book should be the shape of what it's about. If the screen is to correspond exactly to the human build then we should have vertical CinemaScope. If to the human face, it should be square (if not oval), and the most common criticism of Scope was, indeed, that it made the close-up impossible: it no longer "fits" the screen. As Gavin Lambert said, "A face squashed across a concave screen is clearly an unedifying prospect." (In CinemaScope, unlike Cinerama, the screen is seldom noticeably curved, and clearly the objection is more to the dimensions than to the curvature itself.)

The argument is effectively a circular one. I think one can sum up the development of the close-up roughly like this: the natural subject for the film is man-in-a-situation. But the frame was too narrow for this to be shown comfortably: also, it was difficult to organize from scratch, without some experience of the cinema and what could be done with it. So man-in-situation came to be conveyed by man + situation: close-up of a face, intercut with shots defining his experience and/or surroundings.

Certain film-makers welcomed this because it was more manageable and also more clearly "creative." At the same time, the process was rejected by others as being mechanical. One can look at this first from the point of view of actor and director. There is a loss of spontaneity, which is reflected in the film. "If you isolate a detail, that means that you have to take it up again from cold, to resuscitate the emotion" (Vincente Minnelli). "The close-up in the cinema is essentially a reconstruction, something pre-fabricated, carefully worked up" (Jean Renoir).

This in turn affects the spectator, who has to take on trust the connection between the close-up and the rest of the scene; man + situation tends to become a formula, a cruder digest of a reality which is continuous and complex. "If I were to throw in ten more details, everything in my films would suddenly become extremely clear. But those ten details are just what I don't want to add. Nothing could be easier than to take a close-up; I don't take any, lest I be tempted to use them" (Roberto Rossellini).

Directors like these worked out a more integral style presenting man-*in*-situation. This involved compensating for the narrowness of the frame by moving the camera laterally and composing the scene in depth. If the actors were brought close to the camera they would fill the screen, and blot out the background; therefore they were seldom brought close. This style is associated mainly with Renoir, who in 1938 wrote: "The more I advance in my craft, the more I feel it necessary to have the scene set in depth in relation to the screen; and the less can I stand actors placed carefully before the camera, as if they were posing for their photograph. It suits me rather to set my actors freely at different distances from the camera, to make them move about." This can be traced back to *Boudu Sauvé des Eaux* (1932) and even to his silent films; and there are others in the 'thirties like Hawks and Ophuls who, while not applying any formal principle of composition in depth, concentrate on the organization of the space within the image, and avoid the detached close-up—see especially *The Criminal Code* and *Liebelei*.

164

These, together with *Boudu*, make up a marvelous trio of early sound films, which if one relied upon historians one would scarcely know existed, for according to most theories they oughtn't to.

The most spectacular application of these ideas is undoubtedly Antonioni's *Le Amiche* (made in 1955 but in the 1:1.33 ratio), of which he said: "I wanted to show my characters in their context, not to separate them, by montage, from their daily environment. You will find no cross-cutting whatever in *Le Amiche*: this technique expresses nothing." There are no close-ups in this film, and the average length of shot is 30 seconds, which is a lot. Antonioni realizes, and demonstrates, that the interaction of people with each other and with their surroundings is much more subtly expressed by showing them simultaneously. To dissociate them by montage tends to dissociate them altogether. The difference is not one of degree but of kind.

How does this relate to CinemaScope? Many of the directors who thus "anticipate" it do not in fact use it; partly this is chance, partly that they can get along without. But while I would not quite agree with the magazine *Présence du Cinéma*, which states that everything is automatically better in Scope, I think that, other things being equal, Scope refines this style. The director can now afford to bring a character closer to the lens without shutting out the context, and this flexibility is useful. He can have two faces in close shot together, instead of having to cut from one to the other, or to squeeze them in unnaturally close together. (Antonioni, although he has not worked in Scope, has taken advantage of the 1:1.85 screen in this way. Ian Cameron discusses this apropos of *L'Avventura* in *Film Quarterly*, Fall, 1962).

In CinemaScope the close-up, so far from being impossible, is for the first time fully acceptable: it *cannot* be a mechanical, all-purpose CU like the one of Mosjoukine, and it cannot be detached, it must include a genuine and not just a token background. I say "cannot": at least, if it is done this way, it is patently absurd. The image is too open, its space too palpable, to accommodate the "dead object" and give it spurious life. A lifeless film is twice as lifeless in Scope, as certain directors continue to demonstrate by building up scenes in the cutting-room out of the most perfunctory of component-shots. The most grotesque example is *The Lion*, but *The Left Hand of God*, *The Barbarian and the Geisha*, *Bus*

The astronauts (Gary Lockwood and Keir Dullea) discuss Hal's problems while Hal listens in the rearground in *2001: A Space Odyssey* (1968). "The director . . . can have two faces in close shot together, instead of having to cut from one to the other, or to squeeze them in unnaturally close together" (BARR, page 165).

Stop, and *The Deep Blue Sea* are also instructively inept. (I don't suggest that Scope *makes* them bad; they would have been anyway, but Scope shows them up more clearly. Over-all, and with certain clear exceptions like the didactic and the animated film, Scope makes the bad film worse and the good film better: it should gradually separate the sheep among directors from the goats.)

Look at the Scope close-up, as before, from both angles, how it is shot, and how we see it. If it is to pass, it must be analytic rather than synthetic: instead of taking an insert CU, then, against a neutral background, the director will have to recreate the ambience of the whole, and this helps the actor. The actor at the same time is freer to move within the frame, and thus within his surroundings, instead of being "placed carefully before the camera". Mariette Hartley, the girl in *Ride the High Country*, stands at the window of her house, talking to a boy: Scope close-up: she moves around nervously while she talks, and the director (Sam Peckinpah) doesn't have to worry about keeping her fixed to any chalk-marks because there is room enough within the frame; the effect is marvelously spontaneous.

Kazan's *Wild River* (about the evacuation of a remote community by the Tennessee Valley Authority) is a film where environment, and its effect on different people, is as significant as in *Le Amiche* and *The Magnificent Ambersons*. Because it is in Scope it doesn't matter that it is full of close-ups and crosscut sequences. Antonioni's reservations no longer apply; Kazan can concentrate on a single face without dissociating it from its context and "dislocating" the spectator.

Finally, a not unusual CinemaScope scene (from Ray's *Bitter Victory*) which contradicts most of the facile generalizations about Scope, made alike by those against and those in favor. The three main characters sit around a table, talking. The atmosphere is important — a military club in Africa, during the war, a nervous, falsely cheerful environment. The scene is taken in a series of full or medium close-ups, each of the three in turn, as they talk, sometimes two together. The normal theoretical attitude is that this would be fine on the old-ratio screen but clumsy if not impossible in Scope. If anything, the reverse is true, and it works brilliantly *because* it is in Scope: the cutting does not disorient us, the close-ups do not wholly isolate the characters, we know where we are

167

all through. At the edges of the frame there is décor and space and perhaps some casual detail; thus when the camera is on one of the men, Richard Burton, we can see a couple dancing, and an Arab guard, and a general background of the room; we are completely situated at each moment, and accept the scene as real, while getting the full concentration on each face which Ray intends. So far from distracting this awareness of environment and of the characters' relation in space is necessary.

In talking about the close-ups in *Bitter Victory* I am talking about the montage. The two have always been lumped together, by people condemning Scope ("the close-up and montage become impossible") and by those welcoming it ("but montage and the close-up are not essential anyway"); the implications of Scope are identical for both. Montage is at once less necessary and more acceptable. Bazin and Roger Leenhardt, two of the few who approved of Scope from the start, imagined it would come to eliminate cutting within a sequence, and that this was no bad thing, but fortunately the medium is more flexible: some directors cut more in Scope, some less. There is no need to fragment reality, but there is less harm in fragmenting it because the different bits can be fitted together more satisfactorily. . . .

1963

CHRISTIAN METZ
FROM FILM LANGUAGE

SOME POINTS IN
THE SEMIOTICS OF THE CINEMA

The purpose of this text is to examine some of the problems and difficulties confronting the person who wants to begin undertaking, in the field of "cinematographic language," de Saussure's project of a general semiotics: to study the ordering and functionings of the main signifying units used in the filmic message. Semiotics, as de Saussure conceived it, is still in its childhood, but any work bearing on one of the nonverbal "languages," provided that it assumes a resolutely semiological relevance and does not remain satisfied with vague considerations of "substance," brings its contribution, whether modest or important, to that great enterprise, the general study of significations.

The very term "cinematographic *language*" already poses the whole problem of the semiotics of film. It would require a long justification, and strictly speaking it should be used only after the in-depth study of the semiological mechanisms at work in the filmic message had been fairly well advanced. Convenience, however, makes us retain, right from the start, that frozen syntagma — "language" — which has gradually assumed a place in the special vocabulary of film theoreticians and aestheticians. Even from a strictly semiological point of view, one can perhaps at this time give a preliminary justification for the expression "cinematographic language" (not to be confused with "cinematographic *langue*" (language system), which does not seem to me acceptable) — a justification that, in the present state of semiological investigations, can only be very general. I hope to outline it in this essay. . . .

169

CINEMA AND NARRATIVITY

A first choice confronts the "film semiologist": Is the corpus to be made up of feature films *(narrative films)* or, on the contrary, of short films, documentaries, technological, pedagogical, or advertising films, etc.? It could be answered that it depends simply on what one wants to study—that the cinema possesses various "dialects," and that each one of these "dialects" can become the subject of a specific analysis. This is undoubtedly true. Nevertheless, there is a hierarchy of concerns (or, better yet, a methodological urgency) that favors—in the beginning at least—the study of the narrative film. We know that, in the few years immediately before and after the Lumière brothers' invention in 1895, critics, journalists, and the pioneer cinematographers disagreed considerably among themselves as to the *social function* that they attributed to, or predicted for, the new machine: whether it was a means of preservation or of making archives, whether it was an auxiliary technography for research and teaching in sciences like botany or surgery, whether it was a new form of journalism, or an instrument of sentimental devotion, either private or public, which could perpetuate the living image of the dear departed one, and so on. That, over all these possibilities, the cinema could evolve into a machine for telling stories had never been really considered. From the very beginnings of the cinematograph there were various indications and statements that suggested such an evolution, but they had no common measure with the magnitude that the narrative phenomenon was to assume. The merging of the cinema and of narrativity was a great fact, which was by no means predestined—nor was it strictly fortuitous. It was a historical and social fact, a fact of civilization (to use a formula dear to the sociologist Marcel Mauss), a fact that in turn conditioned the later evolution of the film as a semiological reality, somewhat in the same way—indirect and general,* though effective —that "external" linguistic events (conquests, colonizations, transformations of language) influence the "internal" functioning of idioms. In the realm of the cinema, all nonnarrative genres—the documentary, the technical film, etc.—have become marginal

---

*Except, of course, for specific lexical facts.

provinces, border regions so to speak, while the *feature-length film of novelistic fiction*, which is simply called a "film"—the usage is significant†—has traced more and more clearly the king's highway of filmic expression.

This purely numerical and social superiority is not the only fact concerned. Added to it is a more "internal" consideration: Non-narrative films for the most part are distinguished from "real" films by their social purpose and by their content much more than by their "language processes." The basic figures of the semiotics of the cinema—montage, camera movements, scale of the shots, relationships between the image and speech, sequences, and other large syntagmatic units—are on the whole the same in "small" films and in "big" films. It is by no means certain that an independent semiotics of the various nonnarrative genres is possible other than in the form of a series of discontinuous remarks on the points of difference between these films and "ordinary" films. To examine fiction films is to proceed more directly and more rapidly to the heart of the problem.

There is, moreover, an encouraging diachronic consideration. We know, since the observations of Béla Balázs, André Malraux, Edgar Morin, Jean Mitry, and many others, that the cinema was not a specific "language" from its inception. Before becoming the means of expression familiar to us, it was a simple means of mechanical recording, preserving, and reproducing moving visual spectacles—whether of life, of the theater, or even of small *mises-en-scène*, which were specially prepared and which, in the final analysis, remained theatrical—in short, a "means of reproduction," to use André Malraux's term. Now, *it was precisely to the extent that the cinema confronted the problems of narration* that, in the course of successive gropings, it came to produce a body of specific signifying procedures. Historians of the cinema generally agree in dating the beginning of the "cinema" as we know it in the period 1910–15. Films like *Enoch Arden, Life for the Czar, Quo Vadis?, Fantômas, Cabiria, The Golem, The Battle of Gettysburg,* and above all *Birth of a Nation* were among the first films, in the acceptation we now give this word when we use it without a determinant: Narration of

---

†As in statements like "The short was terrible, but the film was great" or "What are they showing tonight? a series of shorts or a film?" etc.

a certain magnitude based on procedures that are supposed to be specifically cinematographic. It so happens that these procedures were perfected in the wake of the narrative endeavor. The pioneers of "cinematographic language"—Méliès, Porter, Griffith—couldn't care less about "formal" research conducted for its own sake; what is more (except for occasional naïve and confused attempts), they cared little about the symbolic, philosophical or human "message" of their films. Men of denotation rather than of connotation, they wanted above all to tell a story; they were not content unless they could subject the continuous, analogical material of photographic duplication to the *articulations*—however rudimentary—of a narrative discourse. Georges Sadoul has indeed shown how Méliès, in his story-teller's naïveté, was led to invent double exposure, the device of multiple exposures with a mask and a dark backdrop, the dissolve and the fade-in, and the pan shot. Jean Mitry, who has written a very precise synthesis of these problems, examines the first occurrences of a certain number of procedures of filmic language—the close-up, the pan shot, the tracking shot, parallel montage, and interlaced, or alternate, montage—among the film primitives. I will summarize the conclusions he reaches: The principal "inventions" are credited to the Frenchmen Méliès and Promio, to the Englishmen G. A. Smith and J. Williamson, and to the American E. S. Porter; it was Griffith's role to define and to stabilize—we would say, to codify—the *function* of these different procedures in relation to the filmic *narrative*, and thereby unify them up to a certain point in a coherent "syntax" (note that it would be better to use the term *syntagmatic category;* Jean Mitry himself avoids the word syntax). Between 1911 and 1915, Griffith made a whole series of films having, more or less consciously, the value of experimental probings, and *Birth of a Nation*, released in 1915, appears as the crowning work, the sum and the public demonstration of investigations that, however naïve they may have been, were nonetheless systematic and fundamental. Thus, it was in a single motion that the cinema became narrative and took over some of the attributes of a language.

Today, still, the so-called filmic procedures are in fact filmic-narrative. This, to my mind, justifies the priority of the narrative film in the filmosemiological enterprise—a priority that must not of course become an exclusivity.

STUDIES OF DENOTATION AND STUDIES OF CONNOTATION IN THE SEMIOTICS OF THE CINEMA

The facts I have just reviewed lead to another consequence. The semiotics of the cinema can be conceived of either as a semiotics of connotation or as a semiotics of denotation. Both directions are interesting, and it is obvious that on the day when the semiological study of film makes some progress and begins to form a body of knowledge, it will have considered connotative and denotative significations together. The study of connotation brings us closer to the notion of the cinema as an art (the "seventh art"). As I have indicated elsewhere in more detail, the art of film is located on the same semiological "plane" as literary art: The properly aesthetic orderings and constraints—versification, composition, and tropes in the first case; framing, camera movements, and light "effects" in the second—serve as the connoted instance, which is superimposed over the denoted meaning. In literature, the latter appears as the purely linguistic signification, which is linked, in the employed idiom, to the units used by the author. In the cinema, it is represented by the literal (that is, perceptual) meaning of the spectacle reproduced in the image, or of the sounds duplicated by the soundtrack. As for connotation, which plays a major role in all aesthetic languages,* its significate is the literary or cinematographic "style," "genre" (the epic, the western, etc.), "symbol" (philosophical, humanitarian, ideological, and so on), or "poetic atmosphere"— and its signifier is the whole denotated semiological material, whether signified or signifying. In American gangster movies, where, for example, the slick pavement of the waterfront distills an impression of anxiety and hardness (significate of the connotation), the scene represented (dimly lit, deserted wharves, with stacks of crates and overhead cranes, the significate of denotation), and the technique of the shooting, which is dependent on the effects of lighting in order to produce a certain *picture* of the docks (signifier of denotation), converge to form the signifier of connotation. The

---

* Aesthetic language practices a kind of promotion of connotation, but connotation occurs as well in various phenomena of expressiveness proper to ordinary language, like those studied by Charles Bally (*Le Langage et la vie*, Geneva, Payot, 1926).

same scene filmed in a different light would produce a different impression; and so would the same technique used on a different subject (for example, a child's smiling face). Film aestheticians have often remarked that filmic effects must not be "gratuitous," but must remain "subordinate to the plot." This is another way of saying that the significate of connotation can establish itself only when the corresponding signifier brings into play *both* the signifier and the significate of denotation.

The study of the cinema as an art—the study of cinematographic expressiveness—can therefore be conducted according to methods derived from linguistics. For instance, there is no doubt that films are amenable to analyses comparable *(mutatis mutandis)* to those Thomas A. Sebeok has applied to Cheremis songs, or to those Samuel R. Levin has proposed. But there is another task that requires the careful attention of the film semiologist. For also, and even first of all, through its procedures of *denotation*, the cinema is a specific language. The concept of *diegesis* is as important for the film semiologist as the idea of art. The word is derived from the Greek διήγησις, "narration" and was used particularly to designate one of the obligatory parts of judiciary discourse, the recital of facts. The term was introduced into the framework of the cinema by Étienne Souriau. It designates the film's *represented* instance (which Mikel Dufrenne contrasts to the expressed, properly aesthetic, instance)—that is to say, the sum of a film's denotation: the narration itself, but also the fictional space and time dimensions implied in and by the narrative, and consequently the characters, the landscapes, the events, and other narrative elements, in so far as they are considered in their denoted aspect. How does the cinema indicate successivity, precession, temporal breaks, causality, adversative relationships, consequence, spatial proximity, or distance, etc.? These are central questions to the semiotics of the cinema.

One must not indeed forget that, from the semiological point of view, the cinema is very different from still photography whence its technique is derived. In photography, as Roland Barthes has clearly shown, the denoted meaning is secured entirely through the automatic process of photochemical reproduction; denotation is a visual transfer,* which is not codified and has no inherent organiza-

---

*I am speaking here as a semiologist and not as a psychologist. Comparative studies of visual perception, both in "real" and in filmic conditions, have indeed isolated all the optical distortions that differentiate between the photograph and the tion. Human intervention, which carries some elements of a proper semiotics, affects only the level of connotation (lighting, camera angle, "photographic effects," and so on). And, in point of fact, there is no specifically photographic procedure for designating the significate "house" in its denotated aspect, unless it is by showing a house. In the cinema, on the other hand, a whole semiotics of denotation is possible and necessary, for a film is composed of *many* photographs (the concept of montage, with its myriad consequences)—photographs that give us mostly only partial views of the diegetic referent. In film a "house" would be a shot of a staircase, a shot of one of the walls taken from the outside, a close-up of a window, a brief establishing shot of the building,† etc. Thus a kind of filmic *articulation* appears, which has no equivalent in photography: It is the denotation itself that is being constructed, organized, and to a certain extent codified *(codified,* not necessarily *encoded).* Lacking absolute laws, filmic intelligibility nevertheless depends on a certain number of dominant habits: A film put together haphazardly would not be understood.

I return to my initial observations: "Cinematographic language" is first of all the literalness of a plot. Artistic effects, even when they are substantially inseparable from the semic act by which the film tells us its story, nevertheless constitute another level of signification, which from the methodological point of view must come "later."

PARADIGMATIC AND SYNTAGMATIC CATEGORIES

There is a danger that the semiotics of the cinema will tend to develop along the syntagmatic rather than along the paradigmatic

---

object. But these transformations, which obey the laws of optical physics, of the chemistry of emulsions and of retinal physiology, do not constitute a signifying system.

†Even if this over-all view is the only one shown us in the film, it is still the result of a choice. We know that the modern cinema has partially abandoned the practices of visual fragmentation and excessive montage in favor of the continuous shot (cf. the famous "shot-sequence" controversy). This condition *modifies* to the same extent the semiotics of filmic denotation, but it in no way dismisses it. Simply, cinematographic language, like other languages, has a diachronic side. A single "shot" itself contains several elements (example: switching from one view to another through a camera movement, and without montage).

axis. It is not that there is no filmic paradigm: At specific points along the chain of images the number of units liable to occur is limited, so that, in these circumstances, the unit that does appear derives its meaning in relation to the other members of the paradigm. This is the case with the "fade-dissolve" duality within the framework of the "conjunction of two sequences":* a simple commutation, which the users—that is to say, the spectators—perform spontaneously, makes it possible to isolate the corresponding significates: a spatiotemporal break with the establishing of an underlying transitive link (dissolve), and a straightforward spatiotemporal break (fade). But in most of the *positions* of the filmic chain, the number of units liable to appear is very much open (though not infinite). Much more open, in any case, than the series of lexemes that, by their nonfinite nature, are nonetheless opposed to the series of grammatical monemes in linguistics. For, despite the difficulty, already emphasized by Joseph Vendryes in *Le Langage*, of accurately enumerating the words of an idiom, it is at least possible to indicate the maximum and minimum limits, thus arriving at the approximate order of magnitude (for example, in French the lexeme *"lav-"* exists, but the lexeme *"patouf"* does not†). The case is different in the cinema, where the number of images is indefinite. Several times indefinite, one should say. For the "pro-filmic" spectacles‡ are themselves unlimited in number; the exact nature of lighting can be varied infinitely and by quantities that are nondiscrete; the same applies to the axial distance between the subject and the camera (in variations which are said to be scalar—that is, scale of the shot),§ to the camera angle, to the properties of the film and

---

*Fades, or dissolves, can also occur in other settings, especially at the center of sequences. In such cases, their value is different.

†The lexemic unit *"lav-"* corresponds to *"wash-"* in English; *"patouf"* is no more of a lexeme in English than it is in French.—TRANSLATOR.

‡As defined by Étienne Souriau. The "profilmic" spectacle is whatever is placed in front of the camera, or whatever one places the camera in front of, in order to "shoot" it.

§In *Le Langage cinématographique* (Paris, 1962), Francois Chevassu maintains (p. 14) that the "scale of shots" is coded. I would say instead that it is the technical terminology ("close-up," "thirty-degree angle shot," "medium shot," etc.) that is coded. The actual scale of the shots constitutes a continuous gradation, from the closest to the furthest shot. Codification intervenes at the metalinguistic level (studio jargon) in this case, and not on that of the language object (that is, cinematographic language).

the focal length of the lens, and to the exact trajectory of the camera movements (including the stationary shot, which represents zero degree in this case). It suffices to vary one of these elements by a perceptible quantity to obtain *another* image. The shot is therefore not comparable to the word in a lexicon; rather it resembles a complete statement (of one or more sentences), in that it is already the result of an essentially free combination, a "speech" arrangement. On the other hand the word is a syntagma that is precast by code — a "vertical" syntagma, as R. F. Mikus would say. Let us note in this connection that there is another similarity between the image and the statement: Both are actualized units, whereas the word in itself is a purely potential unit of code. The image is almost always assertive — and assertion is one of the great "modalities" of actualization, of the semic act. It appears therefore that the paradigmatic category in film is condemned to remain partial and fragmentary, at least as long as one tries to isolate it on the level of the *image*. This is naturally derived from the fact that *creation* plays a larger role in cinematographic language than it does in the handling of idioms: To "speak" a language is to use it, but to "speak" cinematographic language is to a certain extent to invent it. The speakers of ordinary language constitute a group of users; film-makers are a group of creators. On the other hand, movie *spectators* in turn constitute a group of users. That is why the semiotics of the cinema must frequently consider things from the point of view of the spectator rather than of the film-maker. Étienne Souriau's distinction between the filmic point of view and the *"cinéastique,"* or film-making, point of view is a very useful concept; film semiotics is mainly a *filmic* study. The situation has a rough equivalent in linguistics: Some linguists connect the speaker with the message, while the listener in some way "represents" the code, since he requires it to understand what is being said to him, while the speaker is presumed to know beforehand what he wants to say.

But, more than paradigmatic studies, it is the syntagmatic considerations that are at the center of the problems of filmic denotation. Although each image is a free creation, the arrangement of these images into an intelligible sequence — cutting and montage — brings us to the heart of the semiological dimension of film. It is a rather paradoxical situation: Those proliferating (and not very discrete!) units — the *images* — when it is a matter of composing a film, suddenly accept with reasonably good grace the constraint of

177

a few large syntagmatic structures. While no image ever entirely resembles another image, the great majority of narrative films resemble each other in their principal syntagmatic figures. *Filmic narrativity*—since it has again crossed our path—by becoming stable through convention and repetition over innumerable films, has gradually shaped itself into forms that are more or less fixed, but certainly not immutable. These forms represent a synchronic "state" (that of the present cinema), but if they were to change, it could only be through a complete positive evolution, liable to be challenged—like those that, in spoken languages, produce diachronic transformations in the distribution of aspects and tenses. Applying de Saussure's thought to the cinema, one could say that the large syntagmatic category of the narrative film *can change*, but that no single person can make it change over night.* A failure of intellection among the viewers would be the automatic sanctioning of a purely individual innovation, which the system would refuse to confirm. The originality of creative artists consists, here as elsewhere, in tricking the code, or at least in *using* it ingeniously, rather than in attacking it directly or in violating it—and still less in ignoring it.

AN EXAMPLE: THE ALTERNATING SYNTAGMA

It is not within the scope of this paper to analyze the principal types of *large* filmic *syntagma*. Instead, as an example, I will simply indicate some of the characteristics of one type, the *alternating syntagma* (for example, image of a mother-image of her daughter-image of the mother, etc.). The alternating syntagma rests on the principle of alternating distribution of two or more diegetic elements. The images thus fall into two or more *series*, each one of which, if shown continuously, would constitute a normal sequence. The alternating syntagma is, precisely, a rejection of the grouping by continuous series (which remains potential), for reasons of connotation—the search for a certain "construction" or a certain "effect." This type of syntagma apparently made its first appearance in 1901 in England, in a film by Williamson, *Attack on a*

---

* But then, I should have added, by the same token, that this syntagmatic category contains a paradigmatic category, and consequently I should have shown less skepticism as to the possibilities of a paradigmatic category in the cinema.

Mission in China, one of those "re-enacted news reels" that were popular at the time. In it, one saw images of a mission surrounded by Boxers (during the rebellion of that name) alternating with shots of marines coming to the rescue.* Subsequently the procedure becomes more or less usual.

The alternation defines the form of the signifier, but not necessarily, as we shall see, that of the significate—which amounts to saying that the relationship between the signifier and the significate is not always analogous in the alternating syntagma. If one takes the nature of the *significate of temporal denotation* as a relevant basis, one can distinguish three cases of alternating syntagma. In the first case (which might be called the *alternator*), the alternation of the signifiers refers to a parallel alternation of the significates (analogous relationship). Example: two tennis players framed alternately, at the moment each one is returning the ball. In the second case (which would be the *alternate syntagma*), the alternating of the signifiers corresponds to a simultaneity of the significates. Example: the pursuers and the pursued. Every spectator understands that he is seeing two chronological series which are contemporaneous at each instant, and that, while he is seeing the pursued galloping away (locus of the signifier, on the screen), the pursuers are nonetheless continuing the chase (locus of the signifier, in the diegesis). Thus the semiotic *nexus*—alternating simultaneity—is no longer analogous. But it does not become "arbitrary" because of that: It remains motivated (remember that analogy is one of the forms of motivation), and the understanding of this kind of syntagma by the viewer is relatively "natural." The motivation must be explained by the spontaneous psychological mechanisms of filmic perception. Anne Souriau has shown that sequences of the "pursued-pursuing" variety are readily understood, with little previous exposure, by the spectator (on the condition, only, that the rhythm of the alternation not be too slow), for he "interpolates spontaneously" the visual material that the film presents. He guesses that series 1 continues to unfold in the plot while he is seeing series 2 in the image. The third case could be called *parallel syntagma:* Two series of events are mixed together through montage without having any relevant temporal relationships on the level

---

* "Alternation" means simultaneity here. It pertains therefore to the alternate *syntagma*, as I am about to define that term.

of the significate (diegesis), at least with respect to denotation. It is this variety of syntagma that film theoreticians sometimes refer to with expressions like "neutral temporal relationships." Example: a sinister urban landscape at night, alternating with a sunny pastoral view. There is nothing to indicate whether the two scenes are simultaneous or not (and if not, which precedes and which follows). It is simply a matter of two motifs brought together for "symbolic" reasons by montage (the rich and the poor, life and death, reaction and revolution, etc.) and without their literal location in time as a pertinent factor. It is as if the denoted temporal relationship had yielded to the rich, multiple values of connotation, which depend on the context as well as on the substance of the significate.

The three varieties of alternating syntagma constitute a small system whose internal configuration recalls somewhat the structure of verbal grammatical persons as conceived by Émile Benveniste. A first correlation (presence or absence of relevant temporal denotation) allows us to distribute parallel montage to one side (absence), and alternate and alternator montage to the other (presence). Within the second term, another correlation (nature of the significate of temporal denotation) distinguishes between the alternate (significate equals simultaneity) and the alternator (significate equals alternation).*

---

*I have retained this passage because it gives a simple example of what commutation can be in the filmic corpus, but the factual conclusions presented here no longer correspond to the current state of my investigations of the considered point. First of all, the study of various passages of films has made it appear that the "alternator" cannot always be distinguished from the "alternate" syntagma (or, in rarer cases, from the parallel syntagma) by any really probing difference: In the example of the tennis players, it can also be considered that the two partners are both supposed to be engaged in action continuously and simultaneously (i.e., alternate syntagma). Thus—and although certain cases seem to subsist where the alternate syntagma appears, more clearly than in other cases, as a *variant* similar to what I have called here the "alternator"—I have not retained the alternator as a separate type or subtype. Then, there are cases where the alternating of images on the screen corresponds to temporal relationships not mentioned in this article: For example, one finds "alternating syntagmas" that interweave a "present" series with a "past" series (a kind of alternating flashback), and in which consequently the relationship of the two series can be defined neither by simultaneity nor by the term "neutral temporal relationship." One will note also that the concept of "alternating syntagma" has a certain obscure correspondence to that of the "frequentative syntagma." . . . In the final analysis, however, the reason I have dropped the "alternator" *as a general category*

OTHER PROBLEMS

These very brief remarks provided an example of what the syntagmatic study of filmic denotation could be. There are important differences between the semiotics of the cinema and linguistics itself. Without repeating those mentioned elsewhere, let me recall some of the main points: Film contains nothing corresponding to the purely distinctive units of the second articulation; all of its units—even the simplest, like the dissolve and the wipe—are directly significant (and moreover, as I have already pointed out, they only occur in the actualized state). The commutations and other manipulations by which the semiotics of the cinema proceeds therefore affect the large significatory units. The "laws" of cinematographic language call for *statements* within a narrative, and not monemes within a statement, or still less phonemes within a moneme.

Contrary to what many of the theoreticians of the silent film declared or suggested ("*Ciné langue,*" "visual Esperanto," etc.), the cinema is certainly not a language system *(langue)*. It can, however, be considered as a *language*, to the extent that it orders signifying elements within ordered arrangements different from those of spoken idioms—and to the extent that these elements are not traced on the perceptual configurations of reality itself (which does not tell stories). Filmic manipulation transforms what might have been a mere visual transfer of reality into discourse. Derived from a kind of signification that is purely analogous and continuous —animated photography, cinematography—the cinema gradually shaped, in the course of its diachronic maturation, some elements of a proper semiotics, which remain scattered and fragmentary within the open field of simple visual duplication.*

---

of classification is less because of the drawbacks I have just pointed out (and which various adjustments could suppress) than because of an over-all *reformulation* of the table of the main types of filmic arrangement. Taken separately, the analysis developed above remains partially valid.

* But I should have added here that the significations that analogy and mechanical duplication yield—although they do not pertain to *cinematographic* language as a specific system—nevertheless do have the effect of bringing structures and elements that belong to *other* systems which are also cultural, which also carry meaning and which are also more or less organized, into the cinema (as a whole).

181

The "shot"—an already complex unit, which must be studied—remains an indispensable reference for the time being, in somewhat the same way that the "word" was during a period of linguistic research. It might be somewhat adventurous to compare the shot to the *taxeme*, in Louis Hjelmslev's sense, but one can consider that it constitutes the largest *minimum segment* (the expression is borrowed from André Martinet), since at least one shot is required to make a film, or part of a film—in the same way, a linguistic statement must be made up of at least one phoneme. To isolate several shots from a sequence is still, perhaps, to analyze the sequence; to remove several frames from a shot is to destroy the shot. If the shot is not the smallest unit of filmic *signification* (for a single shot may convey several informational elements), it is at least the smallest unit of the filmic chain.*

One cannot conclude, however, that every minimum filmic segment is a shot. Besides shots, there are other minimum segments, *optical devices*—various dissolves, wipes, and so on—that can be defined as visual but not photographic elements. Whereas images have the objects of reality as referents, optical procedures, which do not represent anything, have images as referents (those contiguous in the syntagma). The relationship of these procedures to the actual shooting of the film is somewhat like that of morphemes to lexemes; depending on the context, they have two main functions: as "trick" devices (in this instance, they are sorts of semiological exponents influencing contiguous images), or as "punctuation." The expression "filmic punctuation," which use has ratified, must not make us forget that optical procedures separate large, complex statements and thus correspond to the articulations of the literary narrative (with its pages and paragraphs, for example), whereas actual punctuation—that is to say, typographical punctuation—separates sentences (period, exclamation mark, question mark, semicolon), and clauses (comma, semicolon, dash), possibly even "verbal bases," with or without characteristics (apostrophe, or dash, between two "words," and so on).

---

* Similarly, the phoneme is not the minimum distinctive unit, since the latter is the "feature," but it is the minimum element of the spoken *sequence*, the threshold below which an order of consecutiveness yields to an order of simultaneity.

IN CONCLUSION

The concepts of linguistics can be applied to the semiotics of the cinema only with the greatest caution. On the other hand, the methods of linguistics—commutation, analytical breakdown, strict distinction between the significate and the signifier, between substance and form, between the relevant and the irrelevant, etc.—provide the semiotics of the cinema with a constant and precious aid in establishing units that, though they are still very approximate, are liable over time (and, one hopes, through the work of many scholars) to become progressively refined. . . .

1968

ALFRED GUZZETTI
CHRISTIAN METZ
AND THE SEMIOLOGY
OF THE CINEMA

The three books[1] and numerous articles that Christian Metz has written since 1964 give him fair claim to be considered the most important film theorist since André Bazin. To Bazin's question *What is Cinema?* he has replied cinema is a language. Though he is not the first to give this answer, he is the first to inform it with a sophisticated understanding of modern linguistics. Using models drawn from this discipline, his work attempts to confer on film theory the virtues of systematization, objectivity, and precision.

Metz is, to use his own term, a semiologist, and, as such, groups natural language with signifying systems as diverse as those of myth, dress, food, cinema, kinship, politeness, painting, poetry, and cartography. These systems are taken not simply to serve a function analogous to natural language but to be open to the sort of analysis developed in its study. For these reasons, linguistics plays a double role in semiology. As the source of method, it is the parent discipline; and as the study of a single signifying system, it is a branch of the more general, though still embryonic, science.

Since neither semiology nor the school of linguistics on which it is based is very well known in the United States, I

---

[1] These are *Essais sur la Signification au Cinéma* (Paris, 1968), *Langage et Cinéma* (Paris, 1971), and *Propositions Methodologiques pour l'analyse du Film* (Universitatsverlag Boehum, Germany, 1970), the last of which I have not been able to locate. My translations of quotations from the first two of these books (abbreviated as *Essais* and *Langage*) are incorporated in the text of this essay.

shall try to give a brief outline of its premises and the place of Metz's work with relation to them. Semiology derives its linguistic framework from Ferdinand de Saussure, who furnished the indispensable distinction between the general term *langage* (e.g., French, English, Russian, etc.) and *langue*, the system within a *langage* that comprises such elements as the phonetic, syntactic, and semantic sub-systems, which together permit the intelligibility and multiplicity of utterances. For the term *langue*, which refers specifically to natural language, Metz substitutes the less prejudicial word "code," which is defined in opposition to the complementary term "message." The code is composed of signifying elements and the message of signified elements, called respectively *signifiers* and *signifieds*. A code, to merit the name, must be instanced in more than one *texte*, a word that I shall leave in French in order to indicate its pertinence to any division of any discourse, whether a poem, a painting, or all the films of Jerry Lewis. A *texte* may embody a single code, many codes, or no code at all. In any case, the respective messages will be the counterparts of the codes and not coextensive with the *texte*. Although code and message are complementary terms, their signifiers and signified may not be isomorphic. Metz illustrates this point by citing Gilbert Ryle's observation that the division of the verbal signifier "Fido" into its four constituent phonemes does not entail a corresponding division of the signified, which is, of course, a mental response to the signifier, not the real animal. By contrast, in the case of the cinematic image, a signifier which shows a dog will, if divided, effect a corresponding division of the signified; that is, it will signify a portion of a dog. Thus the relation of signifier to signified, and of code to message is a complex matter informed by problems specific to particular *textes* and languages.

Finally, there is the distinction between *syntagm* and *paradigm*. Following Roland Barthes's suggestion in *Elements of Semiology*, this may be envisioned as a pair of Cartesian coordinates in which the syntagm is the horizontal dimension and the paradigm the vertical. The syntagm is the dimension, whether temporal as in the case of music or a-temporal as in painting, along which the message unfolds, and the paradigm is the system of alternatives that comprise the code. The paradigm portrays the code as a system in which a given signifier takes its meaning through opposition to others which are possible but absent in a given place on the syntagm. Semiologists prefer to organize these oppositions in binary or bifurcating structures.

Metz's use of this general theory is characterized by his resistance to a literal interpretation of the analogy between natural and cinematic language. From the outset he has denied that there is anything in cinema resembling a *langue*. However, he also denies that the intelligibility of the cinema can be entirely explained through its iconicity, that is, the resemblance of the sound and image to the perceived world. Cinema is a discourse and as such must depend on codes. Metz has tried to show that these codes are irreducibly multiple and that no one of them occupies a central or definitive place. Yet they can be, at least initially, divided into those which are found only in films and those which are also found elsewhere. The first group he calls cinematic ("cinématographique") and the second filmic ("filmique"). Among the second group there is a sort of heirarchy, since there exist codes that cinema shares with its double, television, and others with the novel, and still others which it embodies uniquely. Metz denies, however, that this heirarchy suffices to give any of the codes a place like that of the *langue* in natural language.

This position has consequences both for the semiologic study of the cinema and for non-semiologic efforts at theory and criticism. In the first case, it puts a decisive end to fruitless attempts to identify the *langue* of cinema, to isolate its minimal units, and to enumerate the cinematic equivalents of the phoneme, morpheme, sentence, and grammar. In the second, it shows the futility of trying to base normative definitions of the cinema on arguments about the nature of the medium. Metz is firm in his insistence that the medium, or in his terms the *matière de l'expression*, is manifest only through the codes it will support and permit, and that it is only in terms of these codes that cinema as a signifying system can be defined. Since no one or group of these occupies a controlling position, the semiologic study of the cinema will not authorize

a normative position, thus superseding "theories" like Eisenstein's and Bazin's, which are at best criticism in disguise.

More now needs to be said about the seminal concepts *code*
and *système*. The code is defined in relation to the message:
"The code is that which is not the message" (*Langage* . . . , p.
65). The opposition *code/message* is parallel to *système/texte:*
"The word 'système' for us has no sense other than that given
by its opposition to 'texte' " (*Langage* . . . , p. 65). The *système* is the code-like configuration, the formal principle of a
texte. Every code is a *système* and every message a *texte*, but
not the reverse, since a *système* is a singular instance bound to
a given *texte* while the code occurs in more than one *texte*.
Both *système* and code are abstract entities: "A code (in theory)
is defined exclusively as a relationship of logic, as pure form"
(*Langage* . . . , p. 165). The "relationship of logic" obtains between the elements of the paradigm, the signifiers. The *système* has a similar definition: "What defines the *systématique*
(that is, the non-textual) is its character as an ideal object constructed by analysis; the *système* has no material existence, it is
nothing more than a logic, a principle of coherence; it is the
intelligibility of the *texte:* what one must suppose in order that
the *texte* be comprehensible" (*Langage* . . . , p. 57).
Using this vocabulary, Metz distinguishes the work of the
semiologist from that of both film-maker and viewer. The semiologist's task begins where the film-maker's finishes; it does
not lead toward the film, but away from it, toward its *systèmes*.
This movement parallels that of the viewer but differs in one
respect: while the viewer wishes to understand the film, the
semiologist wishes to know in addition how the film is understood ("en outre comprehendre comment le film est compris").
His reading is a "méta-lecture" as opposed to the "lecture
'naïve' (en fait: à la lecture *culturelle*)" of the viewer.
In the passages quoted, Metz's own text supports two distinct readings. In the first, *système* is the name given to the fact
of intelligibility in the *texte*. It is the process of comprehension
("comment le film est compris") and is pictured as the interaction of reader and *texte* within the culture that they share. The
semiologist makes a naive—that is, cultural—reading and a

simultaneous *méta-lecture;* he is the reader who, as he comprehends, enunciates the process of comprehension. This enunciation is the *système* or, in the case of multiple *textes,* the code. Both terms refer not to the *texte,* which can be isolated from its cultural context, but to the *lecture,* which cannot. The *méta-lecture* does not displace but rather subsumes the *lecture.* Therefore, the analysis remains *culturelle,* and the propositions of the semiologist are linked on some level to psychology, sociology, or political theory, as Chomsky's linguistics is to psychology.

In the second reading, the *système* is a fact logically (though not chronologically) prior to the intelligibility and comprehension of the *texte.* It is not implied by the *texte* but constructed ("construit") by the analyst in opposition to the *texte.* To accomplish this, the semiologist must first pass through and discard a cultural *lecture* in order to achieve an analytical *méta-lecture,* the *système.* Thus the *système,* and the code along with it, liberated from its cultural circumstances, becomes an "objet idéal."

Despite hints of the first interpretation, it is the second that prevails in *Langage et Cinéma.* Whatever the validity of this position, it has several inescapable consequences for the central concepts code and *système.* First, it weakens the meaning of "intelligibilité," "lecture," and comprehension by locating these processes exclusively within the *texte.* Though the *lecture* is required and presupposed, only the *méta-lecture* is expressed, or even reflected, at the level of the achieved theory. This isolation of *méta-lecture* from *lecture* requires an opposition that Metz willingly accepts of "analytique" to "culturelle." The analytic statement, the *système* or code, can therefore be tested only against the *texte,* within which the processes of the *lecture* have, somehow, been subsumed. In addressing the *texte,* the semiologist can dismiss as "cultural" the problems of how its messages were encoded and how they are to be decoded. The process of signification thus becomes a synchronic textual fact whose author is superfluous, his work finished, and whose "reader" is demoted to the role of witness.

The abstract, difficult concept of a code that emerges from

this analysis can perhaps be better understood through two examples. The first, drawn from the *Essais sur la Signification au Cinéma* (pp. 121–146 and 105–107), is Metz's most ambitious attempt to describe a particular cinematic code. According to his scheme, the image in fiction film can be sorted into eight categories, or syntagms.[2] One of these, the *montage alterné* or alternating syntagm, is sufficient here to suggest the character and structure of the code as a whole. It is defined at the level of the signifier by two types of shots, called, in *Langage et Cinéma*, A and B. The alternating of the signifiers A and B yields at least three signifieds with respect to temporal denotation. It may indicate that the two signifieds are continuous in time (e.g., alternating views of the two tennis players in a game of singles), or simultaneous (alternating views of fugitives and their pursuers in a chase), or a-temporal (the alternating shots of the situation comedy and singing auditions in Milos Forman's *Taking Off*). The syntagm "A^1-B^1-A^2-B^2-A^1-B^1-etc." is made possible by the sorting of the shots into two classes according to a criterion like "pursuer versus pursued," that is, by a paradigmatic relation "A/B." This relation obtains not between shots or types of shots but between two classes defined by their mutual opposition. Its basis is logic, not the *texte* of a given sequence.

The second example, described in *Langage et Cinéma* (pp. 149–150), is based on Bazin's essay "La meilleure femme ne vaut pas un bon cheval." Bazin describes the well-known pattern in Westerns in which the figures of woman and horse are charged with symbolic meanings (domesticity versus freedom, for example) and presented to the hero for choice. This configuration, according to Metz, is a genuine code since it is common to numerous texts and depends not simply on the presence of a woman and a horse in the story but on the condition of their co-presence, which qualifies the opposition woman/horse as a paradigm. The modest code thus formed, unlike that of the eight syntagmatic categories, is extra-cinematic, or filmic, because it occurs in novels and songs as well as films.

---

[2]The eight syntagms are described in "Film and Language, Film and Literature," JNH 11 (September 1971), 154–160.

It is true by definition that a code is common to multiple *textes*, but the claim that those *textes* may belong to different "languages"—one a song and another a film—requires some discussion, particularly concerning the concepts of the message and the signified. It should be recalled that the message is not the global meaning of the *texte*, but the set of meanings produced by a single code. A *texte* may be the locus of more than one code (for example, as Metz points out, the sentence "Voudriez-vous tenir ceci, s'il vous plaît?" ["would you hold this please?"] displays, among others, a code of phonemes and a code of politeness) and hence of more than one message. In this respect the message, like the code, is a function of the point of view of the analysis.

I admit to some confusion on the question of exactly where or what the signified and message are. In the case of the alternating syntagm one of the possible signifieds is "simultaneity." But it is not, evidently, the word I have written on the page nor what was projected on the screen to provoke it—since these can only be signifiers. It is rather the *idea* of simultaneity within what Metz calls the *diegesis*, that is, the fictional world of the film. Metz assures us that one cannot speak of the *diegesis* or its constituent signifieds directly or in isolation from their signifiers. In other words, the message and its signifieds belong neither to the *texte* nor in the head of its reader, but to the explanatory abstraction of the *lecture*.

Since the signified can be approached only through its signifiers, which are, in turn, bound to a particular signifying system, how can it be said that two or more languages may embody one and the same code? This problem is approached through a complex argument entitled "Interférences Sémiologiques entre Langages" (*Langage* . . . , p. 160ff). Its premise is that a code, and hence a message, is by definition a logical relation without physical existence. However, this premise has a limiting condition: namely, that codes always occur in a *matière de l'expression*, a physical material, which affects and restricts their possible configuration. Thus it is impossible for a code with temporal signifiers (though not temporal signifieds) to exist in a *matière* like painted canvas which does not extend through time. This limiting condition is outlined by three paradigm cases. The first, relatively inconsequential for semiology, concerns the borrowing by one language of a fragment of a code belonging to another. Metz's example is Faulkner's use in prose fiction of a narrative technique resembling *montage alterné*, which is, as explained earlier, a fragment of the code of the image in narrative cinema. The second, and most important case is the manifestation of one and the same code in two languages (or arts). Metz's example is the code of chiaroscuro, light and dark, in painting and color photography. These languages, like any two, necessarily differ with respect to their sensory base, or *matière de l'expression*. The critical point—and the one that distinguishes this category from the third—is "that the differences between the two *matières* concern traits not pertinent to the code in question" (*Langage*, p. 163). The third category fails to meet this condition and hence is a weaker version of the second; it concerns two languages (or arts) whose differences of *matière* will not permit the manifestation of the same code, but only of similar, or "isomorphic," codes. For example, the code of light versus dark may be shown directly in a painting, but in a novel its signifiers must be translated into words, which render the code in a similar, though by no means identical, form.

Can the condition of the second category be met in reality? I have difficulty considering this in the context of Metz's example, since I do not know precisely what the code of chiaroscuro is, unless it is the opposition between light and dark. It seems true enough that such an opposition is possible equally in a color photograph and a painting. Yet the two languages cannot have the same signifiers, since analine dye is not the same as oil paint, nor therefore the same signifieds. Metz's contention, I think, would be either that the differences between these *matières* would not truly change the signifiers (any more than speaking French with an American accent does) or that the opposition of signifiers, which is *logique relationnelle,* remains identical *despite* changes in the signifiers. This identity, however, is postulated, rather than proved; hence the argument is circular. As logic, codes may be exempted from the material conditions which embody them, but is it true that one may perform analogous surgery on the *matière de l'expres-*

191

sion, taking from it only the traits relevant to the codes? Standing before a particular painting and a particular color photograph, is it possible to regard the two systems of light-dark opposition apart from their material context? This may be conceivable as a mental operation, but is this operation other than a thesis whose meaning consists in a continuing relation and return to the *matière?* In the absence of this relation, how is the code capable of signifying? If the code is severed by definition from the *matière*, this does indeed authorize the erection of the second category, but does it not at the same time annul its power as an analytic tool?

Perhaps a more central question is why Metz needs such a category in the first place. His position in the *Essais* is that cinema is a *langage* without a *langue*, and his argument throughout is keyed to this denial. Apart from a few hesitant hypotheses, the work is unremittingly critical and distrustful of any wide-reaching claims for the role of codes in cinema. Cinematic imagery is "a rich message with a poor code, a rich *texte* with a poor *système*" (*Essais*, p. 74). Or "Goodbye, paradigm! Its poverty is the counterpart of a richness distributed elsewhere: the film-maker, different in this respect from the speaker of a language, can express himself by showing us directly the variety of the world; in this way the paradigm is quickly overwhelmed" (*Essais*, p. 75).

Langage et Cinéma gives these denials the positive terms of a theory by pursuing to its conclusion the definition of cinematic language as an "ensemble" of codes. To do this, the three categories of "interférence" are by themselves insufficient, since they only serve to indicate the further problem of describing the limiting conditions imposed by the *matière de l'expression*. Metz's response is to classify the languages bordering on cinema—still photography, painting, the photoroman, comic strip, radio and television—according to such traits of *matière* as iconicity, temporality, and provenance of the image. The resulting taxonomy, in conjunction with the crucial second category of "interférence," suggests a method of defining the relations between languages in terms of their shared codes. In this way, it is possible to identify the set of codes common to, say, cinema and the photo-roman and distinguish it from the set common to cinema and still photography. This network of inter-relations replaces the dichotomy "specific/non-specific," which is the descriptive basis for such normative statements as "Cinema is the art of movement." The analysis also implies that the "ensemble" of codes comprising a given language is not simply an inventory, but has a structure that may, Metz suggests, itself be code-like. Thus, one could complete the definition of cinematic language by writing the "formule codique de sa spécificité"—a prospect that both resolves and reflects the skepticism of the *Essais* concerning the explanatory power of codes regarded individually. However, *Langage et Cinéma* stops short of attempting such a definition since Metz's position is sufficiently established simply by indicating the possibility.

Is this theory truly without norms? To approach this question, I want to sketch an alternative explanation of the syntagm of the film image and compare Metz's to it. In my account, the telecast image of a football game may stand as a paradigm case. In order to understand what he sees, the viewer must know that the syntagm on his TV screen alternates among the views of a small, fixed number of cameras. It is—with apologies to Chomsky—a surface-structure whose deep structure may be visualized as the configuration of monitors in the control room, each of which displays the view of a single camera. It is unnecessary for the viewer to have the slightest knowledge of the circumstances of production in order to understand either this structure or the rules that link it with what appears on his screen at home—just as the native speaker of a language is said to know its deep structures even if he cannot describe them. The proof that this understanding is at work is that when the program deviates from the rules that transform the deep structure into the surface structure, this must be signalled; for instance, an instant replay must be identified either with superimposed titles, spoken comment, or the clear presence of slow motion, so as not to be confused with the live transmission; otherwise, the telecast lapses into unintelligibility.

The film-image is a more complex, but similar case. Again,

the structure has two layers: one which appears on the screen, and its deeper counterpart, which may be represented by the unedited footage. Here too it may be said that the viewer understands the deeper structure even if he knows nothing about the production of motion pictures. If he did not infer it while watching films, he would, like certain early audiences, be confused and disoriented by every disjuncture of time and space, even when they are masked by the continuity of action within the *diegesis*. To understand the deep structure means, in part, to know that the syntagm is not a transmission, but an assemblage of pieces filmed discontinuously in time and space. This knowledge is reflected in the word "cut," which signifies not simply a change like the switch between television cameras, but a joint. To object that the deep structure is here a superfluous concept because the viewer only "knows" the portions of it that reach the surface is to miss the point; the viewer's ability to comprehend consists of his knowledge of the rules that connect the two. The *lecture,* therefore, in certain respects parallels the composition of the film, rather than occurring after it, as in Metz's model.

To take the simplest example, consider a dialogue scene in which bits of two camera-shots, or takes, *A* and *B*, alternate. Undoubtedly the viewer infers, as Metz maintains, on the basis of continuity in the dialogue that the alternating image signifies continuity in time. However, neither this observation nor its implied oppositions between temporal continuity and simultaneity and between alternating and linear syntagms accounts for the structure of alternation. It explains, so to speak, how the structure is absent, but not how it is present. One must add that the viewer also understands the provenance of the alternating shots, the model of which is the unedited takes *A* and *B*. If this were not so, dialogue scenes articulated by jump-cuts, like those in *Breathless*, would be, at least for the original audience, not simply novel or shocking, but unintelligible, or—what comes to the same thing—they would require a new category in the taxonomy of the image-syntagm. In fact, they are intelligible because their relation to the deep structure is intelligible. The role of this deep structure in the specific case of the alternating syntagm is demonstrated clearly by the "dialogue" scene in *Persona* in which the camera-takes *A* and *B*, which show in one-shot Liv Ullmann and Bibi Andersson respectively, are not intercut and do not alternate, but run in their entirety one after the other: *A*, then *B*. This repetition in the *diegesis* does not, however, impair the intelligibility of the sequence. Rather, its effect is to point to and illuminate the deep structure in a way that is not only locally intelligible, but indicative of the director's concern elsewhere in this work with the processes of cinema and representation.

Metz is also aware that exceptions test the rule, and in the *Essais* (pp. 213–215) he cites an image-sequence from *Pierrot le Fou* which does not fit any of his eight categories; it is the sequence, consisting of many short shots, in which the protagonists, Jean-Paul Belmondo and Anna Karina, flee Paris. For Metz, the problem is two-fold: first, the shots are out of chronological order, though the glimpses of the action that they permit allows the viewer to reconstruct the likely chronology, and second, they show some bits of the action more than once and in slightly differing versions. Metz takes the sequence to be an instance of the diachronic processes of history at work, altering and adding to one of the codes of cinema. His response as a semiologist is to give the excerpt the provisional name of a "potential" syntagm, since it allows neither a definitive nor chronological version of the action.

Whatever the paraphrasable meaning of its structure, the sequence is intelligible. As in the much simpler scene from *Persona*, the viewer is referred to the deep structure of the shots, which is, as always, open to an organization that contradicts the chronology of the diegesis. Godard goes further than Bergman, however, when he includes corresponding bits from different camera-takes in which the action happens to differ slightly. Though few viewers would describe this process as I have, in terms of shooting and cutting, everyone would, I think, recognize the director's gesture toward the deep structure and would understand that our normally unconscious knowledge of it is here being invoked. Presumably Godard makes such a gesture because at this moment he sees no alternative but to ask us to participate in his work of examining the world by means of the cinema, not because he is unsure how things happened and can give only a "potential" account. For after all, nothing "happened"; the story is made up, and its author would seem intolerably pretentious if he demanded that we forget this fact in the midst of a sequence that so clearly shows his hand.

The differences between my account of this sequence and Metz's suggest, among other things, the extent to which his thinking is bound to the narrative film. In all of his writing, I could not cite a single example from another source. In the *Essais* (pp. 96ff.) he defends the historical basis of this commitment. His recognition of the relevance of this diachronic question is remarkable in light of his usual contention that his is an exclusively synchronic discipline. His attitude elsewhere toward writing history is the same as toward the creation of individual *textes:* the semiologist begins his work where the film-maker, and likewise the film-historian, finish theirs. He minimizes the importance of the movements at which the work of production, history, and semiology must touch a common point; he maintains, for example, that the semiologist's choice of a *texte* for study may be influenced by the problems currently seen as urgent within his discipline, but is in itself as indifferent as the linguist's decision to study a particular dialect; and, as I have tried to show, his notion of significance neither incorporates nor permits reference to the composition of the *texte.*

The version of film history given in the *Essais* stresses the centrality of "la rencontre du cinéma et de la narrativité," the meeting of cinema and narrative. It holds that in the beginning film was purely iconic—that is, it signified exclusively by means of the resemblance between its imagery and the visible world—and that its association with narrative resulted in the gradual invention and superimposition of various codes over its iconic mechanisms. The repertory of codes pertaining to the image was complete by the time of D. W. Griffith, and those of image and sound formulated during the thirties, stabilizing in the style Bazin called "découpage classique." In this view, the Soviet school of the twenties, despite the magnificence of its production, is a cul-de-sac. Metz is clearly hostile (though respectful) both to Eisenstein's attempt to give

196

montage the status of a "langue" (though, of course, Eisenstein would not use the term) and to his reading of film history, which groups Griffith with the Soviets as the dominant school. In short, Metz's history is like Bazin's, except that he does not acknowledge Bazin's characterization of the two warring tendencies in film history. Nor does he concede that the reliance of his synchronic theory on this version of history in any way compromises its claim of objectivity.

What is at stake here is not simply the importance of narrative film but the controlling place of narrative within film theory. The contrast between Metz's account of the articulation of the image and the alternative that I sketched should make this clear. The basis of his analytical method is to refer the structure of the image to the narrative. In cases where the practice of the cinema itself challenges the explanatory power of the narrative, as does the sequence from *Pierrot le Fou*, his response is to avoid the problem by inventing a new narrative category. The history of film as he rehearses it conveniently minimizes examples of this kind and at the same time authorizes his methods of dealing with them. Supported by this version of history, his synchronic theory affirms a notion of signification in which the spectator, in order to understand the structure of the image, refers not to the real world where films are financed, shot, cut, printed, sold, projected and criticized, but to the fantasy world that the films present—what is clinically called the "diegesis."

At first glance, this tendency is less clear in the vastly more abstract text of *Langage et Cinéma*. There (pp. 142–143) Metz denies that the syntagmatic categories of the image in narrative film merit the status of a *langue*, or even an especially important code, of the cinema. The denial harmonizes with the book's argument that the codes of cinema form an "ensemble," to which the notions of hierarchy, centrality, or specificity are simply not applicable. On the surface, this seems a neutral, a-historical, and objective definition. Yet on examination it turns out, I believe, to be only the position of the *Essais* slightly modified and projected into more abstract terms.

To support this contention, let me reopen the discussion of the crucial second category of "interférence," the instance of one code in two languages, by adducing an example from the *Essais*. Though in context the example relates to some notions of Pasolini's that seem remote from "interférence," it presents issues that are, I think, easier to grasp than those of the light-dark code in paintings and color photographs:

> Certainly, the total comprehension of any film would be impossible if we did not carry within us this vague but quite real dictionary of "im-segni" of which Pasolini speaks, if we did not know—to take only one example—that Jean Claude Brialy's car in *Les Cousins* is a sports-car, with everything that this signifies in twentieth-century France, the diegetic period of the film. But we would know all the same, because we would see it, that it is a car, and this would be sufficient for the comprehension of the *denoted* meaning of the passage. One may not object that an Eskimo with no prior contact with industrial civilization would not even recognize it as a car! For what that Eskimo would need is acculturation, not translation . . . (*Essais*, pp. 209–210)

To analyze this example in terms of Metz's scheme of "interférence," we may note that the sports-car belongs both to a "language" of consumer items in twentieth-century France, like those described by Roland Barthes in *Mythologies*, and to the filmic language of *Les Cousins*. The *matières de l'expression* of these two languages, in the first case the visual, three-dimensional presence of the real objects and in the second their two-dimensional image on film, do not differ in the traits relevant to the code in question. For example, the paradigm sports-car/sedan, in which the sports-car signifies luxury, is possible equally in twentieth-century France and in a film. Like most of the visual codes of culture, the one that includes this paradigm can be rendered in the iconic terms of the cinematic image, and thus is an instance of the second category of "interférence": the manifestation of one and the same code in two languages.

The argument that establishes this instance also—and more importantly—opposes the notion that Metz calls "cinématographisation." His analysis of "interférence" implies that a code like the one of our example does not become "cinematic" by virtue of its mere presence in a film; it is an instance of the second category, not the third. The sports-car in *Les Cousins* not only has the significance it would also have in twentieth-century France—at least in part—but obtains this significance by the same means: "Thus is it necessary to insist on the fact that filmic code is not necessarily cinematic, since a code (in theory) is defined exclusively as a relationship of logic, as pure form, and is therefore not tied to a particular *matière de l'expression*, for example, the cinema's" (*Langage* . . . , p. 165).

Although it is a subtle and difficult matter to say how looking at a painting differs from looking at a color photograph, everyone can tell the difference between a sports-car and a picture of one. Metz does not deny this difference. Rather, he passes over it in silence, speaking only about the place the object occupies in a discourse. This silence is the counterpart of his contention elsewhere that one can sever the code from its *matière* and hence that none of its meaning consists in, or arises from, its situation in the *matière*. Here the difficulties begin. For—to return to the example—when we are before the actual automobile, the paradigm sports-car/sedan and the code which subsumes it can hardly be said to inhere exclusively in "logique relationnelle," but belongs at least partly to the concrete relation between the object and us. We are in the world where we may not address the object except as, say, an owner, customer, envier, producer or viewer—all relations in which the code, admittedly abstract, is at work. None of these relationships can enter unaltered into a film, where there is no longer the possibility of—to keep to the example—an economic relation between us and the object, but only the quite different opportunity to project this relationship onto, or extract it from, the world that is represented.

Yet filming is not simply the loss of a certain sort of relationship. The object filmed, it is true, is in one sense reduced to a phantom. But at the same time it becomes another sort of object—a picture. The code that describes our relation to an actual automobile has a proper analogy only in our relation to the commodity we call a movie, not to what is signified by the movie. Going to the movies and buying a sports-car can even be said to form a paradigm, since they have, as an opposition, the power to signify, and there exist situations in which such a choice may be read as a discourse. I do not mean to insist on

199

the economic basis of this analysis (it is only an illustration chosen to suit Metz's example), but rather on the centrality in signification of the relation between the viewer and the *matière*, from which the code as a signifying mechanism is not detachable. Consequently, all codes, even those of natural language, are "cinematographized" when they pass into films; hence Metz's second category is without true examples.

This argument does not deny the points of similarity between, say, a film and a song that share the theme "The best woman isn't worth a good horse." Rather, it refuses such similarities the status of language, as that term is understood by Metz. This disagreement is reproduced and elaborated in Metz's critique of Pasolini's semiotics, from which the discussion of *Les Cousins* is taken. Pasolini maintains that cinematic language has two articulations, the second more or less equivalent to Metz's specific codes, and the first a rather ill-defined and partly to-be-invented lexicon of "im-segni" (image-signs), which have meanings within culture and therefore comprise a kind of language prior to the intervention of the film-maker. Metz argues that this first articulation is not only questionable but superfluous, since it can be adequately replaced by the concept of iconic analogy; he insists on "the *perceptual* and *cultural* status of these 'im-segni,' opposing it to the language-like character of the codes that are properly cinematic" (*Essais* . . . , p. 210n).

I do not wish to associate myself with Pasolini's position, least of all with the problematical concept of the "im-segno." But I do sympathize with Pasolini's motive, which is, I think, less to introduce economies into the semiologic study of cinema than to place its most fundamental premise, and hence the discipline itself, within a perceptual, cultural, and ultimately political context. Metz is not only unpersuaded of the necessity of this step, but sees an antithesis between the terms "cultural and perceptual" on the one hand and "language" on the other.

In thus opposing the signifying process to its cultural and perceptual setting, Metz exposes the basis of his conception of the cinema. Though his approach to particular questions is always distinguished by the sophisticated application of linguistic methodology, the effect of these methods is to attribute to the cinema a sort of transparency, to imagine it as a glass distinct from culture but through which culture is visible. Cinema emerges in his portrait as an instrument that is as indifferent to ideology and value as he supposes natural language to be, as a system whose workings are logical rather than material and whose history is the immaterial accretion of these processes in the realm of pure logic and pure form. It is a conception that, despite the linguistic vocabulary in which it is stated, recalls Bazin. For Bazin bequeathed to Metz not simply the question *What is Cinema?* but an answer of his own, namely that cinema is an image and substitute for reality, whose history is the gradual aesthetic and technological perfection of the power of illusion. He discards its normative arguments, fills in its silences on the structure of cinematic discourse, and banishes its aesthetic of illusionism if not from the description of particular codes, then at least from the higher, more abstract levels of the theory. Yet, despite all this, he preserves and elaborates Bazin's assumption that the cinema is something one looks through but not at and studies in isolation from the circumstances where it is made and seen.

This shared assumption indicates what is truly at issue in Metz's distinction of his work from that of other theorists and critics. For example, Eisenstein's concept of *montage*, which Metz patronizingly calls, "montage-roi," is, unlike any of the seminal concepts of Metz's theory, rooted in the material world of culture and perception. It locates the process of signification in the interaction of spectator and screen. The relation of frame to frame, of image to image, and of the parts of an image to each other is not merely a fact of the *texte*, but a relation which the film-maker creates and which produces ideas, emotions, and comprehension only by acting on, and being re-enacted by, the viewer. In a comparable way, Pasolini, whose conception is in other respects close to Metz's own, maintains that from the outset the discourse of cinema is entangled in its cultural origins, from which not even the image, for all its iconicity, can be entirely extricated.

Faced with such profound and consequential disagreements, no reader can ignore either the need for judgment or the search for criteria on which a judgment may be based. Despite the subordinate place habitually given to the discussion of particular films and parts of films in Metz's writing, and despite his repeated denial that such discussions are either urgent or germane to his work as a semiologist, I would argue that it is not only inevitable but fair that they should stand as a measure of his theory. Must one not ask what light is shed on the sequence from *Pierrot le Fou* by giving it the name of "potential" or by testing it against the eight supposed syntagmatic categories one at a time? Are we told any more about *The Outlaw* by calling its theme of woman-versus-horse a code? Or can any plausible rationale be conceived for preferring the long analysis of *Intolerance* in *Langage et Cinéma* (pp. 81ff.) to Eisenstein's supposedly unscientific and normative discussion of the same work in "Dickens, Griffith, and the Film Today"? Can one deny that Metz's detailed description of Griffith's parallel montage is simply *less* than Eisenstein's effort to relate it to the film's ideology, than to submit that ideology to a critique based on a reading of history? Whatever the talent of these two men as critics, and whatever one's attitude toward what they value, is there any possible conclusion but that Metz's ideas produce what is by comparison to Eisenstein a diminution and abortion?

But Eisenstein is not to be taken as the measure of Metz's writing. The point is rather that Metz's effort to excise from cinema the process of signification and, in the name of language, to set it in a realm of abstract logical relations is in the end both meaningless and futile. The analogy between natural and cinematic language is not perfect enough in itself to authorize or sustain such an effort. Cinema as a signifying system lacks, as Metz concedes, both arbitrariness in Saussure's sense and the paired systems that permit both distinctive and significative articulation. Moreover, it is, unlike natural language, the outcome of industrial production—a fact with inescapable consequences for its means of signification. When the world, whether coded or not, passes into the sounds and images of cinema, it is not merely reduced to the configurations of an abstract system, but transformed into a concrete object of another kind. The difference between these sounds and images and the objects and codes that they reflect, though it has no stable meaning, nonetheless always and of necessity enters into the process of signification. It is not within the power of the film-maker's intentions, or of their reflection in the film's style, to dissolve this difference. Even if it were, we as spectators are not simply prisoners of those intentions, but are free and co-present in the world where the images and sounds exist as objects. The conditions of this world, its social, economic, and political structure, impose on us, spectators, critics, theorists, and film-makers alike, the obligation to analyze, interpret, and criticize the cinema as it reflects and embodies these conditions. In this light, Metz's retreat to the realm of logic and abstraction that he calls "language" can be seen as not simply anti-normative, but, despite its methodological precision, anti-critical and anti-analytical as well.

1973

GILBERT HARMAN
SEMIOTICS AND THE
CINEMA: METZ AND
WOLLEN

Some film theorists advocate what they call a semiotics or semiology of the cinema. I will discuss two somewhat different proposals of this sort here, one by Christian Metz[1] and another by Peter Wollen.[2]

The term *semiotics* (and, equivalently, the term *semiology*) means theory of signs. Linguistics is one such theory, since it is the theory of language-as-a-system-of-signs. The semiotics of the cinema is, similarly, the theory of film-as-a-system-of-signs. The idea is that we are to think of film as a kind of language and are to try to develop a linguistics of this language of film.

This means, according to Christian Metz, that we will only be interested in certain aspects of film. We will be concerned only with the various ways in which particular films can have meaning and significance for normal spectators. We will be directly concerned with the nature of the film image, the relation between sound and image, and the effect of various kinds of editing. We will not be directly concerned with such things as camera mechanisms, the process of developing and printing films, or the technological structure of the film industry.

---

[1]*Film Language: A Semiotics of the Cinéma.* New York: Oxford University Press, 1974, a translation of *Essais sur la Signification au Cinema* Tome I. Paris: Klinksieck, 1968, 2nd ed. 1971. *Language and Cinema.* The Hague: Mouton, 1974, a translation of *Langage et Cinéma.* Paris: Larousse, 1971.

[2]*Signs and Meaning in the Cinema.* London: Indiana University Press, 3rd revised edition 1972.

There are, of course, very different kinds of films: narrative feature films, documentaries, travel films, advertising films, instructional films, abstract underground films, and so forth. Metz argues, however, that in the first instance we should restrict our study to narrative feature films and ignore the other type of film. According to Metz, before the narrative film existed, the cinema was conceived as a mere technological resource, a recorder of events, and "it was precisely to the extent that the cinema confronted the problems of narration that . . . it came to produce a body of specific signifying procedures." Narrative feature films are, furthermore, what we first think of as films. Shorts of various kinds inhabit "border regions"; their signifying procedures are, for the most part, derived from those in narrative films. We will therefore not go wrong, Metz thinks, if we restrict our attention to the signifying procedures that are used in feature length narrative films.

Moreover, Metz says, we should study denotation before connotation. We should study, that is, the ways in which various aspects of plot are presented before we study how symbolic, philosophical, and human messages are presented and before we study such things as style, genre, and poetic mood. Denotation is basic, according to Metz, because, in the first instance, the basic materials of the film—its sounds and images—present a series of events that constitute the plot or story. That is what is denoted. In other words, the basic material of the film is directly a sign of the denotation, according to Metz. Connotation is secondary in the sense that it is not directly presented by the basic materials of the film in the way that the denotation or plot is. Connotation is, in fact, partly indicated by the denotation. What happens in the film has a certain significance, given the way in which it is presented. This significance is connotation. The connotation is what is signified by a sign when the sign combines aspects of the basic materials of the film and the story that those aspects denote.

We are, therefore, to ask first how narrative films present their plots. In particular, "How does the cinema indicate successivity, precession, temporal breaks, causality, adversative relationships, consequence, spatial proximity or distance, etc.? These are central questions to the semiotics of the cinema."

A similar group of questions can be raised about language. How does language indicate one or another state of affairs or series of events? Linguistics seeks in the first instance to answer that question. Only after considerable progress has been made on that front in understanding linguistic denotation could linguistics hope to be able to investigate style, atmosphere, and other aspects of linguistic connotation. The same thing is true in the semiotics of the cinema, according to Metz.

One big difference, though, as Metz observes, is that linguistic denotation is largely conventional. The word *horse* denotes horses and *man* denotes men; but it could have been otherwise. The word *man* could have denoted horses and *horse* could have denoted men. The sentence *the man is on the horse* has a conventional meaning which depends on its grammatical structure and the meanings of its words. It denotes a situation in which a man is on a horse. If different conventions were in force it might denote a situation in which a horse is on a man. The sentence by itself has no natural meaning, apart from convention, and it can be understood only by someone who is acquainted with the relevant conventions. In the case of film, the situation is quite different. A shot of a man on a horse has an immediate and natural interpretation that does not depend on any filmic conventions.

There is, furthermore, according to Metz, an important sense in which film does not have a syntax. No significant unit in film corresponds to the word in language. The smallest unit of film—the image—is already at the level of the sentence or paragraph. A shot of a revolver does not correspond to the word *revolver* but to the sentence *here is a revolver* or even to a description of the revolver. There cannot be an ungrammatical shot, in the way that there can be an ungrammatical sequence of words.

There are, nevertheless, certain rules and conventions, or "codes," which narrative feature films exploit in order to indicate their denotations, and it is the task of film semiotics, as Metz conceives it, to specify these codes and say how they work. There are certain conventions of filmic punctuation, concerning the interpretation of a fade as opposed to a dissolve, for example. Or, to take another example, Metz suggests that films are made up of a series of minimal sequences that he calls "syntagmas." Syntagmas can be distinguished on the basis of montage and what that montage signifies. A series of different views of a house, for example, might constitute what Metz calls a "descriptive syntagma"—showing what the house is like and not presenting an event unfolding in time. Another series of shots showing various effects of war would constitute what he calls a "bracket syntagma"—in which a number of things are grouped together because of a certain association among those things. A third series might show alternating shots of two different actions, indicating that they are happening simultaneously, for example, alternating shots of the two parties at the opposite ends of a telephone conversation —or alternating shots of pursuer and pursued. And so on. According to Metz, there are only a small number of other possible syntagmas.

Having gone this far, Metz sees the following tasks on the immediate horizon. First, we must attempt to discover the various denotative codes that are exploited in films; and we must classify these codes in terms of their generality. Some of them are relevant to narration in general; some to any sort of depiction, including painting; some only to photographic images; some only to sequences of images, as in comic strips; some only to sequences of moving photographic images correlated with sound; and so forth. As film semioticists, we are to be particularly concerned with codes that are specific to film. These, as previously indicated, will concern mainly such things as filmic punctuation, the various syntagmas, and the meanings of close-ups, zoom shots, and so on.

Second, having carried out that part of our study, we can then begin to investigate questions of style and genre by seeing what subcodes out of the codes available are used in works of that style or genre. We might consider, for example, the codes of dress, behavior, and landscape, that define the western. Or we can study the sorts of codes a particular director or group of directors tends to use.

This summarizes Metz's proposal. What can we say about it? One immediate difficulty is that his order of priorities depends to a considerable extent on his distinction between denotation and connotation. We are to study denotation first, ignoring connotation for the time being. The difficulty is that Metz's definition of the denotation-connotation distinction does not work and it is unclear that there is any way to fix up his definition so as to support his program. He says that the denotation—the series of events of plot portrayed—is what is signified directly by the raw material—images and sound—of the film, whereas connotation is what is signified by the events portrayed plus the way they are signified. But, typically, in order to understand what is happening in the film even at the level of plot, you need to have some understanding of what else has been happening at that level. Most aspects of the plot—who a depicted person is, where the person is going, whom he loves, whom he is betraying, etc.—are indicated not just by image and sound but by other aspects of plot as well. Metz's definition would make these aspects part of connotation rather than denotation. These are, moreover, central aspects of plot, in Metz's own terms, not just aspects suggested or hinted at. Consider, for example, how we are to identify one or another of Metz's syntagmas. A simple scene depicting a conversation with alternating shots of whoever is speaking, coheres as a simple scene rather than as one of Metz's bracket syntagmas, say, not because of aspects of image and sound alone but because the denotation of the various shots allows us to suppose that we are seeing shots of a single event. In order to determine what sort of syntagma is occurring, you need to know not only how many shots there are and what sorts of characteristics the shots have as visual and auditory images but also what the denotations of the shots are. So Metz's definition of the connotation/denotation distinction cannot be used for his purposes.

Nor can he say simply that he wants, first, to restrict himself to examining the semiotic mechanisms by which the story of the film is indicated. That is arbitrary unless there is a clear distinction between the ways in which plot is indicated and the ways in which other aspects of meaning are indicated. Metz's own limited investigations cast doubt on this, since, for example, one of his syntagmas, the bracket syntagma, is a series of shots showing things between which some relationship holds and not showing something that would normally be considered part of plot. The relation presented in this way cannot clearly be distinguished from the sorts of suggestions and human and philosophical messages that Metz counts as part of connotation.

Nor is this criticism of Metz merely theoretical. For, in fact, although Metz has been developing his account of "film language" for over a decade in many articles and in three large books, his analysis remains almost entirely programmatic. The only substantive results that he has achieved concern his classification of syntagmas, a classification that is in my opinion of minimal interest. A theoretical program that leads to so little in practice is clearly suspect.

This suggests that there are practical as well as theoretical reasons for the film semioticist to study exactly those aspects of film signification that Metz assigns to connotation, and this is what Peter Wollen proposes to do. Wollen believes, as Metz does, that the study of film should take the form of a semiotics of the cinema. But he disagrees with Metz's priorities. He suggests that Metz's emphasis on how plot is presented is due to a commitment to realism in the cinema and, furthermore, that this commitment reflects a mistake in semiotics. In order to bring out the nature of this error, we must, according to Wollen, develop semiotics in accordance with the theory of signs envisioned by the American philosopher C. S. Peirce. In particular, we must recall Peirce's distinction between three aspects of a sign: iconic, indexical, and symbolic.

A sign is an *icon* to the extent that its significance depends on the inner nature of the sign—typically, some sort of qualitative or structural resemblance between the sign and what it signifies. Paintings, diagrams, and color samples are predominantly icons. A sign is an *index* to the extent that its significance depends on a real connection between the sign and what it signifies. Proper names, demonstrative pronouns, evidence at the scene of a crime, and symptoms of a disease are predominantly indices. Finally, a sign is a *symbol*, in Peirce's special sense of this term, to the extent that its significance

FILM IMAGE AND FILM LANGUAGE

depends on human convention or an arbitrary decision. Labels
on diagrams, Chinese ideograms, and English words are pre-
dominently symbols in this sense.

Most signs have more than one aspect. A sentence of English will have a symbolic aspect because of the conventions
on which the meanings of its words depend. It will have an
indexical aspect if it contains proper nouns, which have the
significance they do because of a real connection between
name and thing named. And, according to Peirce, the sentence
will have an iconic aspect since its significance depends in
part on its logical-grammatical structure, which is an internal
property of the sentnce and is relevant to what other sentences
logically imply or are implied by it.

A photograph has an indexical aspect; what it pictures depends to a large extent on a real connection between the picture and the object photographed. It also has an iconic aspect
because of the resemblance between the picture and what is
pictured. There may also be a symbolic aspect to the photograph if, for example, the subject matter is identifiable by appeal to some sort of convention or stipulation.

So far, this is simply Peirce's classification of signs. Given
this classification Wollen observes, "In the cinema, it is quite
clear, indexical and iconic aspects are by far the most powerful. The symbolic is limited and secondary." But, it is, according to Wollen, exactly the "submerged" secondary aspects of
signs that assume importance in art. Since in the cinema "it is
the symbolic which is the submerged dimension, we should
therefore expect that in the 'poetry' of the cinema, this aspect
will be manifested more palpably."

Metz's error, according to Wollen, is to take the linguistic
analogy too seriously, thus overlooking the fact that film is
primarily iconic and indexical rather than symbolic. Metz
looks for conventions in film that bear some resemblance to
the conventions of language. But that is to miss the point that
the role of conventional symbols or codes in film is different
from its role in language. The basic linguistic codes are needed
for literal significance. The relevant codes in cinema primarily
concern the poetic rather than the literal.

Wollen's first conclusion is, therefore, the opposite of

Metz's. As film semioticists, our primary task must be to un-cover the codes exploited in films in producing the sort of po-etry that films can produce. We must do this, moreover, re-membering that signs combine all three of Peirce's aspects of significance, iconic, indexical, and symbolic.

Wollen's next point is that although signs are often used to communicate messages, they are not always used in that way and are not used that way in films. A scientist working out the implications of a theory, a mathematician doing a calculation, and a traveller planning an itinerary are all using signs, but not to communicate with anyone. They are, as it were, seeing the implications of certain signs. Similarly, a poet, an artist, and a film director are using signs but not to communicate any sort of message. To suppose that they are is simply to make a mis-take about what they are doing. They, like the mathematician, scientist, and traveller, are using signs for a different purpose. Like them, they are constructing signs in order to see what the implications of those signs are.

Wollen therefore rejects Metz's idea that the purpose of film semiotics is "to study the ordering and functionings of the main signifying units used in the filmic message." Metz's pro-posal is due to his linguistic analogy. Language is often used to communicate messages but film is not normally used in that way. Films have meaning and significance but they do not carry messages—any more than other works of art.

According to Wollen, works of art exploit and call attention to various codes. The greatest works "interrogate" their own codes by pitting them against each other. "We know that *Don Quixote* was destructive of the chivalric romance . . . that *Ulysses* or *Finnegans Wake* are destructive of the nineteenth century novel. . . . A valuable work, a powerful work, at least, is one which challenges codes, overthrows established ways of reading or looking, not simply to establish new ones, but to compel an unending dialogue, not at random but pro-ductively." Wollen goes on to argue that an analysis along these lines can enable us to see what is great about a director like Godard.

Both Metz and Wollen believe, then, that the theory of film must become part of semiotics, although they disagree slightly

211

about the nature of semiotics. For Metz, "the methods of linguistics . . . provide the semiotics of the cinema with a constant and precious aid in establishing units that, although they are still very approximate, are liable over time (and, one hopes, through the work of many scholars) to become progressively refined." For Wollen, this appeal to linguistics is an error. We must rely, rather, on Peirce's general theory of signs, which allows us to see that filmic significance is very different from linguistic signification, and allows us to understand why the role of codes in films is different from the primary role that linguistic codes play in the everyday use of language. Still, Wollen endorses the idea that we ought "to dissolve cinema criticism and cinema aesthetics into a special province of the general science of signs." The differences between Wollen and Metz are then really matters of emphasis rather than anything else. Their first priorities are different. But Metz would agree with Wollen that it is important to discover the various symbolic codes that give film its importance as a work of art; and Wollen can agree that there is *some* point to specifying the significance of close-ups, zoom shots, filmic punctuation, and Metz's syntagmas.

I now want to look more closely at the idea, endorsed by both Metz and Wollen, that films exploit certain codes. What do they mean by codes?

The word *code* as it is ordinarily used is ambiguous. It can mean either cipher or standards. We speak in one sense of messages in code and in another sense of the military code and of codes of dress. Metz and Wollen use the term in a way that appears to combine both of these senses. On the one hand, they speak of decoding works of art and they take codes to be systems of signs with meanings. Here *code* would seem to mean cipher. To decode is to decipher. What would it mean to decode (in this sense) actions done in accordance with the military code? On the other hand, Metz and Wollen also speak, without any sign that they are using the term in a different sense, of codes of dress and even musical codes.

Now, in what sense are there musical codes? Certainly not in the sense of ciphers. Instrumental music does not encode messages. A piano solo does not in any obvious way have meaning. It does not represent, indicate, or signify anything.

There are various musical structures, of course, and we might speak of these or of the principles of structure as codes, but that is certainly stretching a point. We would not normally speak of symphonic or fugal codes.

But then what counts as decoding music? Apparently that is supposed to be figuring out what the structure of a piece of music is, hearing it as having a certain structure, hearing what there is to hear in the music. Similarly, to decode a style of dress—the style of dress in westerns, for example—is first to uncover the dress code that is involved and then, perhaps, to indicate the meaning or significance of that code.

In this usage, then, any sort of system or structure might be called a code; to decode a work is to uncover the various structures that are relevant to it and appreciate their significance for the work in question. Furthermore, any system of assumptions, beliefs, ideology, or stereotypes that is relied on or alluded to in a film or other work of art can be called a code. For, to "decode" the work is also to see how its significance is affected by such things.

What is the point of this usage? Why call all these different things codes, especially when they are not all codes in the same sense of the term and some are not codes at all in any ordinary sense of the term? The answer is that Metz and Wollen are cheating. Their usage disguises the fact that much of aesthetics and criticism is properly concerned with something other than the significance of signs. Instrumental music is not a language, a system of signs. It has no meaning. It does not represent or signify anything. An understanding of musical structure plays a role in our appreciation of music, but that is not to say that an understanding of the significance of musical signs plays a role in our appreciation of music.

Much the same is true of our understanding and appreciation of films. To appreciate something about the structure of a film is not necessarily to appreciate something that functions as a sign. To say, for example, that the love triangle functions as a specific code in the films of Max Ophuls[3] is to say no more than that the love triangle is a feature of many of Max

---

[3]E.g., Dudley Andrew. "Semiology and Film: A Discussion of Metz," University Film Study Center Newsletter Supplement, Cambridge, Mass. 5:3, p. 4.

Ophuls's films and to say it in a way that wrongly suggests that you are saying something semiotic. Once this is clear, it is obvious that neither Metz nor Wollen has given any reason at all for identifying film theory with film semiotics—indeed it is or should be clear that there is nothing to be said for such an identification.

Of course, even if film theory cannot be *identified* with the semiotics of the cinema, the semiotics of the cinema might be a useful subject in its own right. But there are ample reasons for skepticism about this. Both Metz and Wollen envision a science of signs. What makes them think that there is such a science or could be one? What are its laws? Its principles? To be sure, there is Peirce's distinction between the iconic, indexical, and symbolic aspects of signs. You can spend a considerable amount of time separating out the relevant components in various cases. That can be fun, for a while, but it does not constitute a science.

Part of the problem is that Peirce's use of the term *sign* is a technical one, which counts as signs rather different sorts of things. Words are not normally signs in any ordinary sense of the term *sign,* nor are pictures or diagrams; and the sense in which road signs are signs is different from the sense in which smoke is a sign of fire. It is by no means obvious that there is a unitary phenomenon to be captured in a theory of signs in Peirce's sense.

Smoke means fire and the word *combustion* means fire, but not in the same sense of *means.* The word *mean* is ambiguous. To say smoke means fire is to say that smoke is a symptom, sign, indication, or evidence of fire. To say that the word *combustion* means fire is to say that people use the word to mean fire. The word is not normally a symptom, sign, indication, or evidence of fire; on the other hand, people do not normally use smoke to mean fire. Furthermore, there is no ordinary sense of the word *mean* in which a picture of a man means a man or means that man. This suggests that Peirce's theory of signs would comprise at least three rather different subjects: a theory of intended meaning, a theory of evidence, and a theory of pictorial depiction. There is no reason to think that these theories must contain common principles.

214

A fourth and different subject is also relevant—the study of representation. In our scientific, practical, and aesthetic thinking, we often let certain things stand for or represent others, so that relations among the first things can represent corresponding relations among the others. We do this for several reasons—to see the implications of a theory, to see how a battle went, or might go, and so forth. This sort of representation may seem to be exactly what Peirce had in mind when he spoke of signs, since the relation that leads us to let one thing stand for another might be iconic, indexical, conventional, or just arbitrary choice. But, in fact, this sort of representation is a much narrower phenomenon than what Peirce had in mind. Pictures do not ordinarily in this sense "stand for" what they depict; words do not "stand for" their meanings; and evidence does not "stand for" what it indicates.

Metz observes that in the film *M*, a loose balloon caught in overhead wires symbolizes the death of a girl whom we earlier saw always holding a balloon. Now, the earlier photographic images of the girl holding a balloon *depict* a girl holding a balloon but do not stand for or represent a girl with a balloon. The loose balloon by itself, without the wires, would be evidence of her capture and therefore her death, given the filmic context, but the balloon would not in that case stand for or represent her, her capture, or her death. The capturing of the balloon by the wires does stand for the capturing of the girl. The balloon stands for the girl in this context. It is not clear whether the wires stand for the man who captures her; I am inclined to think not. The capturing of the balloon by the wires does not directly stand for the death of the girl. It symbolizes the death because it represents the capture which leads to her death.

Sometimes we arbitrarily let one thing stand for another; sometimes, as in the example just described, we find that it is "natural" to take a particular thing to stand for another. We might try to discover under what conditions such representation seems "natural," although there is, in fact, no reason to suppose that we will ever be able to do this.

In conclusion, let me summarize briefly. Metz and Wollen advocate replacing film theory and criticism with a semiotics of the cinema. I have tried to suggest several reasons for being doubtful about this. Many aspects of film aesthetics appear to be part of semiotics only because of an equivocation in the use of the word *code*. The theory of signs, in Peirce's sense, contains no laws or general principles; at best it contains a few categories of classification. Semiotics is really a collection of three or four disparate subjects. It is not obvious that a close study of any of these subjects will be particularly fruitful for the study of film.

1975

UMBERTO ECO
ON THE CONTRIBUTION
OF FILM TO SEMIOTICS

Many discussions of the semiotics of film (as well as the semiotics of music or of painting) are confused because they try to answer two different questions. First question: "To what extent can semiotics help one to understand film?" Second question: "To what extent can filmic experience help one better understand semiotic problems?" Frequently such confusion has been increased by another ambiguity. Is one studying the elementary mechanisms of film as a medium of communication or rather the complex mechanisms of a movie as a work of art?

I shall want to make just a few statements about the contribution of filmic experience to a semiotic enquiry and about the semiotic nature of film images. It goes without saying that I believe that any film student could rely on those remarks in order to insert them into the framework of his own specific methodology, but I refuse the responsibility of proposing to someone a new key for the understanding of the artistic problems of film. Let me only surreptitiously add that I do not believe it is possible to understand the social relevance and the aesthetic functioning of a movie without focusing on it from a semiotic point of view. But, according to a popular Italiian joke, "qui l'ho detto e qui lo nego," in this precise moment I say this and in this precise moment I deny having said it.

Nobody here has denied the existence of such a phenomenon as cinema, and nobody has denied that good movies exist. But Professor Harman says that he is not sure that a science of signs exists and that, if this science has to be identified with Peirce's trichotomies, this "can be fun, for a while, but it does not constitute a science." Since I believe that there does exist a discipline studying the various types of signs, that many of the things said by Peirce constitute a science, and that those things are not fun at all, let me try to outline some basic requirements of a general approach and to illustrate them by some examples referring to the filmic experience. Naturally I cannot propose a satisfactory semiotic theory within present limitations. Therefore I ask you to consider my statements as a tentative summary of a more elaborated approach. By accident it happens that this approach is outlined in my book *A Theory of Semiotics.* Since there are of course other semiotic theories, I suggest that the organizers of the symposium on Film and the University devote the next one to Semiotics and the University. There has recently been a Charles Sanders Peirce Symposium in Baltimore. By the way, some one hundred years ago, someone in Baltimore considered Peirce neither scientific nor fun, and they fired him. Fortunately people in Baltimore have changed their minds and I hope the same thing will happen in New York.

According to Peirce, a sign is something which stands for something (else) to somebody in some respect or capacity. This definition has some consequences:

1. We have a sign when a material occurrence stands for something else to us. Since a word, a medical symptom, and a movie image are material occurrences sending us back to something else, all those phenomena are signs.

2. In order for an occurrence to be a sign, it is not necessary that the occurrence be intentionally produced by a human agent. According to Morris "something is a sign only because it is interpreted as a sign of something else by some interpreter. . . . Semiotics, then, is not concerned with the study of a particular kind of object, but with ordinary objects insofar (and only insofar) as they participate in semiosis." It is true that the word "smoke" and smoke are not the same kind of entity (and in fact the word sends us back to smoke while

smoke sends us back to fire) and it is true that the way the word stands for smoke is not the way smoke stands for fire: but a science has to choose its own level of pertinence. Physical differences between the word "smoke" and smoke are pertinent to a phonologist and to a fireman; from the semiotic point of view one is obliged to realize that they have at least one feature in common: a physical occurrence sends us back to something which is not present. Any further difference should be isolated on the basis of this identity. To ignore a deep functional identity because of superficial evidence of differences displays a poor scientific attitude. Therefore, between a drawing (intentionally produced by a human being) and an imprint (unintentionally left by an animal agent) there is no semiotic difference as far as a human receiver connects both of them with an absent entity.

3. Signs stand for something else in some respect or capacity. "In some respect" means that they are not a mere duplicate of the thing they stand for; "in some capacity" means that signs represent something else because of some correlated features that must be thoroughly described. Let me say for the moment that signs are correlated with what they stand for on the basis of a rule or a convention. [I shall demonstrate that even the so called natural, iconic, analogic signs, like movie images (supposedly possessing some of the properties of the things they represent) are ruled by conventions.] A conventional relationship is not necessarily an arbitrary one. A sign can be motivated by something else and nevertheless be conventionally correlated with it.

4. The notion of "sign" is an oversimplification. Let me substitute for it, following Hjelmslev, the notion of sign-function. A sign-function is the correlation, posited by a rule of equivalence, between an expression (that is a material occurrence) and its content.

5. A repertoire or a system of sign-functions is a code.

6. Since a sign-function is a posited correlation, its functives (expression and content) are independent of each other. This means that the same expression, on the basis of another rule, can be correlated with a different content. A gold star on the epaulet of a soldier means "lieutenant," while on a striped

flag it means "state of the Union." It could be the same star, graphically realized in the same way, at the interior of a frame, twice inserted in two different contexts (image of the soldier and image of the flag).

This shows that a particular iconological system of correlation (or code) establishes, among its rules, some contextual principles of the type "when inserted in the context x it means. . . ."

7. A sign function becomes possible when both its functives are produced by a system of variously articulated pertinent elements. There are various ways of articulating expressions and the way followed by verbal languages is only one of them. The articulation of content is the one provided by the cultural system of a given society and in principle it does not vary through the possible substitutions of the expression system. In other words, our culture makes available the entity "star" defined as a shining heavenly body and opposed to other bodies such as the planets: this available element of the content system can be expressed either by the words /star/, /étoile/, or /stella/ or by the conventional drawing resulting from different arrangements of intersecting triangles (naturally other types of expression are available).

Different expression systems can have one, two, or more articulations. As we shall see later, so called iconic signs do not have the same kind of articulation as verbal languages.

8. Sign-functions are used in order to mention things or states of the world (in other words we take signs to refer to objects or other entities); but the referential use of a sign-function does not constitute the sign-function as such. This means that the content of an expression is not the referent of the sign. Signs can refer to their possible referent just because they are expressions sending us back to a content. The content of expressions can be analyzed and described by means of a semantic compositional analysis independent of the corresponding referent and also of the correlated expression. Only in this way is it possible to justify theoretically the double phenomenon of signs referring to nonexistent entities and of the use of languages in order to lie. The possibility of signifying nonexistent objects (and therefore of lying) is not only

220

connected with the existence of highly conventionalized and arbitrary sign-functions, as happens with verbal language: drawings, photographs, and cinematographic icons can also signify nonexistent entities, so they cannot be referential indices. As for filmic expressions, through montage two persons can be shown as if they were meeting each other even though this event has never happened. Through various modes of trucage images can be alternated so as to display nonexistent or aberrant shapes; ghosts can appear between real men; a fictitious character can appear to be pointing towards a precise person existing in our physical world while the signified content belongs only to a "possible" world; etc. (One could object that there is at least one instance in which the movie image not only sends back to, but also points directly to, and is motivated by, the real presence of a physical entity: that the image is a sort of imprint of the human body of the actor. I shall discuss the complexities involved here later, when speaking of the semiotic nature of imprints.)

9. When speaking of the coded correlation between an expression and a content we are not obliged to think of a unit-to-unit correlation. In verbal language units of second articulation, phonemes, are combined in order to form units of first articulation, morphemes; these morphemes are usually correlated to cultural units, i.e., to units of content which can in their turn be analyzed into minor semantic units (a "star" is a unit of content that can be analyzed as a "body," as "celestial," as "shining" or "burning," as "rotating," and so on). However, the minor units of the corresponding morpheme, the phonemes, do not refer back to the minor units of the cultural units of sememe—in other words, the elementary components of the word /star/ do not represent the elementary components of the sememe "star." Thus language does not represent a code in which the correlation is posited unit to unit: one could rather speak of a cluster-to-cluster correlation. Morse code represents a case of correlation string to unit (a series of dots and dashes is referred to a precise alphabetic unit not otherwise decomposable). On the contrary, on a watch every movement of the main hand corresponds to a step of the apparent movement of the sun around the earth (or vice

221

versa). Notice that even in this case the movement of the hand does not directly refer back to the real movement of the real celestial body but rather to the way in which our culture has rendered it evident and pertinent: the organization of the expression sends us back to an organization of the content and only in this way can it be used as something pointing towards a real state of the world. (The problem of how the organization of the content has been motivated by the real state of the world is at this stage an extra-semiotic one.) In any case, one should admit that the code of the measurement of time is different from the one of verbal language. We can say that in the former the features of the expression are in some way determined or motivated by the features of the content, while in the latter they are not. Nevertheless, a watch could exist and function even if our astronomic system were by chance totally different. This cannot be said of the sundial: here not only the movements of the shadow reproduce (or are made pertinent in the same way as) the movements of the sun, but the movement of the sun directly causes the movement of the shadow. In this sense one can say that the shadow is an index of the sun. I would like, however, to stress the fact that even in this case there is a sign-function correlating an expression to a content, and the proof is that I can lie with a sundial, producing the shadow by means of an artificial light source. (I can undoubtedly do it in a movie but in principle I can also do it in everyday life, provided that the one I want to cheat is sufficiently naive.) The conclusion of the preceding tentative typology of different sign-functions shows in any case that it is impossible to apply the laws of verbal language to every system of sign-function. The rules of semiotics are not necessarily the same as the rules of linguistics.

10. An expression is correlated to a first content which is denoted by it. I mean by denotation (in a nonreferential framework) the immediate posited correlation between an expression and a given content. I mean by connotation any other content that finds a vehicle only in a preceding sign-function, i.e., that can be expressed through the mediation of a previous content. Consider the word /murderer/: it denotes a man who has killed, or who is killing, another man; by means of this

222

denotation it also connotes a "bad" man or a man doing something against the law. The connotation is associated with the previous denotation by another convention or a subcode. To a secret service planning the assassination of a foreign leader, the word /murderer/ still denotes a man who is killing another man but does not necessarily connote "bad guy." Secret services have connotative codes different from ours. Suppose now that a movie, let us say *War and Peace* shows a small fat man, but does not necessarily show his face; the image denotes "man." But if this man wears a particular coat and a particular hat, and if he is polishing his ears with his little finger, we detect the connotation "Napoleon Bonaparte." A certain iconographic subcode establishes the right connotation. Suppose now that we see another man who, from a window, tries to shoot Napoleon with a gun; denotatively speaking the image tells us no more than that. Nevertheless, a previous verbal denotation has told us that this possible murderer is a Russian nobleman called Pierre Besuchov. Through other indications in the context we know that Pierre connotes some psychological and sociological values (for instance the enlightened liberal aristocracy). Through the contextual pressure, by means of inferences and presuppositions which have not been previously coded, we can arrive at an interpretation of the gesture of Pierre as the manifestation of a wish for justice. We are therefore tempted to dissociate from the denotation of murdering the usual connotation of "bad guy" and to add to the gesture (and to the person who performs it) other and more complex connotations. These connotations are not culturally coded. They represent a sort of semiotic initiative taken by the addressee of such a complex message. The addressee tries to institute a new subcode. This subcode lasts "l'espace d'un matin," the message itself represses, so to speak, the initiative of the addressee, since it tells him that Pierre gives up. But when a different text introduces and reinforces a new connotation (for instance, when in "Citizen Kane" the word—and the sled— /rosebud/ succeeds in connoting the memory of childhood and maternal tenderness) this connotation can last beyond the text that has imposed it and gain acceptance by a cultural milieu as an established metaphor or an emblem.

Please note that in the preceding example I have cited a case in which:

a) the filmic image has no referential index (in any case the real world in which Napoleon has lived is not the possible world in which Pierre lives) and what has been denoted by the message is not a real state of the world (a referent) but pure content;

b) what is connoted has no less consistency (from the referential point of view) than what has been denoted: simply, connotations need previous denotations in order to be grasped;

c) something is directly denoted by the images, something else acquires its denotative consistency through the support of other signs, words, or noises;

d) something is denoted not only by a simple image or a frame but also by a continuous chain of events.

Sometimes signs, that from the iconic point of view are highly imprecise, acquire their denotative power through the impact of the narrative context and of other denotations.

In Antonioni's *Blow Up*, for example, a photographer, after having taken numerous photos in a park, returns to his studio where he succeeds, by means of successive enlargements, in identifying a human form stretched out behind a tree: a man killed by a hand armed with a revolver which, in another section of the enlargement, appears in the middle of the foliage of a hedge.

But this narrative element (which, in the film—and in the critical commentaries about it—assumes the weight of a recalling to reality, and to the total and implacable stare of the photographic lens) only functions if the iconic code interacts with a code of narrative functions. In fact, if the enlargement were shown to someone unfamiliar with its context in the film, it would be very difficult for him to recognize the distorted and granular areas which supposedly denote "a stretched out human form" and "a hand with revolver." The signified "corpse" and "hand with revolver" are only attributed to the signifying form on the basis of the narrative context of the film which, by building the suspense, prepares the spectator (and the protagonist in the film) *to see those things*. The context

224

functions as an ideolect, assigning given values within the code to signals which might otherwise appear as mere noise.

Another example taken from an Antonioni movie can clarify the difference between denotative and connotative conventions. You probably know that Antonioni's *China-Chung Kuo*, a movie the artist directed in a genuinely sympathetic mood, has been interpreted by Chinese critics as an unbearably denigratory pamphlet directed against the Chinese people. Now if one analyzes frame by frame and sequence by sequence all the cases in which Chinese critics and authorities charge Antonioni with unfriendly attitudes, one realizes that they are all cases in which Chinese addressees have superimposed different connotative subcodes on the ones foreseen by the author. Among the sequences which have most offended Chinese audiences is one in which the camera shows the Nanking Bridge. The Chinese say that Antonioni has tried to give the impression that the bridge is unstable and on the verge of collapsing. If you look at the movie you can see that the director has shown the bridge, by passing underneath it moving the camera in a circular manner, from a sort of "expressionistic" point of view. This has the effect of privileging oblique angles, transverse perspectives, and asymmetric frames, as any western movie-maker does when he wants to suggest power and architectural impact. But present Chinese iconographic subcodes are obviously different, as anybody can see when looking at a Chinese movie like *The Girl of the Red Guards Detachment*, or a propaganda mural painting: Chinese iconography is based on symmetrical and frontal frames with a sort of neoclassical mood and they express power, stability, monumentality only by frontal and symmetric shots. The denotation was the same (it was for the Nanking Bridge) but the connotations were based on different subcodes.

11. I have so far outlined some basic definitions of a semiotic discipline and I have given some examples taken from cinematographic practice. But a possible unanswered objection is the following: there is no homology between the definition of sign-function as applied to the arbitrary correlation between a word and its content and as applied to the motivated or iconic correlation between an image and the corresponding object.

Cinema can make people believe that a given person is Napoleon or that Pierre Besuchov has the same kind of referentiality as Napoleon, but in order to do so it has nevertheless to start from physically existing bodies of which it "reflects" some properties at the same time acting as an index, since the traces on the screen demonstrate that there was something which has motivated them. Is this relationship a coded one? And if it is can one speak of "code" both in the case of a word and of an icon without resorting to a mere metaphorical transference?

Since a discipline can control many objects provided it can describe them using the same categories, if the categories of code and sign-function show a lack of univocity, then semiotics is not entitled to speak of such diverse phenomena.

We have said that the proper object of semiotics is the relationship of standing for or of sending-back-to, and it is evident that the cinematographic image of a train stands for a train just as the word /train/ stands for the same content-unit, or sememe. But one could observe that the way in which a word stands for the sememe is not the same as the way in which an image does. What I have to demonstrate (or at least to suggest) is that those different ways of standing for can be methodologically defined by resorting to the same precise set of theoretical tools. The Peircian trichotomy of symbol, index, and icon describes very well the fact that there are different modes of sending-back-to, but it fails in its attempt to unify those three modes. At most, Peirce shows, *et pour cause,* that in every sign phenomenon those three modes interact and that there is never a pure iconic or a pure indexical sign, but that every concrete occurrence of an act of signification relies on all these three modes. But in doing so he stops at the observation that every sign is composed of three mutually incompatible semiotic features. And he does not answer the objection that iconic and indexical signs are in fact uncoded signs (therefore escaping our definition of sign-function) which obey natural rather than cultural laws.

If one undertakes a careful analysis of the notion of iconism and indexicality one can easily see that these are umbrella-notions covering a disparate range of different semiotic phenomena. (I have undertaken this task in two of my books and the critical revision of the notion of iconism is presently being pursued in many semiotic circles. I am obliged to spare you such a complicated argument. Let me only suggest a possible line of solution.) I think that the entire problem becomes clearer if, instead of listing types of signs, one lists the different modalities in which a sign-function is established, that is, the different ways in which one can manipulate a given material continuum in order to produce expressions and to correlate them to a given content. In *A Theory of Semiotics* I have therefore proposed a typology of modes of sign-production according to four parameters, namely a) the material continuum used, b) the complexity of its articulation, c) the arbitrary or the motivated relationship between the form of the expression and the form of the content and, d) the kind of physical labor performed in order to generate the expression. Let me consider for the moment only the last two parameters. From the point of view of physical labor an expression can be produced starting from the minimal physical effort and proceeding to the maximum one: thus we can list *recognition, ostension, combination,* and *invention.*

In *recognition,* on the basis of a cultural convention, I use a natural event (or a mechanical result) as the expression of a given content: instances of this type of labor are imprints, medical symptoms, and clues. In *ostension* I can use an existing object, isolating it and showing it as the representative of the class to which it belongs: I can show a cigarette or its image as the *example* of all existing cigarettes: I can show a handful of tobacco as a *sample* of the entire product of a tobacco factory; and I can reproduce the gesture of a man smoking a cigarette as the *fictive sample* sending us back either to "cigarette" or to "smoking" (according to some previous indications or contextual clues). In *combination* I can reproduce ready-made types of expression in order to compose them in major strings (as it happens with the pre-established expression proposed by any structured verbal language). In all those three cases (recognition, ostension, and combination) the expressions can be chosen or produced according to a preestablished type and are correlated to a content which is already known. The fourth case is the one of *inventions:* one has to invent a sign-function when the broken expression has to be elaborated along with its type since a given culture has not provided a workable model; and it has not been produced because the content to be expressed has not yet been defined. Thus the sign producer has at the same time to propose a new expression, a new content, and a new way of correlating both. Cases of invention are not cases of performance of a given code but rather cases of invention of a new code.

I shift on many minor distinctions and subcategories, but I would like to stress the fact that these modes of sign production do not correspond to different types of signs. Rather, in every sign-function two or more of these productive modes are at work.

Let me now consider a typical instance of imprint, the trace left on the ground by the hoof of a horse. Apparently the imprint, insofar as it has been physically motivated by the passage of the horse, is an index of its passage and an icon of its horseshoe.

One has now to answer the following questions: how can such a hoof be falsified so as to lie? Why is it recognizable even if reproduced on a reduced scale? Why is the horseshoe recognizable although the hoof reproduces, among its properties, only its outline and although the imprint is larger than the horseshoe? The answer is that imprints also send us back to a cultural content; they are produced by individual agents but stand for a cultural notion ("horse," or "hoof," or "a horse has passed here going in that direction"). When the expression is falsely produced by means of a vicarious imprinter and has no real indexical properties, the process of signification takes place equally; the so called similarity between the trace on the ground and the cultural notion of a hoof is recognized only on the basis of some rules of *similitude*. I am expressly using the geometrical term: similitude is not a vague resemblance, it is a system of geometrical transformation ruled by laws of proportionality and by a precise selection of features to be transformed or projected, while other features are completely disregarded. Therefore the correlatoion between expression and content is governed by some technical conventions. Moreover if one has no previous knowledge of the features characterizing a horseshoe one will never be able to project backward from the imprint to the imprinter.

To speak of rules of similitude and of projection devices means to recognize that the expression must realize or embody certain pertinent features by articulation of which a significant shape takes place. Articulations in imprints are not the same as in language: they are not combined in a temporal succession but in a spatial coexistence; they projectively reproduce the articulations of the content type to which they refer, so that the correlation is not only unit to unit, but point to point. But there are nevertheless features and articulations. Suppose I want to produce (perhaps in order to cheat someone) the imprint of a glass of wine upon a table. There are four and no more than four pertinent features: a circular form, the length of the radius, a cue of red, and the characteristic of being wet. Only by familiarity with previous imprints of this type can one detect from this one the past presence of a glass of wine. And only if one knows the transformation rule for passing from the size of the imprint to the supposed size of the glass, can the detection be correct. At the end of such a process what one has detected is not the referent (this or that glass of wine) but only the content "glass of wine." Only by a work of circumstantial inference (for instance, the presence of a given glass on another table) can one use this imprint to refer to that precise glass of wine.

We can undoubtedly consider an imprint as the functive of a sign-function where the correlation has been posited on the basis of some rules. Since a sign-function is the atomic element of a code, we can speak of a code of imprints, a code that for instance is more familiar to hunters and boy scouts than to philosophy professors. Despite their presumed iconism, I would be pretty embarrassed in distinguishing the paw of a dog from the paw of a wolf. Now, the difference between the way in which a word and a hoof are correlated to their content consists in their *type-token* ratio. As for the word, the expression type is independent of the content type; as for the hoof, both types realize the same features. I call those two different cases of type-token ratio, *ratio facilis*, and *ratio difficilis*. But in many cases this opposition is not so straight. A medical symptom is a case of recognition as well as an imprint, but while the imprint relies on a *ratio difficilis* the symptom relies on a *ratio facilis* (like a word): in fact, a symptom is motivated by the corresponding organic disease but has not the form of the disease it signifies. So we could isolate a sort of continuum of differences in the mode of correlation, but all these cases are definable in the terms I have proposed to define a standard sign-function.

Now, what kind of sign-function is realized by the graphic film image of a human being who stands for Napoleon? The reproduction of the form of a human body is an *imprint*. The imprint disregards a lot of the features of the real body (color, third dimension, texture of the skin, and so on) and retains only those which are considered pertinent for a recognizable transformation. As in geometrical similitude, size is not pertinent (we are able to recognize a man projected upon a cinerama screen without believing he is a giant). Understanding images must be learned. But let us consider the man himself, the actor acting in front of the camera. As such it is an *ostensive* sign, a prepared material for the shooting: he and all the surrounding objects stand for the class to which they belong. This man acts and makes gestures: these gestures are elements of a kinesic code and as such they are the significant result of the *combination* of preestablished units. The man moves left to right meeting another man: there are at work *"vectorial"* features (that can be classified half way between imprints and combinational units); by these features the expression sends us back to vectorial features of the content for which it serves as the vehicle. In the same way the verbal difference between /Mary gives something to John/ and /John gives something to Mary/ is given by another vectorial feature, the temporal or spatial succession (before-after, or left-right) embodied in the uttered or written phrase. Since the real purport of the movement of men is reinforced, usually, by words and other sounds, the global denotation of the sequence is supported by many modes of sign production and by many sign-functions. Perhaps at a certain point the actor expresses something by an unheard-of expression of the face or an uncoded gesture: we are witnessing in this case an instance of *invention*. But the acceptance of this new way of coding is undoubtedly supported by the contextual pressure of other already coded sign-functions.

I could continue in this kind of analysis, but a typology of modes of sign production is just at its beginning. I think that it can prove itself very useful in the definition of filmic signification. It could destroy the temptation to analyze movie images as if they were words, duly articulated in minor recognizable units. Someone has, in fact, naively tried to say that the image of a man is the equivalent of a verbal sentence, his eyes and his nose being the equivalent of words, and so on, desperately fishing for nosemes, mouthemes, beardemes, footemes, and so on.

A semiotic of film is possible if one accepts that semiotics is neither a province nor a byproduct of linguistics. But one should at the same time accept the hypothesis that movie images "say" something and, since not everybody understands them, there must be semiotic rules governing this kind of communication.

Once this is accepted, many other problems arise. A movie is a text. As such it is governed by textual rules. All the paraphernalia of a text grammar, presently elaborated mainly at a level of verbal communication, should be applied to the study of film. All the problems approached by the study of cultural interaction, the conversational rules studied by ethnomethodology and sociolinguistics, all interactional laws approached by proxemics and kinesics, should support the study of those visual texts called films. In the same sense the logic of narrative function and the logic of presuppositions should become indispensable tools for the right understanding of the narrative arrangement of a film.

One should indicate, at this stage, when something is understood by means of coded denotation; or by means of a complex inferential labor, which partially relies on coded narrative rules (therefore releasing presuppositions, anaphors, narrative syllogisms, and enthymemes); or when something becomes conventionally coded by force of the contextual pressure of the text itself. When Metz observes that in *M* a loose balloon caught in overhead wires symbolizes the death of the girl whom we earlier saw holding a balloon, I would analyze this in a way which partially differs from the one proposed by Gilbert Harman. The earlier photographic image of the girl holding the balloon *denotes* a girl holding a balloon; at this stage I would draw no distinction between "depicting" a girl and "standing for a girl": on the basis of some conventions the addressee understands that those traces upon the screen send us back to the content "a girl holding a balloon." Until the word "depicts" or some other expression like it has been scientifically analyzed, I prefer to rely on my own definition of the so called iconic relationship: a sign-function based on a visual transformation, a coded projection. When the balloon is seen in isolation, among wires, it is taken as a metonymy for the girl and the correlation girl-balloon is *posited* by the context, it is inferred by the addressee, and it is not necessarily inserted into a code: it represents the provisional and transitory positing of a sign-function, ready to dissolve as soon as the film has accomplished its communicative task. The image of the balloon is ready, so to speak, to become the functive of other sign-functions, and at the end of the movie it is restored to its immediate denotative function: a balloon is a balloon is a balloon is a balloon. It is a girl only for a moment and within a precise context.

The capture of the balloon by the wires may or may not stand for the capture of the girl. Probably the director wished the image to be understood in this way: it was a form of semiotic gambling. Since we are speaking of this interpretation, Fritz Lang has won. The relationship between capture and murder is another metonymy. It too is not coded: this means that outside the film wires do not represent murderers. But culturally speaking wires recall ropes, ropes capture, and so on. The film is playing a risky game between the coded and the uncoded. It supports daring suggestions by coded connotations. Culture acts as a glue to amalgamate the invention of unheard-of relationships. In all this nothing is really "natural." Semiotic laws are at work at every level. A movie is the meeting point of many semiotic phenomena. It carries preexisting codes and it is carried by its own specific codes. Sometimes it establishes new codes and often these new correlations produced by a given film will not be accepted by cinema. A semiotics of cinema and film is still to be completely outlined. But its laws lie outside cinema and film, they are the laws of signification in general.

But nobody can discover laws unless he is guided by the hypothesis that there are laws. It is very dangerous to refuse to recognize semiotic laws acting in cinematographic and filmic phenomena. In this way films are believed to be the spontaneous reproduction of reality, they are polluted by a sort of referential and indexical fallacy and it becomes impossible to detect the plots of culture under the supposed spontaneity of nature. Without a semiotic awareness films are viewed as magic spells. One believes that things make films. On the contrary, frequently, films make things. The semiotic approach is not only a criticism of the illusions of reality, it is also a continuous criticism of the ideological shaping of the reality on the part of the processes of semiosis.

1975

GILBERT HARMAN
ECO-LOCATION

Umberto Eco's semiotic theory[1] provides a good illustration of the emptiness of work done under the labels "semiotics" and "semiology." In part, his theory is a curious compromise between Metz's view and Wollen's. Like Wollen, Eco explicitly rejects Metz's linguistic model in favor of Peirce's theory of signs. But surprisingly, like Metz and unlike Wollen, Eco writes as if signs were used only in communication (which would seem to misrepresent the way signs are used by a traveller planning an itinerary, a mathematician, or a scientist, to say nothing of a film director, artist, or poet). On the other hand, Eco appears to disagree with both Metz and Wollen about convention. Eco sees convention everywhere. Where Metz and Wollen hold that it is by virtue of linguistic convention that, say, the word *combustion* means fire, in contrast to what they take to be the nonconventional way in which smoke means fire or a photographic image of a burning building depicts fire, Eco says that convention is involved in all three cases, since one can take smoke to be a sign of fire only if one knows a rule relating them, and one can interpret the photographic image as an image of fire only if one can recognize it as such an image.

---

[1]"On the Contribution of Film to Semiotics," *Quarterly Review of Film Studies* 2:1 (February 1977), pp. 1–14. *A Theory of Semiotics*, Bloomington, Indiana; Indiana University Press (1976). [Reprinted here, pp. 217 – 33.]

I say that Eco *appears* to disagree with Metz and Wollen in this regard because the issue turns out to be a purely verbal one. Eco is simply using the term "convention" in an unconventional way so as to count as conventions regularities that are not conventions in any ordinary sense, such as the known relation between smoke and fire. To say that it is by convention in the ordinary sense of "convention" that the word *combustion* means fire is to say, roughly, that one takes the word to mean fire simply because that is what others do, and one would take this word to mean something else if others were to do so; one wants to use and understand the word in the same way that others do.[2] One does not similarly take smoke to mean fire simply because others do, and one would not stop taking smoke to be a sign of fire just because others failed to see the connection; in this case it is not true that one wants to take smoke to mean whatever it is that others take it to mean— rather one wants to take it to mean whatever it is that it actually does mean.

Now it is characteristic of those who do what they call "semiotics" or "semiology" to use terms in special new senses for no discernable reason, as in Eco's technical use of the term "convention." Nor is this a harmless practice that simply makes semiotics seem more interesting than it really is, because it is a practice that can obscure important issues. Eco's technical use of the term "convention" makes it almost impossible for him to address issues concerning the extent to which convention (in the ordinary sense of "convention") is involved in certain cases. To take his own example, consider the Chinese reaction to Antonioni's *China-Chung Kuo*. Was this reaction based on a reliance on iconographic conventions (in the ordinary sense of "conventions") of which Antonioni was unaware? Or did it derive merely from unfamiliarity with the effects of certain sorts of camera movement, the use of oblique angles, etc.? There is an interesting and difficult issue here

---

[2]See David Lewis, *Convention*, Cambridge, Harvard University Press (1969). In his *Theory of Semiotics*, Eco claims that he accepts Lewis' account of convention, but Lewis' analysis clearly implies that it is *not* by convention that smoke means fire.

that Eco cannot even pose, given his special use of the term "convention."

Like other semioticists and semiologists, Eco writes a great deal about "semiotic laws," which he says are "at work at every level" and must be understood if we are to appreciate "filmic signification." But neither Eco nor anyone else has ever stated any substantive laws of semiotics. Those working in semiotics or semiology invariably offer instead innumerable technical definitions and distinctions, as if that was a worthwhile activity in itself. Now technical definitions and distinctions are worthwhile only to the extent that they (a) provide a basis for the statement of substantive laws or principles that do not simply follow from the definitions or at least (b) provide a termiology that can be used in giving illuminating descriptions and analyses of particular cases. Since neither Eco nor anyone else states any substantive semiotic laws or principles, such technical distinctions and definitions are going to be worthwhile only to the extent that they make possible improved descriptions and analyses of particular cases. Here questions of the sort that Guzzetti raises for Metz[3] must also be asked of Eco and other proponents of semiotics. What, for example, is the point of saying that a certain photographic image "denotes" rather than depicts a girl holding a balloon. What do we learn when we are told that in appreciating this image one relies on certain "conventions" (in a technical sense) rather than that one simply recognizes the image as an image of a girl holding a balloon. It would certainly seem that in these as in many other instances nothing is gained and often much is lost through the use of semiotic terminology.

1978

---

[3] Alfred Guzzetti, "Christian Metz and the Semiology of the Cinema," *Journal of Modern Literature* 3:2 (April 1973), pp. 307–306. [Reprinted here, pp. 184–203.]

III
The Film Medium

Film theory and film criticism have been largely concerned with one central issue: What is "cinematic?" Which paths should the cinema follow? Which should it reject? Attempts to answer this question inevitably take their lead from Lessing's classic essay, *Laocoon*, in which the eighteenth century German dramatist and essayist attempted to demonstrate that the visual arts organize their materials spatially while the poetic arts organize their materials temporally. The materials, procedures, subjects, and effects of these two different forms (or "media") of artistic organization are therefore necessarily different. In this spirit, film theorists have attempted to discover the characteristics of the film medium, declaring those subjects, materials, procedures, and effects that "exploit" the characteristics of the medium proper, legitimate, and truly cinematic and those subjects, materials, procedures, and effects that "violate" the characteristics of the medium barren, misleading and fundamentally uncinematic.

The concept of a medium is, of course, a difficult one. Is the medium to be defined in purely physical terms (that is, the projection of images at twenty-four frames per second on a screen) or rather in terms of an artistic language (angle and distance of shots, rhythms and patterns of editing, and so forth)? Does it include the main structural features of the art (such as plot) and its main historical conventions (say, its genres)? And how are we to determine which possibilities of

237

the medium are legitimate? Is it legitimate to pursue any possibility inherent in the medium, or only those for which the
medium has a special affinity? And how are we to judge what
those special affinities are? May two different artistic media
share those affinities or must an art confine itself, as certain
purists urge, to realizing only those possibilities that it shares
with no other art?

Erwin Panofsky, the great art historian who was a contemporary of both Arnheim and Kracauer, has written the most
influential discussion of the subject. He argues that an art
ought to exploit the "unique and specific" possibilities of its
medium; and in the film medium these can be defined as the
"dynamization of space" and the "spatialization of time."
Both these features are visual ones, and Panofsky's primarily
visual conception of the film medium is vulnerable to the objection that it accords an undue priority to the silent film, placing unwise restrictions on the use of speech in films. According to Panofsky's principle of "co-expressibility," "the sound,
articulate or not, cannot express any more than is expressed, at
the same time, by visible movement." Panofsky claims that
the Shavian dialogue in the film version of Shaw's *Pygmalion*
falls flat and suggests that Olivier's monologues in *Henry V* are
successful only to the extent that Olivier's face becomes "a
huge field of action" in oblique "close-up." But those who admire the brilliant Hollywood "dialogue" comedies of the 30s
and early 40s and who recall that Olivier does not deliver the
"St. Crispin's Day" speech in *Henry V* in close-up will receive
these views with a measure of skepticism. Indeed, Panofsky
modified them in the revised version of his essay that appears
in this anthology.

Siegfried Kracauer acknowledges the difficulty of defining
the film medium but believes, nevertheless, that cinema has
certain "inherent affinities." There are, in particular, certain
subjects in the physical world that may be termed "cinematic"
because they exert a peculiar attraction on the medium. Kracauer argues that cinema is predestined and even eager to exhibit them. Like Panofsky, Kracauer accepts the use of sound
in films only under certain very restrictive conditions, and he
especially dislikes the development of the "theatrical" film:

"What even the most theatrical minded silent film could not incorporate—pointed controversiees, Shavian witticisms, Hamlet's soliloquies—has been annexed to the screen." But Kracauer finds this annexation unfortunate; it in no way proves that such theatrical speeches are legitimate possibilities of the cinematic medium, for "popularity," in Kracauer's view, has no bearing on questions of aesthetic legitimacy.

Kracauer calls the comedies of Frank Capra and Preston Sturges border-line cases, but only on the ground that their witty dialogue is "complemented and compensated for" by "visuals of independent interest" (he means that they include slapstick sequences). Just as witty dialogue violates the visual requirements of the medium and requires "compensation," surrealistic projections of inner realities, expressionist dreams and visions, and experimental abstractions violate the realist requirements of the medium. On the other hand, certain types of movement—the chase and dancing—and certain types of objects—those that are normally too big or too small to be seen—are peculiarly appropriate subjects of cinema. But does the dance really have a greater affinity for the film than it does for the stage? Must the film avoid what is normally seen simply because it is the subject matter of other arts? One can agree with Kracauer that the close-up is a peculiarly cinematic technique, and even with the influential Hungarian theorist, scenarist, and filmmaker, Béla Balázs, that the close-up is responsible for the "discovery of the human face," without supposing that the film must devote itself exclusively to the exploitation of these "unique" potentialities.

Rudolph Arnheim shares Panofsky's and Kracauer's view that the film ought to stress the peculiar possibilities of the cinematic medium. But he feels obligated to refute the view that cinema is a mere mechanical reproduction of physical reality. If it were, it would not be an art. Arnheim therefore insists on the various discrepancies between the film image and the standard perception of physical reality. The film image suffers a reduction of depth, a distortion of perspective, an accentuation of perspective overlapping and, in the past, an absence of color and articulate speech. Arnheim asserts that the true task of cinema is to exploit these very "defects" and turn them

239

to an advantage, just as painting exploits the fact that it is a two-dimensional, enclosed object. Perhaps a great art can be devised that confines itself to exploiting these defects (the silent film may have been such an art), but can we accept the suggestion that film must avoid exploiting the affinities with physical reality that Kracauer mentions, just because they conform to, rather than deviate from, reality? And should we regret the fact that we can remedy some of the "defects" of a medium rather than exploit them? Should we regret the development of sound, as all three of these theorists do?

Gerald Mast rejects the problem of defining the distinctively cinematic medium as any function of the method of recording moving images—photographic or otherwise. Instead, he regards the projection of images by light as the essential feature of any cinematic work. And the fact of projection permits him to distinguish the experience of cinema from that of theater, television, and painting. He also argues that a careful investigation of the characteristics of projected images undermines a number of commonly held opinions, among them the view that one must project photographic images—upon which Kracauer's theory (and that of all realist cinema theory) is founded, and the view that the projected image is two-dimensional and perceived as flat—claims upon which Arnheim's theory (and that of most puristic and modernistic cinema theory) is based.

Stanley Cavell, the American philosopher and aesthetician, also places great emphasis on the importance of projection and, more particularly, on the fact of projection onto a screen. The projected image is the image of a world, and of a world which, in contrast to the world of a painting, exists beyond the frame. Indeed, the only difference between the projected world and reality is that the projected world does not exist now. It is simultaneously absent and present. One function of the movie screen, then, is to screen that world from the audience. Another is to screen the audience from the projected world. Unlike the audience in a theater which is not present to the actors on stage by convention, the film medium renders the audience absent mechanically and automatically. By this enforced invisibility, movies give expression to our modern experience of privacy and anonymity. Man has longed for invisibility and the absence of responsibility it confers, and film satisfies precisely this wish. In watching a film we view a magically reproduced world while remaining invisible to it. This condition makes the experience of film essentially voyeuristic and even pornographic. It permits the audience a magical-sexual contact with the hypnotic Garbos, Dietrichs, and Gables of the screen.

However, unlike Panofsky and many other theorists, Cavell does not think that the aesthetic possibilities of the movie medium can be deduced from its physical or technical properties. A medium, in his unconventional construal, is simply something through which or by means of which something specific gets said or done in particular ways. In his view, only the art itself, and not a mere consideration of its physical medium, can discover its aesthetic possibilities.

Cavell argues that the issues of genre and of medium are inseparable, and that the classical Hollywood world was composed of three such media—stories or structures that revolve about the Military Man, the Dandy, and the Woman. The Military Man conquers evil for the sake of society (James Stewart in *The Man Who Shot Liberty Valance,* Gary Cooper in *Mr. Deeds Goes to Town*); the Dandy pursues his own interests, values, and self-respect (John Wayne in *Red River,* Cary Grant in anything); and the Woman attracts men as flames attract the moth (Garbo, Dietrich, Davis). With the loss of conviction in these genres, film reached (very belatedly in comparison to the other arts of the twentieth century) the condition of modernism, in which the self-conscious artist seeks to produce a new genre, a new medium, rather than simply producing more instances of a familiar one.

Finally, Francis Sparshott, a contemporary philosopher and aesthetician, challenges the assumptions to which the Lessing tradition has given rise. Sparshott regards many of the views expressed by Panofsky, Kracauer, and Arnheim as dogmas. "Whatever can be done with a medium is among its possibilities and hence 'true to' it in a sense that has yet to be shown to be illegitimate." Sparshott offers an account of the film medium which indicates both its great range and its special fea-

241

tures—its unique way of representing space, time, and motion. This analysis provides the foundation for his conclusion: "Film is unique in its capacity for visual recording and analysis, in its ability to convey the unique present reality of things, in its ability to reveal the qualities of lives; but also in its formal freedom, its capacity for realizing fantasy and developing abstract forms." Sparshott's essay implies that a definition of the film medium ought not to be some simple assertion of dogma or a naked attempt to establish as law the dictates of individual taste or the surmises of personal experience.

ERWIN PANOFSKY
STYLE AND MEDIUM
IN THE MOTION PICTURES

Film art is the only art the development of which men now living
have witnessed from the very beginnings; and this development is
all the more interesting as it took place under conditions contrary
to precedent. It was not an artistic urge that gave rise to the discovery and gradual perfection of a new technique; it was a technical
invention that gave rise to the discovery and gradual perfection of
a new art.

From this we understand two fundamental facts. First, that the
primordial basis of the enjoyment of moving pictures was not an
objective interest in a specific subject matter, much less an aesthetic interest in the formal presentation of subject matter, but the
sheer delight in the fact that things seemed to move, no matter what
things they were. Second, that films—first exhibited in "kineto-
scopes," viz., cinematographic peep shows, but projectable to a
screen since as early as 1894—are, originally, a product of genuine
folk art (whereas, as a rule, folk art derives from what is known as
"higher art"). At the very beginning of things we find the simple
recording of movements: galloping horses, railroad trains, fire engines, sporting events, street scenes. And when it had come to the
making of narrative films these were produced by photographers
who were anything but "producers" or "directors," performed by
people who were anything but actors, and enjoyed by people who
would have been much offended had anyone called them "art
lovers."

The casts of these archaic films were usually collected in a "café" where unemployed supers or ordinary citizens possessed of a suitable exterior were wont to assemble at a given hour. An enterprising photographer would walk in, hire four or five convenient characters and make the picture while carefully instructing them what to do: "Now, you pretend to hit this lady over the head"; and (to the lady): "And you pretend to fall down in a heap." Productions like these were shown, together with those purely factual recordings of "movement for movement's sake," in a few small and dingy cinemas mostly frequented by the "lower classes" and a sprinkling of youngsters in quest of adventure (about 1905, I happen to remember, there was only one obscure and faintly disreputable *kino* in the whole city of Berlin, bearing, for some unfathomable reason, the English name of "The Meeting Room"). Small wonder that the "better classes," when they slowly began to venture into these early picture theaters, did so, not by way of seeking normal and possibly serious entertainment, but with that characteristic sensation of self-conscious condescension with which we may plunge, in gay company, into the folkloristic depths of Coney Island or a European kermis; even a few years ago it was the regulation attitude of the socially or intellectually prominent that one could confess to enjoying such austerely educational films as *The Sex Life of the Starfish* or films with "beautiful scenery," but never to a serious liking for narratives.

Today there is no denying that narrative films are not only "art" —not often good art, to be sure, but this applies to other media as well—but also, besides architecture, cartooning and "commercial design," the only visual art entirely alive. The "movies" have reestablished that dynamic contact between art production and art consumption which, for reasons too complex to be considered here, is sorely attenuated, if not entirely interrupted, in many other fields of artistic endeavor. Whether we like it or not, it is the movies that mold, more than any other single force, the opinions, the taste, the language, the dress, the behavior, and even the physical appearance of a public comprising more than 60 per cent of the population of the earth. If all the serious lyrical poets, composers, painters and sculptors were forced by law to stop their activities, a rather small fraction of the general public would become aware of the fact and a still smaller fraction would seriously regret it. If the same thing were to happen with the movies the social consequences would be catastrophic.

244

In the beginning, then, there were the straight recordings of movement no matter what moved, viz., the prehistoric ancestors of our "documentaries"; and, soon after, the early narratives, viz., the prehistoric ancestors of our "feature films." The craving for a narrative element could be satisfied only by borrowing from older arts, and one should expect that the natural thing would have been to borrow from the theater, a theater play being apparently the *genus proximum* to a narrative film in that it consists of a narrative enacted by persons that move. But in reality the imitation of stage performances was a comparatively late and thoroughly frustrated development. What happened at the start was a very different thing. Instead of imitating a theatrical performance already endowed with a certain amount of motion, the earliest films added movement to works of art originally stationary, so that the dazzling technical invention might achieve a triumph of its own without intruding upon the sphere of higher culture. The living language, which is always right, has endorsed this sensible choice when it still speaks of a "moving picture" or, simply, a "picture," instead of accepting the pretentious and fundamentally erroneous "screen play."

The stationary works enlivened in the earliest movies were indeed pictures: bad nineteenth-century paintings and postcards (or waxworks à la Madame Tussaud's), supplemented by the comic strips—a most important root of cinematic art—and the subject matter of popular songs, pulp magazines and dime novels; and the films descending from this ancestry appealed directly and very intensely to a folk art mentality. They gratified—often simultaneously—first, a primitive sense of justice and decorum when virtue and industry were rewarded while vice and laziness were punished; second, plain sentimentality when "the thin trickle of a fictive love interest" took its course "through somewhat serpentine channels," or when Father, dear Father returned from the saloon to find his child dying of diphtheria; third, a primordial instinct for bloodshed and cruelty when Andreas Hofer faced the firing squad, or when (in a film of 1893–94) the head of Mary Queen of Scots actually came off; fourth, a taste for mild pornography (I remember with great pleasure a French film of *ca.* 1900 wherein a seemingly but not really well-rounded lady as well as a seemingly but not really slender one were shown changing to bathing suits—an honest, straightforward *porcheria* much less objectionable than the

245

now extinct Betty Boop films and, I am sorry to say, some of the more recent Walt Disney productions); and, finally, that crude sense of humor, graphically described as "slapstick," which feeds upon the sadistic and the pornographic instinct, either singly or in combination.

Not until as late as *ca.* 1905 was a film adaptation of *Faust* ventured upon (cast still "unknown," characteristically enough), and not until 1911 did Sarah Bernhardt lend her prestige to an unbelievably funny film tragedy, *Queen Elizabeth of England.* These films represent the first conscious attempt at transplanting the movies from the folk art level to that of "real art"; but they also bear witness to the fact that this commendable goal could not be reached in so simple a manner. It was soon realized that the imitation of a theater performance with a set stage, fixed entries and exits, and distinctly literary ambitions is the one thing the film must avoid.

The legitimate paths of evolution were opened, not by running away from the folk art character of the primitive film but by developing it within the limits of its own possibilities. Those primordial archetypes of film productions on the folk art level—success or retribution, sentiment, sensation, pornography, and crude humor—could blossom forth into genuine history, tragedy and romance, crime and adventure, and comedy, as soon as it was realized that they could be transfigured—not by an artificial injection of literary values but by the exploitation of the unique and specific possibilities of the new medium. Significantly, the beginnings of this legitimate development antedate the attempts at endowing the film with higher values of a foreign order (the crucial period being the years from 1902 to *ca.* 1905), and the decisive steps were taken by people who were laymen or outsiders from the viewpoint of the serious stage.

These unique and specific possibilities can be defined as *dynamization of space* and, accordingly, *spatialization of time.* This statement is self-evident to the point of triviality but it belongs to that kind of truths which, just because of their triviality, are easily forgotten or neglected.

In a theater, space is static, that is, the space represented on the stage, as well as the spatial relation of the beholder to the spectacle, is unalterably fixed. The spectator cannot leave his seat, and the setting of the stage cannot change, during one act (except for such incidentals as rising moons or gathering clouds and such illegitimate reborrowings from the film as turning wings or gliding backdrops). But, in return for this restriction, the theater has the advantage that time, the medium of emotion and thought conveyable by speech, is free and independent of anything that may happen in visible space. Hamlet may deliver his famous monologue lying on a couch in the middle distance, doing nothing and only dimly discernible to the spectator and listener, and yet by his mere words enthrall him with a feeling of intensest emotional action.

With the movies the situation is reversed. Here, too, the spectator occupies a fixed seat, but only physically, not as the subject of an aesthetic experience. Aesthetically, he is in permanent motion as his eye identifies itself with the lens of the camera, which permanently shifts in distance and direction. And as movable as the spectator is, as movable is, for the same reason, the space presented to him. Not only bodies move in space, but space itself does, approaching, receding, turning, dissolving and recrystallizing as it appears through the controlled locomotion and focusing of the camera and through the cutting and editing of the various shots — not to mention such special effects as visions, transformations, disappearances, slow-motion and fast-motion shots, reversals and trick films. This opens up a world of possibilities of which the stage can never dream. Quite apart from such photographic tricks as the participation of disembodied spirits in the action of the *Topper* series, or the more effective wonders wrought by Roland Young in *The Man Who Could Work Miracles*, there is, on the purely factual level, an untold wealth of themes as inaccessible to the "legitimate" stage as a fog or a snowstorm is to the sculptor; all sorts of violent elemental phenomena and, conversely, events too microscopic to be visible under normal conditions (such as the life-saving injection with the serum flown in at the very last moment, or the fatal bite of the yellow-fever mosquito); full-scale battle scenes; all kinds of operations, not only in the surgical sense but also in the sense of any actual construction, destruction or experimentation, as in *Louis Pasteur* or *Madame Curie;* a really grand party, moving through many rooms of a mansion or a palace. Features like these, even the mere shifting of the scene from

247

one place to another by means of a car perilously negotiating heavy traffic or a motorboat steered through a nocturnal harbor, will not only always retain their primitive cinematic appeal but also remain enormously effective as a means of stirring the emotions and creating suspense. In addition, the movies have the power, entirely denied to the theater, to convey psychological experiences by directly projecting their content to the screen, substituting, as it were, the eye of the beholder for the consciousness of the character (as when the imaginings and hallucinations of the drunkard in the otherwise overrated *Lost Weekend* appear as stark realities instead of being described by mere words). But any attempt to convey thought and feelings exclusively, or even primarily, by speech leaves us with a feeling of embarrassment, boredom, or both.

What I mean by thoughts and feelings "conveyed exclusively, or even primarily, by speech" is simply this: Contrary to naïve expectation, the invention of the sound track in 1928 has been unable to change the basic fact that a moving picture, even when it has learned to talk, remains a picture that moves and does not convert itself into a piece of writing that is enacted. Its substance remains a series of visual sequences held together by an uninterrupted flow of movement in space (except, of course, for such checks and pauses as have the same compositional value as a rest in music), and not a sustained study in human character and destiny transmitted by effective, let alone "beautiful," diction. I cannot remember a more misleading statement about the movies than Mr. Eric Russell Bentley's in the spring number of the *Kenyon Review*, 1945: "The potentialities of the talking screen differ from those of the silent screen in adding the dimension of dialogue—which could be poetry." I would suggest: "The potentialities of the talking screen differ from those of the silent screen in integrating visible movement with dialogue which, therefore, had better not be poetry."

All of us, if we are old enough to remember the period prior to 1928, recall the old-time pianist who, with his eyes glued on the screen, would accompany the events with music adapted to their mood and rhythm; and we also recall the weird and spectral feeling overtaking us when this pianist left his post for a few minutes and the film was allowed to run by itself, the darkness haunted by the monotonous rattle of the machinery. Even the silent film, then, was never mute. The visible spectacle always required, and received, an audible accompaniment which, from the very beginning, distinguished the film from simple pantomime and rather classed it—*mutatis mutandis*—with the ballet. The advent of the talkie meant not so much an "addition" as a transformation: the transformation of musical sound into articulate speech and, therefore, of quasi pantomime into an entirely new species of spectacle which differs from the ballet, and agrees with the stage play, in that its acoustic component consists of intelligible words, but differs from the stage play and agrees with the ballet in that this acoustic component is not detachable from the visual. In a film, that which we hear remains, for good or worse, inextricably fused with that which we see; the sound, articulate or not, cannot express any more than is expressed, at the same time, by visible movement; and in a good film it does not even attempt to do so. To put it briefly, the play—or, as it is very properly called, the "script"—of a moving picture is subject to what might be termed the *principle of coexpressibility*.

Empirical proof of this principle is furnished by the fact that, wherever the dialogical or monological element gains temporary prominence, there appears, with the inevitability of a natural law, the "close-up." What does the close-up achieve? In showing us, in magnification, either the face of the speaker or the face of the listeners or both in alternation, the camera transforms the human physiognomy into a huge field of action where—given the qualification of the performers—every subtle movement of the features, almost imperceptible from a natural distance, becomes an expressive event in visible space and thereby completely integrates itself with the expressive content of the spoken word; whereas, on the stage, the spoken word makes a stronger rather than a weaker impression if we are not permitted to count the hairs in Romeo's mustache.

This does not mean that the scenario is a negligible factor in the making of a moving picture. It only means that its artistic intention differs in kind from that of a stage play, and much more from that of a novel or a piece of poetry. As the success of a Gothic jamb figure depends not only upon its quality as a piece of sculpture but also, or even more so, upon its integrability with the architecture of the portal, so does the success of a movie script—not unlike that of an opera libretto—depend, not only upon its quality as a piece of literature but also, or even more so, upon its integrability with the events on the screen.

As a result—another empirical proof of the coexpressibility principle—good movie scripts are unlikely to make good reading and have seldom been published in book form; whereas, conversely, good stage plays have to be severely altered, cut, and, on the other hand, enriched by interpolations to make good movie scripts. In Shaw's *Pygmalion*, for instance, the actual process of Eliza's phonetic education and, still more important, her final triumph at the grand party, are wisely omitted; we see—or, rather, hear—some samples of her gradual linguistic improvement and finally encounter her, upon her return from the reception, victorious and splendidly arrayed but deeply hurt for want of recognition and sympathy. In the film adaptation, precisely these two scenes are not only supplied but also strongly emphasized; we witness the fascinating activities in the laboratory with its array of spinning disks and mirrors, organ pipes and dancing flames, and we participate in the ambassadorial party, with many moments of impending catastrophe and a little counterintrigue thrown in for suspense. Unquestionably these two scenes, entirely absent from the play, and indeed unachievable upon the stage, were the highlights of the film; whereas the Shavian dialogue, however severely cut, turned out to fall a little flat in certain moments. And wherever, as in so many other films, a poetic emotion, a musical outburst, or a literary conceit (even, I am grieved to say, some of the wisecracks of Groucho Marx) entirely lose contact with visible movement, they strike the sensitive spectator as, literally, out of place. It is certainly terrible when a soft-boiled he-man, after the suicide of his mistress, casts a twelve-foot glance upon her photograph and says something less-than-coexpressible to the effect that he will never forget her. But when he recites, instead, a piece of poetry as sublimely more-than-coexpressible as Romeo's monologue at the bier of Juliet, it is still worse. Reinhardt's *Midsummer Night's Dream* is probably the most unfortunate major film ever produced; and Olivier's *Henry V* owes its comparative success, apart from the all but providential adaptability of this particular play, to so many *tours de force* that it will, God willing, remain an exception rather than set a pattern. It combines "judicious pruning" with the interpolation of pageantry, nonverbal comedy and melodrama;

it uses a device perhaps best designated as "oblique close-up" (Mr. Olivier's beautiful face inwardly listening to but not pronouncing the great soliloquy); and, most notably, it shifts between three levels of archaeological reality: a reconstruction of Elizabethan London, a reconstruction of the events of 1415 as laid down in Shakespeare's play, and the reconstruction of a performance of this play on Shakespeare's own stage. All this is perfectly legitimate; but, even so, the highest praise of the film will always come from those who, like the critic of the *New Yorker*, are not quite in sympathy with either the movies *au naturel* or Shakespeare *au naturel*.

As the writings of Conan Doyle potentially contain all modern mystery stories (except for the tough specimens of the Dashiell Hammett school), so do the films produced between 1900 and 1910 pre-establish the subject matter and methods of the moving picture as we know it. This period produced the incunabula of the Western and the crime film (Edwin S. Porter's amazing *Great Train Robbery* of 1903) from which developed the modern gangster, adventure, and mystery pictures (the latter, if well done, is still one of the most honest and genuine forms of film entertainment, space being doubly charged with time as the beholder asks himself not only "What is going to happen?" but also "What has happened before?"). The same period saw the emergence of the fantastically imaginative film (Méliès) which was to lead to the expressionist and surrealist experiments (*The Cabinet of Dr. Caligari, Sang d'un Poète,* etc.), on the one hand, and to the more superficial and spectacular fairy tales à la Arabian Nights, on the other. Comedy, later to triumph in Charlie Chaplin, the still insufficiently appreciated Buster Keaton, the Marx Brothers and the pre-Hollywood creations of René Clair, reached a respectable level in Max Linder and others. In historical and melodramatic films the foundations were laid for movie iconography and movie symbolism, and in the early work of D. W. Griffith we find, not only remarkable attempts at psychological analysis *(Edgar Allan Poe)* and social criticism *(A Corner in Wheat)* but also such basic technical innovations as the long shot, the flashback and the close-up. And modest trick films and cartoons paved the way to Felix the Cat, Popeye the Sailor, and Felix's prodigious offspring, Mickey Mouse.

Within their self-imposed limitations the earlier Disney films, and certain sequences in the later ones,* represent, as it were, a chemically pure distillation of cinematic possibilities. They retain the most important folkloristic elements—sadism, pornography, the humor engendered by both, and moral justice—almost without dilution and often fuse these elements into a variation on the primitive and inexhaustible David-and-Goliath motif, the triumph of the seemingly weak over the seemingly strong; and their fantastic independence of the natural laws gives them the power to integrate space with time to such perfection that the spatial and temporal experiences of sight and hearing come to be almost interconvertible. A series of soap bubbles, successively punctured, emits a series of sounds exactly corresponding in pitch and volume to the size of the bubbles; the three uvulae of Willie the Whale—small, large and medium—vibrate in consonance with tenor, bass and baritone notes; and the very concept of stationary existence is completely

---

*I make this distinction because it was, in my opinion, a fall from grace when *Snow White* introduced the human figure and when *Fantasia* attempted to picturalize The World's Great Music. The very virtue of the animated cartoon is to animate, that is to say endow lifeless things with life, or living things with a different kind of life. It effects a metamorphosis, and such a metamorphosis is wonderfully present in Disney's animals, plants, thunderclouds and railroad trains. Whereas his dwarfs, glamourized princesses, hillbillies, baseball players, rouged centaurs and *amigos* from South America are not transformations but caricatures at best, and fakes or vulgarities at worst. Concerning music, however, it should be borne in mind that its cinematic use is no less predicated upon the principle of coexpressibility than is the cinematic use of the spoken word. There is music permitting or even requiring the accompaniment of visible action (such as dances, ballet music and any kind of operatic compositions) and music of which the opposite is true; and this is, again, not a question of quality (most of us rightly prefer a waltz by Johann Strauss to a symphony by Sibelius) but one of intention. In *Fantasia* the hippopotamus ballet was wonderful, and the Pastoral Symphony and "Ave Maria" sequences were deplorable, not because the cartooning in the first case was infinitely better than in the two others (*cf.* above), and certainly not because Beethoven and Schubert are too sacred for picturalization, but simply because Ponchielli's "Dance of the Hours" is coexpressible while the Pastoral Symphony and the "Ave Maria" are not. In cases like these even the best imaginable music and the best imaginable cartoon will impair rather than enhance each other's effectiveness.

Experimental proof of all this was furnished by Disney's recent *Make Mine Music* where The World's Great Music was fortunately restricted to Prokofieff. Even among the other sequences the most successful ones were those in which the human element was either absent or reduced to a minimum; Willie the Whale, the Ballad of Johnny Fedora and Alice Blue-Bonnet, and, above all, the truly magnificent Goodman Quartet.

252

abolished. No object in creation, whether it be a house, a piano, a tree or an alarm clock, lacks the faculties of organic, in fact anthropomorphic, movement, facial expression and phonetic articulation. Incidentally, even in normal, "realistic" films the inanimate object, provided that it is dynamizable, can play the role of a leading character as do the ancient railroad engines in Buster Keaton's *General* and *Niagara Falls*. How the earlier Russian films exploited the possibility of heroizing all sorts of machinery lives in everybody's memory; and it is perhaps more than an accident that the two films which will go down in history as the great comical and the great serious masterpiece of the silent period bear the names and immortalize the personalities of two big ships: Keaton's *Navigator* (1924) and Eisenstein's *Potemkin* (1925).

The evolution from the jerky beginnings to this grand climax offers the fascinating spectacle of a new artistic medium gradually becoming conscious of its legitimate, that is, exclusive, possibilities and limitations—a spectacle not unlike the development of the mosaic, which started out with transposing illusionistic genre pictures into a more durable material and culminated in the hieratic supernaturalism of Ravenna; or the development of line engraving, which started out as a cheap and handy substitute for book illumination and culminated in the purely "graphic" style of Dürer.

Just so the silent movies developed a definite style of their own, adapted to the specific conditions of the medium. A hitherto unknown language was forced upon a public not yet capable of reading it, and the more proficient the public became the more refinement could develop in the language. For a Saxon peasant of around 800 it was not easy to understand the meaning of a picture showing a man as he pours water over the head of another man, and even later many people found it difficult to grasp the significance of two ladies standing behind the throne of an emperor. For the public of around 1910 it was no less difficult to understand the meaning of the speechless action in a moving picture, and the producers employed means of clarification similar to those we find in medieval art. One of these were printed titles or letters, striking equivalents of the medieval *tituli* and scrolls (at a still earlier date there even used to be explainers who would say, *viva voce*, "Now he thinks his wife is dead but she isn't" or "I don't wish to offend the ladies in the audience but I doubt that any of them would have done that much for her child"). Another, less obtrusive method of explanation was the introduction of a fixed iconography which from the outset informed the spectator about the basic facts and characters, much as the two ladies behind the emperor, when carrying a sword and a cross respectively, were uniquely determined as Fortitude and Faith. There arose, identifiable by standardized appearance, behavior and attributes, the well-remembered types of the Vamp and the Straight Girl (perhaps the most convincing modern equivalents of the medieval personifications of the Vices and Virtues), the Family Man, and the Villain, the latter marked by a black mustache and walking stick. Nocturnal scenes were printed on blue or green film. A checkered tablecloth meant, once for all, a "poor but honest" milieu; a happy marriage, soon to be endangered by the shadows from the past, was symbolized by the young wife's pouring the breakfast coffee for her husband; the first kiss was invariably announced by the lady's gently playing with her partner's necktie and was invariably accompanied by her kicking out with her left foot. The conduct of the characters was predetermined accordingly. The poor but honest laborer who, after leaving his little house with the checkered tablecloth, came upon an abandoned baby could not but take it to his home and bring it up as best he could; the Family Man could not but yield, however temporarily, to the temptations of the Vamp. As a result these early melodramas had a highly gratifying and soothing quality in that events took shape, without the complications of individual psychology, according to a pure Aristotelian logic so badly missed in real life.

Devices like these became gradually less necessary as the public grew accustomed to interpret the action by itself and were virtually abolished by the invention of the talking film. But even now there survive—quite legitimately, I think—the remnants of a "fixed attitude and attribute" principle and, more basic, a primitive or folkloristic concept of plot construction. Even today we take it for granted that the diphtheria of a baby tends to occur when the parents are out and, having occurred, solves all their matrimonial problems. Even today we demand of a decent mystery film that the butler, though he may be anything from an agent of the British Secret Service to the real father of the daughter of the house, must not turn out to be the murderer. Even today we love to see Pasteur, Zola or Ehrlich win out against stupidity and wickedness, with their

254

respective wives trusting and trusting all the time. Even today we much prefer a happy finale to a gloomy one and insist, at the very least, on the observance of the Aristotelian rule that the story have a beginning, a middle and an ending—a rule the abrogation of which has done so much to estrange the general public from the more elevated spheres of modern writing. Primitive symbolism, too, survives in such amusing details as the last sequence of *Casablanca* where the delightfully crooked and right-minded *préfet de police* casts an empty bottle of Vichy water into the wastepaper basket; and in such telling symbols of the supernatural as Sir Cedric Hardwicke's Death in the guise of a "gentleman in a dustcoat trying" *(On Borrowed Time)* or Claude Rains's Hermes Psychopompos in the striped trousers of an airline manager *(Here Comes Mister Jordan).*

The most conspicuous advances were made in directing, lighting, camera work, cutting and acting proper. But while in most of these fields the evolution proceeded continuously—though, of course, not without detours, breakdowns and archaic relapses—the development of acting suffered a sudden interruption by the invention of the talking film; so that the style of acting in the silents can already be evaluated in retrospect, as a lost art not unlike the painting technique of Jan van Eyck or, to take up our previous simile, the burin technique of Dürer. It was soon realized that acting in a silent film neither meant a pantomimic exaggeration of stage acting (as was generally and erroneously assumed by professional stage actors who more and more frequently condescended to perform in the movies), nor could dispense with stylization altogether; a man photographed while walking down a gangway in ordinary, everyday-life fashion looked like anything but a man walking down a gangway when the result appeared on the screen. If the picture was to look both natural and meaningful the acting had to be done in a manner equally different from the style of the stage and the reality of ordinary life; speech had to be made dispensable by establishing an organic relation between the acting and the technical procedure of cinephotography—much as in Dürer's prints color had been made dispensable by establishing an organic relation between the design and the technical procedure of line engraving. This was precisely what the great actors of the silent period accomplished, and it is a significant fact that the best of them did not come from the stage, whose crystallized tradition prevented Duse's only film, *Cenere*, from being more than a priceless record of Duse. They came instead from the circus or the variety, as was the case of Chaplin, Keaton and Will Rogers; from nothing in particular, as was the case of Theda Bara, of her greater European parallel, the Danish actress Asta Nielsen, and of Garbo; or from everything under the sun, as was the case of Douglas Fairbanks. The style of these "old masters" was indeed comparable to the style of line engraving in that it was, and had to be, exaggerated in comparison with stage acting (just as the sharply incised and vigorously curved *tailles* of the burin are exaggerated in comparison with pencil strokes or brushwork), but richer, subtler and infinitely more precise. The advent of the talkies, reducing if not abolishing this difference between screen acting and stage acting, thus confronted the actors and actresses of the silent screen with a serious problem. Buster Keaton yielded to temptation and fell. Chaplin first tried to stand his ground and to remain an exquisite archaist but finally gave in, with only moderate success *(The Great Dictator)*. Only the glorious Harpo has thus far successfully refused to utter a single articulate sound; and only Greta Garbo succeeded, in a measure, in transforming her style in principle. But even in her case one cannot help feeling that her first talking picture, *Anna Christie*, where she could ensconce herself, most of the time, in mute or monosyllabic sullenness, was better than her later performances; and in the second, talking version of *Anna Karenina*, the weakest moment is certainly when she delivers a big Ibsenian speech to her husband, and the strongest when she silently moves along the platform of the railroad station while her despair takes shape in the consonance of her movement (and expression) with the movement of the nocturnal space around her, filled with the real noises of the trains and the imaginary sound of the "little men with the iron hammers" that drives her, relentlessly and almost without her realizing it, under the wheels.

Small wonder that there is sometimes felt a kind of nostalgia for the silent period and that devices have been worked out to combine the virtues of sound and speech with those of silent acting, such as the "oblique close-up" already mentioned in connection with *Henry V;* the dance behind glass doors in *Sous les Toits de Paris;* or, in the

Histoire d'un Tricheur, Sacha Guitry's recital of the events of his youth while the events themselves are "silently" enacted on the screen. However, this nostalgic feeling is no argument against the talkies as such. Their evolution has shown that, in art, every gain entails a certain loss on the other side of the ledger; but that the gain remains a gain, provided that the basic nature of the medium is realized and respected. One can imagine that, when the cavemen of Altamira began to paint their buffaloes in natural colors instead of merely incising the contours, the more conservative cavemen foretold the end of paleolithic art. But paleolithic art went on, and so will the movies. New technical inventions always tend to dwarf the values already attained, especially in a medium that owes its very existence to technical experimentation. The earliest talkies were infinitely inferior to the then mature silents, and most of the present technicolor films are still inferior to the now mature talkies in black and white. But even if Aldous Huxley's nightmare should come true and the experiences of taste, smell and touch should be added to those of sight and hearing, even then we may say with the Apostle, as we have said when first confronted with the sound track and the technicolor film, "We are troubled on every side, yet not distressed; we are perplexed, but not in despair."

From the law of time-charged space and space-bound time, there follows the fact that the screenplay, in contrast to the theater play, *has no aesthetic existence independent of its performance, and that its characters have no aesthetic existence outside the actors.*

The playwright writes in the fond hope that his work will be an imperishable jewel in the treasure house of civilization and will be presented in hundreds of performances that are but transient variations on a "work" that is constant. The script-writer, on the other hand, writes for one producer, one director and one cast. Their work achieves the same degree of permanence as does his; and should the same or a similar scenario ever be filmed by a different director and a different cast there will result an altogether different "play."

Othello or Nora are definite, substantial figures created by the playwright. They can be played well or badly, and they can be "interpreted" in one way or another; but they most definitely exist, no matter who plays them or even whether they are played at all. The character in a film, however, lives and dies with the actor.

It is not the entity "Othello" interpreted by Robeson or the entity "Nora" interpreted by Duse; it is the entity "Greta Garbo" incarnate in a figure called Anna Christie or the entity "Robert Montgomery" incarnate in a murderer who, for all we know or care to know, may forever remain anonymous but will never cease to haunt our memories. Even when the names of the characters happen to be Henry VIII or Anna Karenina, the king who ruled England from 1509 to 1547 and the woman created by Tolstoy, they do not exist outside the being of Garbo and Laughton. They are but empty and incorporeal outlines like the shadows in Homer's Hades, assuming the character of reality only when filled with the lifeblood of an actor. Conversely, if a movie role is badly played there remains literally nothing of it, no matter how interesting the character's psychology or how elaborate the words.

What applies to the actor applies, *mutatis mutandis*, to most of the other artists, or artisans, who contribute to the making of a film: the director, the sound man, the enormously important cameraman, even the make-up man. A stage production is rehearsed until everything is ready, and then it is repeatedly performed in three consecutive hours. At each performance everybody has to be on hand and does his work; and afterward he goes home and to bed. The work of the stage actor may thus be likened to that of a musician, and that of the stage director to that of a conductor. Like these, they have a certain repertoire which they have studied and present in a number of complete but transitory performances, be it *Hamlet* today and *Ghosts* tomorrow, or *Life with Father per saecula saeculorum*. The activities of the film actor and the film director, however, are comparable, respectively, to those of the plastic artist and the architect, rather than to those of the musician and the conductor. Stage work is continuous but transitory; film work is discontinuous but permanent. Individual sequences are done piecemeal and out of order according to the most efficient use of sets and personnel. Each bit is done over and over again until it stands; and when the whole has been cut and composed everyone is through with it forever. Needless to say that this very procedure cannot but emphasize the curious consubstantiality that exists between the person of the movie actor and his role. Coming into existence piece by piece, regardless of the natural sequence of events, the "character" can grow into a unified whole only if the actor manages to be, not merely to play, Henry VIII or Anna Karenina throughout the entire wearisome period of shooting. I have it on the best of authorities that Laughton was really difficult to live with in the particular six or eight weeks during which he was doing—or rather being—Captain Bligh.

It might be said that a film, called into being by a co-operative effort in which all contributions have the same degree of permanence, is the nearest modern equivalent of a medieval cathedral; the role of the producer corresponding, more or less, to that of the bishop or archbishop; that of the director to that of the architect in chief; that of the scenario writers to that of the scholastic advisers establishing the iconographical program; and that of the actors, cameramen, cutters, sound men, make-up men and the divers technicians to that of those whose work provided the physical entity of the finished product, from the sculptors, glass painters, bronze casters, carpenters and skilled masons down to the quarry men and woodsmen. And if you speak to any one of these collaborators he will tell you, with perfect *bona fides*, that his is really the most important job—which is quite true to the extent that it is indispensable.

This comparison may seem sacrilegious, not only because there are, proportionally, fewer good films than there are good cathedrals, but also because the movies are commercial. However, if commercial art be defined as all art not primarily produced in order to gratify the creative urge of its maker but primarily intended to meet the requirements of a patron or a buying public, it must be said that noncommercial art is the exception rather than the rule, and a fairly recent and not always felicitous exception at that. While it is true that commercial art is always in danger of ending up as a prostitute, it is equally true that noncommercial art is always in danger of ending up as an old maid. Noncommercial art has given us Seurat's "Grande Jatte" and Shakespeare's sonnets, but also much that is esoteric to the point of incommunicability. Conversely, commercial art has given us much that is vulgar or snobbish (two aspects of the same thing) to the point of loathsomeness, but also Dürer's prints and Shakespeare's plays. For, we must not forget that Dürer's prints were partly made on commission and partly intended to be sold in the open market; and that Shakespeare's plays—in contrast to the earlier masques and intermezzi which were produced at court by aristocratic amateurs and could afford to be so incomprehensible that even those who described them in printed monographs occasionally failed to grasp their intended significance—were meant to appeal, and did appeal, not only to the select few but also to everyone who was prepared to pay a shilling for admission.

It is this requirement of communicability that makes commercial art more vital than noncommercial, and therefore potentially much more effective for better or for worse. The commercial producer can both educate and pervert the general public, and can allow the general public—or rather his idea of the general public—both to educate and to pervert himself. As is demonstrated by a number of excellent films that proved to be great box office successes, the public does not refuse to accept good products if it gets them. That it does not get them very often is caused not so much by commercialism as such as by too little discernment and, paradoxical though it may seem, too much timidity in its application. Hollywood believes that it must produce "what the public wants" while the public would take whatever Hollywood produces. If Hollywood were to decide for itself what it wants it would get away with it—even if it should decide to "depart from evil and do good." For, to revert to whence we started, in modern life the movies are what most other forms of art have ceased to be, not an adornment but a necessity.

That this should be so is understandable, not only from a sociological but also from an art-historical point of view. The processes of all the earlier representational arts conform, in a higher or lesser degree, to an idealistic conception of the world. These arts operate from top to bottom, so to speak, and not from bottom to top; they start with an idea to be projected into shapeless matter and not with the objects that constitute the physical world. The painter works on a blank wall or canvas which he organizes into a likeness of things and persons according to his idea (however much this idea may have been nourished by reality); he does not work with the things and persons themselves even if he works "from the model." The same is true of the sculptor with his shapeless mass of clay or his untooled block of stone or wood; of the writer with his sheet of paper or his dictaphone; and even of the stage designer with his empty and sorely limited section of space. It is the movies, and only

Laurence Olivier in *Henry V* (1944). The film "uses a device perhaps best designated as 'oblique close-up' (Mr. Olivier's beautiful face inwardly listening to but not pronouncing the great soliloquy)." (PANOFSKY, page 251).

Caligari (Werner Krauss) feeding Cesare (Conrad Veidt) in *The Cabinet of Doctor Caligari* (1919). "The expressionist settings . . . could exert but little influence upon the general course of events. To prestylize reality prior to tackling it amounts to dodging the problem" (PANOFSKY, page 263). "Films of this type are not only intended as autonomous wholes but frequently ignore physical reality or exploit it for purposes alien to photographic veracity" (KRACAUER, page 21).

the movies, that do justice to that materialistic interpretation of the universe which, whether we like it or not, pervades contemporary civilization. Excepting the very special case of the animated cartoon, the movies organize material things and persons, not a neutral medium, into a composition that receives its style, and may even become fantastic or pretervoluntarily symbolic, not so much by an interpretation in the artist's mind as by the actual manipulation of physical objects and recording machinery. The medium of the movies is physical reality as such: the physical reality of eighteenth-century Versailles—no matter whether it be the original or a Hollywood facsimile indistinguishable therefrom for all aesthetic intents and purposes—or of a suburban home in Westchester; the physical reality of the Rue de Lappe in Paris or of the Gobi Desert, of Paul Ehrlich's apartment in Frankfurt or of the streets of New York in the rain; the physical reality of engines and animals, of Edward G. Robinson and Jimmy Cagney. All these objects and persons must be organized into a work of art. They can be arranged in all sorts of ways ("arrangement" comprising, of course, such things as make-up, lighting and camera work); but there is no running away from them. From this point of view it becomes evident that an attempt at subjecting the world to artistic prestylization, as in the expressionist settings of *The Cabinet of Dr. Caligari* (1919), could be no more than an exciting experiment that could exert but little influence upon the general course of events. To prestylize reality prior to tackling it amounts to dodging the problem. The problem is to manipulate and shoot unstylized reality in such a way that the result has style. This is a proposition no less legitimate and no less difficult than any proposition in the older arts.

1934; revised 1947

263

SIEGFRIED KRACAUER
FROM THEORY OF FILM

THE ESTABLISHMENT OF
PHYSICAL EXISTENCE

In establishing physical existence, films differ from photographs in two respects: they represent reality as it evolves in time; and they do so with the aid of cinematic techniques and devices.

Consequently, the recording and revealing duties of the two kindred media coincide only in part. And what do they imply for film in particular? The hunting ground of the motion picture camera is in principle unlimited; it is the external world expanding in all directions. Yet there are certain subjects within that world which may be termed "cinematic" because they seem to exert a peculiar attraction on the medium. It is as if the medium were predestined (and eager) to exhibit them. The following pages are devoted to a close examination of these cinematic subjects. Several lie, so to speak, on the surface; they will be dealt with under the title "recording functions." Others would hardly come to our attention or be perceptible were it not for the film camera and/or the intervention of cinematic techniques; they will be discussed in the subsequent section "revealing functions." To be sure, any camera revelation involves recording, but recording on its part need not be revealing.

RECORDING FUNCTIONS

Movement

At least two groups of quite common external phenomena are naturals for the screen. As might be expected, one is made up of all kinds of movements, these being cinematic because only the motion picture camera is able to record them. Among them are three types which can be considered cinematic subjects par excellence.

The Chase

"The chase," says Hitchcock, "seems to me the final expression of the motion picture medium." This complex of interrelated movements is motion at its extreme, one might almost say, motion as such—and of course it is immensely serviceable for establishing a continuity of suspenseful physical action. Hence the fascination the chase has held since the beginning of the century. The primitive French comedies availed themselves of it to frame their space-devouring adventures. Gendarmes pursued a dog who eventually turned the tables on them (*Course des sergeants de ville*); pumpkins gliding from a cart were chased by the grocer, his donkey, and passers-by through sewers and over roofs (*La Course des potirons*, *1907*; English title: *The Pumpkin Race*). For any Keystone comedy to forgo the chase would have been an unpardonable crime. It was the climax of the whole, its orgiastic finale—a pandemonium, with onrushing trains telescoping into automobiles and narrow escapes down ropes that dangled above a lion's den.

But perhaps nothing reveals the cinematic significance of this reveling in speed more drastically than D. W. Griffith's determination to transfer, at the end of all his great films, the action from the ideological plane to that of his famous "last-minute rescue," which was a chase pure and simple. Or should one say, a race? In any case, the rescuers rush ahead to overwhelm the villains or free their victims at the very last moment, while simultaneously the inner emotion which the dramatic conflict has aroused yields to a state of acute physiological suspense called forth by exuberant physical motion and its immediate implications. Nor is a genuine Western imaginable without a pursuit or a race on horseback. As Flaherty put it, Westerns are popular "because people never get tired of seeing a horse gallop across the plains." Its gallop seems still to gain momentum by contrast with the immense tranquility of the far-away horizon.

Dancing

The second type of specifically cinematic movement is dancing. This does not apply, of course, to the stage ballet which evolves in a space-time outside actuality proper. Interestingly enough, all attempts at "canning" it adequately have so far failed. Screen reproductions of theatrical dancing either indulge in a completeness which is boring or offer a selection of attractive details which confuse in that they dismember rather than preserve the original. Dancing attains to cinematic eminence only if it is part and parcel of physical reality. René Clair's early sound films have judiciously been called ballets. True, they are, but the performers are real-life Parisians who just cannot help executing dance movements when going about their love adventures and minor quarrels. With infinite subtlety Clair guides them along the divide between the real and unreal. Sometimes it appears as though these delivery boys, taxi drivers, girls, clerks, shopkeepers, and nondescript figures are marionettes banding together and parting from each other according to designs as delicate as lacework; and then again they are made to look and behave like ordinary people in Paris streets and bistros. And the latter impression prevails. For, even granted that they are drawn into an imaginary universe, this universe itself reflects throughout our real world in stylizing it. What dancing there is, seems to occur on the spur of the moment; it is the vicissitudes of life from which these ballets issue.

Fred Astaire too prefers apparent impromptu performances to stage choreography; he is quite aware that this type of performance is appropriate to the medium. "Each dance," says he, "ought to spring somehow out of character or situation, otherwise it is simply a vaudeville act." This does not mean that he would dispense with theatrical production numbers. But no sooner does he perform in vaudeville fashion than he breaks out of the prison of prearranged stage patterns and, with a genius for improvisation, dances over tables and gravel paths into the everyday world. It is a one-way route which invariably leads from the footlights to the heart of camera-reality. Astaire's consummate dancing is meant to belong among the real-life events with which he toys in his musicals; and it is so organized that it imperceptibly emerges from, and disappears, in the flow of these happenings. . . .

Nascent Motion

The third type of motion which offers special interest cinematically is not just another group of interrelated movements but movement as contrasted with motionlessness. In focusing upon this contrast, films strikingly demonstrate that objective movement—any movement, for that matter—is one of their choice subjects. Alexander Dovzhenko in both *Arsenal* and *Earth* frequently stops the action to resume it after a short lull. The first phase of this procedure—characters or parts of them abruptly ceasing to move—produces a shock effect, as if all of a sudden we found ourselves in a vacuum. The immediate consequence is that we acutely realize the significance of movement as an integral element of the external world as well as film.

But this is only part of the story. Even though the moving images on the screen come to a standstill, the thrust of their movement is too powerful to be discontinued simultaneously. Accordingly, when the people in *Arsenal* or *Earth* are shown in the form of stills, the suspended movement nevertheless perpetuates itself by changing from outer motion into inner motion. Dovzhenko has known how to make this metamorphosis benefit his penetrations of reality. The immobile lovers in *Earth* become transparent; the deep happiness which is moving them turns inside out. And the spectator on his part grasps their inward agitation because the cessation of external motion moves him all the more intensely to commune with them. Yet despite these rewarding experiences he cannot help feeling a certain relief when eventually the characters take on life again—an event which marks the second and final phase of the procedure. It is a return to the world of film, whose inherent motion alone renders possible such excursions into the whirlpool of the motionless. . . .

Inanimate Objects

Since the inanimate is featured in many paintings, one might question the legitimacy of characterizing it as a cinematic subject. Yet it is a painter—Fernand Léger—who judiciously insists that only film is equipped to sensitize us, by way of big close-ups, to the possibilities that lie dormant in a hat, a chair, a hand, and a foot. Similarly Cohen-Séat: "And I? says the leaf which is falling.—And we? say the orange peel, the gust of wind. . . . Film, whether intentionally or not, is their mouthpiece." Nor should it be forgotten that the camera's ability to single out and record the orange peel or the hand marks a decisive difference between screen and stage, so close to each other in some respects. Stage imagery inevitably centers on the actor, whereas film is free to dwell on parts of his appearance

267

and detail the objects about him. In using its freedom to bring the inanimate to the fore and make it a carrier of action, film only protests its peculiar requirement to explore all of physical existence, human or nonhuman. Within this context it is of interest that in the early 'twenties, when the French cinema was swamped with theatrical adaptations and stage-minded dramas, Louis Delluc tried to put the medium on its own feet by stressing the tremendous importance of objects. If they are assigned the role due to them, he argued, the actor too "is no more than a detail, a fragment of the matter of the world."

Actually, the urge to raise hats and chairs to the status of full-fledged actors has never completely atrophied. From the malicious escalators, the unruly Murphy beds, and the mad automobiles in silent comedy to the cruiser Potemkin, the oil derrick in *Louisiana Story* and the dilapidated kitchen in *Umberto D.*, a long procession of unforgettable objects has passed across the screen—objects which stand out as protagonists and all but overshadow the rest of the cast. Or remember the powerful presence of environmental influences in *The Grapes of Wrath*, the part played by nocturnal Coney Island in *Little Fugitive*, the interaction between the marshland and the guerilla fighters in the last episode of *Paisan*. Of course, the reverse holds true also: films in which the inanimate merely serves as a background to self-contained dialogue and the closed circuit of human relationships are essentially uncinematic.

REVEALING FUNCTIONS

"I ask that a film *discover* something for me" declares Luis Buñuel, who is himself a fiery pathfinder of the screen. And what are films likely to discover? The evidence available suggests that they assume three kinds of revealing functions. They tend to reveal things normally unseen; phenomena overwhelming consciousness; and certain aspects of the outer world which may be called "special modes of reality."

Things Normally Unseen

The many material phenomena which elude observation under normal circumstances can be divided into three groups. The first includes objects too small to be readily noticed or even perceived by the naked eye and objects so big that they will not be fully taken in either.

The Small and the Big

The small. The small is conveyed in the form of close-ups. D. W. Griffith was among the first to realize that they are indispensable for cinematic narration. He initiated their use, as we now know it, in *After Many Years* (1908), an adaptation of Tennyson's *Enoch Arden*. There his memorable first close-up appeared within contexts which Lewis Jacobs describes as follows: "Going further than he had ventured before, in a scene showing Annie Lee brooding and waiting for her husband's return, Griffith daringly used a large close-up of her face. . . . He had another surprise, even more radical, to offer. Immediately following the close-up of Annie, he inserted a picture of the object of her thoughts—her husband cast away on a desert isle."

On the surface, this succession of shots seems simply designed to lure the spectator into the dimension of her intimate preoccupations. He first watches Annie from a distance and then approaches her so closely that he sees only her face; if he moves on in the same direction, as the film invites him to do, it is logical that he should penetrate Annie's appearance and land inside her mind. Granting the validity of this interpretation, the close-up of her face is not an end in itself; rather, along with the subsequent shots, it serves to suggest what is going on behind that face—Annie's longing for reunion with her husband. A knowingly chosen detail of her physique thus would help establish the whole of her being in a dramatic interest.

The same obviously holds true of another famous Griffith close-up: Mae Marsh's clasped hands in the trial episode of *Intolerance*. It almost looks as if her huge hands with the convulsively moving fingers were inserted for the sole purpose of illustrating eloquently her anguish at the most crucial moment of the trial; as if, generally speaking, the function of any such detail exhausted itself in intensifying our participation in the total situation. This is how Eisenstein conceives of the close-up. Its main function, says he, is "not so much to *show* or to *present* as to *signify*, to *give meaning*, to *designate*." To designate what? Evidently something of importance to the narrative. And montage-minded as he is, he immediately adds that the significance of the close-up for the plot accrues to it less from its own content than from the manner in which it is juxtaposed with the surrounding shots. According to him, the close-up is primarily a montage unit.

But is this really its only function? Consider again the combination of shots with the close-up of Annie's face: the place assigned to the latter in the sequence intimates that Griffith wanted us also to absorb the face for its own sake instead of just passing through and beyond it; the face appears before the desires and emotions to which it refers have been completely defined, thus tempting us to get lost in its puzzling indeterminacy. Annie's face is also an end in itself. And so is the image of Mae Marsh's hands. No doubt it is to impress upon us her inner condition, but besides making us experience what we would in a measure have experienced anyway because of our familiarity with the characters involved, this close-up contributes something momentous and unique—it reveals how her hands behave under the impact of utter despair.

Eisenstein criticizes the close-ups in Griffith films precisely for their relative independence of the contexts in which they occur. He calls them isolated units which tend "to show or to present"; and he insists that to the extent that they indulge in isolation they fail to yield the meanings which the interweaving processes of montage may elicit from them. Had Eisenstein been less possessed with the magic powers of montage he would certainly have acknowledged the cinematic superiority of the Griffith close-up. To Griffith such huge images of small material phenomena are not only integral components of the narrative but disclosures of new aspects of physical reality. In representing them the way he does, he seems to have been guided by the conviction that the cinema is all the more cinematic if it acquaints us with the physical origins, ramifications, and connotations of all the emotional and intellectual events which comprise the plot; that it cannot adequately account for these inner developments unless it leads us through the thicket of material life from which they emerge and in which they are embedded. . . .

The big. Among the large objects, such as vast plains or panoramas of any kind, one deserves special attention: the masses. No doubt imperial Rome already teemed with them. But masses of people in the modern sense entered the historical scene only in the wake of the industrial revolution. Then they became a social force of first magnitude. Warring nations resorted to levies on an un-heard-of scale and identifiable groups yielded to the anonymous multitude which filled the big cities in the form of amorphous crowds. Walter Benjamin observes that in the period marked by the rise of photography the daily sight of moving crowds was still a spectacle to which eyes and nerves had to get adjusted. The testimony of sensitive contemporaries would seem to corroborate this sagacious observation: The Paris crowds omnipresent in Baude-laire's *Les Fleurs du mal* function as stimuli which call forth irritating kaleidoscopic sensations; the jostling and shoving passers-by who, in Poe's *Man of the Crowd*, throng gas-lit London provoke a succession of electric shocks.

At the time of its emergence the mass, this giant animal, was a new and upsetting experience. As might be expected, the traditional arts proved unable to encompass and render it. Where they failed, photography easily succeeded; it was technically equipped to portray crowds as the accidental agglomerations they are. Yet only film, the fulfillment of photography in a sense, was equal to the task of capturing them in motion. In this case the instrument of reproduction came into being almost simultaneously with one of its main subjects. Hence the attraction which masses exerted on still and motion picture cameras from the outset. It is certainly more than sheer coincidence that the very first Lumière films featured a crowd of workers and the confusion of arrival and departure at a railway station. Early Italian films elaborated upon the theme; and D. W. Griffith, inspired by them, showed how masses can be represented cinematically. The Russians absorbed his lesson, applying it in ways of their own. . . .

The Transient

The second group of things normally unseen comprises the transient. Here belong, first, fleeting impressions—"the shadow of a cloud passing across the plain, a leaf which yields to the wind." Evanescent, like dream elements, such impressions may haunt the moviegoer long after the story they are called upon to implement has sunk into oblivion. The manes of the galloping horses— flying threads or streamers rather than manes—in the chariot race episode of Fred Niblo's *Ben Hur* are as unforgettable as the fiery traces of the projectiles that tear the night in *Desert Victory*. The motion picture camera seems to be partial to the least permanent components of our environment. It may be anticipated that the street in the broadest sense of the word is a place where impressions of this kind are bound to occur. "The cinema," says Aragon, delighting in its snapshot-like predilection for the ephemeral, "has taught us more about man in a few years than centuries of painting have taught: fugitive expressions, attitudes scarcely credible yet real, charm and hideousness"

Second, there are movements of so transitory a nature that they would be imperceptible were it not for two cinematic techniques: accelerated-motion, which condenses extremely slow and, hence, unobservable developments, such as the growth of plants, and slow-motion, which expands movements too fast to be registered. Like the big close-up, these correlated techniques lead straight into "reality of another dimension." Pictures of stalks piercing the soil in the process of growing open up imaginary areas, and racing legs shown in slow-motion do not just slow down but change in appearance and perform bizarre evolutions—patterns remote from reality as we know it. Slow-motion shots parallel the regular close-ups; they are, so to speak, temporal close-ups achieving in time what the close-up proper is achieving in space. That, unlike the latter, they are used rather infrequently, may be traced to the fact that the enlargement of spatial phenomena, as effected by the close-up, seems more "natural" to us than the expansion of a given time interval. (On the other hand, it appears that film makers draw more readily on slow-motion than on the reverse technique— perhaps simply because it does not require so lengthy preparations.)

As contrived-reality pictures, the deviant images gained by both techniques, especially slow-motion, may well figure in nonrealistic experimental films. Yet they live up to the cinematic approach only if they are made to fulfill a revealing function within contexts focusing on physical existence. The late Jean Epstein, who felt so immensely attracted by "reality of another dimension," considered this their true destination. Referring to waves in slow-motion and clouds in accelerated-motion, he declared that for all their "startling physics and strange mechanics" they "are but a portrait—seen in a certain perspective—of the world in which we live."

Blind Spots of the Mind

The third and last group of things normally unseen consists of phenomena which figure among the blind spots of the mind; habit and prejudice prevent us from noticing them. The role which cultural standards and traditions may play in these processes of elimination is drastically illustrated by a report on the reactions of African natives to a film made on the spot. After the screening the spectators, all of them still unacquainted with the medium, talked volubly about a chicken they allegedly had seen picking food in the mud. The film maker himself, entirely unaware of its presence, attended several performances without being able to detect it. Had it been dreamed up by the natives? Only by scanning his film foot by foot did he eventually succeed in tracing the chicken: it appeared for a fleeting moment somewhere in a corner of a picture and then vanished forever.

The following types of objects are cinematic because they stubbornly escape our attention in everyday life.

Unconventional complexes. Film may bare real-life complexes which the conventional figure-ground patterns usually conceal from view. Imagine a man in a room: accustomed as we are to visualize the human figure as a whole, it would take us an enormous effort to perceive instead of the whole man a pictorial unit consisting, say, of his right shoulder and arm, fragments of furniture and a section of the wall. But this is exactly what photography and, more powerfully, film may make us see. The motion picture camera has a way of disintegrating familiar objects and bringing to the fore—often just in moving about—previously invisible interrelationships between parts of them. These newly arising complexes lurk behind the things known and cut across their easily identifiable contexts. *Jazz Dance*, for instance, abounds with shots of ensembles built from human torsos, clothes, scattered legs, and what not—shapes which are almost anonymous. In rendering physical existence, film tends to reveal configurations of semi-abstract phenomena. Sometimes these textures take on an ornamental character. In the Nazi propaganda film *Triumph of the Will* moving banners fuse into a very beautiful pattern at the moment when they begin to fill the screen.

The refuse. Many objects remain unnoticed simply because it

273

never occurs to us to look their way. Most people turn their backs on garbage cans, the dirt underfoot, the waste they leave behind. Films have no such inhibitions; on the contrary, what we ordinarily prefer to ignore proves attractive to them precisely because of this common neglect. Ruttmann's *Berlin* includes a wealth of sewer grates, gutters, and streets littered with rubbish; and Cavalcanti in his *Rien que les heures* is hardly less garbage-minded. To be sure, shots in this vein may be required by the action, but intrigues inspired by a sense of the medium are often so devised that they offer the camera ample opportunity to satisfy its inborn curiosity and function as a rag-picker; think of the old silent comedies— e.g. Chaplin's *A Dog's Life*— or pictures which involve crime, war, or misery. Since sights of refuse are particularly impressive after spectacles extolling the joy of living, film makers have repeatedly capitalized on the contrast between glamorous festivities and their dreary aftermath. You see a banquet on the screen and then, when everybody has gone, you are made to linger for a moment and stare at the crumpled tablecloth, the half-emptied glasses, and the unappetizing dishes. The classical American gangster films indulged in this effect. *Scarface* opens on a restaurant at dawn, with the remnants of the nocturnal orgy strewn over floors and tables; and after the gangsters' ball in Sternberg's *Underworld* Bancroft totters through a maze of confetti and streamers left over from the feast.

The familiar. Nor do we perceive the familiar. It is not as if we shrank from it, as we do in the case of refuse; we just take it for granted without giving it a thought. Intimate faces, streets we walk day by day, the house we live in—all these things are part of us like our skin, and because we know them by heart we do not know them with the eye. Once integrated into our existence, they cease to be objects of perception, goals to be attained. In fact, we would be immobilized if we focused on them. This is confirmed by a common experience. A man entering his room will immediately feel disturbed if during his absence something has been changed in it. But in order to find out about the cause of his uneasiness he must discontinue his routine occupations; only in deliberately scrutinizing, and thus estranging, the room will he be able to discover what it actually is that has been changed. Proust's narrator is acutely aware of this very estrangement when he suddenly sees his grandmother not as he always believed her to be but as she really is or at

274

least as she would appear to a stranger—a snapshot likeness severed from his dreams and memories.

Films make us undergo similar experiences a thousand times. They alienate our environment in exposing it. One ever-recurrent film scene runs as follows: Two or more people are conversing with each other. In the middle of their talk the camera, as if entirely indifferent to it, slowly pans through the room, inviting us to watch the faces of the listeners and various furniture pieces in a detached spirit. Whatever this may mean within the given context, it invariably dissolves a well-known total situation and thereby confronts the spectator with isolated phenomena which he previously neglected or overlooked as matter-of-course components of that situation. As the camera pans, curtains become eloquent and eyes tell a story of their own. The way leads toward the unfamiliar in the familiar. How often do we not come across shots of street corners, buildings, and landscapes with which we were acquainted all our life; we naturally recognize them and yet it is as if they were virgin impressions emerging from the abyss of nearness. The opening sequence of Vigo's *Zéro de conduite* shows two boys traveling back to school by train. Is it just an ordinary night trip? Vigo manages to transform a familiar railway compartment into a magic wigwam in which the two, drunk from their boasts and pranks, are floating through the air.

This transformation is partly achieved with the aid of a device, both photographic and cinematic, which deserves some attention—the use of uncommon camera angles. Vigo occasionally represents the railway compartment slantwise and from below so that the whole room seems to drift along in the haze from the cigars which the high-strung schoolboys are smoking, while little toy balloons hover to and fro before their pale faces. Proust knew about the alienating effect of this device. After having mentioned that certain photographs of scenery and towns are called "admirable," he continues: "If we press for a definition of what their admirers mean by that epithet, we shall find that it is generally applied to some unusual picture of a familar object, a picture different from those that we are accustomed to see, unusual and yet true to nature, and for that reason doubly impressive because it startles us, makes us emerge from our habits, and at the same time brings us back to ourselves by recalling to us an earlier impression." And to concretize this definition, he refers to the picture of a cathedral which does not render it as it is normally seen—namely, in the middle of the town—but is taken from a point of view from which the building "will appear thirty times the height of the houses." . . .

Phenomena Overwhelming Consciousness

Elemental catastrophes, the atrocities of war, acts of violence and terror, sexual debauchery, and death are events which tend to overwhelm consciousness. In any case, they call forth excitements and agonies bound to thwart detached observation. No one witnessing such an event, let alone playing an active part in it, should therefore be expected accurately to account for what he has seen. Since these manifestations of crude nature, human or otherwise, fall into the area of physical reality, they range all the more among the cinematic subjects. Only the camera is able to represent them without distortion.

Actually the medium has always shown a predilection for events of this type. There is practically no newsreel that would not indulge in the ravages of an inundation, a hurricane, an airplane crash, or whatever catastrophe happens to be at hand. The same applies to feature films. One of the first film strips ever made was *The Execution of Mary Queen of Scots* (1895); the executioner cuts off her head and then holds it in his uplifted hand so that no spectator can possibly avoid looking at the frightful exhibit. Pornographic motifs also emerged at a very early date. The path of the cinema is beset with films reveling in disasters and nightmarish incidents. Suffice it to pick out, at random, the war horrors in Dovzhenko's *Arsenal* and Pabst's *Westfront 1918;* the terrible execution sequence at the end of *Thunder over Mexico,* a film based on Eisenstein's Mexican material; the earthquake in *San Francisco;* the torture episode in Rossellini's *Open City;* the depiction of a Polish Nazi concentration camp in *The Last Stop;* the scene with the young hoodlums wantonly mistreating a blind man in Buñuel's *Los Olvidados.*

Because of its sustained concern with all that is dreadful and off limits, the medium has frequently been accused of a penchant for cheap sensationalism. What lends support to this verdict is the indisputable fact that films have a habit of dwelling on the sensational much longer than any moral purpose would seem to justify;

276

it often is as if that purpose served merely as a pretext for rendering a savage murder or the like.

In defense of the medium one might argue that it would not be the mass medium it is if it failed to provide stunning sensations; and that, in offering them, it only follows a venerable tradition. Since time immemorial, people have craved spectacles permitting them vicariously to experience the fury of conflagrations, the excesses of cruelty and suffering, and unspeakable lusts—spectacles which shock the shuddering and delighted onlooker into unseeing participation.

Yet this argument misses the point. The point is, rather, that the cinema does not simply imitate and continue the ancient gladiator fights or the *Grand Guignol* but adds something new and momentous: it insists on rendering visible what is commonly drowned in inner agitation. Of course, such revelations conform all the more to the cinematic approach if they bear on actual catastrophes and horrors. In deliberately detailing feats of sadism in their films, Rossellini and Buñuel force the spectator to take in these appalling sights and at the same time impress them on him as real-life events recorded by the imperturbable camera. Similarly, besides trying to put across their propaganda messages, the Russian films of the 'twenties convey to us the paroxysmal upheavals of real masses which, because of their emotional *and* spatial enormity, depend doubly upon cinematic treatment to be perceptible.

The cinema, then, aims at transforming the agitated witness into a conscious observer. Nothing could be more legitimate than its lack of inhibitions in picturing spectacles which upset the mind. Thus it keeps us from shutting our eyes to the "blind drive of things."

Special Modes of Reality

Finally films may expose physical reality as it appears to individuals in extreme states of mind generated by such events as we have mentioned, mental disturbances, or any other external or internal causes. Supposing such a state of mind is provoked by an act of violence, then the camera often aspires to render the images which an emotionally upset witness or participant will form of it. These images also belong among the cinematic subjects. They are distorted from the viewpoint of a detached observer; and they differ from each other according to the varying states of mind in which they originate.

In his *Ten Days That Shook the World*, for instance, Eisenstein composes a physical universe reflecting exultation. This episode runs as follows: At the beginning of the October Revolution, worker delegates succeed in bringing a contingent of Cossacks over to their side; the Cossacks put their half-drawn swords with the ornamented pommels back into their sheaths, and then the two groups boisterously fraternize in a state of euphoria. The ensuing dance scene is represented in the form of an accelerated montage sequence which pictures the world as experienced by the overjoyed. In their great joy, dancers and onlookers who constantly mingle cannot help perceiving incoherent pieces of their immediate environment in motion. It is a whirling agglomerate of fragments that surrounds them. And Eisenstein captures this jumble to perfection by having follow each other—in a succession which becomes ever faster with the growing ecstasy—shots of Cossack boots executing the *krakoviak*, worker legs dancing through a puddle, clapping hands, and faces inordinately broadened by laughter.

In the world of a panic-stricken individual laughter yields to grimacing and dazzling confusion to fearful rigidity. At any rate, this is how Ernö Metzner conceived of that world in his *Ueberfall*. Its "hero" is a wretched little fellow who gets a lucky break thanks to a coin he furtively picks up in the street and then stakes in a crap game. As he walks away with his wallet stuffed, a thug follows him at a steadily diminishing distance. The man is scared. No sooner does he take to his heels than all the objects about him make common cause with his pursuer. The dark railway underpass turns into a sinister trap; frozen threats, the dilapidated slum houses close ranks and stare at him. (It is noteworthy that these effects are largely due to accomplished photography.) Temporarily saved by a streetwalker, who puts him up in her room, the man knows that the thug continues to lie in wait for him down in the street. The curtain moves, and he feels that the room itself harbors dangers. There is no escape wherever he looks. He looks into the mirror: what shines out of it are distorted reflections of his mask-like features.

1960

278

RUDOLF ARNHEIM
FROM FILM AS ART

FILM AND REALITY

Film resembles painting, music, literature, and the dance in this respect—it is a medium that may, but need not, be used to produce artistic results. Colored picture post cards, for instance, are not art and are not intended to be. Neither are a military march, a true confessions story, or a strip tease. And the movies are not necessarily film art.

There are still many educated people who stoutly deny the possibility that film might be art. They say, in effect: "Film cannot be art, for it does nothing but reproduce reality mechanically." Those who defend this point of view are reasoning from the analogy of painting. In painting, the way from reality to the picture lies via the artist's eye and nervous system, his hand and, finally, the brush that puts strokes on canvas. The process is not mechanical as that of photography, in which the light rays reflected from the object are collected by a system of lenses and are then directed onto a sensitive plate where they produce chemical changes. Does this state of affairs justify our denying photography and film a place in the temple of the Muses?

It is worth while to refute thoroughly and systematically the charge that photography and film are only mechanical reproductions and that they therefore have no connection with art—for this is an excellent method of getting to understand the nature of film art.

With this end in view, the basic elements of the film medium will be examined separately and compared with the corresponding characteristics of what we perceive "in reality." It will be seen how fundamentally different the two kinds of image are; and that it is just these differences that provide film with its artistic resources. We shall thus come at the same time to understand the working principles of film art.

THE PROJECTION OF SOLIDS
UPON A PLANE SURFACE

Let us consider the visual reality of some definite object such as a cube. If this cube is standing on a table in front of me, its position determines whether I can realize its shape properly. If I see, for example, merely the four sides of a square, I have no means of knowing that a cube is before me, I see only a square surface. The human eye, and equally the photographic lens, acts from a particular position and from there can take in only such portions of the field of vision as are not hidden by things in front. As the cube is now placed, five of its faces are screened by the sixth, and therefore this last only is visible. But since this face might equally well conceal something quite different—since it might be the base of a pyramid or one side of a sheet of paper, for instance—our view of the cube has not been selected characteristically.

We have, therefore, already established one important principle: If I wish to photograph a cube, it is not enough for me to bring the object within range of my camera. It is rather a question of my position relative to the object, or of where I place it. The aspect chosen above gives very little information as to the shape of the cube. One, however, that reveals three surfaces of the cube and their relation to one another, shows enough to make it fairly unmistakable what the object is supposed to be. Since our field of vision is full of solid objects, but our eye (like the camera) sees this field from only one station point at any given moment, and since the eye can perceive the rays of light that are reflected from the object only by projecting them onto a plane surface—the retina—the reproduction of even a perfectly simple object is not a mechanical process but can be set about well or badly.

The second aspect gives a much truer picture of the cube than the first. The reason for this is that the second shows more than the first—three faces instead of only one. As a rule, however, truth does not depend on quantity. If it were merely a matter of finding which aspect shows the greatest amount of surface, the best point of view could be arrived at by purely mechanical calculation. There is no formula to help one choose the most characteristic aspect: it is a question of feeling. Whether a particular person is "more himself" in profile than full face, whether the palm or the outside of the hand is more expressive, whether a particular mountain is better taken from the north or the west cannot be ascertained mathematically—they are matters of delicate sensibility.

Thus, as a preliminary, people who contemptuously refer to the camera as an automatic recording machine must be made to realize that even in the simplest photographic reproduction of a perfectly simple object, a feeling for its nature is required which is quite beyond any mechanical operation. We shall see later, by the way, that in artistic photography and film, those aspects that best show the characteristics of a particular object are not by any means always chosen; others are often selected deliberately for the sake of achieving specific effects.

REDUCTION OF DEPTH

How do our eyes succeed in giving us three-dimensional impressions even though the flat retinae can receive only two-dimensional images? Depth perception relies mainly on the distance between the two eyes, which makes for two slightly different images. The fusion of these two pictures into one image gives the three-dimensional impression. As is well known, the same principle is used in the stereoscope, for which two photographs are taken at once, about the same distance apart as the human eyes. This process cannot be used for film without recourse to awkward devices, such as colored spectacles, when more than one person is to watch the projection. For a single spectator it would be easy to make a stereoscopic film. It would only mean taking two simultaneous shots of the same incident a couple of inches apart and then showing one of them to each eye. For display to a larger number of spectators, however, the problem of stereoscopic film has not yet been solved satisfactorily—and hence the sense of depth in film pictures is extraordinarily small. The movement of people or objects from front to back makes a certain depth evident—but it is only necessary to glance into a stereoscope, which makes everything stand out most realistically, to recognize how flat the film picture is. This is another example of the fundamental difference between visual reality and film.

The effect of film is neither absolutely two-dimensional nor absolutely three-dimensional, but something between. Film pictures are at once plane and solid. In Ruttmann's film *Berlin* there is a scene of two subway trains passing each other in opposite directions. The shot is taken looking down from above onto the two trains. Anyone watching this scene realizes, first of all, that one train is coming toward him and the other going away from him (three-dimensional image). He will then also see that one is moving from the lower margin of the screen toward the upper and the other from the upper toward the lower (plane image). This second impression results from the projection of the three-dimensional movement onto the screen surface, which, of course, gives different directions of motion.

The obliteration of the three-dimensional impression has as a second result a stronger accentuation of perspective overlapping. In real life or in a stereoscope, overlapping is accepted as due merely to the accidental arrangement of objects, but very marked cuts result from superimpositions in a plane image. If a man is holding up a newspaper so that one corner comes across his face, this corner seems almost to have been cut out of his face, so sharp are the edges. Moreover, when the three-dimensional impression is lost, other phenomena, known to psychologists as the constancies of size and shape, disappear. Physically, the image thrown onto the retina of the eye by any object in the field of vision diminishes in proportion to the square of the distance. If an object a yard distant is moved away another yard, the area of the image on the retina is diminished to one-quarter of that of the first image. Every photographic plate reacts similarly. Hence in a photograph of someone sitting with his feet stretched out far in front of him the subject comes out with enormous feet and much too small a head. Curiously enough, however, we do not in real life get impressions to accord with the images on the retina. If a man is standing three feet away and another equally tall six feet away, the area of the image of the second does not appear to be only a quarter of that of the first. Nor if a man stretches out his hand toward one does it look disproportionately large. One sees the two men as equal in size and the hand as normal. This phenomenon is known as the constancy of size. It is impossible for most people—excepting those accustomed to drawing and painting, that is, artificially trained—to see according to the image on the retina. This fact, incidentally, is one of the reasons the average person has trouble copying things "correctly." Now an essential for the functioning of the constancy of size is a clear three-dimensional impression; it works excellently in a stereoscope with an ordinary photograph, but hardly at all in a film picture. Thus, in a film picture, if one man is twice as far from the camera as another, the one in front looks very considerably the taller and broader.

It is the same with the constancy of shape. The retinal image of a table top is like the photograph of it; the front edge, being nearer to the spectator, appears much wider than the back; the rectangular surface becomes a trapezoid in the image. As far as the average person is concerned, however, this again does not hold good in practice: he *sees* the surface as rectangular and draws it that way too. Thus the perspective changes taking place in any object that extends in depth are not observed but are compensated unconsciously. That is what is meant by the constancy of form. In a film picture it is hardly operative at all—a table top, especially if it is near the camera, looks very wide in front and very narrow at the back.

These phenomena, as a matter of fact, are due not only to the reduction of three-dimensionality but also to the unreality of the film picture altogether—an unreality due just as much to the absence of color, the delimitation of the screen, and so forth. The result of all this is that sizes and shapes do not appear on the screen in their true proportions but distorted in perspective. . . .

THE MAKING OF A FILM

It has been shown above that the images we receive of the physical world differ from those on the movie screen. This was done in order to refute the assertion that film is nothing but the feeble mechanical reproduction of real life. The analysis has furnished us with the data from which we can hope to derive now the principles of film art.

By its very nature, of course, the motion picture tends to satisfy the desire for faithful reports about curious, characteristic, exciting things going on in this world of ours. The first sensation provided by film in its early music-hall days was to depict everyday things in a lifelike fashion on the screen. People were greatly thrilled by the sight of a locomotive approaching at top speed or the emperor in person riding down *Unter den Linden*. In those days, the pleasure given by film derived almost entirely from the subject matter. A film art developed only gradually when the movie makers began consciously or unconsciously to cultivate the peculiar possibilities of cinematographic technique and to apply them toward the creation of artistic productions. To what extent the use of these means of expression affects the large audiences remains a moot question. Certainly box-office success depends even now much more on what is shown than on whether it is shown artistically.

The film producer himself is influenced by the strong resemblance of his photographic material to reality. As distinguished from the tools of the sculptor and the painter, which by themselves produce nothing resembling nature, the camera starts to turn and a likeness of the real world results mechanically. There is serious danger that the film maker will rest content with such shapeless reproduction. In order that the film artist may create a work of art it is important that he consciously stress the peculiarities of his medium. This, however, should be done in such a manner that the character of the objects represented should not thereby be destroyed but rather strengthened, concentrated, and interpreted. . . .

People who did not understand anything of the art of film used to cite silence as one of its most serious drawbacks. These people regard the introduction of sound as an improvement or completion of silent film. This opinion is just as senseless as if the invention of three-dimensional oil painting were hailed as an advance on the hitherto known principles of painting.

From its very silence film received the impetus as well as the power to achieve excellent artistic effects. Charles Chaplin wrote somewhere that in all his films there was not a single scene where he "spoke," that is, moved his lips. Hundreds of the most various situations in human relationships are shown in his films, and yet he did not feel the need to make use of such an ordinary faculty as speech. And nobody has missed it. The spoken word in Chaplin's films is as a rule replaced by pantomime. He does not *say* that he is pleased that some pretty girls are coming to see him, but performs the silent dance, in which two bread rolls stuck on forks act as dancing feet on the table *(The Gold Rush)*. He does not argue, he fights. He avows his love by smiling, swaying his shoulders, and moving his hat. When he is in the pulpit he does not preach in words, but acts the story of David and Goliath *(The Pilgrim)*. When he is sorry for a poor girl, he stuffs money into her handbag. He shows renunciation by simply walking away (finale of *The Circus*). The incredible visual concreteness of every one of his scenes makes for a great part of Chaplin's art; and this should not be forgotten when it is said—as is often done and of course not without foundation—that his films are not really "filmic" (because his camera serves mainly as a recording machine).

Mention has already been made of the scene from Sternberg's *The Docks of New York* in which a revolver shot is illustrated by the rising of a flock of birds. Such an effect is not just a contrivance on the part of a director to deal with the evil of silence by using an indirect visual method of explaining to the audience that there has been a bang. On the contrary, a positive artistic effect results from the paraphrase. Such indirect representation of an event in a material that is strange to it, or giving not the action itself but only its consequences, is a favorite method in all art. To take an example at random: when Francesca da Rimini tells how she fell in love with the man with whom she was in the habit of reading, and only says "We read no more that day," Dante thereby indicates indirectly, simply by giving the consequences, that on this day they kissed each other. And this indirectness is shockingly impressive.

In the same way, the rising of the birds is particularly effective, and probably more so than if the actual sound of the pistol shot were heard. And then another factor comes in: the spectator does not simply *infer* that a shot has been fired, but he actually *sees* something of the quality of the noise—the suddenness, the abruptness of the rising birds, give visually the exact quality that the shot possesses acoustically. In Jacques Feyder's *Les Nouveaux Messieurs* a political meeting becomes very uproarious, and in order to calm the rising emotions Suzanne puts a coin into a mechanical piano. Immediately the hall is lit up by hundreds of electric bulbs, and now the music chimes in with the agitative speech. The music is not heard: it is a silent film. But Feyder shows the audience excitedly listening to the speaker; and suddenly the faces soften and relax; all the heads begin quite gently to sway in time to the music. The rhythm grows more pronounced until at last the spirit of the dance has seized them all; and they swing their bodies gaily from side to side as if to an unheard word of command. The speaker has to give way to the music. Much more clearly than if the music were actually heard, this shows the power that suddenly unites all these discontented people, puts them into the same merry mood; and indicates as well the character of the music itself, its sway and rhythm. What is particularly noteworthy in such a scene is not merely how easily and cleverly the director makes visible something that is not visual, but by so doing, actually strengthens its effect. If the music were really heard, the spectator might simply realize that music was sounding, but by this indirect method, the particular point, the important part of this music—its rhythm, its power to unite and "move" men—is conspicuously brought out. Only these special attributes of the music are given, and appear as the music itself. Similarly the fact that a pistol shot is sudden, explosive, startling, becomes doubly impressive by transposition into the visible, because only these particular attributes and not the shot itself are given. Thus silent film derives definite artistic potentialities from its silence. What it wishes particularly to emphasize in an audible occurrence is transposed into something visual; and thus instead of giving the occurrence "itself," it gives only some of its telling characteristics, and thereby shapes and interprets it.

Owing to its insubstantiality silent film does not in any way give the effect of being dumb pantomime. Its silence is not noticed, unless the action happens to culminate in something acoustic for which nothing can be substituted, and which is therefore felt as missing—or unless one is accustomed to sound film. Because of sound film, in the future it will be possible only with great difficulty to show speech in a silent way. Yet this is a most effective artistic device. For if a man is heard speaking, his gestures and facial expression only appear as an accompaniment to underline the sense of what is said. But if one does not hear what is said, the meaning becomes indirectly clear and is artistically interpreted by muscles of the face, of the limbs, of the body. The emotional quality of the conversation is made obvious with a clarity and definiteness which are hardly possible in the medium of actual speech. Moreover, the divergence between reality and dumb show gives the actor and his director plenty of leeway for artistic invention. (The creative power of the artist can only come into play where reality and the medium of representation do not coincide.)

Dialogue in silent film is not simply the visible part of a real spoken dialogue. If a real dialogue is shown without the sound, the spectator will often fail to grasp what it is all about; he will find the facial expression and the gestures unintelligible. In silent film, the lips are no longer word-forming physical organs but a means of visual expression—the distortion of an excited mouth or the fast chatter of lips are not mere by-products of talking; they are communications in their own right. Silent laughter is often more effective than if the sound is actually heard. The gaping of the open mouth gives a vivid, highly artistic interpretation of the phenomenon "laughter." If, however, the sound is also heard, the opening of the mouth appears obvious and its value as a means of expression is almost entirely lost. This opportunity of the silent film was once used by the Russians in a most unusual and effective manner. A shot of a soldier who had gone mad in the course of a battle and was laughing hideously with his mouth wide open was joined with a shot of the body of a soldier who had died of poison gas, and whose mouth was fixed in death in a ghastly, rigid grin.

The absence of the spoken word concentrates the spectator's attention more closely on the visible aspect of behavior, and thus the whole event draws particular interest to itself. Hence it is that very ordinary shots are often so impressive in silent films—such as a documentary shot of an itinerant hawker crying his wares with grandiose gestures. If his words could be heard the effect of the gestures would not be half as great, and the whole episode might attract very little attention. If, however, the words are omitted, the spectator surrenders entirely to the expressive power of the gestures. Thus by merely robbing the real event of something—the sound—the appeal of such an episode is greatly heightened. . . .

1933

BÉLA BALÁZS
FROM THEORY OF THE FILM

THE CLOSE-UP

THE FACE OF THINGS

The first new world discovered by the film camera in the days of
the silent film was the world of very small things visible only from
very short distances, the hidden life of little things. By this the
camera showed us not only hitherto unknown objects and events:
the adventures of beetles in a wilderness of blades of grass, the
tragedies of day-old chicks in a corner of the poultry-run, the erotic
battles of flowers and the poetry of miniature landscapes. It
brought us not only new themes. By means of the close-up the
camera in the days of the silent film revealed also the hidden main-
springs of a life which we had thought we already knew so well.
Blurred outlines are mostly the result of our insensitive short-
sightedness and superficiality. We skim over the teeming substance
of life. The camera has uncovered that cell-life of the vital issues in
which all great events are ultimately conceived; for the greatest
landslide is only the aggregate of the movements of single particles.
A multitude of close-ups can show us the very instant in which
the general is transformed into the particular. The close-up has not
only widened our vision of life, it has also deepened it. In the days
of the silent film it not only revealed new things, but showed us the
meaning of the old.

VISUAL LIFE

The close-up can show us a quality in a gesture of the hand we
never noticed before when we saw that hand stroke or strike something, a quality which is often more expressive than any play of the

features. The close-up shows your shadow on the wall with which you have lived all your life and which you scarcely knew; it shows the speechless face and fate of the dumb objects that live with you in your room and whose fate is bound up with your own. Before this you looked at your life as a concert-goer ignorant of music listens to an orchestra playing a symphony. All he hears is the leading melody, all the rest is blurred into a general murmur. Only those can really understand and enjoy the music who can hear the contrapuntal architecture of each part in the score. This is how we see life: only its leading melody meets the eye. But a good film with its close-ups reveals the most hidden parts in our polyphonous life, and teaches us to see the intricate visual details of life as one reads an orchestral score.

LYRICAL CHARM OF THE CLOSE-UP

The close-up may sometimes give the impression of a mere naturalist preoccupation with detail. But good close-ups radiate a tender human attitude in the contemplation of hidden things, a delicate solicitude, a gentle bending over the intimacies of life-in-the-miniature, a warm sensibility. Good close-ups are lyrical; it is the heart, not the eye, that has perceived them.

Close-ups are often dramatic revelations of what is really happening under the surface of appearances. You may see a medium shot of someone sitting and conducting a conversation with icy calm. The close-up will show trembling fingers nervously fumbling a small object—sign of an internal storm. Among pictures of a comfortable house breathing a sunny security, we suddenly see the evil grin of a vicious head on the carved mantelpiece or the menacing grimace of a door opening into darkness. Like the *leitmotif* of impending fate in an opera, the shadow of some impending disaster falls across the cheerful scene.

Close-ups are the pictures expressing the poetic sensibility of the director. They show the faces of things and those expressions on them which are significant because they are reflected expressions of our own subconscious feeling. Herein lies the art of the true cameraman.

In a very old American film I saw this dramatic scene: the bride at the altar suddenly runs away from the bridegroom whom she detests, who is rich and who has been forced on her. As she rushes away she must pass through a large room full of wedding presents. Beautiful things, good things, useful things, things radiating plenty and security smile at her and lean towards her with expressive faces. And there are the presents given by the bridegroom: faces of things radiating touching attention, consideration, tenderness, love— and they all seem to be looking at the fleeing bride, because she looks at them; all seem to stretch out hands towards her, because she feels they do so. There are ever more of them—they crowd the room and block her path—her flight slows down more and more, then she stops and finally turns back. . . .

Having discovered the soul of things in the close-up, the silent film undeniably overrated their importance and sometimes succumbed to the temptation of showing "the hidden little life" as an end in itself, divorced from human destinies; it strayed away from the dramatic plot and presented the "poetry of things" instead of human beings. But what Lessing said in his *Laokoon* about Homer—that he never depicted anything but human actions and always described objects only inasmuch as they took part in the action—should to this day serve as a model for all epic and dramatic art as long as it centres around the presentation of man.

THE FACE OF MAN

Every art always deals with human beings, it is a human manifestation and presents human beings. To paraphrase Marx: "The root of all art is man." When the film close-up strips the veil of our imperceptiveness and insensitivity from the hidden little things and shows us the face of objects, it still shows us man, for what makes objects expressive are the human expressions projected on to them. The objects only reflect our own selves, and this is what distinguished art from scientific knowledge (although even the latter is to a great extent subjectively determined). When we see the face of things, we do what the ancients did in creating *gods* in man's image and breathing a human soul into them. The close-ups of the film are the creative instruments of this mighty visual anthropomorphism.

What was more important, however, than the discovery of the

physiognomy of things, was the discovery of the human face. Facial
expression is the most subjective manifestation of man, more subjective even than speech, for vocabulary and grammar are subject
to more or less universally valid rules and conventions, while the
play of features, as has already been said, is a manifestation not
governed by objective canons, even though it is largely a matter of
imitation. This most subjective and individual of human manifestations is rendered objective in the close-up.

A NEW DIMENSION

If the close-up lifts some object or some part of an object out of
its surroundings, we nevertheless perceive it as existing in space;
we do not for an instant forget that the hand, say, which is shown
by the close-up, belongs to some human being. It is precisely this
connection which lends meaning to its every movement. But when
Griffith's genius and daring first projected gigantic "severed heads"
on to the cinema screen, he not only brought the human face closer
to us in space, he also transposed it from space into another dimension. We do not mean, of course, the cinema screen and the patches
of light and shadow moving across it, which being visible things,
can be conceived only in space; we mean the expression on the face
as revealed by the close-up. We have said that the isolated hand
would lose its meaning, its expression, if we did not know and
imagine its connection with some human being. The facial expression on a face is complete and comprehensible in itself and therefore
we need not think of it as existing in space and time. Even if we had
just seen the same face in the middle of a crowd and the close-up
merely separated it from the others, we would still feel that we have
suddenly been left alone with this one face to the exclusion of the
rest of the world. Even if we have just seen the owner of the face in
a long shot, when we look into the eyes in a close-up, we no longer
think of that wide space, because the expression and significance of
the face has no relation to space and no connection with it. Facing
an isolated face takes us out of space, our consciousness of space is
cut out and we find ourselves in another dimension: that of physiognomy. The fact that the features of the face can be seen side by
side, i.e. in space—that the eyes are at the top, the ears at the sides
and the mouth lower down—loses all reference to space when we

see, not a figure of flesh and bone, but an expression, or in other words when we see emotions, moods, intentions and thoughts, things which although our eyes can see them, are not in space. For feelings, emotions, moods, intentions, thoughts are not themselves things pertaining to space, even if they are rendered visible by means which are.

MELODY AND PHYSIOGNOMY

We will be helped in understanding this peculiar dimension by Henri Bergson's analysis of time and duration. A melody, said Bergson, is composed of single notes which follow each other in sequence, i.e. in time. Nevertheless a melody has no dimension in time, because the first note is made an element of the melody only because it refers to the next note and because it stands in a definite relation to all other notes down to the last. Hence the last note, which may not be played for some time, is yet already present in the first note as a melody-creating element. And the last note completes the melody only because we hear the first note along with it. The notes sound one after the other in a time-sequence, hence they have a real duration, but the coherent line of melody has no dimension in time; the relation of the notes to each other is not a phenomenon occurring in time. The melody is not born gradually in the course of time but is already in existence as a complete entity as soon as the first note is played. How else would we know that a melody is begun? The single notes have duration in time, but their relation to each other, which gives meaning to the individual sounds, is outside time. A logical deduction also has its sequence, but premise and conclusion do not follow one another in time. The process of thinking as a psychological process may have duration; but the logical forms, like melodies, do not belong to the dimension of time.

Now facial expression, physiognomy, has a relation to space similar to the relation of melody to time. The single features, of course, appear in space; but the significance of their relation to one another is not a phenomenon pertaining to space, no more than are the emotions, thoughts and ideas which are manifested in the facial expressions we see. They are picture-like and yet they seem outside space; such is the psychological effect of facial expression.

SILENT SOLILOQUY

The modern stage no longer uses the spoken soliloquy, although without it the characters are silenced just when they are the most sincere, the least hampered by convention: when they are alone. The public of today will not tolerate the spoken soliloquy, allegedly because it is "unnatural." Now the film has brought us the silent soliloquy, in which a face can speak with the subtlest shades of meaning without appearing unnatural and arousing the distaste of the spectators. In this silent monologue the solitary human soul can find a tongue more candid and uninhibited than in any spoken soliloquy, for it speaks instinctively, subconsciously. The language of the face cannot be suppressed or controlled. However disciplined and practisedly hypocritical a face may be, in the enlarging close-up we see even that it is concealing something, that it is looking a lie. For such things have their own specific expressions superposed on the feigned one. It is much easier to lie in words than with the face and the film has proved it beyond doubt.

In the film the mute soliloquy of the face speaks even when the hero is not alone, and herein lies a new great opportunity for depicting man. The poetic significance of the soliloquy is that it is a manifestation of mental, not physical, loneliness. Nevertheless, on the stage a character can speak a monologue only when there is no one else there, even though a character might feel a thousand times more lonely if alone among a large crowd. The monologue of loneliness may raise its voice within him a hundred times even while he is audibly talking to someone. Hence the most deep-felt human soliloquies could not find expression on the stage. Only the film can offer the possibility of such expression, for the close-up can lift a character out of the heart of the greatest crowd and show how solitary it is in reality and what it feels in this crowded solitude.

The film, especially the sound film, can separate the words of a character talking to others from the mute play of features by means of which, in the middle of such a conversation, we are made to overhear a mute soliloquy and realize the difference between this soliloquy and the audible conversation. What a flesh-and-blood actor can show on the real stage is at most that his words are insincere and it is a mere convention that the partner in such a conversa-

293

tion is blind to what every spectator can see. But in the isolated close-up of the film we can see to the bottom of a soul by means of such tiny movements of facial muscles which even the most observant partner would never perceive.

A novelist can, of course, write a dialogue so as to weave into it what the speakers think to themselves while they are talking. But by so doing he splits up the sometimes comic, sometimes tragic, but always awe-inspiring, unity between spoken word and hidden thought with which this contradiction is rendered manifest in the human face and which the film was the first to show us in all its dazzling variety.

"POLYPHONIC" PLAY OF FEATURES

The film first made possible what, for lack of a better description, I call the "polyphonic" play of features. By it I mean the appearance on the same face of contradictory expressions. In a sort of physiognomic chord a variety of feelings, passions and thoughts are synthesized in the play of the features as an adequate expression of the multiplicity of the human soul.

Asta Nielsen once played a woman hired to seduce a rich young man. The man who hired her is watching the results from behind a curtain. Knowing that she is under observation, Asta Nielsen feigns love. She does it convincingly: the whole gamut of appropriate emotion is displayed in her face. Nevertheless we are aware that it is only play-acting, that it is a sham, a mask. But in the course of the scene Asta Nielsen really falls in love with the young man. Her facial expression shows little change; she had been "registering" love all the time and done it well. How else could she now show that this time she was really in love? Her expression changes only by a scarcely perceptible and yet immediately obvious nuance— and what a few minutes before was a sham is now the sincere expression of a deep emotion. Then Asta Nielsen suddenly remembers that she is under observation. The man behind the curtain must not be allowed to read her face and learn that she is now no longer feigning, but really feeling love. So Asta now pretends to be pretending. Her face shows a new, by this time threefold, change. First she feigns love, then she genuinely shows love, and as she is not permitted to be in love in good earnest, her face again registers a sham, a pretence of love. But now it is this pretence that is a lie. Now she is lying that she is lying. And we can see all this clearly in her face, over which she has drawn two different masks. At such times an invisible face appears in front of the real one, just as spoken words can by association of ideas conjure up things unspoken and unseen, perceived only by those to whom they are addressed.

In the early days of the silent film Griffith showed a scene of this character. The hero of the film is a Chinese merchant. Lillian Gish, playing a beggar-girl who is being pursued by enemies, collapses at his door. The Chinese merchant finds her, carries her into his house and looks after the sick girl. The girl slowly recovers, but her face remains stone-like in its sorrow. "Can't you smile?" the Chinese asks the frightened child who is only just beginning to trust him. "I'll try," says Lillian Gish, picks up a mirror and goes through the motions of a smile, aiding her face muscles with her fingers. The result is a painful, even horrible mask which the girl now turns towards the Chinese merchant. But his kindly friendly eyes bring a real smile to her face. The face itself does not change; but a warm emotion lights it up from inside and an intangible nuance turns the grimace into a real expression.

In the days of the silent film such a close-up provided an entire scene. A good idea of the director and a fine performance on the part of the actor gave as a result an interesting, moving, new experience for the audience.

MICROPHYSIOGNOMY

In the silent film facial expression, isolated from its surroundings, seemed to penetrate to a strange new dimension of the soul. It revealed to us a new world—the world of microphysiognomy which could not otherwise be seen with the naked eye or in everyday life. In the sound film the part played by this 'microphysiognomy' has greatly diminished because it is now apparently possible to express in words much of what facial expression apparently showed. But it is never the same—many profound emotional experiences can never be expressed in words at all.

Not even the greatest writer, the most consummate artist of the pen, could tell in words what Asta Nielsen tells with her face in close-up as she sits down to her mirror and tries to make up for the last time her aged, wrinkled face, raddled with poverty, misery, disease and prostitution, when she is expecting her lover, released after ten years in jail; a lover who has retained his youth in captivity because life could not touch him there.

ASTA AT THE MIRROR

She looks into the mirror, her face pale and deadly earnest. It expresses anxiety and unspeakable horror. She is like a general who, hopelessly encircled with his whole army, bends once more, for the last time, over his maps to search for a way out and finds there is no escape. Then she begins to work feverishly, attacking that disgustingly raddled face with a trembling hand. She holds her lipstick as Michelangelo might have held his chisel on the last night of his life. It is a life-and-death struggle. The spectator watches with bated breath as this woman paints her face in front of her mirror. The mirror is cracked and dull, and from it the last convulsions of a tortured soul look out on you. She tries to save her life with a little rouge! No good! She wipes it off with a dirty rag. She tries again. And again. Then she shrugs her shoulders and wipes it all off with a movement which clearly shows that she has now wiped off her life. She throws the rag away. A close-up shows the dirty rag falling on the floor and after it has fallen, sinking down a little more. This movement of the rag is also quite easy to understand— it is the last convulsion of a death agony.

In this close-up "microphysiognomy" showed a deeply moving human tragedy with the greatest economy of expression. It was a great new form of art. The sound film offers much fewer opportunities for this kind of thing, but by no means excludes it and it would be a pity if such opportunities were to be neglected, unnecessarily making us all the poorer. . . .

MUTE DIALOGUES

In the last years of the silent film the human face had grown more and more visible, that is, more and more expressive. Not only had "microphysiognomy" developed but together with it the faculty of understanding its meaning. In the last years of the silent film we saw not only masterpieces of silent monologue but of mute dialogue as

The accusers and Joan (Falconetti) in *The Passion of Joan of Arc* (1928). In "Dreyer's film . . . we move in the spiritual dimension of facial expression alone" (BALÁZS, page 298). "It is a documentary of faces" (BAZIN, page 391).

well. We saw conversations between the facial expressions of two human beings who understood the movements of each others' faces better than each others' words and could perceive shades of meaning too subtle to be conveyed in words.

A necessary result of this was . . . that the more space and time in the film was taken up by the inner drama revealed in the "microphysiognomic" close-up, the less was left of the predetermined 8,000 feet of film for all the external happenings. The silent film could thus dive into the depths—it was given the possibility of presenting a passionate life-and-death struggle almost exclusively by close-ups of faces.

Dreyer's film *Jeanne d'Arc* provided a convincing example of this in the powerful, lengthy, moving scene of the Maid's examination. Fifty men are sitting in the same place all the time in this scene. Several hundred feet of film show nothing but big close-ups of heads, of faces. We move in the spiritual dimension of facial expression alone. We neither see nor feel the space in which the scene is in reality enacted. Here no riders gallop, no boxers exchange blows. Fierce passions, thoughts, emotions, convictions battle here, but their struggle is not in space. Nevertheless this series of duels between looks and frowns, duels in which eyes clash instead of swords, can hold the attention of an audience for ninety minutes without flagging. We can follow every attack and riposte of these duels on the faces of the combatants; the play of their features indicates every stratagem, every sudden onslaught. The silent film has here brought an attempt to present a drama of the spirit closer to realization than any stage play has ever been able to do. . . .

1945

GERALD MAST
FROM FILM/CINEMA/MOVIE

PROJECTION

An obvious assumption of the preceding chapter is that the *aesthetic event* of cinema is the projection of the finished work—analogous to the reading of the type that is a novel, the attending to the motion and conversation that are a play, the listening to the sound that is a piece of music, or the looking at the color on canvas that is a painting. The creative process of shooting and assembling film is certainly a worthy subject of study—as are the notebooks of Henry James or the Georges Seurat sketches for *A Sunday Afternoon on the Island of La Grande Jatte.* To study this process reveals both the artist's specific choices and the general way he viewed his art and his craft. But it nonetheless studies the means to the end, and that end is experiencing the work of art itself, which remains its own testament and as solid a piece of evidence as any. With the cinema art it is perhaps an even solider piece of evidence than its maker's recollections of the creative process, since the memories of moviemakers are at least as prone to error as any, since the movie business encourages self-congratulation, and since the creative process of moviemaking is such an admittedly collective one.*

---

*Movie directors are notoriously unreliable. Frank Capra claims he watched Leo McCarey direct Laurel and Hardy at the Hal Roach studio in 1924 (L & H never worked together until 1927); Mack Sennett went to his grave claiming Buster Keaton was one of his Keystone Cops (never); Groucho Marx is under the impression that there are no musical numbers in *A Night at the Opera*

This emphasis on projection necessarily excludes certain interesting kinds of questions, among them some of the classic problems of film, cinema, and movie theory. It denies the notion of "the cinematic" altogether, since it assumes that any finished piece of cinema is indisputably a piece of cinema. The precise meaning of "cinematic" is "of or pertaining to the cinema," and its essence is merely that a succession of frames moves forward through the projector. You can, of course, then discuss whether that succession of frames is interesting or boring, beautiful or ugly, good or bad. True, the primitive film strips of Edison, Lumière, and most of their pre-Griffith contemporaries might properly be called "uncinematic," simply because they had no notion at all of one of the three principles of temporal succession (imagistic succession) and a very clumsy and undeveloped notion of another (structural succession). One of today's experimental, minimal films is certainly not uncinematic in the same way, for its maker was aware of all the possible principles of succession, but deliberately tried to extend or eliminate the use of some of them.

The insistence on projection has certain theoretical advantages. First, it clearly distinguishes cinema from a live theatrical performance, on the one hand, and from television on the other. The fact that film is projected alters its tense (it must necessarily *have been* photographed and processed in the past), whereas the tense of a live theatrical performance (dance, drama, opera) is the now. The fact that film is projected also means that it will be perceived and received differently from a live performance, particularly since projections are perceived and received as a series of different kinds of successions. In a live performance, although plot might parallel structural succession, there are no equivalents to the literal and imagistic successions of cinema; the stage movement is

---

(poor Kitty Carlisle and Allan Jones; or rather, poor us—because Groucho is unfortunately wrong). One of the consistent mistakes of film historians is to quote the recollections of moviemakers as gospel; the American Film Institute has invested both time and money in the recording of some four-hundred "oral histories" of their recollections. To preserve these thoughts and voices for posterity is undeniably valuable, but gospel it isn't.

continuous, not successive. The visual power and concentration of cinema's successiveness (coupled with the kinetic power of the individual images) give the force of the spoken word a different (and lighter) "weight" in the cinema than in the drama (as noted and developed by Bazin). Television transmission is not a projection at all; nor is its literal succession identical to cinema's. These differences produce the reduced clarity, subtlety, luminosity, density, and (for the present anyway) size of the television image. This reduction also guarantees a different emotional response and reaction to our perception of the weakened kinesis of the television image.

Indeed, the emphasis on projection as the aesthetic event consistently forces our attention on how a work of cinema is received and perceived rather than on what cinema is. Arnheim gets into all kinds of trouble with this problem since he constantly explores the ways in which the cinema image differs physically from natural vision. What he never unscrambles, however, is whether the cinema makes us perceive its differences from nature or whether it fools us by erasing those physical differences so that we perceive the image as apparently quite natural. For example, Arnheim's first principle is that photography converts three-dimensional space into a two-dimensional plane. He then develops the ways that this "fact" can be exploited artistically, some of those exploitations based on the way that the focal lengths of various lenses can alter the way we perceive relative distances between objects. One of his examples is that a newspaper appears to be "cut out" of the face of the person reading it; the converse effect would be the way that a wide-angle lens can make a hand holding a gun in the foreground appear ten times larger than the assailant's face, only an arm's length away.

But do we perceive the projected image as two-dimensional at all? The very fact that we call one object in the projected image apparently close to or far away from another implies that there is some kind of mental translation of the two-dimensional image into three-dimensional terms. In the cinema, when we see large and small, we translate our perception either into close and far (based on our awareness of relative distances and the sizes of objects in life) or into not so close or far but deliberately distorted for some effect by the lens (as in that hand-face example, which we know is based on an impossible relationship of size and distance in nature). We perceive the projected image as a kind of three-dimensional system, once we have learned to translate it (which means that we must learn to watch cinema, just as we must learn any system of translation—and just as we learn to translate sizes into distances in life).

The occasional 3-D movie (or the re-release of one from the Great Flurry of '52) proves that our perception of the projected three-dimensional image is nothing like that of the natural three-dimensional one either. The whole tendency of the 3-D image is to push the action and motion at us; not simply the deliberately hurled objects that sail toward our heads, but even the horizontal movement of walking from left to right feels as if it were thrusting toward us. Even the stationary walls seem to loom out at us, in a way that I do not usually perceive walls to do in life.

The projected cinema image does not appear to be flat; light on a screen is not perceived the same way as paint on canvas. Why not? First, paint is itself a hard, physical material that refracts light. That refraction is the physical stimulus that produces the effect of the painting (since light produces our perception of color by refraction); but it also reminds us of the flatness of the canvas and the material on it (because light bounces off the paint material itself, and that bouncing is perceived as a kind of surface refraction). Those painters who became self-conscious about the flatness of paint on canvas (for example, the evolving rough-textured brush strokes of Van Gogh) simply called attention to the essential flatness of the art by trying to avoid or exploit it. And what else was the development of perspective but a response to the flatness of canvas and paint? It was not the modernist response, however, as was Van Gogh's.

But the "material" of projected images is the immaterial operation of light itself; the images of cinema are produced by light's bouncing off the beaded surfaced of a screen, a refraction that is not, however, perceived as a refractive bouncing of light off a surface, but as the images themselves. The screen seems more to absorb the images (like a sponge) than to refract and bounce them, although such a refraction is literally what we see (but not perceive). The immateriality of light itself and the perception that the screen is a kind of translucent sponge (yet another cinema illusion) militate against the flatness of the projected image, convincing us that the image has a kind of depth (which it obviously does not).

Second, paintings are still and projected images are not. The two physical forms of cinema succession work upon the eye by keeping the photographed subjects constantly in motion. Not only is this motion a further diversion from any consciousness of the screen's flatness, but it is also a way of defining distance and dimensionality. The enlarging or shrinking of an object over a period of time or the length of time required to travel between two points are two familiar ways of defining terms like "close" and "far." One of the striking effects of halting the cinema's motion—of the "freeze frame"—is the sudden reduction of the screen's apparent depth. Only by freezing the movement that is the essence of cinema's succession does one convert the photographed image into a truly two-dimensional plane.

The projection of successive images does not convert three-dimensional nature into a two-dimensional pattern, but changes three-dimensional nature into a different three-dimensional system using two-dimensional symbols. As always, there are exceptional films that attempt to make the projected image appear as flat as possible (the Zagreb animation films, any experimental films that deliberately use the static flatness of lettering and title cards, the films of Len Lye, Norman McLaren, Robert Breer, or anyone else who uses drawn figures of any kind). Walt Disney's entire career in animation can be chronicled as a progressive war against the flatness of cinema cartooning, as a struggle to make the drawn image as apparently three-dimensional as the photographed one. Like so many valuable cinema experiments, these uses or denials of two-dimensionality are ironic reversals or revelations of traits that seem inherent to cinema.

This insistence on projection also addresses whether cinema

is or is not an "automatic" art (is for Bazin, Kracauer, Cavell, and their followers; is not for Arnheim, Eisenstein, and theirs). Projection is obviously "automatic," but is the shooting of a film equally "automatic"? And these theories of film as "automatic" art are all based on the recording, not the projection, process. There is *something* about the shooting of a film that is certainly automatic—the precise moment of etching the light on the film material itself. Other than that moment of recording, however, almost nothing about the shooting of a film is automatic. The creators control the intensity and quality of the light; even outdoor sequences use key lights, floodlights, reflectors, and scrims, as well as selecting the precise type and time of day for shooting—as Antonioni did in *Red Desert* or Mizoguchi did in all his films). They control the action within the shot, the setting, the colors, the objects, the details of décor. They control the specific lens that will be used, and the filters for it (if any), and the speed and type of film itself. To reduce the question to the absurd, could you call the shooting of an animated film automatic? Yes, the film captures the light automatically when the single frame is exposed. But no, the entire world that is so captured is the project of a human imagination.

The primacy of projection also solves the nature-nurture controversy in the cinema, since that controversy is a corollary of considering the shooting process as automatic (i.e., cinema automatically records the integrity of nature) or not (i.e., cinema is the artificial project of human choices, not a mechanical recording of nature). Obviously, the projection of a reel of film has nothing to do with nature—no more than does the reading of a novel or the looking at a painting. There may be a good deal of nature (or human life, or natural experience) in the work's succession of frames, images, and events, but there may also be a good deal of this same kind of nature in the content of a novel or the subject of a painting. To emphasize projection is to reiterate that the work of cinema is necessarily as artificial as any work of any art.

To emphasize projection is also to reiterate that an essential condition of the cinema experience is viewing flickering light in an enveloping darkness. This piercing of darkness by projected light is the source of cinema's hypnotic power, paralleling the way that the professional hypnotist entrances a subject by focusing attention on a bright and rhythmically flickering source of light. This light-in-darkness also generates several paradoxes that infuse and influence our experiencing of cinema: we both sit in darkness and are bathed in light; the experience is both private and public at the same time; the projected images both speak to our personal dreams and fantasies and seem to depict the most public and familiar realities. Projection gives us both the concreteness of visual images and the abstract play of light itself.

1977

STANLEY CAVELL
FROM THE WORLD VIEWED

PHOTOGRAPH AND SCREEN

Let us notice the specific sense in which photographs are of the world, of reality as a whole. You can always ask, pointing to an object in a photograph—a building, say—what lies behind it, totally obscured by it. This only accidentally makes sense when asked of an object in a painting. You can always ask, of an area photographed, what lies adjacent to that area, beyond the frame. This generally makes no sense asked of a painting. You can ask these questions of objects in photographs because they have answers in reality. The world of a painting is not continuous with the world of its frame; at its frame, a world finds its limits. We might say: A painting *is* a world; a photograph is *of* the world. What happens in a photograph is that *it* comes to an end. A photograph is cropped, not necessarily by a paper cutter or by masking but by the camera itself. The camera crops it by predetermining the amount of view it will accept; cutting, masking, enlarging, predetermine the amount after the fact. (Something like this phenomenon shows up in recent painting. In this respect, these paintings have found, at the extremest negation of the photographic, media that achieve the condition of photographs.) The camera, being finite, crops a portion from an indefinitely larger field; continuous portions of that field could be included in the photograph in fact taken; in principle, it could all be taken. Hence objects in photographs that run past the edge do not feel cut; they are aimed at, shot, stopped live. When a photograph is cropped, the rest of the world is cut *out*. The implied presence of the rest of the world, and its explicit rejection, are as essential in the experience of a photograph as what it explicitly presents. A camera is an opening in a box: that is the best emblem of the fact that a camera holding on an object is holding the rest of the world away. The camera has been praised for extending the senses; it may, as the world goes, deserve more praise for confining them, leaving room for thought.

The world of a moving picture is screened. The screen is not a support, not like a canvas; there is nothing to support, that way. It holds a projection, as light as light. A screen is a barrier. What does the silver screen screen? It screens me from the world it holds—that is, makes me invisible. And it screens that world from me—that is, screens its existence from me. That the projected world does not exist (now) is its only difference from reality. (There is no feature, or set of features, in which it differs. Existence is not a predicate.) Because it is the field of a photograph, the screen has no frame; that is to say, no border. Its limits are not so much the edges of a given shape as they are the limitations, or capacity, of a container. The screen *is* a frame; the frame is the whole field of the screen—as a frame of film is the whole field of a photograph, like the frame of a loom or a house. In this sense, the screen-frame is a mold, or form.

The fact that in a moving picture successive film frames are fit flush into the fixed screen frame results in a phenomenological frame that is indefinitely extendible and contractible, limited in the smallness of the object it can grasp only by the state of its technology, and in largeness only by the span of the world. Drawing the camera back, and panning it, are two ways of extending the frame; a close-up is of a part of the body, or of one object or small set of objects, supported by and reverberating the whole frame of nature. The altering frame is the image of perfect attention. Early in its history the cinema discovered the possibility of *calling* attention to persons and parts of persons and objects; but it is equally a possibility of the medium not to call attention to them but, rather, to let the world happen, to let its parts draw attention to themselves according to their natural weight. This possibility is less ex-

307

plored than its opposite. Dreyer, Flaherty, Vigo, Renoir, and Antonioni are masters of it.

AUDIENCE, ACTOR, AND STAR

The depth of the automatism of photography is to be read not alone in its mechanical production of an image of reality, but in its mechanical defeat of our presence to that reality. The audience in a theater can be defined as those to whom the actors are present while they are not present to the actors. But movies allow the audience to be mechanically absent. The fact that I am invisible and inaudible to the actors, and fixed in position, no longer needs accounting for; it is not part of a convention I have to comply with; the proceedings do not have to make good the fact that I do nothing in the face of tragedy, or that I laugh at the follies of others. In viewing a movie my helplessness is mechanically assured: I am present not at something happening, which I must confirm, but at something that has happened, which I absorb (like a memory). In this, movies resemble novels, a fact mirrored in the sound of narration itself, whose tense is the past.

It might be said: "But surely there is the obvious difference between a movie house and a theater that is not recorded by what has so far been said and that outweighs all this fiddle of differences. The obvious difference is that in a theater we are in the presence of an actor, in a movie house we are not. You have said that in both places the actor is in our presence and in neither are we in his, the difference lying in the mode of our absence. But there is also the plain fact that in a theater a real man is *there,* and in a movie no real man is there. That is obviously essential to the differences between our responses to a play and to a film." What that means must not be denied; but the fact remains to be understood. Bazin meets it head on by simply denying that "the screen is incapable of putting us 'in the presence of' the actor"; it, so to speak, relays his presence to us, as by mirrors. Bazin's idea here really fits the facts of live television, in which the thing we are presented with is happening simultaneously with its presentation. But in live television, what is present to us while it is happening is not the world, but an event standing out from the world. Its point is not to reveal, but to cover (as with a gun), to keep something on view.

It is an incontestable fact that in a motion picture no live human being is up there. But a human *something* is, and something unlike anything else we know. We can stick to our plain description of that human something as "in our presence while we are not in his" (present *at* him, because looking at him, but not present *to* him) and still account for the difference between his live presence and his photographed presence to us. We need to consider what is present or, rather, since the topic is the human being, *who* is present.

One's first impulse may be to say that in a play the character is present, whereas in a film the actor is. That sounds phony or false: one wants to say that both are present in both. But there is more to it, ontologically more. Here I think of a fine passage of Panofsky's:

> Othello or Nora are definite, substantial figures created by the playwright. They can be played well or badly, and they can be "interpreted" in one way or another; but they most definitely exist, no matter who plays them or even whether they are played at all. The character in a film, however, lives and dies with the actor. It is not the entity "Othello" interpreted by Robeson or the entity "Nora" interpreted by Duse, it is the entity "Greta Garbo" incarnate in a figure called Anna Christie or the entity "Robert Montgomery" incarnate in a murderer who, for all we know or care to know, may forever remain anonymous but will never cease to haunt our memories.

If the character lives and dies with the actor, that ought to mean that the actor lives and dies with the character. I think that is correct, but it needs clarification. Let us develop it slightly.

For the stage, an actor works himself into a role; for the screen, a performer takes the role onto himself. The stage actor explores his potentialities and the possibilities of his role simultaneously; in performance these meet at a point in spiritual space—the better the performance, the deeper the point. In this respect, a role in a play is like a position in a game, say,

third base: various people can play it, but the great third base-
man is a man who has accepted and trained his skills and instincts most perfectly and matches them most intimately with
his discoveries of the possibilities and necessities of third
base. The screen performer explores his role like an attic and
takes stock of his physical and temperamental endowment; he
lends his being to the role and accepts only what fits; the rest
is nonexistent. On the stage there are two beings, and the
being of the character assaults the being of the actor; the actor
survives only by yielding. A screen performance requires not
so much training as planning. Of course, both the actor and
the performer require, or can make use of, experience. The actor's role is his subject for study, and there is no end to it. But
the screen performer is essentially not an actor at all: he *is* the
subject of study, and a study not his own. (That is what the
content of a photograph is—its subject.) On a screen the study
is projected; on a stage the actor is the projector. An exemplary
stage performance is one which, for a time, most fully creates a
character. After Paul Scofield's performance in *King Lear,* we
know who King Lear is, we have seen him in flesh. An exemplary screen performance is one in which, at a time, a star is
born. After *The Maltese Falcon* we know a new star, only dis-
tantly a person. "Bogart" *means* "the figure created in a given
set of films." His presence in those films is who he is, not
merely in the sense in which a photograph of an event is that
event; but in the sense that if those films did not exist, Bogart
would not exist, the name "Bogart" would not mean what it
does. The figure it names is not only in our presence, we are
in his, in the only sense we could ever be. That is all the
"presence" he has.

But it is complicated. A full development of all this would
require us to place such facts as these: Humphrey Bogart was a
man, and he appeared in movies both before and after the
ones that created "Bogart." Some of them did not create a new
star (say, the stable groom in *Dark Victory*), some of them
defined stars—anyway meteors—that may be incompatible
with Bogart (e.g., Duke Mantee and Fred C. Dobbs) but that
are related to that figure and may enter into our later experience of it. And Humphrey Bogart was both an accomplished

actor and a vivid subject for a camera. Some people are, just as some people are both good pitchers and good hitters; but there are so few that it is surprising that the word "actor" keeps on being used in place of the more beautiful and more accurate word "star"; the stars are only to gaze at, after the fact, and their actions divine our projects. Finally, we must note the sense in which the creation of a (screen) performer is also the creation of a character—not the kind of character an author creates, but the kind that certain real people are: a type.

TYPES; CYCLES AS GENRES

Our attention turns from the physical medium of cinema in general to the specific forms or genres the medium has taken in the course of its history.

Both Panofsky and Bazin begin at the beginning, noting and approving that early movies adapt popular or folk arts and themes and performers and characters: farce, melodrama, circus, music hall, romance, etc. And both are gratifyingly contemptuous of intellectuals who could not come to terms with those facts of life. (Such intellectuals are the alter egos of the film promoters they so heartily despise. Roxy once advertised a movie as "Art, in every sense of the word"; his better half declaims, "This is not art, in any sense of the word.") Our question is, why did such forms and themes and characters lend themselves to film? Bazin, in what I have read of him, is silent on the subject, except to express gratitude to film for revivifying these ancient forms, and to justify in general the legitimacy of adaptation from one art to another. Arnold Hauser, if I understand him, suggests wrong answers, in a passage that includes the remark "Only a young art can be popular," a remark that not only is in itself baffling (did Verdi and Dickens and Shakespeare and Chaplin and Frank Loesser work in young arts?) but suggests that it was only natural for the movies to pick up the forms they did. It *was* natural—anyway it happened fast enough—but not because movies were destined to popularity (they were at first no more popular than other forms of entertainment). In any case, popular arts are likely to pick up the forms and themes of high art for their material—popular theater naturally *burlesques*. And it means next to nothing to say that movies are young, because we do not know what the normal life span of an art is supposed to be, nor what would count as a unit of measure. Panofsky raises the question of the appropriateness of these original forms, but his answer is misleading.

> The legitimate paths of evolution [for the film] were opened, not by running away from the folk art character of the primitive film but by developing it within the limits of its own possibilities. Those primordial archetypes of film productions on the folk art level— success or retribution, sentiment, sensation, pornography, and crude humor—could blossom forth into genuine history, tragedy and romance, crime and adventure, and comedy, as soon as it was realized that they could be transfigured—not by an artificial injection of literary values but by the exploitation of the unique and specific possibilities of the new medium.

The instinct here is sound, but the region is full of traps. What are "the unique and specific possibilities of the new medium"? Panofsky defines them as dynamization of space and spatialization of time—that is, in a movie things move, and you can be moved instantaneously from anywhere to anywhere, and you can witness successively events happening at the same time. He speaks of these properties as "self-evident to the point of triviality" and, because of that, "easily forgotten or neglected." One hardly disputes this, or its importance. But we still do not understand what makes these properties "the possibilities of the medium." I am not now asking how one would know that these are *the* unique and specific possibilities (though I will soon get back to that); I am asking what it means to call them possibilities at all.

Why, for example, didn't the medium begin and remain in the condition of home movies, one shot just physically tacked on to another, cut and edited simply according to subject? (Newsreels essentially did, and they are nevertheless valuable, enough so to have justified the invention of moving pictures.) The answer seems obvious: narrative movies emerged because someone "saw the possibilities" of the medium—cutting and editing and taking shots at different distances from the subject. But again, these are mere actualities of film mechanics: every home movie and newsreel contains them. We could say: to make them "possibilities of the medium" is to realize what will give them *significance*—for example, the narrative and physical rhythms of melodrama, farce, American comedy of the 1930s. It is not as if film-makers saw these possibilities and then looked for something to apply them to. It is truer to say that someone with the wish to make a movie saw that certain established forms would give point to certain properties of film.

This perhaps sounds like quibbling, but what it means is that the aesthetic possibilities of a medium are not givens. You can no more tell what will give significance to the unique and specific aesthetic possibilities of projecting photographic images by thinking about them or seeing some, than you can tell what will give significance to the possibilities of paint by thinking about paint or by looking some over. You have to think about painting, and paintings; you have to think about motion pictures. What does this "thinking about them" consist in? Whatever the useful criticism of an art consists in. (Painters before Jackson Pollock had dripped paint, even deliberately. Pollock made dripping into a medium of painting.) I feel like saying: The first successful movies—i.e., the first moving pictures accepted as motion pictures—were not applications of a medium that was defined by given possibilities, but the *creation of a medium* by their giving significance to specific possibilities. Only the art itself can discover its possibilities, and the discovery of a new possibility is the discovery of a new medium. A medium is something through which or by means of which something specific gets done or said in particular ways. It provides, one might say, particular ways to get through to someone, to make sense; in art, they are forms, like forms of speech. To discover ways of making sense is always a matter of the relation of an artist to his art, each discovering the other.

Panofsky uncharacteristically skips a step when he describes the early silent films as an "unknown language . . . forced upon a public not yet capable of reading it." His notion is (with good reason, writing when he did) of a few industrialists forcing their productions upon an addicted multitude. But from the beginning the language was not "unknown"; it was known to its creators, those who found themselves speaking it; and in the beginning there was no "public" in question; there were just some curious people. There soon was a public, but that just proves how easy the thing was to know. If we are to say that there was an "unknown" something, it was less like a language than like a fact—in particular,

313

the fact that something is intelligible. So while it may be true, as Panofsky says, that "for a Saxon peasant of around 800 it was not easy to understand the meaning of a picture showing a man as he pours water over the head of another man," this has nothing special to do with the problems of a moviegoer. The meaning of that act of pouring in certain communities is still not easy to understand; it was and is impossible to understand for anyone to whom the practice of baptism is unknown. Why did Panofsky suppose that comparable understanding is essential, or uniquely important, to the reading of movies? Apparently he needed an explanation for the persistence in movies of "fixed iconography"—"the well-remembered types of the Vamp and the Straight Girl . . . the Family Man, and the Villain," characters whose conduct was "predetermined accordingly"—an explanation for the persistence of an obviously primitive or folkloristic element in a rapidly developing medium. For he goes on, otherwise inexplicably, to say that "devices like these became gradually less necessary as the public grew accustomed to interpret the action by itself and were virtually abolished by the invention of the talking film." In fact such devices persist as long as there are still Westerns and gangster films and comedies and musicals and romances. *Which* specific iconography the Villain is given will alter with the times, but that his iconography remains specific (i.e., operates according to a "fixed attitude and attribute" principle) seems undeniable: if Jack Palance in *Shane* is not a Villain, no honest home was ever in danger. Films have changed, but that is not because we don't need such explanations any longer; it is because we can't *accept* them.

These facts are accounted for by the actualities of the film medium itself: types are exactly what carry the forms movies have relied upon. These media created new types, or combinations and ironic reversals of types; but there they were, and stayed. Does this mean that movies can never create individuals, only types? What it means is that this is the movies' way of creating individuals: they create *individualities*. For what makes someone a type is not his similarity with other members of that type but his striking separateness from other people.

Until recently, types of black human beings were not created in film: black people were stereotypes—mammies, shiftless servants, loyal retainers, entertainers. We were not given, and were not in a position to be given, individualities that projected particular *ways* of inhabiting a social role; we recognized only the role. Occasionally the humanity behind the role would manifest itself; and the result was a revelation not of a human individuality, but of an entire realm of humanity becoming visible. When in *Gone With the Wind* Vivien Leigh, having counted on Butterfly McQueen's professed knowledge of midwifery, and finding her as ignorant as herself, slaps her in rage and terror, the moment can stun us with a question: What was the white girl assuming about blackness when she believed the casual claim of a black girl, younger and duller and more ignorant than herself, to know all about the mysteries of childbirth? The assumption, though apparently complimentary, is dehumanizing—with such creatures knowledge of the body comes from nowhere, and in general they are to be trusted absolutely or not at all, like lions in a cage, with whom you either do or do not know how to deal. After the slap, we are left with two young girls equally frightened in a humanly desperate situation, one limited by a distraction which expects and forgets that it is to be bullied, the other by an energetic resourcefulness which knows only how to bully. At the end of Michael Curtiz' *Breaking Point*, as the wounded John Garfield is carried from his boat to the dock, awaited by his wife and children and, just outside the circle, by the other woman in his life (Patricia Neal), the camera pulls away, holding on the still waiting child of his black partner, who only the unconscious Garfield knows has been killed. The poignance of the silent and unnoticed black child overwhelms the yarn we had been shown. Is he supposed to symbolize the fact of general human isolation and abandonment? Or the fact that every action has consequences for innocent bystanders? Or that children are the real sufferers from the entangled efforts of adults to straighten out their lives? The effect here is to rebuke Garfield for attaching so much importance to the loss of his arm, and generally to blot out attention to individual suffering by invoking a massive social evil about which this film has nothing to say.

The general difference between a film type and a stage type is that the individuality captured on film naturally takes precedence over the social role in which that individuality gets expressed. Because on film social role appears arbitrary or incidental, movies have an inherent tendency toward the democratic, or anyway the idea of human equality. (But because of film's equally natural attraction to crowds, it has opposite tendencies toward the fascistic or populistic.) This depends upon recognizing film types as inhabited by figures we have met or may well meet in other circumstances. The recognized recurrence of film performers will become a central idea as we proceed. At the moment I am emphasizing only that in the case of black performers there was until recently no other place for them to recur in, except just the role within which we have already met them. For example, we would not have expected to see them as parents or siblings. I cannot at the moment remember a black person in a film making an ordinary purchase—say of a newspaper, or a ticket to a movie or for a train, let alone writing a check. (*Pinky* and *A Raisin in the Sun* prove the rule: in the former, the making of a purchase is a climactic scene in the film; in the latter, it provides the whole subject and structure.)

One recalls the list of stars of every magnitude who have provided the movie camera with human subjects—individuals capable of filling its need for individualities, whose individualities in turn, whose inflections of demeanor and disposition were given full play in its projection. They provided, and still provide, staples for impersonators: one gesture or syllable of mood, two strides, or a passing mannerism was enough to single them out from all other creatures. They realized the myth of singularity—that we can still be found, behind our disguises of bravado and cowardice, by someone, perhaps a god, capable of defeating our self-defeats. This was always more important than their distinction by beauty. Their singularity made them more like us—anyway, made their difference from us less a matter of metaphysics, to which we must accede, than a matter of responsibility, to which we must bend. But then that made them even more glamorous. That they should be able to stand upon their singularity! If one did that, one might be found, and called out, too soon, or at an inconvenient moment.

What was wrong with type-casting in films was not that it displaced some other, better principle of casting, but that factors irrelevant to film-making often influenced the particular figures chosen. Similarly, the familiar historical fact that there are movie cycles, taken by certain movie theorists as in itself a mark of unscrupulous commercialism, is a possibility internal to the medium; one could even say, it is the best emblem of the fact that a medium had been created. For a cycle is a genre (prison movies, Civil War movies, horror movies, etc.); and a genre is a medium.

316

TYPES; CYCLES AS GENRES

As Hollywood developed, the original types ramified into individualities as various and subtle, as far-reaching in their capacities to inflect mood and release fantasy, as any set of characters who inhabited the great theaters of our world. We do not know them by such names as Pulcinella, Crispin, Harlequin, Pantaloon, the Doctor, the Captain, Columbine; we call them the Public Enemy, the Priest, James Cagney, Pat O'Brien, the Confederate Spy, the Army Scout, Randolph Scott, Gary Cooper, Gable, Paul Muni, the Reporter, the Sergeant, the Sheriff, the Deputy, the D.A., the Quack, the Shyster, the Other Woman, the Fallen Woman, the Moll, the Dance Hall Hostess. Hollywood was the theater in which they appeared, because the films of Hollywood constituted a world, with recurrent faces more familiar to me than the faces of the neighbors of all the places I have lived.

The great movie comedians—Chaplin, Keaton, W. C. Fields— form a set of types that could not have been adapted from any other medium. Its creation depended upon two conditions of the film medium mentioned earlier. These conditions seem to be necessities, not merely possibilities, so I will say that two necessities of the medium were discovered or expanded in the creation of these types. First, movie performers cannot project, but are projected. Second, photographs are of the world, in which human beings are not ontologically favored over the rest of nature, in which objects are not props but natural allies (or enemies) of the human character. The first necessity—projected visibility—permits the sublime comprehensibility of Chaplin's natural choreography; the second—ontological equality—permits his Proustian or Jamesian relationships with Murphy beds and flights of stairs and with vases on runners on tables on rollers: the heroism of momentary survival, Nietzsche's man as a tightrope across an abyss. These necessities permit not merely the locales of Keaton's extrications, but the philosophical mood of his countenance and the Olympic resourcefulness of his body; permit him to be perhaps the only constantly beautiful and continuously hilarious man ever seen, as though the ugliness in laughter should be redeemed. They permit Fields to mutter and suffer and curse obsessively, but heard and seen only by us; because his attributes are those of the gentleman (confident swagger and elegant manners, gloves, cane, outer heartiness), he can manifest continuously with the remorselessness of nature, the psychic brutalities of bourgeois civilization.

317

IDEAS OF ORIGIN

It is inevitable that in theorizing about film one at some point speculate about its origins, because despite its recentness, its origin remains obscure. The facts are well enough known about the invention and the inventors of the camera, and about improvements in fixing and then moving the image it captures. The problem is that the invention of the photographic picture is not the same thing as the creation of photography as a medium for making sense. The historical problem is like any other: a chronicle of the facts preceding the appearance of this technology does not explain why it happened when and as it did. Panofsky opens his study of film by remarking, "It was not an artistic urge that gave rise to the discovery and gradual perfection of a new technique; it was a technical invention that gave rise to the discovery and gradual perfection of a new art." We seem to understand this, but do we understand it? Panofsky assumes we know what it is that at any time has "given rise" to a "new art." He mentions an "artistic urge," but that is hardly a candidate to serve as an explanation; it would be about as useful as explaining the rise of modern science by appealing to "a scientific urge." There may be such urges, but they are themselves rather badly in need of explanation. Panofsky cites an artistic urge explicitly as the occasion for a new "technique." But the motion picture is not a new *technique*, any more than the airplane is. (What did we use to do that such a thing enables us to do better?) Yet some idea of flying, and an urge to do it, preceded the mechanical invention of the airplane. What is "given rise to" by such inventions as movable type or the microscope or the steam engine or the pianoforte?

It would be surprising if the history of the establishment of an artistic medium were less complex a problem for the historical understanding than (say) the rise of modern science. I take Bazin to be suggesting this when he reverses the apparent relation between the relevant technology and the idea of cinema, emphasizing that the idea preceded the technology, parts of it by centuries, and that parts of the technology preceded the invention of movies, some of it by centuries. So what has to be explained is not merely how the feat was technically accomplished but, for example, what

318

stood in the way of its happening earlier. Surprisingly, Bazin, in the selection of essays I have read, does not include the contemporary condition of the related arts as a part of the ideological superstructure that elicited the new material basis of film. But it is certainly relevant that the burning issue during the latter half of the nineteenth century, in painting and in the novel and in the theater, was realism. And unless film captured possibilities opened up by the arts themselves, it is hard to imagine that its possibilities as an artistic medium would have shown up as, and as suddenly as, they did.

The idea of and wish for the world re-created in its own image was satisfied *at last* by cinema. Bazin calls this the myth of total cinema. But it had always been one of the myths of art; each of the arts had satisfied it in its own way. The mirror was in various hands held up to nature. In some ways it was more fully satisfied in.theater. (Since theater is on the whole not now a major art for us, it on the whole no longer makes contact with its historical and psychological sources; so we are rarely gripped by the trauma we must once have suffered when the leader of the chorus stopped contributing to a narrative or song and turned to face the others, suffering incarnation.)

What is cinema's way of satisfying the myth? Automatically, we said. But what does that mean—mean mythically, as it were? It means satisfying it without *my* having to do anything, satisfying it *by* wishing. In a word, *magically*. I have found myself asking: How could film be art, since all the major arts arise in some way out of religion? Now I can answer: Because movies arise out of magic; from *below* the world.

The better a film, the more it makes contact with this source of its inspiration; it never wholly loses touch with the magic lantern behind it. This suggests why movies of the fantastic *(The Cabinet of Dr. Caligari, Blood of a Poet)* and filmed scenes of magic (say, materialization and dematerialization), while they have provided moods and devices, have never established themselves as cinematic media, however strongly this "possibility" is suggested by the physical medium of film: they are technically and psychologically trivial compared with the medium of magic itself. It is otherwise if the presented magic is itself made technically or physically interesting *(The Invisible Man, Dr. Jekyll and Mr. Hyde, Frankenstein, 2001: A Space Odyssey)*, but then that becomes another way of confirming the physicality of our world. Science presents itself, in movies, as magic, which was indeed one source of science. In particular, projected science retains magic's mystery and forbiddenness. Science-fiction films exploit not merely certain obvious aspects of adventure, and of a physicality that special effects specialize in, but also the terrific mumbo-jumbo of hearsay science: "My God, the thing is impervious to the negative beta ray! We must reverse the atom recalcitration spatter, before it's too late!" The dialogue has the surface of those tinbox-and-lever contraptions that were sufficiently convincing in prime *Flash Gordon*. These films are carried by the immediacy of the fantasy that motivates them (say, destruction by lower or higher forms of life, as though the precariousness of human life is due to its biological stage of development); together with the myth of the one way and last chance in which the (external) danger can be averted. And certainly the beauty of forms and motions in Frankenstein's laboratory is essential to the success of *Frankenstein;* computers seem primitive in comparison. It always made more sense to steal from God than to try to outwit him.

How do movies reproduce the world magically? Not by literally presenting us with the world, but by permitting us to view it unseen. This is not a wish for power over creation (as Pygmalion's was), but a wish not to need power, not to have to bear its burdens. It is, in this sense, the reverse of the myth of Faust. And the wish for invisibility is old enough. Gods have profited from it, and Plato tells it at the end of the *Republic* as the Myth of the Ring of Gyges. In viewing films, the sense of invisibility is an expression of modern privacy or anonymity. It is as though the world's projection explains our forms of unknownness and of our ability to know. The explanation is not so much that the world is passing us by, as that we are displaced from our natural habitation within it, placed at a distance from it. The screen overcomes our fixed distance; it makes displacement appear as our natural condition.

1971

320

F. E. SPARSHOTT
BASIC FILM AESTHETICS

The basic aesthetics of film as of any other art must be descriptive and analytic, giving an account of the relevant variables and their means of variation. And any such account must be rooted in some notion, however imprecise, of what a work of the art in question is. What, then, is a film? It seems to be characteristic of the art that acceptable definitions need to specify not only the nature of the work itself but also the means essential to its production and its characteristic effects. A sample definition might go like this: "A film is a series of motionless images projected onto a screen so fast as to create in the mind of anyone watching the screen an impression of continuous motion, such images being projected by a light shining through a corresponding series of images arranged on a continuous band of flexible material." Much variation in detail and in emphasis is possible, but no definition can dispense with two important features: a succinct description of at least the basic features of the *mechanism* employed, and an allusion to the creation of an *illusion* of motion. Let us consider these necessary features in turn.

MECHANISM

More than any other art, film is technologically determined. Music, dance, drawing, painting, sculpture, poetry, even architecture need for their original and rudimentary forms either no materials or materials lying everywhere at hand, but cinematography cannot begin without laboriously invented and precisely constructed equipment. The history of film is the history of the invention of its means. Aestheticians of the cinema may often be differentiated by how they react to various aspects of its technology: the properties of lenses and emulsions, the conditions of production and display. Thus the most notorious dogmas about how films ought to be made are demands for truth to the supposed tendencies of some aspect of the medium: to the clarity and convincingness of photographic images, or to the impartial receptivity of a film camera to whatever may be put before it, or to the camera's way of reducing whatever is put before it to a homogeneous image, or to the ease with which assorted scraps of film may be so cemented as to suggest a common provenance, and so on. It is characteristic of such dogmas that they fasten on one such aspect and tendency and ignore the rest. All of them ignore one very important factor: just because the means of cinema are so complex, anyone who has mastered them (and, equally rare and difficult, who has regular access to them) will naturally use them to convey whatever message or vision he may wish to convey, whether or not it is "cinematic" by any plausible definition. People use their languages to say what they wish to say, not what the language makes it easy to say. Most theorists of cinema insist that the outcome of this natural tendency is bound to be a bad film, but one hardly sees why. Whatever can be done with a medium is among its possibilities and hence "true to" it in a sense that has yet to be shown to be illegitimate. A person may become (or may train himself to be) sensitive to the degree in which films exploit or ignore some possibility of the medium, and then may govern his taste or regulate his critical judgment accordingly, but one does not see why such arbitrary selective systems should be imposed on those who would reject them. It is one thing to show that it is almost impossible to make a good film by photographing a stage performance of a play, by enumerating the probable sources of boredom and irritation; it is quite another to declare that all filmed plays are necessarily nonfilmic and on that account bad films.

ILLUSION

The second necessary feature of our sample definition was its reference to an illusion. Perhaps alone among the arts, and certainly in a way quite different from any of the other major arts, film is necessarily an art of illusion from the very beginning; and illusion, like technology, serves as a focal point around which aesthetic disputes arrange themselves. On the one hand, it may be taken as an opportunity to be exploited. Both by fabricating the images to be projected and by manipulating the speed and sequence of their projection, films can and do revel in the creation of the most elaborate illusions. On the other hand, illusion may be seen as the temptation to be resisted. The motion on the screen has to be unreal, but can and should faithfully portray a motion that really took place just so in the real world. Both tendencies go back to the earliest days of cinema, in the work of the realist Lumière and the fantasist Méliès. But that does not mean that film-makers have to choose between embracing and eschewing illusion: quite usually, and in the films of at least some acknowledged masters, fantasy is put at the service of realism (e.g. the stone lions in *Potemkin*) or realism at the service of fantasy (e.g. the homecoming in *Ugetsu*).

To speak broadly of "illusion" as we have done is misleading. While the basic illusion of motion is an automatic and unavoidable function of the mechanism of human vision, what I shall call the "secondary illusions" constructed upon it, to the effect that an event or movement of a certain sort is taking place, are not automatic but depend on the filmgoer's knowledge and his ability or willingness to acquiesce in a pretense. Writers on film often mention a scene in which an Indian villager is pursued by a tiger. The pursuit is shown entirely by intercut shots of scared man and slavering beast until, at the very end, pursuer and pursued at last appear together in a single shot. For Bazin, this saves the scene: previously one had assumed that the propinquity of man and beast was an illusion created by cutting, now one suddenly sees that it was not. For Montagu, it is stupid: the effect was created by the cutting, the concluding two-shot is a banal assertion. And of course on reflection one realizes that either it was a tame tiger or we are being served another trick shot. It seems obvious that different audiences will differ in their susceptibilities to such effects; trying to decide the proprieties (as both writers do) by invoking ultimate principles is surely a waste of time.

THE BIAS OF EXPOSITION

As the example we have just given shows, the secondary illusions of film relate not to what is projected on the screen but to the supposed provenance of the image. No more than when attending a stage play does anyone at the movies feel as if an event were really taking place before his eyes. But why should there be illusions of provenance? The answer seems to lie in the complex relations between cinematography and photography, and the peculiar nature of photographic images themselves. A clue to these relations may be found in the fact that all but one of the demands of "truth to the medium" that we used as examples mentioned some aspect of photography, although our sample definition of a film made no allusion to photography at all.

The images whose successive projection makes a film are most easily produced by photography; but they can be drawn directly on the film stock. A photograph to represent an object is most easily made by aiming a camera at an object of the appropriate kind; but what is photographed may also be a model or a drawing or even another photograph made for the purpose. A photograph of an event or happening is most easily made by finding one and photographing it; but scenes may be enacted and scenery constructed for the purpose. The required succession of images is most easily produced by using a device that will take a lot of photographs in rapid succession and fix them in the right order; but it can be (and in animated cartoons is) drawn or photographed frame by frame. And the obvious way to work the film camera (though not necessarily the easiest; rather it is synchronization that requires care) is to run it at the same speed as you will run your projector; but it can be run faster or slower. Film thus has a bias, quite strong though readily resistible, towards its simplest form, that in which the projector repeats a camera event; and one tends if not on one's guard to assume, wherever nothing in the film suggests the contrary, that what is shown on the screen represents such a repetition, as if the projector copied a camera that enacted the spectator's eye.

An eye is not a camera, and a photographic image does not show what eyes see. As you look around you, your eye constantly adjusts its iris as brightness changes and alters its focus as depth changes. The parallax effect of the use of two eyes gives everything you see a shifting and unstable character, since everything not focused on at the moment yields a vague doubled image. The eye in nature is therefore restless; in looking at a photograph, all in one plane and with a relatively small range of luminosity, the eye is spared much of its labor. However, though a photographic image is not at all like the visible world, it does have precisely the quality that old theorists used to ascribe to that venerable phantom of optics, the retinal image. A photographic image represents a sort of ideal projection, the way we normalize in imagination what we see. What the invention of photography did was not to reproduce vision but to achieve a dream of ideal vision. A photographic image is not so much a true one as a convincing one. Photographs tend to carry an irresistible sense of authenticity. Looking at a good photograph is not like looking at the photographed thing (this is so far from being the case that Peter Ustinov's famous remark, that he made *Billy Budd* in black-and-white because it was more realistic than color, hardly seems paradoxical); it is like looking at a faithful record.

The basic illusion of movement by itself gives an impression not of reality but of a sort of unattributable vivacity. This becomes evident when one watches an animated cartoon. Verisimilitude adds nothing to the lifelikeness of such films, and the elaborate devices used by Disney in his later years to suggest a third dimension have been abandoned as futile (as well as expensive). The sense of reality elicited by such films is akin to that of painting: we attribute the actions we see neither to the real world nor to the screen image, but to Donald Duck and the cartoon world created for him. It is not the illusion of movement, then, that moves us to attribute what we see to the world of experience; rather it is the photographic character of the image that lends films their characteristic bias of exposition, and to the extent that it is present and uncontradicted by the nature of what is presented encourages us to take what we see as the record of something that took place as we see it taking place. The viewer tends to normalize in this sense his perception of films made in the most diverse ways.

Many theories about how films ought to be made represent attitudes to the bias of exposition just described. The Soviet filmmakers of the twenties claimed that the whole art of film lay in exploiting its tendency by the use of montage or associative cutting, joining strips of photographed film in such a way as to synthesize in the spectator's mind an experiential reality that went beyond the images shown. Siegfried Kracauer urged on the contrary that the best use of film is an honest reliance on its capacity to convey authenticity, to preserve and celebrate the sense of reality. His argument was not that a film should actually be a record or chronicle, but that it should celebrate and "redeem," as no other medium can, the radiant actuality of the physical world, eschewing alike fantasies and superimposed formal arrangements. Other critics, noting that film bestows verisimilitude on the deserving and the undeserving alike, urge that film includes among its unique capacities that of making "dreams come true." Only film can *show* the impossible happening and thus make fantasy convincing. In the opposite direction, some exponents of contemporary "underground" film go beyond Kracauer (and beyond Rossellini and the Italian neorealists) in urging that to cut film at all is to falsify: the finished film should consist of all that the camera took in the order it was taken in, and if this means that some shots are out-of-focus, ill-exposed or irrelevant, they will thereby only be truer to the film experience. On this view, a film records not what happened in front of the camera but what happened to the film *in* the camera. And finally, some extremists might urge that the only honest way to make a film is to set a camera up somewhere and let it just run, taking in whatever may happen along. But at that point the urge to honesty would surely defeat itself by suggesting a standard it cannot fulfill. Films are not natural events, and it is pointless to prevaricate about the selective intervention of the film-maker.

FILM SPACE

That the realism of film is that of a graphic record and not that of an illusive actuality is apparent in the peculiar nature of film space, the actual and suggested spatial relations between elements of the film and between film and spectator. Many writers imply that a film-goer ordinarily feels himself to be in the same relation to the filmed scene as the camera was (or purports to have been). On this basis such trick shots as those showing a room through the flames of a fire in the fireplace are condemned on the ground that the audience know that nobody would be in that position. But this seems to be mistaken. Spectators seem to identify themselves with the camera viewpoint only when some such process as Cinerama is used which makes the screen approximate to the total visual environment. Otherwise, shots taken looking straight downward do not give one a sense of vertigo (though they may do to persons extremely susceptible in this regard), and even the most rapid changes in camera position do not produce in an experienced filmgoer any sense of nausea or disorientation. If one really accepted a change in camera position as a change in one's personal viewpoint, rapid intercutting between different viewpoints would obviously be intolerable. There is certainly a sense in which one has a feeling of spatial presence at the filmed scene (which is not to be confused with psychological involvement in the action), construing the scene as a three-dimensional space in which one is involved and has a viewpoint. This depth and inclusiveness of cinema space owes much to parallax, the differential motion and occlusion of distant objects as the viewpoint changes. It follows that when, as often happens nowadays, action is interrupted by stop-motion, the whole nature of the space in which the action takes place is instantly transformed (a striking instance is the concluding scene of *The Strawberry Statement*). This little-noted factor is important. Without such a change in spatiality, stop-motion might give the impression that the world had suddenly come to a halt; as it is, it confronts us rather with a transition to a different mode of representation, and hence perhaps a different mode of being.

The more one reflects on one's sense of cinema space, the more it seems to be one peculiar to cinema. The use of a zoom lens increasing the (objective) size of the image does have the effect of bringing the action nearer; but walking towards the screen, though it produces a (subjectively) larger image and does bring the screen nearer, does not bring the action nearer at all. One's sense of spatial involvement in a scene does not depend on one's occupying any particular seat, but only on one's being neither too close nor too far to see the screen properly. Similar considerations apply to all the distortions of space that result from the use of various lenses. The resulting plasticity of space relations is accepted as a narrative device or as an invitation to an imaginary viewpoint, it does not disorient the audience. The use of a deep-focus lens for Miss Havisham's room in *Great Expectations* certainly has a "magnifying" effect, but a curious one: we do not feel that we are in a big room, but that "this is how it must have seemed to Pip." Again, in the scene where the girl runs toward the airplane in *Zabriskie Point* the scale-relations between girl and low horizon are such that for a second or two we accept what we see as an ordinary medium-shot; then we notice that for all her running the girl is not receding much, and realize that it is a typical telephoto shot. But the effect of this realization on me was not to alter my feeling of where I was in relation to the scene, but to change my interpretation of that relation. In fact, a telephoto shot answers to no possible real spatial relationship between spectator and event: there is a viewing angle, but no possible viewpoint. Yet this never disturbs anyone.

Phenomena of the sort we have been mentioning suggest that one's sense of space in film is somehow bracketed or held in suspense: one is aware of one's implied position and accepts it, but is not existentially committed to it. A simple explanation of this is that most of the time one is simultaneously aware of a film (as one is of a painting) both as a two-dimensional arrangement on the screen and as a three-dimensional scene, so that neither aspect dominates the mind except in moments of excitement or disaffection. A subtler explanation is that cinema vision is alienated vision. A man's sense of where he is depends largely on his sense of balance and his muscular senses, and all a filmgoer's sensory cues other than those of vision and hearing relate firmly to the theater and seat in which he sits. In the scene with the epileptic doctor in *Carnet du Bal*, which is taken with a consistently tilted camera, what one sees on the screen insists that one is off balance, but one's body insists that it is not; and the effect on me is the one Duvivier surely intended, a feeling of malaise accompanied by a sense of *vicarious* disorientation on behalf of the protagonist.

Some of the spatial ambiguity of film is shared with still photography. No matter how one moves a photograph around in relation to oneself, it continues to function as a faithful record implying a viewpoint from which it was taken: and there is a sense in which one continues to be "at" this viewpoint no matter what angle the photograph is inspected from. What differentiates film from still photography is not only the sense of vivacity and hence spatial reality that motion imparts, but also the great size and contrasting illumination of the film image in the darkened theater, whereby it comes much closer to dominating the visual sense, and the relatively invariant relation between screen and spectator.* The di-

---

*Note that in being transferred to the domestic television screen a film loses all three characteristics: size, luminosity, and audience immobility. It becomes an object rather than an experience.

rector determines the audience's spatial relation to his films, but what he determines remains an imaginary space; we are within the film's space but not part of its world; we observe from a viewpoint at which we are not situated.

It is the alienation of the visual sense in cinema space that makes possible many of the uses and special effects of film that work against its function as record. Being deprived of so many sensory cues, the spectator loses all sense of absolute scale, so that back-projections and painted backgrounds may wear a convincing air of reality, and the apparent size of any object may be varied by placing it in a magnified or diminished setting, or simply (as when storms and wrecks are shot using models in tanks) by trading on the spectator's narrative assumptions.

FILM AND DREAM

Unique as it is, the alienated spatiality of film, in which the spectator participates without contact, and which he observes from a viewpoint that contrives to be both definite and equivocal or impossible, presents striking analogies to the space of dreams. Or perhaps, since different people seem to have widely varying dream perceptions, I should limit myself to saying that my own spatial relation to my dream worlds is like nothing in waking reality so much as it is like my relation to film worlds. In my dreams, too, I see from where I am not, and move helplessly in a space whose very nature is inconstant, and may see beside me the being whose perceptions I share. There are indeed many ways in which film-going is like dreaming; but the likeness is always qualified. Films are like dreams in involving one in a world whose course one cannot control, but unlike them in that their world does not incorporate the dream of effort and participation. Filmed reality shares with dreamed reality (as nothing else does) its tolerance of limitlessly inconsequent transitions and transformations; but it lacks that curious conceptual continuity of dreams in which what is a raven may become a writing-desk or may simultaneously *be* a writing-desk, and in which one *knows* that what looks like one person is really a quite different person. The conceptual equivalences essayed by film-makers (e.g. Eisenstein's equation of Kerensky with a peacock in *October*), which usually proceed by intercutting shots of the two entities to be equated, seem rather to be the visual equivalent of similes or metaphors than equivalents of the dream carryover, which depends on a dream-interpretation imposed on the dream-percept and not (as must be the case in film) on an interpretation suggested by the percept itself.

The dreamlikeness of film has often been noted. Usually the recognition takes the form of a loose analogy with daydreaming (which is quite different), but Susanne Langer for one has made the formal analogy with dreaming the basis of her account of the nature of film. The analogy must not be pushed too far. A quite fundamental difference between a filmgoer and a dreamer is that the former remains in control of his faculties, capable of sustained and critical attention. A dream-like inconsequentiality is thus far from typical of film, though it remains among filmic possibilities and the filmgoing public at large acquiesces in a degree of cheerful incoherence (as in *Casino Royale*) that in other arts is acceptable only to the sophisticate.

To the extent that the analogy between film and dream is taken seriously, it seems to invite Freudians to apply their methods of symbolic interpretation with even more confidence than they do to other arts. But they seem not to have accepted the invitation (except in so far as Freudian methodology lies behind the auteur theory of criticism), perhaps because not enough film-makers are safely dead yet. In any case, before we reach that level of interpretation we have to complete our survey of the basic attributes of the film world.

FILM TIME AND FILM REALITY

The same confusion between an actual event and a convincing record that has made critics write of the camera as a surrogate for the spectator's eye leads them to say that film time is present time, that in watching a film one seems to see things happening *now*, as though one were present not at the film but at the filmed event. But this contention is vulnerable to the same sort of objection that refutes the doctrine of the camera eye. In one sense it is true but trivial: of course what one sees is always here and now, because "here" and "now" are defined by one's presence. In any other sense it is false, or we should not be able to take in our stride the flashbacks and flash-forwards, the accelerations and decelerations,

330

that are part of film's stock in trade. Rather, it is as though we were spectators of the temporality of the films we see. Film time has a quality analogous to that dreamlike floating between participation and observation, between definite and indeterminate relationships, that gives film space its pervasive character. Granted, the fundamental illusion of motion combines with the convincingness of a photographic record to ensure that we ordinarily do read the presented motion as continuous and as taking just as much time to happen as it takes us to observe it; but this supposition is readily defeated by any counterindication. D. W. Griffith, challenged on his early use of spatiotemporal discontinuities, justified himself by appealing to the example of Dickens, and surely he was right to do so. The time of a novel is filmic, as its space is not. Events can be filmed, as they can be narrated, with equal facility in any order, at any speed, with any degree of minuteness. Unlike the novelist, however, the film-maker has no language proper to his medium in which to specify temporal relations. He may use titles, trick dissolves, a narrator's voice, or datable visual clues to establish his temporal relations; but some directors seem to feel that such devices are clumsy or vulgar, and prefer to trust the public's acumen or simply to leave the relations indeterminate.

The dream-relationships of film space and the narrative nature of film time combine to encourage an ambiguity that may be fruitful or merely irritating. One often does not know whether one is seeing what in the film's terms is real, or only what is passing through the mind of one of the film's characters. This ambiguity becomes acute whenever there is a temporal jump, for time (as Kant observed) is the form of subjectivity. A flash-back may represent a character's memory, or may simply be a narrative device; a flash-forward may stand for a character's premonition, or simply an anticipation by the film-maker,* and, where the temporally displaced scene is recalled or foreseen, it may stand either for the event as it was or would be, or for the way it is (perhaps falsely) conjured up. The

---

*The terms "flash-back" and "flash-forward" are often used in such a way as to suggest that every film has a normal time from which all sequences assignable to other times are to be regarded as deviations. But why should this be so? The terms are better taken as marking temporal discontinuities rather than displacements.

status of film events thus becomes equivocal, and such uncertainty may pervade an entire film. Thus in *8½* some scenes are remembered, some dreamed, some imagined, and some belong to the reality of the film's story. There are many scenes whose status is unclear at the time, and some whose status never becomes clear. Does the opening scene of the closed car in the traffic jam show a seizure which makes the cure necessary (as Arnheim seems to think), or is it a dream of a patient already undergoing treatment (as most critics suppose)? Nothing in the version of the film I saw determined either answer. A more striking equivocation occurs in *Easy Rider*, when a brief glimpse of an unexplained roadside fire is identified at the end of the film as the burning of the hero's motorcycle. Was that first glimpse a premonition of the hero's (and if so, just what did he foresee?), or a *memento mori* by the director, or just a pointless interjection to which no meaning can be assigned? In such a self-indulgent piece of hokum, who can say? In general, the tolerability of such unresolved ambiguities is likely to depend partly on the handling of "reality" in the film as a whole, partly on one's confidence in the director's control over his medium, and partly on one's own tolerance of ambiguity. In any case, one must not suppose that such questions as we have just posed need have a single "right" answer (perhaps what the director "meant"). All the director has done is to splice celluloid, and if he has not provided enough clues to determine a reading then no meaning is determined. What the director may have had in mind is not the same as what he put on film, and directors sometimes have nothing at all in mind. The flexibility of film technique is a standing invitation to meaningless trickery, and the complexities of production involve endless risks of inadvertent nonsense.

As the apparent time of the action changes, then, so changes the subjectivity/objectivity rating of what we see; and so too may vary our degree of confidence in our ability to assign a rating. Nor are such ambiguities the prerogative of highbrow excursions like *Last Year at Marienbad*. They occur quite naturally in unsophisticated films. For example, in Jerry Lewis's Jekyll-and-Hyde fantasy *The Nutty Professor* the transformation scene in the laboratory slips onto a plane of witty extravagance quite removed from the surface naturalism of the rest of the film. Are we witnessing the event or a metaphor for the event? Who knows? One could spend a long time figuring out possible meanings for it, but in fact it comes across as just a happy episode and the popcorn-grinding jaws do not miss a beat.

FILM MOTION

The ambiguities of space and time combine to give film motion an endless complexity that we have no space to explore here. Let us confine our attention to some additional complications. In the earliest movies, each scene was taken with a fixed camera, so that the motion shown took place within a fixed frame and against an unchanging background. A scene in a modern film is likely to be enriched or muddled with three different kinds of camera motion. The camera may be shifted from place to place, turned horizontally or vertically to alter its field of reception, or modified by changing the focal length of its lens so as to take in a greater or smaller area. This third kind of camera shot is often dismissed as the equivalent of a tracking shot, moving the camera viewpoint toward or away from the scene, but it is not; it retains much of the sense of getting a different view from the same position. A camera can also be rotated on its focal axis, or joggled and steadied, but these can be set aside for now as occasional effects.

Even a shot of immobile objects taken with an immobile camera need not be devoid of movement, for there is also movement of light: illumination may change in direction, in intensity, in color, in sharpness. And even when the light remains unchanged, the much-used prints that most audiences see have a sort of constant surface shimmer, a vibrant presence derived from the random stains and lesions hard use imparts, that has a good deal to do with the "film experience" and is exploited by some film-makers in much the same spirit that furniture-makers fake a "distressed finish." The free combinations of all the kinds of film motion can impart to a single scene a plastic, balletic quality, a unique kind of formal beauty that is at once abstract and realistic and has no parallel in any other medium.

The mobility of the frame combines with the camera's typical neglect of natural boundaries to produce a marked contrast between the actions of theater and cinema. The stage world is a closed world; an actor who goes offstage loses all determinate existence for the audience; but the edge of a cinema screen functions like a window frame through which we glimpse part of a world to which we attribute infinite continuity. This sense of infinity adds an implicit freedom of movement to the actual freedom that the camera's mobility affords.

Because film space and time are observed rather than lived, film motion can be speeded up or slowed down within scenes in a way denied to theater, in which events take their proper time. (Conversely, theater has a way of achieving temporal plasticity denied to film, by exploiting the stage-unreality of the offstage world: in theater, but not in film, offstage actions are often performed in the course of a scene in an incongruously short time.) The effects of such variations in time depend on context, in a way that becomes easier to understand when we reflect that motion photography was invented to serve not one realistic purpose but two: not only to observe and record movements, but also to study and examine them. And of course very fast movements are best studied by slowing down their representation, very slow ones by speeding it up. Nature films are quite regularly made at unnatural speeds, accelerating plant growth and decelerating bird flight, and replays of crucial movements in sport are usually in slow motion. In this context of study the spectator has no sense of unreality at all: he feels simply that he is getting a better look. But in narrative contexts things are different. Acceleration was early discovered to have a reliably comic effect. But deceleration is more variable, for it may produce an impression of joy, or unreality, or obsessiveness, or solemnity, or inevitability. Its effects often evade description, but directors find them reliable enough for regular use, and they have hardened into more than one cliché. One such is the flash-back reverie, where the slow motion seems to work by suggesting weightlessness and hence ethereality (as in *The Pawnbroker*). Another is the use of weightlessness as a metaphor for lightheartedness (as in many TV commercials). A third is the slow-motion death by shooting (as in *Bonnie and Clyde*), partly an appeal to voyeurism but partly a symbolization of death through the transposition of the action into another key of reality.

One can think of acceleration and deceleration as a sort of pre-editing, the equivalent of adding or subtracting frames in a film taken at projector speed. It is basic to film that editing can produce an impression of motion by intercutting suitably spaced shots of the same object in different positions (as by successive still photographs). The impression does not depend on the basic illusion of continuity: provided that the mind can supply a possible trajectory, all that is needed is that the object should appear to be the same and that its position in successive shots should appear to be different. But beyond this, the effect of *any* sustainedly rapid cutting is to produce an impression of rapid motion, even if the intercut shots have no common content and one cannot say what (apart from "things") is moving. An intermediate sort of effect produced by editing is a two-dimensional movement of light, where the continuity of light and dark areas in successive shots is enough to entice the mind to complete a *Gestalt*; but this effect is of limited application, in that it draws attention away from the filmed world to the screen surface.

Cinema's repertory of motions both presented and psychologically suggested is so extensive and so essential that one might think that what film shares with still photography is unimportant, and specifically that two-dimensional composition within the frame can play no significant part in film at all. But that would be going too far. Not only does the awareness of the screen and its flat pattern play an essential part in grounding the ambiguous nature of film space, but directors in practice often do envisage their scenes statically. They make sketches for their key scenes beforehand, and use viewfinders to compose a scene before shooting it. A film no less than a play may proceed from tableau to tableau. Nonetheless, the tableau is insidiously misleading in more than one way. The more one reads about films the more clearly one sees how each film is invariably illustrated by a handful of constantly recurring still shots: *Potemkin* comes to be represented by half a dozen stills, *Caligari* by two, *Nosferatu* by one. Most of these are not even frames taken from the actual film, but photographs taken on a still camera before or after shooting. And they are chosen for their pictorial qualities. What I most vividly recall from *Bicycle Thieves* is the mountain of bundled clothing in the pawnshop, but that image would be nothing without the camera's movement and the action of adding one's own bundle to the mountain; and what the stills show me is a pretty, pathetic picture of the hero and his son sitting on the sidewalk. Thus in time one's recollection of what a film was like becomes distorted.

335

SOUND

We have been discussing film in visual terms. But for rather more than half its history film has been fully an art of sound as well as sight in the sense that the associated sound has been determined by the same celluloid strip that carries the image. The justification of our procedure is that sight remains primary. It is the requirements of the visual image that call for the elaboration of equipment and the circumstances of display that are fundamental to cinema. Film sound has no distinctive qualities in itself, and can be meaningfully discussed only as an adjunct to the visual.

Though a sound track for a film can be made directly at the time of shooting simply by hanging microphones near the action and recording on the film whatever they pick up, this is neither necessary nor usual. The sound track is usually made separately and combined with the visual film later. The resulting complexities for sound film are theoretically immense, though in practice the technology is not intimidating. The use of magnetic tape has made the recording, inventing, blending, splicing and modification of sounds easy and inexpensive as the analogous procedures for visual film can never be.

The fundamental classification of film sounds is that enunciated by Kracauer. A sound may belong to the world of the film (e.g. the dialogue of its characters) or it may be extraneous (e.g. background music or a commentary). In the former case, it may belong to the very scene being shown on the screen or it may ot (you may hear what is happening elsewhere from what you see, or be reminded by the sound track of a previous scene; as a marginal case, what you hear may be a sound remembered by one of the characters). If the sound does belong to the scene being shown, its provenance may be on or off camera (as you hear someone talk, you may see him, or the person he is addressing, or someone who overhears him, or an opening door that he fails to notice). Thus sound may (and in a slackly made film often does) merely duplicate or reinforce what is visible, but it may play an independent structural or narrative role, and may affect the interpretation or emotional tone of what is seen. For example, distortions, fadings, and swellings of voices can be used to overcome one of the difficulties of film narrative, that of economically revealing to the audience a state of mind that someone is successfully hiding from those around him. Background music may supply an ironic comment, as when the refueling of aircraft in *Dr. Strangelove* is accompanied by a love song—a Russian film of the silent days would have made the point by intercutting shots of animals mating, and what a bore it would have been. One can even try to use a musical score to supplement narrative deficiencies, or even to contradict the apparent tendency of what is seen to be happening, though such techniques have some notorious fiascos to their credit.

When determinate sound was first introduced, many film-lovers were opposed to it. In principle, the objection was invalid, for films had never been shown without accompanying (and would-be relevant) sound (a "silent" film shown in silence is a curiosity rather than a significant experience), and in principle the change only guaranteed that from now on the sound would indeed be relevant. But in practice what was feared was the "talking film," in which the sound track merely enabled the audience to hear what they could already see. And the use of sound does indeed make sloppy and mindless film-making easier. But sound can be and properly is used not merely to add another dimension to the film experience but to add an extra perspective to the visual experience itself.

As an alternative to the mindless use of attached sound that they dreaded, the Russian theorists of the late twenties proposed that their favorite device of associative or metaphorical montage should be extended to sound: intercut images should form a counterpoint against intercut sounds. This did not happen. For one thing, auditory comprehension has a much slower tempo than visual; for another, sounds tend to blend whereas images contrast. The proposed contrapuntal montage would have been impossibly overloaded, if not unintelligible. What montage requires from sound, it turns out, is not a contrapuntal pattern but a chordal backing for its visual melody, a continuous equivalent for or commentary on the character of the whole episode. In any case, the possibility of using sound effects as commentary on the visual images has made elaborate visual montage an obsolete device. This can be thought of as a catastrophic and uncompensated loss to the art of film, but the matter is open to question. Although Eisenstein and others made the use of associative intercutting into a Marxist aesthetic dogma (inasmuch as the conflict of contrasting shots forms a "dialectic" from which the realist truth is synthesized), others have pointed out that the device endears itself to totalitarian regimes by lending itself to lying propaganda: the associations it creates are entirely irrational. Partly, too, the reliance on cutting was enforced by the use of heavy and inflexible camera equipment. Conversely, the decreasing reliance on editing in scene construction is partly due to the introduction of ever more mobile and flexible equipment, partly to the familiarity of multicamera television procedures, partly to difficulties in synchronizing dialogue, but partly also to the fact that commercial directors tend not to do their own cutting anyway, losing effective control over their films as soon as shooting stops.

STRUCTURE

We have been dealing with the materials of film. To make a movie, the materials must somehow be organized. A film can be made simply by linking images and sounds in abstract rhythmic concatenation (as in McLaren's films), or by loosely arranging them around a theme (as in travelogues). But these straightforward methods, though in some ways they represent an ideal of pure cinema, seem to work well only for quite short films, and (especially since the decline of vaudeville) the staple of film production is the "feature," long enough to give the cash customers their money's worth. There are no theoretical limits to the length of a clearly articulated pattern of imagery, but most abstract films are short. The closest actual approximation to an abstract or purely formal method of organizing images is to associate them with extended musical forms, since the latter constitute long formal sequences of a kind that audiences already know and accept; but Disney's *Fantasia*, though often and lucratively revived, has not aroused emulation and in any case supplemented the musical structure with at least an illusion of parallel narrative form. More usually, coherence is sought through the organization of the subject matter of the imagery: by exploring a problem, or an object, or a place, or a situation, or an event (documentary), or, commonest of all, by constructing a fictitious or historical story. The contrast between documentary and the regular "feature" is not so much that between fact

338

and fiction, for features may be factual and most documentaries have fictional aspects, as between exploratory and narrative methods of organization. The reason for the dominance of the narrative feature lies partly in the flexibility of the film medium, which makes it especially suitable for a free-running narrative whose closest affinities are with novels and biographies, but partly in the assumption that the "mass audience" will associate exploration with instruction and hence with tedium. Now that the mass audience is safely shut away with its TV set things may change: *Woodstock* is a portent. Meanwhile, writers on cinema are bound to assume that the narrative feature remains the norm.

It is from the normal narrative form that the customary description of the articulation of film is derived. In a sense, and from the editor's viewpoint, the unit is the frame, but this does not exist for perception. Aesthetically, a film consists of shots organized into scenes which are themselves articulated into sequences. This structure corresponds, very roughly, to an analysis of activity into movements (shots), actions (scenes), and episodes (sequences). Accordingly, shots cohere into scenes through relevance, each shot being experienced as relevant to expectations aroused earlier in the scene (ideally, I suppose, by the preceding shot). Scenes are divided by jump-cuts or dissolves marking a change of subject; sequences are divided by such more emphatic punctuation as fade-out and fade-in. But (as with novel and theater) no rules or firm conventions demand such articulation: the determining changes are discontinuities of place, time, participants or activities (in abstract films, changes in the kind of image or movement; in documentaries, changes of aspect or style). The film-maker's use of punctuating devices is merely incidental to these. Actually, the very concept of a "shot" becomes nebulous and archaic as cameras become more mobile: the distinction between scene and shot takes on a vagueness such as infects the distinction between an action and its constituent movements.

The plasticity of camera viewpoint is such that films, like novels and unlike plays, can focus one's attention precisely. Only what is irreducibly relevant to the story need to be shown. A raised eyebrow can fill the screen. In theater, perception follows attention: one looks at the relevant part of what is visible on stage and ignores the rest. In film, attention follows perception: whatever is not relevant is either not screened or thrown into shadow or out of focus. Hence, film storytelling can and sometimes does achieve great elegance and economy. Styles change, however. The introduction of the wide screen has made the use of close-ups to isolate relevant detail seem rather blatant, and encourages a more fluid and relaxed style of presentation in which more use is made of the simultaneous presence on the screen of more than one focus for attention.

The focusing habit of the camera and the necessary priority of the visual might make one think that the most filmic and hence the best film story was one in which the *precise* content of each shot set up the story through its dynamic connection with the next. One might further infer from this that tragedy with its overriding architectonic goes against the grain of film, which has a special affinity for such episodic forms as picaresque comedy. There is something in that, but we warned at the start against the facile assumption that the best works in any medium are those which take its most obvious opportunities as procedural rules, and an overly filmic film might have the mechanized aggressiveness of a "well-made play." One could more reasonably infer that the least filmic and hence dullest films would be those in which the dialogue carried the story and the camera just coasted along. And yet that is how most films seem to be made. One can see why. Many films are adapted from literary works in which the dialogue alone can be borrowed without alteration. But in any case the logistics of making a full-scale film are such that it more or less has to be constructed from a detailed shooting-script. Films are largely *written* before they are shot. But writers are bound to be word-oriented. Besides, dialogue is the only part of the script that contributes directly to determining the actual quality of the finished film: specifications of visual images cannot include what will differentiate the effective from the flat, the fine from the clumsy. Perhaps most important, to throw responsibility for the story onto the dialogue is to play safe and easy. So long as the actors mouth the lines the story will somehow come through, and the director can content himself with the most perfunctory and generalized camera work. If the story depends on what can be seen, much greater care must be taken over exactly what is shown, and that will add to the shooting time which is the variable on which the cost of a film chiefly depends.

ART, COMMERCE, AND CRITICISM

Now the cat is out of the bag. Films are traditionally about money, and film as most people know it is commercial film. Film did not begin as high art or as folk art, but as the offspring of technological curiosity and showmanship. It got into the public eye by way of peep-show and vaudeville, and its first exponents did not think of themselves as artists. The structural analogies between film and novel, and the superficial likenesses between film and drama, suggest affiliations that took some time to develop. A glance at the advertisements in your local newspaper should convince you that film has yet to free itself from the hectic world and accent of the fairground.

Though cheap and flexible sound and camera equipment has done much to effect what Andrew Sarris has called "demystifying the medium," the financial structure of the film industry has still some claim to be considered as part of the technological conditions that we have recognized to be paramount in cinema. The decisive factors here are that the initial costs of making even a cheap film are high, but the printing, distribution, and exhibition costs are low. So the costs can be recovered if enough people are willing to see the film—which they will be able to do only if enough people are willing to show it. Nor is this a consequence of the sickness of western bourgeois society. No one, socialist or capitalist, is going to be allowed to tie up so much of other people's labor and equipment unless there is some reasonable assurance that there will be something to show for it: if not money, then prestige or the approved performance of some supposed social function. By the same token, the complexities of the arrangements for distributing or showing films are almost certain to deprive the director of control over the final condition and destiny of his work. A film critic is seldom commenting on the work of an individual or a cohesive group so much as on the upshot of a loosely connected series of independent decisions. He may thus succumb to feelings of irrelevance.

There are three plausible lines a critic can take here. One is to confine his attention to noncommercial films. Of course, these are atypical, but the critic can say (as Parker Tyler says) that it is not typical for a film to be a work of art. Most drawings, to take a parallel case, are not works of art but advertisements or sources of technical information or doodles, and no one expects a critic to waste his time on such objects.

A second critical line is to accept that most films, both commercial and "underground," are junk, to be greeted with silence or a dismissive gesture, but that any kind of interest or excellence may turn up in any sort of film. Such a rejection of all commitments to styles and cultural traditions is in the line of twentieth-century critical orthodoxy, but may find it hard to steer between the Scylla of an empty formalistic aestheticism and the Charybdis of a relativism that accepts everything equally because everything succeeds in being what it is.

A third critical line is to accept cinema as a demotic art and devise a critical system appropriate to such an art. George Orwell has shown the way. His exemplary study of Frank Richards devoted itself to describing the "world" depicted or implied by the ensemble of Richard's work, and exploring the repertory of mannerisms which gave that world a facile coherence. Students of Jung and Frye have enlarged this critical armory by showing how to expose the underlying mythical archetypes and patterns in popular fiction. These methods have been applied to Hollywood films in what is misnamed the "auteur theory" of criticism (which is a policy rather than a theory). Whatever a studio does to a film, a strong-minded director can impregnate it indelibly with his own basic textures, his view of human relationships, his favorite narrative devices, and obsessive images. In fact, the measure of a director's stature may be the extent to which he can retain these elements of his own style when working on an uncongenial assignment from his studio. And by comparing a director's different films, which taken in isolation had been thought undistinguished if no worse, one can educe a complex world full of ironies and unexpected insights.

Some auteur critics seem to assume that any director whose work is susceptible to their methods is thereby proved to be an artist, and his films shown to be good films. This is a strange assumption. Critics of other arts are far from supposing that to show that a work is recognizable and typical of its author has any tendency to show that it is a good work. In fact, the analogue in other arts is a form of criticism specifically devised for handling material incapable of yielding anything of interest to a more searching critique. Auteur criticism may work best as a heuristic device: armed with his comparisons and with his trained eye for manners and genres, a critic can show us meaning where we saw none; but when we have been shown we must be able to see for ourselves. In other arts we accept that one may not understand any work by an innovating artist until one has familiarized oneself with his style; but it is strange to have a similar esoteric status claimed for the output of a studio work-horse. The paradox of auteur criticism is that while its methods are devised to handle cinema as a demotic art, it relies on a view of that art which is inaccessible to most of its normal public. How many people are going to get to see a Raoul Walsh festival?

In so far as the normal film is about human affairs, it is susceptible to criticism on the same basis as literary or dramatic works or figurative paintings, in terms of its verisimilitude, psychological richness, moral maturity, social significance, political viability, relations to the divine and the unconscious and so on. The fact that such topics are not specific to film does not make them trivial or irrelevant*: on the contrary, most actual serious discussion of films centers on this human side, and so it should. But we need say nothing about such criticism here. In practice we all know what we want to say; in theory the basic moves are familiar from discussions of criticism in the older arts. From this point of view, the art of film criticism would lie in knowledge of and sensitivity to the ways in which such human qualities can be conveyed by such cinematic means as we have been discussing.

The salient feature of film is the enormous range of its specific effects. Film is unique in its capacity for visual recording and analysis, in its ability to convey the unique present reality of things, in its ability to reveal the qualities of lives; but also in its formal freedom, its capacity for realizing fantasy and developing abstract forms. In view of this inexhaustible flexibility of the medium, it is ludicrous to lay down general principles as to what is a good film.

---

*It has become fashionable among practitioners of the visual arts to apply the term "literary" to all humanistic or nonformal aspects of works of art, thus suggesting that in being a picture *of* something a work is somehow untrue of the visual. This implies that seeing or hearing something happen is an indirect way of reading about it. In fact, of course, scenes convey meaning as naturally and directly as words.

Those critics who do so are in most cases obviously fixated on the kind of film that was around when they were first moved by movies. A judicious critic will equip himself with the most exhaustive possible grasp of the variables and variations accessible to filmmakers, and note just which of these the director is exploiting and how he is doing it. So much can be done in a film that it requires close attention and knowledge to discern what is actually being done. Technical assessment and appreciation can almost be read off from the roll of specific opportunities opened up by the director's initial options and then seized or missed: take care of the facts and the values will take care of themselves. Beyond that, the moral and cultural side of a critique must depend on the maturity and sensitivity of the critic's social and moral awareness. If you could teach someone to be a critic, you could teach him to be a man.

1971

344

IV

Film, Theater, and Literature

Theorists have often attempted to discover the characteristics of the film medium by comparing it with other media. Panofsky, for example, contrasts the theater's static use of space and its independence of the principle of co-expressibility with cinema's more dynamic use of space and its rigorous subjection to that principle. For Panofsky, this difference explains why film adaptations of plays are so unlikely to succeed. Any attempt to transfer theater's essentially verbal resources to the cinema violates the principle that no more should be expressed verbally than can be expressed visually. The cinema's business is not the photographing of theatrical decor, a prestylized reality, but the photographing of actual physical reality so that it has style. Panofsky finds cinema the only medium that does justice to the materialistic interpretation of the universe which pervades contemporary civilization.

Like Panofsky, Hugo Munsterberg, the Harvard psychologist and philosopher who was a colleague of both William James and George Santayana, attempted in 1916 to delineate the features of the silent "photoplay" by contrasting it with the theater. For Munsterberg, the representation of physical reality is the concern not of cinema, but of theater. In true cinema, "the massive outer world has lost its weight, it has been freed from space, time and causality, and it has been clothed in the forms of our consciousness." Theater is bound by the same laws that govern nature, but the cinema is free to be shaped by the inner movements of the mind. Theater therefore trespasses on the realm of cinema when it employs any analogue of the close-up or the flash-back, and Munsterberg is as harsh a critic of "cinematified" theater as Panofsky is of "theatricalized" film.

For Munsterberg the true function of the close-up is not to provide a closer view of nature but to reproduce the mental act of attention. Similarly, the cut-back provides a cinematic equivalent of human memory and is alien to theater, which is bound by the laws of nature and the necessities of temporal succession. In the theater, "men of flesh and blood with really plastic bodies stand before us. They move like any moving body in our surroundings. Moreover, those happenings on the stage, just like events in life, are independent of our subjective attention and memory and imagination. They go their objective course." If it were the object of cinema, then, to "imitate" nature, film could hardly compete with theater. "The color of the world has disappeared, the persons are dumb, no sound reaches our ears. The depth of the scene appears unreal, the motion has lost its natural character. Worst of all, the objective course of events is falsified . . ." The genius of cinema is not, then, to "imitate" nature; rather it is to display the triumph of mind over matter.

The essay by Susan Sontag, the influential American writer and director, may be read as a critique of both Panofsky and Munsterberg. Despite their many and important differences, both "insist on a single model for film" and for theater, too. Their conception of the stage derives from notions of realism based on Ibsen and the French well-made play more than it does on the epic use of the stage by Shakespeare, the Russian constructivists, or Brecht. Similarly, their views of film display a strong prejudice in favor of the methods of the silent film. They are all too ready to confine cinema within rigid boundaries and to insist on maintaining artistic "purity," a separation of the various arts. Although Sontag understands the impulse to purity, she also understands a contrasting artistic ideal, one descending from Wagner rather than Lessing, which takes as its ideal a comprehensive "mixed-media" art form in the tradition of Greek theater and the Wagnerian music-drama. She does not choose between puristic and anti-puristic conceptions of the cinema or of the theater, but suggests awaiting future developments without prejudice.

Sontag accepts both the fact that many successful films have been "adapted" from plays and the fact that cinematic effects have been employed successfully in the theater. Andre Bazin, too, insists

346

on the value of adaptations. He thinks that Cocteau's *Les Parents Terrible* and Olivier's *Henry V* are superb films. But he does not feel that one should "cinematify," simply "open up" the original play by moving around outdoors, in order to make a successful adaptation. Rather, "a good adaptation should result in a restoration of the essence and spirit" of the original play. Indeed, in films like Cocteau's and Olivier's, one is "no longer adapting, one is staging a play by means of cinema."

Bazin realizes that if the living actor's presence were essential to the effects of theater, the successful staging of a play by means of cinema would be impossible. He therefore argues that there is a sense in which the actor is present on the screen just as a person is "present" in a mirror. Although Bazin's refutation of the importance of presence is not very convincing (Stanley Cavell treats the issue much more systematically in *The World Viewed*), it allows him to assert that the primary difference between stage and screen is not one of living beings but of architecture. Bazin thinks that theatrical speech often fails in a film not because it was written for living speakers but because it was written to be uttered in a particular kind of world. The problem of filming a play is to find a decor that preserves the closed, microcosmic qualities of theatrical architecture for which the dialogue was written and which at the same time preserves the natural realism of the screen. The screen is not a world in itself but a window on the world which consistently dwarfs and dissipates theatrical speech. Bazin believes this problem is worth solving, for even if original film scripts are preferable to adaptations, truly distinguished ones are rare. The cinema cannot afford to ignore its theatrical heritage, any more than the drama can afford the loss of the audiences that film can bring it.

Eisenstein too insists on the cultural heritage of cinema. He argues that Griffith even learned montage, which Eisenstein considers the essence of film, from the pages of Dickens. Eisenstein plainly sees no theoretical bar to adapting novels successfully to the screen, as proved by his own attempt to adapt Drieser's *An American Tragedy*. Indeed, it is not implausible to argue, as Bazin and Sontag have, that the film's deepest affinities are with the novel, not with the play. The novel is "cinematic" in its fluid handling of time and space, in its "focused" narrative control, in its ability to alternate description with dialogue, and even in the privacy and isolation of its audiences. The film has adapted more fiction than drama.

347

In contrast, George Bluestone, a contemporary American scholar, argues that film and novel are fundamentally different. The novel (like the stage in Panofsky's view) is fundamentally a linguistic medium, while the film is primarily visual. Although both D. W. Griffith and Joseph Conrad state that their purpose is to make us "see," Bluestone contends that while we literally "see" films (we perceive the images themselves), we do not literally see anything in a sentence except the words (which we apprehend conceptually). The film, therefore, "necessarily leaves behind those characteristic contents of thought which only language can approximate: tropes, dreams, memories, conceptual consciousness." The adapter must treat the novel merely as raw material and create for the film its own form and content, which will be sensual and perceptual, rather than conceptual and discursive as was the original novel.

Like Eisenstein and Bazin, Robert Scholes, the contemporary American literary scholar, believes that story-telling in film is comparable to story-telling in any medium. And, like Bluestone, Scholes differentiates between the perceptual apprehension of film stories and the conceptual apprehension of written narrative texts. But Scholes locates the primary difference between written and filmed stories not in the texts themselves but in the way that "readers read" those texts. His central term, "narrativity," borrowed from recent French narrative theory, refers to the way that the "reader" reconstructs the story in his or her own mind, in effect puts the events and description of the story together into a coherent pattern of expectations and gratifications, based on a recognition of temporality and causality. The word "narrativity" refers to "the process by which a perceiver actively constructs a story from the fictional data provided by any narrative medium."

For Scholes, the written narrative, conveyed by the more abstract sign-system of words, requires and rewards a narrativity that concretizes and pictorializes the verbal images into more specific mental pictures of persons, places, actions, and things. But the concrete pictorialization of the filmed image requires and rewards precisely the opposite kind of narrativity—the abstracting of highly specific stimuli into more general patterns of structure and theme. "The cinematic world invites—even requires—conceptualization." By implication, any film that attempted to adapt a written narrative (or, conversely, any "novelization" of a film, making a novel from an original screenplay,—an increasingly common practice in the 1970s) would need to take account of the different kinds of narrativity the two media generate.

HUGO MUNSTERBERG
FROM THE FILM:
A PSYCHOLOGICAL STUDY
THE MEANS OF THE PHOTOPLAY

We have now reached the point at which we can knot together all our threads, the psychological and the esthetic ones. If we do so, we come to the true thesis of this whole book. Our esthetic discussion showed us that it is the aim of art to isolate a significant part of our experience in such a way that it is separate from our practical life and is in complete agreement within itself. Our esthetic satisfaction results from this inner agreement and harmony, but in order that we may feel such agreement of the parts we must enter with our own impulses into the will of every element, into the meaning of every line and color and form, every word and tone and note. Only if everything is full of such inner movement can we really enjoy the harmonious coöperation of the parts. The means of the various arts, we saw, are the forms and methods by which this aim is fulfilled. They must be different for every material. Moreover the same material may allow very different methods of isolation and elimination of the insignificant and reënforcement of that which contributes to the harmony. If we ask now what are the characteristic means by which the photoplay succeeds in overcoming reality, in isolating a significant dramatic story and in presenting it so that we enter into it and yet keep it away from our practical life and enjoy the harmony of the parts, we must remember all the results to which our psychological discussion in the first part of the book has led us.

We recognized there that the photoplay, incomparable in this respect with the drama, gave us a view of dramatic events which was completely shaped by the inner movements of the mind. To be sure, the events in the photoplay happen in the real space with its depth. But the spectator feels that they are not presented in the three dimensions of the outer world, that they are flat pictures which only the mind molds into plastic things. Again the events are seen in continuous movement; and yet the pictures break up the movement into a rapid succession of instantaneous impressions. We do not see the objective reality, but a product of our own mind which binds the pictures together. But much stronger differences came to light when we turned to the processes of attention, of memory, of imagination, of suggestion, of division of interest and of emotion. The attention turns to detailed points in the outer world and ignores everything else: the photoplay is doing exactly this when in the close-up a detail is enlarged and everything else disappears. Memory breaks into present events by bringing up pictures of the past: the photoplay is doing this by its frequent cutbacks, when pictures of events long past flit between those of the present. The imagination anticipates the future or overcomes reality by fancies and dreams; the photoplay is doing all this more richly than any chance imagination would succeed in doing. But chiefly, through our division of interest our mind is drawn hither and thither. We think of events which run parallel in different places. The photoplay can show in intertwined scenes everything which our mind embraces. Events in three or four or five regions of the world can be woven together into one complex action. Finally, we saw that every shade of feeling and emotion which fills the spectator's mind can mold the scenes in the photoplay until they appear the embodiment of our feelings. In every one of these aspects the photoplay succeeds in doing what the drama of the theater does not attempt.

If this is the outcome of esthetic analysis on the one side, of psychological research on the other, we need only combine the results of both into a unified principle: *the photoplay tells us the human story by overcoming the forms of the outer world, namely, space, time, and causality, and by adjusting the events to the forms of the inner world, namely, attention, memory, imagination, and emotion.*

We shall gain our orientation most directly if once more, under this point of view, we compare the photoplay with the performance on the theater stage. We shall not enter into a discussion of the character of the regular theater and its drama. We take this for granted. Everybody knows that highest art form which the Greeks created and which from Greece has spread over Asia, Europe, and America. In tragedy and in comedy from ancient times to Ibsen, Rostand, Hauptmann, and Shaw we recognize one common purpose and one common form for which no further commentary is needed. How does the photoplay differ from a theater performance? We insisted that every work of art must be somehow separated from our sphere of practical interests. The theater is no exception. The structure of the theater itself, the framelike form of the stage, the difference of light between stage and house, the stage setting and costuming, all inhibit in the audience the possibility of taking the action on the stage to be real life. Stage managers have sometimes tried the experiment of reducing those differences, for instance, keeping the audience also in a fully lighted hall, and they always had to discover how much the dramatic effect was reduced because the feeling of distance from reality was weakened. The photoplay and the theater in this respect are evidently alike. The screen too suggests from the very start the complete unreality of the events.

But each further step leads us to remarkable differences between the stage play and the film play. In every respect the film play is further away from the physical reality than the drama and in every respect this greater distance from the physical world brings it nearer to the mental world. The stage shows us living men. It is not the real Romeo and not the real Juliet; and yet the actor and the actress have the ringing voices of true people, breathe like them, have living colors like them, and fill physical space like them. What is left in the photoplay? The voice has been stilled: the photoplay is a dumb show. Yet we must not forget that this alone is a step away from reality which has often been taken in the midst of the dramatic world. Whoever knows the history of the theater is aware of the tremendous rôle which the pantomime has played in the development of mankind. From the old half-religious pantomimic and suggestive dances out of which the beginnings of the real drama grew to the fully religious pantomimes of medieval ages and, further on, to many silent mimic elements in modern performances, we find a continuity of conventions which make the pantomime almost the real background of all dramatic development. We know how popular the pantomimes were among the Greeks, and how they stood in the foreground in the imperial period of Rome. Old

Rome cherished the mimic clowns, but still more the tragic panto-mimics. "Their very nod speaks, their hands talk and their fingers have a voice." After the fall of the Roman empire the church used the pantomime for the portrayal of sacred history, and later centuries enjoyed very unsacred histories in the pantomimes of their ballets. Even complex artistic tragedies without words have triumphed on our present-day stage. *L'Enfant Prodigue* which came from Paris, *Sumurun* which came from Berlin, *Petroushka* which came from Petrograd, conquered the American stage; and surely the loss of speech, while it increased the remoteness from reality, by no means destroyed the continuous consciousness of the bodily existence of the actors.

Moreover the student of a modern pantomime cannot overlook a characteristic difference between the speechless performance on the stage and that of the actors of a photoplay. The expression of the inner states, the whole system of gestures, is decidedly different: and here we might say that the photoplay stands nearer to life than the pantomime. Of course, the photoplayer must somewhat exaggerate the natural expression. The whole rhythm and intensity of his gestures must be more marked than it would be with actors who accompany their movements by spoken words and who express the meaning of their thoughts and feelings by the content of what they say. Nevertheless the photoplayer uses the regular channels of mental discharge. He acts simply as a very emotional person might act. But the actor who plays in a pantomime cannot be satisfied with that. He is expected to add something which is entirely unnatural, namely a kind of artificial demonstration of his emotions. He must not only behave like an angry man, but he must behave like a man who is consciously interested in his anger and wants to demonstrate it to others. He exhibits his emotions for the spectators. He really acts theatrically for the benefit of the by-standers. If he did not try to do so, his means of conveying a rich story and a real conflict of human passions would be too meager. The photoplayer, with the rapid changes of scenes, has other possibilities of conveying his intentions. He must not yield to the temptation to play a pantomime on the screen, or he will seriously injure the artistic quality of the reel.

The really decisive distance from bodily reality, however, is created by the substitution of the actor's picture for the actor himself. Lights and shades replace the manifoldness of color effects and mere perspective must furnish the suggestion of depth. We traced it when we discussed the psychology of kinematoscopic perception. But we must not put the emphasis on the wrong point. The natural tendency might be to lay the chief stress on the fact that those people in the photoplay do not stand before us in flesh and blood. The essential point is rather that we are conscious of the flatness of the picture. If we were to see the actors of the stage in a mirror, it would also be a reflected image which we perceive. We should not really have the actors themselves in our straight line of vision; and yet this image would appear to us equivalent to the actors themselves, because it would contain all the depth of the real stage. The process which leads from the living men to the screen is more complex than a mere reflection in a mirror, but in spite of the complexity in the transmission we do, after all, see the real actor in the picture. The photograph is absolutely different from those pictures which a clever draughtsman has sketched. In the photoplay we see the actors themselves and the decisive factor which makes the impression different from seeing real men is not that we see the living persons through the medium of photographic reproduction but that this reproduction shows them in a flat form. The bodily space has been eliminated. We said once before that stereoscopic arrangements could reproduce somewhat this plastic form also. Yet this would seriously interfere with the character of the photoplay. We need there this overcoming of the depth, we want to have it as a picture only and yet as a picture which strongly suggests to us the actual depth of the real world. We want to keep the interest in the plastic world and want to be aware of the depth in which the persons move, but our direct object of perception must be without the depth. That idea of space which forces on us most strongly the idea of heaviness, solidity and substantiality must be replaced by the light flitting immateriality.

But the photoplay sacrifices not only the space values of the real theater; it disregards no less its order of time. The theater presents its plot in the time order of reality. It may interrupt the continuous flow of time without neglecting the conditions of the dramatic art. There may be twenty years between the third and the fourth act, inasmuch as the dramatic writer must select those elements spread over space and time which are significant for the development of his story. But he is bound by the fundamental principle of real time, that it can move only forward and not backward. Whatever the theater shows us now must come later in the story than that which it showed us in any previous moment. The strict classical demand for complete unity of time does not fit every drama, but a drama would give up its mission if it told us in the third act something which happened before the second act. Of course, there may be a play within a play, and the players on the stage which is set on the stage may play events of old Roman history before the king of France. But this is an enclosure of the past in the present, which corresponds exactly to the actual order of events. The photoplay, on the other hand, does not and must not respect this temporal structure of the physical universe. At any point the photoplay interrupts the series and brings us back to the past. We studied this unique feature of the film art when we spoke of the psychology of memory and imagination. With the full freedom of our fancy, with the whole mobility of our association of ideas, pictures of the past flit through the scenes of the present. Time is left behind. Man becomes boy; today is interwoven with the day before yesterday. The freedom of the mind has triumphed over the unalterable law of the outer world.

It is interesting to watch how playwrights nowadays try to steal the thunder of the photoplay and experiment with time reversals on the legitimate stage. We are esthetically on the borderland when a grandfather tells his grandchild the story of his own youth as a warning, and instead of the spoken words the events of his early years come before our eyes. This is, after all, quite similar to a play within a play. A very different experiment is tried in *Under Cover*. The third act, which plays on the second floor of the house, ends with an explosion. The fourth act, which plays downstairs, begins a quarter of an hour before the explosion. Here we have a real denial of a fundamental condition of the theater. Or if we stick to recent products of the American stage, we may think of *On Trial*, a play which perhaps comes nearest to a dramatic usurpation of the rights of the photoplay. We see the court scene and as one witness after another begins to give his testimony the courtroom is replaced by the scenes of the actions about which the witness is to report. Another clever play, *Between the Lines*, ends the first act with a postman bringing three letters from the three children of the house.

The second, third, and fourth acts lead us to the three different homes from which the letters came and the action in the three places not only precedes the writing of the letters, but goes on at the same time. The last act, finally, begins with the arrival of the letters which tell the ending of those events in the three homes. Such experiments are very suggestive but they are not any longer pure dramatic art. It is always possible to mix arts. An Italian painter produces very striking effects by putting pieces of glass and stone and rope into his paintings, but they are no longer pure paintings. The drama in which the later event comes before the earlier is an esthetic barbarism which is entertaining as a clever trick in a graceful superficial play, but intolerable in ambitious dramatic art. It is not only tolerable but perfectly natural in any photoplay. The pictorial reflection of the world is not bound by the rigid mechanism of time. Our mind is here and there, our mind turns to the present and then to the past: the photoplay can equal it in its freedom from the bondage of the material world.

But the theater is bound not only by space and time. Whatever it shows is controlled by the same laws of causality which govern nature. This involves a complete continuity of the physical events: no cause without following effect, no effect without preceding cause. This whole natural course is left behind in the play on the screen. The deviation from reality begins with that resolution of the continuous movement which we studied in our psychological discussions. We saw that the impression of movement results from an activity of the mind which binds the separate pictures together. What we actually see is a composite; it is like the movement of a fountain in which every jet is resolved into numberless drops. We feel the play of those drops in their sparkling haste as one continuous stream of water, and yet are conscious of the myriads of drops, each one separate from the others. This fountainlike spray of pictures has completely overcome the causal world.

In an entirely different form this triumph over causality appears in the interruption of the events by pictures which belong to another series. We find this whenever the scene suddenly changes. The processes are not carried to their natural consequences. A movement is started, but before the cause brings its results another scene has taken its place. What this new scene brings may be an effect for which we saw no causes. But not only the processes are interrupted. The intertwining of the scenes which we have traced in detail is itself such a contrast to causality. It is as if different objects could fill the same space at the same time. It is as if the resistance of the material world had disappeared and the substances could penetrate one another. In the interlacing of our ideas we experience this superiority to all physical laws. The theater would not have even the technical means to give us such impressions, but if it had, it would have no right to make use of them, as it would destroy the basis on which the drama is built. We have only another case of the same type in those series of pictures which aim to force a suggestion on our mind. We have spoken of them. A certain effect is prepared by a chain of causes and yet when the causal result is to appear the film is cut off. We have the causes without the effect. The villain thrusts with his dagger—but a miracle has snatched away his victim.

While the moving pictures are lifted above the world of space and time and causality and are freed from its bounds, they are certainly not without law. We said before that the freedom with which the pictures replace one another is to a large degree comparable to the sparkling and streaming of the musical tones. The yielding to the play of the mental energies, to the attention and emotion, which is felt in the film pictures, is still more complete in the musical melodies and harmonies in which the tones themselves are merely the expressions of the ideas and feelings and will impulses of the mind. Their harmonies and disharmonies, their fusing and blending, is not controlled by any outer necessity, but by the inner agreement and disagreement of our free impulses. And yet in this world of musical freedom, everything is completely controlled by esthetic necessities. No sphere of practical life stands under such rigid rules as the realm of the composer. However bold the musical genius may be he cannot emancipate himself from the iron rule that his work must show complete unity in itself. All the separate prescriptions which the musical student has to learn are ultimately only the consequences of this central demand which music, the freest of the arts, shares with all the others. In the case of the film, too, the freedom from the physical forms of space, time, and causality does not mean any liberation from this esthetic bondage either. On the contrary, just as music is surrounded by more technical rules than literature, the photoplay must be held together by the esthetic demands still more firmly than is the drama. The arts which are subordinated to the conditions of space, time, and causality find a certain firmness of structure in these material forms which contain an element of outer connectedness. But where these forms are given up and where the freedom of mental play replaces their outer necessity, everything would fall asunder if the esthetic unity were disregarded.

This unity is, first of all, the unity of action. The demand for it is the same which we know from the drama. The temptation to neglect it is nowhere greater than in the photoplay where outside matter can so easily be introduced or independent interests developed. It is certainly true for the photoplay, as for every work of art, that nothing has the right to existence in its midst which is not internally needed for the unfolding of the unified action. Wherever two plots are given to us, we receive less by far than if we had only one plot. We leave the sphere of valuable art entirely when a unified action is ruined by mixing it with declamation, and propaganda which is not organically interwoven with the action itself. It may be still fresh in memory what an esthetically intolerable helter-skelter performance was offered to the public in *The Battlecry of Peace*. Nothing can be more injurious to the esthetic cultivation of the people than such performances which hold the attention of the spectators by ambitious detail and yet destroy their esthetic sensibility by a complete disregard of the fundamental principle of art, the demand for unity. But we recognized also that this unity involves complete isolation. We annihilate beauty when we link the artistic creation with practical interests and transform the spectator into a selfishly interested bystander. The scenic background of the play is not presented in order that we decide whether we want to spend our next vacation there. The interior decoration of the rooms is not exhibited as a display for a department store. The men and women who carry out the action of the plot must not be people whom we may meet tomorrow on the street. All the threads of the play must be knotted together in the play itself and none should be connected with our outside interests. A good photoplay must be isolated and complete in itself like a beautiful melody. It is not an advertisement for the newest fashions.

This unity of action involves unity of characters. It has too often been maintained by those who theorize on the photoplay that the development of character is the special task of the drama, while the photoplay, which lacks words, must be satisfied with types. Probably this is only a reflection of the crude state which most photoplays of today have not outgrown. Internally, there is no reason why the means of the photoplay should not allow a rather subtle depicting of complex character. But the chief demand is that the characters remain consistent, that the action be developed according to inner necessity and that the characters themselves be in harmony with the central idea of the plot. However, as soon as we insist on unity we have no right to think only of the action which gives the content of the play. We cannot make light of the form. As in music the melody and rhythms belong together, as in painting not every color combination suits every subject, and as in poetry not every stanza would agree with every idea, so the photoplay must bring action and pictorial expression into perfect harmony. But this demand repeats itself in every single picture. We take it for granted that the painter balances perfectly the forms in his painting, groups them so that an internal symmetry can be felt and that the lines and curves and colors blend into a unity. Every single picture of the sixteen thousand which are shown to us in one reel ought to be treated with this respect of the pictorial artist for the unity of the forms.

The photoplay shows us a significant conflict of human actions in moving pictures which, freed from the physical forms of space, time, and causality, are adjusted to the free play of our mental experiences and which reach complete isolation from the practical world through the perfect unity of plot and pictorial appearance.

1916

SUSAN SONTAG
FILM AND THEATRE

The big question is whether there is an unbridgeable division, even opposition, between the two arts. Is there something genuinely "cinematic"?

Almost all opinion holds that there is. A commonplace of discussion has it that film and theatre are distinct and even antithetical arts, each giving rise to its own standards of judgment and canons of form. Thus Erwin Panofsky argues, in his celebrated essay "Style and Medium in the Motion Pictures" (1934, rewritten in 1946), that one of the criteria for evaluating a movie is its freedom from the impurities of theatricality. To talk about film, one must first define "the basic nature of the medium." Those who think prescriptively about the nature of live drama, less confident in the future of their art than the *cinéphiles* in theirs, rarely take a comparably exclusivist line.

The history of cinema is often treated as the history of its emancipation from theatrical models. First of all from theatrical "frontality" (the unmoving camera reproducing the situation of the spectator of a play fixed in his seat), then from theatrical acting (gestures needlessly stylized, exaggerated—needlessly, because now the actor could be seen "close up"), then from theatrical furnishings (unnecessary "distancing" of the audience's emotions, disregarding the opportunity to immerse the audience in reality). Movies are regarded as advancing from theatrical stasis to cinematic fluidity, from theatrical artificiality to cinematic naturalness and immediacy. But this view is far too simple.

Such over-simplification testifies to the ambiguous scope of the camera eye. Because the camera *can* be used to project a relatively passive, unselective kind of vision—as well as the highly selective ("edited") vision generally associated with movies—cinema is a "medium" as well as an art, in the sense that it can encapsulate any of the performing arts and render it in a film transcription. (This "medium" or non-art aspect of film attained its routine incarnation with the advent of television. There, movies themselves became another performing art to be transcribed, miniaturized on film.) One *can* film a play or ballet or opera or sporting event in such a way that film becomes, relatively speaking, a transparency, and it seems correct to say that one is seeing the event filmed. But theatre is never a "medium." Thus, because one can make a movie "of" a play but not a play "of" a movie, cinema had an early but, I should argue, fortuitous connection with the stage. Some of the earliest films were filmed plays. Duse and Bernhardt and Barrymore are on film—marooned in time, absurd, touching; there is a 1913 British film of Forbes-Robertson playing Hamlet, a 1923 German film of *Othello* starring Emil Jannings. More recently, the camera has "preserved" Helene Weigel's performance of *Mother Courage* with the Berliner Ensemble, the Living Theatre production of *The Brig* (filmed by the Mekas brothers), and Peter Brook's staging of Weiss's *Marat/Sade*.

But from the beginning, even within the confines of the notion of film as a "medium" and the camera as a "recording" instrument, a great deal other than what occurred in theatres was taken down. As with still photography, some of the events captured on moving photographs were staged but others were valued precisely because they were *not* staged—the camera being the witness, the invisible spectator, the invulnerable voyeuristic eye. (Perhaps public happenings, "news," constitute an intermediate case between staged and unstaged events; but film as "newsreel" generally amounts to using film as a "medium.") To create on film a *document* of a transient reality is a conception quite unrelated to the purposes of theatre. It only appears related when the "real event" being recorded is a theatrical performance. And the first use of the motion picture camera was to make a documentary record of unstaged, casual reality: Louis Lumière's films of crowd-scenes in Paris and New York made in the 1890's antedate any use of film in the service of plays.

The other paradigmatic non-theatrical use of film, which dates from the earliest activity of the motion-picture camera, is for the creation of *illusion*, the construction of fantasy. The pioneer figure here is, of course, Georges Méliès. To be sure, Méliès (like many directors after him) conceived of the rectangle of the screen on analogy with the proscenium stage. And not only were the events staged; they were the very stuff of invention: imaginary journeys, imaginary objects, physical metamorphoses. But this, even adding the fact that Méliès situated his camera "in front of" the action and hardly moved it, does not make his films theatrical in an invidious sense. In their treatment of persons as things (physical objects) and in their disjunctive presentation of time and space, Méliès' films are quintessentially "cinematic"—so far as there is such a thing.

The contrast between theatre and films is usually taken to lie in the materials represented or depicted. But exactly where does the difference lie? It's tempting to draw a crude boundary. Theatre deploys artifice while cinema is committed to reality, indeed to an ultimately physical reality which is "redeemed," to use Siegfried Kracauer's striking word, by the camera. The aesthetic judgment that follows this bit of intellectual map-making is that films shot in real-life settings are better (*i.e.*, more cinematic) than those shot in a studio (where one can detect the difference). Obviously, if Flaherty and Italian neo-realism and the *cinema verité* of Vertov, Rouch, Marker, and Ruspoli are the preferred models, one would judge rather harshly the period of 100% studio-made films inaugurated around 1920 by *The Cabinet of Dr. Caligari*, films with ostentatiously artificial landscapes and decor, and deem the right direction to be that taken at the same period in Sweden, where many films with strenuous natural settings were being shot "on location." Thus, Panofsky attacks *Dr. Caligari* for "prestylizing reality," and urges upon cinema "the problem of manipulating and shooting unstylized reality in such a way that the result has style."

But there is no reason to insist on a single model for film. And it is helpful to notice that, for the most part, the apotheosis of realism, the prestige of "unstylized reality," in cinema is actually a covert political-moral position. Films have been rather too often acclaimed as the democratic art, the art of mass society. Once one takes this description very seriously, one tends (like Panofsky and Kracauer) to want movies to continue to reflect their origins in a vulgar level of the arts, to remain loyal to their vast uneducated audience. Thus, a vaguely Marxist orientation jibes with a fundamental tenet of romanticism. Cinema, at once high art and popular art, is cast as the art of the authentic. Theatre, by contrast, means dressing up, pretense, lies. It smacks of aristocratic taste and the class society. Behind the objection of critics to the stagy sets of *Dr. Caligari*, the improbable costumes and florid acting of Renoir's *Nana*, the talkiness of Dreyer's *Gertrud*, as "theatrical," lay the feeling that such films were false, that they exhibited a sensibility both pretentious and reactionary which was out-of-step with the democratic and more mundane sensibility of modern life.

Anyway, whether aesthetic defect or not in the particular case, the synthetic look in films is not necessarily a misplaced theatricalism. From the beginning of film history, there were painters and sculptors who claimed that cinema's true future resided in artifice, construction. It lay not in figurative narration or story-telling of any kind (either in a relatively realistic or in a "surrealistic" vein), but in abstraction. Thus, Theo van Doesburg in his essay of 1929, "Film as Pure Form," envisages film as the vehicle of "optical poetry," "dynamic light architecture," "the creation of a moving ornament." Films will realize "Bach's dream of finding an optical equivalent for the temporal structure of a musical composition." Today, a few film-makers—for example, Robert Breer—continue to pursue this conception of film, and who is to say it is not cinematic?

Could anything be farther from the scope of theatre than such a degree of abstraction? It's important not to answer that question too quickly.

Some locate the division between theatre and film as the difference between the play and the filmscript. Panofsky derives this difference from what he takes to be the most profound one: the difference between the *formal* conditions of seeing a play and those of seeing a movie. In the theatre, says Panofsky, "space is static, that is, the space represented on the stage, as well as the spatial relation of the beholder to the spectacle, is unalterably fixed," while in the cinema "the spectator occupies a fixed seat, but only physically, not as the subject of an aesthetic experience." In the cinema, the spectator is "aesthetically . . . in permanent motion as his eye identifies with the lens of the camera, which permanently shifts in distance and direction."

True enough. But the observation does not warrant a radical dissociation of theatre from film. Like many critics, Panofsky is assuming a "literary" conception of theatre. To a theatre which is conceived of basically as dramatized literature, texts, words, he contrasts cinema which is, according to the received phrase, primarily "a visual experience." In effect, we are being asked to acknowledge tacitly the period of silent films as definitive of cinematic art and to identify theatre with "plays," from Shakespeare to Tennessee Williams. But many of the most interesting movies today are not adequately described as images with sound added. And what if theatre is conceived of as more than, or something different from, plays?

Panofsky may be over-simplifying when he decries the theatrical taint in movies, but he is sound when he argues that, historically, theatre is only one of the arts that feeds into cinema. As he remarks, it is apt that films came to be known popularly as moving *pictures* rather than as "photoplays" or "screen plays." Movies derive less from the theatre, from a performance art, an art that already moves, than they do from works of art which were stationary. Bad nineteenth-century paintings and postcards, wax-works à la Madame Tussaud, and comic strips are the sources Panofsky cites. What is surprising is that he doesn't connect movies with earlier narrative uses of still photography—like the family photo-album. The narrative techniques developed by certain nineteenth-century novelists, as Eisenstein pointed out in his brilliant essay on Dickens, supplied still another prototype for cinema.

Movies are images (usually photographs) that move, to be sure. But the distinctive unit of films is not the image but the principle of connection between the images, the relation of a "shot" to the one that preceded it and the one that comes after. There is no peculiarly "cinematic" as opposed to "theatrical" mode of linking images.

Panofsky tries to hold the line against the infiltration of theatre by cinema, as well as vice versa. In the theatre, not only can the spectator not change his angle of vision but, unlike movies, "the settings of the stage cannot change during one act (except for such incidentals as rising moons or gathering clouds and such illegitimate reborrowings from film as turning wings or gliding backdrops)." Were we to assent to this, the ideal play would be *No Exit*, the ideal set a realistic living room or a blank stage.

No less dogmatic is the complementary dictum about what is illegitimate in films—according to which, since films are "a visual

363

experience," all components must be demonstrably subordinate to the image. Thus, Panofsky asserts: "Wherever a poetic emotion, a musical outburst, or a literary conceit (even, I am grieved to say, some of the wisecracks of Groucho Marx) entirely lose contact with visible movement, they strike the sensitive spectator as, literally, out of place." What, then, of the films of Bresson and Godard, with their allusive, densely thoughtful texts and their characteristic refusal to be visually beautiful? How could one explain the extraordinary rightness of Ozu's relatively immobilized camera?

The decline in average quality of films in the early sound period (compared with the level reached by films in the 1920's) is undeniable. Although it would be facile to call the sheer uninterestingness of most films of this period simply a regression to theatre, it is a fact that film-makers did turn more frequently to plays in the 1930's than they had in the preceding decade. Countless stage successes like *Outward Bound, Dinner at Eight, Blithe Spirit, Faisons un Rêve, Twentieth Century, Boudu Sauvé des Eaux, She Done Him Wrong, Anna Christie, Marius, Animal Crackers, The Petrified Forest*, were filmed. The success of movie versions of plays is measured by the extent to which the script rearranges and displaces the action and deals less than respectfully with the spoken text—as do certain films of plays by Wilde and Shaw, the Olivier Shakespeare films (at least *Henry V*), and Sjöberg's *Miss Julie*. But the basic disapproval of films which betray their origins in plays remains. A recent example: the outright hostility which greeted Dreyer's latest film, *Gertrud*. Not only does *Gertrud*, which I believe to be a minor masterpiece, follow a turn-of-the-century play that has characters conversing at length and quite formally, but it is filmed almost entirely in middle-shot.

Some of the films I have just mentioned are negligible as art; several are first-rate. (The same for the plays, though no correlation between the merits of the movies and those of the "original" plays can be established.) However, their virtues and faults cannot be sorted out as a cinematic versus a theatrical element. Whether derived from plays or not, films with complex or formal dialogue, films in which the camera is static or in which the action stays indoors, are not necessarily theatrical. *Per contra*, it is no more part of the putative "essence" of movies that the camera must rove over a large physical area, than it is that movies ought to be silent.

Though most of the action of Kurosawa's *The Lower Depths*, a fairly faithful transcription of Gorki's play, is confined to one large room, it is as cinematic as the same director's *Throne of Blood*, a very free and laconic adaptation of *Macbeth*. The quality of Melville's claustrophobic *Les Enfants Terribles* is as peculiar to the movies as Ford's *The Searchers* or a train journey in Cinerama.

What does make a film theatrical in an invidious sense is when the narration becomes coy or self-conscious: compare Autant-Lara's *Occupe-Toi d'Amélie*, a brilliant cinematic use of the conventions and materials of theatricality, with Ophuls' clumsy use of similar conventions and materials in *La Ronde*.

Allardyce Nicoll, in his book *Film and Theatre* (1936), argues that the difference may be understood as a difference in kinds of characters. "Practically all effectively drawn stage characters are types [while] in the cinema we demand individualization and impute greater power of independent life to the figures on the screen." (Panofsky, it might be mentioned, makes exactly the opposite point: that the nature of films, in contrast to plays, requires flat or stock characters.)

Nicoll's thesis is not as arbitrary as it may at first appear. I would relate it to the fact that often the indelible moments of a film, and the most potent elements of characterization, are precisely the "irrelevant" or unfunctional details. (A random example: the ping-pong ball the schoolmaster toys with in Ivory's *Shakespeare Wallah*.) Movies thrive on the narrative equivalent of a technique familiar from painting and photography, off-centering. It is this that creates the pleasing disunity of fragmentariness (what Nicoll means by "individualization"?) of the characters of many of the greatest films. In contrast, linear "coherence" of detail (the gun on the wall in the first act that must go off by the end of the third) is the rule in Occidental narrative theatre, and gives rise to the sense of the unity of the characters (a unity that may appear like the statement of a "type").

But even with these adjustments, Nicoll's thesis seems less than appealing when one perceives that it rests on the idea that "When we go to the theatre, we expect theatre and nothing else." What is this theatre-and-nothing-else? It is the old notion of artifice. (As if art were ever anything else. As if some arts were artificial but others not.) According to Nicoll, when we are in a theatre "in every way the 'falsity' of a theatrical production is borne in upon us, so that we are prepared to demand nothing save a theatrical truth." In the cinema, however, every member of the audience, no matter how sophisticated, is on essentially the same level; we all believe that the camera cannot lie. As the film actor and his role are identical, so the image cannot be dissociated from what is imaged. Cinema, therefore, gives us what is experienced as the truth of life.

Couldn't theatre dissolve the distinction between the truth of artifice and the truth of life? Isn't that just what the theatre as ritual seeks to do? Isn't that what is being sought when theatre is conceived as an *exchange* with an audience?—something that films can never be.

If an irreducible distinction between theatre and cinema does exist, it may be this. Theatre is confined to a logical or *continuous* use of space. Cinema (through editing, that is, through the change of shot—which is the basic unit of film construction) has access to an alogical or *discontinuous* use of space. In the theatre, people are either in the stage space or "off." When "on," they are always visible or visualizable in contiguity with each other. In the cinema, no such relation is necessarily visible or even visualizable. (Example: the ·last shot of Paradjanov's *In the Shadows of Our Ancestors*.) Some films considered objectionably theatrical are those which seem to emphasize spatial continuities, like Hitchcock's virtuoso *Rope* or the daringly anachronistic *Gertrud*. But closer analysis of both these films would show how complex their treatment of space is. The longer and longer "takes" toward which sound films have been moving are, in themselves, neither more nor less cinematic than the short "takes" characteristic of silents.

Thus, cinematic virtue does not reside in the fluidity of the positioning of the camera nor in the mere frequency of the change of shot. It consists in the arrangement of screen images and (now) of sounds. Méliès, for example, though he didn't get beyond the static positioning of his camera, had a very striking conception of how to link screen images. He grasped that editing offered an equivalent to the magician's sleight of hand—thereby suggesting that one of the features of film (as distinct from theatre) is that *anything* can happen, that there is nothing that can't be represented convincingly.

Through editing, Méliès presents discontinuities of physical substance and behavior. In his films, the discontinuities are, so to speak, practical, functional; they accomplish a transformation of ordinary reality. But the continuous *re*invention of space (as well as the option of temporal indeterminacy) peculiar to film narration does not pertain only to the cinema's ability to fabricate "visions," to show us a radically altered world. The most "realistic" use of the motion-picture camera also involves a discontinuous account of space.

Film narration has a "syntax," composed of the rhythm of associations and disjunctions. As Cocteau has written, "My primary concern in a film is to prevent the images from flowing, to oppose them to each other, to anchor them and join them without destroying their relief." (But does such a conception of film syntax entail, as Cocteau thinks, our disavowal of movies as "mere entertainment instead of a vehicle for thought"?)

In drawing a line of demarcation between theatre and films, the issue of the continuity of space seems to me more fundamental than the difference that might be pointed out between theatre as an organization of movement in three-dimensional space (like dance) versus cinema as an organization of plane space (like painting). The theatre's capacities for manipulating space and time are, simply, much cruder and more labored than film's. Theatre cannot equal the cinema's facilities for the strictly-controlled repetition of images, for the duplication or matching of word and image, and for the juxtaposition and over-lapping of images. (Through advanced lighting techniques, one can now "dissolve" on the stage. But as yet there is no equivalent, not even through the most adept use of scrim, of the "lap dissolve.")

Theatre has been described as a mediated art, presumably because it usually consists of a pre-existent play mediated by a particular performance which offers one of many possible interpretations of the play. Film, in contrast, is regarded as unmediated—because of its larger-than-life scale and more unrefusable impact on the eye, and because (in Panofsky's words) "the medium of the movies is physical reality as such" and the characters in a movie "have no aesthetic existence outside the actors." But there is an equally valid sense which shows movies to be the mediated art and theatre the unmediated one. We see what happens on the stage with our own

367

eyes. We see on the screen what the camera sees. In the cinema, narration proceeds by ellipsis (the "cut" or change of shot); the camera eye is a unified point of view that continually displaces itself. But the change of shot can provoke questions, the simplest of which is: from *whose* point of view is the shot seen? And the ambiguity of point of view latent in all cinematic narration has no equivalent in the theatre.

Indeed, one should not neglect to emphasize the aesthetically positive role of disorientation in the cinema. Examples: Busby Berkeley dollying back from an ordinary-looking stage already established as some thirty feet deep to disclose a stage area three hundred feet square. Resnais planning from character X's point of view a full 360°, to come to rest upon X's face.

Much may be made of the fact that, in its concrete existence, cinema is an *object* (a *product*, even) while theatre is a *performance*. Is this so important? In a way, no. Whether objects (like films or paintings) or performances (like music or theatre), all art is first a mental act, a fact of consciousness. The object aspect of film, the performance aspect of theatre are merely means—means to the experience, which is not only "of" but "through" the film and the theatre-event. Each subject of an aesthetic experience shapes it to his own measure. With respect to any *single* experience, it hardly matters that a film is usually identical from one projection of it to another while theatre performances are highly mutable.

The difference between object-art and performance-art lies behind Panofsky's observation that "the screenplay, in contrast to the theatre play, has no aesthetic existence independent of its performance," and characters in movies *are* the stars who enact them. It is because the film is an object, a totality that is set, that movie roles are identical with the actors' performances; while in the theatre (in the West, an additive rather than an organic art?) only the written play is "fixed," an object and therefore existing apart from any staging of it. Yet this dichotomy is not beyond dispute. Just as movies needn't necessarily be designed to be shown in theatres at all (they can be intended for more continuous and casual looking), a movie *may* be altered from one projection to the next. Harry Smith, when he runs off his own films, makes each projection an unrepeatable performance. And, again, it is not true that all theatre is only about written plays which may be given a good or a bad production. In Happenings and other recent theatre-events, we are precisely being offered "plays" identical with their productions in the same sense as the screenplay is identical with the film.

Yet, a difference remains. Because the film is an object, it is totally manipulable, totally calculable. A film is like a book, another portable art-object; making a film, like writing a book, means constructing an inanimate thing, every element of which is determinate. Indeed, in films, this determinacy has or can have a quasi-mathematical form, like music. (A shot lasts a certain number of seconds, a change of angle of so many degrees is required to "match" two shots.) Given the total determinacy of the result on celluloid (whatever the extent of the director's conscious intervention), it was inevitable that some film directors would want to devise schemas to make their intentions more exact. Thus, it was neither perverse nor primitive of Busby Berkeley to have used only one camera to shoot the whole of each of his mammoth dance numbers. Every "set-up" was designed to be shot from only one exactly calculated angle. Bresson, working on a far more self-conscious level of artistry, has declared that, for him, the director's task is to find the single correct way of doing each shot. An image cannot be justified in itself, according to Bresson; it has an exactly specifiable relation to the temporally adjacent images, which relation constitutes its "meaning."

But the theatre allows only the loosest approximation to this sort of formal concern. (And responsibility. Justly, French critics speak of the director of a film as its "author.") Because they are performances, something always "live," theatre-events are not subject to a comparable degree of control, do not admit a comparably exact integration of effects.

It would be foolish to conclude that the best films are those which arise from the greatest amount of conscious planning; the plan may be faulty; and with some directors, instinct works better than any plan. Besides, there is an impressive body of "improvised" cinema. (To be distinguished from the work of some film-makers, notably Godard, who have become fascinated with the "look" of improvised cinema.) Nevertheless, it seems indisputable that cinema, not only potentially but by its nature, is a more rigorous art than theatre.

Thus, not merely a failure of nerve accounts for the fact that theatre, this seasoned art, occupied since antiquity with all sorts of local offices—enacting sacred rites, reinforcing communal loyalty, guiding morals, provoking the therapeutic discharge of violent emotions, conferring social status, giving practical instruction, affording entertainment, dignifying celebrations, subverting established authority—is now on the defensive before movies, this brash art with its huge, amorphous, passive audience. Meanwhile, movies continue to maintain their astonishing pace of formal articulation. (Take the commercial cinema of Europe, Japan, and the United States simply since 1960, and consider what audiences have become habituated to in the way of increasingly elliptical story-telling and visualization.)

But note: this youngest of the arts is also the one most heavily burdened with memory. Cinema is a time machine. Movies preserve the past, while theatres—no matter how devoted to the classics, to old plays—can only "modernize." Movies resurrect the beautiful dead; present intact vanished or ruined environments; employ, without irony, styles and fashions that seem funny today; solemnly ponder irrelevant or naïve problems. The historical flavor of anything registered on celluloid is so vivid that practically all films older than two years or so are saturated with a kind of pathos. (The pathos I am describing, which overtakes animated cartoons and drawn, abstract films as well as ordinary movies, is not simply that of old photographs.) Films age (being objects) as no theatre-event does (being always new). There is no pathos of mortality in theatre's "reality" as such, nothing in our response to a good performance of a Mayakovsky play comparable to the aesthetic role the emotion of nostalgia has when we see a film by Pudovkin.

Also worth noting: compared with the theatre, innovations in cinema seem to be assimilated more efficiently, seem altogether to be more shareable—and not only because new films are quickly and widely circulated. Also, partly because virtually the entire body of accomplishment in film can be consulted in the present, most film-makers are more knowledgeable about the history of their art than most theatre directors are about the recent past of theirs.

The key word in many discussions of cinema is "possibility." A merely classifying use of the word occurs, as in Panofsky's engaging judgment that, "within their self-imposed limitations the earlier Disney films . . . represent, as it were, a chemically pure distillation of cinematic possibilities." But behind this relatively neutral sense lurks a more polemical sense of cinema's "possibility." What is regularly intimated is the obsolescence of theatre, its supercession by films.

Thus, Panofsky describes the mediation of the camera eye as opening "up a world of possibility of which the stage can never dream." Artaud, earlier, thought that motion pictures may have made the theatre obsolete. Movies "possess a sort of virtual power which probes into the mind and uncovers undreamt of possibilities. . . . When this art's exhilaration has been blended in the right proportions with the psychic ingredient it commands, it will leave the theatre far behind and we will relegate the latter to the attic of our memories."

Meyerhold, facing the challenge head on, thought the only hope for theatre lay in a wholesale emulation of the cinema. "Let us 'cinematify' the theatre," he urged. The staging of plays must be "industrialized," theatres must accommodate audiences in the tens of thousands rather than in the hundreds, etc. Meyerhold also seemed to find some relief in the idea that the coming of sound signalled the downfall of movies. Believing that their international appeal depended entirely on the fact that screen actors didn't speak any particular language, he couldn't imagine in 1930 that, even if that were so, technology (dubbing, sub-titling) could solve the problem.

Is cinema the successor, the rival, or the revivifier of the theatre?

Art forms *have* been abandoned. (Whether because they became obsolete is another question.) One can't be sure that theatre is not in a state of irremediable decline, spurts of local vitality notwithstanding. But why should it be rendered obsolete by movies? It's worth remembering that predictions of obsolescence amount to declaring that a something has one peculiar task (which another something may do as well or better). Has theatre one peculiar task or aptitude?

Those who predict the demise of the theatre, assuming that cinema has engulfed its function, tend to impute a relation between films and theatre reminiscent of what was once said about photography and painting. If the painter's job had been no more than fabricating likenesses, the invention of the camera might indeed have made painting obsolete. But painting is hardly just "pictures," any more than cinema is just theatre for the masses, available in portable standard units.

In the naïve tale of photography and painting, painting was reprieved when it claimed a new task, abstraction. As the superior realism of photography was supposed to have liberated painting, allowing it to go abstract, cinema's superior power to represent (not merely to stimulate) the imagination may appear to have emboldened the theatre in a similar fashion, inviting the gradual obliteration of the conventional "plot."

Actually, painting and photography evidence parallel developments rather than a rivalry or a supercession. And, at least in principle, so have theatre and film. The possibilities for theatre that lie in going beyond psychological realism, in seeking greater abstractness, are not less germane to the future of narrative films. Conversely, the notion of movies as witness to real life, testimony rather than invention, the treatment of collective situations rather than the depiction of personal "dramas," is equally relevant to the stage. Not surprisingly, what follows some years after the rise of *cinema verité*, the sophisticated heir of documentary films, is a documentary theatre, the "theatre of fact." (Cf. Hochhuth, Weiss's *The Investigation*, recent projects of the Royal Shakespeare Company in London.)

The influence of the theatre upon films in the early years is well known. According to Kracauer, the distinctive lighting of *Dr. Caligari* (and of many subsequent German silents) can be traced to an experiment with lighting Max Reinhardt made shortly before, in his production of Sorge's play, *The Beggar*. Even in this period, however, the impact was reciprocal. The accomplishments of the "Expressionist film" were immediately absorbed by the Expressionist theatre. Stimulated by the cinematic technique of the "iris-in," stage lighting took to singling out a lone player, or some segment of the scene, masking out the rest of the stage. Rotating sets tried to approximate the instantaneous displacement of the camera eye. (More recently, reports have come of ingenious lighting techniques used by the Gorki Theatre in Leningrad, directed since 1956 by Georgi Tovstonogov, which allow for incredibly rapid scene changes taking place behind a horizontal curtain of light.)

Today traffic seems, with few exceptions, entirely one way: film to theatre. Particularly in France and in Central and Eastern Europe, the staging of many plays is inspired by the movies. The aim of adapting neo-cinematic devices for the stage (I exclude the outright use of films within the theatre production) seems mainly to tighten up the theatrical experience, to approximate the cinema's absolute control of the flow and location of the audience's attention. But the conception can be even more directly cinematic. Example: Josef Svoboda's production of *The Insect Play* by the Capek brothers at the Czech National Theatre in Prague (recently seen in London) which frankly attempted to install a mediated vision upon the stage, equivalent to the discontinuous intensifications of the camera eye. According to a London critic's account, "the set consisted of two huge, faceted mirrors slung at an angle to the stage, so that they reflect whatever happens there defracted as if through a decanter stopper or the colossally magnified eye of a fly. Any figure placed at the base of their angle becomes multiplied from floor to proscenium; farther out, and you find yourself viewing it not only face to face but from overhead, the vantage point of a camera slung to a bird or a helicopter."

Perhaps the first to propose the use of film itself as *one* element in a theatre experience was Marinetti. Writing between 1910 and 1914, he envisaged the theatre as a final synthesis of all the arts; and as such it had to use the newest art form movies. No doubt the cinema also recommended itself for inclusion because of the priority Marinetti gave to the use of existing forms of popular entertainment, such as the variety theatre and the *café-chantant*. (He called his projected art form "the Futurist Variety Theatre.") And cinema, at that time, was not considered as anything other than a vulgar art.

Soon after, the idea begins to occur frequently. In the total-theatre projects of the Bauhaus group in the 1920's (Gropius, Piscator, etc.), film had a regular place. Meyerhold insisted on its use in the theatre. (He described his program as fulfilling Wagner's once "wholly utopian" proposals to "use all means available from

373

the other arts.") Film's actual employment has by now a fairly long history, which includes "the living newspaper," "epic theatre," and "happenings." This year marked the introduction of a film sequence into Broadway-type theatre. In two highly successful musicals, London's *Come Spy with Me* and New York's *Superman*, both parodic in tone, the action is interrupted to lower a screen and run off a movie showing the pop-art hero's exploits.

Thus far, the use of film within live theatre-events has tended to be stereotyped. Film is employed as *document*, supportive of or redundant to the live stage events (as in Brecht's productions in East Berlin). Or else it is employed as *hallucinant*; recent examples are Bob Whitman's Happenings, and a new kind of nightclub situation, the mixed-media discothèque (Andy Warhol's The Plastic Inevitable, Murray the K's World). The interpolation of film into the theatre-experience may be enlarging from the point of view of theatre. But in terms of what film is capable of, it seems a reductive, monotonous use of film.

Every interesting aesthetic tendency now is a species of radicalism. The question each artist must ask is: What is *my* radicalism, the one dictated by *my* gifts and temperament? This doesn't mean all contemporary artists believe that art progresses. A radical position isn't necessarily a forward-looking position.

Consider the two principal radical positions in the arts today. One recommends the breaking down of distinctions between genres: the arts would eventuate in one art, consisting of many different kinds of behavior going on at the same time, a vast behavioral magma or synaesthesis. The other position recommends the maintaining and clarifying of barriers between the arts, by the intensification of what each art distinctively is; painting must use only those means which pertain to painting, music only those which are musical, novels those which pertain to the novel and to no other literary form, etc.

The two positions are, in a sense, irreconcilable. Except that both are invoked to support a perennial modern quest—the quest for the definitive art form. An art may be proposed as definitive because it is considered the most rigorous, or most fundamental. For these reasons, Schopenhauer suggested and Pater asserted that all art aspires to the condition of music. More recently, the thesis that all the arts are leading toward one art has been advanced by enthusiasts of the cinema. The candidacy of film is founded on its being so exact and, potentially, so complex—a rigorous combination of music, literature, and the image.

Or, an art may be proposed as definitive because it is the most inclusive. This is the basis of the destiny for theatre held out by Wagner, Marinetti, Artaud, John Cage—all of whom envisage theatre as nothing less than a total art, potentially conscripting all the arts into its service. And as the ideas of synaesthesia continue to proliferate among painters, sculptors, architects, and composers, theatre remains the favored candidate for the role of summative art. So conceived, of course, theatre's claims do contradict those of cinema. Partisans of theatre would argue that while music, painting, dance, cinema, the speaking of words, etc. can all converge on a "stage," the film-object can only become bigger (multiple screens, 360° projection, etc.) or longer in duration or more internally articulated and complex. Theatre can be anything, everything; in the end, films can only be more of what they specifically (that is to say, cinematically) are.

Underlying the competing apocalyptic expectations for both arts, one detects a common animus. In 1923 Béla Balázs, anticipating in great detail the thesis of Marshall McLuhan, described movies as the herald of a new "visual culture" that will give us back our bodies, and particularly our faces, which have been rendered illegible, soulless, unexpressive by the centuries-old ascendancy of "print." An animus against literature, against "the printing press" and its "culture of concepts," also informs most of the interesting thinking about the theatre in our time.

What's important is that no definition or characterization of theatre and cinema, even the most self-evident, be taken for granted.

For instance: both cinema and theatre are temporal arts. Like music (and unlike painting), everything is *not* present all at once.

Could this be modified? The allure of mixed-media forms in theatre suggests not only a more elongated and more complex "drama" (like Wagnerian opera) but also a more compact theatre-experience which approaches the condition of painting. This prospect of increased compactness is broached by Marinetti; he calls it simultaneity, a leading idea of Futurist aesthetics. In becoming a final synthesis of all the arts, says Marinetti, theatre "would use the new twentieth-century devices of electricity and the cinema; this would enable plays to be extremely short, since all these technical means would enable the theatrical synthesis to be achieved in the shortest possible space of time, as all the elements could be presented simultaneously."

A pervasive notion in both advanced cinema and theatre is the idea of art as an act of violence. Its source is to be found in the aesthetics of Futurism and of Surrealism; its principal "texts" are, for theatre, the writings of Artaud and, for cinema, the two classic films of Luis Buñuel, *L'Age d'Or* and *Un Chien Andalou*. (More recent examples: the early plays of Ionesco, at least as conceived; the "cinema of cruelty" of Hitchcock, Clouzot, Franju, Robert Aldrich, Polanski; work by the Living Theatre; some of the neocinematic lighting techniques used in experimental theatres; the sound of late Cage and LaMonte Young.) The relation of art to an audience understood to be passive, inert, surfeited, can only be assault. Art becomes identical with aggression.

This theory of art as assault on the audience—like the complementary notion of art as ritual—is understandable, and precious. Still, one must not neglect to question it, particularly in the theatre. For it can become as much a convention as anything else; and end, like all theatrical conventions, by reinforcing the deadness of the audience. (As Wagner's ideology of a total theatre played its role in confirming the stupidity and bestiality of German culture.)

Moreover, the depth of the assault must be assessed honestly. In the theatre, this entails not "diluting" Artaud. Artaud's writings represent the demand for a totally open (therefore, flayed, self-cruel) consciousness of which theatre would be *one* adjunct or instrument. No work in the theatre has yet amounted to this. Thus, Peter Brook has astutely and forthrightly disclaimed that his company's work in London in the "Theatre of Cruelty," which culminated in his celebrated production of Weiss's *Marat/Sade*, is genuinely Artaudian. It is Artaudian, he says, in a trivial sense only. (Trivial from Artaud's point of view, not from ours.)

376

For some time, all useful ideas in art have been extremely sophisticated. Like the idea that everything is what it is, and not another thing. A painting is a painting. Sculpture is sculpture. A poem is a poem, not prose. Etcetera. And the complementary idea: a painting can be "literary" or sculptural, a poem can be prose, theatre can emulate and incorporate cinema, cinema can be theatrical.

We need a new idea. It will probably be a very simple one. Will we be able to recognize it?

1966

ANDRÉ BAZIN
FROM WHAT IS CINEMA?

THEATRE AND CINEMA

The leitmotiv of those who despise filmed theater, their final and apparently insuperable argument, continues to be the unparalleled pleasure that accompanies the presence of the actor. "What is specific to theater," writes Henri Gouhier, in *The Essence of Theater*, "is the impossibility of separating off action and actor." Elsewhere he says "the stage welcomes every illusion except that of presence; the actor is there in disguise, with the soul and voice of another, but he is nevertheless there and by the same token space calls out for him and for the solidity of his presence. On the other hand and inversely, the cinema accommodates every form of reality save one —the physical presence of the actor." If it is here that the essence of theater lies then undoubtedly the cinema can in no way pretend to any parallel with it. If the writing, the style, and the dramatic structure are, as they should be, rigorously conceived as the receptacle for the soul and being of the flesh-and-blood actor, any attempt to substitute the shadow and reflection of a man on the screen for the man himself is a completely vain enterprise. There is no answer to this argument. The successes of Laurence Olivier, of Welles, or of Cocteau can only be challenged—here you need to be in bad faith—or considered inexplicable. They are a challenge both to critics and philosophers. Alternatively one can only explain them by casting doubts on that commonplace of theatrical criticism "the irreplacable presence of the actor."

THE CONCEPT OF PRESENCE

At this point certain comments seem called for concerning the concept of "presence," since it would appear that it is this concept,

378

as understood prior to the appearance of photography, that the cinema challenges.

Can the photographic image, especially the cinematographic image, be likened to other images and in common with them be regarded as having an existence distinct from the object? Presence, naturally, is defined in terms of time and space. "To be in the presence of someone" is to recognize him as existing contemporaneously with us and to note that he comes within the actual range of our senses—in the case of cinema of our sight and in radio of our hearing. Before the arrival of photography and later of cinema, the plastic arts (especially portraiture) were the only intermediaries between actual physical presence and absence. Their justification was their resemblance which stirs the imagination and helps the memory. But photography is something else again. In no sense is it the image of an object or person, more correctly it is its tracing. Its automatic genesis distinguishes it radically from the other techniques of reproduction. The photograph proceeds by means of the lens to the taking of a veritable luminous impression in light—to a mold. As such it carries with it more than mere resemblance, namely a kind of identity—the card we call by that name being only conceivable in an age of photography. But photography is a feeble technique in the sense that its instantaneity compels it to capture time only piecemeal. The cinema does something strangely paradoxical. It makes a molding of the object as it exists in time and, furthermore, makes an imprint of the duration of the object.

The nineteenth century with its objective techniques of visual and sound reproduction gave birth to a new category of images, the relation of which to the reality from which they proceed requires very strict definition. Even apart from the fact that the resulting aesthetic problems cannot be satisfactorily raised without this introductory philosophical inquiry, it would not be sound to treat the old aesthetic questions as if the categories with which they deal had in no way been modified by the appearance of completely new phenomena. Common sense—perhaps the best philosophical guide in this case—has clearly understood this and has invented an expression for the presence of an actor, by adding to the placards announcing his appearance the phrase "in flesh and blood." This means that for the man in the street the word "presence," today, can be ambiguous, and thus an apparent redundancy is not out of place in this age of cinema. Hence it is no longer as certain as it was that there is no middle stage between presence and absence. It is likewise at the ontological level that the effectiveness of the cinema has its source. It is false to say that the screen is incapable of putting us "in the presence of" the actor. It does so in the same way as a mirror—one must agree that the mirror relays the presence of the person reflected in it—but it is a mirror with a delayed reflection, the tin foil of which retains the image.* It is true that in the theater Molière can die on the stage and that we have the privilege of living in the biographical time of the actor. In the film about Manolete however we are present at the actual death of the famous matador and while our emotion may not be as deep as if we were actually present in the arena at that historic moment, its nature is the same. What we lose by way of direct witness do we not recapture thanks to the artificial proximity provided by photographic enlargement? Everything takes place as if in the time-space perimeter which is the definition of presence. The cinema offers us effectively only a measure of duration, reduced but not to zero, while the increase in the space factor reestablishes the equilibrium of the psychological equation.

OPPOSITION AND IDENTIFICATION

An honest appraisal of the respective pleasures derived from theater and cinema, at least as to what is less intellectual and more direct about them, forces us to admit that the delight we experience

---

*Television naturally adds a new variant to the "pseudopresences" resulting from the scientific techniques for reproduction created by photography. On the little screen during live television the actor is actually present in space and time. But the reciprocal actor-spectator relationship is incomplete in one direction. The spectator sees without being seen. There is no return flow. Televised theater, therefore, seems to share something both of theater and of cinema: of theater because the actor is present to the viewer, of cinema because the spectator is not present to the actor. Nevertheless, this state of not being present is not truly an absence. The television actor has a sense of the millions of ears and eyes virtually present and represented by the electronic camera. This abstract presence is most noticeable when the actor fluffs his lines. Painful enough in the theater, it is intolerable on television since the spectator who can do nothing to help him is aware of the unnatural solitude of the actor. In the theater in similar circumstances a sort of understanding exists with the audience, which is a help to an actor in trouble. This kind of reciprocal relationship is impossible on television.

at the end of a play has a more uplifting, a nobler, one might perhaps say a more moral, effect than the satisfaction which follows a good film. We seem to come away with a better conscience. In a certain sense it is as if for the man in the audience all theater is "Corneillian." From this point of view one could say that in the best films something is missing. It is as if a certain inevitable lowering of the voltage, some mysterious aesthetic short circuit, deprived us in the cinema of a certain tension which is a definite part of theater. No matter how slight this difference it undoubtedly exists, even between the worst charity production in the theater and the most brilliant of Olivier's film adaptations. There is nothing banal about this observation and the survival of the theater after fifty years of cinema, and the prophecies of Marcel Pagnol, is practical proof enough. At the source of the disenchantment which follows the film one could doubtless detect a process of depersonalization of the spectator. As Rosenkrantz wrote in 1937, in *Esprit*, in an article profoundly original for its period, "The characters on the screen are quite naturally objects of identification, while those on the stage are, rather, objects of mental opposition because their real presence gives them an objective reality and to transpose them into beings in an imaginary world the will of the spectator has to intervene actively, that is to say, to will to transform their physical reality into an abstraction. This abstraction being the result of a process of the intelligence that we can only ask of a person who is fully conscious." A member of a film audience tends to identify himself with the film's hero by a psychological process, the result of which is to turn the audience into a "mass" and to render emotion uniform. Just as in algebra if two numbers equal a third, then they are equal to one another, so here we can say, if two individuals identify themselves with a third, they identify themselves with one another. Let us compare chorus girls on the stage and on the screen. On the screen they satisfy an unconscious sexual desire and when the hero joins them he satisfies the desire of the spectator in the proportion to which the latter has identified himself with the hero. On the stage the girls excite the onlooker as they would in real life. The result is that there is no identification with the hero. He becomes instead an object of jealousy and envy. In other words, Tarzan is only possible on the screen. The cinema calms the spectator, the theater excites him. Even when it appeals to the lowest

381

instincts, the theater up to a certain point stands in the way of the creation of a mass mentality.* It stands in the way of any collective representation in the psychological sense, since theater calls for an active individual consciousness while the film requires only a passive adhesion.

These views shed a new light on the problem of the actor. They transfer him from the ontological to the psychological level. It is to the extent to which the cinema encourages identification with the hero that it conflicts with the theater. Put this way the problem is no longer basically insoluble, for it is a fact that the cinema has at its disposal means which favor a passive position or on the other hand, means which to a greater or lesser degree stimulate the consciousness of the spectator. Inversely the theater can find ways of lessening the psychological tension between spectator and actor. Thus theater and cinema will no longer be separated off by an unbridgeable aesthetic moat, they would simply tend to give rise to two attitudes of mind over which the director maintains a wide control.

Examined at close quarters, the pleasure derived from the theater not only differs from that of the cinema but also from that of the novel. The reader of a novel, physically alone like the man in the dark movie house, identifies himself with the character. That is why after reading for a long while he also feels the same intoxication of an illusory intimacy with the hero. Incontestably, there is in the pleasure derived from cinema and novel a self-satisfaction, a concession to solitude, a sort of betrayal of action by a refusal of social responsibility.

The analysis of this phenomenon might indeed be undertaken from a psychoanalytic point of view. Is it not significant that the psychiatrists took the term catharsis from Aristotle? Modern pedagogic research on psychodrama seems to have provided fruitful insights into the cathartic process of theater. The ambiguity existing in the child's mind between play and reality is used to get him to free himself by way of improvised theater from the repressions from which he suffers. This technique amounts to creating a kind of vague theater in which the play is of a serious nature and the

*Crowd and solitude are not antinomies: the audience in a movie house is made up of solitary individuals. Crowd should be taken here to mean the opposite of an organic community freely assembled.

actor is his own audience. The action that develops on these occasions is not one that is divided off by footlights, which are undoubtedly the architectural symbol of the censor that separates us from the stage. We delegate Oedipus to act in our guise and place him on the other side of a wall of fire—that fiery frontier between fantasy and reality which gives rein to Dionysiac monsters while protecting us from them. These sacred beasts will not cross this barrier of light beyond which they seem out of place and even sacrilegious—witness the disturbing atmosphere of awe which surrounds an actor still made up, like a phosphorescent light, when we visit him in his dressing room. There is no point to the argument that the theater did not always have footlights. These are only a symbol and there were others before them from the cothurnus and mask onwards. In the seventeenth century the fact that young nobles sat up on the stage is no denial of the role of the footlights, on the contrary, it confirms it, by way of a privileged violation so to speak, just as when today Orson Welles scatters actors around the auditorium to fire on the audience with revolvers. He does not do away with the footlights, he just crosses them. The rules of the game are also made to be broken. One expects some players to cheat.* With regard to the objection based on presence and on that alone, the theater and the cinema are not basically in conflict. What is really in dispute are two psychological modalities of a performance. The theater is indeed based on the reciprocal awareness of the presence of audience and actor, but only as related to a performance. The theater acts on us by virtue of our participation in a theatrical action across the footlights and as it were under the protection of their censorship. The opposite is true in the cinema.

---

*Here is a final example proving that presence does not constitute theater except in so far as it is a matter of a performance. Everyone either at his own or someone else's expense has known the embarrassment of being watched without knowing it or in spite of knowing it. Lovers who kiss on public benches offer a spectacle to the passerby, but they do not care. My concierge who has a feeling for the *mot juste* says, when she sees them, that it is like being at the movies. Each of us has sometimes found himself forced to his annoyance to do something absurd before other people. On those occasions we experience a sense of angry shame which is the very opposite of theatrical exhibitionism. Someone who looks through a keyhole is not at the theater; Cocteau has rightly demonstrated in *Le sang d'un poète* that he was already at the cinema. And nevertheless there are such things as "shows," when the protagonists are present to us in flesh and blood but one of the two parties is ignorant of the fact or goes through with it reluctantly. This is not "play" in the theatrical sense.

Alone, hidden in a dark room, we watch through half-open blinds a spectacle that is unaware of our existence and which is part of the universe. There is nothing to prevent us from identifying ourselves in imagination with the moving world before us, which becomes *the* world. It is no longer on the phenomenon of the actor as a person physically present that we should concentrate our analysis, but rather on the ensemble of conditions that constitute the theatrical play and deprive the spectator of active participation. We shall see that it is much less a question of actor and presence than of man and his relation to the decor.

BEHIND THE DECOR

The human being is all-important in the theater. The drama on the screen can exist without actors. A banging door, a leaf in the wind, waves beating on the shore can heighten the dramatic effect. Some film masterpieces use man only as an accessory, like an extra, or in counterpoint to nature which is the true leading character. Even when, as in *Nanook* and *Man of Aran*, the subject is man's struggle with nature, it cannot be compared to a theatrical action. The mainspring of the action is not in man but nature. As Jean-Paul Sartre, I think it was, said, in the theater the drama proceeds from the actor, in the cinema it goes from the decor to man. This reversal of the dramatic flow is of decisive importance. It is bound up with the very essence of the *mise-en-scène*. One must see here one of the consequences of photographic realism. Obviously, if the cinema makes use of nature it is because it is able to. The camera puts at the disposal of the director all the resources of the telescope and the microscope. The last strand of a rope about to snap or an entire army making an assault on a hill are within our reach. Dramatic causes and effects have no longer any material limits to the eye of the camera. Drama is freed by the camera from all contingencies of time and space. But this freeing of tangible dramatic powers is still only a secondary aesthetic cause, and does not basically explain the reversal of value between the actor and the decor. For sometimes it actually happens that the cinema deliberately deprives itself of the use of setting and of exterior nature—we have already seen a perfect instance of this in *Les Parents terribles*—while the theater in contrast uses a complex machinery to give a feeling of ubiquity to

Theater in Cinema. Jean Marais, Yvonne de Bray, Gabrielle Dorziat, Marcel André, and Josette Day in *Les Parents Terribles* (1948). It "deliberately deprives itself of the use of setting and of exterior nature" (BAZIN, page 384). Anna Magnani onstage in the *commedia dell'arte* of *The Golden Coach* (1952). Renoir incorporates the artifice of the theater into the cinema without destroying "that realism of space without which moving pictures do not constitute cinema" (BAZIN, page 393).

the audience. Is *La Passion de Jeanne d'Arc* by Carl Dreyer, shot entirely in close-up, in the virtually invisible and in fact theatrical settings by Jean Hugo, less cinematic than *Stagecoach?* It seems to me that quantity has nothing to do with it, nor the resemblance to certain theater techniques. The ideas of an art director for a room in *Les Dames aux camélias* would not noticeably differ whether for a film or a play. It's true that on the screen you would doubtless have some close-ups of the blood-stained handkerchief, but a skillful stage production would also know how to make some play with the cough and the handkerchief. All the close-ups in *Les Parents terribles* are taken directly from the theater where ;our attention would spontaneously isolate them. If film direction only differed from theater direction because it allows us a closer view of the scenery and makes a more reasonable use of it, there would really be no reason to continue with the theater and Pagnol would be a true prophet. For it is obvious that the few square yards of the decor of Vilar's *La Danse de la mort* contributed as much to the drama as the island on which Marcel Cravene shot his excellent film. The fact is that the problem lies not in the decor itself but in its nature and function. We must therefore throw some light on an essentially theatrical notion, that of the dramatic place.

There can be no theater without architecture, whether it be the cathedral square, the arena of Nîmes, the palace of the Popes, the trestle stage on a fairground, the semicircle of the theater of Vicenza that looks as if it were decorated by Bérard in a delirium, or the rococo amphitheaters of the boulevard houses. Whether as a performance or a celebration, theater of its very essence must not be confused with nature under penalty of being absorbed by her and ceasing to be. Founded on the reciprocal awareness of those taking part and present to one another, it must be in contrast to the rest of the world in the same way that play and reality are opposed, or concern and indifference, or liturgy and the common use of things. Costume, mask, or make-up, the style of the language, the footlights, all contribute to this distinction, but the clearest sign of all is the stage, the architecture of which has varied from time to time without ever ceasing to mark out a privileged spot actually or virtually distinct from nature. It is precisely in virtue of this *locus dramaticus* that decor exists. It serves in greater or less degree to set the place apart, to specify. Whatever it is, the decor constitutes the walls of this three-sided box opening onto the auditorium, which we call the stage. These false perspectives, these façades, these arbors, have another side which is cloth and nails and wood. Everyone knows that when the actor "retires to his apartment" from the yard or from the garden, he is actually going to his dressing room to take off his make-up. These few square feet of light and illusion are surrounded by machinery and flanked by wings, the hidden labyrinths of which do not interfere one bit with the pleasure of the spectator who is playing the game of theater. Because it is only part of the architecture of the stage, the decor of the theater is thus an area materially enclosed, limited, circumscribed, the only discoveries of which are those of our collusive imagination.

Its appearances are turned inward facing the public and the footlights. It exists by virtue of its reverse side and of anything beyond, as the painting exists by virtue of its frame. Just as the picture is not to be confounded with the scene it represents and is not a window in a wall. The stage and the decor where the action unfolds constitute an aesthetic microcosm inserted perforce into the universe but essentially distinct from the Nature which surrounds it.

It is not the same with cinema, the basic principle of which is a denial of any frontiers to action.

The idea of a *locus dramaticus* is not only alien to, it is essentially a contradiction of the concept of the screen. The screen is not a frame like that of a picture but a mask which allows only a part of the action to be seen. When a character moves off screen, we accept the fact that he is out of sight, but he continues to exist in his own capacity at some other place in the decor which is hidden from us. There are no wings to the screen. There could not be without destroying its specific illusion, which is to make of a revolver or of a face the very center of the universe. In contrast to the stage the space of the screen is centrifugal. It is because that infinity which the theater demands cannot be spatial that its area can be none other than the human soul. Enclosed in this space the actor is at the focus of a two-fold concave mirror. From the auditorium and from the decor there converge on him the dim lights of conscious human beings and of the footlights themselves. But the fire with which he burns is at once that of his inner passion and of that focal point at which he stands. He lights up in each member of his audience an accomplice flame. Like the ocean in a sea shell the dramatic infinities of the human heart moan and beat between the enclosing walls of the theatrical sphere. This is why this dramaturgy is in its essence human. Man is at once its cause and its subject.

On the screen man is no longer the focus of the drama, but will become eventually the center of the universe. The impact of his action may there set in motion an infinitude of waves. The decor that surrounds him is part of the solidity of the world. For this reason the actor as such can be absent from it, because man in the world enjoys no a priori privilege over animals and things. However there is no reason why he should not be the mainspring of the drama, as in Dreyer's *Jeanne d'Arc*, and in this respect the cinema may very well impose itself upon the theater. As actions *Phèdre* or *King Lear* are no less cinematographic than theatrical, and the visible death of a rabbit in *La Règle du jeu* affects us just as deeply as that of Agnès' little cat about which we are merely told.

But if Racine, Shakespeare, or Molière cannot be brought to the cinema by just placing them before the camera and the microphone, it is because the handling of the action and the style of the dialogue were conceived as echoing through the architecture of the auditorium. What is specifically theatrical about these tragedies is not their action so much as the human, that is to say the verbal, priority given to their dramatic structure. The problem of filmed theater at least where the classics are concerned does not consist so much in transposing an action from the stage to the screen as in transposing a text written for one dramaturgical system into another while at the same time retaining its effectiveness. It is not therefore essentially the action of a play which resists film adaptation, but above and beyond the phases of the intrigue (which it would be easy enough to adapt to the realism of the screen) it is the verbal form which aesthetic contingencies or cultural prejudices oblige us to respect. It is this which refuses to let itself be captured in the window of the screen. "The theater," says Baudelaire, "is a crystal chandelier." If one were called upon to offer in comparison a symbol other than this artificial crystal-like object, brilliant, intricate, and circular, which refracts the light which plays around its center and holds us prisoners of its aureole, we might say of the cinema that it is the little flashlight of the usher, moving like an uncertain comet across the night of our waking dream, the diffuse space without shape or frontiers that surrounds the screen.

The story of the failures and recent successes of theater on film will be found to be that of the ability of directors to retain the dramatic force of the play in a medium that reflects it or, at least, the ability to give this dramatic force enough resonance to permit a film audience to perceive it. In other words, it is a matter of an aesthetic that is not concerned with the actor but with decor and editing. Henceforth it is clear that filmed theater is basically destined to fail whenever it tends in any manner to become simply the photographing of scenic representation even and perhaps most of all when the camera is used to try and make us forget the footlights and the backstage area. The dramatic force of the text, instead of being gathered up in the actor, dissolves without echo into the cinematic ether. This is why a filmed play can show due respect to the text, be well acted in likely settings, and yet be completely worthless. This is what happened, to take a convenient example, to *Le Voyageur sans baggages*. The play lies there before us apparently true to itself yet drained of every ounce of energy, like a battery dead from an unknown short. But over and beyond the aesthetic of the decor we see clearly both on the screen and on the stage that in the last analysis the problem before us is that of realism. This is the problem we always end up with when we are dealing with cinema.

THE SCREEN AND THE REALISM OF SPACE

The realism of the cinema follows directly from its photographic nature. Not only does some marvel or some fantastic thing on the screen not undermine the reality of the image, on the contrary it is its most valid justification. Illusion in the cinema is not based as it is in the theater on convention tacitly accepted by the general public; rather, contrariwise, it is based on the inalienable realism of that which is shown. All trick work must be perfect in all material respects on the screen. The "invisible man" must wear pyjamas and smoke a cigarette.

Must we conclude from this that the cinema is dedicated entirely to the representation if not of natural reality at least of a plausible reality of which the spectator admits the identity with nature as he knows it? The comparative failure of German expressionism would seem to confirm this hypothesis, since it is evident that *Caligari* attempted to depart from realistic decor under the influence of the theater and painting. But this would be to offer an oversimplified explanation for a problem that calls for more subtle answers. We are prepared to admit that the screen opens upon an artificial world provided there exists a common denominator between the cinematographic image and the world we live in. Our experience of space is the structural basis for our concept of the universe. We may say in fact, adapting Henri Gouhier's formula, "The stage welcomes every illusion except the illusion of presence," that "the cinematographic image can be emptied of all reality save one—the reality of space."

It is perhaps an overstatement to say "all reality" because it is difficult to imagine a reconstruction of space devoid of all reference to nature. The world of the screen and our world cannot be juxtaposed. The screen of necessity substitutes for it since the very concept of universe is spatially exclusive. For a time, a film is the Universe, the world, or if you like, Nature. We will see how the films that have attempted to substitute a fabricated nature and an artificial world for the world of experience have not all equally succeeded. Admitting the failure of *Caligari* and *Die Nibelungen* we then ask ourselves how we explain the undoubted success of *Nosferatu* and *La Passion de Jeanne d'Arc*, the criterion of success being that these films have never aged. Yet it would seem at first sight that the methods of direction belong to the same aesthetic family, and that viewing the varieties of temperament and period, one could group these four films together as expressionist as distinct from realist. However, if we examine them more closely we see that there are certain basic differences between them. It is clear in the case of R. Wiene and Murnau. *Nosferatu* plays, for the greater part of the time, against natural settings whereas the fantastic qualities of *Caligari* are derived from deformities of lighting and decor. The case of Dreyer's *Jeanne d'Arc* is a little more subtle since at first sight nature plays a nonexistent role. To put it more directly, the decor by Jean Hugo is no whit less artificial and theatrical than the settings of *Caligari*; the systematic use of close-ups and unusual angles is well calculated to destroy any sense of space. Regular cinéclub goers know that the film is unfailingly introduced with the famous story of how the hair of Falconetti was actually cut in the

390

interest of the film and likewise, the actors, we are told, wore no make-up. These references to history ordinarily have no more than gossip value. In this case, they seem to me to hold the aesthetic secret of the film; the very thing to which it owes its continued survival. It is precisely because of them that the work of Dreyer ceases to have anything in common with the theater, and indeed one might say, with man. The greater recourse Dreyer has exclusively to the human "expression," the more he has to reconvert it again into Nature. Let there be no mistake, that prodigious fresco of heads is the very opposite of an actor's film. It is a documentary of faces. It is not important how well the actors play, whereas the pockmarks on Bishop Cauchon's face and the red patches of Jean d'Yd are an integral part of the action. In this drama-through-the-microscope the whole of nature palpitates beneath every pore. The movement of a wrinkle, the pursing of a lip are seismic shocks and the flow of tides, the flux and reflux of this human epidermis. But for me Dreyer's brilliant sense of cinema is evidenced in the exterior scene which every other director would assuredly have shot in the studio. The decor as built evoked a Middle Ages of the theater and of miniatures. In one sense, nothing is less realistic than this tribunal in the cemetery or this drawbridge, but the whole is lit by the light of the sun and the gravedigger throws a spadeful of real earth into the hole.*

It is these "secondary" details, apparently aesthetically at odds with the rest of the work, which give it its truly cinematic quality.

If the paradox of the cinema is rooted in the dialectic of concrete and abstract, if cinema is committed to communicate only by way of what is real, it becomes all the more important to discern those elements in filming which confirm our sense of natural reality and those which destroy that feeling. On the other hand, it certainly argues a lack of perception to derive one's sense of reality from these accumulations of factual detail. It is possible to argue that *Les Dames du Bois de Boulogne* is an eminently realistic film, though

---

*This is why I consider the graveyard scene in *Hamlet* and the death of Ophelia bad mistakes on Olivier's part. He had here a chance to introduce sun and soil by way of counterpoint to the setting of Elsinore. Does the actual shot of the sea during the soliloquy of Hamlet show that he had sensed the need for this? The idea, excellent in itself, is not well handled technically.

everything about it is stylized. Everything, except for the rarely noticeable sound of a windshield-wiper, the murmur of a waterfall, or the rushing sound of soil escaping from a broken vase. These are the noises, chosen precisely for their "indifference" to the action, that guarantee its reality.

The cinema being of its essence a dramaturgy of Nature, there can be no cinema without the setting up of an open space in place of the universe rather than as part of it. The screen cannot give us the illusion of this feeling of space without calling on certain natural guarantees. But it is less a question of set construction or of architecture or of immensity than of isolating the aesthetic catalyst, which it is sufficient to introduce in an infinitesimal dose, to have it immediately take on the reality of nature.

The concrete forest of *Die Nibelungen* may well pretend to be an infinite expanse. We do not believe it to be so, whereas the trembling of just one branch in the wind, and the sunlight, would be enough to conjure up all the forests of the world.

If this analysis be well founded, then we see that the basic aesthetic problem of filmed theater is indeed that of the decor. The trump card that the director must hold is the reconversion into a window onto the world of a space oriented toward an interior dimension only, namely the closed and conventional area of the theatrical play.

It is not in Laurence Olivier's *Hamlet* that the text seems to be rendered superfluous or its strength diminished by directorial interpretations, still less in Welles' *Macbeth*, but paradoxically in the stage productions of Gaston Baty, to the precise extent that they go out of their way to create a cinematographic space on the stage; to deny that the settings have a reverse side, thus reducing the sonority of the text simply to the vibration of the voice of the actor who is left without his "resonance box" like a violin that is nothing else but strings. One would never deny that the essential thing in the theater is the text. The latter conceived for the anthropocentric expression proper to the stage and having as its function to bring nature to it cannot, without losing its raison d'être, be used in a space transparent as glass. The problem then that faces the film-maker is to give his decor a dramatic opaqueness while at the same time reflecting its natural realism. Once this paradox of space has been dealt with, the director, so far from hesitating to bring theatrical conventions and faithfulness to the text to the screen will find himself now, on the contrary, completely free to rely on them. From that point on it is no longer a matter of running away from those things which "make theater" but in the long run to acknowledge their existence by rejecting the resources of the cinema, as Cocteau did in *Les Parents terribles* and Welles in *Macbeth*, or by putting them in quotation marks as Laurence Olivier did in *Henry V*. The evidence of a return to filmed theater that we have had during the last ten years belongs essentially to the history of decor and editing. It is a conquest of realism—not, certainly, the realism of subject matter or realism of expression but that realism of space without which moving pictures do not constitute cinema.

1951

SERGEI EISENSTEIN
FROM DICKENS, GRIFFITH, AND THE FILM TODAY

The most thrilling figure was Griffith, for it was in his works that the cinema made itself felt as more than an entertainment or pastime. The brilliant new methods of the American cinema were united in him with a profound emotion of story, with human acting, with laughter and tears, and all this was done with an astonishing ability to preserve all that gleam of a filmically dynamic holiday, which had been captured in *The Gray Shadow* and *The Mark of Zorro* and *The House of Hate*. That the cinema could be incomparably greater, and that this was to be the basic task of the budding Soviet cinema—these were sketched for us in Griffith's creative work, and found ever new confirmation in his films.

Our heightened curiosity of those years in *construction and method* swiftly discerned wherein lay the most powerful affective factors in this great American's films. This was in a hitherto unfamiliar province, bearing a name that was familiar to us, not in the field of art, but in that of engineering and electrical apparatus, first touching art in its most advanced section—in cinematography. This province, this method, this principle of building and construction was *montage*.

This was the montage whose foundations had been laid by American film-culture, but whose full, completed, conscious use' and world recognition was established by our films. Montage, the rise of which will be forever linked with the name of Griffith. Montage, which played a most vital rôle in the creative work of Griffith and brought him his most glorious successes.

Griffith arrived at it through the method of parallel action. And, essentially, it was on this that he came to a standstill. But we mustn't run ahead. Let us examine the question of how montage came to Griffith or—how Griffith came to montage.

Griffith arrived at montage through the method of parallel action, and he was led to the idea of parallel action by—Dickens! . . .

What were the novels of Dickens for his contemporaries, for his readers? There is one answer: they bore the same relation to them that the film bears to the same strata in our time. They compelled the reader to live with the same passions. They appealed to the same good and sentimental elements as does the film (at least on the surface); they alike shudder before vice, they alike mill the extraordinary, the unusual, the fantastic, from boring, prosaic and everyday existence. And they clothe this common and prosaic existence in their special vision.

Illumined by this light, refracted from the land of fiction back to life, this commonness took on a romantic air, and bored people were grateful to the author for giving them the countenances of potentially romantic figures.

This partially accounts for the close attachment to the novels of Dickens and, similarly, to films. . . .

Perhaps the secret lies in Dickens's (as well as cinema's) creation of an extraordinary plasticity. The observation in the novels is extraordinary—as is their optical quality. The characters of Dickens are rounded with means as plastic and slightly exaggerated as are the screen heroes of today. The screen's heroes are engraved on the senses of the spectator with clearly visible traits, its villains are remembered by certain facial expressions, and all are saturated in the peculiar, slightly unnatural radiant gleam thrown over them by the screen.

It is absolutely thus that Dickens draws his characters—this is the faultlessly plastically grasped and pitilessly sharply sketched gallery of immortal Pickwicks, Dombeys, Fagins, Tackletons, and others. . . .

Analogies and resemblances cannot be pursued too far—they lose conviction and charm. They begin to take on the air of machination or card-tricks. I should be very sorry to lose the conviction of the affinity between Dickens and Griffith, allowing this abundance of common traits to slide into a game of anecdotal semblance of tokens.

All the more that such a gleaning from Dickens goes beyond the limits of interest in Griffith's individual cinematic craftsmanship and widens into a concern with film-craftsmanship in general. This is why I dig more and more deeply into the film-indications of Dickens, revealing them through Griffith—for the use of future film-exponents. So I must be excused, in leafing through Dickens, for having found in him even—a "dissolve." . . .

However, let us turn to the basic montage structure, whose rudiment in Dickens's work was developed into the elements of film composition in Griffith's work. Lifting a corner of the veil over these riches, these hitherto unused experiences, let us look into *Oliver Twist*. Open it at the twenty-first chapter. Let's read its beginning:

CHAPTER XXI*

1. It was a cheerless morning when they got into the street; blowing and raining hard; and the clouds looking dull and stormy.

The night had been very wet: for large pools of water had collected in the road: and the kennels were overflowing.

There was a faint glimmering of the coming day in the sky; but it rather aggravated than relieved the gloom of the scene: the sombre light only serving to pale that which the street lamps afforded, without shedding any warmer or brighter tints upon the wet housetops, and dreary streets.

There appeared to be nobody stirring in that quarter of the town; for the windows of the houses were all closely shut; and the streets through which they passed, were noiseless and empty.

2. By the time they had turned into the Bethnal Green Road, the day had fairly begun to break. Many of the lamps were already extinguished;

a few country waggons were slowly toiling on, towards London;

and now and then, a stage-coach, covered with mud, rattled briskly by:

the driver bestowing, as he passed, an admonitory lash upon the heavy waggoner who, by keeping on the wrong side of the road, had endangered his arriving at the office, a quarter of a minute after his time.

---

*For demonstration purposes I have broken this beginning of the chapter into smaller pieces than did its author; the numbering is, of course, also mine.

The public-houses, with gas-lights burning inside, were already open.

By degrees, other shops began to be unclosed; and a few scattered people were met with.

Then, came straggling groups of labourers going to their work;
then, men and women with fish-baskets on their heads:
donkey-carts laden with vegetables;
chaise-carts filled with live-stock or whole carcasses of meat;
milk-women with pails;
and an unbroken concourse of people, trudging out with various supplies to the eastern suburbs of the town.

3. As they approached the City, the noise and traffic gradually increased;
and when they threaded the streets between Shoreditch and Smithfield, it had swelled into a roar of sound and bustle.

It was as light as it was likely to be, till night came on again; and the busy morning of half the London population had begun. . . .

4. It was market-morning.
The ground was covered, nearly ankle-deep, with filth and mire;
and a thick steam, perpetually rising from the reeking bodies of the cattle,
and mingling with the fog,
which seemed to rest upon the chimney-tops, hung heavily above.
. . .
Countrymen,
butchers,
drovers,
hawkers,
boys,
thieves,
idlers,
and vagabonds of every low grade,
were mingled together in a dense mass;

5. the whistling of drovers,
the barking of dogs,
the bellowing and plunging of oxen,
the bleating of sheep,
the grunting and squeaking of pigs;
the cries of hawkers,
the shouts, oaths and quarrelling on all sides;

397

the ringing of bells
and roar of voices, that issued from every public-house;
the crowding, pushing, driving, beating,
whooping and yelling;
the hideous and discordant din that resounded from every corner
of the market;
and the unwashed, unshaven, squalid, and dirty figures constantly
running to and fro, and bursting in and out of the throng; rendered
it a stunning and bewildering scene, which quite confounded the
senses.

How often have we encountered just such a structure in the work
of Griffith? This austere accumulation and quickening tempo, this
gradual play of light: from burning street-lamps, to their being
extinguished; from night, to dawn; from dawn, to the full radiance
of day *(It was as light as it was likely to be, till night came on
again);* this calculated transition from purely visual elements to an
interweaving of them with aural elements: at first as an indefinite
rumble, coming from afar at the second stage of increasing light,
so that the rumble may grow into a roar, transferring us to a purely
aural structure, now concrete and objective (section 5 of our break-
down); with such scenes, picked up *en passant*, and intercut into the
whole—like the driver, hastening towards his office; and, finally,
these magnificently typical details, the reeking bodies of the cattle,
from which the steam rises and mingles with the over-all cloud of
morning fog, or the close-up of the legs in the almost ankle-deep
filth and mire, all this gives the fullest cinematic sensation of the
panorama of a market. . . .

If in the above-cited examples we have encountered prototypes
of characteristics for Griffith's *montage exposition*, then it would
pay us to read further in *Oliver Twist*, where we can find another
montage method typical for Griffith—the method of a *montage
progression of parallel scenes, intercut into each other.*

For this let us turn to that group of scenes in which is set forth
the familiar episode of how Mr. Brownlow, to show faith in Oliver
in spite of his pick-pocket reputation, sends him to return books
to the book-seller, and of how Oliver again falls into the clutches
of the thief Sikes, his sweetheart Nancy, and old Fagin.

These scenes are unrolled absolutely à la Griffith: both in their
inner emotional line, as well as in the unusual sculptural relief and

delineation of the characters; in the uncommon full-bloodedness of the dramatic as well as the humorous traits in them; finally, also in the typical Griffith-esque montage of parallel interlocking of all the links of the separate episodes. Let us give particular attention to this last peculiarity, just as unexpected, one would think, in Dickens, as it is characteristic for Griffith!

CHAPTER XIV

COMPRISING FURTHER PARTICULARS OF OLIVER'S STAY AT MR. BROWNLOW'S, WITH THE REMARKABLE PREDICTION WHICH ONE MR. GRIMWIG UTTERED CONCERNING HIM, WHEN HE WENT OUT ON AN ERRAND.

. . . "Dear me, I am very sorry for that," exclaimed Mr. Brownlow; "I particularly wished those books to be returned tonight."

"Send Oliver with them," said Mr. Grimwig, with an ironical smile; "he will be sure to deliver them safely, you know."

"Yes; do let me take them, if you please, Sir," said Oliver. "I'll run all the way, Sir."

The old gentleman was just going to say that Oliver should not go out on any account; when a most malicious cough from Mr. Grimwig determined him that he should; and that, by his prompt discharge of the commission, he should prove to him the injustice of his suspicions: on this head at least: at once.

[Oliver is prepared for the errand to the bookstall-keeper.]

"I won't be ten minutes, Sir," replied Oliver, eagerly.

[Mrs. Bedwin, Mr. Brownlow's housekeeper, gives Oliver the directions, and sends him off.]

"Bless his sweet face!" said the old lady, looking after him. "I can't bear, somehow, to let him go out of my sight."

At this moment, Oliver looked gaily round, and nodded before he turned the corner. The old lady smilingly returned his salutation, and, closing the door, went back to her own room.

"Let me see; he'll be back in twenty minutes, at the longest," said Mr. Brownlow, pulling out his watch, and placing it on the table. "It will be dark by that time."

"Oh! you really expect him to come back, do you?" inquired Mr. Grimwig.

"Don't you?" asked Mr. Brownlow, smiling.

The spirit of contradiction was strong in Mr. Grimwig's breast, at the moment; and it was rendered stronger by his friend's confident smile.

"No," he said, smiting the table with his fist, "I do not. The boy has a new suit of clothes on his back; a set of valuable books under his arm; and a five-pound note in his pocket. He'll join his old friends the thieves, and laugh at you. If ever that boy returns to this house, Sir, I'll eat my head."

With these words he drew his chair closer to the table; and there the two friends sat, in silent expectation, with the watch between them.

This is followed by a short "interruption" in the form of a digression:

It is worthy of remark, as illustrating the importance we attach to our own judgments, and the pride with which we put forth our most rash and hasty conclusions, that, although Mr. Grimwig was not by any means a bad-hearted man, and though he would have been unfeignedly sorry to see his respected friend duped and deceived, he really did most earnestly and strongly hope, at that moment, that Oliver Twist might not come back.

And again a return to the two old gentlemen:

It grew so dark, that the figures on the dial-plate were scarcely discernible; but there the two old gentlemen continued to sit, in silence: with the watch between them.

Twilight shows that only a little time has passed, but the *close-up* of the watch, *already twice* shown lying between the old gentlemen, says that a great deal of time has passed already. But just then, as in the game of "will he come? won't he come?", involving not only the two old men, but also the kind-hearted reader, the worst fears and vague forebodings of the old housekeeper are justified by the cut to the new scene—Chapter XV. This begins with a short scene in the public-house, with the bandit Sikes and his dog, old Fagin and Miss Nancy, who has been obliged to discover the whereabouts of Oliver.

"You are on the scent, are you, Nancy?" inquired Sikes, proffering the glass.

"Yes, I am, Bill," replied the young lady, disposing of its contents; "and tired enough of it I am, too. . . ."

Then, one of the best scenes in the whole novel—at least one that since childhood has been perfectly preserved, along with the evil figure of Fagin—the scene in which Oliver, marching along with the books, is suddenly

> startled by a young woman screaming out very loud, "Oh, my dear brother!" And he had hardly looked up, to see what the matter was, when he was stopped by having a pair of arms thrown tight round his neck.

With this cunning maneuver Nancy, with the sympathies of the whole street, takes the desperately pulling Oliver, as her "prodigal brother," back into the bosom of Fagin's gang of thieves. This fifteenth chapter closes on the now familiar montage phrase:

> The gas-lamps were lighted; Mrs. Bedwin was waiting anxiously at the open door; the servant had run up the street twenty times to see if there were any traces of Oliver; and still the two old gentlemen sat, perseveringly, in the dark parlour: with the watch between them.

In Chapter XVI Oliver, once again in the clutches of the gang, is subjected to mockery. Nancy rescues him from a beating:

> "I won't stand by and see it done, Fagin," cried the girl. "You've got the boy, and what more would you have? Let him be—let him be, or I shall put that mark on some of you, that will bring me to the gallows before my time."

By the way, it is characteristic for both Dickens and Griffith to have these sudden flashes of goodness in "morally degraded" characters and, though these sentimental images verge on hokum, they are so faultlessly done that they work on the most skeptical readers and spectators!

At the end of this chapter, Oliver, sick and weary, falls "sound asleep." Here the physical time unity is interrupted—an evening and night, crowded with events; but the montage unity of the episode is not interrupted, tying Oliver to Mr. Brownlow on one side, and to Fagin's gang on the other.

Following, in Chapter XVIII, is the arrival of the parish beadle, Mr. Bumble, in response to an inquiry about the lost boy, and the appearance of Bumble at Mr. Brownlow's, again in Grimwig's company. The content and reason for their conversation is revealed by the very title of the chapter: OLIVER'S DESTINY CONTINUING UNPROPITIOUS, BRINGS A GREAT MAN TO LONDON TO INJURE HIS REPUTATION . . .

"I fear it is all too true," said the old gentleman sorrowfully, after looking over the papers. "This is not much for your intelligence; but I would gladly have given you treble the money, if it had been favourable to the boy."

It is not at all improbable that if Mr. Bumble had been possessed of this information at an earlier period of the interview, he might have imparted a very different coloring to his little history. It was too late to do it now, however; so he shook his head gravely; and, pocketing the five guineas, withdrew. . . .

"Mrs. Bedwin," said Mr. Brownlow, when the housekeeper appeared; "that boy, Oliver, is an impostor."

"It can't be, Sir. It cannot be," said the old lady energetically. . . . "I never will believe it, Sir. . . . Never!"

"You old women never believe anything but quack-doctors, and lying story-books," growled Mr. Grimwig. "I knew it all along. . . ."

"He was a dear, grateful, gentle child, Sir," retorted Mrs. Bedwin, indignantly. "I know what children are, Sir; and have done these forty years; and people who can't say the same, shouldn't say anything about them. That's my opinion!"

This was a hard hit at Mr. Grimwig, who was a bachelor. As it extorted nothing from that gentleman but a smile, the old lady tossed her head, and smoothed down her apron preparatory to another speech, when she was stopped by Mr. Brownlow.

"Silence!" said the old gentleman, feigning an anger he was far from feeling. "Never let me hear the boy's name again. I rang to tell you that. Never. Never, on any pretence, mind! You may leave the room, Mrs. Bedwin. Remember! I am in earnest."

And the entire intricate montage complex of this episode is concluded with the sentence:

There were sad hearts in Mr. Brownlow's that night.

It was not by accident that I have allowed myself such full extracts, in regard not only to the composition of the scenes, but also to the delineation of the characters, for in their very modeling, in their characteristics, in their behavior, there is much typical of Griffith's manner. This equally concerns also his "Dickens-esque" distressed, defenseless creatures (recalling Lillian Gish and Richard Barthelmess in *Broken Blossoms* or the Gish sisters in *Orphans of the Storm*), and is no less typical for his characters like the two old gentlemen and Mrs. Bedwin; and finally, it is entirely characteristic of him to have such figures as are in the gang of "the merry old Jew" Fagin.

In regard to the immediate task of our example of Dickens's montage progression of the story composition, we can present the results of it in the following table:

1. *The old gentlemen.*
2. Departure of Oliver.
3. *The old gentlemen and the watch. It is still light.*
4. Digression on the character of Mr. Grimwig.
5. *The old gentlemen and the watch. Gathering twilight.*
6. Fagin, Sikes and Nancy in the public-house.
7. Scene on the street.
8. *The old gentlemen and the watch. The gas-lamps have been lit.*
9. Oliver is dragged back to Fagin.
10. Digression at the beginning of Chapter XVII.
11. The journey of Mr. Bumble.
12. *The old gentlemen* and Mr. Brownlow's command to forget Oliver forever.

As we can see, we have before us a typical and, for Griffith, a model of parallel montage of two story lines, where one (the waiting gentlemen) emotionally heightens the tension and drama of the other (the capture of Oliver). It is in "rescuers" rushing along to save the "suffering heroine" that Griffith has, with the aid of parallel montage, earned his most glorious laurels!

Most curious of all is that in the *very center* of our breakdown of the episode, is wedged another "interruption"—a whole digression at the beginning of Chapter XVII, on which we have been purposely silent. What is remarkable about this digression? It is Dickens's own "treatise" on the principles of this montage construction of the story which he carries out so fascinatingly, and which passed into the style of Griffith. Here it is:

> It is the custom on the stage, in all good murderous melodramas, to present the tragic and the comic scenes, in as regular alternation, as the layers of red and white in a side of streaky well-cured bacon. The hero sinks upon his straw bed, weighed down by fetters and misfortunes; and, in the next scene, his faithful but unconscious squire regales the audience with a comic song. We behold, with throbbing bosoms, the heroine in the grasp of a proud and ruthless baron: her virtue and her life alike in danger; drawing forth her dagger to preserve the one at the cost of the other; and just as our expectations are wrought up to the highest pitch, a whistle is heard: and we are straightway transported to the great hall of the castle: where a grey-headed seneschal sings a funny chorus with a funnier body of vassals, who are free of all sorts of places from church vaults to palaces, and roam about in company, carolling perpetually.
>
> Such changes appear absurd; but they are not so unnatural as they would seem at first sight. The transitions in real life from well-spread boards to death-beds, and from mourning-weeds to holiday garments, are not a whit less startling; only, there, we are busy actors, instead of passive lookers-on; which makes a vast difference. The actors in the mimic life of the theatre, are blind to violent transitions and abrupt impulses of passion of feeling, which, presented before the eyes of mere spectators, are at once condemned as outrageous and preposterous.
>
> As sudden shiftings of the scene, and rapid changes of time and place, are not only sanctioned in books by long usage, but are by many considered as the great art of authorship: an author's skill in his craft being, by such critics, chiefly estimated with relation to the dilemmas in which he leaves his characters at the end of every chapter: this brief introduction to the present one may perhaps be deemed unnecessary. . . .

There is another interesting thing in this treatise: in his own words, Dickens (a life-long amateur actor) defines his direct relation to the theater melodrama. This is as if Dickens had placed himself in the position of a connecting link between the future, unforeseen art of the cinema, and the not so distant (for Dickens) past—the traditions of "good murderous melodramas."

This "treatise," of course, could not have escaped the eye of the patriarch of the American film, and very often his structure seems to follow the wise advice, handed down to the great film-maker of the twentieth century by the great novelist of the nineteenth. And Griffith, hiding nothing, has more than once acknowledged his debt to Dickens's memory. . . .

I don't know how my readers feel about this, but for me personally it is always pleasing to recognize again and again the fact that our cinema is not altogether without parents and without pedigree, without a past, without the traditions and rich cultural heritage of the past epochs. It is only very thoughtless and presumptous people who can erect laws and an esthetic for cinema, proceeding from premises of some incredible virgin-birth of this art!

Let Dickens and the whole ancestral array, going back as far as the Greeks and Shakespeare, be superfluous reminders that both Griffith and our cinema prove our origins to be not solely as of Edison and his fellow inventors, but as based on an enormous cultured past; each part of this past in its own moment of world history has moved forward the great art of cinematography. Let this past be a reproach to those thoughtless people who have displayed arrogance in reference to literature, which has contributed so much to this apparently unprecedented art and is, in the first and most important place: the art of viewing—not only the *eye*, but *viewing*—both meanings being embraced in this term. . . .

1944

GEORGE BLUESTONE
FROM NOVELS INTO FILM
LIMITS OF THE NOVEL AND THE FILM

THE MODES OF CONSCIOUSNESS

It is a commonplace by now that the novel has tended to retreat more and more from external action to internal thought, from plot to character, from social to psychological realities. Although these conflicting tendencies were already present in the polarity of Fielding and Sterne, it was only recently that the tradition of *Tristram Shandy* superseded the tradition of *Tom Jones*. It is this reduction of the novel to experiences which can be verified in the immediate consciousness of the novelist that Mendilow has called modern "inwardness" and E. M. Forster the "hidden life." Forster suggests the difference when he says that "The hidden life is, by definition, hidden. The hidden life that appears in external signs is hidden no longer, has entered the realm of action. And it is the function of the novelist to reveal the hidden life at its source." But if the hidden life has become the domain of the novel, it has introduced unusual problems.

In a recent review of Leon Edel's *The Psychological Novel: 1900–1950*, Howard Mumford Jones sums up the central problems which have plagued the modern novelist: the verbal limitations of nonverbal experience; the dilemma of autobiographical fiction in which the novelist must at once evoke a unique consciousness and yet communicate it to others; the difficulty of catching the flux of time in static language. The summary is acutely concise in picking out the nerve centers of an increasingly subjective novel where "after images fished out of the stream of past time . . . substitute a kind of smoldering dialectic for the clean impact of drama."

Béla Balázs has shown us how seriously we tend to underestimate the power of the human face to convey subjective emotions and to suggest thoughts. But the film, being a presentational medium (except for its use of dialogue), cannot have direct access to the power of discursive forms. Where the novel discourses, the film must picture. From this we ought not to conclude like J. P. Mayer that "our eye is weaker than our mind" because it does not "*hold* sight impressions as our imagination does." For sense impressions, like word symbols, may be appropriated into the common fund of memory. Perceptual knowledge is not necessarily different in strength; it *is* necessarily different in kind.

The rendition of mental states—memory, dream, imagination—cannot be as adequately represented by film as by language. If the film has difficulty presenting streams of consciousness, it has even more difficulty presenting states of mind which are defined precisely by the absence in them of the visible world. Conceptual imaging, by definition, has no existence in space. However, once I cognize the signs of a sentence through the conceptual screen, my consciousness is indistinguishable from nonverbal thought. Assuming here a difference between *kinds* of images—between images of things, feelings, concepts, words—we may observe that conceptual images evoked by verbal stimuli can scarcely be distinguished in the end from those evoked by nonverbal stimuli. The stimuli, whether they be the signs of language or the sense data of the physical world, lose their spatial characteristics and become components of the total ensemble which is consciousness.

On the other hand, the film image, being externalized in space, cannot be similarly converted through the conceptual screen. We have already seen how alien to the screen is the compacted luxuriance of the trope. For the same reasons, dreams and memories, which exist nowhere but in the individual consciousness, cannot be adequately represented in spatial terms. Or rather, the film, having only arrangements of space to work with, cannot rende thought, for the moment thought is externalized it is no longer thought. The film, by arranging external signs for our visual perception, or by presenting us with dialogue, can lead us to *infer* thought. But it cannot show us thought directly. It can show us characters thinking, feeling, and speaking, but it cannot show us their thoughts and feelings. A film is not thought; it is perceived.

That is why pictorial representations of dreams or memory on the screen are almost always disappointing. The dreams and memories of *Holiday for Henrietta* and *Rashomon* are spatial referents to dreams and memories, not precise renditions. To show a memory or dream, one must balloon a separate image into the frame (Gypo remembering good times with Frankie in *The Informer*); or superimpose an image (Gypo daydreaming about an ocean voyage with Katie); or clear the frame entirely for the visual equivalent (in *Wuthering Heights*, Ellen's face dissolving to the house as it was years ago). Such spatial devices are always to some degree dissatisfying. Acting upon us perceptually, they cannot render the conceptual feel of dreams and memories. The realistic tug of the film is too strong. If, in an effort to bridge the gap between spatial representation and nonspatial experience, we accept such devices at all, we accept them as cinematic conventions, not as renditions of conceptual consciousness.

Given the contrasting abilities of film and novel to render conceptual consciousness, we may explore further the media's handling of time. . . .

PSYCHOLOGICAL TIME: THE TIME-FLUX

As soon as we enter the realm of time-in-flux, we not only broach all but insoluble problems for the novel but we also find a sharp divergence between prose and cinema. The transient, sequential, and irreversible character of language is no longer adequate for this type of time experience. For in the flux, past and present lose their identity as discrete sections of time. The present becomes "specious" because on second glance it is seen as fused with the past, obliterating the line between them.

Discussing its essential modernity, Mendilow lends support to the idea that the whole of experience is implicit in every moment of the present by drawing from Sturt's *Psychology of Time*. For Sturt tries to work out the sense in which we are caught by a perpetual present permeated by the past:

408

One of the reasons for the feeling of pastness is that we are familiar with the things or events that we recognize as past. But it remains true that this feeling of familiarity is a *present* experience, and therefore logically should not arouse a concept of the past. On the other hand, a present impression (or memory) of something which is past is different from a present impression of something which is present but familiar from the past.

How this seeming contradiction operates in practice may be seen when we attempt to determine precisely which of two past events is prior, and in what manner the distinction between the memory of a past thing and the impression of a present thing is to be made. At first glance, we seem perfectly able to deduce which of two remembered events is prior. For example, on the way to the store this morning, I met a group of children going to school. I also mailed my letter just as the postman came by. I know that ordinarily the children go to school at nine o'clock and the postman comes by at eleven. Therefore, I deduce that I went to the store *before* I mailed my letter. Although I have not been able to give the act of my going to the store an exact location in the past, I have been able to establish its priority.

On second thought, however, it seems as if (apart from the deductions one makes by deliberate attention to relationships) the memory of a past event comes to me with its pastness already intended. The image I have of my friend *includes* the information that this is the way he looked the year before he died. Similarly, if I have a mental image of myself on a train to Kabul, then summon up an image of myself eating chestnuts, I know that the first is an image of a past thing and the second an image of a present thing because the image of myself on the train includes the information that the event took place last year. At the same time, I know that I am eating chestnuts right now. Here the perceptual witnessing of my present action checks and defines my mental images, confirming both the priority of the train ride and the presentness of the eating.

But suppose I bring my attention to bear on an object which is present now and which was also present yesterday at the same time, in the same place, in the same light. If, for example, I look at the lamp in my room, which fulfills all these requirements, then close my eyes and behold the mental image, how am I to know if that image refers to the lamp which was there yesterday or to the lamp which is there today? In this instance, which is tantamount to fusing a thing's past with its present, my present image, for all practical purposes, no longer respects the distinction between past and present. It offers me no way of knowing the exact location of its temporal existence.

This obliteration between past and present is precisely the problem which faces the novelist who wishes to catch the flux in language. If he is faced with the presentness of consciousness on the one hand, and the obliteration of the discrete character of past and present on the other, how is he to express these phenomena in a language which relies on tenses?

Whether we look at William James' "stream of consciousness," Ford Madox Ford's "chronological looping," or Bergson's *"durée,"* we find the theorists pondering the same problem: language, consisting as it does of bounded, discrete units cannot satisfactorily represent the unbounded and continuous. We have a sign to cover the concept of a thing's "becoming"; and one to cover the concept of a thing's "having become." But "becoming" is a *present* participle, "become" a *past* participle, and our language has thus far offered no way of showing the continuity between them.

So elusive has been the *durée* that the novelist has submitted to the steady temptation of trying to escape time entirely. But here, too, the failure has served to dramatize the medium's limitations. Speaking of Gertrude Stein's attempt to emancipate fiction from the tyranny of time, E. M. Forster notes the impasse: "She fails, because as soon as fiction is completely delivered from time it cannot express anything at all."

To be sure, there seem to be intuitive moments of illumination in Proust and Wolfe during which a forgotten incident floats up from oblivion in its pristine form and seems thereby to become free of time. Proust's involuntary memory fuses the experience of his mother's madeleine cake with the former experience of Aunt Léonie's, and the intervening time seems, for the moment, obliterated. But it is the precise point of Proust's agonizing effort that— despite our ability, through involuntary memory, to experience simultaneously events "with countless intervening days between" —there is always a sense in which these events remain "widely separated from one another in Time." The recognition of this conflict helps us understand why every formulation which attempts to define a "timeless" quality in a novel seems unsatisfactory, why Mendilow's attempt to find an "ideal time" in Kafka seems to say little more than that Kafka was not plagued by the problem. In the end, the phrase "timeless moment" poses an insuperable contradiction in terms.

We can see the problem exemplified concretely in a passage from Thomas Wolfe's *The Hills Beyond*. The passage describes Eugene Gant's visit to the house in St. Louis where his family had lived thirty years before. Eugene can remember the sights, shapes, sounds, and smells of thirty years ago, but something is missing — a sense of absence, the absence of his brother Grover, of his family away at the fair:

> And he felt that if he could sit there on the stairs once more, in solitude and absence in the afternoon, he would be able to get it back again. Then would he be able to remember all that he had seen and been — that brief sum of himself, the universe of his four years, with all the light of Time upon it — that universe which was so short to measure, and yet so far, so endless, to remember. Then would he be able to see his own small face again, pooled in the dark mirror of the hall, and discover there in his quiet three years' self the lone integrity of "I," knowing: "Here is the House, and here House listening; here is Absence, Absence in the afternoon; and here in this House, this Absence, is my core, my kernel — here am I!"

The passage shows the characteristic, almost obsessive longing of the modern novel to escape the passage of time by memory; the recognition that the jump, the obliteration, cannot be made; the appropriation of non-space as a reality in the novel — not the feeling of absence alone, but the absence of absence.

We arrive here at the novel's farthest and most logical remove from the film. For it is hard to see how any satisfactory film equivalents can be found for such a paragraph. We can show Eugene waiting in the house, then superimpose an image of the boy as he might have looked thirty years before, catch him watching a door as if waiting for Grover to return. But as in all cinematic attempts to render thought, such projection would inevitably fail. How are we to capture that combination of past absence and present longing, if both are conditions contrary to spatial fact?

The film-maker, in his own and perhaps more acute way, also

faces the problem of how to render the flux of time. "Pictures have no tenses," says Balázs. Unfolding in a perpetual present, like visual perception itself, they cannot express either a past or a future. One may argue that the use of dialogue and music provides a door through which a sense of past and future may enter. Dialogue, after all, is language, and language does have referential tenses. A character whose face appears before us may *talk* about his past and thereby permeate his presence with a kind of pastness. Similarly, as we saw in our discussion of sound in editing, music may be used to counterpoint a present image (as in *High Noon* and *Alexander Nevsky*) and suggest a future event. In this way, apparently, a succession of present images may be suffused with a quality of past or future.

At best, however, sound is a secondary advantage which does not seriously threaten the primacy of the spatial image. When Ellen, the housekeeper, her withered face illumined by the fire, begins telling her story to Lockwood in *Wuthering Heights*, we do sense a certain tension between story-teller and story. But in the film we can never fully shake our attention loose from the teller. The image of her face has priority over the sound of her voice. When Terry Malone tells Edie about his childhood in *On the Waterfront*, the present image of his face so floods our consciousness that his words have the thinnest substance only. The scars around his eyes tell us more about his past than any halting explanation. This phenomenon is essentially what Panofsky calls the "principle of coexpressibility," according to which a moving picture—even when it has learned to talk—remains a picture that moves, and does not convert itself into a piece of writing that is enacted. That is why Shakesperian films which fail to adapt the fixed space of the stage to cinematic space so often seem static and talky.

In the novel, the line of dialogue stands naked and alone; in the film, the spoken word is attached to its spatial image. If we try to convert Marlon Brando's words into our own thought, we leave for a moment the visual drama of his face, much as we turn away from a book. The difference is that, whereas in the book we miss nothing, in the film Brando's face has continued to act, and the moment we miss may be crucial. In a film, according to Panofsky, "that which we hear remains, for good or worse, inextricably fused with that which we see." In that fusion, our seeing (and therefore our sense of the present) remains primary.

If, however, dialogue and music are inadequate to the task of capturing the flux, the spatial image itself reveals two characteristics which at least permit the film to make a tentative approach. The first is the quality of familiarity which attaches itself to the perceptual image of a thing after our first acquaintance. When I first see Gelsomina in *La Strada*, I see her as a stranger, as a girl with a certain physical disposition, but without a name or a known history. However, once I identify her as a character with a particular relationship to other characters, I am able to include information about her past in the familiar figure which now appears before me. I do not have to renew my acquaintance at every moment. Familiarity, then, becomes a means of referring to the past, and this past reference fuses into the ensemble which is the present Gelsomina. The spatial image of Gelsomina which I see toward the end of the film includes, in its total structure, the knowledge that she has talked to the Fool and returned to Zampano. In a referential sense, the pastness is built in.

That the film is in constant motion suggests the second qualification of film for approximating the time-flux. At first glance, the film seems bound by discrete sections, much as the novel is bound by discrete words. At the film's outer limit stands the frame; and within the frame appear the distinct outlines of projected objects, each one cut as by a razor's edge. But the effect of running off the frames is startlingly different from the effect of running off the sentence. For whether the words in a novel come to me as non-verbal images or as verbal meanings, I can still detect the discrete units of subject and predicate. If I say, "The top spins on the table," my mind assembles first the top, then the spinning, then the table. (Unless, of course, I am capable of absorbing the sentence all at once, in which case the process may be extended to a paragraph composed of discrete sentences.) But on the screen, I simply perceive a shot of a top spinning on a table, in which subject and predicate appear to me as *fused*. Not only is the top indistinguishable from its spinning, but at every moment the motion of the top seems to contain the history of its past motion. It is true that the top-image stimulated in my mind by the sentence resembles the top-image stimulated by the film in the sense that both contain the illusion of continuous motion. Yet this resemblance does not appear in the *process* of cognition. It appears only after the fact, as it were, only after the component words have been assembled. Although the mental and filmic images do meet in rendering the top's continuity of motion, it is in the mode of apprehending them that we find the qualitative difference.

In the cinema, for better or worse, we are bound by the forward looping of the celluloid through the projector. In that relentless unfolding, each frame is blurred in a total progression. Keeping in mind Sturt's analysis of the presentness of our conceptions, a presentness permeated by a past and therefore hardly ruled by tense at all, we note that the motion in the film's *present* is unique. Montage depends for its effects on instantaneous successions of different spatial entities which are constantly exploding against each other. But a succession of such variables would quickly become incomprehensible without a constant to stabilize them. In the film, that constant is motion. No matter how diverse the moving spaces which explode against each other, movement itself pours over from shot to shot, binding as it blurs them, reinforcing the relentless unrolling of the celluloid.

Lindgren advances Abercrombie's contention that completeness in art has no counterpart in real life, since natural events are never complete: "In nature nothing at any assignable point begins and nothing at any assignable point comes to an end: all is perfect continuity." But Abercrombie overlooks both our ability to perceive spatial discreteness in natural events and the film's ability to achieve "perfect continuity." So powerful is this continuity, regardless of the *direction* of the motion, that at times we tend to forget the boundaries of both frame and projected object. We attend to the motion only. In those moments when motion alone floods our attention and spatial attributes seem forgotten, we suddenly come as close as the film is able to fulfilling one essential requirement of the time-flux—the boundaries are no longer perceptible. The transience of the shot falls away before the sweeping permanence of its motion. Past and present seem fused, and we have accomplished before us a kind of spatial analogue for the flux of time.

If the film is incapable of maintaining the illusion for very long, if its spatial attributes, being primary, presently assert themselves,

414

if the film's spatial appeal to the eye overwhelms its temporal appeal to the mind, it is still true that the film, above all other non-verbal arts, comes closest to rendering the time-flux. The combination of familiarity, the film's linear progression, and what Panofsky calls the "Dynamization of Space" permits us to intuit the *durée* insofar as it can, in spatial art, be intuited at all.

The film, then, cannot render the attributes of thought (metaphor, dream, memory); but it can find adequate equivalents for the kind of psychological time which is characterized by variations in rate (distension, compression; speed-up, *ralenti*); and it approaches, but ultimately fails, like the novel, to render what Bergson means by the time-flux. The failure of both media ultimately reverts to root differences between the structures of art and consciousness.

Our analysis, however, permits a usable distinction between the two media. Both novel and film are time arts, but whereas the formative principle in the novel is time, the formative principle in the film is space. Where the novel takes its space for granted and forms its narrative in a complex of time values, the film takes its time for granted and forms its narrative in arrangements of space. Both film and novel create the illusion of psychologically distorted time and space, but neither destroys time or space. The novel renders the illusion of space by going from point to point in time; the film renders time by going from point to point in space. The novel tends to abide by, yet explore, the possibilities of psychological law; the film tends to abide by, yet explore, the possibilities of physical law.

Where the twentieth-century novel has achieved the shock of novelty by explosions of words, the twentieth-century film has achieved a comparable shock by explosions of visual images. And it is a phenomenon which invites detailed investigation that the rise of the film, which preëmpted the picturing of bodies in nature, coincides almost exactly with the rise of the modern novel which preëmpted the rendition of human consciousness.

Finally, to discover distinct formative principles in our two media is not to forget that time and space are, for artistic purposes, ultimately inseparable. To say that an element is contingent is not to say that it is irrelevant. Clearly, spatial effects in the film would be impossible without concepts of time, just as temporal effects

415

in the novel would be impossible without concepts of space. We are merely trying to state the case for a system of priority and emphasis. And our central claim—namely that time is prior in the novel, and space prior in the film—is supported rather than challenged by our reservations.

1957

ROBERT SCHOLES
NARRATION AND
NARRATIVITY IN FILM

Let us assume that there is something called narrative that can exist apart from any particular method of narration or any particular narrative utterance, as we assume that there is something called the English language that exists apart from any particular form of discourse or any individual speech act in English. Narration is, first of all, a kind of human behavior. It is specifically a mimetic or representative behavior, through which human beings communicate certain kinds of messages. The modes of narration may vary extraordinarily. (In passing, I should say that I am aware of our customary distinction between what is told and what is enacted, which leads us to oppose narrative representation to dramatic enactment. In this case, however, I am using the word narration in its broadest sense to include both plays and stories, along with other forms of imitation.) A narrative, then, may be recounted orally, committed to writing, acted out by a group of actors or a single actor, presented in wordless pantomime, represented as a sequence of visual images, with or without words, or as a cinematic flow of moving pictures, with or without sounds, speech, music, and written language.

All of these mimetic kinds of behavior have certain features in common, which enable us to consider them together as narrative. First of all, they belong to a special class of symbolic activity which forces the interpreter to make a distinction between his own immediate situation and some other situation which is being presented to him through the medium of narration. In narrative there is always a spectator or interpreter who is situated in a space/time reference different from that of the events narrated. The *process* of narration culminates in the interpreter's immediate frame of reference, but it *refers* to events outside of that immediate situation. This is as true for my dinner-time recital of the little events of my day as it is for a performance of *King Lear* or *Swan Lake,* or a reading of *War and Peace.* Narration, then, rests upon the presence of a narrator or narrative medium (actors, book, film, etc.) and the absence of the events narrated. These events are present as fictions but absent as realities. Given this situation, it is possible to distinguish different kinds and qualities of narration by the varying extents to which they emphasize either that immediate process of narration (as an actor may draw attention to himself as performer or a writer to himself as stylist) or, on the other hand, emphasize those mediated events themselves. Using our common critical terminology, it is possible to say that a narration is more fictional as it emphasizes the events narrated, and more lyrical as it emphasizes its own language, and more rhetorical as it uses either language or events for some persuasive end.

Before looking more closely at the processes of narration, it may be useful to pause here and consider the relationship of narrative to theories of literature and literary value. The Russian formalists and the Prague school of structuralists, and in particular Roman Jakobson, have attempted to isolate the quality of "literariness" as a feature added to ordinary language. They have defined literariness as language calling attention to itself, or as a kind of message in which emphasis is placed on the form of the utterance rather than on its referential capacity. For the student of narrative, however, it is clear that this notion is applicable only to the lyrical dimension of an utterance. If narratives may be considered to be literary, they must be literary also in a way which is more purely narrative. Let me try to put this problem in a more concrete fashion.

We can begin by considering a question: what distinguishes a literary narrative from my recital of the events of my day? Is it a matter of the style of my performance—my language, voice, gesture, as opposed to those of a literary raconteur—or is it a matter of the events themselves—the trivial, loosely ordered events of my day, as opposed to events of greater consequence shaped to a more aesthetically satisfying pattern? The question—which need not be answered—reinforces the notion that there are two distinct formal dimensions to narrative utterances: a presentational form which is immediate (language, gesture, etc.), and a represented form which is at one remove from the level of performance itself. In a novel, for instance, there is the language of the author at one level, and the representation of character, situation, and event at another. In a play, there is the language of the author, the performance of the actor, and the deeds of the character to consider: three easily discerned levels at which form is perceptible. And film adds at least one level to these, just through the processes of photography itself: camera-angle, lighting, focus, etc.

In a sense, each of these formal levels adds a certain amount of literariness to the process simply by existing. Take, for instance, a text which can be read as a book, enacted on a stage, or filmed and projected on a screen—like Shakespeare's *Henry V*. Each of the added levels of presentational style intensifies the literariness of the experience by its own artifice: language plus enactment plus photography. And the achieved fiction is *there* with a specificity which the printed text alone can never hope to match. The price for this intensity is a reduction in the interpretive richness of the written text—and this happens as every level is added. When the play is staged, each performance makes interpretive choices for the reader—but no two performances make all the same choices. When the story is filmed, all choices are final. Which suggests that one ought to be very careful about confusing interpretive richness with the quality of literariness in any given work. Life itself, with all its quotidian contingency, provides the richest possible field for interpretation. Art reduces this field drastically. And that is why we value it—not the only reason why, but perhaps the main one. My example, of course, being a film based on an enactment of a particularly rich verbal text, is oversimple and may even be misleading in certain respects. Certainly I do not wish to suggest that verbal texts are rich and cinematic ones impoverished with respect to interpretability. Rather, it is my ultimate intention to indicate the different kinds of interpretation that verbal and cinematic texts entail, and to illustrate this with some brief examples drawn from recent American films. But first it will be necessary to return to some consideration of the general aspects of narrative behavior.

Any telling or recounting of a string of events may be called narration. But not every narration yields a narrative, and not every narrative makes a story. By becoming a story, or pretending to be a story, a narration arrives at literariness of the fictive kind. A story is a narration that attains a certain degree of completeness, and even a fragment of a story or an unfinished story will imply that completeness as an aspect of its informing principle—the intentionality that governs its construction. Given its linear, consecutive character, it is not surprising that film has come to be a predominantly narrative medium. That it should be dominated by stories, however, is somewhat more surprising, but dominated by stories it is, to a much greater extent than printed books are dominated by novels.

At this point it may be useful to review some terminology. A *narration* is a process of enactment or recounting which is a common feature of our cultural experience. We all do some of it every day. When this process is sufficiently coherent and developed to detach itself from the flux of cultural interchange, we perceive it as a *narrative*. As a perceived narrative begins to imply a special kind of pointedness or teleology, we recognize that it is a *story*, and we regard it with a certain set of expectations about its expressive patterning and its semantic content. We have a continuum here, like the color spectrum, which our perceptual mechanism breaks into discrete levels. And the level we recognize as "story" is distinguished by certain structural features in presentation which in turn require of the perceiver an active participation which I should like to call "narrativity." This word is presently used, by French critics primarily, to refer to a property of films themselves—their narrative quality. But the word seems a trifle misleading in English, in that it implies a more sentient character than we generally allow to an artifact. For this reason and some others, I should like to suggest that we employ the word "narrativity" to refer to the process by which a perceiver actively constructs a story from the fictional data provided by any narrative medium. A fiction is presented to us in the form of a narration which guides us as our own active narrativity seeks to complete the process that will achieve a story.

The nature of narrativity is, to some extent, culture-bound. It is a matter of learned or acquired behavior, like the acquisition of a particular language, but it is based on a predisposition or potential of the human species to acquire this particular kind of behavior. In the contemporary Western world, the culture of narrativity appears to be sufficiently homogeneous so that it may be considered in the way that a single language may be—as a systematic whole. We are only beginning to study "readers reading," as opposed to the texts that they read, so my remarks on narrativity will have to be rough and ready, based, to a certain extent, on intuitive extrapolations from my own experience as a reader and a teacher of reading. But it is also possible to base a study of narrativity at least partially upon texts, if we consider texts in various media. That is, things that are left to the reader's narrativity in some media are presented directly in others. The arrival of film on the narrative scene has enabled us to perceive certain features of fiction more clearly because they are part of the narration in film while they have only been part of the reader's narrativity in fiction. To take the most obvious instance, the visual quality of film reminds us forcibly of how much of fictional narrativity involves the supplying of physical details or the translating of verbal signs into images. Readers who are feeble at such visualizing often fail to realize important aspects of fictional texts. Film, of course, does not raise such problems of visualization. It raises other problems, however, which I shall consider later on. For the moment, it may be useful to break down a bit further the processes of aesthetic interpretation.

The activities of readers and spectators in the face of artistic or recreational texts involve both a passive or automatic translation of semiotic conventions into intelligible elements and an active or interpretive rearrangement of textual signs into significant structures. The automatic part of these operations is a matter of linguistic or semiotic competence and not of special interest to us upon this occasion. The interpretive part concerns us here. The interpreter of lyric poetry, for example, must of course know the language and the verbal conventions in which a poem is cast. But he must go beyond this level of competence to understand the poem. In particular, he must construct a situational structure from clues in the poem—who speaks, to whom, under what circumstances, etc.—and he must also decompose the special linguistic features of the poetic lexicon, grammar, and syntax in order to comprehend them. He must measure poetic structures against the prosaic structures he needs to understand the deviant features of poetic utterance. He must supply missing parts of metaphors; he must acknowledge the ordinary words replaced by unusual ones in order to grasp the functions of the usual ones; he must discover the fundamental syntactic structures in sentences that conceal aspects of those structures. In order to understand, he must explicate or unfold what is implicated or folded into the poem. And the poetic text must be designed to reward such interpretive activity. This activity is a matter of supplying semiotic features that the text requires for interpretation, a matter of building a hermeneutic structure around the text itself. The poem is not the text alone but the text used to construct a complete and intelligible interpretation of it. A poem is a text which requires and rewards poetic procedures (or "poeticity") in its interpretation.

Similarly, a narrative is a text which requires and rewards narrativity. Narrativity involves a number of procedures of interpretive constructing, but one of these may be singled out as the most characteristic feature of this activity. Just as the lyric is characterized by the need to simplify its verbal constructions for interpretation, the narrative is characterized by a need to simplify certain elements in narration. We "make sense" of a poem by perceiving familiar sentence patterns within its unique verbal structure. We make sense of narration in a similar fashion, but at a different level of the text. In a story it is the order of events that concerns us, more than the order of words. And our primary effort in attending to a narration is to construct a satisfying order of events. To do this we

422

must locate or provide two features: temporality and causality.

Narrativity is based upon a mental operation similar to a logical fallacy: *post hoc ergo propter hoc*. What is a fallacy in logic is a principle of fiction: that a cause and effect relationship links the temporal elements in any narrative sequence. I am not suggesting that fiction itself is fallacious in some way, but rather that it is constructed so as to make this fallacy a feature of the fictional world. When we say that a work is "episodic," for instance, we mean that the work frustrates the narrativitous urge for causal connection and we consider this a fictional deficiency (though obviously there may be other non-fictional compensations in any given work). Above all, when we recognize a work as a story, we regard it as having a temporal sequentiality based on cause and effect. This means that if the events in a story are presented in their temporal sequence, much of our narrativity is devoted to establishing the causal connections between one event and the next. It means further that if the events themselves are presented out of temporal sequence, we seek first to arrive at an understanding of the true temporal sequence in order then to grasp the causal sequence informing the temporal. In the course of following even a simple fiction, the processes of narrativity can be quite complex, as we separate the causal from the merely descriptive or contingent, as we seek to anticipate the future events in the causal patterns we discern, and we reconsider past events based on present understandings. The extraordinary popularity of detective fiction since its invention by Poe is based upon the way in which this fictional form incorporates the principles of narrativity within the narration itself. We follow the detective moving through time from crime to solution, while he, in turn, is in the process of constructing a narration of the crime itself from a set of clues encountered without their temporal and causal situations having been clarified. From discrete clues, he constructs a criminal narrative, which finally provides a verification or correction for our own narrativity. Something like this pattern is as old as *Oedipus*, and is at least adumbrated in much drama and in melodramatic fiction. In the theater, the chronology of on stage events tends toward brevity and direct temporal flow, but frequently generates revelations that belong to the time before the play began. There is often a story in a play which includes important events that precede the plot enacted on stage.

The strength of the human disposition toward simple narrativity can be measured in part through the mounting assaults upon that disposition in various modern and post-modern media. Pirandello and Brecht represent in theater two ways of trying to work against the spectator's impulse towards narrativity. Pirandello breaks illusion for aesthetic reasons, to demonstrate the power of illusion, and finally to urge upon us the view that life itself is a matter of enactment and illusion. Brecht seeks to subvert narrativity to allow his theater ideological scope for the realization of ethical ends. And in film, Resnais and Godard represent positions similar to Pirandello and Brecht in theater. We could find fictional analogues for these figures as well, in the labyrinths of Robbe-Grillet, or the novelistic journalism of Norman Mailer. Yet all these assaults on narrativity—and their ancestors in Cervantes, Calderon, Diderot, Sterne, etc.—depend upon narrativity and could not function without it. It may even be that no long form of discourse can be received by a reader, spectator, or auditor unless it allows and encourages a certain amount of narrativity in its audience.

The nature of narrativity can be seen in another way. It is not only based upon what is a fallacy in logic, but upon behavior that in psychology must be seen as neurotic or psychotic. Narrativity is a form of licensed and benign paranoia. (How many school children refer to the author of a book as "they" or "them"?) The interpreter of a narrative process assumes a purposefulness in the activities of narration which, if it existed in the world would be truly destructive of individuality and personality as we know them. (I leave aside the question of whether this would be an improvement.) The spectator or reader of a narrative assumes that he is in the grip of a process controlled outside himself, designed to do things to him which he will be powerless to resist, and that all his struggles will only enmesh him further in the author's toils. Much of our impatience with inferior fiction comes from our loss of faith in the author's power. When he fails to anticipate our reactions and to lay traps for us into which we delightedly stumble, we begin to wonder if he is in control at all and to fear that we may have to move out of narrativity and into narration itself—or else simply return to entirely non-narrative behavior.

A feature of narrativity is our desire to abandon certain dimensions of existence, certain quotidian responsibilities, and place ourselves under the illusionary guidance of a maker of narratives, upon whom we rely because we respect his powers. There is something very undemocratic about all this, and uncritical as well. Criticism begins when narrativity ceases. Life resumes when narrativity ceases. Call it escape or call it transcendence, narrativity is a pleasurable state of consciousness which is as different from other states as the dreaming part of sleep is from the other parts. This element of narrativity, which is perhaps its most fundamental and most primitive dimension, is a source of dissatisfaction to many contemporary writers and filmmakers. This quality of submission and abandon, which is so characteristic of narrativitous activity, has led some creators of narrative artifacts to try forcing the reader out of his familiar patterns of narrativity and into some more dynamic and tendentious attitude toward the text. The search for a "zero degree" of writing, in which the writer simply provides materials out of which a reader constructs a text, is, in the terms I have been using, an attempt to turn narrativity into narration itself. The ultimate form of this tendency would be a book with blank pages, or a silent concert (which John Cage has given us), an empty picture frame, a motion-picture screen lit by the lamp of the projector but showing only its own texture and perhaps the motes in the middle distance or the specks on the lens. These anti-forms all have been or will be tried, but they are capable of little development. Even an encore to a silent concert presents a problem. And the zero degree of life is death.

I should like to suggest that the proper way for narrative artists to provide for their audiences an experience richer than submissive stupefaction is not to deny them the satisfactions of story, but to generate for them stories which reward the most energetic and rigorous kinds of narrativity. It is possible, as Shakespeare knew, to provide some plain satisfactions for the simple or the weary while also rewarding those who are ready to give a narrative the fullest attention of their mental and emotional powers. In the remaining portion of this paper, I wish to turn my attention to the way film, in particular, can achieve this and is achieving this at present, even in works of what might be called the middle range, that do not aspire to the summits of aesthetic approbation. In order to do this—and at the risk of covering over-familiar ground for some of my audience—I shall begin with a brief review of the nature of cinematic signs.

As Christian Metz has made abundantly clear, film and narrative have such a powerful affinity that their relationship assumes a supreme naturalness. When, in the eighteenth century, Lessing sought so elaborately to contrast the mimetic possibilities of verbal narration and pictorial representation, he neatly (too neatly, doubtless) divided the world between them—assigning to the sequential, arbitrary signs of fiction the narration of actions, and to the simultaneous, motivated signs of painting, the description of objects and persons. If he were brought back to life today he would recognize in cinema the reconciliation of the parts of his divided world. For the motion-picture film gives us objects and persons moving and enacting in a visual system of narration which combines the powers of poetry and painting in an extraordinary synthesis.

The product of this synthesis, however, is a very different thing from verbal narration, more different than we sometimes realize, and it is different in a way that Lessing would understand—different because the signs in cinema function differently from the signs of verbal fiction. In the language of verbal narration, each sign is first interpreted as a concept or category, and then, where this is relevant and possible, connected to a referent of some sort. Thus, if I say to you, "There's a dog on the lawn," you translate the sound-image "dog" into some canine category of your own, and if you are moved to look out the window and see for yourself, you may finally perceive a specific referent which will supplant the conceptual category in your interpretive operation. If I provide you with a fictional dog, however, your concretization of the

426

empty category will depend on an interaction between my narration and your narrativity. If I say, "He's lifting his leg," your image must lift a leg, preferably a hind leg, but the choice of leg is left up to you, unless and until I provide you with new verbal data which forces you to correct your image.

If, on the other hand, I present you with a cinematic dog— the signifying process is entirely different. You are confronted with a sign tightly tied to a specific referent, which you then may relate to a categorial concept or a set of such concepts by a process which may be partly conscious and partly not. I may misdirect you, if I can use words in my film, calling a male dog "Lassie," and if the dog is sufficiently wooly or the camera work and editing sufficiently adroit, you may never detect the imposture, and thus assign the referent to a category which is fictionally correct but factually false—a problem which can hardly come up in verbal narration, where if I call a dog Lassie you are obliged to provide her with all the proper equipment or to leave parts of her blank until I direct your attention to them.

The point of this excursion into sign language is to suggest that though the "same narrative" may be presented in both verbal and cinematic form, the narration and the narrativity will be extremely different. This is why my earlier example of *Henry V* was misleading to a certain extent. Since the verbal part of a play is entirely oral, it may be completely reproduced in a film. In a novel, however, much of the language is busy with description and reflection, which must be eliminated in cinematic translation. Even voice-over narration in films made from novels, which is used very effectively in a good film like *Farewell My Lovely* or a great one like *Jules et Jim*, is highly selective when compared to the total verbiage of the book. These differences in narration correspond to important differences in narrativity. The reader's narrative processes in dealing with printed fiction are mainly oriented toward visualization. This is what the reader must supply for a printed text. But in cinematic narrative, the spectator must supply a more categorial and abstract narrativity. This is one reason why film criticism is frequently more interesting than literary criticism. A well-made film requires interpretation while a well-made novel may only need understanding. There is a redundancy in providing a verbal gloss for a verbal object which does not apply when the object is significantly visual.

Some movements in contemporary fiction can be seen as attempts to acquire a cinematic opacity and freedom from conceptual thinking. Alain Robbe-Grillet has tried very hard to be a camera and produced some interesting verbal *tours de force*. But these experiments in writing against the grain of verbal narration are limited in their developmental possibilities. A writer who wants to be a camera should probably make a movie. Makers of narrative films can also work against the grain, and films have been made which try to conceptualize so much that they founder in seas of rhetoric. These two different narrative media require and must encourage two different kinds of narrativity—though both admit of great intensity and great complexity. Before concluding, I should like to explore some aspects of narrativity in recent American films—as an illustration of the processes I have been discussing perhaps too abstractly. These processes involve the conceptualization of images and the construction of frameworks of causality and value around such concepts.

In the past year I found myself moved in very different ways to different kinds of narrativity by the images of America presented in three films: *The Great Waldo Pepper, Godfather II,* and *The Parallax View.* Having seen each film only once, I am in no position to argue their merits vigorously or to analyze them with any pretensions to depth and rigor. But each of them proved striking to me, and left me with residues of narrativity that have become a part of my cognitive apparatus. *Waldo Pepper* is a charming film, perhaps too conscious of its charm. It summons up an America already coded for us by Norman Rockwell—but it transcends this quality on several occasions. In the crowd scenes around the fatal plane crash we find Rockwell's world metamorphosed into something like Nathaniel West's—with an economy and power far beyond the ponderous Westian fidelities of the cinematic *Day of the Locust.* Suddenly, the blood lust, the brutality behind the placid surface of mid-America bursts through the Rockwellian facade, and it is all the more convincing because of the sincerity with which that facade has been established in the film. In the processes of my own narrativity, continuing long after the viewing itself was completed, still continuing, joining the images of the great meta-film I am constructing in my mind, other images have come to dominate my recollection of that film. Not the Rockwellian faces, not even the marvellous aerial acrobatics, but features of landscape and humanity which are closer to Grant Wood than to Rockwell. In particular, I see a frame house, a tree, a person or two at home in these surroundings, and beyond them the fields and the sky. The camera is stationary or moving slowly, and the sense of peace, of man's harmony with nature, is overwhelming. These images generate in me the same feeling I experience when I go back to Iowa, where you can smell the fertility of the land and understand how people can love it, and how that farmer's love for the earth must transcend national boundaries and go back for centuries to beyond the beginning of history. That this sense of land should be so strong in a film about the sky, about restlessness, about people who find no resting place on the ground, is important. It is a measure of a kind of complexity in a film which is in many respects simple, and it is a complexity that comes from a loving attention to images which invite us to go through them to the meanings behind them.

Our narrativity with respect to a film like *Waldo Pepper* begins with a simple attempt to register the images, to categorize them and assign them value according to whatever cultural codes we have available. Where I use Norman Rockwell and Grant Wood, someone else might operate with different paradigms, which might not carry any labels at all. But in any case, as we proceed along the narrative track of the film, we construct the story of Waldo himself from the incidents presented to us, and we charge that story with value and emotion in very complex ways. What I wish to suggest here is that a part of that vital and complex process by which we accomplish this energizing of the narration depends upon such things as our codifying and assigning value to particular images. In this case, Waldo's fate is as it is because his life is torn between the placidity of that prairie landscape, tamed by man, and the pettiness and cruelty of man as a social being.

Waldo cannot accept the placidity of the one side of his culture and he despises the mundane cupidity and sensationalism of the other. His lies and his flights are both attempts to transcend these realities, to construct a mythic world which he can comfortably inhabit. But one way or another, planes must come down. Myths may be created but they cannot be lived.

Some devotees of film may object to my discussion as moving too far from the reality of dissolves and jump cuts to some airy realm of thematic speculation. But my point is that this is precisely what we must do in the realization of a narrative film. The cinematic world invites—even requires—conceptualization. The images presented to us, their arrangement and juxtapositioning, are narrational blueprints for a fiction that must be constructed by the viewer's narrativity.

The images of America in *Godfather II* are different from those of *Waldo Pepper*, of course, as different as Little Italy from Nebraska or Las Vegas from Keokuk. But the images evoke similar processes of narrativity in our minds. For me, the scenes of Ellis Island were worth a stack of history books. One long shot in particular, the camera tracking slowly past the immigrant hordes, labeled and herded like cattle, brought the dream and reality of America into vertiginous proximity. Some of my ancestors stood in those lines, and I felt closer to them as I watched than I had ever felt before. The slow camera, the warm lighting, the hopeful patience of the crowds provided an image closer to the heart of this country than any Mayflower or Plymouth Rock. The film, of course, is about the betrayal of this dream: the mafioso in his fortress, the senator in his whorehouse, the conference of thugs and politicians in Batista's Cuba. These images must be set next to those patient lines of immigrants for the film's full irony to be achieved. But once we grasp them they remain with us for a long time.

The final film I wish to mention is less highly regarded than the other two and was, I believe, less successful commercially. But for me it is a film of extraordinary interest, despite its weaknesses—and to a certain extent because of them. *The Parallax View* attempted two remarkable narrative feats. It took the paranoia that lies benevolently at the heart of the narrative process itself and the other paranoia that threatens to overwhelm our national life, and tried to make them congruent. And it undertook a single scene requiring the most intense narrativity I can recall encountering in a film. The picture provides a story that postulates a conspiracy behind the assassinations of various liberal political figures and satirizes the complacency or complicity of the inquiries into those assassinations. All the characters in the film who begin to perceive this plot against America die violently, and the last heroic defender is trapped into a situation where he is himself taken to be an assassin and is finally killed by those truly guilty who are pretending to aid in his arrest. It is a chilling film, pointedly and scandalously close to actual contemporary events. It shares a view of America with the frighteningly irrational readers of scandal magazines and the uncritical devotees of paranoid conspiracy theories. As a film, its lack of popular success probably stems from the fact that its audience could not accept the slaughter of their protagonist. In the formulas of popular fiction, this film called for a victorious hero who saved the country from a wicked gang of conspirators. By accepting the paranoia latent in a part of the mass audience while rejecting the power fantasy and wish fulfillment that regularly accompany it, the film alienated its most likely audience. And, of course, those who consider themselves above such things were disqualified from the beginning.

The film had other problems—in pacing and in the logic of its story-telling, leaning too heavily on the invisible masters of conspiracy to tie together the loose ends of its plot, encouraging a sloppy and careless narrativity in the viewer. But it did give us one extraordinary scene. In this episode, the intrepid protagonist, who is trying to infiltrate the conspiracy, faces a futuristic personality test. To qualify as an apprentice assassin, he must demonstrate that he has the emotional profile of an extremely psychotic individual. The test consists of his being strapped into an electronic chair which monitors his reactions while he is shown slides calculated to produce strong emotional effects upon him: authority figures, sex objects, flags, scenes of violence and brutality, mom-type ladies, homosexuals, apple pie, Captain America—all in a rapid sequence of repetitions and juxtapositions. Our protagonist, to pass the test, must try to generate the appropriate involuntary reactions for a paranoid psychopath, and we, in our own chairs watching the same slides, are inevitably drawn to assist him empathetically by trying to force the appropriate reactions out of our own nervous systems. The result is a kind of mind-blowing sensory overload, a short-circuiting of a narrativity asked to accomplish too much too fast. The vagueness of the monitoring itself, the absence of rules for this game, indicates that the makers of the film were not in imaginative control of their own conception. Thus, the film repeatedly attempts to allow a real and malevolent paranoia to substitute for the benign paranoia at the heart of narrative activity. The film tries to hide its own imaginative inadequacies behind one of its inadequately conceived fictions. This is truly an instructive failure, for we see ideas that might have functioned powerfully reduced to the level of sensational gimmicks before our eyes.

In these three glances into the processes of cinematic narrativity, I have been trying to suggest the power and importance of conceptualization by the viewer in the realization of narrative films. There is, of course, much more to cinematic narrative than this. And there is much less too. Some aspects of narrative film are simply matters of stimulus and response, in which conceptualization is held to a minimum. This, I take it, is a useful definition of pornography, whether it is the pornography of pleasure or of pain. We need no very elaborate concepts of erotic or brutal acts to be "moved" by enactments of them—and even more "moved" by photographs of the actuality. But such motion, however violent, is not derived from any narrative process. Presumably, to see someone tortured or gratified sexually before our eyes would be even more "moving," and to play the principal role in such a situation ourselves would be the most "moving" condition of all. And this would not be a narrative experience any more. It would be life, not fiction.

Film, because it excels all other narrative media in its rendition of material objects and the actions of creatures, is the closest to actuality, to undifferentiated thoughtless experience. Literature, beginning in language, must exert extraordinary pains to achieve some impression of the real. For this reason, written fiction has almost always used some notion of realism or verisimilitude as an evaluative standard. For film, the problem is different. It must achieve some level of reflection, or conceptualization, in order to reach its optimum condition as narrative. The best narrative films have always accomplished this, and they have done so cinematically, through scenes and images that induce an appropriate narrativity in their audiences.

1975

V

Kinds of Film

The study of artistic genres is as old as Aristotle, and at least one of his generic terms, "comedy," has been regularly applied to films. (Significantly, tragedy has not established itself as a film genre.) The generic approach to art has frequently been attacked, however, for its terms are often imprecise and its methods of categorization unclear. What, precisely, is a documentary film or a screwball comedy? Are films to be classified by their physical properties (silent, color), by their subject matter (gangster, western), or by their purpose or effect (comic, educational)? Further, are these categories legitimate? Of what interest is a category like the "educational" film? In any case, is it even proper to arrange works of art in classes, viewing them as instances of types? Benedetto Croce, the influential Italian philosopher and critic, argued that generic criticism was necessarily incompatible with an aesthetic point of view, which always treats works of art as individual and unique. Croce's views have not prevailed, however, and the concept of genre continues to be employed in film theory and criticism, as it is in all art theory and criticism, and with important results.

The most familiar system by which films are generically classified distinguishes between the different kinds of fictional narrative (almost inevitably American) feature films: westerns, gangster films, newspaper pictures, detective dramas, screwball comedies, courtroom dramas, *films noirs*, musicals, war films, spy films, prison films, horror films, science fictions, fantasies, thrillers. An obvious difficulty with such commonly used categories is that they overlap; a film might combine gangsters, detectives, newspapermen, a courtroom, a prison, suspense, and a bleak, *"noir"* atmosphere; a film might combine screwball comedy, newspapermen, and prisons (as *His Girl Friday* does), or screwball comedy, the western, and the musical (as *Calamity Jane* and *Annie Get Your Gun* do). In classifying such a film one would have to rely on a judgment about what is important. Or one might decide to employ a compound category. But this sort of adjustment does not present genre criticism with an insoluble difficulty, for to be able to speak of a compound genre at all implies that elemental genres existed in order to be compounded.

Another problem of classifying fictional narrative films in this way arises when we ask if such categories have any impact on the making of films or our responses to films. Are they critical and commercial conveniences, designed merely to help market a film or to describe a film for those who have not seen it? How conscious are filmmakers of their use of generic conventions? How conscious are audiences of these conventions? How do we recognize that a film does indeed represent a particular genre? How do the conventions of a genre evolve over the history of film? Are such evolutions the result of changing artistic conventions in films, of developing cultural standards in society, or both? Despite these questions, there can be no doubt that treating a film as a representative of a familiar and perceptively formulated genre is often essential to a proper understanding of it.

For Leo Braudy, the contemporary American film and literary critic, the concept of genre must first be rescued from the presumption that it can only describe a debased and degraded kind of art. "Genre films offend our most common definition of artistic excellence: the uniqueness of the art object, whose value can in part be defined by its desire to be uncaused and unfamiliar, as much as possible unindebted to any tradition, popular or otherwise." After tracing this critical prejudice to its roots in the aesthetic and literary theories of the Romantic Era, Braudy posits the two kinds of connection which genre films achieve. First, genre films forge a deliberate connection between each new instance of the genre and its past tradition and manifestations. Second, genre films, because of their popularity and familiarity, have a more powerful impact on their audience—and a highly democratic one—converting that audience into a unified cultural force: "Genre films strike beneath our intellectual appreciation of high art and make us one with a large mass audience, often despite our more articulate and elitist views." His specific look at musicals of the 1930s and 1940s demonstrates the way that the genre, especially as embodied in the contrast between Fred Astaire and Gene Kelly, sought to interject energy and spontaneity into the repetitiveness of everyday social reality, either by Astaire's escape into the perfect world of dance or by Kelly's making the imperfect world more perfect by making it dance.

Robert Warshow, the influential American analyst of the popular arts in the era just after World War II, would agree with Braudy's observation that the popular genre film makes connections both with its filmic past and with the temperaments of its contemporary viewers. Although he would be less willing to grant the general artistic excellence and importance to genre films that Braudy does, he does consider the gangster and the westerner as the two most important creations of American movies. The power of both genres derives from their concern with the problem of violence. The hero of the Western asserts his honor and demonstrates the possibility of "style" in the face of inevitable defeat. He asserts that even in killing and being killed we are not freed from the necessity of establishing an admirable mode of behavior. Because the pattern of the classical Western is so firmly fixed, our pleasure is that of the connoisseur. We must appreciate minor variations in the characteristics of the actors who play the hero's role, and it is only in virtue of the film's ability to record such variations that these films can remain interesting to us. Any attempt to break the set pattern (to violate the "rules" of the genre), either by turning the Western into a "social drama" (as in *The Ox-Bow Incident*) or by aestheticizing it (as in *Shane*), destroys its power. According to Warshow, part of our pleasure in this kind of complete and self-contained art derives precisely from its contrast with the more complex, uncertain, and self-conscious creations of modernism. The art of the

Western is not an art that precedes modernism (as it is for Stanley Cavell), but one that is contemporary with it and draws strength from the contrast.

Susan Sontag also sees the relationship of a genre, the science fiction fantasy that emerged in the 1950s, to the most important issues of modernist works. She shows how, because of the differences in the media, the science fiction film differs from the science fiction novel, and her account of the genre indicates the relationship, recognized by Braudy and Warshow as well, between the rise and fall of genres and the social realities they reflect. Like the Western, the science fiction film has a typical hero and a recurrent structure. It too is concerned with the anxieties of contemporary life. But its fear of "depersonalization" is ambivalent and its attitude toward destruction is aesthetic; it fails to make the kind of authentic response to the contemporary situation that can be found in the best modernist works.

For Braudy, Warshow, and Sontag there is an implicit connection between a popular genre and the social attitudes of contemporary audiences who respond to it. But Molly Haskell, the contemporary film critic, defines one important genre as an explicit manifestation of social attitudes. Although for years the "Woman's Film" was a bread-and-butter staple of the Hollywood diet—one of the most profitable of film genres for the major studios in their most golden eras—these films were consistently disparaged by critics as trivial, sentimental tear-jerkers. Haskell sees these critical reactions as symptomatic of the totally male circle of film critics who responded to male films as "psychological" and to male-centered melodramas—westerns, adventures, gangsters—as dynamic and important, but to female-centered melodramas as mere "weepers." For Haskell, the "Woman's Film" was the one Hollywood genre that the totally male movie industry made exclusively for women and about the social, moral, emotional, and psychological problems of women. "Its recurrent themes represent the closest thing to an expression of collective drives, conscious and unconscious, of American women." The conflicts familiar to the "Woman's Film's" protagonists—the choice between marriage and lover, marriage and career, sexual love and maternal love; the inevitability of compromise and sacrifice—make the genre both the embodiment of the era's social stereotyping of woman's role and a revealing indication of the limited number of choices that American women could make.

As we have seen, Braudy regards Fred Astaire and Gene Kelly as significant figures, and their musicals as among Hollywood's greatest successes, while Warshow grants such places of honor to the gangster and the westerner. Others, however, would reserve that honor for the comedies of the silent period, a genre to which James Agee, the most celebrated film critic of the last generation, calls attention in his affectionate tribute. For Agee, however, sound comedy reveals a radical deterioration, which he is inclined to attribute to an incompatibility between comic style and speech. No doubt there is such an incompatibility between some comic styles (particularly the most physical ones) and speech, but the Hollywood dialogue comedies of the 1930s and early 1940s have themselves come to be considered a genre, the screwball comedy, that look as good in retrospect as many of the silent classics (partially because they also sound so good).

John Cawelti, the contemporary academic analyst of American popular culture, treats the issue of genre in a much broader context. On the one hand, he traces a familiar film genre—the private-eye, detective film—back to its roots as a popular genre of American mass-market fiction. For Cawelti, the generic categories of American studio films have their analogues and ancestors in American popular fictions. On the other, he notes a new attitude toward genre that has dominated many American films of the past decade, particularly the most interesting and important ones—the generic transformation. This deliberately self-conscious transforming of familiar film genres might be seen as an American compromise between the modernist art-films of post-war Europe and the traditional American tendency toward generic plots and characters. Cawelti sees these contemporary generic transformations, though a manifestation of a single spirit, as having four emphases. The film can parody a familiar genre (as Mel Brooks's films do), can nostalgically evoke a familiar genre (as a film like *Farewell, My Lovely* does), can demythologize the familiar genre (as *Chinatown* and Arthur Penn's films do), or can recog-

439

nize its artificiality but deliberately choose to sustain the myth of the familiar genre (as Sam Peckinpah's films do). Of these four transformations, Cawelti finds the demythologizing film the richest, most complex, and most challenging to its audience's values and responses, approaching the complexity of response required for European art-films. Like Braudy, Warshow, Sontag, and Haskell, Cawelti sees this contemporary attitude toward genre as not merely a manifestation of evolving aesthetic tastes but of underlying social attitudes as well.

To categorize fictional narrative films as representatives of particular genres is only one way to classify possible kinds of films. According to a much broader system of classification, fictional films are themselves only one type of film. One might divide the history of film into four major traditions: fiction, nonfiction (or documentary), animation, and experimental. Although these categories are, like those of fictional genres, widely recognized and accepted, they are also highly problematic. If fictional narrative films tell stories by presenting an *imitation* of a human action, one might claim that nonfiction films (or documentary films) document or present a *real* human action. But what if the nonfiction filmmaker uses actors (as Lionel Rogosin's *On the Bowery* does) to impersonate real persons performing a real process or event? What if the filmmaker uses a real person (as Robert Flaherty used Nanook) to enact his performing a real event (say, building his igloo), when he is building his igloo for the camera and not for himself as a place to live? And if we must assign a purpose to a nonfiction film, is it merely to record a real human action, or is it to teach the audience something about that action?

The animated film scrambles the problem still more, for this classification is not determined by the relation of a film to reality but simply by the manner of making it—the mechanical way the film has been shot, a single frame at a time. Animated films can both tell stories (whether in short cartoons or feature-length ones, not to mention the combination of animation and live action in films such as *Anchors Aweigh* and *Song of the South*) and demonstrate real processes (as in the animated series produced by Frank Capra, "Hemo the Magnificent," which demonstrates the ways in which blood cells convert ox-

440

ygen into nutriment). Finally, experimental films can only be defined according to a vague, spiritual desire—"to experiment." In fact, films commonly accepted as experimental have told stories (albeit poetic stories, like Jean Cocteau's *Blood of a Poet*, Maya Deren's *Meshes of the Afternoon*, and Kenneth Anger's *Fireworks*), have documented real processes (such as Alberto Cavalcanti's *Rien que les heures*, Dziga-Vertov's *The Man with the Movie Camera*, and Ralph Steiner's H_2O), and have used animation (for example, Hans Richter, Oskar Fischinger, Robert Breer, and Stan VanDerBeek). Despite these difficulties, which can be overcome by theories and conceptions which are sufficiently complex, genre studies have provided some of the richest and most suggestive contributions to film criticism—among them studies of the nonfiction film, the animated film, and the experimental film.

If one argues (as Kracauer does) that film is photographic by nature and that it has a special affinity with the physical world, then the nonfiction film (Richard Barsam's more precise term for what is commonly called "documentary film") necessarily holds a special and privileged place among film genres. Barsam, a contemporary analyst of the nonfiction film tradition, argues that the appeal of the nonfiction film comes directly from its relationship to the realist aesthetic, as propounded by Kracauer and Bazin: the desire "to record life as it is," in order "to understand its complexities by showing us that even the most complex social issues come from conflicting needs of individual human beings." Barsam divides the nonfiction film tradition into its own system of six genres—the factual film, the documentary, direct cinema, the travel film, the instructional film, and the newsreel—revealing that nonfiction films can be grouped according to classes and categories, just as fictional narrative films can.

On the other hand, Gilbert Seldes, an American student of popular culture, and Joe Adamson, a young American critic and animator, reject the realistic bias as dogmatic and untenable in view of the brilliant success of animated cartoons which, in Adamson's words, create "a new outpost of reality," a world "with its own set of physical laws and behavioral properties." Film, after all, is not essentially a photographic medium. A filmmaker can draw directly on celluloid, and even his photographs can be of drawings or of other photographs.

Annette Michelson, a contemporary art critic and film aesthetician, also looks beyond the traditional issues raised by realism in identifying the class of films that interests her most. Instead, she groups a series of films and filmmakers according to their modernist "aspiration" that spans the entire history of film. She does not believe modernism came to the film (as it did for Cavell) with the decline of Hollywood. Nor does she see modernism as a threat to the film, as Cavell does. On the contrary, Hollywood, and the triumph of the commercialism and mass culture which it represents, brought the first and classic phase of film modernism to an end. Never again would we see the combination of formal and political radicalism that reached its consummation in the Soviet film of the 1920s.

But Michelson discerns a re-emergence of the radical spirit in a new kind of film, the film of radical aspiration. In Europe the post-Eisensteinian film accepts this "Fall from Grace," this "dissociation" of formal experimentation and radical political commitment, but attempts to exploit the divorce for valid aesthetic purposes. European filmmakers like Resnais and Godard have accepted the conventions of commercial Hollywood cinema and made it the basis for their radical political inquiries. Godard's *Alphaville*, for instance, uses the genre of the Hitchcock suspense story to meditate on the agony and death of love, liberty, and language, on the fate of a society trapped in the self-perpetuating dialectic of terrified progress. The American "independent" filmmakers, on the contrary, have been forced to separate formal and political radicalism in a different way. The best recent work, such as Stan Brakhage's and Michael Snow's, is marked by a rejection of radical political content, turning exclusively to the filmmaker's questioning and exposing the ways that the cinema creates its illusions of reality, space, depth, and motion. In both its European and American forms, the film of radical aspiration makes a kind of response to our situation that is closest to the demythologizing transformation described by Cawelti, but which the Western, as described by Warshow, and the science-fiction film, as described by Sontag, do not succeed in making.

442

LEO BRAUDY
FROM
THE WORLD IN A FRAME

GENRE:
THE CONVENTIONS
OF CONNECTION

Actually I do not think that there are any wrong reasons for liking a statue or a picture . . . There are wrong reasons for disliking a work of art.

E. H. GOMBRICH,
The Story of Art

No part of the film experience has been more consistently cited as a barrier to serious critical interest than the existence of forms and conventions, whether in such details as the stereotyped character, the familiar setting, and the happy ending, or in those films that share common characteristics—westerns, musicals, detective films, horror films, escape films, spy films—in short, what have been called *genre* films. Films in general have been criticized for their popular and commercial appeal, seemingly designed primarily for entertainment and escape rather than enlightenment. Genre films especially are criticized because they seem to appeal to a pre-existing audience, while the film "classic" creates its own special audience through the unique power of the filmmaking artist's personal creative sensibility. Too often in genre films the creator seems gone and only the audience is present, to be attacked for its bad taste and worse politics for even appreciating this debased art.

The critical understanding of genre films therefore becomes

a special case of the problem of understanding films in general. Genre films offend our most common definition of artistic excellence: the uniqueness of the art object, whose value can in part be defined by its desire to be uncaused and unfamiliar, as much as possible unindebted to any tradition, popular or otherwise. The pure image, the clear personal style, the intellectually respectable content are contrasted with the impurities of convention, the repetitions of character and plot. We undervalue their attractions and inner dynamics because there seems to be no critical vocabulary with which to talk about them without condescending, and therefore no aesthetic criteria by which to judge them, no way of understanding why one horror film scares us and another leaves us cold, why one musical is a symphony of style and another a clashing disarray.

Critics have ignored genre films because of their prejudice for the unique. But why should art be restricted only to works of self-contained intensity, while many other kinds of artistic experience are relegated to the closet of aesthetic pleasure, unfit for the daylight? Genre films, in fact, arouse and complicate feelings about the self and society that more serious films, because of their bias toward the unique, may rarely touch. Within film the pleasures of originality and the pleasures of familiarity are at least equally important. Following Marcel Duchamp and Antonin Artaud, Andy Warhol in the early 1960s announced "no more classics." In painting and sculpture this meant an attack on the canonization of museum art and the acceptance of previously unacceptable, often popular, forms. For films, the problem has usually been the other way around. "No more classics" for film might mean no more films defined as separate from the popular forms that are the great energy of film, artistically as well as thematically.

The modern prejudice against genre in art can be traced to the aesthetic theories of the Romantic period. In the later eighteenth century the older idea of poetic inspiration began to be expanded into a major literary theory by works like Edward Young's *Conjectures on Original Composition* (1759). Poetic "imitation," the building of creativity on the achievements of the past, began to fade as the standard of personal vision became

444

more important. Only conventions that could be understood literally survived, and the eighteenth-century unwillingness to accord imaginative sympathy to convention received its most famous expression in Samuel Johnson's attack on John Milton's *Lycidas*, a poem in the form of a pastoral elegy, which drew upon a tradition of lament that went back to Theocritus and Vergil. The English and German Romantic writers consolidated this trend by establishing originality not only as a criterion of art, but, in their crudest statements, the *only* criterion of art. Art could owe nothing to tradition or the past because that debt qualified the power and originality of the individual creator. The poet was inspired by what he saw and experienced, and the intervention of any prior categories for that experience doomed the work to secondary value unless the forms that intervened were primitive forms—the folktale or the ballad—that had none of the hated sophistication of the art of the previous age. Any use of genre and convention as such necessarily debarred a work and its author from the status of true art. If poetry were defined as the spontaneous outpouring of strong feelings, how could a work that employed stock characters and stock situations, stock images and stock resolutions, have any art or originality in it? Folk art or popular art could be used because it was generally assumed that serious art was the purity of which popular art was the degeneracy, and that purity necessarily precedes degeneracy.* Poetic inspiration and self-sufficiency occupied the higher peaks of art, while hack work and despised formulas inhabited the more populated and bourgeois valleys. Genre and convention were the fare of the multitudes, while originality and storming self-as-

---

*Ballad-collectors like Bishop Percy or Sir Walter Scott could therefore argue that their rewritings were an effort to restore the ballads to the form in which the "Bard" originally created them, before they were passed on to the fumbling brains of the folk. Pop Art has revived this theory in a somewhat different form. Ostensibly making us look at the common objects of the world with new intensity, Pop Art also conveys the idea that serious art and artists make popular themes and motifs worthy (read "self-conscious") by putting them into museum settings and charging high prices. Warhol may have first done this to satirize the whole elitist-popular division, but the joke seems to have run thin.

sertion, without a past, without any controls, was the caviar of the truly aware audience.

Until the eighteenth century, artists had generally been distinguished by their class, their education, and their patrons. But, with the growth of a mass society and a mass culture, the hierarchy shifted from distinctions in genealogy to distinctions in sensibility. Almost all of the great eighteenth-century English novelists and essayists had spent some time in Grub Street, that world created to serve the new hunger for the printed word. But the Romantic sensibility turned Grub Street into a synonym for the convention-ridden enemies of art. The true artist was noncommercial, struggling on the fringes of human existence, with neither society nor companions (and hardly any publishers), alone with his indomitable self. Only Byron, the most eighteenth-century of the Romantics, could have said, "I awoke to find myself famous" (on the publication of *Childe Harold*); such an obvious interest in the approval of a book-buying public was disdained in the Romantics' image of their calling. And Byron himself preoccupied much of his writing with the depiction of solitary heroes, striding mountainsides to challenge gloomy fates. The Romantic artist tried to make his work unique to escape from the dead hand of traditional form. The only serious use of the past was the contemplation of vanished greatness, to raise the artist out of what he believed to be an uncultured present and establish for himself a continuity with what has been best before the triumph of modern degeneracy. Like T. S. Eliot in *The Wasteland,* the serious, unpopular artist was the only one in a corrupt age who could summon up the artistic Eden of the past and collect its fragments into some coherence.

Such absolute creativity is finally a fraud because all art must exist in some relation to the forms of the past, whether in contrast or continuation. Both the generic work and the more self-contained work expand our sense of the possibilities of art. But the nineteenth-century stress on literary originality and freedom has inhibited our responses, both intellectual and emotional, to works that try to complicate our appreciation of tradition and form, works that may in fact embody a more radical critique of the past than those which ignore it. More people dislike westerns or musicals because such film genres outrage their inherited and unexamined sense of what art *should* be than because the films are offensive in theme, characterization, style, or other artistic quality. Every lover of musicals, for example, has heard the complaint that musicals are unrealistic and the viewer gets embarrassed when people start singing or dancing. But the relationship between realism and stylization is a central issue in musicals, not an absurd convention. When auteur critics applaud the studio director for triumphing over his material and point to the glimmers of original style shining through the genre assignment, they may awaken us to the merits of an individual artist. But they also fall into the Romantic trap of searching for only what is obviously original and personal in a work. In auteur theory, genre directors with large popular audiences become transformed into embattled Romantic artists trying to establish their personal visions in the face of an assembly-line commercialism. Frank Capra has pointed out the opposite possibility: in the days of big studio monopoly, there was a great deal of freedom to experiment because every film had guaranteed distribution, whereas now, with increased independent production, films have become more uniform and compromised, because each has to justify itself financially. Underground and avant-garde films with their emphasis on the individual creative sensibility above all, are naturally enough the most hostile to genre. But the bulk of films fall between pure personal expression and pure studio exploitation, mingling the demands of art and culture, creativity and talent. By their involvement in collective creativity, film directors have, at least practically, moved away from the image of the isolated Romantic artist, no matter how they may indulge that image in their public statements.

Instead of dismissing genre films from the realm of art, we should therefore examine what they accomplish. Genre in films can be the equivalent of conscious reference to tradition in the other arts—the invocation of past works that has been so important a part of the history of literature, drama, and painting. Miró's use of Vermeer, Picasso's use of Delacroix are efforts to distinguish their view of the proper ends of paint-

447

ing. Eliot's use of Spenser or Pynchon's of Joyce make similar assertions of continuity and difference. The methods of the western, the musical, the detective film, or the science-fiction film are also reminiscent of the way Shakespeare infuses old stories with new characters to express the tension between past and present. All pay homage to past works even while they vary their elements and comment on their meaning.

Perhaps the main difference between genre films and classic films is the way that genre films invoke past forms while classic films spend time denying them. The joy in genre is to see what can be dared in the creation of a new form or the creative destruction and complication of an old one. The ongoing genre subject therefore always involves a complex relation between the compulsions of the past and the freedoms of the present, an essential part of the film experience. The single, unique work tries to be unforgettable by solving the whole world at once. The genre work, because of its commitment to pre-existing forms, explores the world more slowly. Its hallmark is less the flash of inspiration than the deep exploration of craft. Like Ford's *Stagecoach* or Aldrich's *Ulzana's Raid* (1972) it can exist both in itself and as the latest in a line of works like it, picking and choosing among possible conventions, refusing one story or motif to indulge another, avoiding one "cliché" in order to show a self-conscious mastery of the cliché that has not been avoided. After all, the reason that an artistic element becomes a cliché is that it answers so well to the experience, intelligence, and feelings of the audience. Subsequent artists, perceiving the same aptness, want to exercise its power themselves, even in a potentially hostile new context, to discover if all the possibilities of the form have thoroughly been explored. The only test is its continuing relevance, and a genre will remain vital, as the western has, and the musical has not, so long as its conventions still express themes and conflicts that preoccupy its audience. When either minority or majority art loses contact with its audience, it becomes a mere signpost in history, an aesthetic rather than an art.

Genre films affect their audience especially by their ability to express the warring traditions in society and the social importance of understanding convention. When Irene Dunne, in

448

The Awful Truth (Leo McCarey, 1937), disguises herself as Cary Grant's (fictitious) sister and arrives drunk and raucous at a society gathering where Grant is trying to establish himself, we can open a critical trapdoor and say that the other people at the party, who already know her, don't recognize her in her flimsy disguise because of the necessities of plot and comic form. But we must go on to say that this particular convention, used with all its force, allows McCarey, without dropping the general humorous tone, to point out that she is recognized because the upper classes base their estimates and knowledge of character on dress, voice, and manners—a theme supported by the rest of the film as well. The conflict between desire and etiquette can define both a social comedy like *The Awful Truth* and even a more obviously stylized genre work like *Dr. Jekyll and Mr. Hyde* (Rouben Mamoulian, 1932); it parallels in the plot the aesthetic contrast between the individual film and the conventions to which it plays a complex homage.

Genre demands that we know the dynamics of proper audience response and may often require a special audience because of the need to refer the latest instance to previous versions. But response is never invariable. Convention isn't only whatever we don't have to pay attention to. Explaining Shakespeare's use of soliloquies by observing that the practice was an Elizabethan dramatic convention tells us as little as saying that Picasso used blue because it was cheap or that Edward Everett Horton appeared in so many Fred Astaire-Ginger Rogers films because comic relief was needed. Why a soliloquy *now?* What does Horton's presence mean *here?* The possibility exists in all art that convention and comment coexist, that overlapping and even contradictory assumptions and conventions may be brought into play to test their power and make the audience reflect on why they were assumed. The genre film lures its audience into a seemingly familiar world, filled with reassuring stereotypes of character, action, and plot. But the world may actually be not so lulling, and, in some cases, acquiescence in convention will turn out to be bad judgment or even a moral flaw—the basic theme of such Hitchcock films as *Blackmail* (1929), *Rear Window* (1954), and *Psycho*. While avant-garde and original works congratulate the audience by

449

implying it has the capacity to understand them, genre films can exploit the automatic conventions of response for the purposes of pulling the rug out from under their viewers. The very relaxing of the critical intelligence of the audience, the relief that we need not make decisions—aesthetic, moral, metaphysical—about the film, allows the genre film to use our expectations against themselves, and, in the process, reveal to us expectations and assumptions that we may never have thought we had. They can potentially criticize the present, because it too automatically *accepts* the standards of the past, to build subversion within received forms and thereby to criticize the forms instead of only setting up an alternate vision.*

Through a constant interplay between the latest instance and the history of a particular form, genre films can call upon a potential of aesthetic complexity that would be denied if the art defined itself only in terms of its greatest and most inimitable works. Because of the existence of generic expectations— how a plot "should" work, what a stereotyped character "should" do, what a gesture, a location, an allusion, a line of dialogue "should" mean—the genre film can step beyond the moment of its existence and play against its own aesthetic history. Through genre, movies have drawn upon their own tradition and been able to reflect a rich heritage unavailable to the "high" arts of the twentieth century which are so often intent upon denying the past and creating themselves totally anew each time out. Within the world of genre films one finds battles, equivalent to those in the history of literature, drama, and painting, between artists who are willing to reproduce a

---

*The three main American critics who appreciated such films before the New Wave popularized them critically—Otis Ferguson, James Agee, and Manny Farber—were less interested in them for their formal qualities than for their action and unpretentiousness, aspects of energy related to their formal self-consciousness. But both Agee and Farber (and Pauline Kael is their true heir in this) wanted to protect at all costs their beloved movies from any charge of art. As far as the definition of art they were attacking goes, they were right. But to continue such attacks now confuses where it once illuminated. One virtue of the French New Wave critics was that they didn't have to defend themselves simultaneously against pompous ideas of high art, the myth of the American tough guy artist, and the specter of Hollywood commercialism.

tradition through their own vision because they believe it still has the ability to evoke the emotional response that made it a satisfying artistic form to begin with, and those who believe the form has dried up and needs an injection, usually of "realism." Poets, for example, may contrast the city and the country because that opposition answers to some real beliefs in their audience and because the choice of the rural virtues of the country satisfactorily resolves the conflict. Others might question the authenticity of the traditional materials: did shepherds really play their pipes in singing contests? isn't the elaborate language untrue to rural idioms? or, to extend the analogy, did cowboys really respect law and justice so much? do people really break into dances on the street when they're happy, and does the neighborhood automatically join in? The later generations may feel an emotional pull in the form, but they might want to destylize it and make it more real. The directors of the "adult" western of the 1950s accepted the vitality of the western but thought that a more realistic treatment would strengthen its inherent virtues. If controversy were part of film tradition, we might have an argument between John Ford and Fred Zinnemann on the essence of the western like that between Alexander Pope and Ambrose Phillips on the pastoral, Ford and Pope arguing for the value of form and style, while Zinnemann and Phillips press the need to make the characters of art as close as possible to the real persons who live or lived in that place.

Genre films share many of the characteristics of the closed films I have described in the previous chapter. But, instead of being framed visually, genre films are primarily *closed by convention*. Of course, they may be visually enclosed as well, as, for example, are horror films and 1930s musicals; but the more important enclosure is the frame of pre-existing motifs, plot turns, actors, and situations—in short everything that makes the film a special place with its own rules, a respite from the more confusing and complicated worlds outside. The frame of genre, the existence of expectations to be used in whatever way the intelligence of the filmmaker is capable, allows freedoms within the form that more original films cannot have because they are so committed to a parallel between form and

451

content. The typical genre situation is a contrast between form and content. With the expectations of stock characters, situations, or narrative rhythms, the director can choose areas of free aesthetic play within. In genre films the most obvious focus of interest is neither complex characterization nor intricate visual style, but pure story. Think about the novel we can't put down. That rare experience in literature is the common experience in film, where we stay only because we want to, where we often must be intrigued by the first five minutes or not at all, and where we know that once we leave the spell is broken. Like fairy tales or classical myths, genre films concentrate on large contrasts and juxtapositions. Genre plots are usually dismissed with a snide synopsis (a process that is never very kind to drama that employs conventions, like Shakespeare's plays). But, amid the conventions and expectations of plot, other kinds of emphasis can flourish. To the unsympathetic eye, the pleasures of variation are usually invisible, whether they appear in the medieval morality play, the Renaissance sonnet, the Restoration comedy, the eighteenth-century portrait, the Chopinesque etude, the horror film, the romantic comedy, the musical, or the western. When we can perceive the function of vampire-film conventions in *Persona* or boxing-film conventions in *On the Waterfront* as clearly as we note the debt of Kurosawa's samurai films to American westerns, or that of the New Wave films to American crime films of the 1950s, then we will be able to appreciate more fully the way in which films can break down the old visions between elite and popular art to establish, almost unbeknown to aesthetics and criticism, a vital interplay between them. . . .*

---

*The way in which television "cannibalizes" material therefore has less to do with its constant demand than with the speed with which such material becomes outdated. When the audience accepts material as generic and ritualistic—situation comedy, talk shows, sports, news, weather—the form can include an infinite variety of nuance. But when the paradigms are no longer emotionally appealing, formal variety will do no good and there arises a desperate, cannibalizing, attempt to discover the new form of audience solace, whether the subject matter is Dick Cavett or the Vietnam War. Thus the whole process of cultural history is speeded up through successive purgations of used-up subject matter and style.

The epic sweep of the early westerns could be conveyed by the silent screen, but musicals necessarily begin their real film career with sound (and sound films begin, appropriate enough, with *The Jazz Singer*). The Charleston sequences of the silent *Our Dancing Daughters* (Harry Beaumont, 1928) look oddly impersonal and detached today, hardly more real than the bunny-costumed Rockettes. Sound not only individualizes the performer, but also provides a bridge of music between otherwise separate visual moments, a continuity against which the image can play, potentially freeing the film from a strict adherence to a one-to-one relation between sight and sound. Once sound frees image from the necessity to appear logical and casual, the director can experiment with different kinds of nonlogical, noncausal narrative. But, after the first years of sound and such experiments with the new form as René Clair's *Under the Roofs of Paris* (1929), Lang's *M* (1931), Renoir's *Boudu Saved from Drowning* (1932), and Ernst Lubitsch's *Trouble in Paradise* (1932), primarily musicals explored its possibilities. The western may be self-conscious about its myths, but the musical is self-conscious about its stylization, the heightened reality that is its norm. The games with continuous narrative that Busby Berkeley plays in the musical numbers of *Footlight Parade* (1933), *42nd Street* (1933), or *Gold Diggers of 1935* are hardly attempted by nonmusical directors until the jumpcutting achronicity of the New Wave.

Berkeley's films show how the stylistic self-consciousness of musicals directly concerns the relation of their art to the everyday world outside the confines of the film. His camera presses relentlessly forward, through impossible stages that open up endlessly, expanding the inner space of film and affirming the capacity of the world of style to mock the narrowness of the "real" world outside the theater walls, populated by bland tenors, greedy producers, and harried directors. Ford uses theater in *Liberty Valance* to purify his genre vision. But Berkeley uses theater, the impossible theater available to film artifice, to give a sense of exuberance and potential. Playing with space, Berkeley in *Footlight Parade* creates an incredible extravaganza supposedly taking place in miniature within a waterfall, with pyramids of swimming girls, diving cameras, and fifty-foot fountains.

453

Berkeley's real problem, however, is his concentration on the production number and the spectacle. The sense of play and opulence he brought to the musical, his effort to make its stage artifice a source of strength, was, if we look back upon the direction the musical took, a minor stream in its history. His influence appears in the show business biography (*A Star Is Born*, 1937; *The Jolson Story*, 1946; *Funny Girl*, 1968), the production story (*Summer Stock*, 1950; *The Band Wagon*, 1953), and that great amalgam of realized style and stylized realism, *Singin' in the Rain* (1952). There is also a darker side apparent in a film like *All About Eve* (1950), in which the urge to theater is considered to be manipulative, a reduction of the self rather than an expansion. The dark side may be the truer side of Berkeley's inheritance, because his musicals lack any sense of the individual. The strange melancholy of the "Lullaby of Broadway" number from *Gold Diggers of 1935*, in which, after some elaborately uplifting production numbers, an unsuccessful showgirl commits suicide, combines comedy and the tragedy of sentimental realism in a way that only penetrated serious films in the late 1940s. It presages the urbane tragedies of fatality in a theatrical setting that mark the late films of Julien Duvivier (*Flesh and Fantasy*, 1943) and Max Ophuls (*La Ronde*, 1950; *Lola Montès*, 1955). The showgirl commits suicide in "Lullaby of Broadway" in part because the Berkeley ensemble of faceless dancers holds no place for her at all, perhaps because of her lack of talent, but more clearly because her individuality is contrary to the demands of the uniform musical group. Like Eisenstein or the Lang of *Metropolis*, Berkeley magisterially juxtaposes sequences and articulates crowds with ritual symmetry. Berkeley's atttitude toward individuals is that of a silent film director, iconographic and symmetric. The community of the Berkeley girls is cold and anonymous, like Lang's workers, a community created by a nonparticipating choreographer-director. But the kind of musical that had the greatest popular strength, spawned the largest number of descendants, and historically defined the American musical film, is the musical in which the dancer-choreographer himself was a participant, in which an individual man danced with an individual woman, and in which the theme of the individual energy of the dance, the relation of the dancer to his own body, became the main theme of the film. Obviously I am referring to the films of Fred Astaire and Ginger Rogers.*

Shall We Dance (1937, songs by George and Ira Gershwin), the last film of the basic Astaire-Rogers series, is a model of their films, perhaps not least because it contains a final sequence that seems to be an implicit attack against the Berkeley emphasis on anonymous spectacle. Astaire plays the Great Petrov, star of the Russian ballet, who is in reality Peter P. Peters, from Philadelphia. The basic conflict of the film is established in the first scene, when Petrov's manager Jeff (Edward Everett Horton) comes into his rehearsal room to find Petrov improvising a dance to a jazz record. "The Great Petrov doesn't dance for fun," he tells him, emphasizing that ballet is a serious business to which the artist must devote his full time. "But I do," responds Astaire. "Remember me? Pete Peters from Philadelphia, P.A.?" Horton points to the taps on Astaire's ballet shoes and continues his insistence that whatever Astaire is doing, it's not art. "Maybe it's just the Philadelphia in me," says Astaire, and begins dancing again. The forces have been set in motion: the dancing that Astaire likes to do when he is alone directly expresses his personal emotions as well as his real identity—the American tap dancer under the high-culture disguise of the Russian ballet dancer. Horton, as he usually does in these films, comically combines a commitment to high culture (and high society) with a definite antagonism to emotion and feeling. When Astaire falls in love with Linda Keene (Ginger Rogers), a nightclub dancer, after seeing a series of movie-like flip cards of her dancing, Horton speaks darkly of the danger to Astaire's "serious" career and the need to be personally pure (i.e., nonsexual and nonemotional) for art. Like so many musicals, *Shall We Dance* contrasts the emotionally detached and formal patterns of high

---

*Rouben Mamoulian in *Love Me Tonight* (1932, songs by Rodgers and Hart) focuses on individuals (Jeanette MacDonald and Maurice Chevalier), but the style of the film is still one of directional control rather than a performer's energy. The most impressive song settings are those in which parts of the song are sung and played by people in isolated places, visually linked by the director's wit and style (for example, "Isn't It Romantic?").

art with the involved and spontaneous forms of popular art. (Vincente Minnelli's *Meet Me in St. Louis*, 1944, for example, establishes the same relationship between serious music and popular music, and many musicals include parodies of serious theater by vaudevillians.) The 1930s musical may have its historical roots in the silent-film urge to the respectability of theater, the importation of theatrical performers both to give the young industry tone and to banish the generally lower-class associations that film had from its vaudeville beginnings. But the sound musical—like so many genres of the 1930s, comedies and horror films included—begins to mock this respect for older forms just as it parodies the upper class in general. Tap dancing is superior to ballet as movies are superior to drama, not merely because they are more popular, but because they contain more life and possibility. The flip-card stills that turn into a sequence of Rogers dancing present her as a creature of the film, not the stage. Like Astaire in the film, Rogers is also an American, but more proudly: she doesn't like the "hand-kissing heel-clickers of Paris" and rejects Peters when he attempts to impress her by coming on as the formal Petrov. Berkeley attacks theater in favor of film and dance by destroying the limits of theatrical space. But Astaire and Rogers (and their directors, especially Mark Sandrich and choreographer Hermes Pan) attack all high art in favor of the new dancing forms of spontaneity, American style. The Berkeleyan world spawns the myth of show-business biography that success on stage buys only unhappiness in one's personal life. But the silvery world of Astaire and Rogers celebrates the ability of individual energy to break away from the dead hand of society, class and art as well. The open space of the western that offers a chance to build becomes in the musical the endless inner energy released in dance.

Shall We Dance is defined by the collision between the forces of inertia and stasis and the forces of vitality, between Astaire as Petrov—the commitment to high art and personal repression—and Astaire as Peters—the commitment to an art that attempts to structure individual energy instead of excluding it. Musical comedy therefore also attacks any theories of acting in which character comes from the past. Character in musical

456

comedy is physiological and external: the ability to dance and the way dancing functions in specific situations becomes a direct expression of the tensions within the self. In the first scene Astaire dances along at the proper speed; and then, when the machine needs to be wound up again, he slows down as the record itself slows down. On the ship that takes him and Rogers back to America, he descends into the engine room and dances there in time to the pistons while black members of the crew who are taking a musical break play for him. In both sequences the energy of the dance—the personal emphasis in the first, the relation to jazz and black music in the second ("Slap That Bass")—draws upon the analogy between body and machine. But here, unlike literary attacks against the machine, the film, true to its mechanical and technological origins, celebrates the machine as a possible element in the liberation of the individual rather than in his enslavement (similar to the ambivalence about machines that characterizes *Metropolis*). Machines are outside class, purifiers of movement. The real threat to individual energy and exuberance is not the machine, but the forces of society and respectability—the impresario Jeff, the rich suitor Jim with the weak chin (William Brisbane), who wants to take Rogers away from show business, and the punctilious hotel manager Cecil Flintridge (Eric Blore). Here they are comic, but they nevertheless play the same repressive roles as they would in the more melodramatic world of the western.*

At the end of *Shall We Dance*, the comically hostile forces (including an outside world of publicity and gossip) are reconciled by Astaire's typical process of self-realization—the search for the perfect partner. The perfect partner is always a dancing partner, since it is within the world of dance that true communication and complementarity can be achieved: the male-female dance duo is a model of male-female relationship

---

*The positive interpretation of the machine analogy to the body is a constant theme in musicals, most recently expressed in the Ken Russell film of *Tommy* (1975, words and music by Peter Townshend and The Who), in which the deaf, dumb, and blind boy first discovers his real nature through his symbiotic relation with pinball machines.

457

in general. Dancing isn't a euphemism for sex; in Astaire-Rogers films at least, dancing is much better. Two sequences in *Shall We Dance* constitute the dance of courtship and they appear after the first dancing sequences, which establish the separate personalities of Astaire and Rogers. In the first, "They All Laughed," Astaire begins with ballet-like steps while Rogers stands still. Then she begins to tap, and he responds, first with a ballet version of the tapping, then a straight tap. In the second such number, "Let's Call the Whole Thing Off," the importance of the dancing situation to their relationship is further underlined. They are taking a walk in a stage-set Central Park and decide to go skating, even though neither of them has skated in a long time. They begin very haltingly, with frequent stumbles. But, as soon as the music starts, they skate perfectly together. Then, at the end of the song, as the music ends, they hit the grass outside the skating rink and fall down. Once the magic world of dance and its ability to idealize personal energy into a model of relationship has vanished, Astaire and Rogers again become separate and even bickering individuals. "Let's Call the Whole Thing Off" memorializes their differences, even while it provides a context for their relationship. The next musical number, "They Can't Take That Away from Me," contains no dancing. It takes place at night on a ferry between New Jersey and New York and emphasizes the problems of their relationship, especially the seeming conflict between their real feelings, which can be expressed at night, and the public and social demands on them that the daylight world of the rest of the film exerts. Like Astaire and Rogers themselves, who feel the pressure to continue their successful film partnership despite their own wishes, Peter Peters and Linda Keene have been forced into marriage primarily so they can get divorced. The publicity generated by their managers is meant to connect them, but it succeeds only in driving them apart, as aesthetic as well as emotional partners.

Astaire solves the conflict and rejoins Rogers in the remarkable final sequence. In a theatrical setting reminiscent of the roof of the Winter Garden, an open space within the city, Astaire stages a show that summarizes the main elements of the film. In the early sequences Astaire plays a Russian ballet dancer; Rogers appears; he loses her. Meanwhile, the real Rogers, the comic Claudius in this mousetrap, sits in a box, part of the audience, but separate from it. Astaire reprises "You Can't Take That Away from Me" to lead into a sequence in which a whole group of dancing partners appear—all wearing a mask with Rogers' face on it. The song then becomes ironic, since the memory of her uniqueness that it celebrates has been confused in the many Rogers of the present. Ruby Keeler is obviously pleased to be multiplied into many images for the adoration of Dick Powell in Berkeley's *Dames* (1934), but the Ginger Rogers in the audience of *Shall We Dance* cannot take this anonymous crowd of Busby Berkeley chorus girls all wearing her face. Astaire's message makes the same plea: deliver me from the life of a single man amid innumerable faceless girls by asserting the perfection of our relationship. Rogers goes backstage and puts on one of the masks. She comes onstage, briefly reveals herself to Astaire, and then glides back into the anonymity of the many Rogers. Which is the real Rogers among the false, the reality and energy of the individual beneath the generalized artifice of the image? Astaire finds her and together they sing and dance the final song, "Shall We Dance," an invitation to let the dancing, emotional energetic self out, to reject depression and the forms of society, and to accept the frame of theater that allows one, through the exuberance of dance, to be free.

The figure of Fred Astaire implies that dance is the perfect form, the articulation of motion that allows the self the most freedom at the same time that it includes the most energy. The figure of Gene Kelly implies that the true end of dance is to destroy excess and attack the pretensions of all forms in order to achieve some new synthesis. Kelly the sailor teaching Jerry the Mouse to dance in *Anchors Aweigh* (George Sidney, 1945) stands next to Bill Robinson teaching Shirley Temple to dance in *The Little Colonel* (David Butler, 1935). Astaire may move dance away from the more formal orders of the ballet, but Kelly emphasizes its appeal to the somewhat recalcitrant, not quite socialized part of the self, where the emotions are hidden. Astaire and Kelly are part of the same continuum of

459

Fred Astaire among the many masks of Ginger Rogers in *Shall We Dance* (1937). "Which is the real Rogers among the false, the reality and energy of the individual beneath the generalized artifice of the image? Astaire finds her and together they sing and dance, 'Shall We Dance', an invitation to let the dancing, emotional energetic self out . . ." (BRAUDY, page 459). Gene Kelly in *Singin' in the Rain* (1952) at the climax of "the great set piece of 'Gotta Dance', another statement of Kelly's belief that dancing is a compulsion from within, more authentic than the forms imposed from without" (BRAUDY, page 468).

themes and motifs in musicals (an interesting study could be done of the interaction of their images in the 1940s and 1950s). There are many contrasts that can be made between the way they use dance and the way they appear in their films, but the basic fact of their continuity should be remembered. The question of personal energy, which I have characterized as the musical's basic theme, once again appears centrally. The social world against which Astaire defined himself in the 1930s no longer had the same attraction to movie audiences in the 1940s; it was a hangover from the early days of film and their simultaneous fascination with 1920s high life and the higher seriousness of theater, in a double effort both to imitate and to mock. Astaire is the consummate theatrical dancer, while Kelly is more interested in the life outside the proscenium. The energy that Astaire defines within a theatrical and socially formal framework Kelly takes outside, into a world somewhat more "real" (that is, similar to the world of the audience) and therefore more recalcitrant. Kelly's whole presence is therefore more rugged and less ethereal than Astaire's. Both Astaire and Kelly resemble Buster Keaton, their prime ancestor in dancing's paean to the freedom and confinement of the body. But Astaire is the spiritual Keaton while Kelly is the combative, energetic Keaton, compounded with the glee of Douglas Fairbanks. Kelly has more obvious physical presence than Astaire, who hides his well-trained body in clothes that give the impression he has nothing so disruptive as muscles, so that the form of his dancing is even more an ideal and a mystery. Astaire often wears suits and tuxedos, while Kelly generally wears open-collared shirts, slacks, white socks, and loafers—a studied picture of informality as opposed to Astaire's generally more formal dress. Astaire wears the purified Art Deco makeup of the 1930s, but Kelly keeps the scar on his cheek visible—an emblem of the interplay between formal style and disruptive realism in his definition of the movie musical.*

---

*I have been using Astaire and Kelly to represent the change in the movie musical as much as I have been describing what they do themselves. A full account would also have to include a close consideration of Eleanor Powell, whose fantastic exuberance and bodily freedom often threatened to destroy

461

Astaire may mock social forms for their rigidity, but Kelly tries to explode them. Astaire purifies the relation between individual energy and stylized form, whereas Kelly tries to find a new form that will give his energy more play. Astaire dances onstage or in a room, expanding but still maintaining the idea of enclosure and theater; Kelly dances on streets, on the roofs of cars, on tables, in general bringing the power of dance to bear on a world that would ordinarily seem to exclude it. (Astaire absorbs this ability of Kelly's to reorganize normal space and integrates it with his own lighter-than-air quality in the dancing on the walls sequence in *Royal Wedding*, 1951, directed by Kelly's favorite collaborator Stanley Donen.) Astaire usually plays a professional dancer; Kelly sometimes does and sometimes does not, although he is usually an artist of some kind, often, as in *The Pirate*, a popular artist, or, as in *Summer Stock*, a director, associated with the stage but not totally inside it. Kelly therefore merges the director emphasis of Berkeley with the performer emphasis of Astaire. To complement the distance from theatrical form Kelly maintains, his whole style of acting is self-mocking, while Astaire's is almost always serious and heartfelt, as far as comedy will allow. Because the film attitude toward serious art is less defensive in the 1940s than in the 1930s, Kelly can include ballet and modern dance in his films, although always in a specifically theatrical setting (the pirate dream ballet in *The Pirate*, the gangster ballet in *Les Girls*). Theater and style in Astaire's films reconcile the conflict between personal life and social pressures, and allow the self to repair and renovate its energy. Many of his films have more or less autobiographical elements in them, not the autobiography of Astaire's private life, but the autobiography of Astaire's professional life: the effect to get a new partner after Ginger Rogers decided to do dramatic films instead (*Easter Parade*, Charles Walters, 1948, with Judy Garland), the celebration of Rogers' return to dance after several

---

the generally theatrical plots in which she was encased. The most important film for these purposes might be *Broadway Melody of 1940* (Norman Taurog), in which she and Astaire dance together with an equality of feeling and ability that presages the teaming of Kelly and Judy Garland.

"serious" films (*The Barkleys of Broadway*, Charles Walters, 1949). Kelly, however, far from taking refuge in theater, wants to make theater take over daily life. His films are hardly ever autobiographical; unlike Astaire's, they have stories in which Kelly plays a role. Astaire may dance by himself, with a partner, or with a company of dancers. Kelly wants to galvanize a community of nondancers as well. Astaire and his partner are professionals; Kelly and his partner are often amateurs, but everyone they meet knows the steps to their dances and the words to their songs.*

A Kelly film that highlights the differences and similarities between the two great definers of the American musical comedy is Vincent Minnelli's *The Pirate* (1948, songs by Cole Porter, story by Frances Goodrich and Albert Hackett). In the beginning of *The Pirate*, Manuela (Judy Garland), the poor niece of a wealthy family on an eighteenth-century Caribbean island, is leafing through a book detailing the highly romanticized adventures of the pirate Macoco. She dreamily desires the embraces of Macoco but is realistically resigned to marrying the unromantic, fat town mayor (Walter Slezak), who courts her with propriety and respect. One of her companions tells her that the life of Macoco is pure fantasy and she responds by expressing the sense of separate worlds she feels within her: "I realize there's a practical world and a dream world. I won't mix them"‡ Enter Serafin (Gene Kelly), the head of a traveling company of players. He flirts with Manuela, and falls in love with her. By accidental hypnosis the reserved Manuela changes into a manic performer, and she

---

*It is worth mentioning that Astaire and Kelly are appropriately enough the two supreme examples of Hollywood stars who never really gave their private lives in any way over to the fan magazines or the mechanism of offscreen publicity, since their screen presences are personal enough.

‡Observers of Vincente Minnelli have often pointed out the constant interest in the clash of reality and dream in his films. Here, of course, I am considering these themes in terms of the larger issue of the history of musicals as a genre. The way specific directors, with their own thematic and stylistic preoccupations, interact with pre-existing conventions to change those conventions and clarify their own interests at the same time is a topic that requires much more minute examination that I can give it here.

and Serafin dance and sing together in a funny scene in which Serafin thinks he's tricked this pretty girl into dancing with him, while the exuberance released in Manuela by the hypnosis threatens to knock him off the stage. Horrified at what she's done, Manuela leaves for her hometown away from the big city to prepare for her marriage to the mayor. Serafin follows her and recognizes the mayor as the real Macoco. He threatens to expose him unless the mayor allows Serafin to pretend that he is Macoco, since Serafin knows of Manuela's hero-worship. The mayor agrees, until he sees that Manuela's attraction to Serafin is increased by the impersonation. The mayor then arrests Serafin and is about to hang him when Serafin, asking for the opportunity to do a last act on stage, plays a scene with Manuela that reveals to the mayor her actual love for Macoco the Pirate. Unaware of the game, the mayor announces that he is the real Macoco and therefore Manuela should love him. He is arrested, and the united Kelly and Garland appear in the last scene as stage partners singing "Be a Clown" to the audience.

Through the personalities of Garland and Kelly, *The Pirate* explores the theme of identity I have discussed in Astaire's films in a very different way. Serafin's courtship of Manuela reveals that her desire for Macoco is a desire for a romantic individualism outside society—a theme made especially strong by setting the film in an eighteenth-century Spanish Roman Catholic country with all its elaborate social forms and ceremonies. Kelly hypnotizes her with a spinning mirror—an image of the many possible selves. The Manuela that is released, the self below the social surface, is a singing, dancing self. Her exuberance indicates that Serafin has in fact released more than he expects or may want. He is a professional artist. But she gets her art directly from her inner life, untamed by society or by learned craft. Garland is perfect for this kind of role because she projects so clearly the image of a restrained, almost mouse-like person until she begins to sing and dance. (Her first important film, *The Wizard of Oz*, Victor Fleming, 1939, solidified this tension in Garland between the acceptance of daily life in a world of drabness and moral boredom, and the possibility of escape to an exuberant singing, dancing world of dream. It appeared as well in *Meet Me in St. Louis,* 1944, another Minnelli film, where the pattern of stability and release is more parallel to that of *The Pirate.*)

Serafin is the alternative to Macoco in more ways than one. The real pirate has changed from an antisocial adventurer to a socially dictatorial mayor, thus rejecting the Macoco side of himself to become almost the opposite. But Kelly instead tries to mediate individuality and community. His first song in the film is "Niña," a typical Kelly dance in a street fair, where he sings and dances with half the surprised people there to weave together a kind of community of otherwise isolated individuals and objects through the catalyst of his own personality and artistic ability. The song relates how he calls every girl he meets "niña," that is, little girl. At the end of the song Garland appears and the amazed Kelly asks her what her name is. Like Rogers at the end of *Shall We Dance,* she stands apart from communal anonymity. Serafin is the articulate adventurer, the popular artist, who sees his art to be part of a creation of community; she is the individual artist, whose art is less craft than a swelling sense of herself from within. We admire and feel friendly to him because he includes us in his dance. But we identify with her, for she, like us, is not professional, even in the loose sense in which Serafin is professional. Serafin realizes this and therefore pretends to be Macoco to win her. In the climactic moment, when he is plotting to get the real Macoco to reveal himself and brings out the mirror to rehypnotize Garland, Slezak breaks the mirror. But it doesn't matter. Manuela is willing to go along with Serafin's plot, as Garland accepts Kelly's choreography and control. Her energy, once released, can be controlled, especially within the context of love and theater. *The Pirate* is therefore a next step from the themes of the Astaire-Rogers films. Kelly makes the perfect couple the center of an ideal community created by dance, a world of harmony where everyone on the street not only sympathizes with the exuberance you feel because you're in love, but also knows all the words and dance steps that express your feelings.

The context of the ideal, the place where the true self can be revealed, is still theatrical space. The final song, "Be a Clown," emphasizes the responsible escape of art, especially popular

art, in a way very reminiscent of the title song at the end of
Shall We Dance. But the inclusion of the Garland figure—the
nonprofessional dancer from the heart—indicates the direction that Kelly has taken the musical, as does the fact that
Kelly and Garland are not elegant in their world of theater, but
clownish and self-mocking, more willing than Astaire and
Rogers to include the potential disruptiveness of the world
outside them and the world within. Astaire and Rogers dance
for us, looking at each other primarily to integrate their dancing. Kelly and Garland convey a much friendlier and more
personal relationship. We may watch Astaire and Rogers. But
we empathize with Kelly and Garland.*

Kelly in *The Pirate* is an entertainer. But the emphasis of the
film is less on his dancing and singing than on the world that
dance and theater can create together. The stylization and historical setting of *The Pirate* emphasize the release from the
stultifying social self dance allows; the contemporary setting of
most other Kelly films further highlights Kelly's effort to bring
his dancing out of the enclosed world of theater and make the
whole world a theater, responsive to and changed by his energy. Astaire's dances define a world of perfect form, while
Kelly's often reach out to include improvisation, spontaneity,
and happenstance. The scene that contrasts best with Astaire's
imitation of the record player and the machines in *Shall We
Dance* is Kelly's marvelous interweaving of a creaky board and
a piece of paper left on the stage in *Summer Stock* (1950).
Kelly's self-mocking smile reflects the way most of his films
continue the attack of Astaire's films against artistic preten-
sion. Embodying the catalytic possibilities of dance to create a

---

*The strength of Minnelli's own vision obviously has its place in under-
standing *The Pirate* (1948), although the comparative visual stasis and the commitment to the values of stability that characterize *Meet Me in St. Louis* (1944)
indicate the importance of Kelly in changing his style and his ideas. Minnelli's
musicals may try to celebrate the triumph of the individual through art, but
just as often (for example, in *The Band Wagon,* 1953) they catch a tint of gloom
from his more melancholic nonmusical films, which often deal with artistic
compromise and disintegration, either in the context of the world of film (*The
Bad and the Beautiful,* 1952; *Two Weeks in Another Town,* 1962) or the other arts
(*Lust for Life,* 1956; *Some Came Running,* 1958). Only in the pure world of the
musical can art and individuality succeed without compromise.

new coherence for the nontheatrical world, Kelly journeys through parody and realism, attacking formal excesses on the one hand and transforming everyday reality on the other.

Singin' in the Rain (Kelly and Stanley Donen, 1952), is one aspect of his effort and *On the Town* (Kelly and Stanley Donen, 1949) is the other. The frame of *Singin' in the Rain* is a full-scale parody of the early days of sound film (an appropriate subject for the musical), complete with an attack on artistic high seriousness in favor of the comic exuberance of popular art. The essential scene is Donald O'Connor's incredible acrobatic dance "Make 'Em Laugh" (unfortunately often cut for television), like "Be a Clown" a description of the popular artist's relation to his audience. But this time, instead of being on a stage, the number is done amid a welter of different film sets depicting different worlds, with stagehands moving through the scene. O'Connor's partner for a while is a featureless, uncostumed dummy that he makes seem alive (a reminiscence of the Ginger Rogers dummy in *Shall We Dance*), and for a finale he starts walking up the set walls and finally jumps right through them. In the early scenes of the film, Kelly, the phony silent-screen lover, needs to set up a sound stage and props before he can tell Debbie Reynolds he loves her and sings "You Were Meant for Me." But the declaration becomes acceptable as real emotion only when, in the next scene, he and Donald O'Connor parody the demands of their diction coach in "Moses Supposes." By this time, to parallel his change from form to substance, Kelly has left his suits and tuxedoes behind and dresses in the more familiar open-collared shirt and loafers. Once again, the scar on his cheek is an emblem of the reality that will emerge. In *Singin' in the Rain* silent films are artificial in their stylized actions and hoked-up emotions; only sound is real. The discovery of communication with an audience changes clearly from "Shall We Dance" to "Be a Clown" to "Make 'Em Laugh," with an increasing emphasis on the place of informality and personal style. The solution of the plot of *Singin' in the Rain* is to make the bad serious film into the parodic musical; almost all the dances in the film contain parodies of earlier dances and dancers, in the same somewhat mocking homage that characterizes the attitude to Impressionism in *An American in Paris* (Minnelli, 1951). This is the es-

sence of the kind of energy Kelly's film embodies: theater, like
the ability to dance, is a manner of inner perspective on the
world outside. The reality of sound film that Kelly discovers
follows his own curve of increased dancing in the film until
the great set piece of "Gotta Dance," another statement of
Kelly's belief that dancing is a compulsion from within more
authentic than the forms imposed from without. The final
scene, in which Debbie Reynolds is revealed as the voice of
Jean Hagen from behind the curtain, repeats on still another
level the basic theme of outer form and inner reality. Music
and dance are the real spirit of film in the same way they are
the real soul and energy of New York in *On the Town,* or Paris
in *An American in Paris.*

Kelly's dancing tries not to be the aesthetic escape of Astaire's. It is more utopian because it aims to bring the world
together. Astaire's films often imply that dance and therefore
energy itself can be a refuge from a stuffy world of social
forms; Kelly's films imply that dance and the individual can
change the world. The three sailors on leave in *On the Town*—
Kelly, Frank Sinatra, and Jules Munshin—are searching for
the perfect partner and all find their girls, not in a purified
world of dance, but in a real New York (the first musical made
on location) that embraces both their dancing and their search.
The women—Vera-Ellen, Ann Miller, and Betty Garrett—are
all at least the equals of the men in exuberance, energy, and
wit. They make their own space in a public world, like Kelly
in the "Singin' in the Rain" sequence, splashing through pud-
dles of chance and nature. The great pretenders in *On the
Town* are Kelly and Vera-Ellen, the small-town kids who come
on to each other as sophisticates. The moral is that of almost
all Kelly films: don't worry about the true self; it will turn out
to be better than the one you're pretending to be. Kelly's kind
of musical doesn't retreat from reality. It tries to subvert reality
through its new energy, an energy available to everyone in the
audience through Kelly's insistence on the nonprofessional
character, the musical self that wells from inside instead of
being imposed from without, whether by training, tradition,
or society. . . .

1976

468

ROBERT WARSHOW
MOVIE CHRONICLE: THE WESTERNER

They that have power to hurt and will do none,
That do not do the thing they most do show,
Who, moving others, are themselves as stone,
Unmoved, cold, and to temptation slow;
They rightly do inherit heaven's graces,
And husband nature's riches from expense;
They are the lords and owners of their faces,
Others but stewards of their excellence.

The two most successful creations of American movies are the gangster and the Westerner: men with guns. Guns as physical objects, and the postures associated with their use, form the visual and emotional center of both types of films. I suppose this reflects the importance of guns in the fantasy life of Americans; but that is a less illuminating point than it appears to be.

The gangster movie, which no longer exists in its "classical" form, is a story of enterprise and success ending in precipitate failure. Success is conceived as an increasing power to work injury, it belongs to the city, and it is of course a form of evil (though the gangster's death, presented usually as "punishment," is perceived simply as defeat). The peculiarity of the gangster is his unceasing, nervous activity. The exact nature of his enterprises may remain vague, but his commitment to enterprise is always clear, and all the more clear because he operates outside the field of utility. He is without culture, without manners, without leisure, or at any rate his leisure is likely to be spent in debauchery so compulsively aggressive as to seem only another aspect of his "work." But he is graceful, moving like a dancer among the crowded dangers of the city.

Like other tycoons, the gangster is crude in conceiving his ends but by no means inarticulate; on the contrary, he is usually expansive and noisy (the introspective gangster is a fairly recent development), and can state definitely what he wants: to take over the North Side, to own a hundred suits, to be Number One. But new "frontiers" will present themselves infinitely, and by a rigid convention it is understood that as soon as he wishes to rest on his gains, he is on the way to destruction.

The gangster is lonely and melancholy, and can give the impression of a profound worldly wisdom. He appeals most to adolescents with their impatience and their feeling of being outsiders, but more generally he appeals to that side of all of us which refuses to believe in the "normal" possibilities of happiness and achievement; the gangster is the "no" to that great American "yes" which is stamped so big over our official culture and yet has so little to do with the way we really feel about our lives. But the gangster's loneliness and melancholy are not "authentic"; like everything else that belongs to him, they are not honestly come by: he is lonely and melancholy not because life ultimately demands such feelings but because he has put himself in a position where everybody wants to kill him and eventually somebody will. He is wide open and defenseless, incomplete because unable to accept any limits or come to terms with his own nature, fearful, loveless. And the story of his career is a nightmare inversion of the values of ambition and opportunity. From the window of Scarface's bulletproof apartment can be seen an electric sign proclaiming: "The World Is Yours," and, if I remember, this sign is the last thing we see after Scarface lies dead in the street. In the end it is the gangster's weakness as much as his power and freedom that appeals to us; the world is not ours, but it is not his either, and in his death he "pays" for our fantasies, releasing us momentarily both from the concept of success, which he denies by caricaturing it, and from the need to succeed, which he shows to be dangerous.

The Western hero, by contrast, is a figure of repose. He resembles the gangster in being lonely and to some degree melancholy. But his melancholy comes from the "simple" recognition that life is unavoidably serious, not from the disproportions of his own temperament. And his loneliness is organic, not imposed on him by his situation but belonging to him intimately and testifying to his completeness. The gangster must reject others violently or draw them violently to him. The Westerner is not thus compelled to seek love; he is prepared to accept it, perhaps, but he never asks of it more than it can give, and we see him constantly in situations where love is at best an irrelevance. If there is a woman he loves, she is usually unable to understand his motives; she is against killing and being killed, and he finds it impossible to explain to her that there is no point in being "against" these things: they belong to his world.

Very often this woman is from the East and her failure to understand represents a clash of cultures. In the American mind, refinement, virtue, civilization, Christianity itself, are seen as feminine, and therefore women are often portrayed as possessing some kind of deeper wisdom, while the men, for all their apparent self-assurance, are fundamentally childish. But the West, lacking the graces of civilization, is the place "where men are men"; in Western movies, men have the deeper wisdom and the women are children. Those women in the Western movies who share the hero's understanding of life are prostitutes (or, as they are usually presented, barroom entertainers)—women, that is, who have come to understand in the most practical way how love can be an irrelevance, and therefore "fallen" women. The gangster, too, associates with prostitutes, but for him the important things about a prostitute are her passive availability and her costliness: she is part of his winnings. In Western movies, the important thing about a prostitute is her quasi-masculine independence: nobody owns her, nothing has to be explained to her, and she is not, like a virtuous woman, a "value" that demands to be protected. When the Westerner leaves the prostitute for a virtuous woman—for love—he is in fact forsaking a way of life, though the point of the choice is often obscured by having the prostitute killed by getting into the line of fire.

The Westerner is *par excellence* a man of leisure. Even when he wears the badge of a marshal or, more rarely, owns a ranch, he appears to be unemployed. We see him standing at a bar, or playing poker—a game which expresses perfectly his talent for remaining

Easterners and Westerners. Paul Muni in *Scarface* (1932); John Carradine, Andy Devine, Chris Martin, George Bancroft, Louise Platt, Donald Meek, Claire Trevor, and John Wayne in *Stagecoach* (1939). "The two most successful creations of American movies are the gangster and the Westerner: men with guns. . . . The land and the horses have . . . a moral significance: the physical freedom they represent belongs to the moral 'openness' of the West—corresponding to the fact that guns are carried where they can be seen. . . . The gangster's world is less open . . ." (WARSHOW, pages 469, 473).

relaxed in the midst of tension—or perhaps camping out on the plains on some extraordinary errand. If he does own a ranch, it is in the background; we are not actually aware that he owns anything except his horse, his guns, and the one worn suit of clothing which is likely to remain unchanged all through the movie. It comes as a surprise to see him take money from his pocket or an extra shirt from his saddlebags. As a rule we do not even know where he sleeps at night and don't think of asking. Yet it never occurs to us that he is a poor man; there is no poverty in Western movies, and really no wealth either: those great cattle domains and shipments of gold which figure so largely in the plots are moral and not material quantities, not the objects of contention but only its occasion. Possessions too are irrelevant.

Employment of some kind—usually unproductive—is always open to the Westerner, but when he accepts it, it is not because he needs to make a living, much less from any idea of "getting ahead." Where could he want to "get ahead" to? By the time we see him, he is already "there": he can ride a horse faultlessly, keep his countenance in the face of death, and draw his gun a little faster and shoot it a little straighter than anyone he is likely to meet. These are sharply defined acquirements, giving to the figure of the Westerner an apparent moral clarity which corresponds to the clarity of his physical image against his bare landscape; initially, at any rate, the Western movie presents itself as being without mystery, its whole universe comprehended in what we see on the screen.

Much of this apparent simplicity arises directly from those "cinematic" elements which have long been understood to give the Western theme its special appropriateness for the movies: the wide expanses of land, the free movement of men on horses. As guns constitute the visible moral center of the Western movie, suggesting continually the possibility of violence, so land and horses represent the movie's material basis, its sphere of action. But the land and the horses have also a moral significance: the physical freedom they represent belongs to the moral "openness" of the West—corresponding to the fact that guns are carried where they can be seen. (And, as we shall see, the character of land and horses changes as the Western film becomes more complex.)

The gangster's world is less open, and his arts not so easily identifiable as the Westerner's. Perhaps he too can keep his countenance, but the mask he wears is really no mask: its purpose is precisely to make evident the fact that he desperately wants to "get ahead" and will stop at nothing. Where the Westerner imposes himself by the appearance of unshakable control, the gangster's pre-eminence lies in the suggestion that he may at any moment lose control; his strength is not in being able to shoot faster or straighter than others, but in being more willing to shoot. "Do it first," says Scarface expounding his mode of operation, "and keep on doing it!" With the Westerner, it is a crucial point of honor *not* to "do it first"; his gun remains in its holster until the moment of combat.

There is no suggestion, however, that he draws the gun reluctantly. The Westerner could not fulfill himself if the moment did not finally come when he can shoot his enemy down. But because that moment is so thoroughly the expression of his being, it must be kept pure. He will not violate the accepted forms of combat though by doing so he could save a city. And he can wait. "When you call me that—smile!"—the villain smiles weakly, soon he is laughing with horrible joviality, and the crisis is past. But it is allowed to pass because it must come again: sooner or later Trampas will "make his play," and the Virginian will be ready for him.

What does the Westerner fight for? We know he is on the side of justice and order, and of course it can be said he fights for these things. But such broad aims never correspond exactly to his real motives; they only offer him his opportunity. The Westerner himself, when an explanation is asked of him (usually by a woman), is likely to say that he does what he "has to do." If justice and order did not continually demand his protection, he would be without a calling. Indeed, we come upon him often in just that situation, as the reign of law settles over the West and he is forced to see that his day is over; those are the pictures which end with his death or with his departure for some more remote frontier. What he defends, at bottom, is the purity of his own image—in fact his honor. This is what makes him invulnerable. When the gangster is killed, his whole life is shown to have been a mistake, but the image the Westerner seeks to maintain can be presented as clearly in defeat as in victory: he fights not for advantage and not for the right, but to state what he is, and he must live in a world which permits that statement. The Westerner is the last gentleman, and the movies which over and over again tell his story are probably the last art form in which the concept of honor retains its strength.

Of course I do not mean to say that ideas of virtue and justice and courage have gone out of culture. Honor is more than these things: it is a style, concerned with harmonious appearances as much as with desirable consequences, and tending therefore toward the denial of life in favor of art. "Who hath it? he that died o' Wednesday." On the whole, a world that leans to Falstaff's view is a more civilized and even, finally, a more graceful world. It is just the march of civilization that forces the Westerner to move on; and if we actually had to confront the question it might turn out that the woman who refuses to understand him is right as often as she is wrong. But we do not confront the question. Where the Westerner lives it is always about 1870—not the real 1870, either, or the real West—and he is killed or goes away when his position becomes problematical. The fact that he continues to hold our attention is evidence enough that, in his proper frame, he presents an image of personal nobility that is still real for us.

Clearly, this image easily becomes ridiculous: we need only look at William S. Hart or Tom Mix, who in the wooden absoluteness of their virtue represented little that an adult could take seriously; and doubtless such figures as Gene Autry or Roy Rogers are no better, though I confess I have seen none of their movies. Some film enthusiasts claim to find in the early, unsophisticated Westerns a "cinematic purity" that has since been lost; this idea is as valid, and finally as misleading, as T. S. Eliot's statement that *Everyman* is the only play in English that stays within the limitations of art. The truth is that the Westerner comes into the field of serious art only when his moral code, without ceasing to be compelling, is seen also to be imperfect. The Westerner at his best exhibits a moral ambiguity which darkens his image and saves him from absurdity; this ambiguity arises from the fact that, whatever his justifications, he is a killer of men.

In *The Virginian*, which is an archetypal Western movie as *Scarface* or *Little Caesar* are archetypal gangster movies, there is a lynching in which the hero (Gary Cooper), as leader of a posse, must supervise the hanging of his best friend for stealing cattle. With the growth of American "social consciousness," it is no longer possible to present a lynching in the movies unless the point is the illegality and injustice of the lynching itself; *The Ox-Bow Incident*, made in 1943, explicitly puts forward the newer point of view and can be regarded as a kind of "anti-Western." But in 1929, when

475

The Virginian was made, the present inhibition about lynching was not yet in force; the justice, and therefore the necessity, of the hanging is never questioned—except by the school-teacher from the East, whose refusal to understand serves as usual to set forth more sharply the deeper seriousness of the West. The Virginian is thus in a tragic dilemma where one moral absolute conflicts with another and the choice of either must leave a moral stain. If he had chosen to save his friend, he would have violated the image of himself that he had made essential to his existence, and the movie would have had to end with his death, for only by his death could the image have been restored. Having chosen instead to sacrifice his friend to the higher demands of the "code"—the only choice worthy of him, as even the friend understands—he is none the less stained by the killing, but what is needed now to set accounts straight is not his death but the death of the villain Trampas, the leader of the cattle thieves, who had escaped the posse and abandoned the Virginian's friend to his fate. Again the woman intervenes: Why must there be *more* killing? If the hero really loved her, he would leave town, refusing Trampas's challenge. What good will it be if Trampas should kill him? But the Virginian does once more what he "has to do," and in avenging his friend's death wipes out the stain on his own honor. Yet his victory cannot be complete: no death can be paid for and no stain truly wiped out; the movie is still a tragedy, for though the hero escapes with his life, he has been forced to confront the ultimate limits of his moral ideas.

This mature sense of limitation and unavoidable guilt is what gives the Westerner a "right" to his melancholy. It is true that the gangster's story is also a tragedy—in certain formal ways more clearly a tragedy than the Westerner's—but it is a romantic tragedy, based on a hero whose defeat springs with almost mechanical inevitability from the outrageous presumption of his demands: the gangster is *bound* to go on until he is killed. The Westerner is a more classical figure, self-contained and limited to begin with, seeking not to extend his dominion but only to assert his personal value, and his tragedy lies in the fact that even this circumscribed demand cannot be fully realized. Since the Westerner is not a murderer but (most of the time) a man of virtue, and since he is always prepared for defeat, he retains his inner invulnerability and his story need not end with his death (and usually does not); but what we finally respond to is not his victory but his defeat.

Up to a point, it is plain that the deeper seriousness of the good Western films comes from the introduction of a realism, both physical and psychological, that was missing with Tom Mix and William S. Hart. As lines of age have come into Gary Cooper's face since *The Virginian*, so the outlines of the Western movie in general have become less smooth, its background more drab. The sun still beats upon the town, but the camera is likely now to take advantage of this illumination to seek out more closely the shabbiness of buildings and furniture, the loose, worn hang of clothing, the wrinkles and dirt of the faces. Once it has been discovered that the true theme of the Western movie is not the freedom and expansiveness of frontier life, but its limitations, its material bareness, the pressures of obligation, then even the landscape itself ceases to be quite the arena of free movement it once was, but becomes instead a great empty waste, cutting down more often than it exaggerates the stature of the horseman who rides across it. We are more likely now to see the Westerner struggling against the obstacles of the physical world (as in the wonderful scenes on the desert and among the rocks in *The Last Posse*) than carelessly surmounting them. Even the horses, no longer the "friends" of man or the inspired chargers of knight-errantry, have lost much of the moral significance that once seemed to belong to them in their careering across the screen. It seems to me the horses grow tired and stumble more often than they did, and that we see them less frequently at the gallop.

In *The Gunfighter*, a remarkable film of a couple of years ago, the landscape has virtually disappeared. Most of the action takes place indoors, in a cheerless saloon where a tired "bad man" (Gregory Peck) contemplates the waste of his life, to be senselessly killed at the end by a vicious youngster setting off on the same futile path. The movie is done in cold, quiet tones of gray, and every object in it—faces, clothing, a table, the hero's heavy mustache—is given an air of uncompromising authenticity, suggesting those dim photographs of the nineteenth-century West in which Wyatt Earp, say, turns out to be a blank untidy figure posing awkwardly before some uninteresting building. This "authenticity," to be sure, is only aesthetic; the chief fact about nineteenth-century photographs, to my eyes at any rate, is how stonily they refuse to yield up the truth. But that limitation is just what is needed: by preserving some hint of the rigidity of archaic photography (only in tone and décor,

477

never in composition), *The Gunfighter* can permit us to feel that we are looking at a more "real" West than the one the movies have accustomed us to—harder, duller, less "romantic"—and yet without forcing us outside the boundaries which give the Western movie its validity.

We come upon the hero of *The Gunfighter* at the end of a career in which he has never upheld justice and order, and has been at times, apparently, an actual criminal; in this case, it is clear that the hero has been wrong and the woman who has rejected his way of life has been right. He is thus without any of the larger justifications, and knows himself a ruined man. There can be no question of his "redeeming" himself in any socially constructive way. He is too much the victim of his own reputation to turn marshal as one of his old friends has done, and he is not offered the sentimental solution of a chance to give up his life for some good end; the whole point is that he exists outside the field of social value. Indeed, if we were once allowed to see him in the days of his "success," he might become a figure like the gangster, for his career has been aggressively "anti-social" and the practical problem he faces is the gangster's problem: there will always be somebody trying to kill him. Yet it is obviously absurd to speak of him as "anti-social," not only because we do not see him acting as a criminal, but more fundamentally because we do not see his milieu as a society. Of course it has its "social problems" and a kind of static history: civilization is always just at the point of driving out the old freedom; there are women and children to represent the possibility of a settled life; and there is the marshal, a bad man turned good, determined to keep at least his area of jurisdiction at peace. But these elements are not, in fact, a part of the film's "realism," even though they come out of the real history of the West; they belong to the conventions of the form, to that accepted framework which makes the film possible in the first place, and they exist not to provide a standard by which the gunfighter can be judged, but only to set him off. The true "civilization" of the Western movie is always embodied in an individual, good or bad is more a matter of personal bearing than of social consequences, and the conflict of good and bad is a duel between two men. Deeply troubled and obviously doomed, the gunfighter is the Western hero still, perhaps all the more be-

478

The aging Westerner—Gary Cooper (with Mary Brian) in *The Virginian* (1929) and (with Grace Kelly) in *High Noon* (1952). "As lines of age have come into Gary Cooper's face since *The Virginian*, so the outlines of the Western movie in general have become less smooth, its background more drab. . . . In *High Noon* we find Gary Cooper still the upholder of order that he was in *The Virginian*, but twenty-four years older, stooped, slower moving . . . the flesh sagging . . ." (WARSHOW, pages 477, 481).

cause his value must express itself entirely in his own being—in his presence, the way he holds our eyes—and in contradiction to the facts. No matter what he has done, he *looks* right, and he remains invulnerable because, without acknowledging anyone else's right to judge him, he has judged his own failure and has already assimilated it, understanding—as no one else understands except the marshal and the barroom girl—that he can do nothing but play out the drama of the gun fight again and again until the time comes when it will be he who gets killed. What "redeems" him is that he no longer believes in this drama and nevertheless will continue to play his role perfectly: the pattern is all.

The proper function of realism in the Western movie can only be to deepen the lines of that pattern. It is an art form for connoisseurs, where the spectator derives his pleasure from the appreciation of minor variations within the working out of a pre-established order. One does not want too much novelty: it comes as a shock, for instance, when the hero is made to operate without a gun, as has been done in several pictures (e.g., *Destry Rides Again*), and our uneasiness is allayed only when he is finally compelled to put his "pacifism" aside. If the hero can be shown to be troubled, complex, fallible, even eccentric, or the villain given some psychological taint or, better, some evocative physical mannerism, to shade the colors of his villainy, that is all to the good. Indeed, that kind of variation is absolutely necessary to keep the type from becoming sterile; we do not want to see the same movie over and over again, only the same form. But when the impulse toward realism is extended into a "reinterpretation" of the West as a developed society, drawing our eyes away from the hero if only to the extent of showing him as the one dominant figure in a complex social order, then the pattern is broken and the West itself begins to be uninteresting. If the "social problems" of the frontier are to be the movie's chief concern, there is no longer any point in reexamining these problems twenty times a year; they have been solved, and the people for whom they once were real are dead. Moreover, the hero himself, still the film's central figure, now tends to become its one unassimilable element, since he is the most "unreal."

The Ox-Bow Incident, by denying the convention of the lynching, presents us with a modern "social drama" and evokes a corresponding response, but in doing so it almost makes the Western setting irrelevant, a mere backdrop of beautiful scenery. (It is significant that *The Ox-Bow Incident* has no hero; a hero would have to stop the lynching or be killed in trying to stop it, and then the "problem" of lynching would no longer be central.) Even in *The Gunfighter* the women and children are a little too much in evidence, threatening constantly to become a real focus of concern instead of simply part of the given framework; and the young tough who kills the hero has too much the air of juvenile criminality: the hero himself could never have been like that, and the idea of a cycle being repeated therefore loses its sharpness. But the most striking example of the confusion created by a too conscientious "social" realism is in the celebrated *High Noon*.

In *High Noon* we find Gary Cooper still the upholder of order that he was in *The Virginian*, but twenty-four years older, stooped, slower moving, awkward, his face lined, the flesh sagging, a less beautiful and weaker figure, but with the suggestion of greater depth that belongs almost automatically to age. Like the hero of *The Gunfighter*, he no longer has to assert his character and is no longer interested in the drama of combat; it is hard to imagine that he might once have been so youthful as to say, "When you call me that—smile!" In fact, when we come upon him he is hanging up his guns and his marshal's badge in order to begin a new, peaceful life with his bride, who is a Quaker. But then the news comes that a man he had sent to prison has been pardoned and will get to town on the noon train; three friends of this man have come to wait for him at the station, and when the freed convict arrives the four of them will come to kill the marshal. He is thus trapped; the bride will object, the hero himself will waver much more than he would have done twenty-four years ago, but in the end he will play out the drama because it is what he "has to do." All this belongs to the established form (there is even the "fallen woman" who understands the marshal's position as his wife does not). Leaving aside the crudity of building up suspense by means of the clock, the actual Western drama of *High Noon* is well handled and forms a good companion piece to *The Virginian*, showing in both conception and technique the ways in which the Western movie has naturally developed.

But there is a second drama along with the first. As the marshal sets out to find deputies to help him deal with the four gunmen, we are taken through the various social strata of the town, each group in turn refusing its assistance out of cowardice, malice, irresponsibility, or venality. With this we are in the field of "social drama"—of a very low order, incidentally, altogether unconvincing and displaying a vulgar anti-populism that has marred some other movies of Stanley Kramer's. But the falsity of the "social drama" is less important than the fact that it does not belong in the movie to begin with. The technical problem was to make it necessary for the marshal to face his enemies alone; to explain *why* the other townspeople are not at his side is to raise a question which does not exist in the proper frame of the Western movie, where the hero is "naturally" alone and it is only necessary to contrive the physical absence of those who might be his allies, if any contrivance is needed at all. In addition, though the hero of *High Noon* proves himself a better man than all around him, the actual effect of this contrast is to lessen his stature: he becomes only a rejected man of virtue. In our final glimpse of him, as he rides away through the town where he has spent most of his life without really imposing himself on it, he is a pathetic rather than a tragic figure. And his departure has another meaning as well; the "social drama" has no place for him.

But there is also a different way of violating the Western form. This is to yield entirely to its static quality as legend and to the "cinematic" temptations of its landscape, the horses, the quiet men. John Ford's famous *Stagecoach* (1938) had much of this unhappy preoccupation with style, and the same director's *My Darling Clementine* (1946), a soft and beautiful movie about Wyatt Earp, goes further along the same path, offering indeed a superficial accuracy of historical reconstruction, but so loving in execution as to destroy the outlines of the Western legend, assimilating it to the more sentimental legend of rural America and making the hero a more dangerous Mr. Deeds. (*Powder River*, a recent "routine" Western shamelessly copied from *My Darling Clementine*, is in most ways a better film; lacking the benefit of a serious director, it is necessarily more concerned with drama than with style.)

The highest expression of this aestheticizing tendency is in George Stevens' *Shane*, where the legend of the West is virtually reduced to its essentials and then fixed in the dreamy clarity of a fairly tale. There never was so broad and bare and lovely a land-

482

The lawyer from the East learns the law of the West: John Wayne and James Stewart in John Ford's *The Man Who Shot Liberty Valance* (1962). "Ford's . . . preoccupation with style" has the tendency "to destroy the outlines of the Western legend, assimilating it to the more sentimental legend of rural America and making the hero a more dangerous Mr. Deeds . . ." (WARSHOW, page 482).

scape as Stevens puts before us, or so unimaginably comfortless a "town" as the little group of buildings on the prairie to which the settlers must come for their supplies and to buy a drink. The mere physical progress of the film, following the style of *A Place in the Sun*, is so deliberately graceful that everything seems to be happening at the bottom of a clear lake. The hero (Alan Ladd) is hardly a man at all, but something like the Spirit of the West, beautiful in fringed buckskins. He emerges mysteriously from the plains, breathing sweetness and a melancholy which is no longer simply the Westerner's natural response to experience but has taken on spirituality; and when he has accomplished his mission, meeting and destroying in the black figure of Jack Palance a Spirit of Evil just as metaphysical as his own embodiment of virtue, he fades away again into the more distant West, a man whose "day is over," leaving behind the wondering little boy who might have imagined the whole story. The choice of Alan Ladd to play the leading role is alone an indication of this film's tendency. Actors like Gary Cooper or Gregory Peck are in themselves, as material objects, "realistic," seeming to bear in their bodies and their faces mortality, limitation, the knowledge of good and evil. Ladd is a more "aesthetic" object, with some of the "universality" of a piece of sculpture; his special quality is in his physical smoothness and serenity, unworldly and yet not innocent, but suggesting that no experience can really touch him. Stevens has tried to freeze the Western myth once and for all in the immobility of Alan Ladd's countenance. If *Shane* were "right," and fully successful, it might be possible to say there was no point in making any more Western movies; once the hero is apotheosized, variation and development are closed off.

Shane is not "right," but it is still true that the possibilities of fruitful variation in the Western movie are limited. The form can keep its freshness through endless repetitions only because of the special character of the film medium, where the physical difference between one object and another—above all, between one actor and another—is of such enormous importance, serving the function that is served by the variety of language in the perpetuation of literary types. In this sense, the "vocabulary" of films is much larger than that of literature and falls more readily into pleasing and significant arrangements. (That may explain why the middle levels of excellence are more easily reached in the movies than in literary forms, and perhaps also why the status of the movies as art is constantly being called into question.) But the advantage of this almost automatic particularity belongs to all films alike. Why does the Western movie especially have such a hold on our imagination?

Chiefly, I think, because it offers a serious orientation to the problem of violence such as can be found almost nowhere else in our culture. One of the well-known peculiarities of modern civilized opinion is its refusal to acknowledge the value of violence. This refusal is a virtue, but like many virtues it involves a certain willful blindness and it encourages hypocrisy. We train ourselves to be shocked or bored by cultural images of violence, and our very concept of heroism tends to be a passive one: we are less drawn to the brave young men who kill large numbers of our enemies than to the heroic prisoners who endure torture without capitulating. In art, though we may still be able to understand and participate in the values of the Iliad, a modern writer like Ernest Hemingway we find somewhat embarrassing: there is no doubt that he stirs us, but we cannot help recognizing also that he is a little childish. And in the criticism of popular culture, where the educated observer is usually under the illusion that he has nothing at stake, the presence of images of violence is often assumed to be in itself a sufficient ground for condemnation.

These attitudes, however, have not reduced the element of violence in our culture but, if anything, have helped to free it from moral control by letting it take on the aura of "emancipation." The celebration of acts of violence is left more and more to the irresponsible: on the higher cultural levels to writers like Céline, and lower down to Mickey Spillane or Horace McCoy, or to the comic books, television, and the movies. The gangster movie, with its numerous variations, belongs to this cultural "underground" which sets forth the attractions of violence in the face of all our higher social attitudes. It is a more "modern" genre than the Western, perhaps even more profound, because it confronts industrial society on its own ground—the city—and because, like much of our advanced art, it gains its effects by a gross insistence on its own narrow logic. But it is anti-social, resting on fantasies of irresponsible freedom. If we are brought finally to acquiesce in the denial of these fantasies, it is only because they have been shown to be dangerous, not because they have given way to a better vision of behavior.*

In war movies, to be sure, it is possible to present the uses of violence within a framework of responsibility. But there is the disadvantage that modern war is a co-operative enterprise; its violence is largely impersonal, and heroism belongs to the group more than to the individual. The hero of a war movie is most often simply a leader, and his superiority is likely to be expressed in a denial of the heroic: you are not supposed to be brave, you are supposed to get the job done and stay alive (this too, of course, is a kind of heroic posture, but a new—and "practical"—one). At its best, the war movie may represent a more civilized point of view than the Western, and if it were not continually marred by ideological sentimentality we might hope to find it developing into a higher form of drama. But it cannot supply the values we seek in the Western.

Those values are in the image of a single man who wears a gun on his thigh. The gun tells us that he lives in a world of violence, and even that he "believes in violence." But the drama is one of self-restraint: the moment of violence must come in its own time and according to its special laws, or else it is valueless. There is little cruelty in Western movies, and little sentimentality; our eyes are not focused on the sufferings of the defeated but on the deportment of the hero. Really, it is not violence at all which is the "point" of the Western movie, but a certain image of man, a style, which expresses itself most clearly in violence. Watch a child with his toy guns and you will see: what most interests him is not (as we so much fear) the fantasy of hurting others, but to work out how a man might look when he shoots or is shot. A hero is one who looks like a hero.

Whatever the limitations of such an idea in experience, it has always been valid in art, and has a special validity in an art where appearances are everything. The Western hero is necessarily an

---

* I am not concerned here with the actual social consequences of gangster movies, though I suspect they could not have been so pernicious as they were thought to be. Some of the compromises introduced to avoid the supposed bad effects of the old gangster movies may be, if anything, more dangerous, for the sadistic violence that once belonged only to the gangster is now commonly enlisted on the side of the law and thus goes undefeated, allowing us (if we wish) to find in the movies a sort of "confirmation" of our fantasies.

archaic figure; we do not really believe in him and would not have him step out of his rigidly conventionalized background. But his archaicism does not take away from his power; on the contrary, it adds to it by keeping him just a little beyond the reach both of common sense and of absolutized emotion, the two usual impulses of our art. And he has, after all, his own kind of relevance. He is there to remind us of the possibility of style in an age which has put on itself the burden of pretending that style has no meaning, and, in the midst of our anxieties over the problem of violence, to suggest that even in killing or being killed we are not freed from the necessity of establishing satisfactory modes of behavior. Above all, the movies in which the Westerner plays out his role preserve for us the pleasures of a complete and self-contained drama—and one which still effortlessly crosses the boundaries which divide our culture—in a time when other, more consciously serious art forms are increasingly complex, uncertain, and ill-defined.

1954

SUSAN SONTAG
THE IMAGINATION
OF DISASTER

The typical science fiction film has a form as predictable as a Western, and is made up of elements which, to a practiced eye, are as classic as the saloon brawl, the blonde schoolteacher from the East, and the gun duel on the deserted main street.

One model scenario proceeds through five phases.

(1) The arrival of the thing. (Emergence of the monsters, landing of the alien spaceship, etc.) This is usually witnessed or suspected by just one person, a young scientist on a field trip. Nobody, neither his neighbors nor his colleagues, will believe him for some time. The hero is not married, but has a sympathetic though also incredulous girl friend.

(2) Confirmation of the hero's report by a host of witnesses to a great act of destruction. (If the invaders are beings from another planet, a fruitless attempt to parley with them and get them to leave peacefully.) The local police are summoned to deal with the situation and massacred.

(3) In the capital of the country, conferences between scientists and the military take place, with the hero lecturing before a chart, map, or blackboard. A national emergency is declared. Reports of further destruction. Authorities from other countries arrive in black limousines. All international tensions are suspended in view of the planetary emergency. This stage often includes a rapid montage of news broadcasts in various languages, a meeting at the UN, and more conferences between the military and the scientists. Plans are made for destroying the enemy.

(4) Further atrocities. At some point the hero's girl friend is in

grave danger. Massive counter-attacks by international forces, with brilliant displays of rocketry, rays, and other advanced weapons, are all unsuccessful. Enormous military casualties, usually by incineration. Cities are destroyed and/or evacuated. There is an obligatory scene here of panicked crowds stampeding along a highway or a big bridge, being waved on by numerous policemen who, if the film is Japanese, are immaculately white-gloved, preternaturally calm, and call out in dubbed English, "Keep moving. There is no need to be alarmed."

(5) More conferences, whose motif is: "They must be vulnerable to something." Throughout the hero has been working in his lab to this end. The final strategy, upon which all hopes depend, is drawn up; the ultimate weapon—often a super-powerful, as yet untested, nuclear device—is mounted. Countdown. Final repulse of the monster or invaders. Mutual congratulations, while the hero and girl friend embrace cheek to cheek and scan the skies sturdily. "But have we seen the last of them?"

The film I have just described should be in color and on a wide screen. Another typical scenario, which follows, is simpler and suited to black-and-white films with a lower budget. It has four phases.

(1) The hero (usually, but not always, a scientist) and his girl friend, or his wife and two children, are disporting themselves in some innocent ultra-normal middle-class surroundings—their house in a small town, or on vacation (camping, boating). Suddenly, someone starts behaving strangely; or some innocent form of vegetation becomes monstrously enlarged and ambulatory. If a character is pictured driving an automobile, something gruesome looms up in the middle of the road. If it is night, strange lights hurtle across the sky.

(2) After following the thing's tracks, or determining that It is radioactive, or poking around a huge crater—in short, conducting some sort of crude investigation—the hero tries to warn the local authorities, without effect; nobody believes anything is amiss. The hero knows better. If the thing is tangible, the house is elaborately barricaded. If the invading alien is an invisible parasite, a doctor or friend is called in, who is himself rather quickly killed or "taken possession of" by the thing.

(3) The advice of whoever further is consulted proves useless. Meanwhile, It continues to claim other victims in the town, which remains implausibly isolated from the rest of the world. General helplessness.

(4) One of two possibilities. Either the hero prepares to do battle alone, accidentally discovers the thing's one vulnerable point, and destroys it. Or, he somehow manages to get out of town and succeeds in laying his case before competent authorities. They, along the lines of the first script but abridged, deploy a complex technology which (after initial setbacks) finally prevails against the invaders.

Another version of the second script opens with the scientist-hero in his laboratory, which is located in the basement or on the grounds of his tasteful, prosperous house. Through his experiments, he unwittingly causes a frightful metamorphosis in some class of plants or animals which turn carnivorous and go on a rampage. Or else, his experiments have caused him to be injured (sometimes irrevocably) or "invaded" himself. Perhaps he has been experimenting with radiation, or has built a machine to communicate with beings from other planets or transport him to other places or times.

Another version of the first script involves the discovery of some fundamental alteration in the conditions of existence of our planet, brought about by nuclear testing, which will lead to the extinction in a few months of all human life. For example: the temperature of the earth is becoming too high or too low to support life, or the earth is cracking in two, or it is gradually being blanketed by lethal fallout.

A third script, somewhat but not altogether different from the first two, concerns a journey through space—to the moon, or some other planet. What the space-voyagers discover commonly is that the alien terrain is in a state of dire emergency, itself threatened by extra-planetary invaders or nearing extinction through the practice of nuclear warfare. The terminal dramas of the first and second scripts are played out there, to which is added the problem of getting away from the doomed and/or hostile planet and back to Earth.

I am aware, of course, that there are thousands of science fiction novels (their heyday was the late 1940s), not to mention the transcriptions of science fiction themes which, more and more, provide the principal subject-matter of comic books. But I propose to discuss science fiction films (the present period began in 1950 and continues, considerably abated, to this day) as an independent subgenre, without reference to other media—and, most particularly, without reference to the novels from which, in many cases, they were adapted. For, while novel and film may share the same plot, the fundamental difference between the resources of the novel and the film makes them quite dissimilar.

Certainly, compared with the science fiction novels, their film counterparts have unique strengths, one of which is the immediate representation of the extraordinary: physical deformity and mutation, missile and rocket combat, toppling skyscrapers. The movies are, naturally, weak just where the science fiction novels (some of them) are strong—on science. But in place of an intellectual workout, they can supply something the novels can never provide—sensuous elaboration. In the films it is by means of images and sounds, not words that have to be translated by the imagination, that one can participate in the fantasy of living through one's own death and more, the death of cities, the destruction of humanity itself.

Science fiction films are not about science. They are about disaster, which is one of the oldest subjects of art. In science fiction films disaster is rarely viewed intensively; it is always extensive. It is a matter of quantity and ingenuity. If you will, it is a question of scale. But the scale, particularly in the wide-screen color films (of which the ones by the Japanese director Inoshiro Honda and the American director George Pal are technically the most convincing and visually the most exciting), does raise the matter to another level.

Thus, the science fiction film (like that of a very different contemporary genre, the Happening) is concerned with the aesthetics of destruction, with the peculiar beauties to be found in wreaking havoc, making a mess. And it is in the imagery of destruction that the core of a good science fiction film lies. Hence, the disadvantage of the cheap film—in which the monster appears or the rocket lands in a small dull-looking town. (Hollywood budget needs usually dictate that the town be in the Arizona or California desert. In *The Thing From Another World* [1951] the rather sleazy and confined set is supposed to be an encampment near the North Pole.)

491

Still, good black-and-white science fiction films have been made. But a bigger budget, which usually means color, allows a much greater play back and forth among several model environments. There is the populous city. There is the lavish but ascetic interior of the spaceship—either the invaders' or ours—replete with streamlined chromium fixtures and dials and machines whose complexity is indicated by the number of colored lights they flash and strange noises they emit. There is the laboratory crowded with formidable boxes and scientific apparatus. There is a comparatively old-fashioned-looking conference room, where the scientists unfurl charts to explain the desperate state of things to the military. And each of these standard locales or backgrounds is subject to two modalities—intact and destroyed. We may, if we are lucky, be treated to a panorama of melting tanks, flying bodies, crashing walls, awesome craters and fissures in the earth, plummeting spacecraft, colorful deadly rays; and to a symphony of screams, weird electronic signals, the noisiest military hardware going, and the leaden tones of the laconic denizens of alien planets and their subjugated earthlings.

Certain of the primitive gratifications of science fiction films—for instance, the depiction of urban disaster on a colossally magnified scale—are shared with other types of films. Visually there is little difference between mass havoc as represented in the old horror and monster films and what we find in science fiction films, except (again) scale. In the old monster films, the monster always headed for the great city, where he had to do a fair bit of rampaging, hurling busses off bridges, crumpling trains in his bare hands, toppling buildings, and so forth. The archetype is King Kong, in Schoedsack and Cooper's great film of 1933, running amok, first in the native village (trampling babies, a bit of footage excised from most prints), then in New York. This is really no different in spirit from the scene in Inoshiro Honda's *Rodan* (1957) in which two giant reptiles—with a wingspan of 500 feet and supersonic speeds—by flapping their wings whip up a cyclone that blows most of Tokyo to smithereens. Or the destruction of half of Japan by the gigantic robot with the great incinerating ray that shoots forth from his eyes, at the beginning of Honda's *The Mysterians* (1959). Or, the devastation by the rays from a fleet of flying saucers of New York, Paris, and Tokyo, in *Battle in Outer Space* (1960). Or, the inundation of New York in *When Worlds Collide* (1951). Or, the end of London in 1966 depicted in George Pal's *The Time Machine* (1960). Neither do these sequences differ in aesthetic intention from the destruction scenes in the big sword, sandal, and orgy color spectaculars set in Biblical and Roman times—the end of Sodom in Aldrich's *Sodom and Gomorrah*, of Gaza in De Mille's *Samson and Delilah*, of Rhodes in *The Colossus of Rhodes*, and of Rome in a dozen Nero movies. Griffith began it with the Babylon sequence in *Intolerance*, and to this day there is nothing like the thrill of watching all those expensive sets come tumbling down.

In other respects as well, the science fiction films of the 1950s take up familiar themes. The famous 1930s movie serials and comics of the adventures of Flash Gordon and Buck Rogers, as well as the more recent spate of comic book super-heroes with extraterrestrial origins (the most famous is Superman, a foundling from the planet Krypton, currently described as having been exploded by a nuclear blast), share motifs with more recent science fiction movies. But there is an important difference. The old science fiction films, and most of the comics, still have an essentially innocent relation to disaster. Mainly they offer new versions of the oldest romance of all—of the strong invulnerable hero with a mysterious lineage come to do battle on behalf of good and against evil. Recent science fiction films have a decided grimness, bolstered by their much greater degree of visual credibility, which contrasts strongly with the older films. Modern historical reality has greatly enlarged the imagination of disaster, and the protagonists—perhaps by the very nature of what is visited upon them—no longer seem wholly innocent.

The lure of such generalized disaster as a fantasy is that it releases one from normal obligations. The trump card of the end-of-the-world movies—like *The Day the Earth Caught Fire* (1962)—is that great scene with New York or London or Tokyo discovered empty, its entire population annihilated. Or, as in *The World, The Flesh, and The Devil* (1957), the whole movie can be devoted to the fantasy of occupying the deserted metropolis and starting all over again, a world Robinson Crusoe.

Another kind of satisfaction these films supply is extreme moral simplification—that is to say, a morally acceptable fantasy where one can give outlet to cruel or at least amoral feelings. In this re-

493

spect, science fiction films partly overlap with horror films. This is the undeniable pleasure we derive from looking at freaks, beings excluded from the category of the human. The sense of superiority over the freak conjoined in varying proportions with the titillation of fear and aversion makes it possible for moral scruples to be lifted, for cruelty to be enjoyed. The same thing happens in science fiction films. In the figure of the monster from outer space, the freakish, the ugly, and the predatory all converge—and provide a fantasy target for righteous bellicosity to discharge itself, and for the aesthetic enjoyment of suffering and disaster. Science fiction films are one of the purest forms of spectacle; that is, we are rarely inside anyone's feelings. (An exception is Jack Arnold's *The Incredible Shrinking Man* [1957].) We are merely spectators; we watch.

But in science fiction films, unlike horror films, there is not much horror. Suspense, shocks, surprises are mostly abjured in favor of a steady, inexorable plot. Science fiction films invite a dispassionate, aesthetic view of destruction and violence—a *technological* view. Things, objects, machinery play a major role in these films. A greater range of ethical values is embodied in the décor of these films than in the people. Things, rather than the helpless humans, are the locus of values because we experience them, rather than people, as the sources of power. According to science fiction films, man is naked without his artifacts. *They* stand for different values, they are potent, they are what get destroyed, and they are the indispensable tools for the repulse of the alien invaders or the repair of the damaged environment.

The science fiction films are strongly moralistic. The standard message is the one about the proper, or humane, use of science, versus the mad, obsessional use of science. This message the science fiction films share in common with the classic horror films of the 1930s, like *Frankenstein*, *The Mummy*, *Island of Lost Souls*, *Dr. Jekyll and Mr. Hyde*. (George Franju's brilliant *Les Yeux Sans Visage* [1959], called here *The Horror Chamber of Doctor Faustus*, is a more recent example.) In the horror films, we have the mad or obsessed or misguided scientist who pursues his experiments against good advice to the contrary, creates a monster or monsters, and is himself destroyed—often recognizing his folly himself, and dying

494

in the successful effort to destroy his own creation. One science fiction equivalent of this is the scientist, usually a member of a team, who defects to the planetary invaders because "their" science is more advanced than "ours."

This is the case in *The Mysterians*, and, true to form, the renegade sees his error in the end, and from within the Mysterian spaceship destroys it and himself. In *This Island Earth* (1955), the inhabitants of the beleaguered planet Metaluna propose to conquer earth, but their project is foiled by a Metalunan scientist named Exeter who, having lived on earth a while and learned to love Mozart, cannot abide such viciousness. Exeter plunges his spaceship into the ocean after returning a glamorous pair (male and female) of American physicists to earth. Metaluna dies. In *The Fly* (1958), the hero, engrossed in his basement-laboratory experiments on a matter-transmitting machine, uses himself as a subject, exchanges head and one arm with a housefly which had accidentally gotten into the machine, becomes a monster, and with his last shred of human will destroys his laboratory and orders his wife to kill him. His discovery, for the good of mankind, is lost.

Being a clearly labeled species of intellectual, scientists in science fiction films are always liable to crack up or go off the deep end. In *Conquest of Space* (1955), the scientist-commander of an international expedition to Mars suddenly acquires scruples about the blasphemy involved in the undertaking, and begins reading the Bible mid-journey instead of attending to his duties. The commander's son, who is his junior officer and always addresses his father as "General," is forced to kill the old man when he tries to prevent the ship from landing on Mars. In this film, both sides of the ambivalence toward scientists are given voice. Generally, for a scientific enterprise to be treated entirely sympathetically in these films, it needs the certificate of utility. Science, viewed without ambivalence, means an efficacious response to danger. Disinterested intellectual curiosity rarely appears in any form other than caricature, as a maniacal dementia that cuts one off from normal human relations. But this suspicion is usually directed at the scientist rather than his work. The creative scientist may become a martyr to his own discovery, through an accident or by pushing things too far. But the implication remains that other men, less imaginative—in short, technicians—could have administered the same discovery better and more safely. The most ingrained contemporary mistrust of the intellect is visited, in these movies, upon the scientist-as-intellectual.

The message that the scientist is one who releases forces which, if not controlled for good, could destroy man himself seems innocuous enough. One of the oldest images of the scientist is Shakespeare's Prospero, the overdetached scholar forcibly retired from society to a desert island, only partly in control of the magic forces in which he dabbles. Equally classic is the figure of the scientist as satanist (*Doctor Faustus*, and stories of Poe and Hawthorne). Science is magic, and man has always known that there is black magic as well as white. But it is not enough to remark that contemporary attitudes — as reflected in science fiction films — remain ambivalent, that the scientist is treated as both satanist and savior. The proportions have changed, because of the new context in which the old admiration and fear of the scientist are located. For his sphere of influence is no longer local, himself or his immediate community. It is planetary, cosmic.

One gets the feeling, particularly in the Japanese films but not only there, that a mass trauma exists over the use of nuclear weapons and the possibility of future nuclear wars. Most of the science fiction films bear witness to this trauma, and, in a way, attempt to exorcise it.

The accidental awakening of the super-destructive monster who has slept in the earth since prehistory is, often, an obvious metaphor for the Bomb. But there are many explicit references as well. In *The Mysterians*, a probe ship from the planet Mysteroid has landed on earth, near Tokyo. Nuclear warfare having been practiced on Mysteroid for centuries (their civilization is "more advanced than ours"), ninety percent of those now born on the planet have to be destroyed at birth, because of defects caused by the huge amounts of Strontium 90 in their diet. The Mysterians have come to earth to marry earth women, and possibly to take over our relatively uncontaminated planet. . . . In *The Incredible Shrinking Man*, the John Doe hero is the victim of a gust of radiation which blows over the water, while he is out boating with his wife; the radiation causes him to grow smaller and smaller, until at the end of the movie he steps through the fine mesh of a window screen to become "the infinitely small." . . . In *Rodan,* a horde of monstrous carnivorous prehistoric insects, and finally a pair of giant flying reptiles (the prehistoric Archeopteryx), are hatched from dormant eggs in the depths of a mine shaft by the impact of nuclear test explosions, and go on to destroy a good part of the world before they are felled by the molten lava of a volcanic eruption. . . . In the English film, *The Day the Earth Caught Fire,* two simultaneous hydrogen bomb tests by the United States and Russia change by 11 degrees the tilt of the earth on its axis and alter the earth's orbit so that it begins to approach the sun.

Radiation casualties—ultimately, the conception of the whole world as a casualty of nuclear testing and nuclear warfare—is the most ominous of all the notions with which science fiction films deal. Universes become expendable. Worlds become contaminated, burnt out, exhausted, obsolete. In *Rocketship X-M* (1950) explorers from the earth land on Mars, where they learn that atomic warfare has destroyed Martian civilization. In George Pal's *The War of the Worlds* (1953), reddish spindly alligator-skinned creatures from Mars invade the earth because their planet is becoming too cold to be inhabitable. In *This Island Earth,* also American, the planet Metaluna, whose population has long ago been driven underground by warfare, is dying under the missile attacks of an enemy planet. Stocks of uranium, which power the force field shielding Metaluna, have been used up; and an unsuccessful expedition is sent to earth to enlist earth scientists to devise new sources for nuclear power. In Joseph Losey's *The Damned* (1961), nine icy-cold radioactive children are being reared by a fanatical scientist in a dark cave on the English coast to be the only survivors of the inevitable nuclear Armageddon.

There is a vast amount of wishful thinking in science fiction films, some of it touching, some of it depressing. Again and again, one detects the hunger for a "good war," which poses no moral problems, admits of no moral qualifications. The imagery of science fiction films will satisfy the most bellicose addict of war films, for a lot of the satisfactions of war films pass, untransformed, into science fiction films. Examples: the dogfights between earth "fighter rockets" and alien spacecraft in the *Battle in Outer Space* (1960); the escalating firepower in the successive assaults upon the invaders in *The Mysterians*, which Dan Talbot correctly described as a non-stop holocaust; the spectacular bombardment of the underground fortress of Metaluna in *This Island Earth*.

Yet at the same time the bellicosity of science fiction films is neatly channeled into the yearning for peace, or for at least peaceful coexistence. Some scientist generally takes sententious note of the fact that it took the planetary invasion to make the warring nations of the earth come to their senses and suspend their own conflicts. One of the main themes of many science fiction films—the color ones usually, because they have the budget and resources to develop the military spectacle—is this UN fantasy, a fantasy of united warfare. (The same wishful UN theme cropped up in a recent spectacular which is not science fiction, *Fifty-Five Days in Peking* [1963]. There, topically enough, the Chinese, the Boxers, play the role of Martian invaders who unite the earthmen, in this case the United States, England, Russia, France, Germany, Italy, and Japan.) A great enough disaster cancels all enmities and calls upon the utmost concentration of earth resources.

Science—technology—is conceived of as the great unifier. Thus the science fiction films also project a Utopian fantasy. In the classic models of Utopian thinking—Plato's Republic, Campanella's City of the Sun, More's Utopia, Swift's land of the Houyhnhnms, Voltaire's Eldorado—society had worked out a perfect consensus. In these societies reasonableness had achieved an unbreakable supremacy over the emotions. Since no disagreement or social conflict was intellectually plausible, none was possible. As in Melville's *Typee*, "they all think the same." The universal rule of reason meant universal agreement. It is interesting, too, that societies in which reason was pictured as totally ascendant were also traditionally pictured as having an ascetic or materially frugal and economically simple mode of life. But in the Utopian world community projected by science fiction films, totally pacified and ruled by scientific consensus, the demand for simplicity of material existence would be absurd.

Yet alongside the hopeful fantasy of moral simplification and international unity embodied in the science fiction films lurk the deepest anxieties about contemporary existence. I don't mean only the very real trauma of the Bomb—that it has been used, that there are enough now to kill everyone on earth many times over, that those new bombs may very well be used. Besides these new anxieties about physical disaster, the prospect of universal mutilation and even annihilation, the science fiction films reflect powerful anxieties about the condition of the individual psyche.

For science fiction films may also be described as a popular mythology for the contemporary *negative* imagination about the impersonal. The other-world creatures that seek to take "us" over are an "it," not a "they." The planetary invaders are usually zombie-like. Their movements are either cool, mechanical, or lumbering, blobby. But it amounts to the same thing. If they are non-human in form, they proceed with an absolutely regular, unalterable movement (unalterable save by destruction). If they are human in form—dressed in space suits, etc.—then they obey the most rigid military discipline, and display no personal characteristics whatsoever. And it is this regime of emotionlessness, of impersonality, of regimentation, which they will impose on the earth if they are successful. "No more love, no more beauty, no more pain," boasts a converted earthling in *The Invasion of the Body Snatchers* (1956). The half-earthling, half-alien children in *The Children of the Damned* (1960) are absolutely emotionless, move as a group and understand each others' thoughts, and are all prodigious intellects. They are the wave of the future, man in his next stage of development.

These alien invaders practice a crime which is worse than murder. They do not simply kill the person. They obliterate him. In *The War of the Worlds*, the ray which issues from the rocket ship disintegrates all persons and objects in its path, leaving no trace of them but a light ash. In Honda's *The H-Man* (1959), the creeping blob melts all flesh with which it comes in contact. If the blob, which looks like a huge hunk of red Jello and can crawl across floors and up and down walls, so much as touches your bare foot, all that is left of you is a heap of clothes on the floor. (A more articulated, size-multiplying blob is the villain in the English film *The Creeping Unknown* [1956].) In another version of this fantasy, the body is preserved but the person is entirely reconstituted as the automatized servant or agent of the alien powers. This is, of course, the vampire fantasy in new dress. The person is really dead, but he doesn't know it. He is "undead," he has become an "unperson." It

499

Attack of the Space Ship Invaders in *The War of the Worlds* (1953). "In *The War of the Worlds*, the ray which issues from the rocket ship disintegrates all persons and objects in its path, leaving no trace of them but a light ash" (SONTAG, page 499).

happens to a whole California town in *The Invasion of the Body Snatchers*, to several earth scientists in *This Island Earth*, and to assorted innocents in *It Came From Outer Space*, *Attack of the Puppet People* (1958), and *The Brain Eaters* (1958). As the victim always backs away from the vampire's horrifying embrace, so in science fiction films the person always fights being "taken over"; he wants to retain his humanity. But once the deed has been done, the victim is eminently satisfied with his condition. He has not been converted from human amiability to monstrous "animal" bloodlust (a metaphoric exaggeration of sexual desire), as in the old vampire fantasy. No, he has simply become far more efficient—the very model of technocratic man, purged of emotions, volitionless, tranquil, obedient to all orders. (The dark secret behind human nature used to be the upsurge of the animal—as in *King Kong*. The threat to man, his availability to dehumanization, lay in his own animality. Now the danger is understood as residing in man's ability to be turned into a machine.)

The rule, of course, is that this horrible and irremediable form of murder can strike anyone in the film except the hero. The hero and his family, while greatly threatened, always escape this fate and by the end of the film the invaders have been repulsed or destroyed. I know of only one exception, *The Day That Mars Invaded Earth* (1963), in which after all the standard struggles the scientist-hero, his wife, and their two children are "taken over" by the alien invaders—and that's that. (The last minutes of the film show them being incinerated by the Martians' rays and their ash silhouettes flushed down their empty swimming pool, while their simulacra drive off in the family car.) Another variant but upbeat switch on the rule occurs in *The Creation of the Humanoids* (1964), where the hero discovers at the end of the film that he, too, has been turned into a metal robot, complete with highly efficient and virtually indestructible mechanical insides, although he didn't know it and detected no difference in himself. He learns, however, that he will shortly be upgraded into a "humanoid" having all the properties of a real man.

Of all the standard motifs of science fiction films, this theme of dehumanization is perhaps the most fascinating. For, as I have indicated, it is scarcely a black-and-white situation, as in the old vampire films. The attitude of the science fiction films toward depersonalization is mixed. On the one hand, they deplore it as the ultimate horror. On the other hand, certain characteristics of the dehumanized invaders, modulated and disguised—such as the ascendancy of reason over feelings, the idealization of teamwork and the consensus-creating activities of science, a marked degree of moral simplification—are precisely traits of the savior-scientist. It is interesting that when the scientist in these films is treated negatively, it is usually done through the portrayal of an individual scientist who holes up in his laboratory and neglects his fiancée or his loving wife and children, obsessed by his daring and dangerous experiments. The scientist as a loyal member of a team, and therefore considerably less individualized, is treated quite respectfully.

There is absolutely no social criticism, of even the most implicit kind, in science fiction films. No criticism, for example, of the conditions of our society which create the impersonality and dehumanization which science fiction fantasies displace onto the influence of an alien It. Also, the notion of science as a social activity, interlocking with social and political interests, is unacknowledged. Science is simply either adventure (for good or evil) or a technical response to danger. And, typically, when the fear of science is paramount—when science is conceived of as black magic rather than white—the evil has no attribution beyond that of the perverse will of an individual scientist. In science fiction films the antithesis of black magic and white is drawn as a split between technology, which is beneficent, and the errant individual will of a lone intellectual.

Thus, science fiction films can be looked at as thematically central allegory, replete with standard modern attitudes. The theme of depersonalization (being "taken over") which I have been talking about is a new allegory reflecting the age-old awareness of man that, sane, he is always perilously close to insanity and unreason. But there is something more here than just a recent, popular image which expresses man's perennial, but largely unconscious, anxiety about his sanity. The image derives most of its power from a supplementary and historical anxiety, also not experienced *consciously* by most people, about the depersonalizing conditions of modern urban life. Similarly, it is not enough to note that science fiction allegories are one of the new myths about—that is, one of the ways of accommodating to and negating—the perennial human anxiety about death. (Myths of heaven and hell, and of ghosts, had the same function.) For, again, there is a historically specifiable twist which intensifies the anxiety. I mean, the trauma suffered by everyone in the middle of the 20th century when it became clear that, from now on to the end of human history, every person would spend his individual life under the threat not only of individual death, which is certain, but of something almost insupportable psychologically—collective incineration and extinction which could come at any time, virtually without warning.

From a psychological point of view, the imagination of disaster does not greatly differ from one period in history to another. But from a political and moral point of view, it does. The expectation of the apocalypse may be the occasion for a radical disaffiliation from society, as when thousands of Eastern European Jews in the 17th century, hearing that Sabbatai Zevi had been proclaimed the Messiah and that the end of the world was imminent, gave up their homes and businesses and began the trek to Palestine. But people take the news of their doom in diverse ways. It is reported that in 1945 the populace of Berlin received without great agitation the news that Hitler had decided to kill them all, before the Allies arrived, because they had not been worthy enough to win the war. We are, alas, more in the position of the Berliners of 1945 than of the Jews of 17th century Eastern Europe; and our response is closer to theirs, too. What I am suggesting is that the imagery of disaster in science fiction is above all the emblem of an *inadequate response*. I don't mean to bear down on the films for this. They themselves are only a sampling, stripped of sophistication, of the inadequacy of most people's response to the unassimilable terrors that infect their consciousness. The interest of the films, aside from their considerable amount of cinematic charm, consists in this intersection between a naïve and largely debased commercial art product and the most profound dilemmas of the contemporary situation.

Ours is indeed an age of extremity. For we live under continual threat of two equally fearful, but seemingly opposed, destinies: unremitting banality and inconceivable terror. It is fantasy, served out in large rations by the popular arts, which allows most people to cope with these twin specters. For one job that fantasy can do is to lift us out of the unbearably humdrum and to distract us from

503

terrors—real or anticipated—by an escape into exotic, dangerous situations which have last-minute happy endings. But another of the things that fantasy can do is to normalize what is psychologically unbearable, thereby inuring us to it. In one case, fantasy beautifies the world. In the other, it neutralizes it.

The fantasy in science fiction films does both jobs. The films reflect world-wide anxieties, and they serve to allay them. They inculcate a strange apathy concerning the processes of radiation, contamination, and destruction which I for one find haunting and depressing. The naïve level of the films neatly tempers the sense of otherness, of alien-ness, with the grossly familiar. In particular, the dialogue of most science fiction films, which is of a monumental but often touching banality, makes them wonderfully, unintentionally funny. Lines like "Come quickly, there's a monster in my bathtub," "We must do something about this," "Wait, Professor. There's someone on the telephone," "But that's incredible," and the old American stand-by, "I hope it works!" are hilarious in the context of picturesque and deafening holocaust. Yet the films also contain something that is painful and in deadly earnest.

There is a sense in which all these movies are in complicity with the abhorrent. They neutralize it, as I have said. It is no more, perhaps, than the way all art draws its audience into a circle of complicity with the thing represented. But in these films we have to do with things which are (quite literally) unthinkable. Here, "thinking about the unthinkable"—not in the way of Herman Kahn, as a subject for calculation, but as a subject for fantasy—becomes, however inadvertently, itself a somewhat questionable act from a moral point of view. The films perpetuate clichés about identity, volition, power, knowledge, happiness, social consensus, guilt, responsibility which are, to say the least, not serviceable in our present extremity. But collective nightmares cannot be banished by demonstrating that they are, intellectually and morally, fallacious. This nightmare—the one reflected, in various registers, in the science fiction films—is too close to our reality.

1965

504

MOLLY HASKELL
FROM
FROM REVERENCE TO RAPE

THE WOMAN'S FILM

What more damning comment on the relations between men and women in America than the very notion of something called the "woman's film"? And what more telling sign of critical and sexual priorities than the low caste it has among the highbrows? Held at arm's length, it is indeed, the untouchable of film genres. The concept of a "woman's film" and "women's fiction" as a separate category of art (and/or kitsch), implying a generically shared world of misery and masochism the individual work is designed to indulge, does not exist in Europe. There, affairs of the heart are of importance to both men and women and are the stuff of literature. In England, the woman's film occupies a place somewhere between its positions in France and in America; *Brief Encounter* and *The Seventh Veil* are not without soap opera elements, but they are on a slightly higher plane than their American counterparts.

Among the Anglo-American critical brotherhood (and a few of their sisters as well), the term "woman's film" is used disparagingly to conjure up the image of the pinched-virgin or little-old-lady writer, spilling out her secret longings in wish fulfillment or glorious martyrdom, and transmitting these fantasies to the frustrated housewife. The final image is one of wet, wasted afternoons. And if strong men have also cried their share of tears over the weepies, that is all the more reason (goes the argument) we should be suspicious, be on our guard against the flood of "unearned" feelings released by these assaults, unerringly accurate, on our emotional soft spots.

As a term of critical opprobrium, "woman's film" carries the implication that women, and therefore women's emotional problems, are of minor significance. A film that focuses on male relationships is not pejoratively dubbed a "man's film" (indeed, this term, when it is used, confers—like "a man's man"—an image of brute strength), but a "psychological drama." European films, too, are automatically exempted from the "woman's film" caste; thus, the critical status of *Mayerling* over *Love Affair*, *Le Carnet du Bal* over *Angel*, *Jules and Jim* over *Design for Living*, *My Night at Maud's* over *Petulia*, and *The Passion of Anna* over Bergman's English-language *The Touch*. Also exempted are films with literary prestige, like *Carrie* or *Sunday, Bloody Sunday*.

In the thirties and forties, the heyday of the "woman's film," it was as regular an item in studio production as the crime melodrama or the Western. Like any routine genre, it was subject to its highs and lows, and ranged from films that adhered safely to the formulae of escapist fantasy, films that were subversive only "between the lines" and in retrospect, and the rare few that used the conventions to undermine them. At the lowest level, as soap opera, the "woman's film" fills a masturbatory need, it is soft-core emotional porn for the frustrated housewife. The weepies are founded on a mock-Aristotelian and politically conservative aesthetic whereby women spectators are moved, not by pity and fear but by self-pity and tears, to accept, rather than reject, their lot. That there should be a need and an audience for such an opiate suggests an unholy amount of real misery. And that a term like "woman's film" can be summarily used to dismiss certain films, with no further need on the part of the critic to make distinctions and explore the genre, suggests some of the reasons for this misery.

In the woman's film, the woman—*a* woman—is at the center of the universe. Best friends and suitors, like Bette Davis' satellites (Geraldine Fitzgerald and George Brent) in *Dark Victory*, live only for her pleasure, talk about her constantly, and cease to exist when she dies. In the rare case

where a man's point of view creeps in, as screenwriter Howard Koch's did in *No Sad Songs for Me*, it is generally reconciled with the woman's point of view. Thus, after Margaret
Sullavan dies, the husband (Wendell Corey) will marry the
woman (Viveca Lindfors) he almost had an affair with. But it
is with the dead wife's blessing (she has actually chosen the
woman who will replace her as wife and mother), and with the
knowledge that when the chips were down, he preferred the
wife to the "other woman." The result is the same as that of
Dark Victory: The two loved ones—the remainders—may
unite out of loneliness, but always with the shadow and memory of the "great woman" (vivid and in her prime) between
them. If woman hogs this universe unrelentingly, it is perhaps
her compensation for all the male-dominated universes from
which she has been excluded: the gangster film, the Western,
the war film, the *policier*, the rodeo film, the adventure film.
Basically, the woman's film is no more maudlin and self-pity-
ing than the male adventure film (what British critic Raymond
Durgnat calls the "male weepies"), particularly in the male
film's recent mood of bronco-busting buddies and bleary-eyed
nostalgia. The well of self-pity in both types of films, though
only hinted at, is bottomless, and in their sublimation or eva-
sion of adult reality, they reveal, almost by accident, real attitudes toward marriage—disillusionment, frustration, and con-
tempt--beneath the sunny-side-up philosophy congealed in
the happy ending.

The underlying mystique of the man's film is that these are
(or were) the best of times, roaming the plains, or prowling
the city, in old clothes and unshaven, the days before settling
down or going home, days spent battling nature or the enemy.
In such films, the woman becomes a kind of urban or frontier
Xantippe with rather limited options. She can be a meddling
moralist who wants the hero to leave off his wandering; or a
last resort for him, after his buddies have died or departed; or
an uptight socialite to whom the hero can never confess his
criminal, or even just shadowy, past; or a nagging nice-girl
wife, who pesters the hero to spend more time with her, instead of always working, working, working or killing, killing,
killing. The most common pattern is probably the wife com-

peting with her husband's other life—business, crime, or crime detection; and since these activities are the dramatic focus and lifeblood of the film, the wife becomes a killjoy, distracting not only the hero but the audience from the fun and danger.

Marriage becomes the heavy. The implication is clear: All the excitement of life—the passion, the risk—occurs outside marriage rather than within it. Marriage is a deadly bore, made to play the role of the spoilsport, the ugly cousin one has to dance with at the ball. An excruciating example, and they abound, occurs in *The Big Clock*, in the husband-wife relationship of Ray Milland and Maureen O'Sullivan. Milland, an advertising executive, has been framed for murder; he is in life-or-death danger as he tries to track down the real culprit. Meanwhile O'Sullivan—naturally, as the wife, the last to be informed—keeps complaining of Milland's long hours at the office and his failure to take her on a promised wedding trip. Indeed, the murderer (Charles Laughton) is by far a more sympathetic character than the wife. By intruding on and sometimes interfering with the melodrama, such women become harpies even when they aren't meant to—*The Big Clock*, after all, was directed by Maureen O'Sullivan's husband, John Farrow.

That love is woman's stuff is a hoary Anglo-Saxon idea, devolving from the (American) tough guy and (British) public school etiquette that to show emotion is bad form, a sign of effeminacy, and that being tender in love is the equivalent of doing the dishes or darning socks. The association takes. For the housewife, betrayed by her romantic ideals, the path of love leads to, becomes, the dead end of household drudgery. The domestic and the romantic are entwined, one redeeming the other, in the theme of self-sacrifice, which is the mainstay and oceanic force, high tide and low ebb, of the woman's film. The equation of time and Tide is not so risible as it seems, just as the emphasis in the women's movement on domestic arrangements is not a trivializing of "larger issues." Rather, it is an intuitive recognition that the essence of salvation is not in the single leap of the soul, but in the day-to-day struggle to keep the best of oneself afloat—the discovery that perdition is not the moment of Faustian sellout, but the gradual dribbling of self-esteem, and self, down the drain of meaningless activity.

To the view that women's concerns, and the films that depict them, are of minor significance in the drama of life and art, women themselves have acquiesced, and critics have led the way. James Agee was almost alone among critics in not dismissing the woman's film summarily. In a favorable review of *Brief Encounter*, he wrote that when he associated the film with the best of women's magazine fiction, he did not intend a backhand compliment. "For it seems to me that few writers of supposedly more serious talent even undertake themes as simple and important any more: so that, relatively dinky and sentimental as it is—a sort of vanity-sized *Anna Karenina*—*Brief Encounter* is to be thoroughly respected."

But for every Agee, there have been critics whose voices dripped sarcasm and whose pens went lax when they came to review a woman's film. In his 1946 book *On Documentary*, the late John Grierson, the father of the "serious subject" critics, interrupted his anti-Hollywood and prosocial-realism diatribe to deplore Anthony Asquith's waste of time and talent on *Dance, Pretty Lady*. Grierson, admitting the film was "a delight to the eye," nonetheless deplored its subject: "This is it, bless you. Claptrap about a virginity. Why the entire sentiment that makes a plot like that possible went into discard with the good, prosperous, complacent Victoria. It was, relatively, an important matter then. But it is mere infant fodder now when you consider the new problems we carry in our bellies, and think of the new emphases we must in mercy to ourselves create out of our different world." Apparently the way to a socially conscious critic's heart is through his stomach. A woman's virginity (infant fodder, indeed!), and where and how she lost it, is at least as important as the high and mighty manly themes of the films Grierson approved of.

The deprecation of women's films takes a different form among critics who are not socially conscious—the aesthetically open, "movie-movie critics" represented, in the thirties and forties, by Agee, Otis Ferguson, Robert Warshow, and Manny Farber. There, the prejudice is more subtle: It is not that they

509

love women less, but that they admire men more. Even Ferguson and Agee, who were enraptured with certain female presences on the screen, reserved their highest accolades for the
films that showed men doing things and that captured the look
and feel of down-at-heel losers, criminals, or soldiers, men
battling nature or big-city odds. Agee never avoided the emotional or sentimental side of film (in the forties, who could?),
but like the others, he had a slight case of Hemingwayitis.
This infatuation with the masculine mystique was the paleface New York intellectual's compensation for life in a cubicle,
a *nostalgie de la boue* for the real grit and grime, as opposed to
synthetic smudge—the kind that rubs off on your hands from
typewriter erasures or newspapers.

There has been a corollary blindness on the part of most film
critics to the achievements of the "woman's director," to the
mixture of seriousness and high style that Europeans like Max
Ophuls, Douglas Sirk, Otto Preminger, and Lubitsch bring to
women's subjects, not just enhancing but transforming them;
or to the commitment of a John Stahl or Edmund Goulding to
material from which other directors withdraw in tasteful disdain (as did Wyler and Stevens, "graduating" as soon as they
got the opportunity from the woman's film subjects of their
early and best work to the bloated seriousness of their later
work); or to the complete identification of a director like
George Cukor with the woman's point of view, so that the attitude expressed is not his so much as hers.

Central to the woman's film is the notion of middle-classness, not just as an economic status, but as a state of mind and
a relatively rigid moral code. The circumscribed world of the
housewife corresponds to the state of woman in general, confronted by a range of options so limited she might as well inhabit a cell. The persistent irony is that she is dependent for
her well-being and "fulfillment" on institutions—marriage,
motherhood—that by translating the word "woman" into
"wife" and "mother," end her independent identity. She then
feels bound to adhere to a morality which demands that she
stifle her own "illicit" creative or sexual urges in support of a
social code that tolerates considerably more deviation on the
part of her husband. She is encouraged to follow the lead of
her romantic dreams, but when they expire she is stuck.

Beyond this common plight of a generic nature, there are as many kinds of woman's film as there are kinds of women. One division, providing the greatest tension with conventions of the genre, is between the upper-middle-class elite and the rest of the world, between women as models and women as victims. There are the "extraordinary" women—actresses like Marlene Dietrich, Katharine Hepburn, Rosalind Russell, Bette Davis, and characters like Scarlett O'Hara and Jezebel—who are the exceptions to the rule, the aristocrats of their sex. Their point of view is singular, and in calling the shots they transcend the limitations of their sexual identities. But their status as emancipated women, based as it is on the very quality of being exceptional, weakens their political value as demonstration-model victims and makes them, in their independence, unpopular with a majority of men and women.

Then there are the "ordinary" women—women whose options have been foreclosed by marriage or income, by children or age, who are, properly speaking, the subject of women's films at their lowest and largest common denominator. As audience surrogates, their heroines are defined negatively and collectively by their mutual limitations rather than by their talents or aspirations. Their point of view is not singular but plural, political rather than personal. They embrace the audience as victims, through the common myths of rejection and self-sacrifice and martyrdom as purveyed by the mass media. These—the media—have changed over the years, from magazines like *Good Housekeeping, Cosmopolitan, The Saturday Evening Post*, and from novels like those of Fannie Hurst, Edna Ferber, and Kathleen Norris, through the movies of the twenties, thirties, and forties, to television soap opera today. But the myths have not changed, nor has the underlying assumption: that these women are stuck, and would rather be stuck than sorry. The purpose of these fables is not to encourage "woman" to rebel or question her role, but to reconcile her to it, and thus preserve the status quo. The fictions are her defense not only against "man," but against the "extraordinary woman." For the average housewife, who has not quite gotten around to sex therapy or sensitivity training or group grope, prostitution, drugs, or even drink, these matinee myths are her alcoholic afternoons.

511

Between these two, there is a third category, one to which the better women's films aspire: It is the fiction of the "ordinary woman who becomes extraordinary," the woman who begins as a victim of discriminatory circumstances and rises, through pain, obsession, or defiance, to become mistress of her fate. Between the suds of soap opera we watch her scale the heights of Stendhalian romance. Her ascent is given stature and conviction not through a discreet contempt for the female sensibility, but through an all-out belief it it, through the faith, expressed in directorial sympathy and style, that the swirling river of a woman's emotions is as important as anything on earth. The difference between the soap opera palliative and the great woman's film (*Angel, Letter from an Unknown Woman*) is like the difference between masturbatory relief and mutually demanding love.

All women begin as victims. Anna Karenina is a victim of the double standard no less than is Laura in *Brief Encounter;* Emma Bovary is as much a casualty of middle-class morality as is Ruby Gentry. Anna and Emma cease to be victims, cease to be easy identification figures, as they become increasingly complex and cruel, as they take fate into their own hands. As with all his characters, Tolstoy kept Anna at arm's length, in "middle shot," finding external correlatives to suggest her inner state. But movie heroines are in close-up; they have a narrower context in which to operate, and they must achieve stature in a different way. They cannot afford to alienate us (if the movie *Madame Bovary* had ended like the novel it would have been more catastrophic than courageous), because there is no wider field of vision, no social context or alternate major characters to claim our attention and absorb the shock. The movie of *Anna Karenina* is not, like the novel, about [Anna + Vronsky + Karenin + Levin + Kitty; country + city; society + art + religion] but about Garbo—or, in the later version, Vivien Leigh. (Sometimes the producers' reluctance to have a star alienate or disappoint the audiences goes too far; in the first, silent version of *Anna Karenina* which was called *Love,* and starred Garbo, an alternate happy ending was provided with the print sent to theaters; in it, according to a synopsis, "Anna and Vronsky are happily reunited three years later, after her husband's opportune death.'') The movie *Madame Bovary* is not about [Emma + French provincial society + the art form itself] but about Jennifer Jones' rapt romanticism as envisioned by Vincente Minnelli. But in the distinguished women's films, the combination of director and star serve the same function as the complex perspective of the novelist: They take the woman out of the plural into the singular, out of defeat and passivity and collective identity into the radical adventure of the solitary soul, out of the contrivances of puritanical thinking into enlightened self-interest.

It is this unique combination of actress plus director that makes, for example, one version of *Back Street* better or worse than another, even when the plot is identical. There are stars like Garbo and Marie Dressler and Joan Crawford who are their own genres. There are also distinctions to be made between one decade and another. Still, the bare bones remain remarkably similar, like grammatical models from which linguistical examples are formed. The themes of the woman's film can themselves be reduced to four categories, often found overlapping or in combination: sacrifice, affliction, choice, competition.

In the first, the woman must "sacrifice" (1) herself for her children—e.g., *Madame X, The Sin of Madelon Claudet;* (2) her children for their own welfare—e.g., *The Old Maid, Stella Dallas, To Each His Own;* (3) marriage for her lover—e.g., *Back Street;* (4) her lover for marriage or for his own welfare—e.g., *Kitty Foyle* and *Intermezzo,* respectively; (5) her career for love—e.g., *Lady in the Dark, Together Again;* or (6) love for her career—e.g., *The Royal Family of Broadway, Morning Glory.* The sacrifice film may end happily, with the wife/mother reclaiming her husband/child when her rival dies, or tragically, as mother watches daughter's happiness from afar, or sees son or lover only to lose him once again. In either case, the purgative sensations—the joy of suffering, the pain of joy—are very close. But not identical. Indeed, most of the thirties' and forties' woman's films ended tragically, an indication perhaps of the vision women had of themselves.

In the second category, the heroine is struck by some "affliction" which she keeps a secret and eventually either dies un-

513

blemished (*Dark Victory*), despite the efforts of her doctor-turned-lover, or is cured (*The Magnificent Obsession*) by the efforts of her lover-turned-doctor.

The third category, "choice," has the heroine pursued by at least two suitors who wait, with undivided attention, her decision; on it, their future happiness depends (*The Seventh Veil, Daisy Kenyon, Lydia*).

In the final category, "competition," the heroine meets and does battle with the woman whose husband (fiancé, lover) she loves (*The Great Lie, When Ladies Meet, Love Story* — the forties' English version; *Old Acquaintance*). While deciding the man's fate, the women will discover, without explicitly acknowledging it, that they prefer each other's company to his. The obtuseness of men generally is implied by their inability to perceive love or (in the case of the second category) disease.*

As patently idiotic as these themes sound, how is one to explain the degree to which some of them enthrall us: the mesmerized absorption, the choking, the welling up of tears over some lugubrious rendition of a famous piano concerto that will haunt us forever afterward with the memory of James Mason rapping Ann Todd's knuckles or Margaret Lockwood banging away in Albert Hall?

The Mason-Todd scene comes, of course, from *The Seventh Veil*, coauthored by the husband-and-wife team Muriel and Sydney Box, and directed by Compton Bennett. The title refers, in the pseudo-psychoanalytical idiom of the film, to the last "wall" between a woman and her innermost thoughts. Along with *Daisy Kenyon*, this is a model of the "choice" category, one of the most likable and yet more spurious, the pretense of suffering in a totally pleasurable situation being the height of hypocrisy. It is woman's understandable revenge, and reversal, of the state of affairs in which, as Byron said, "Man's love is of man's life a thing apart/'Tis woman's whole existence." The pattern of such films is to open with a period in which the heroine is soiled and petted (metaphorically, of

---

*Sometimes the categories overlap, as in *No Sad Songs for Me*, in which a dying Margaret Sullavan prepares to turn her husband over to another woman.

514

course) by several devoted males whose infatuation she either does not notice or is aggrieved by, after which she is given an ultimatum. She has to make a decision. At this point, a pretext will be found whereby the suitors are assembled, like characters in an Agatha Christie mystery—preferably at the bottom of a large staircase—to hear the "solution." This is, staircase and all, the arrangement that concludes *The Seventh Veil*. Ann Todd, resting upstairs, having been cured of her traumatic paralysis by psychiatrist Herbert Lom, will shortly descend and select either Hugh McDermott, the boorish American jazz musician whose wife has just divorced him, leaving him free to return to his first love; Albert Lieven, the world-weary Viennese artist who thought no woman could rekindle his dying passion; or James Mason, the witheringly sardonic guardian who trained and tyrannized her, poured his own pent-up talent into her, and couldn't let her go. (Although Lom, too, is undoubtedly in love with her, we can discount him as a contender, this being the modest era before mutual Oedipal transference and doctor-participation therapy.)

It isn't the list of players that tips us off—this is practically James Mason's first noteworthy movie. Nor is it the dime-store Freudianism that attaches to Mason's character (think of the penis envy potential in Todd's fingers and Mason's sadism). Nor is it just that he retains his dignity while those about him begin to fall apart. The choice has to be Mason, as any Anglo-American woman knows instinctively, because he, with his cultivated, misogynous manner, is the paragon of the English lover, the type most irresistible to the puritan woman. Father figure and mentor, Professor Higgins and Pygmalion, he exacts the best from her artistically, intellectually, spiritually, but makes no sexual demands. He never imposes on her; on the contrary, his indifference is the spur to her attraction. He is for most American women, the male ideal—cultured, genteel, refined, repressed, with a slight antagonism toward women that is not congenital but the result of an earlier wound or disillusionment, and therefore curable. But it is curable only by her. About all other women he continues to be cynical and disbelieving, and thus his fidelity is assured. He is, like the celibate clergyman or "confirmed bachelor," a chal-

515

lenge to a woman, and a relief from the sexually aggressive male.

The delicate, well-bred British hero (Mason, Herbert Marshall, the Howards—Trevor and Leslie) has had far more appeal than such matinee idol stock figures as John Boles, John Lund, George Brent, and all the other pretty profiles. Women's preference for the English gentleman—witty, overrefined, unsexual or apparently misogynous, paternal—is rooted in an instinct for self-preservation that expresses itself in the romantic drive. There is a split in a woman's sensibility, revealed over and over again in literature that expresses a woman's point of view, between her romantic interest—elevated, "total" (that is, not total, but psychological, spiritual)—focusing on a hero who will look into her eyes and embrace her soul and demand nothing sexually, and her sexual drive, brute and impersonal, demanding to be ravished "anonymously," that is, taken without asking, almost unawares, so that she will neither be responsible for her surrender nor bound by it afterward. (Even today, studies show that an amazing number of modern women neglect to prepare themselves for intercourse with contraception, indicating that women still prefer to think of sex as a seduction rather than a partnership. The reluctance of women to take responsibility for sex would seem a prime factor in perpetuating the stereotypes of the dominant, active male and the submissive, passive female.) Hence Scarlett's bliss the morning after her "rape" by Rhett Butler, although—and because—she will never love him the way she loves the unavailable, the undemanding Ashley. Her love for Ashley is passionate, but it is that of a tigress for a kitten; and his resistance and general effeteness assure us that even if he were to succumb she would have the upper hand. She is a diabolically strong woman—deceptively so, in the manner of the southern belle—and she fears the loss of her strength and selfhood that a total, "animal" relationship with Rhett would entail.

The "Ashley" figure, the sexually unthreatening male, whether as romantic lover or friend, crops up repeatedly in fiction written by women. The character of Waldo Lydecker, the acid-tongued columnist in Otto Preminger's *Laura*, is a perfect example. In Preminger's coolly perverse melodrama, made from a novel by Vera Caspary, the beautiful, self-possessed heroine has evaded marriage largely through the ritual savaging of her beaux by Clifton Webb's brilliant Lydecker. They make a dazzling team—Gene Tierney's career woman and the epicene, knife-blade-lean New York intellectual who launched her. Lydecker has a hold on Laura that cannot be explained merely by her indebtedness to him, and he is able to influence her further in the way that she is already predisposed. Not wanting to lose her, and expressing his own ambivalent attraction and repulsion, he ridicules her sexually demanding suitors, of whom Dana Andrews' detective is the crudest and therefore the least vulnerable. By making no claims to the chic and cultivation of the Laura–Lydecker world (by entering the battle of wits without a weapon), he emerges unscathed by Lydecker's sword and proves himself Laura's true knight.

Another Preminger gem and quintessential "choice" film is *Daisy Kenyon*, in which Joan Crawford, as a successful dress designer, has to choose between Dana Andrews, the married man who is her lover, and Henry Fonda, her boat-designing beau. Adapted from a novel by Elizabeth Janeway, it is a movie filled with typical "woman's film" scenes: the jangling telephone; the scene in the bar, when the rivals fruitlessly try to bypass Daisy and reach some sort of agreement on their own; or the climactic image of Joan Crawford, having left the two men at her country cabin to await her decision, driving eighty miles an hour through the woods, her chin jutting, her eyes glaring ahead not at the road but into the middle distance of her own self-absorption, in a narcissistic trance that can only be broken (since she can't change expression) by the crash when she drives off the road.

Strictly speaking, the "sacrifice" film constitutes a separate category, but in a broader sense it is, like the idea of "middle-classness," synonymous with the woman's film. The sacrifice film offers relief in, indeed thrives on, a contravention of its own morality: that "you can't have your cake and eat it too." The narrative impetus is based on an either/or ethic, on the universally accepted existence of fixed, life-and-death, in-or-out social rules which it is the film's precise purpose to circumvent. Doomed heroines, by not dying until the last moment, do not (as far as the experience of the film is concerned) really die. Women with fatal diseases receive all the attention and sympathy of an invalid without actually acting or looking sick. A heroine gets moral credit for not telling anyone of her illness . . . while only divulging it to an audience of millions.

Because the woman's film was designed for and tailored to a certain market, its recurrent themes represent the closest thing to an expression of the collective drives, conscious and unconscious, of American women, of their avowed obligations and their unconscious resistance. Children are an obsession in American movies—sacrifice of and for children, the use of children as justification for all manner of sacrifice—in marked contrast to European films about love and romantic intrigue, where children rarely appear at all and are almost never the instruments of judgment they are in American films. (To compare films made from almost-identical stories, Max Ophuls' *Letter from an Unknown Woman* introduces the illegitimate child only to kill him off shortly thereafter, while John Stahl's *Only Yesterday* makes his "legitimization" the culmination of the film and the redemption of the mother.)

But in true having-your-cake-and-eating-it-too fashion, the underlying resentment will have its say. In films where the unmarried or poverty-stricken mother sacrifices her children for their advancement, the children are usually such little monsters that their departure provides secret relief. Where a mother holds on to the kids and sacrifices herself for them, they are even more thankless (*Mildred Pierce* is a good example).

The sacrifice of and for children—two sides of the same coin—is a disease passing for a national virtue, and a constant theme in films that preach one thing and, for anyone who is listening, say another. Whether the totem is challenged, as in the woman's films of European directors like Ophuls and Sirk (*Reckless Moment, There's Always Tomorrow, All That Heaven Allows*), or played straight and heartwarmingly, as in *Penny Serenade, Mildred Pierce, To Each His Own*, all three verions of *Madame X, The Old Maid,* and *That Certain Woman*, the spectacle of a woman owned by her children or consumed by her maternal zeal is as much the mainstay of the woman's film as it is of American culture and middle-class marriage.

Like all obsessions, this one betrays a fear of its opposite, of a hatred so intense it must be disguised as love. The obsession is composed of various related elements: a conviction that children are the reason for getting married (*Penny Serenade*) or the only thing holding marriage together (*The Great Lie*, *The Marrying Kind*), or woman's ultimate *raison d'être*, her only worth-confirming "career." The chain becomes a vicious circle. The woman without a job, without interests, without an absorbing marriage, invests her whole life, her erotic and emotional energy, in the child, who then becomes a divining rod, further drawing off the energy and electricity that should provide a constant current between husband and wife. The child that is seen as the means of shoring up a marriage becomes the wedge that drives a couple apart. But to admit this, to admit any reservations about having children or toward the children themselves, is to commit heresy. The only way to express this hostility is through a noble inversion: the act of sacrifice, of giving them up. Thus, the surrender of the children for their welfare (*Stella Dallas* and *The Old Maid*) is a maneuver for circumventing the sacred taboo, for getting rid of the children in the guise of advancing their welfare. (The sacrifice of oneself for one's children is a more subtle and metaphorical means to the same end: of venting hostility on the children through approved channels.) Both of these transactions represent beautifully masked wish fulfillments, suggesting that the myth of obsession—the love lavished, the attention paid to children, their constant inclusion in narratives where their presence is not required—is compensation for women's guilt, for the deep, inadmissible feelings of not wanting children, or not wanting them unreservedly, in the first place.

This goes some way toward explaining the plot contrivances and emotional excesses to be found in the "sacrifice" film: Martyrdom must be proportionate to guilt, and the greater the aversion to having a child, the greater the sacrifices called for. The inconveniences the child will cause (to an unwed mother, for example) and which are the source of her aversion, become trials actively sought as tests of her mother-love. In *To Each*

519

His Own, Olivia de Havilland has become pregnant as the result of a one-night affair with an aviator who has been killed in the war. She goes to New York to have the child, but instead of staying there, where she could live with the child unquestioned, she returns to the provincial hamlet and gives the baby up to a neighbor, asking only for the privilege of spending one day a week with him. In one sense she "rejects" the child, as her lover, in dying, had "rejected" her; in another sense, the child becomes the object of all her pent-up emotions, a surrogate lover. When an old beau reappears and tries to persuade her to marry him and go away, he mistakes her refusal—and the light in her eyes—for commitment to another. And indeed it is. But it is to her own son, not a suitor, and the misinterpretation which follows revealingly suggests the degree to which an American woman's feelings for son and lover are identical. The loveliest part of the film concerns neither of these passions, but the very touching, adult encounter—the flirtation between two middle-aged air wardens (de Havilland and Roland Culver) in London—that begins and ends the film.

The mother's excessive and covertly erotic attachment to her children leads to a sense of bereavement, of the mistress "spurned," when they grow up and away from her. Once again the "woman's film" provides her with myths to support her sense of betrayal, to give her the sweet taste of revenge. Her sacrifice has spoiled them: When they leave home or "outgrow" their parents, it is not from a child's natural desire to be on his or her own, but because they have adopted "false values." In the materialism with which mothers like Stella Dallas and Mildred Pierce smother their children (a figurative rendering of the cultural advantages, higher education, and "quality" friends, in which the children go beyond their parents), in pushing them to want "more," they are creating monsters who will reject and be "ashamed" of them; simultaneously, the children's heartlessness will vindicate and earn audience sympathy for the mothers.

Less riddled with ambivalence is the "sacrifice-for-lover" film, although it carries a similar sense of pessimism and doom regarding marriage. Love is not lasting under the best of

520

circumstances, such films suggest philosophically, but the best circumstances are not to be found in marriage. Hence the numerous stories of impossible, imaginary, or extramarital love. In the latter category, *Back Street* is perhaps the most familiar, and offers, in its various remakes, a reflection of changing values.

The woman's film underwent a change between the thirties and forties, affecting—and affected by—the change in the image of women themselves. The forties were more emotional and neurotic, alternating between the self-denying passivity of the waiting war wife and the brittle aggressiveness of heroines like Davis and Crawford; thirties' heroines were spunkier and more stoical that their forties' sisters, the difference perhaps between a stiff and a quivering upper lip. Thirties' films unfolded against a normal society, whose set of standards the heroine automatically accepted. The social structure wavered in the forties, with women moving up the employment ladder and down from the pedestal, paying for one with their fall from the other. There is, as a result, a constant ambivalence in forties' films, a sensibility that is alternately hard and squishy, scathing and sentimental.

In the thirties, most heroines were still content with white-collar jobs or life at home. In the 1932 version of *Back Street*, with John Boles and Irene Dunne, Dunne is merely and merrily the town beauty. Even when she transfers to New York, following a missed rendezvous and Boles' marriage to another woman, her job is vague. The emphasis is on her reunion with Boles, who becomes her lover, and the tiny apartment where she waits and suffers. The supreme suffering, which he inflicts on her, is his refusal to let her have a baby. (Naturally she, who wants a baby and has plenty of occasion to conceive, never becomes pregnant, while Olivia de Havilland, like most movie heroines, gets pregnant from a one-night fling. But even the one-night-stand pregnancy, the seemingly silliest of movie conventions, has a source in real life; indifference on the part of women seems practically to insure pregnancy, while desperate longing seems invariably to forestall it.) In the 1941 remake (with Charles Boyer in the Boles role), Margaret Sullavan is an enterprising woman working in the family dry goods store, a buyer who knows her stuff and trades quips with the men. It is, in fact, her sharp tongue that gets her into trouble and precipitates the missed appointment. But the fact that Sullavan is more independent and self-sufficient than Dunne makes her sacrifice for love that much more humiliating; in Dunne's case, that sacrifice gives point and nobility to a life that would have been at best ordinary and conventional. Love *is* Dunne's career, and obsession is its own justification. This is one of the paradoxes basic to the woman's film, a paradox which is promptly undermined by another: The idea of a woman "giving up all" for Charles Boyer is a lot easier on the pride than the idea of "giving up all" for John Boles. But then, Boyer's delicacy and intelligence make it impossible to believe him capable of the insensitive behavior toward a woman that one can believe of Boles. It is part of the double bind of masochistic rationalization triggering the woman's film that what adds to its conviction on one level subtracts from it on another. The intelligence and chemistry of Sullavan–Boyer make them a more exciting and romantic couple than Dunne–Boles, but the ending (in their separate deaths) seems a waste and a letdown, which the fantasy happy ending—in which they meet instead of missing each other at the dock—does nothing to dispel. On the other hand, John Stahl's direction, and the script, of the earlier version become sublime at just this point. In a stunning final sequence, the appointment at the gazebo (a more felicitous location than the dock) is kept, the lovers are united, and in death they gain a beauty they never had in life.

The third version, an inane, jet-setting remake, stars John Gavin as the contemporary answer to Boles (plastic replacing plastic) and Susan Hayward as a globe-trotting fashion executive. Of all, she is the most exalted professionally and the least convincing emotionally, because her success and mobility (and here paradox dissolves in mere contradiction) undercut the closed system of decisions and consequences on which middle-class tragedy depends.

Women's films, particularly those of the thirties, have a stronger sense of social reality than their glossy-magazine or vacuum-sealed television equivalents. Aside from the portrait of American society they give as a matter of course, there are

522

unconscious reflections of misery "in passing," like the image of a drunk or a prostitute reflected on the shiny surface of a parked limousine. The spectacle of perverted child-love is one such image, as are the American obsession with money, status, social climbing and its epiphenomenon, the *faux pas*. Who can forget the horror, and terrible humor, of the birthday party scene in King Vidor's *Stella Dallas,* when Stanwyck and daughter Anne Shirley wait at the place-marked and over-decorated table as first one, then another and another note of regret arrives.

A growing ambivalence and coyness in films began in the thirties and ran into the forties. (Sometimes it wasn't so ambivalent; for example, a strong antifeminist and philistine sentiment runs through Lubitsch's *That Uncertain Feeling,* with its derisive attitude toward the "cultural evening" that opens the film.) Part of the silliness arose from the fact that sexual passion and desire could not be shown: compare the 1929 version of *The Letter,* in which Jeanne Eagels seems to disintegrate before our eyes with the force of her passion, and the 1941 remake, in which Bette Davis has to give a suppressed and largely psychological performance in conformance with code decorum. There was also a retrenchment from the feminism of the twenties and thirties. Women might have better jobs, largely as a result of the war and a shortage of male personnel, but they would pay more heavily for them in the movies. Naturally. They were more of a threat. Men were nervous not so much about women taking their jobs—the firing of women directly after the war and the reinstatement of protective legislation that had been temporarily suspended would take care of that—but about women leaving the home "untended" as they crept back to work. For it was a fact that once women had savored the taste of work and independence, many didn't want to go back to being "just housewives." And so in films working women (who were statistically older than their pre-war counterparts) were given a pseudo-toughness, a facade of steel wool that at a man's touch would turn into cotton candy.

As fixed point of Hollywood and lodestar of the woman's film, managing always to be where it was or vice versa, Joan Crawford provides a running commentary of changing attitudes. In *Susan and God,* her multiple-cause crusading woman, patterned on Eleanor Roosevelt, is subtly mocked for neglecting the home. Professionally, Crawford's roles reflected the American woman's rise up the wage scale: a perfume salesgirl in *The Women,* a chain-restaurateuse in *Mildred Pierce,* a designer in *Daisy Kenyon,* in *The Damned Don't Cry* she goes from being the smalltown wife of a pinchpenny hardhat, to being a "model," to being the rich and powerful "socialite" Lorna Hansen Forbes, and she does it by having more guts than any man ("I wouldn't have had the nerve," says her male protégé; "You don't need it," Crawford snaps back, "I got enough for both of us"). Then as the woman's film began to die, she moved into the neurotic women's roles of off-center *auteurs* like Nicholas Ray and Robert Aldrich. If her move from Mildred of Mildred's franchise to the single saloon-owner, Vienna, of Ray's *Johnny Guitar* was a step down economically, it was something of a leap forward iconographically. Whatever satisfaction Mildred got from Jack Carson's doglike self-abasement, Vienna's prestige was multiplied by that of her employee, Sterling Hayden, as a guitar-playing gunfighter. Vienna's final showdown with malevolent Mercedes McCambridge not only puts Mildred's altercation with her daughter to shame, it rivals such climactic mortal combats as that between Gary Cooper and Walter Huston in *The Virginian.* As the outrageous gun-toting Vienna (a more respectful *reductio ad absurdum* of her persona than Aldrich's *What Ever Happened to Baby Jane?*), Crawford alternates between the masculine and feminine elements of her personality with a bravura that is grand and funny without ever being ludicrous or demeaning.

The all-out perversity and outrageousness of *Johnny Guitar* and *What Ever Happened to Baby Jane?* are to be preferred to the sly, hidden nastiness of a film like *They All Kissed the Bride.* There, Crawford played the head of a trucking firm in conflict with Melvyn Douglas' labor leader. To suggest—leeringly, not openly—that all male-female conflict is sexual and that Crawford is really "just a girl," she goes, literally, weak in the knees every time she sees Douglas and must grab on to something or fall. It would be more humiliating if one believed for a moment that Joan Crawford could really go weak in the knees. But she can't and one doesn't. Her appeal is that she is not "just a girl" underneath; in fact, there is nothing underneath. Her hard-as-nails exterior conceals no heart of gold, or even steel. That's all there is—a sheet-metal facade, intense and glittering.

The unselfconscious luster of the early Joan Crawford hardens into the carefully polished sheen of the star. That she was a woman of many faces and uncommon adaptability is not surprising, perhaps, for a girl who had four names before she was twenty-one. She was christened Billie Cassin by her mother and adoptive father (who, in a curious parallel to Bette Davis' biography, abandoned the family when Joan was seven); she took the name (Lucille) LeSueur from her real father when she learned of his existence; she was rechristened Joan Arden by the M-G-M publicity department when she first got to Hollywood; and finally, when it was discovered that the name Joan Arden had already been assigned, she became Joan Crawford.

Even the leading men she chose to share her life with reflect the evolution of her career. She was the dancing lady of the silents whose marriage to Douglas Fairbanks, Jr., confirmed her as a symbol of flaming youth; the aspiring actress of the thirties whose marriage to Franchot Tone confirmed her seriousness; the businesswoman of the forties whose marriage to Pepsi-Cola chairman Alfred Nu Steele cemented her power and gave her security as a lifetime executive of Pepsi-Cola. The obsessively responsible heroine of *Mildred Pierce* (1945) is a long way from the feckless secretary of *Grand Hotel* (1932), the flapper of the silents, or the beautiful degenerate of *Rain*. Indeed, her performance in *Rain* is one of her loveliest and most appealing, although the 1932 film was poorly received by the press and public, and Crawford herself dislikes it. In her autobiography, she blushes an un-Crawford-like blush over her portrayal of Sadie Thompson, insisting that the critics were indeed right (just this once, is the implication) in accusing her of overacting. But her twisted relationship with the zealous reformer played by Walter Huston—her spiritual conversion, his guilty surrender to the lust against which his whole life's work has been a fortress—is one of those heady, erotic encounters that only the pre-code thirties could produce.

In her transition from the wanton, overly made-up, fluffy-haired Sadie to the severe, self-sacrificing hollow-eyed convert of *Rain*, Crawford curiously prefigured the transition in her own career from the go-go flapper to the glazed icon, from the natural party girl to the star, conscious of the importance of her fan club, of her religious commitment. But in *Rain*, even at her most pious, she has a prodigal luster, the radiance of a woman not yet aware of her powers, or of the fingernail-digging strength she will need to survive.

As she became more of a star, she was less inclined to do anything unpleasant, anything that might antagonize her audience; she thus compounded a weakness already inherent in the woman's film. But it was a paradoxical progression: If she was always morally righteous at the expense of libertine recklessness, it was also a form of security, of self-possession in which she no longer felt the need to flirt with and flatter men. The message behind the progression is not reassuring, for it tells us that a woman can't be both feminine and successful. As Crawford ceases to use her charms, she becomes less "attractive" to men; she becomes tougher and professionally driven. She becomes a "woman's woman," but as such she transgresses the etiquette and basic social laws of woman's dependency; and so her toughness is exaggerated as if to punish her and, in a vicious circle, she becomes even less sexually appealing.

Crawford, in the transition from glamour girl to self-reliant woman, reveals not just what a woman must do once her sexual commodities are no longer in demand, but suggests that a terrible loss is sustained in the process. For a woman trading on her looks, survival and adaptability are gained at a price, the price of the inner self, the core, the continuum that exists in most men unaltered by phases or changes of life. It is something men are born with, or given a sense of almost at birth; it is the bedrock sense of self on which they build. But women, when they gear their lives to men and neglect their own inner resources, are caught short by the aging process and must suddenly develop in ways that could not have been foreseen.

Thus the fragmentation of a woman's character, given symbolical and perhaps not altogether witting expression in Crawford's performance in *Possessed*. As a woman obsessed by her love for a callous architect (Van Heflin), a conscientious nurse to a rich man's wife, wife to that man (Raymond Massey) when the wife dies, suspect in the murder of the wife, mistrusted stepmother of Massey's wild daughter (Geraldine Brooks), and finally distraught murderer of Van Heflin, she encompasses vastly more facets than are strictly required by the "split personality" that is the subject of the film, one of the clinically oriented movies about psychoanalysis that were so popular in the forties. For reasons that are partly the fault of script and direction, but not entirely, we begin to wonder which, if any, is the real Crawford, so perfectly does she become each successive role. There finally seems to be no connecting link, and the madwoman roaming the streets in the film's first sequence becomes a perfect expression of the end of the line, the total confusion and centerlessness for a woman in whom existence has replaced essence.

In *Mildred Pierce*, the lower-middle-class, greasy spoon, California milieu of the James Cain novel was upgraded and much of the point was lost. By refusing to muss herself up, physically and psychologically, Crawford took the guts out of the character and the class crunch out of the mother-daughter conflict. She became a dulcifluous housewife, whose only fault, if it could be so designated, was loving her daughter too much. The obsession with the daughter (Ann Blyth), with its erotic implications, is the most fascinating aspect in the movie, since it is a veiled expression of self-love, and takes on the aspect of narcissism that is the ultimate Crawford posture.

Even Mildred's competence in the business world, radical enough, perhaps, for its time, is not a sign of independence sought for its own sake, but of initiative in the service of family (or of self-love pervertedly disguised). Mildred's ambitions are for some "higher purpose" than self-fulfillment. Her words to Pierce, her first husband, elided into one sesquipedalian word, might stand as the motto of the woman's film: "I'lldoanythingforthosekidsdoyouunderstandanything," she says, packing another homemade pie into a box for delivery.

Eve Arden's role in *Mildred Pierce* also tells us much. In the film she plays her characteristic role of the smart, cheerfully bitter woman, sidekick to the heroine and running commentator on the cruelties and stupidity of men. In many ways, her character is the most treacherously and heart-breakingly sexist of all. Independent, witty, intelligent, a true friend to her own sex and of all women the most apparently "complete" within herself, she is made to talk constantly and longingly of men, to deprecate her own powers of attraction, to place greater emphasis on sex than all the silly ninny sex objects who have nothing else to live for, in short, constantly to bemoan her "incompleteness." She thus becomes the greatest feather in the cap of male vanity. In what is an obvious contradiction of her true nature—for her relationship with Crawford is close, generous, and satisfying—she confirms the male (and, derivatively, female) idea that a bunch of women together are at best incomplete, if not downright silly.

Even more insidious is her portrayal as being "out of the running" romantically and sexually, while she is the most outspoken and least puritanical of women. There is, by implication, something "improper" in the woman (Aline MacMahon often plays the same type) who actually expresses sexual desire, and an ability to handle it, and a light touch, so that she must be denied getting the man, while the coy, hard-to-get virgin wins the prize. There is something as disheartening as it is brave in her acceptance of the status quo, for she is using her brains to deprecate their importance and downgrading her friendships with women as second-best arrangements.

Generally—and typically—the only films that allowed dignity to working woman were those based on historical figures, real-life women, the singularity (and therefore non-applicability) of whose achievement would not make them a threat to men. Or to other women. Mme Curie and Amelia Earhart would hardly start a rush on women scientists and aviatrixes, or, being dead, intimidate the living with their accomplishments. In *Blossoms in the Dust*, Greer Garson's dedicated woman battling to erase the stigma of illegitimacy from birth certificates (based on a historical case) is no problem. Yet, despite the safety of the nineteenth-century milieu, Katharine Hepburn's feminist in *A Woman Rebels* was too threatening. The film flopped and ushered in her period of "box-office poison."

Hepburn was one of the few, if not the only, actresses allowed to sacrifice love for career, rather than the other way around. The explanation usually offered is that her arrogance and eccentricity exempted her: She was neither a "regular guy" (in fact, she never won any popularity prizes in Hollywood) nor a representative of the American woman. Even in *Morning Glory*, where she gave up love for her theatrical career, the implication was that she would turn into a dried-up, defeminized old lady. And even in the hands of a sympathetic director like George Stevens or Cukor or Hawks, there was a cutting edge to her parts as written, a kind of ruthless, upper-class eccentricity, that was more a revenge on, than an expression of, her personality. In *Woman of the Year*, her cosmopolitan political reporter is pitted against Spencer Tracy's no-nonsense, boys-in-the-back-room sports reporter. Their enchanting interplay (this was their first film together) creates a sense of complementary natures and equality which is gradually eroded, then cruelly and dishonestly shattered, as Hepburn's "weaknesses"—her drive, her lack of interest in creating a home and family—are belabored and blackened while Tracy's faults—his philistinism, his "old-fashioned" American values—are softened and colored as virtues by comparison. In *The Philadelphia Story*, she is attacked from all sides for her supposed coldness (for real coldness, see Grace Kelly in the fifties' musical version, *High Society*), of which there is not a shred of evidence. This is the furtive revenge of mediocrity on excellence; she is being convicted merely for being a superior creature. In *Alice Adams*, she is bitten by the most antipathetic and unattractive bug of them all, social climbing, and she manages to make it seem like the most charming of aspirations. In *Bringing Up Baby*, she is impervious to the havoc she wreaks on poor Cary Grant. But through all these films, she refuses to be humiliated or look ugly. Her combined integrity, intelligence, and proud, frank beauty rise to the surface, making us feel, with her, the difficulty and joy of being such a woman. A scene which is consummate Hepburn in its mingling of pride and vulnerability and the young, still-searching-for-herself woman, occurs during the courtship on the porch in *Alice Adams,* when she asks Fred MacMurray what his impression of her is, what he would like her to be. At this moment, as she looks into his eyes, she would willingly become what he wants, just as every girl is always shaping and reshaping her image according to her reflection in a man's eyes. Here she reveals the terrible, chameleon aspect of a woman's life, the necessity of adapting to others' needs, in constant, cosmetic metamorphosis, rather than finding and remaining true to the hard-core changeless being of the inner self. This is the trembling, smiling readiness Hepburn expresses (the terrified eagerness of a woman for psychological rape, as for her first sexual experience), and yet her entire life and persona suggest exactly the opposite and are a victory over this. She evolved, developed, played different parts, and in remaining true to her intractable self, made some enemies. And she made life difficult for those who believed that a woman could not be brilliant and beautiful, and ambitious and feminine at the same time.

Women have been caught between Scylla and Charybdis. Just as Hepburn was ridiculed in *Woman of the Year* for not paying enough attention to the home, Rosalind Russell, the heroine of *Craig's Wife,* was criticized for devoting too much attention to the home, valuing its contents more than people. In *Roughly Speaking,* the Rosalind Russell wife is more ambiguous—a demoness of energy (childbearing and otherwise) beside whom even her second husband (her first, feeling superfluous, left), an indefatigable entrepreneur, pales.

At the other end of the spouse spectrum, no less monstrous in her way, is Dorothy McGuire as *Claudia,* the helpless and adorably incompetent child-wife. Made from the successful Broadway play by Rose Franken, the film, directed by Edmund Goulding, was a hit and inspired a sequel, *Claudia and David,* also starring Dorothy McGuire and Robert Young. McGuire is the neurotic housewife whose arsenal of charms and eccentricities seems an unconscious device to postpone direct contact with her husband, and whose fixation on her mother is transferred, after the mother's death, to her own son. It is impossible to imagine the husband and wife having any real communion, verbal or sexual, "offstage," and the dynamics of both films spring from the relationship between the women: Dorothy McGuire and Ina Claire in the first, Dorothy McGuire and Mary Astor in the second. Claudia's total and loving dependence on her mother, played by Ina Claire, becomes, like child obsession for other "woman's film" heroines, the relationship which takes all the emotional energy from her marital responsibilities (both sexual and spiritual) and from her own, indefinitely postponed growing up. Dorothy McGuire is irresistible in the part. One hears, in her slightly cracked, desperately pleading voice, the admission, for so many American women, of a complete unpreparedness for married life. And, with the fear of sex that has been inculcated in her, and the pressure to be a perfectionist housekeeper, who can blame her for reverting to a state of childlike helplessness in which she will not have to perform sexually or domestically? But these subterfuges only increase her self-contempt. Seeing that she cannot even perform these trivial chores (while her husband has his interesting work and masters "important" challenges), she is quite ready to believe that he could be lured by another, more interesting woman.

With McGuire, as with so many women's film heroines, what moves—even convulses—us is not her self-pity but, on the contrary, her absolute refusal to feel sorry for herself. We supply what these heroines hold back. Who can help weeping all the tears refused by the laughing-on-the-outside bravura of Bette Davis in *Dark Victory* or Margaret Sullavan in everything; the cheerfully stoical Irene Dunne in *Love Affair* or Susan Hayward in *My Foolish Heart*.

Given the fictional necessity of woman's self-sacrifice—a premise we rightly challenge today—the heroine's attitude was often resolute and brave, an act of strength rather than helplessness. Nor did she deal in the eternal hope and the endless postponements of tragedy provided by soap opera. Rather, hers was a more exacting and fatalistic form of "escape," in which certain steps or nonsteps were decisive and irrevocable. In *When Tomorrow Comes*, Irene Dunne plays a waitress to Charles Boyer's concert pianist. For their last dinner together, wearing a dress on which she has spent six months' wages, she sits conversing cheerfully, knowing she will never see him again. In *Only Yesterday*, John Boles has an affair with Margaret Sullavan and, unbeknownst to him, gets her pregnant. He goes off to war, she brings up the child, and that is the last she hears of him . . . until one day years later, she runs into him at a New Year's Eve party and he doesn't remember her at all. The ultimate nightmare of a man's (husband's, lover's) "forgetfulness." She goes and spends the night with him without reminding him.

A similar situation occurs in *Letter from an Unknown Woman*, Max Ophuls' 1949 masterpiece, in which Joan Fontaine loses her head and heart, first as a young girl, then as an adult, over concert pianist Louis Jourdan. The film, adapted by Howard Koch from a novel by Stefan Zweig, is framed by the letter in which a dying Fontaine informs Jourdan of her love for him, and, in awakening his honor, seals his death. They had an affair—one of many for him—but were separated. She has his child and in order to provide the boy with security, makes a comfortable marriage: Jourdan meanwhile continues his life of women and dissipation. One night a long time later, she encounters him after an opera; he asks her to come to his apartment the following night, and she accepts, knowing that if she goes, she will never be able to return to her husband. She arrives at the appointed time, begins talking to him, and, waiting tremulously for the reconciliation, suddenly realizes that he doesn't recognize her, that she is just another pretty woman and he hasn't the faintest idea who she is.

The exquisite pain of this scene, of her humiliating surrender to a love that is so unreciprocated, is balanced, in Ophuls' vision and sublimely sensitive direction, by the sense of Jourdan's general depletion and decline, but mainly by the counterweight of Fontaine's obsessiveness, the stubbornness of her will to love this one man against all reason and logic, her certainty that she can "save" him; by that total defiance of social rules, she becomes not only the architect of her fate, but the precipitator of her downfall, and thus a tragic heroine. She is radical in her refusal to follow the "normal" path of a woman's destiny—to stop dreaming once she has married the proper man and settled down. Similarly the Danielle Darrieux character in Ophuls' great French film, *Madame de* (note the anonymity of the women in both titles, their exemption from names and social identities) forgoes the duties and pleasures of a normal wife, first out of vanity and lovelessness, finally out of the love for which she dies. In their abrogation of ordinary responsibilities, both women become outlaws, militarists of love, heroic and cruel. From the opening of *Madame de,* when Darrieux is examining her clothes and jewels to determine which she will pawn, to the end in which the earrings are consecrated to God and her soul symbolically redeemed, she undergoes the tortures of love and, through the consequences of her habitual frivolity, the loss of that love, finally to attain the stature of a saint, as the movie attains the stature of great art.

What Ophuls shows is that he, like the ceremonial Boyer-Darrieux marriage, like the woman's film itself, is only superficially superficial. For what greater conflict can there be within woman than that between what she conceives of as a biologically rooted duty and her spiritual wish to be free? And, like the greatest directors, Ophuls reveals this deep conflict through surfaces; through the endless movements of camera, and characters within a fixed society, he captures the inner movement of the soul in its rare, solitary passage to tragedy and grace.

The woman's film reaches its apotheosis under Ophuls and Douglas Sirk in the late forties and fifties, at a time when the genre was losing its mass audience to television soap opera. Eventually women-oriented films, like the women-oriented plays from which many of them were adapted, disappeared from the cultural scene. The derisive attitude of the eastern critical establishment won the day and drove them out of business. But at one time the "matinee audience" had considerable influence on movie production and on the popularity of certain stars. This influence has waned to the point that the only films being made for women are the afternoon soaps, and there is very little attempt to appeal to women in either regular films or nighttime television.

Where are the romantic idols who made their reputations on their appeal to women, the John Barrymores and Leslie Howards to whom women offered themselves in marriage? To Robert Redford and Paul Newman, who might conceivably be thought of as their successors, women, when they bother, send only billet-doux. But like most of their colleagues, Redford and Newman would rather be "real people" than actors, and would rather be "real actors" than romantic leads. So instead of playing opposite beautiful women in love stories of civilized narratives, they play opposite each other in *Butch Cassidy and the Sundance Kid* and romance takes on a whole new twist. They are on their way to becoming the Myrna Loy–William Powell of the seventies.

Women respond to them perhaps because they represent the wine of the old romance in a new bottle. It is the rapport between Newman and Redford in *Butch Cassidy* rather than between either one of them and Katharine Ross, that has all the staples—the love and loyalty, the yearning and spirituality, the eroticism sublimated in action and banter, the futility and fatalism, the willingness to die for someone—of women's fantasies as traditonally celebrated by the woman's film.

The woman's film, its themes appropriated by the man's film, has died out, and with it a whole area of heterosexual feeling and fantasy. For the woman's film, like other art forms, pays tribute at its best (and at its worst) to the power of the imagination, to the mind's ability to picture a perfect love triumphing over the mortal and conditional. Fontaine's and Darrieux's obsessions become leaps into immortality. The lovers in *Back Street* are finally united—in the resurrection of filmed time. In *Peter Ibbetson*, Ann Harding and Gary Cooper, separated by prison walls, live their love in their dreams and in the bowery radiance of Lee Garmes' cinematography. They are transfixed at the sublime moment of their love (denying yet improving on reality) by the power of the imagination, by the screen, and by their permanence in our memories.

1973

534

JAMES AGEE
COMEDY'S GREATEST ERA

In the language of screen comedians four of the main grades of laugh are the titter, the yowl, the belly laugh and the boffo. The titter is just a titter. The yowl is a runaway titter. Anyone who has ever had the pleasure knows all about a belly laugh. The boffo is the laugh that kills. An ideally good gag, perfectly constructed and played, would bring the victim up this ladder of laughs by cruelly controlled degrees to the top rung, and would then proceed to wobble, shake, wave and brandish the ladder until he groaned for mercy. Then, after the shortest possible time out for recuperation, he would feel the first wicked tickling of the comedian's whip once more and start up *a new ladder*.

The reader can get a fair enough idea of the current state of screen comedy by asking himself how long it has been since he has had that treatment. The best of comedies these days hand out plenty of titters and once in a while it is possible to achieve a yowl without overstraining. Even those who have never seen anything better must occasionally have the feeling, as they watch the current run or, rather, trickle of screen comedy, that they are having to make a little cause for laughter go an awfully long way. And anyone who has watched screen comedy over the past ten or fifteen years is bound to realize that it has quietly but steadily deteriorated. As for those happy atavists who remember silent comedy in its heyday and the belly laughs and boffos that went with it, they have something close to an absolute standard by which to measure the deterioration.

When a modern comedian gets hit on the head, for example, the

535

most he is apt to do is look sleepy. When a silent comedian got hit on the head he seldom let it go so flatly. He realized a broad license, and a ruthless discipline within that license. It was his business to be as funny as possible physically, without the help or hindrance of words. So he gave us a figure of speech, or rather of vision, for loss of consciousness. In other words he gave us a poem, a kind of poem, moreover, that everybody understands. The least he might do was to straighten up stiff as a plank and fall over backward with such skill that his whole length seemed to slap the floor at the same instant. Or he might make a cadenza of it—look vague, smile like an angel, roll up his eyes, lace his fingers, thrust his hands palms downward as far as they would go, hunch his shoulders, rise on tiptoe, prance ecstatically in narrowing circles until, with tallow knees, he sank down the vortex of his dizziness to the floor and there signified nirvana by kicking his heels twice, like a swimming frog.

Startled by a cop, this same comedian might grab his hatbrim with both hands and yank it down over his ears, jump high in the air, come to earth in a split violent enough to telescope his spine, spring thence into a coattail-flattening sprint and dwindle at rocket speed to the size of a gnat along the grand, forlorn perspective of some lazy back boulevard.

Those are fine clichés from the language of silent comedy in its infancy. The man who could handle them properly combined several of the more difficult accomplishments of the *acrobat*, the *dancer*, the *clown* and the *mime*. Some very gifted comedians, unforgettably Ben Turpin, had an immense vocabulary of these clichés and were in part so lovable because they were deep conservative classicists and never tried to break away from them. The still more gifted men, of course, simplified and invented, finding out new and much deeper uses for the idiom. They learned to show emotion through it, and comic psychology, more eloquently than most language has ever managed to, and they discovered beauties of comic motion which are hopelessly beyond reach of words.

It is hard to find a theater these days where a comedy is playing; in the days of the silents it was equally hard to find a theater which was not showing one. The laughs today are pitifully few, far between, shallow, quiet and short. They almost never build, as they used to, into something combining the jabbering frequency of a machine gun with the delirious momentum of a roller coaster. Saddest of all, there are few comedians now below middle age and there are none who seem to learn much from picture to picture, or to try anything new.

To put it unkindly, the only thing wrong with screen comedy today is that it takes place on a screen which talks. Because it talks, the only comedians who ever mastered the screen cannot work, for they cannot combine their comic style with talk. Because there is a screen, talking comedians are trapped into a continual exhibition of their inadequacy as screen comedians on a surface as big as the side of a barn.

At the moment, as for many years, the chances to see silent comedy are rare. There is a smattering of it on television—too often treated as something quaintly archaic, to be laughed at, not with. Some two hundred comedies—long and short—can be rented for home projection. And a lucky minority has access to the comedies in the collection of New York's Museum of Modern Art, which is still incomplete but which is probably the best in the world. In the near future, however, something of this lost art will return to regular theaters. A thick straw in the wind is the big business now being done by a series of revivals of W. C. Field's memorable movies, a kind of comedy more akin to the old silent variety than anything which is being made today. Mack Sennett now is preparing a sort of potpourri variety show called *Down Memory Lane* made up out of his old movies, featuring people like Fields and Bing Crosby when they were movie beginners, but including also interludes from silents. Harold Lloyd has re-released *Movie Crazy*, a talkie, and plans to revive four of his best silent comedies, *Grandma's Boy*, *Safety Last*, *Speedy* and *The Freshman*. Buster Keaton hopes to remake at feature length, with a minimum of dialogue, two of the funniest short comedies ever made, one about a porous homemade boat and one about a prefabricated house.

Awaiting these happy events, we will discuss here what has gone wrong with screen comedy and what, if anything, can be done about it. But mainly we will try to suggest what it was like in its glory in the years from 1912 to 1930, as practiced by the employees of Mack Sennett, the father of American screen comedy, and by the four most eminent masters: Charlie Chaplin, Harold Lloyd, the late Harry Langdon and Buster Keaton.

Mack Sennett made two kinds of comedy: parody laced with

slapstick, and plain slapstick. The parodies were the unceremonious burial of a century of hamming, including the new hamming in serious movies, and nobody who has missed Ben Turpin in *A Small Town Idol*, or kidding Erich von Stroheim in *Three Foolish Weeks* or as *The Shriek of Araby*, can imagine how rough parody can get and still remain subtle and roaringly funny. The plain slapstick, at its best, was even better: a profusion of hearty young women in disconcerting bathing suits, frisking around with a gaggle of insanely incompetent policemen and of equally certifiable male civilians sporting museum-piece mustaches. All these people zipped and caromed about the pristine world of the screen as jazzily as a convention of water bugs. Words can hardly suggest how energetically they collided and bounced apart, meeting in full gallop around the corner of a house; how hard and how often they fell on their backsides; or with what fantastically adroit clumsiness they got themselves fouled up in folding ladders, garden hoses, tethered animals and each other's headlong cross-purposes. The gestures were ferociously emphatic; not a line or motion of the body was wasted or inarticulate. The reader may remember how splendidly upright wandlike old Ben Turpin could stand for a Renunciation Scene, with his lampshade mustache twittering and his sparrowy chest stuck out and his head flung back like Paderewski assaulting a climax and the long babyish back hair trying to look lionlike, while his Adam's apple, an orange in a Christmas stocking, pumped with noble emotion. Or huge Mack Swain, who looked like a hairy mushroom, rolling his eyes in a manner patented by French romantics and gasping in some dubious ectasy. Or Louise Fazenda, the perennial farmer's daughter and the perfect low-comedy housemaid, primping her spit curl; and how her hair tightened a good-looking face into the incarnation of rampant gullibility. Or snouty James Finlayson, gleefully foreclosing a mortgage, with his look of eternally tasting a spoiled pickle. Or Chester Conklin, a myopic and inebriated little walrus stumbling around in outsize pants. Or Fatty Arbuckle, with his cold eye and his loose, serene smile, his silky manipulation of his bulk and his satanic marksmanship with pies (he was ambidextrous and could simultaneously blind two people in opposite directions).

The intimate tastes and secret hopes of these poor ineligible dunces were ruthlessly exposed whenever a hot stove, an electric fan or a bulldog took a dislike to their outer garments: agonizingly elaborate drawers, worked up on some lonely evening out of some Godforsaken lace curtain; or men's underpants with big round black spots on them. The Sennett sets—delirious wallpaper, megalomaniacally scrolled iron beds, Grand Rapids *in extremis*—outdid even the underwear. It was their business, after all, to kid the squalid braggadocio which infested the domestic interiors of the period, and that was almost beyond parody. These comedies told their stores to the unaided eye, and by every means possible they screamed to it. That is one reason for the India ink silhouettes of the cops, and for convicts and prison bars and their shadows in hard sunlight, and for bare-footed husbands, in tigerish pajamas, reacting like dervishes to stepped-on tacks.

The early silent comedians never strove for or consciously thought of anything which could be called artistic "form," but they achieved it. For Sennett's rival, Hal Roach, Leo McCarey once devoted almost the whole of a Laurel and Hardy two-reeler to pie throwing. The first pies were thrown thoughtfully, almost philosophically. Then innocent bystanders began to get caught into the vortex. At full pitch it was Armageddon. But everything was calculated so nicely that until late in the picture, when havoc took over, every pie made its special kind of point and piled on its special kind of laugh.

Sennett's comedies were just a shade faster and fizzier than life. According to legend (and according to Sennett) he discovered the tempo proper to screen comedy when a green cameraman, trying to save money, cranked too slow. Realizing the tremendous drumlike power of mere motion to exhilarate, he gave inanimate objects a mischievous life of their own, broke every law of nature the tricked camera would serve him for and made the screen dance like a witches' Sabbath. The thing one is surest of all to remember is how toward the end of nearly every Sennett comedy, a chase (usually called the "rally") built up such a majestic trajectory of pure anarchic motion that bathing girls, cops, comics, dogs, cats, babies, automobiles, locomotives, innocent bystanders, sometimes what seemed like a whole city, an entire civilization, were hauled along head over heels in the wake of that energy like dry leaves following an express train.

"Nice" people, who shunned all movies in the early days, condemned the Sennett comedies as vulgar and naive. But millions of less pretentious people loved their sincerity and sweetness, their wild-animal innocence and glorious vitality. They could not put these feelings into words, but they flocked to the silents. The reader who gets back deep enough into that world will probably even remember the theater: the barefaced honky-tonk and the waltzes by Waldteufel, slammed out on a mechanical piano; the searing redolence of peanuts and demirep perfumery, tobacco and feet and sweat; the laughter of unrespectable people having a hell of a fine time, laughter as violent and steady and deafening as standing under a waterfall.

Sennett wheedled his first financing out of a couple of ex-bookies to whom he was already in debt. He took his comics out of music halls, burlesque, vaudeville, circuses and limbo, and through them he tapped in on that great pipeline of horsing and miming which runs back unbroken through the fairs of the Middle Ages at least to ancient Greece. He added all that he himself had learned about the large and spurious gesture, the late decadence of the Grand Manner, as a stage-struck boy in East Berlin, Connecticut, and as a frustrated opera singer and actor. The only thing he claims to have invented is the pie in the face, and he insists, "Anyone who tells you he has discovered something new is a fool or a liar or both."

The silent-comedy studio was about the best training school the movies have ever known, and the Sennett studio was about as free and easy and as fecund of talent as they came. All the major comedians we will mention worked there, at least briefly. So did some of the major stars of the '20s and since—notably Gloria Swanson, Phyllis Haver, Wallace Beery, Marie Dressler and Carole Lombard. Directors Frank Capra, Leo McCarey and George Stevens also got their start in silent comedy; much that remains most flexible, spontaneous and visually alive in sound movies can be traced, through them and others, to this silent apprenticeship. Everybody did pretty much as he pleased on the Sennett lot, and everybody's ideas were welcome. Sennett posted no rules, and the only thing he strictly forbade was liquor. A Sennett story conference was a most informal affair. During the early years, at least, only the most important scenario might be jotted on the back of an envelope. Mainly Sennett's men thrashed out a few primary ideas and carried them in their heads, sure that better stuff would turn up while they were shooting, in the heat of physical action. This put quite a load on the prop man; he had to have the most improbable apparatus on hand—bombs, trick telephones, what not—to implement whatever idea might suddenly turn up. All kinds of things did—and were recklessly used. Once a low-comedy auto got out of control and killed the cameraman, but he was not visible in the shot, which was thrilling and undamaged; the audience never knew the difference.

Sennett used to hire a "wild man" to sit in on his gag conferences, whose whole job was to think up "wildies." Usually he was an all but brainless, speechless man, scarcely able to communicate his idea; but he had a totally uninhibited imagination. He might say nothing for an hour; then he'd mutter, "You take . . ." and all the relatively rational others would shut up and wait. "You take this cloud . . ." he would get out, sketching vague shapes in the air. Often he could get no further; but thanks to some kind of thought transference, saner men would take this cloud and make something of it. The wild man seems in fact to have functioned as the group's subconscious mind, the source of all creative energy. His ideas were so weird and amorphous that Sennett can no longer remember a one of them, or even how it turned out after rational processing. But a fair equivalent might be one of the best comic sequences in a Laurel and Hardy picture. It is simple enough— simple and real, in fact, as a nightmare. Laurel and Hardy are trying to move a piano across a narrow suspension bridge. The bridge is slung over a sickening chasm, between a couple of Alps. Midway they meet a gorilla.

Had he done nothing else, Sennett would be remembered for giving a start to three of the four comedians who now began to apply their sharp individual talents to this newborn language. The one whom he did not train (he was on the lot briefly but Sennett barely remembers seeing him around) wore glasses, smiled a great deal and looked like the sort of eager young man who might have quit divinity school to hustle brushes. That was Harold Lloyd. The others were grotesque and poetic in their screen characters in degrees which appear to be impossible when the magic of silence is broken. One, who never smiled, carried a face as still and sad as a daguerreotype through some of the most preposterously ingenious and visually satisfying physical comedy ever invented. That was Buster Keaton. One looked like an elderly baby and, at times, a baby dope fiend; he could do more with less than any other comedian. That was Harry Langdon. One looked like Charlie Chaplin, and he was the first man to give the silent language a soul.

When Charlie Chaplin started to work for Sennett he had chiefly to reckon with Ford Sterling, the reigning comedian. Their first picture together amounted to a duel before the assembled professionals. Sterling, by no means untalented, was a big man with a florid Teutonic style which, under this special pressure, he turned on full blast. Chaplin defeated him within a few minutes with a wink of the mustache, a hitch of the trousers, a quirk of the little finger.

With *Tillie's Punctured Romance*, in 1914, he became a major star. Soon after, he left Sennett when Sennett refused to start a landslide among the other comedians by meeting the raise Chaplin demanded. Sennett is understandably wry about it in retrospect, but he still says, "I was right at the time." Of Chaplin he says simply, "Oh well, he's just the greatest artist that ever lived." None of Chaplin's former rivals rates him much lower than that; they speak of him no more jealously than they might of God. We will try here only to suggest the essence of his supremacy. Of all comedians he worked most deeply and most shrewdly within a realization of what a human being is, and is up against. The Tramp is as centrally representative of humanity, as many-sided and as mysterious, as Hamlet, and it seems unlikely that any dancer or actor can ever have excelled him in eloquence, variety or poignancy of motion. As for pure motion, even if he had never gone on to make his magnificent feature-length comedies, Chaplin would have made his period in movies a great one singlehanded even if he had made nothing except *The Cure*, or *One A.M.* In the latter, barring one immobile taxi driver, Chaplin plays alone, as a drunk trying to get upstairs and into bed. It is a sort of inspired elaboration on a soft-shoe dance, involving an angry stuffed wildcat, small rugs on slippery floors, a Lazy Susan table, exquisite footwork on a flight of stairs, a contretemps with a huge, ferocious pendulum and the funniest and most perverse Murphy bed in movie history—

A shivering Tramp in *The Gold Rush* (1925). "Of all comedians he worked most deeply and most shrewdly within a realization of what a human being is, and is up against. . . . The finest pantomime, the deepest emotion, the richest and most poignant poetry were in Chaplin's work" (AGEE, pages 542, 544).

and, always made physically lucid, the delicately weird mental processes of a man ethereally sozzled.

Before Chaplin came to pictures people were content with a couple of gags per comedy; he got some kind of laugh every second. The minute he began to work he set standards—and continually forced them higher. Anyone who saw Chaplin eating a boiled shoe like brook trout in *The Gold Rush*, or embarrassed by a swallowed whistle in *City Lights*, has seen perfection. Most of the time, however, Chaplin got his laughter less from the gags, or from milking them in any ordinary sense, than through his genius for what may be called *inflection*—the perfect, changeful shading of his physical and emotional attitudes toward the gag. Funny as his bout with the Murphy bed is, the glances of awe, expostulation and helpless, almost whimpering desire for vengeance which he darts at this infernal machine are even better.

A painful and frequent error among tyros is breaking the comic line with a too-big laugh, then a letdown; or with a laugh which is out of key or irrelevant. The masters could ornament the main line beautifully; they never addled it. In *A Night Out* Chaplin, passed out, is hauled along the sidewalk by the scruff of his coat by staggering Ben Turpin. His toes trail; he is as supine as a sled. Turpin himself is so drunk he can hardly drag him. Chaplin comes quietly to, realizes how well he is being served by his struggling pal, and with a royally delicate gesture plucks and savors a flower.

The finest pantomime, the deepest emotion, the richest and most poignant poetry were in Chaplin's work. He could probably pantomime Bryce's *The American Commonwealth* without ever blurring a syllable and make it paralyzingly funny into the bargain. At the end of *City Lights* the blind girl who has regained her sight, thanks to the Tramp, sees him for the first time. She has imagined and anticipated him as princely, to say the least; and it has never seriously occurred to him that he is inadequate. She recognizes who he must be by his shy, confident, shining joy as he comes silently toward her. And he recognizes himself, for the first time, through the terrible changes in her face. The camera just exchanges a few quiet close-ups of the emotions which shift and intensify in each face. It is enough to shrivel the heart to see, and it is the greatest piece of acting and the highest moment in movies.

544

Harold Lloyd worked only a little while with Sennett. During most of his career he acted for another major comedy producer, Hal Roach. He tried at first to offset Chaplin's influence and establish his own individuality by playing Chaplin's exact opposite, a character named Lonesome Luke who wore clothes much too small for him and whose gestures were likewise as un-Chaplinesque as possible. But he soon realized that an opposite in itself was a kind of slavishness. He discovered his own comic identify when he saw a movie about a fighting parson: a hero who wore glasses. He began to think about those glasses day and night. He decided on horn rims because they were youthful, ultravisible on the screen and on the verge of becoming fashionable (he was to make them so). Around these large lensless horn rims he began to develop a new character, nothing grotesque or eccentric, but a fresh, believable young man who could fit into a wide variety of stories.

Lloyd depended more on story and situation than any of the other major comedians (he kept the best stable of gagmen in Hollywood, at one time hiring six); but unlike most "story" comedians he was also a very funny man from inside. He had, as he has written, "an unusually large comic vocabulary." More particularly he had an expertly expressive body and even more expressive teeth, and out of this thesaurus of smiles he could at a moment's notice blend prissiness, breeziness and asininity, and still remain tremendously likable. His movies were more extroverted and closer to ordinary life than any others of the best comedies: the vicissitudes of a New York taxi driver; the unaccepted college boy who, by desperate courage and inspired ineptitude, wins the Big Game. He was especially good at putting a very timid, spoiled or brassy young fellow through devastating embarrassments. He went through one of his most uproarious Gethsemanes as a shy country youth courting the nicest girl in town in *Grandma's Boy*. He arrived dressed "strictly up to date for the Spring of 1862," as a subtitle observed, and found that the ancient colored butler wore a similar flowered waistcoat and moldering cut-away. He got one wandering, nervous forefinger dreadfully stuck in a fancy little vase. The girl began cheerfully to try to identify that queer smell which dilated from him; Grandpa's best suit was rife with mothballs. A tenacious litter of kittens feasted off the goose grease on his home-shined shoes.

Lloyd was even better at the comedy of thrills. In *Safety Last*, as a rank amateur, he is forced to substitute for a human fly and to climb a medium-sized skyscraper. Dozens of awful things happen to him. He gets fouled up in a tennis net. Popcorn falls on him from a window above, and the local pigeons treat him like a cross between a lunch wagon and St. Francis of Assisi. A mouse runs up his britches leg, and the crowd below salutes his desperate dance on the window ledge with wild applause of the daredevil. A good deal of this full-length picture hangs thus by its eyelashes along the face of a building. Each new floor is like a new stanza in a poem; and the higher and more horrifying it gets, the funnier it gets.

In this movie Lloyd demonstrates beautifully his ability to do more than merely milk a gag, but to top it. (In an old, simple example of topping, an incredible number of tall men get, one by one, out of a small closed auto. After as many have clambered out as the joke will bear, one more steps out: a midget. That tops the gag. Then the auto collapses. That tops the topper.) In *Safety Last* Lloyd is driven out to the dirty end of a flagpole by a furious dog; the pole breaks and he falls, just managing to grab the minute hand of a huge clock. His weight promptly pulls the hand down from IX to VI. That would be more than enough for any ordinary comedian, but there is further logic in the situation. Now, hideously, the whole clockface pulls loose and slants from its trembling springs above the street. Getting out of difficulty with the clock, he makes still further use of the instrument by getting one foot caught in one of these obstinate springs.

A proper delaying of the ultrapredictable can of course be just as funny as a properly timed explosion of the unexpected. As Lloyd approaches the end of his horrible hegira up the side of the building in *Safety Last*, it becomes clear to the audience, but not to him, that if he raises his head another couple of inches he is going to get murderously conked by one of the four arms of a revolving wind gauge. He delays the evil moment almost interminably, with one distraction and another, and every delay is a suspense-tightening laugh; he also gets his foot nicely entangled in a rope, so that when he does get hit, the payoff of one gag sends him careening head downward through the abyss into another. Lloyd was outstanding even among the master craftsmen at setting up a gag clearly, culminating and getting out of it deftly, and linking it smoothly

Harold Lloyd in trouble in *Safety Last* (1923). "Lloyd was outstanding
. . . at setting up a gag clearly, culminating and getting out of it
deftly, and linking it smoothly to the next" (AGEE, pages 546–48).

to the next. Harsh experience also taught him a deep and fundamental rule: Never try to get "above" the audience.

Lloyd tried it in *The Freshman*. He was to wear an unfinished, basted-together tuxedo to a college party, which would gradually fall apart as he danced. Lloyd decided to skip the pants, a low-comedy cliché, and lose just the coat. His gag men warned him. A preview proved how right they were. Lloyd had to reshoot the whole expensive sequence, build it around defective pants and climax it with the inevitable. It was one of the funniest things he ever did.

When Lloyd was still a very young man he lost about half his right hand (and nearly lost his sight) when a comedy bomb exploded prematurely. But in spite of his artificially built-out hand he continued to do his own dirty work, like all of the best comedians. The side of the building he climbed in *Safety Last* did not overhang the street, as it appears to. But the nearest landing place was a roof three floors below him, as he approached the top, and he did everything, of course, the hard way, i.e., the comic way, keeping his bottom stuck well out, his shoulders hunched, his hands and feet skidding over perdition.

If great comedy must involve something beyond laughter, Lloyd was not a great comedian. If plain laughter is any criterion—and it is a healthy counterbalance to the other—few people have equaled him, and nobody has ever beaten him.

Chaplin and Keaton and Lloyd were all more like each other, in one important way, than Harry Langdon was like any of them. Whatever else the others might be doing, they all used more or less elaborate physical comedy; Langdon showed how little of that one might use and still be a great silent-screen comedian. In his screen character he symbolized something as deeply and centrally human, though by no means as rangily so, as the Tramp. There was, of course, an immense difference in inventiveness and range of virtuosity. It seemed as if Chaplin could do literally anything, on any instrument in the orchestra. Langdon had one queerly toned, unique little reed. But out of it he could get incredible melodies.

Like Chaplin, Langdon wore a coat which buttoned on his wishbone and swung out wide below, but the effect was very different:

A childish Harry Langdon (complete with bicycle) tips his hat to a gun moll in *Long Pants* (1927). "Langdon's magic was in his innocence . . . [he] looked like an elderly baby and, at times, a baby dope fiend . . ." (AGEE, pages 542, 551).

he seemed like an outsized baby who had begun to outgrow his clothes. The crown of his hat was rounded and the brim was turned up all around, like a little boy's hat, and he looked as if he wore diapers under his pants. His walk was that of a child which has just got sure on its feet, and his body and hands fitted that age. His face was kept pale to show off, with the simplicity of a nursery school drawing, the bright, ignorant, gentle eyes and the little twirling mouth. He had big moon cheeks, with dimples, and a Napoleonic forelock of mousy hair; the round, docile head seemed large in ratio to the cream-puff body. Twitchings of his face were signals of tiny discomforts too slowly registered by a tinier brain; quick, squirty little smiles showed his almost prehuman pleasures, his incurably premature trustfulness. He was a virtuoso of hesitations and of delicately indecisive motions, and he was particularly fine in a high wind, rounding a corner with a kind of skittering toddle, both hands nursing his hatbrim.

He was as remarkable a master as Chaplin of subtle emotional and mental process and operated much more at leisure. He once got a good three hundred feet of continuously bigger laughs out of rubbing his chest, in a crowded vehicle, with Limburger cheese, under the misapprehension that it was a cold salve. In another long scene, watching a brazen show girl change her clothes, he sat motionless, back to the camera, and registered the whole lexicon of lost innocence, shock, disapproval and disgust, with the back of his neck. His scenes with women were nearly always something special. Once a lady spy did everything in her power (under the Hays Office) to seduce him. Harry was polite, willing, even flirtatious in his little way. The only trouble was that he couldn't imagine what in the world she was leering and pawing at him for, and that he was terribly ticklish. The Mata Hari wound up foaming at the mouth.

There was also a sinister flicker of depravity about the Langdon character, all the more disturbing because babies are premoral. He had an instinct for bringing his actual adulthood and figurative babyishness into frictions as crawly as a fingernail on a slate blackboard, and he wandered into areas of strangeness which were beyond the other comedians. In a nightmare in one movie he was forced to fight a large, muscular young man; the girl Harry loved was the prize. The young man was a good boxer; Harry could scarcely lift his gloves. The contest took place in a fiercely lighted

550

prize ring, in a prodigious pitch-dark arena. The only spectator was the girl, and she was rooting against Harry. As the fight went on, her eyes glittered ever more brightly with blood lust and, with glittering teeth, she tore her big straw hat to shreds.

Langdon came to Sennett from a vaudeville act in which he had fought a losing battle with a recalcitrant automobile. The minute Frank Capra saw him he begged Sennett to let him work with him. Langdon was almost as childlike as the character he played. He had only a vague idea of his story or even of each scene as he played it; each time he went before the camera Capra would brief him on the general situation and then, as this finest of intuitive improvisers once tried to explain his work, "I'd go into my routine." The whole tragedy of the coming of dialogue as far as these comedians were concerned—and one reason for the increasing rigidity of comedy ever since—can be epitomized in the mere thought of Harry Langdon confronted with a script.

Langdon's magic was in his innocence, and Capra took beautiful care not to meddle with it. The key to the proper use of Langdon, Capra always knew, was "the principle of the brick." "If there was a rule for writing Langdon material," he explains, "it was this: His only ally was God. Langdon might be saved by the brick falling on the cop, but it was *verboten* that he in any way motivate the brick's fall." Langdon became quickly and fantastically popular with three pictures, *Tramp, Tramp, Tramp, The Strong Man* and *Long Pants;* from then on he went downhill even faster. "The trouble was," Capra says, "that high-brow critics came around to explain his art to him. Also he developed an interest in dames. It was a pretty high life for such a little fellow." Langdon made two more pictures with highbrow writers, one of which *(Three's a Crowd)* had some wonderful passages in it, including the prizering nightmare; then First National canceled his contract. He was reduced to mediocre roles and two-reelers which were more rehashes of his old gags; this time around they no longer seemed funny. "He never did really understand what hit him," says Capra. "He died broke [in 1944]. And he died of a broken heart. He was the most tragic figure I ever came across in show business."

Buster Keaton started work at the age of three and a half with his parents in one of the roughest acts in vaudeville ("The Three Keatons"); Harry Houdini gave the child the name Buster in admiration for a fall he took down a flight of stairs. In his first movies Keaton teamed with Fatty Arbuckle under Sennett. He went on to become one of Metro's biggest stars and earners; a Keaton feature cost about $200,000 to make and reliably grossed $2 million. Very early in his movie career friends asked him why he never smiled on the screen. He didn't realize he didn't. He had got the deadpan habit in variety; on the screen he had merely been so hard at work it had never occurred to him there was anything to smile about. Now he tried it just once and never again. He was by his whole style and nature so much the most deeply "silent" of the silent comedians that even a smile was as deafeningly out of key as a yell. In a way his pictures are like a transcendent juggling act in which it seems that the whole universe is in exquisite flying motion and the one point of repose is the juggler's effortless, uninterested face.

Keaton's face ranked almost with Lincoln's as an early American archetype; it was haunting, handsome, almost beautiful, yet it was irreducibly funny; he improved matters by topping it off with a deadly horizontal hat, as flat and thin as a phonograph record. One can never forget Keaton wearing it, standing erect at the prow as his little boat is being launched. The boat goes grandly down the skids and, just as grandly, straight on to the bottom. Keaton never budges. The last you see of him, the water lifts the hat off the stoic head and it floats away.

No other comedian could do as much with the deadpan. He used this great, sad, motionless face to suggest various related things: a one-track mind near the track's end of pure insanity; mulish imperturbability under the wildest of circumstances; how dead a human being can get and still be alive; an awe-inspiring sort of patience and power to endure, proper to granite but uncanny in flesh and blood. Everything that he was and did bore out this rigid face and played laughs against it. When he moved his eyes, it was like seeing them move in a statue. His short-legged body was all sudden, machinelike angles, governed by a daft aplomb. When he swept a semaphorelike arm to point, you could almost hear the electrical impulse in the signal block. When he ran from a cop his transitions from accelerating walk to easy jog trot to brisk canter to headlong gallop to flogged-piston sprint— always floating, above this frenzy, the untroubled, untouchable

552

Buster Keaton surveying the situation in *The General* (1926). "He was by his whole style and nature so much the most deeply 'silent' of the silent comedians that even a smile was as deafeningly out of key as a yell" (AGEE, page 552).

face—were as distinct and as soberly in order as an automatic gearshift.

Keaton was a wonderfully resourceful inventor of mechanistic gags (he still spends much of his time fooling with Erector sets); as he ran afoul of locomotives, steamships, prefabricated and over-electrified houses, he put himself through some of the hardest and cleverest punishment ever designed for laughs. In *Sherlock Jr.*, boiling along on the handlebars of a motorcycle quite unaware that he has lost his driver, Keaton whips through city traffic, breaks up a tug-of-war, gets a shovelful of dirt in the face from each of a long line of Rockette-timed ditchdiggers, approaches at high speed a log which is hinged open by dynamite precisely soon enough to let him through and, hitting an obstruction, leaves the handlebars like an arrow leaving a bow, whams through the window of a shack in which the heroine is about to be violated, and hits the heavy feet first, knocking him through the opposite wall. The whole sequence is as clean in motion as the trajectory of a bullet.

Much of the charm and edge of Keaton's comedy, however, lay in the subtle leverages of expression he could work against his nominal deadpan. Trapped in the side wheel of a ferryboat, saving himself from drowning only by walking, then desperately running, inside the accelerating wheel like a squirrel in a cage, his only real concern was, obviously, to keep his hat on. Confronted by Love, he was not as deadpan as he was cracked up to be, either; there was an odd, abrupt motion of his head which suggested a horse nipping after a sugar lump.

Keaton worked strictly for laughs, but his work came from so far inside a curious and original spirit that he achieved a great deal besides, especially in his feature-length comedies. (For plain hard laughter his nineteen short comedies—the negatives of which have been lost—were even better.) He was the only major comedian who kept sentiment almost entirely out of his work, and he brought pure physical comedy to its greatest heights. Beneath his lack of emotion he was also uninsistently sardonic; deep below that, giving a disturbing tension and grandeur to the foolishness, for those who sensed it, there was in his comedy a freezing whisper not of pathos but of melancholia. With the humor, the craftsmanship and the action there was often, besides, a fine, still and sometimes dreamlike beauty. Much of his Civil War picture *The General* is within hailing distance of Mathew Brady. And there is a ghostly, unforgettable moment in *The Navigator* when, on a deserted, softly, rolling ship, all the pale doors along a deck swing open as one behind Keaton and, as one, slam shut, in a hair-raising illusion of noise.

Perhaps because "dry" comedy is so much more rare and odd than "dry" wit, there are people who never much cared for Keaton. Those who do cannot care mildly.

As soon as the screen began to talk, silent comedy was pretty well finished. The hardy and prolific Mack Sennett made the transfer; he was the first man to put Bing Crosby and W. C. Fields on the screen. But he was essentially a silent-picture man, and by the time the Academy awarded him a special Oscar for his "lasting contribution to the comedy technique of the screen" (in 1938), he was no longer active. As for the comedians we have spoken of in particular, they were as badly off as fine dancers suddenly required to appear in plays.

Harold Lloyd, whose work was most nearly realistic, naturally coped least unhappily with the added realism of speech; he made several talking comedies. But good as the best were, they were not so good as his silent work, and by the late '30s he quit acting. A few years ago he returned to play the lead (and play it beautifully) in Preston Sturges' *The Sin of Harold Diddlebock*, but this exceptional picture—which opened, brilliantly, with the closing reel of Lloyd's *The Freshman*—has not yet been generally released.

Like Chaplin, Lloyd was careful of his money; he is still rich and active. Last June, in the presence of President Truman, he became Imperial Potentate of the A.A.O.N.M.S. (Shriners). Harry Langdon, as we have said, was a broken man when sound came in.

Up to the middle '30s Buster Keaton made several feature-length pictures (with such players as Jimmy Durante, Wallace Beery and Robert Montgomery); he also made a couple of dozen talking shorts. Now and again he managed to get loose into motion, without having to talk, and for a moment or so the screen would start singing again. But his dark, dead voice, though it was in keeping with the visual character, tore his intensely silent style to bits and destroyed the illusion within which he worked. He gallantly and correctly refuses to regard himself as "retired." Besides occasional bits, spots and minor roles in Hollywood pictures, he has worked on summer stages, made talking comedies in France and Mexico and clowned in a French circus. This summer he has played the straw hats in *Three Men on a Horse*. He is planning a television program. He also has a working agreement with Metro. One of his jobs there is to construct comedy sequences for Red Skelton.

The only man who really survived the flood was Chaplin, the only one who was rich, proud and popular enough to afford to stay silent. He brought out two of his greatest nontalking comedies, *City Lights* and *Modern Times*, in the middle of an avalanche of talk, spoke gibberish and, in the closing moments, plain English in *The Great Dictator*, and at last made an all-talking picture, *Monsieur Verdoux*, creating for that purpose an entirely new character who might properly talk a blue streak. *Verdoux* is the greatest of talking comedies though so cold and savage that it had to find its public in grimly experienced Europe.

Good comedy, and some that was better than good, outlived silence, but there has been less and less of it. The talkies brought one great comedian, the late, majestically lethargic W. C. Fields, who could not possibly have worked as well in silence; he was the toughest and the most warmly human of all screen comedians, and *It's a Gift* and *The Bank Dick*, fiendishly funny and incisive white-collar comedies, rank high among the best comedies (and best movies) ever made. Laurel and Hardy, the only comedians who managed to preserve much of the large, low style of silence and who began to explore the comedy of sound, have made nothing since 1945. Walt Disney, at his best an inspired comic inventor and teller of fairy stories, lost his stride during the war and has since regained it only at moments. Preston Sturges has made brilliant, satirical comedies, but his pictures are smart, nervous comedy-dramas merely italicized with slapstick. The Marx Brothers were sidesplitters but they made their best comedies years ago. Jimmy Durante is mainly a night-club genius; Abbott and Costello are semiskilled laborers, at best; Bob Hope is a good radio comedian with a pleasing presence, but not much more, on the screen.

There is no hope that screen comedy will get much better than it is without new, gifted young comedians who really belong in movies, and without freedom for their experiments. For everyone who may appear we have one last, invidious comparison to offer as a guidepost.

One of the most popular recent comedies is Bob Hope's *The Paleface*. We take no pleasure in blackening *The Paleface*; we single it out, rather, because it is as good as we've got. Anything that is said of it here could be said, with interest, of other comedies of our time. Most of the laughs in *The Paleface* are verbal. Bob Hope is very adroit with his lines and now and then, when the words don't get in the way, he makes a good beginning as a visual comedian. But only the beginning, never the middle or the end. He is funny, for instance, reacting to a shot of violent whisky. But he does not know how to get still funnier (i.e., how to build and milk) or how to be funniest last (i.e., how to top or cap his gag). The camera has to fade out on the same old face he started with.

One sequence is promisingly set up for visual comedy. In it, Hope and a lethal local boy stalk each other all over a cow town through streets which have been emptied in fear of their duel. The gag here is that through accident and stupidity they keep just failing to find each other. Some of it is quite funny. But the fun slackens between laughs like a weak clothesline, and by all the logic of humor (which is ruthlessly logical) the biggest laugh should come at the moment, and through the way, they finally spot each other. The sequence is so weakly thought out that at that crucial moment the camera can't afford to watch them; it switches to Jane Russell.

Now we turn to a masterpiece. In *The Navigator* Buster Keaton works with practically the same gag as Hope's duel. Adrift on a ship which he believes is otherwise empty, he drops a lighted cigarette. A girl finds it. She calls out and he hears her; each then tries to find the other. First each walks purposefully down the long, vacant starboard deck, the girl, then Keaton, turning the corner just in time not to see each other. Next time around each of them is trotting briskly, very much in earnest; going at the same pace, they miss each other just the same. Next time around each of them is going like a bat out of hell. Again they miss. Then the camera withdraws to a point of vantage at the stern, leans its chin in its hand and just watches the whole intricate superstructure of the ship as the protagonists stroll, steal and scuttle from level

557

to level, up, down and sidewise, always managing to miss each other by hairbreadths, in an enchantingly neat and elaborate piece of timing. There are no subsidiary gags to get laughs in this sequence and there is little loud laughter; merely a quiet and steadily increasing kind of delight. When Keaton has got all he can out of this fine modification of the movie chase he invents a fine device to bring the two together: the girl, thoroughly winded, sits down for a breather, indoors, on a plank which workmen have left across sawhorses. Keaton pauses on an upper deck, equally winded and puzzled. What follows happens in a couple of seconds at most: Air suction whips his silk topper backward down a ventilator; grabbing frantically for it, he backs against the lip of the ventilator, jackknifes and falls in backward. Instantly the camera cuts back to the girl. A topper falls through the ceiling and lands tidily, right side up, on the plank beside her. Before she can look more than startled, its owner follows, head between his knees, crushes the topper, breaks the plank with the point of his spine and proceeds to the floor. The breaking of the plank smacks Boy and Girl together.

It is only fair to remember that the silent comedians would have as hard a time playing a talking scene as Hope has playing his visual ones, and that writing and directing are as accountable for the failure as Hope himself. But not even the humblest journeyman of the silent years would have let themselves off so easily. Like the masters, they knew, and sweated to obey, the laws of their craft.

1949

JOHN G. CAWELTI

CHINATOWN AND GENERIC TRANSFORMATION IN RECENT AMERICAN FILMS

One of the fascinating things about Roman Polanski's *Chinatown* is that it invokes in so many ways the American popular genre of the hard-boiled detective story. Most of us, I suppose, associate this tradition particularly with two films, both of which starred Humphrey Bogart: John Huston's *The Maltese Falcon* (1941) and Howard Hawks' *The Big Sleep* (1946). But these are only the two most-remembered and perhaps the most memorable versions of a narrative formula which has been replicated in hundreds of novels, films, and television programs. Next to the western, the hard-boiled detective story is America's most distinctive contribution to the world's stock of action-adventure stories, our contemporaneous embodiment of the drama of heroic quest which has appeared in so many different cultures in so many different guises. Unlike the western—heroic quest on the frontier—which can perhaps be traced back as far as the Indian captivity narratives of the late seventeenth century, and certainly to Cooper's Leatherstocking saga of the early nineteenth century, the hard-boiled detective story is of quite recent origin. It developed in the twenties through the medium of short action stories in pulp magazines like the famous *Black Mask*. By 1929, Dashiell Hammett had produced in *Red Harvest*, the first hard-boiled detective novel. Before retiring into literary silence in the mid-thirties, Hammett had created a basic core of hard-boiled adventure in his Continental Op stories and his novels—*The*

Maltese Falcon (1930), *The Dain Curse* (1929), *The Glass Key* (1931) and *The Thin Man* (1934). In very short order, the hard-boiled detective made the transition from novel to film. *The Maltese Falcon* appeared in two film versions in the early 30s, before John Huston made the definitive version in 1941. *The Glass Key* was produced in the early 30s and in the 40s; *The Thin Man* became one of the great movie successes of the later 30s, so popular that it led to a number of invented sequels. And while the hard-boiled detective flourished in film, Hammett's example was followed in novels by writers whose literary approach ranged from the subtlety and depth of Raymond Chandler and Ross Macdonald to the sensational—and best-selling—crudity of Mickey Spillane. Radio and television, too, made many series based on the figure of the hard-boiled detective and his quest for justice through the ambiguous landscape of the modern American city. If a myth can be defined as a pattern of narrative known throughout the culture and presented in many different versions by many different tellers, then the hard-boiled detective story is in that sense an important American myth.

Chinatown invokes this myth in many different ways. Its setting in Los Angeles in the 1930s is very much the archetypal "hard-boiled" setting, the place and time of Hammett's and Chandler's novels. While it is true that many hard-boiled novels and films are set in different places and times—Mickey Spillane's Mike Hammer stories in New York City, John D. Macdonald's Travis McGee saga in Florida—the California city setting of Hammett and Chandler and the approximate time of their stories, memorialized in the period furnishings, visual icons, and style of the great hard-boiled films of the 1940s, have become for us the look and the temporal-spacial aura of the hard-boiled myth. It is this aura which Polanski generates, though there is something not quite right, something disturbingly off about it. In this case, it is the color. The world of the hard-boiled myth is preeminently a world of black and white. Its ambience is that compound of angular light and shadow enmeshed in webs of fog which grew out of the visual legacy of German expressionism in drama and film, transformed into what is now usually called *film noir* by its adjustment to Amer-

560

ican locales and stories. Polanski carefully controls his spectrum of hue and tone in order to give it the feel of *film noir*, but it is nonetheless color with occasional moments of rich golden light—as in the scene in the dry riverbed. These moments of warm color often relate to scenes that are outside the usual setting or thematic content—for example, scenes in the natural landscape outside the city—which are themselves generally outside the world of the hard-boiled detective story. The invocation of many other traditional elements of the hard-boiled myth, the *film noir* tone and the 1930s setting cue us to expect the traditional mythical world of the private eye hero. But the presence of color, along with increasing deviations from established patterns of plot, motive and character give us an eerie feeling of one myth colliding with and beginning to give way to others.

Let us begin by examining *Chinatown*'s relation to the traditional myth of the hard-boiled detective. The established narrative formula of the hard-boiled story has as its protaganist a private investigator who occupies a marginal position with respect to the official social institutions of criminal justice. The private eye is licensed by the state, but though he may be a former member of a police force or district attorney's staff, he is not now connected with such an organization. In the course of the story, he is very likely to come into conflict with representatives of the official machinery, though he may also have friends who are police officers. His position on the edge of the law is very important, because one of the central themes of the hard-boiled myth is the ambiguity between institutionalized law enforcement and true justice. The story shows us that the police and the courts are incapable of effectively protecting the innocent and bringing the guilty to appropriate justice. Only the individual of integrity who exists on the margins of society, can solve the crime and bring about a true justice.

The marginal character of the private eye hero is thus crucial to his role in the myth. It is also central to his characterization. We see him not only as a figure outside the institutionalized process of law enforcement, but as the paradoxical combination of a man of character who is also a failure. The private eye is a relatively poor man who operates out of a seedy office and never seems to make very much money by his exploits; he is the most marginal sort of lower-middle class quasi-professional. Yet unlike the usual stereotype of this social class, he is a man of honor and integrity who cannot be made to give up his quest for true justice. He is a compelling American hero type, clearly related to the traditional western hero who manifests many of the same characteristics and conditions of marginality.

The story begins when the hard-boiled hero is given a mission by a client. It is typical that this initial mission is a deceptive one. Either the client is lying, as Brigid O'Shaughnessy lies to Sam Spade in *The Maltese Falcon,* or the client has himself been deceived and does not understand what is really at stake when he gives the detective his case, as with General Sternwood in *The Big Sleep*. Often the detective is being used as a pawn in some larger plot of the client's. Whatever his initial impetus to action, the detective soon finds himself enmeshed in a very complex conspiracy involving a number of people from different spheres of society. The ratiocinative English detective in authors like Dorothy Sayers, Agatha Christie, or Ngaio Marsh, investigates crimes by examining clues, questionning witnesses and then using his intellectual powers of insight and deduction to arrive at the solution. The hardboiled detective investigates through movement and encounter; he collides with the web of conspiracy until he has exposed its outlines. The crime solved by the ratiocinative detective is usually that of a single individual. With this individual's means and motives for the criminal act rationally established he can be turned over to the law for prosecution. But the hard-boiled detective encounters a linked series of criminal acts and responsibilities; he discovers not a single guilty individual, but a corrupt society in which wealthy and respectable people are linked with gangsters and crooked politicians. Because it is society and not just a single individual which is corrupt, the official machinery of law enforcement is unable to bring the guilty to justice. The hard-boiled detective must decide for himself what kind of justice can be accomplished in the ambiguous urban world of modern America, and he must, in many instances, undertake to see

562

this justice through, himself. There have always been two different tendencies within the hard-boiled myth. Some writers, like Mickey Spillane and his many current followers, place their emphasis on the hero as private vigilante avenger. Their stories climax with the hero playing the role of executioner as well as detective and judge. More complex and artistic writers, like Hammett, Chandler and Ross Macdonald, develop instead the theme of the hero's own relationship to the mythical role of lawman- outside-the-law. Their versions of the story rarely end with the detective's execution of the criminal; they prefer instead either to arrange for the criminal's self-destruction as in Chandler's *Farewell, My Lovely*, or simply to bring about the criminal's exposure and confession, as in *The Maltese Falcon*. But this latter trend, though it has produced greater literature, is perhaps best understood as a humane avoidance of the true thrust of the myth which is, I think, essentially toward the marginal hero becoming righteous judge and executioner, culture-hero for a society which has profoundly ambiguous conflicts in choosing between its commitment to legality and its belief that only individual actions are ultimately moral and just.

One further element of the hard-boiled myth needs to be particularly noted: the role of the feminine antagonist. In almost every case, the hard-boiled hero encounters a beautiful and dangerous woman in the course of his investigations and he finds himself very much drawn toward her, even to the point of falling in love. Sometimes the woman is his client, sometimes a figure in the conspiracy. In a surprising number of cases (*The Maltese Falcon, The Big Sleep, Farewell, My Lovely, I, The Jury*, and many others) the woman turns out to be the murderess, and, in Spillane at least, is killed by her detective-lover. This murky treatment of the "romance" between detective and dangerous female is occasionally resolved happily as in the Bogart-Bacall relationship at the end of the film version of *The Big Sleep* (in the novel this romantic culmination does not take place). However, such an outcome is rare. Even if the beautiful woman does not turn out to be a murderess, the detective usually separates from her at the end to return to his marginal situation, basically unchanged by what has happened to him and ready to perform more acts of justice when the occasion arises.

We can see from this brief resumé of the hard-boiled formula how close a resemblance *Chinatown* bears to it. But the film deviates increasingly from the myth until, by the end of the story, the film arrives at an ending almost contrary to that of the myth. Instead of bringing justice to a corrupt society, the detective's actions leave the basic source of corruption untouched. Instead of protecting the innocent, his investigation leads to the death of one victim and the deeper moral destruction of another. Instead of surmounting the web of conspiracy with honor and integrity intact, the detective is overwhelmed by what has happened to him.

True, the action of *Chinatown* increasingly departs from the traditional hard-boiled formula as the story progresses; however, there are, from the very beginning, a number of significant departures from the standard pattern. The choice of Jack Nicholson and Faye Dunaway as leading actors is a good instance of this. Nicholson and Dunaway have certain physical and stylistic resemblances to Bogart and Bacall and these are obviously played up through costume, makeup and gesture. Indeed, there is one early scene in a restaurant between them which is almost eerily reminiscent of the famous horse-racing interchange between Bogart and Bacall in *The Big Sleep*. But much as they echo the archetypal hard-boiled duo in a superficial way, Nicholson and Dunaway play characters which are very different. Dunaway has a neurotic fragility, an underlying quality of desperation which becomes even more apparent as her true situation is revealed. She never generates the sense of independence and courage that Bacall brought to her hard-boiled roles; her qualities of wit and sophistication—those characteristics which made Bacall such an appropriate romantic partner for the hard-boiled detective—are quickly seen to be a veneer covering depths of anguish and ambiguity. Nicholson also portrays, at least early on, a character who is not quite what he seems. His attempt to be the tough, cynical, and humorous private eye is undercut on all sides; he is terribly inept as a wit, as his attempt to tell his assistants the Chinese joke makes clear. Nor is he the tough, marginal man of profes-

564

sional honor he pretends to be at the beginning; actually, he is a successful small businessman who has made a good thing out of exploiting the more sordid needs of his fellowmen. One of the most deeply symbolic clichés of the traditional hard-boiled formula is the hero's refusal to do divorce business, in fact one of the primary functions of the private detective. By this choice the traditional private-eye of the myth established both his personal sense of honor and his transcendent vocation, distinguishing himself from the typical private investigator. However, from the beginning of *Chinatown*, it is clear that the accumulation of evidence of marital infidelity is Jake Gittes' primary business. He is, indeed, drawn into the affairs of Noah Cross, his daughter, and her husband by a commission to document a supposedly clandestine affair between the latter and a much younger woman. The name, J. J. Gittes, which Polanski and Robert Towne, the screenwriter, chose for their protagonist is a good indication of this aspect of his character. Think of the names of the traditional hard-boiled detectives: Sam Spade, with its implication of hardness and digging beneath the surface; Philip Marlowe with its aura of knightliness and chivalry; Lew Archer with its mythical overtones. Gittes, or "Gits" as Noah Cross ironically keeps pronouncing it, connotes selfishness and grasping and has, in addition, a kind of ethnic echo very different from the pure Anglo of Spade, Marlowe and Archer.

Yet, qualified and even "anti-heroic" as he is, Gittes is swept up into the traditional hard-boiled action. His initial and deceptive charge involves him in the investigation of a murder, which in turn leads him to evidence of a large-scale conspiracy involving big business, politics, crime and the whole underlying social and environmental structure of Los Angeles. Like the traditional hard-boiled detective, Gittes begins as a marginal individual, but gradually finds himself becoming a moral agent with a mission. At the same time he becomes romantically involved with a character deeply implicated in the web of conspiracy, the mysterious widow of the man who has been murdered. By the middle of the film Gittes is determined to expose the political conspiracy which he senses beneath the surface, and also to resolve the question of the guilt or innocence of the woman to whom he has been so strongly attracted. Thus far, the situation closely resembles that of *The Maltese Falcon and The Big Sleep*. It is at this point, however, that the action again takes a vast departure from that of the traditional hard-boiled story. Instead of demonstrating his ability to expose and punish the guilty, Gittes steadily finds himself confronting a depth of evil and chaos so great that he is unable to control it. In relation to the social and personal depravity represented by Noah Cross and the world in which he can so successfully operate, the toughness, moral concern, and professional skill of Gittes not only seem ineffectual, but lead to ends that are the very opposite of those intended. At the end of the film, Noah Cross is free to continue his rapacious depredations on the land, the city and the body of his own daughter-granddaughter; and the one person who might have effectively brought Cross to some form of justice—his daughter-mistress—has been destroyed. Gittes' confrontation with a depth of depravity beyond the capacity of the hard-boiled ethos of individualistic justice is, I think, the essential significance of the Chinatown motif in the film. Chinatown becomes a symbol of life's deeper moral enigmas, those unintended consequences of action that are past understanding and control. Gittes has been there before. In another case his attempts at individual moral action had led to the death of a woman he cared for. It is apparently this tragedy that motivated him to leave the police force and set up as a private investigator. Now he has been drawn back into moral action, and it is again, in Chinatown, that his attempt to live out the myth of individualistic justice collides with the power of evil and chance in the world. The result is not heroic confrontation and the triumph of justice, but tragic catastrophe and the destruction of the innocent.

Chinatown places the hard-boiled detective story within a view of the world that is deeper and more catastrophic, more enigmatic in its evil, more sudden and inexplicable in its outbreaks of violent chance. In the end, the image of heroic, moral action embedded in the traditional private-eye myth turns out to be totally inadequate to overcome the destructive realities revealed in the course of this story. This revelation of depths beneath depths is made increasingly evident in the film's relentless movement toward Chinatown, the symbolic locus of darkness, strangeness and catastrophe; but it also appears in the film's manipulation of action and image. The themes of water and drought, which weave through the action, not only reveal the scope of Noah Cross's conspiracy to dominate a city by manipulating its water supply, but create a texture of allusion which resonates with the mythical meanings traditionally associated with water and drought. Polanski's version of Los Angeles in the 1930s reveals the transcendent mythical world of the sterile kingdom, the dying king and the drowned man beneath it—the world, for example, of Eliot's *Wasteland* and before that of the cylical myths of traditional cultures. Another of the film's motifs, its revelation of the rape-incest by which Noah Cross has fathered a daughter on his own daughter and is apparently intending to continue this method of establishing a progeny through the agency of his daughter-granddaughter, is another of the ways in which the hard-boiled myth is thrust into depths beyond itself. Though traditionally an erotically potent figure, the private eye's sexuality seems gentility itself when confronted with the potent perversity embodied in the figure of Noah Cross. Cross is reminiscent of the primal father imagined by Freud in *Totem and Taboo*, but against his overpowering sexual, political and economic power, our hero-Oedipus in the form of J. J. Gittes proves to be tragically impotent, an impotence symbolized earlier in the film by the slashing of his nose and the large comic bandage he wears throughout much of the action.

In its manipulation of a traditional American popular myth and the revelation of the tragic inadequacy of this myth when it collides with a universe that is deeper and more enigmatic in its evil and destructive force, *Chinatown* is one of the richest and most artistically powerful instances of a type of film of which we have seen many striking instances in the last decade. It is difficult to know just what to call this type of film. On one level, it relates to the traditional literary mode of burlesque or parody in which a well-established set of conventions or a style is subjected to some form of ironic or humorous exploitation. Indeed, many of the most striking and successful

567

films of the period have been out and out burlesques of traditional popular genres such as Mel Brooks' *Blazing Saddles* (westerns), *Young Frankenstein* (the Frankenstein horror cycle), and *High Anxiety* (Hitchcock's psychological suspense films). However, burlesque and parody embody a basically humorous thrust, and many of the most powerful generic variations of the last decade or so—films like *Bonnie and Clyde*, *The Wild Bunch*, *The Godfather* and *Nashville*—tend more toward tragedy than comedy in their overall structures. It seems odd to speak of a tragic parody or a doomed burlesque. Therefore, one is at first tempted to conclude that the connection between *Blazing Saddles* and *The Wild Bunch*, or *The Black Bird* and *The Long Goodbye* is only superficial. Yet it is clear that in many of these films the line between comedy and tragedy is not so simply drawn. What, for example, of the extraordinary combination of Keystone Cops chase scenes and tragic carnage in *Bonnie and Clyde*, or the interweaving of sophomoric high jinks and terrible violence in Altman's *MASH?* This puzzling combination of humorous burlesque and high seriousness seems to be a mode of expression characteristic of our period, not only in film, but in other literary forms. It is at the root of much that is commonly described as the literature of the absurd, or of so-called "Black humor," and is, as well, characteristic of the style of major contemporary novelists like Thomas Pynchon. By adopting this mode, American movies have, in a sense, become a more integral part of the mainstream of postmodernist literature, just as, through their frequent allusion to the narrative conventions of American film, contemporary novelists and dramatists have created a new kind of relationship between themselves and the traditions of popular culture.

The linkage between these many different kinds of contemporary literary, dramatic and cinematic expression is their use of the conventions of traditional popular genres. Basically, they do in different ways what Polanski does in *Chinatown*: set the elements of a conventional popular genre in an altered context, thereby making us perceive these traditional forms and images in a new way. It appears to me that we can classify

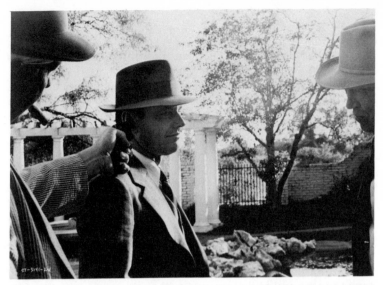

Roy Jenson and John Huston threaten Jack Nicholson in a scene from *Chinatown* (1974) that is "outside the usual setting or thematic content— for example, scenes in the natural landscape outside the city— which are themselves outside the world of the hardboiled detective story." (CAWELTI, page 561). The Black Sheriff (Cleavon Little) encounters the Count Basie band on the prairie in *Blazing Saddles* (1972). "Many of the most striking and successful films of the period have been out and out burlesques of traditional popular genres such as Mel Brooks' *Blazing Saddles* . . ." (CAWELTI, pages 567–68).

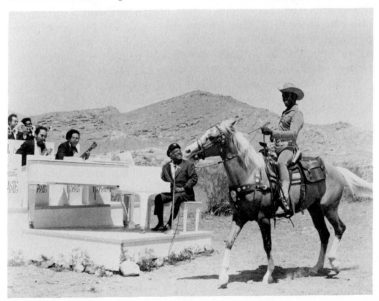

the various relationships between traditional generic elements and altered contexts into four major modes.

First, there is the burlesque proper. In this mode, elements of a conventional formula or style are situated in contexts so incongruous or exaggerated that the result is laughter. There are many different ways in which this can be done. The formulaic elements can be acted out in so extreme a fashion that they come into conflict with our sense of reality forcing us to see these aspects of plot and character as fantastic contrivances. A good example of this is the burlesque image of the gunfighter in *Cat Ballou*. In this film we are shown how, by putting on his gunfighter costume, a process that involves strapping himself into a corset within which he can barely move, an old drunk can become the terror of the bad guys. Or, in a closely related type of altered context, a situation that we are ordinarily accustomed to seeing in rather romanticized terms can be suddenly invested with a sense of reality. This is how the famous campfire scene in *Blazing Saddles* operates. The cowboys sit around a blazing campfire at night, a scene in which we are accustomed to hearing mournful and lyrical cowboy ballads performed by such groups as the Sons of the Pioneers. Instead we are treated to an escalating barrage of flatulence. Anyone who knows the usual effect of canned wilderness fare is likely to be delighted at this sudden exposure of the sham involved in the traditional western campfire scene. Sam Peckinpah's *Ride the High Country* offers another instance of the humorous effect of a sudden penetration of reality into a fantasy when one of his aging heroes attempts to spring gracefully into the saddle and is suddenly halted by a twinge of rheumatism.

In addition to these sudden confrontations with "reality" conventional patterns can be turned into laughter by inverting them. A good example of this is the device of turning a character who shows all the marks of a hero into a coward, or vice versa. A favorite manifestation of this in recent films and novels is what might be called the hard-boiled schlemiehl, the private detective who turns out to be totally unable to solve a crime or resist villains except by accident. This type of burlesque is even more effective when the inverted presentation actually seems to bring out some latent meanings which were lurking all the time in the original convention. Mel Brooks is a particular master of this kind of burlesque. In his *Young Frankenstein*, the monster attacks Frankenstein's fiancee Elizabeth—a moment of tragic violence in the original novel—and the result is complete sexual satisfaction on both sides, something most of us had suspected all along.

These two primary techniques of burlesque, the breaking of convention by the intrusion of reality and the inversion of expected implications, have frequently appeared in the history of literature as a response to highly conventionalized genres. Just as the Greek tragedies gave rise to their burlesque counterparts in the plays of Aristophanes, the western, one of our most formally distinctive genres, has been the inspiration of parody and burlesque throughout its history from Twain and Harte's assaults on James Fenimore Cooper to Brooks' send-up of *Shane* and *High Noon*. Thus, there is nothing particularly new in the penchant toward humorous burlesque so evident in recent films. What is more striking in the films of the last decade is their use of these techniques of generic parody for ultimately serious purposes.

The second major mode of generic transformation is the cultivation of nostalgia. In this mode, traditional generic features of plot, character, setting and style are deployed to recreate the aura of a past time. The power of nostalgia lies especially in its capacity to evoke a sense of warm reassurance by bringing before our mind's eye images from a time when things seemed more secure and full of promise and possibility. Though one can, of course, evoke nostalgia simply by viewing films of the past, a contemporary nostalgia film cannot simply duplicate the past experience, but must make us aware in some fashion of the relationship between past and present. Attempts to evoke nostalgia merely by imitating past forms, as was the case with the television series *City of Angels*, do not generally work because they seem simply obsolescent. A truly successful nostalgia film—like Fred Zinneman's *True Grit*, one of the last highly popular westerns—succeeds because it set its highly traditional generic content in a slightly different context, thereby giving us both a sense of contemporaneity and of pastness. In *True Grit*, this was done in a number of ways. First of all, the central character played by Kim Darby represented an extremely contemporary image of adolescent girlhood. She was independent, aggressive and full of initiative, a shrewd horsetrader and a self-confident, insistent moralist, unlike the shy desert rose of the traditional western. John Wayne, aging and paunchy, did not attempt to cover up the ravages of the years and reaffirm without change the vigorous manhood of his earlier films. Instead, with eyepatch, unshaven face and sagging flesh, he fully enacted his aging. Similarly, the film's images of the western landscape were in many ways deromanticized. But out of this context of contemporaneity there sprang the same old story of adventure and heroism culminating in an exhuberant shootout which seemed to embody everybody's best dreams of Saturday matinees. The same quality of nostalgic reinvocation of the past played an even more powerful role in Peckinpah's *Ride the High Country* in which two tired, aging and obsolescent heroes ride again, and in Dick Richard's recent version of Raymond Chandler's *Farewell, My Lovely* where a sagging Robert Mitchum moves out of the malaise of modernity and reenacts once more the ambiguous heroic quest of the hard-boiled detective of the 1930s and 1940s.

The difference between nostalgic reincarnation of an earlier genre like *Farewell, My Lovely* and the more complex ironies of *Chinatown* and Robert Altman's *The Long Goodbye* is considerable. It is a difference similar to the one between *True Grit* and neo-westerns like Altman's *McCabe and Mrs. Miller* or Arthur Penn's *Little Big Man*. In the former case, nostalgia is the end result of the film. In the latter nostalgia is often powerfully evoked, but as a means of undercutting or ironically commenting upon the generic experience itself. This brings us to the third and, in many respects, the most powerful mode of generic transformation in recent films: the use of traditional generic structures as a means of demythologization. A film like *Chinatown* deliberately invokes the basic characteristics of a traditional genre in order to bring its audience to see that genre as the embodiment of an inadequate and destructive myth. We have seen how this process of demythologization operates in *Chinatown* by setting the traditional model of the hard-boiled detective's quest for justice and integrity over and against Polanski's sense of a universe so steeped in ambiguity, corruption and evil that such individualistic moral enterprises are doomed by their innocent naiveté to end in tragedy and self-destruction.

The work of Arthur Penn has also explored the ironic and tragic aspects of the myths implicit in traditional genres. His *Night Moves*, a transformation of the detective story, was, like *Chinatown*, the ambiguous enactment of a reluctant quest for the truth about a series of crimes. As the detective approaches a solution to the crimes, he becomes morally and emotionally involved in the quest, making it more and more difficult for him to integrate truth, feeling, and morality. In the end, like Polanski's Jake Gittes, he is more dazed than fulfilled by the catastrophe his investigation has brought about.

In other films, such as *The Left-Handed Gun, Bonnie and Clyde* and *Little Big Man*, Penn created a version of the western or the gangster film in which traditional meanings were inverted, but the effect was tragic rather than humorous. In *Little Big Man*, for example, the conventional western opposition between Indians and pioneers serves as the basis of the plot, which embodies two of the most powerful of our western myths, the Indian captivity and the massacre. However, the conventional renderings of these myths pit the humanely civilizing thrust of the pioneers against the savage ferocity and eroticism of the Indians and thereby justify the conquest of the West. Penn reverses these implications. In his film it is the Indians who are humane and civilized, while the pioneers are violent, corrupt, sexually repressed and madly ambitious. By the end, when Custer's cavalry rides forward to attack the Indian villages, our sympathies are all with the Indians. From this perspective, the conquest of the West is demythologized from the triumph of civilization into a historical tragedy of the destruction of a rich and vital human culture.

Despite its many virtues, the film version of *Little Big Man* was less artistically successful than Thomas Berger's novel on which it was based, primarily because as the film proceeds, Penn loses the ironic detachment which Berger successfully

573

maintains throughout the novel. Penn's portrayal of Custer as a lunatic symbol of aggressive American imperialism is overstated, and toward the end the cinematic *Little Big Man* tends to fall back from the serious exploration of mythical meanings into melodramatic burleque. This is an artistic problem common to films in the mode of demythologization of traditional genres. Penn was far more successful in *Bonnie and Clyde*, which will remain one of the major masterpieces of recent American film. Taking off from the traditional gangster film with its opposition between the outlaw and society, *Bonnie and Clyde* establishes a dialectic between conventional and inverted meanings which is far richer and more powerfully sustained throughout the film. In the traditional gangster film, a powerful individual, frustrated by the limitations of his lower-class origin, is driven to a life of crime. Initially the audience is inclined to sympathize and identify with this character, but as he becomes involved in criminal actions, he overreaches himself and becomes a vicious killer who must be tracked down and destroyed by the representatives of society. The underlying myth of this genre affirms the limits of individual aggression in a society which tolerates and even encourges a high degree of personal enterprise and violence. The gangster becomes a tragic figure not because he is inherently evil, but because he fails to recognize these limits. The myth assures us that society is not repressive or violent; instead it shows how criminal violence evokes its own inevitable doom.

It is this comforting myth of proper and improper violence that Penn demythologizes in *Bonnie and Clyde*. As in *Little Big Man*, meanings become inverted. Instead of representing a limit to aggression and violence, society is portrayed as its fountainhead, while the outlaw protagonists are seen as victims of society's bloodlust. Throughout the film, we are shown a society of depression and chaos which yearns for action, and which projects this yearning into a vicarious excitement about the robberies and murders of the Barrow gang. Penn effectively develops this theme through his representation of the newspapers which so avidly report the gang's adventures and by the reactions of witnesses to the gang's attacks on banks. Finally, its lust for the hunt aroused, society itself takes up the pursuit in packs and posses and, in a final ambush which set a new level in explicit screen violence, the doomed Bonnie and Clyde are shot to pieces. But the inversion of generic meanings is still more complex, for Penn refuses to make the opposition between gangster and society a simple reversal of traditional generic meanings as he does in *Little Big Man*. The protagonists of *Bonnie and Clyde* are not simply victims of society. They are themselves very much a part of the society they are attacking. They share its basic aspirations and confusions and they yearn above all to be reintegrated with it. In many respects, their actions reflect a desperate and misconceived attempt to achieve some measure of the status, security and belongingness which ought to be among the basic gifts of a society to its members. Instead of simply reversing the meanings conventionally ascribed to the opposing forces of criminal and society in the gangster genre, *Bonnie and Clyde* expressed a more complex and dark awareness that this basic opposition was itself a mythical simplification, and showed us the deeper and more difficult irony of the twisted and inseparable fates of individuals and their society. This was in its way a recognition of that skein of ambiguous inevitability which Polanski summed up in the symbol of Chinatown, and which Francis Ford Coppola developed through the fateful intertwining of individuals, "families" and society in *The Godfather*.

Though the demythologization of traditional genres has been primarily evident in the work of younger directors, it has also had some influence on the later work of some of the classic filmmakers, most noticeably perhaps in the later westerns of John Ford, particularly *The Searchers, Cheyenne Autumn* and *The Man who Shot Liberty Valance*. Indeed, in the latter film, Ford symbolized the conquest of the West through a story in which the territory's last major outlaw was killed in a shootout by a man destined to lead the territory into the blessings of civilization. In fact, the legend of Senator Stoddard's heroic deed was a myth, the actual shooting of Liberty Valance having been done by another man. Toward the end of the film, the newspaper editor to whom Senator Stoddard confesses the truth about his past, makes the famous and ambiguous comment "when the legend becomes a fact, print the legend." But is this an ironic comment on the falsity of legends and newspapers alike, or is it some kind of affirmation of the significance of myth in spite of its unreality? Ford was apparently inclined to the latter interpretation, for he once told Peter Bogdanovich, "We've had a lot of people who were supposed to be great heroes and you know damn well they weren't. But it's good for the country to have heroes to look up to."*

This brings us to a fourth and final mode of generic transformation which might be described as the affirmation of myth for its own sake. In films in this mode, a traditional genre and its myth are probed and shown to be unreal, but then the myth itself is at least partially affirmed as a reflection of authentic human aspirations and needs. This is the element which becomes dominant in Ford's later westerns in which he seems to see the heroic ethos of the West in critical terms and becomes more and more sympathetic with the Indian victims of the Westward movement. Yet, at the same time that he became more cynical about the reality of the West, he seemed to feel even more strongly the need to affirm its heroic ideals. Thus, in his powerful late film *The Searchers*, Ford turns to the old western theme of Indian captivity, portraying the mad obsessive hatred with which a White man pursues a band of Indians who have captured and adopted his niece. Yet Ford also accepted a change in the ending of the original novel, where this mad Indian hater was finally destroyed by his obsession, in order to reaffirm at the end the heroism and self-sacrifice of this obsessive quest. *The Searchers* is a powerful and beautiful film, yet one feels uncomfortable at the end, as if the gap between Ford's sense of historical reality and his feelings about genre and myth have come into collision.

Sam Peckinpah's *The Wild Bunch*, for all its ugliness and violence, is a more coherent example of the destruction and reaffirmation of myth. Throughout the film, Peckinpah points up the gap between the conventional western's heroic struggle between pioneers and outlaws. His pioneer lawmen are despicable bounty hunters in the employ of the railroad and they kill

---

*Quoted in Jon Tuska, *The Filming of the West*. (Garden City, N.Y.: Doubleday and Co., 1976, p. 519.)

the guilty and the innocent indiscriminately. His outlaws are not much better; they are brutal, coarse, and quite capable of leaving a wounded comrade behind. Moreover, their type of criminal operation has become absurdly obsolescent in the early twentieth-century West of the film. In the end, Peckinpah's outlaw protagonists are drawn into a ridiculously destructive shootout with an entire Mexican village full of troops and are completely wiped out in the process. Yet the film also leaves us with a sense that through their hopeless action these coarse and vicious outlaws have somehow transcended themselves and become embodiments of a myth of heroism that men need in spite of the realities of their world.

While I have separated the four modes of generic transformation—humorous burlesque, evocation of nostalgia, demythologization of generic myth, and the affirmation of myth as myth—into separate categories in order to define them more clearly, it should be clear that most films which employ one of these modes are likely to use another at some point. Probably the best films based on generic transformation employ some combination of several of these modes in the service of one overriding artistic purpose; *Chinatown* uses both humorous burlesque and nostalgic evocation as a basis for its devastating exploration of the genre of the hard-boiled detective and his myth. Some directors seem to have a primary predilection for one of these modes; Brooks is primarily oriented toward burlesque, Bogdanovich toward nostalgia, Penn toward demythologization and Peckinpah toward reaffirmation. Some directors—Robert Altman springs particularly to mind—have, in their best films, worked out a rich and fascinating dialectic between different modes of generic transformation. In films like *McCabe and Mrs. Miller, The Long Goodbye, Thieves Like Us,* and *Nashville* it is quite difficult to decide at the end whether Altman is attacking or reaffirming the genre on which he has based each particular work. In fact, until the last two or three years, Altman's filmography looks almost as if he had planned a systematic voyage through the major traditional film genres. That generic transformation has been so important a source of artistic energy to the most vital

577

younger directors suggests that it is a central key to the current state of the American film.

There are probably many reasons for the importance of these modes of filmmaking in the last decade, but in conclusion, I will comment briefly on what seem to me the most important factors involved in the proliferation of this kind of film. I think it is not primarily the competition of television. Though television has been somewhat more conservative in its use of generic transformation than film, the same modes seem to be turning up with increasing frequency in television series. Instead I would point to the tendency of genres to exhaust themselves, to our growing historical awareness of modern popular culture, and finally, to the decline of the underlying mythology on which traditional genres have been based since the late nineteenth century. Generic exhaustion is a common phenomenon in the history of culture. One can almost make out a life-cycle characteristic of genres as they move from an initial period of articulation and discovery, through a phase of conscious self-awareness on the part of both creators and audiences, to a time when the generic patterns have become so well-known that people become tired of their predictability. It is at this point that parodic and satiric treatments proliferate and new genres gradually arise. Our major traditional genres—the western, the detective story, the musical, the domestic comedy—have, after all, been around for a considerable period of time and it may be they have simply reached a point of creative exhaustion.

In our time, the awareness of the persistence of genres has been intensified by an increasing historical awareness of film. A younger generation of directors has a sense of film history quite different from many of their predecessors who, like Ford and Hawks, were involved with the art of film almost from its beginnings. Similarly, audiences have a kind of sophistication about the history of genres different from earlier film publics because of the tremendous number of past films now regularly shown on television and by college film societies.

But I am inclined to think that there is more to it than that. The present significance of generic transformation as a creative mode reflects the feeling that not only the traditional genres, but the cultural myths they once embodied, are no longer fully adequate to the imaginative needs of our time. It will require another essay to explain and justify this assertion, but if I may hazard a final prediction, I think we will begin to see emerging out of this period of generic transformation a new set of generic constructs more directly related to the imaginative landscape of the second half of the twentieth century. Thus, the present period of American filmmaking will seem in retrospect an important time of artistic and cultural transition. Like many transition periods, it may also turn out to be a time of the highest artistic accomplishment.

1978

579

RICHARD MERAN BARSAM
FROM NONFICTION FILM:
A CRITICAL HISTORY

NONFICTION FILM:
THE REALIST IMPULSE*

The origins of cinema—of cinematography and, indeed, of photography itself—are rooted in the desire to record life as it is. Cinema is actually capable of reproducing the physical world within the formal properties of the work of art. From such eminent theorists as Siegfried Kracauer and André Bazin, who disagree on almost everything but the realism of cinema, we learn that cinematic content takes precedence over form, that the world reproduced through photography—as opposed to the world created through film editing—is the proper concern of the filmmaker. It is also the proper concern of the nonfiction filmmaker. The theoretical basis of nonfiction film is in the realist tradition.

Kracauer proposes that film should both record and reveal the physical world, but in so doing, that it should also redeem it, a moral imperative that implies, to paraphrase what Joseph Conrad said about the novel, an obligation to *make us see.* Through its properties as a visual medium, cinema does make us see, but the nonfiction filmmaker is concerned not only with *what* we see but also with *how* we see it. Far more than Kracauer, Bazin trusted the artist's ability to make us see the significance of people and objects in the world around us. With his emphasis on such familiar cinematic properties as

---

*This article is based on and adapted from *Nonfiction Film: A Critical History,* New York: E. P. Dutton, 1973.

deep-focus photography and the dramatic interrelationships within the frame (what we call *mise-en-scène*), Bazin regards cinema as an inherently realistic medium. And it was Bazin, not Kracauer, who created respect for the work of Robert Flaherty at a time when many critics found his view of the world to be anachronistic, perhaps even antagonistic to the nature of realist cinema itself.

The prevailing theories of realist film were published in the 1950s, long after the first nonfiction film was made. Since the origins of cinema in the 1880s, people have been thinking, if not always theorizing, about the relationship between the filmmaker, the medium, and the raw material of the physical world. Nonfiction film is as old as cinema itself; indeed, the first films in the history of the medium are simple attempts to record reality without a fictional or dramatic framework. The dramatic impulse shortly transformed the new art into the medium we know today, but the realist impulse was undoubtedly the first and remains today as an important one.

From Auguste and Louis Lumière in the 1880s to David and Albert Maysles in the 1970s, from Robert Flaherty in the early 1920s and John Grierson in the early 1930s, the emphasis of the nonfiction filmmaker has been not on form or on content, but on that ineluctable area in which form and content coalesce. It is this concern with form and content, with what people see and how they see it, that helps to distinguish nonfiction film from the more familiar fiction film.

Various definitions of the nonfiction film have been presented and elaborated. The most familiar, but most abused and most misunderstood term in the film lexicon, *documentary*, has been applied to such diverse cinematic forms as propaganda films, newsreels, travelogues, military and classroom training films, and films of rock music concerts. Its meaning has been interpreted differently by film theorists, historians, and critics, as well as by the film audience and by filmmakers joined in groups to promote specific political ideologies. Evidently, there is much disagreement over its meaning. The history of nonfiction film shows that there is little stylistic similarity in the work of the major nonfiction filmmakers: Robert Flaherty, Dziga Vertov, Leni Riefenstahl, John Grierson, Paul

581

Rotha, Alberto Cavalcanti, Humphrey Jennings, Willard Van Dyke, Pare Lorentz, Richard Leacock, Albert and David Maysles, Frederick Wiseman, and Marcel Ophuls, to name only those who have pursued the most distinctive forms. I suggest that the genre is better served by the term *nonfiction film* than by the term *documentary*.

All documentaries are nonfiction films, but not all nonfiction films are documentaries. The nonfiction genre is also the rubric under which one finds various approaches to filmmaking in which fidelity to actuality is the primary goal. But a definition of the nonfiction film must acknowledge that film is an art and that the artist has an individual vision and technique. One way to view the history of art is to see it as the record of different responses to similar phenomena. The history of the nonfiction film is no different, including, for example, Robert Flaherty's *Nanook of the North* (1922) and Michael Wadleigh's *Woodstock* (1970). The former was made on a small budget with a simple hand-cranked camera, while the latter was made with every technical convenience available to the modern filmmaker, including computerized editing equipment. It may be argued that there is a closer relation between these two films than the separation of years would suggest—that they both celebrate life, for instance—but it is apparent that the factors of time, technique, artistic vision, production budget, facilities, and audience are important factors in defining the cinematic art form to which they both belong.

Any definition of nonfiction film would have to be so broad as to include Vertov's *Kino-Pravda*, Flaherty's *Man of Aran*, Ivens' *The Spanish Earth*, Huston's *Let There Be Light*, Anderson's *Every Day Except Christmas*, and the Maysles brothers' *Salesman*. To try to define this spectrum of filmmaking with one term could be self-defeating. Nonetheless, it is possible if *documentary* is placed subordinate to the overall genre of nonfiction film.

Nonfiction Film: Form and Function

The nonfiction filmmaker presents actual physical reality in a form that strives to be faithful to actuality. Unlike the fictional filmmaker, who transforms the world through his or her imaginative conception of it, the nonfiction filmmaker creatively records and interprets the world without substantially altering it. This is not only a matter of genre, but also of degree. Obviously some nonfiction films are more imaginative than others, just as some nonfiction books transcend the traditional guidelines that separate nonfiction from the fiction books on library shelves. Equally obvious is the manner in which the viewer's affective and intellectual responses are elicited. This problem of audience reaction, so basic to aesthetics and so often overlooked in cinema studies, calls for an analysis of the medium that acknowledges both its stylistic range and its significance as a cultural phenomenon. The development of direct cinema since the 1950s helps us to better understand this. For example, Frederick Wiseman's *Meat* (1975) elicits a range of audience reaction that is wide enough to sustain dichotomies. One's reaction to this film may depend upon his or her feelings about such things as food, technology, mass production, work, and the American way of life, as well as on whatever prior knowledge that person might have about the meat packing industry. Consumers, workers, and management all react differently to the film, yet all, including the filmmaker, agree that it faithfully represents reality. Nonfiction film is the art of *re*-presentation.

The nonfiction film responds to immediate moments, and is therefore rooted in a cultural context that should be studied along with the film. It originates in specific social situations: sometimes a problem, sometimes a crisis, sometimes an undramatic and seemingly unimportant person or event. It is usually filmed on the actual scene, with the actual people, without sets, costumes, written dialogue, or created sound effects. It tries to recreate the feeling of "being there," with as much fidelity to fact as the situation allows. The structure of a typical nonfiction film is two or three parts, with an introduction and conclusion, and tends to follow a pattern that moves from statement of problem to advocacy of solution. Even more typically, it is filmed in black-and-white, with direct sound recording (or simulated sound), a musical score written expressly for the film and conceived as part of a cinematic whole,

583

and, as often as not, a spoken narration. Its traditional running time is thirty minutes, but Leni Riefenstahl's *Olympia* (1938) runs for three hours and forty minutes, Marcel Ophuls' *The Sorrow and the Pity* (1971) runs for four hours and thirty minutes, and Louis Malle's *Phantom India* (1968) runs for six hours. The current trend is toward a length that can adequately accommodate the demands imposed by content, not those suggested by tradition.

Nonfiction Film: Three Major Approaches

The nonfiction filmmaker may choose from various approaches to the genre, but in the brief history of the medium these three have been most apparent: the factual approach, the documentary approach, and the direct cinema approach.

The Factual Approach

Contrary to popular belief, the facts do not speak for themselves, especially in cinema. They require structure and interpretation, elements that reflect the filmmaker's vision. Unlike the documentary film, the factual film ordinarily lacks a specific message; however, if it has one, it does not necessarily take precedence over the other cinematic aspects of the film. What is important is the facts, but when we acknowledge that film is an art, we also acknowledge that the purely factual film is something of an impossibility.

Perhaps an analogy to another means of expression will clarify the nature of the factual film. Nonfiction films share many characteristics of journalism, and the difference between the documentary and factual film is roughly the difference between the editorial and news pages of the daily newspaper. The editorial page is labeled as such, so the reader will know that he or she is reading opinions that are based on what might otherwise be considered facts. The news pages, though, are a different thing. Sometimes they contain releases from the wire services, and at other times they contain the signed releases of reporters who have been at the scene about which they write. No matter how "objective" they try to be, the reports must contend with their own subjective responses, even though, for the most part, the facts predominate.

It should be apparent now that to distinguish too precisely between the documentary and the factual approaches would be to formulate inflexible concepts that would tend to defeat any fluent analysis. It is sufficient to remember that documentary films are concerned with facts *and* opinion, and that factual films are primarily concerned with the facts. Leni Riefenstahl's *Olympia* (1938), Lindsay Anderson's *Every Day Except Christmas* (1957), and Michael Wadleigh's *Woodstock* (1970) are all considered factual films, because these filmmakers place a factual recording of reality above an impulse to interpret that reality. But even to the unsophisticated viewer, one viewing of any of them is enough to indicate that it is difficult, if not impossible, to present facts without somehow influencing the viewer's interpretation of them.

Nonfiction films are not primarily intended to be commercial and are not released by commercial distributors unless it is believed that they will be unusually broad in their appeal. During the 1960s and 1970s, rock music enthusiasts comprised a vast audience for films about rock music concerts, but aside from that particular phenomenon, which appears to be following the diminishing vogue for that music, nonfiction films are categorized as nontheatrical, meaning that they are shown without admission charge in schools, colleges, libraries, unions, churches, and in industrial, social, and cultural organizations. Although there are many exceptions, they are exceptions rather than the rule. Some important directors of fiction films, such as Michelangelo Antonioni, Stanley Kubrick, and Lindsay Anderson, began their careers with nonfiction films; many nonfiction films have been shown in large commercial theaters and have made a profit for their producers; but the distinctions between theatrical and nontheatrical distribution help to separate and to explain the two most obvious forms of filmmaking: fiction and nonfiction. When there are films that successfully straddle the two fields, rare as that is—films such as Georges Rouquier's *Farrebique* (1946) or Sidney Meyer's *The Quiet One* (1949)—then we are reminded that cinema resists stratification and that its possibilities are infinite.

585

The Documentary Approach

Nonfiction film was pioneered and developed by the French, the Americans, the Russians, and the British, roughly in that order, but the most influential theories regarding the documentary approach came from the British, notably from John Grierson and Paul Rotha.

John Grierson was truly the father of the documentary film. He was the first to apply the term *documentary* — when reviewing Flaherty's *Moana* in 1926 — and in 1928 he established the first documentary film production unit sponsored by the British government. His views provided the philosophical foundation for the production and development of documentary film. From the beginning, he sought to develop a sense of community, placing his patriotism and commitment to national goals over and above any personal achievement he might have made with his films. The origins of the British documentary movement lay in sociological, not in aesthetic aims, in a belief in film as a means of national communication, not in a feeling for film as art. Filmmakers who were influenced by Grierson realized and extended the aesthetic capabilities of the genre during the 1930s, but Grierson remained preoccupied with message, not medium.

Grierson was convinced that the documentary approach was basically propagandist rather than aesthetic, and, for him, the film medium happened to be the most convenient and the most dramatic means by which to implement his ideas of community and world peace. He was deeply troubled by the two world wars, although his major theories were formulated before World War II and his major influence felt during the 1930s, both in England and in the United States. To make films with a social message was all-important in the context of the world as he knew it. Grierson was determined to prove that the world could be made a better place in which to live through mass education and communication. For him, art and aesthetics were only a means to an end: national education.

Grierson's principles of documentary are fundamental. He believed, first, that the documentary filmmaker could *reveal* the real world; second, that he had — and this is perhaps ironic—a more imaginative degree of control over his material than the maker of fiction films; and, third, that he could make the materials and stories taken from the raw stuff of everyday life more real than the acted article. His theory is not without its problems, but his essential convictions are that documentary film should be a creative treatment of everyday actuality and that the filmmaker should be committed to crystallizing civic sentiments and to furthering national goals. At the core of his theory is the simple belief that "somehow we had to make peace exciting, if we were to prevent wars. Simple notion that it is—that has been my propaganda ever since—to make peace exciting." If that lacks substance as film theory, it more than compensates as a belief in the moral power of art.

Paul Rotha has both produced and directed many documentary films. Like Grierson, he is idealistic, but unlike Grierson, he believes—because he is an artist—in cinematic form and properties. He believes that documentary filmmakers take greater care in the production of their films, that they are more skillful craftsmen, and that they use "more profound reasoning" in their choice of theme and approach than their colleagues in the other branches of filmmaking. The extent of Rotha's influence can be seen in the high cinematic merit of the documentary films produced in England during the late 1930s and after.

In addition to emphasizing cinematic properties, Rotha emphasizes humanistic ideals. He is concerned with issues that transcend time and place, and he is likewise concerned with finding immediate examples in the contemporary world that exemplify these issues. Rotha asks that the documentary filmmaker be both a sociologist and a cinematographer and, whenever possible, a poet, too. In short, the documentary film artist is a man of goodwill, a man who, in Grierson's words, can "make peace exciting." Indeed, he sees the role of the filmmaker much in the same way as Flaherty saw it long before and long after Rotha's influence was greatest—the role of the artist as educator, illuminator, and, finally, of conciliator. Like Shelley, Rotha would have his filmmakers be "legislators of mankind," and in addition he would prefer that they be acknowledged, respected, and supported. The state-supported documentary filmmaking units that flourished in England during the 1930s made this idealistic aim a reachable goal. Rotha's theories and films carry with them the unmistakable marks of a man of faith and vision, and of a man whose art, however biased, was ultimately nonpolitical in its attempts to unite mankind. The social consciousness of the 1930s is reflected in Rotha's vision of a society in which art and science can work together to solve the problems of this world. But we have been to the moon and back since then, and many of the same world problems exist still and with increasingly more deadly consequences. If Rotha's vision of the filmmaker seems outdated today, that is not his fault. Today's filmmakers have almost unanimously turned inward, to individual, rather than social problems; to intimate, rather than public issues; to questions, rather than answers. Those, too, are ways of exploring the world around us. Grierson and Rotha assure us that all nonfiction film, not just the documentary approach, is an art, and that it can serve, as any art, to illuminate the human condition.

The documentary film is distinguished from the factual film by its sociopolitical purpose, its "message." It attempts to fuse two concerns that often prove to be incompatible in art: medium and message. Medium and message are not synonyms for form and content, but rather attest to a different situation in which the medium is regarded by some (unfortunately, Grierson was among them) as less important than the message (distinct from content, a goal to be achieved above all). In its most intimate way, art can create powerful personal reactions and emotions, while in its most public way, it can create powerful group actions and reactions. Art can be an instrument for social influence and change, although it rarely sets out with this intention. However, the documentary film does have this purpose, and the filmmaker who works with this approach wants to use cinema for purposes more important than entertainment. He wants to persuade, influence, and change his audience. The content of the documentary film is more important, at first, than the style by which that content is communicated. Here the distinctions between form and content are important ones, and while it is not my intention to imply that the documentary filmmaker places politics above aesthetics, we should remember that most often he has a sponsor to whom he is responsible and has a specific goal to achieve. While these factors do not preclude great art, they do not always encourage it. As Lindsay Anderson points out: "Documentary should not be—it certainly need not be—synonymous with dullness. It should be one of the most exciting and stimulating of contemporary forms." All filmmakers, including those who make nonfiction films, should be technically proficient in dealing with the cinematic elements available to them and talented enough to understand how best to use those elements to realize their goals. But form and content are not inseparable. When the documentary approach has been synonymous with dullness, that has occurred not because the documentary form is inherently dull, but because the documentary filmmaker placed message above medium.

The Direct Cinema Approach

Direct cinema, or *cinéma vérité* (as it is often called in France and elsewhere), was created in the late 1950s by filmmakers who were frustrated by the inherent limitations of the factual and documentary approaches. Accepting the concept that nonfiction film could be an art form, and that it need not be dull, they searched for a cinematic language that would help them to realize the form. Their achievement reaffirms the fundamental realist impulse behind all nonfiction film.

Aesthetic considerations were one impulse behind the development of direct cinema; technological considerations were another and, perhaps, a more important one. The camera and sound recording equipment used in direct cinema is lightweight and portable, making it possible for the first time for filmmakers to achieve a physical intimacy with the subject and even an emotional relationship with it. With the camera braced on the shoulder and the tape recorder strapped to the back, the filmmaker is an almost self-contained production unit, able to move about freely and to catch events as they are happening. Technology produced the advantages of this new approach, but the artistic characteristics of intimacy and informality derive from the blend of technology and aesthetics that distinguishes cinema from the other arts.

In direct cinema, two kinds of language are important: the

589

cinematic language as it has been affected by the new equipment, and the language (spoken and natural sound) as it is heard on the soundtrack. Unlike the factual and documentary film, direct cinema does not use narration, except in such films as Marcel Ophuls' *The Sorrow and the Pity* (1971) where unobtrusive titles or spoken narration provide essential information and where the interviewer elicits responses from the subject. The words spoken by the Beales in the Maysles' brothers *Grey Gardens* (1975) or by the people in Frederick Wiseman's *Meat* (1975) provide images that are often equally if not more important than the visual images we see. Our intimate relationship to these people, and our realization that they are speaking directly (i.e., not from a script) make these films all the more realistic. Because of this, we respond more fully to the other qualities of language, including nuance, tone, volume, and rhythm. Direct cinema marks the first time in the history of cinema that aural language reaches the communicative power of visual language.

It is this "direct" quality that distinguishes these films. The filmmaker is an intermediary between the viewer and the subject, rather than an obstacle, subservient to the script, to preconceived thematic statement, or to plotted narrative. Motivated by spontaneity, the filmmaker has an obligation to the moment, to presenting as many facets of the actual situation as he or she is able to record with camera and tape recorder. Art presupposes the presence of the artist, but in direct cinema, the artist submerges himself into his material. Establishing his persona is not important, for his consciousness is so intrinsically a part of the film that it does not become an obstacle to our own. The film artist and the film are one, achieving an entity that brings us closer to cinematic realism than we have ever been before.

No artist merely records phenomena, for even the simplest home movie reflects the attitude of the person behind the camera, and in that attitude is the foundation of the creative process. The film art is so highly complicated, so directly and indirectly affected by theories of time and space, by principles of editing, by types of film, lenses, by properties of stock, by weight of equipment, by finances, and by countless other factors, that anything like what the theorists of direct cinema

590

suggest might seem possible only in theory and not in practice. It is, after all, in the presentation and interpretation of events that the process of photography (an art in itself) becomes the art of cinema. But direct cinema is not only possible, but also possibly the logical and desirable end of the impulse that makes filmmakers want to record life as it is.

The filmmakers Jonas Mekas and David Maysles suggest that *nonfiction film* is a better term to apply than *direct cinema*, but they use *nonfiction film* as Truman Capote uses *nonfiction novel*. However successful Capote's concept has proved as an influence on contemporary prose writing, it is a theory more notable for its contradictory quality than for its clarity. The theory behind direct cinema is not confusing. Inherent in the art of filmmaking is the process of selection: the selection of subject, of crew, of images (the editing of sight and sound), and of distribution. But what all these theories about direct cinema neglect to discuss is the importance of selecting the subject. It is easy enough to insist on objectivity once the subject has been chosen, but if the subject is dull, lacking in the energy and originality that must be at the heart of these films, then the film will be dull. No amount of lighting, camera work, sound recording, editing, or music will erase that fact. Once the filmmaker has chosen this kind of subject, and then taken the difficult step of submerging himself in it—perhaps even to the extent of becoming secondary to it, if not totally invisible— then he or she is ready for direct cinema. Instead of making *Grey Gardens* (1975) as they did—with the actual people in their own house—Albert and David Maysles might have taken the fictional approach by writing a script that captured the contrapuntal intensity of their two female characters, and then by directing two actresses (and what extraordinary actresses they would have to be) to achieve a predetermined end. Instead, they took the direct cinema approach, proving not only that life is stranger than fiction, but that a nonfiction film can demand as much from itself, and its audience, as a fiction film.

Other Approaches to Nonfiction Film

As discussed here, nonfiction film includes the factual, documentary, and direct cinema approaches; it also includes travel films; educational, training, or classroom films; and newsreels. Although these minor genres do not always provide distinguished examples of film art, they contain, within their specific limitations, possibilities that have not always been realized. A brief account of each extends our definition.

Travel films, or travelogues, as they are more commonly called, are one of the oldest and most popular forms of film, demonstrating the power of cinema to bring people together. The French used the word *documentaires* to describe early travel films, but the meaning of this word is different from that of the English word *documentary*. Early travel films did create documents, or to be more precise, factual visual records, but they did not function within the overall scope of documentary film as we have defined it. In short, they were not concerned with a message, but with entertainment. The travel film is still popular with the armchair traveller, but the genre has not ever really captured the interest of serious nonfiction filmmakers.

The power of the nonfiction film to attract an audience, engage its attention, and influence its behavior is better demonstrated in that large body of films that teach and train people. These training films are used everywhere, from kindergarten classrooms to battlefield information centers, and within their modest expectations, they are usually successful. Undistinguished in aesthetic terms, they make up in purpose what they lack in art. Children can be introduced to safety rules, teenagers to sex education, soldiers to the prevention of intelligence leaks (as well as how to make their beds), and farmers to the advantages of crop rotation. These training or information films are used extensively by such agencies as UNESCO in their efforts to inform and educate people about such things as health and agriculture. They can be used to teach almost anything to almost anyone, and their quality and success are limited only by the seriousness of the effort and the thoroughness of the approach used in making them.

Newsreels were once a flourishing part of the film industry, but the news digest has all but vanished from the screen. These biweekly or weekly "newspapers of the screen" were sometimes shown in special newsreel theaters in larger cities, or, more often, on the same bill with a cartoon, travel film, and one or two feature films. The "March of Time" and "This is America" series reflected a particular editorial bias, while those of Paramount or Pathé presented more objective reportage.

The newsreel relied on actual events for its raw material, but the public favored the more unusual events that became its staple offering. Newsreels presented their material in simple, descriptive terms, and within a minimum amount of time. Like the films of the Lumière brothers that began film history, they satisfied an audience's curiosity about daily life around them. Although they are still capable of responding to this interest in daily events, their place has been taken by instantaneous television news reports.

The Nonfiction Film Tradition

One of the fundamental impulses of cinema, from its beginnings, has been the realist impulse, the desire to record life as it is. The nonfiction filmmaker not only records life as it is lived, but also helps us to understand its complexities by showing us that even the most complex social issues arise out of the conflicting needs of individual human beings. As with any other film genre, the nonfiction film offers various approaches to its makers and has various effects on its viewers. It may present the facts, it may argue with them, it may show that there are infinite possibilities in any phenomenon by taking the direct cinema approach. But always nonfiction film deals with reality—with real people and real situations—and it is in reality that we find the impulse behind it and our fascination with it.

1973; revised 1978

GILBERT SELDES
THE LOVELY ART: MAGIC

To little children and to aesthetes, the motion picture has always been sheer magic, and one of the complaints the aesthetes have consistently made against Hollywood is that its direction has steadily been toward reducing the magical content of the movies, making them more and more *real*. They are certainly justified in one respect: even the part of the movies which is most magical, the animated cartoon, has been pushed toward photographic realism. It has, however, resisted. Driven out of its natural habitat— sheer fantasy and illusion—by one practitioner, it has slipped out of his hands and returned with a flourish, as naïve-seeming, as saucy, as mystifying as ever, in the hands of another. So here, before we approach the newest technique by which the movies think they can make us forget that they are something more than photographic records of the actual, we can stop to consider the one kind of movie which triumphantly asserts its non- or super-reality.

If we were not so accustomed to it, if it were not on view day by day, we should celebrate, in reverence or by shouting in public places, the incredible wonder of the animated cartoon. Many years ago the aged Henri Matisse came to this country and it was said that, while he wished to see many men, he intended to pay his respects to two: Disney and Thurber. (An irony to which I am not partial: when Thurber came to be done in animations, Disney was off on other concerns and *The Unicorn in the Garden* was beautifully made by the supremely talented group of people who have the most forgettable trade name: UPA.)

THE LOVELY ART: MAGIC

The animated cartoon, the *Silly Symphonies*, the Mickey Mouse series, *Bambi* and *Snow White* and the other full-length features in animation, and the dreadful mistaken concept that let real people be surrounded by cartoon characters—the whole Disney enterprise and whatever went before it and came after can be taken as the typical, focal, symbolic creation in the popular arts. Whoever entirely dislikes this manifestation of money, machinery, and genius sets himself apart from humanity—as a saint perhaps, or a fool; I pass no judgments. Whoever takes them all, without making distinctions, is a happier man, but not the happiest man. For I take my stand on the principle that no harm is done by knowing—and that satisfaction increases with understanding. Or, in the specific instance, I would say that the animated cartoon is one of the three supreme examples of the multiple or diversified nature of these arts, in many respects more typical, purer, and consequently more of a test case than the two others, jazz and the feature picture. For in the animated drawing the use and abuse of the mechanism is perfectly displayed, the pressure of economic necessity, down and up, exists at high intensity, and the entire enterprise cannot come into being without pure genius of the simplest, most universal order.

And I should add that the curve of goodness (that essence which every professional recognizes) is in itself a case history of these dear and exasperating arts to which I am so devoted; should add that the pang of disappointment and the resurgence of delight are also characteristic of these arts, for they seem condemned by their own nature to destroy their sweetest qualities—and to recover. In the special case of the animated cartoon, the recovery has been made by Disney's successors while he has created at least three new careers for himself.

There were animations before Disney, and some of them were good. Even before the Keystone comedies were becoming fantastic, the animators were staking out their claims. To be sure, I can now recall only those bits I recorded at the time: the imp coming out of the inkpot and going back into it, protesting; the cow walking up the side of a barn; and the great, lovely, immortal Krazy Kat, who announced his arrival on the screen with the simple, often quoted words, "Envy me, Mice, I'm going into pictures." The mechanism of the animated cartoon had been known for generations and was used for a mild type of "feelthy pictures"—fifty drawings, packed rather like a paper-match book, when flicked presented the hootchy-kootchy dancer. To transfer the process to film was simple. Presently a disastrous discovery was made: the more single frames drawn for a step or a jump or any other action, the more lifelike it becomes. No one at that moment asked, "Who wants an animated cartoon to be life-like?"

Because the genius and the enchantment of the Disneys were so various, so overwhelming, for a long, long time the master of the business could do anything. Or let us say that at the heart of every-thing an animator does there is an animating principle—which here seems like a pun, but is the essence of the art. It is not the single situation created when Pluto is climbing a mountain, it is the fact that a drawn dog can move at all which captivates us first. After that we want these drawings to entertain us, to make us laugh. No one suggested in the early days that animations might make us do anything but laugh. (In 1923 I asked Picasso whether he would be interested in making some masterdrawings, and we also talked about using the *Goyescas* for a series. Picasso had, however, not seen any good animations, and unfortunately we never took the project up again. In 1953 UPA did *The Telltale Heart*, the first uncomic animation I have seen, outside of industrials and educa-tional films, in the United States.)

To pile up the circumstances of good fortune surrounding Walt Disney is not to imply any lack of genius. Everything was in his favor—but genius was in his favor to begin with. The animated cartoon had followed the normal course of production—it had become routine. Disney arrived, a cartoonist dissatisfied with his own work; he had barely finished a few cartoons on his own when Vitaphone struck. Sound had come—and Disney took it in his stride, as if he had just been waiting for sound before starting his real work. Within a year he was using sound in counterpoint to his drawings; there was a scene in a cave, with icicles: the reverbera-tions of sound were precisely adapted to the movements of the drops of water forming into ice—and the sense of unreality was superb.

And then, as if to challenge Disney's capacities once more, color came to Hollywood. Again there was no hesitation, no perplexity. Color, which was lacking in *Steamboat Willie* and the dance of the Egyptian characters around a frieze, was exactly what the *Silly*

596

THE LOVELY ART: MAGIC

Symphonies required. Let it be said at once that Disney made a few mistakes in the handling of color, slashing it about like a boy with a whitewash brush, but the major errors he never made; he never used color offensively. At worst, he used it without talent, and these occasions were few. He began by using a watercolor palette, a sort of wash in which his characters moved lightly; later he began to use the palette of an oil painter, which got thicker with every feature. I prefer the wash, because it seems to me to be within the tone of fantasy; oil is the medium of the real. But for a long time Disney had the instinctive feel for his work and seemed incapable of making a mistake. (I said this once a little more broadly; I wrote that he had never done a picture I did not like. That same week he released one about Midas, probably *The Golden Touch*, which was plodding and pretentious, and a year later he and I compared notes and I discovered that he disliked the picture almost as much as I did.) In those years he turned out masterpieces—not in comparison with the work of others, but absolutely, works that were perfect in detail as they were simple and, in a magnificent way, grand in their basic concepts. You can tick them off, this title and that, but you will run out of fingers because they came one after another, apparently without end, alternating the sheer magical loveliness of the *Silly Symphonies* and the intricate, ultralogical fantasies of Mickey Mouse and the great character who was to outshine him, Donald Duck, and the dear beasts who peopled the world in which these two lived.

There came a time, a few years after the shine and gaiety had become familiar, when people discovered a streak of cruelty in Disney; and it would be foolish to deny that it was there, as it was in Grimm and Hans Christian Andersen. But we have now the perspective of the years, and we can look at the Disney product as an entity, a single complete thing, and deliver ourselves of a nice judgment. And I think the first element in our judgment is the one no court would allow: it is sheer love. These fifteen-minute games played out in front of our eyes were—and to this day are—like candy and ice cream in our childhood, things about which we say, openly and freely, that we *love* them. They are like holidays about which we say "I can't wait . . ." because in a true sense we could hardly bear the long wait, in the early days, between Disney pictures.

I know that it is my business to say why and how these things occurred, since I am a professional critic, and if pushed, I think I can say why and how. But I think it also a good part of observation, if not of criticism, to utter the innocent childish cry of surprise and admiration with which we greet Roman candles in the summer night, or a moment in the circus when dexterity turns to loveliness. For Disney always had this moment when he was running true to his own form. It might be only the muted croak of a frog after the full chorus, it might be the sudden resemblance he showed us between a mammal and a machine, it might be the flow of one color into another or one sound into another sound, but always there was the special, sweetly knowing touch that skillful men before him had lacked. They had all his elements at their command, they seemed to do what he was doing, but the final ingredient was missing. It was not taste, not imagination, for these things Disney shared with others; and, while he developed a vast complexity in production, with machines as menacing as those that stamp out whole car-bodies in one operation, the difference between him and the others was never purely mechanical. I think that actually it was a moral difference, composed of two attitudes: a mischievous impertinence toward the public and a loving kindness toward his own creations.

I am still speaking of the short pictures, in which violence existed but was somehow held under control, as the fury of the hurricane was magisterially subdued to the beat of the music in *The Band Concert* or the tantrums of Donald Duck were justified and tamed. Since the animated cartoon, even more than the regular movie, can satisfy our wish to be omnipotent, defying the laws of gravitation, defying time and space, endowing animals with human attributes and making men and women into machines (and then giving the machines an apparent will and life of their own)—since these things are so, animations must have their own logic; we must rejoice when the Mouse or the Duck walks over the edge of a precipice and keeps on walking on air; we must rejoice because we would like also to be able to walk on air. And we must not let questions come into our minds, we must be under the spell of the picture. Then when the walker sees what has happened and panics and scrambles back to the cliff or falls and bounces back, we must recognize that also—the kind of morality of the cartoons, the laws by which they live; for it is their law that until we are afraid of what happens to us, we can do anything on earth or in the air or under the seas.

There was an additional quality in these early pictures: they missed completely the dreary quaintness of animal stories. They were partly Aesop with a touch of La Fontaine, perhaps, but they were never children's-book animals. They were carefully created characters with sustained motives, placed in situations which seemed plausible to them and in which they acted according to their lights. They were not Aesopian in any sense of delivering moral lessons, nor were their approaches to the society of human beings as satirical as those of La Fontaine; they were animals with lives of their own to lead.

The strangest thing about the early Disneys is that they did not make money—for Disney. The intricacies of the system of releasing movies can be of interest only to those in the business; they were defeating to Walt Disney, who saw his *Three Little Pigs* become an attraction capable of pulling in more money at the box office than the feature picture, yet was paid a lump sum, so much per week or per day, regardless of the take. This was the customary arrangement; everything except the feature was a filler and excluded from the percentage arrangements. There was a rough justice in this, but in the case of Disney it became intolerable and it compelled him to take the road to corporate enterprise, a big studio, big pictures, and eventually the virtual disappearance of the work that had made him famous.

The making of long pictures is in itself a natural outcome of making short ones. Chaplin had hardly arrived in the Keystone comedies when he was put into the support of Marie Dressler in *Tillie's Punctured Romance*, which some people professed to find pretentious on the silly ground that no comedy could last for seven reels. Actually, Disney waited ten years after the beginning of Mickey Mouse before doing his first feature cartoon: *Snow White and the Seven Dwarfs*. By that time his releasing arrangements were better and his studio was constantly enlarging and endless experiments were being made with color, with sound, and particularly with two qualities that Disney began to value more and more: depth and smoothness of motion, two qualities giving the effect of realness, as if he were in competition with regular movies. Some five years later he went back to a technique with which he had had a small success long before Mickey Mouse, a combination of cartoons and live actors. Eventually he made the picture that, one would have said, he was destined to make, as if the rest of his professional life was a preparation for it: *Alice in Wonderland*. Nothing so marked his fall as the tasteless, elaborate defeat he inflicted on the imagination and logic of the original—and I speak as a non-idolater.

Was it entirely the "curse of bigness" which had overtaken Disney? I am not sure. I know that midway in his work with one of his long features he wanted to call it off, but allowed his staff to go on, withdrawing only his supervision (it was either *Dumbo* or *The Reluctant Dragon*, both up to the Disney standard and, in parts, highly inventive). He had also made teaching films for one or more branches of the armed services which were miracles of inventiveness not only in his own field but in the field of education; the abstractions and fundamental principles and definitions that are so tedious and necessary were simplified, projected, and connected with happy devices, so that a mind positively allergic to ohms and amperes would remember the angle at which an animated and anguished arrow moved into a mass of bubbles, and even eyes not peculiarly observant learned to tell the nose and wing of a friendly plane from those of the enemy. And Disney made a feature in which he came to believe profoundly and passionately: *Victory Through Air Power*. The refusal of the high command to accept the thesis of this picture infuriated Disney. It was virtually that victory could be won by air power *alone*, that all other commitments of men and money and material were wasteful, and in the background was the implication that unless the Seversky principle were accepted, we could never hope for victory at all. Long after the picture was made and even when victory was beginning to be possible Disney spoke of it with a peculiar fanaticism, not with the genial enthusiasm he had for his entertainments. He was in rebellion against the government, and presently a less important event aggravated his feelings. A strike broke out at his studio.

It is hardly worth while to recall the passions of that time, but the effect on Disney was particularly strong because of the general assumption that all strikers were favored by the Administration. Disney was confused by the strike and kept saying to his friends, "I don't understand it. . . . Every one of them calls me Walt. I call them by their first names. . . ." He was back in the early days, the small studio, everybody sitting around the drawing tables, making a crack or a suggestion; he forgot the acres of buildings, the five or ten story boards simultaneously in use, the armory of sound effects, the huge machinery that photographed through several layers of gels to give perspective, the commitments to releasing organizations, the contracts, the income—he did remember the taxes. I have no position on the strike, having nothing to go on beyond Disney's own statements, which were not illuminating; I know that from that time on a certain sweetness left the studio and men of prodigious talent and pleasant natures found it difficult to work there. The last feature that seemed to me to capture anything of the quality of Disney's art was *Saludos Amigos*, which was really a grouping of unconnected shorts. In *Bambi*, which was made the same year, the naturalistic backgrounds and a mixture of the heavy and the arch brought the whole picture down to the level of illustration. The earlier elaborate *Fantasia* gave itself airs, but again, because it was made up of separate sections, seemed to have more brilliant episodes than the full-length single-story films. In addition to putting Carmen Miranda among cartoons, Disney also illustrated and hammed up *Casey at the Bat* as if its simple story needed to be helped to fame, and, laying a rough hand on whatever needed to be treated respectfully—not with reverence but with understanding— he finally came, as noted, to *Alice*.

And it must have been around this time that Stephen Bosustow and a few associates, some of whom had undergone the Disney treatment, began to make cartoons totally different in character— the first challengers to Disney sensible enough to know that they could not compete with him on his ground, the first to go back to basic principles in animations, perhaps the first since Disney to believe in their work and to enjoy it. They made a short, and suddenly everyone became aware of them and for several years they were constantly identified as "the people that made *Gerald McBoing Boing*." The surprise and elation brought by the first Disneys were again in the air, a kind of delight all the more pleasurable because it was remembered as well as new.

The men at UPA had the advantage of Disney's twenty years; they could begin with human figures—squat and round and unreal —where Disney had begun only with animals; they had all the experiments with comic sound to fall back on. The one thing they did not have was Disney's plant. They could not duplicate his backgrounds and perspectives, nor could they afford as many separate drawings per movement or gesture as Disney could give. They had to make flat backgrounds and spasmodic movements acceptable, and their particular stroke of genius was that they turned these two things into positive attractions, making them the essentials of their work. As I said, they reverted to first principles, which wouldn't have helped them if the pictures had not been supremely attractive; it is, however, agreeable to find that on occasion good theory results in practical success.

The theoretical approach is this: a caricature is not a photograph; an animation is exactly what the name implies—it makes a non-alive thing seem alive. The cartoon is not a series of photographs of reality, it is a series of photographs of drawings. A drawing has no real depth, only an appearance, and some drawings (notably cartoons) intentionally avoid even the appearance. So you have flat surfaces upon which a totally unreal movement appears to take place.

As a matter of pure speculation, I would say that without color these UPA pictures would not have succeeded; for color supplied what we might miss and accentuated the good things that we saw. In a wall of neutral color a rectangle of brightest blue was a door; colors distorted in a mirror showed us what the short-sighted Mr. Magoo imagined he saw. Sometimes a house is merely diagramed in white or brown, or with lines of different colors; sometimes all the rainbow is called on for a rich contrast. Color in the first years of UPA had the freshness and the innocence of the early Disneys; it came from a child's colorbox used with discretion and delight. (One thing Disney did which was beyond the UPA resources: when a hurricane or a whirlwind of passion started Donald in pursuit of an enemy, when a cyclone threatened Mickey and Minnie Mouse, these characters would take off, as characters always do in comic strips, in their equivalent of "a cloud of dust." Miraculously the Disney artists made this real, for as the characters moved faster, all the color in them changed and amalgamated until it became like a rubbing of crayons, the whole outline of the figures gone and the quality of the color changing as they gathered speed. The first time I saw this effect I felt that at last I understood the theory of relativity—for here the speed at which an object moved had altered its qualities; since Disney had shown it to me and it seemed perfectly logical, I need no longer worry at the thought of a yardstick being more or less than thirty-six inches long under certain circumstances. As usual, the "omnipotence effect" of the animated cartoon had brought a high degree of satisfaction.)

The satisfactions created by UPA are of two kinds. One is parallel to that of any other cartoon organization—a series in which a familiar figure appears. In UPA's case, it is Mr. Magoo, the myopic gentleman out of whose misfortunes you would have thought no comedy should be drawn. The comedy really lies in Mr. Magoo's sublime confidence and, of course, in his eventual success; it lies in his irascible scolding of other people for not looking where they are going, in his conviction that he has done the right thing when he takes off in the fire truck instead of the examiner's car to demonstrate his right to a driving license. The situations are ingenious, the drawings and the combinations of line and color are enchantments to the eye, and the tone of almost violent high spirits is exhilarating.

The other UPA cartoons are single shots with a wide range. In addition to the famous Gerald, who did things like sound effects with his voice, there was the child who demanded a jet plane under threat of turning himself into a rooster if refused. Another was about a child whose mother was going to have (or perhaps did have) a baby. A remarkably sound psychological lesson was conveyed in this cartoon with astounding virtuosity in its dream sequence, an intelligent use of symbolic images, and a wonderful scene at a circus in which the whole audience was like a painted curtain of faces, moving in unison as faces do at tennis matches at Forest Hills. And, among others, there has been *The Unicorn in the Garden*, a beginning perhaps of a whole series of Thurber. It moved intellectually out of the field of the usual cartoon, having a point, but it stayed well within the mode of comedy. *The Telltale Heart*, macabre in handling to match the material, was not entirely successful, but entire success was not to be looked for, and the question remaining is still whether a medium so "unreal" is suited to material as real in its significance as Poe's story or, to take another example, Orwell's *Animal Farm*. This was done by the British team of Halas and Batchelor, who have at times shown a light palette similar to UPA's, but in this satirical work chose to be somber, to work in semi-darkness much of the time, and to follow too literally a not-too-inspired original story. It was as if Disney's menagerie had suddenly turned pedantic, and I felt all the time that you cannot have animals in cartoons without letting us have at least a little fun out of them.

Outside of the field of entertainment, UPA has done the most entertaining TV commercials and also films for industry; some of these have been so good that they have been shown in regular movie houses. A film on cancer and when to be afraid of it, a film on the oil industry which was a brief history of the United States, and others have been as impressive in their way as the films made for fun.

The coda to the story of the cartoon is that Disney has for several years been making films of the actual lives of animals. At the beginning he insisted on making his animals behave the way his menagerie used to behave; by skillful cutting he could time the movements of a bear scratching his back or a beaver flapping his tail to the beat of a familiar piece of music, or the croaking of frogs, with the pulsation of their throats, would become a male chorus. This trick has been somewhat abated and Disney has gone forward to make serious reports on animal life in America, pictures of restrained power with just enough showmanship to make them popular. These reports grew gradually longer until a full-length feature, *The Living Desert*, was produced, and this held its own in the smaller houses at least. It was nice to know that Disney had found something interesting and important to do. Continuing these features, Disney also turned to television and won a dazzling and deserved success. He used his old materials and developed new ones; he made his television program an advertisement for a playground he had built in California; some of his material was not first-rate. But he was bold and enterprising. Even before he was established, he refused to conform to routine. Into his time period he put different kinds of programs—animation or movie, comedy or fact—until his Davy Crockett series (a straight filmed program) captured the imagination of the country. By that act he told a dreadful truth about the producers of those children's programs which were vile and violent and were presented "because children wouldn't look at anything else"—the truth being that their producers were not only liars but men of no talent whatever.

604

I said at the beginning of this brief history that the animated cartoon could be considered typical of the popular arts. It was typical of the best product in these arts because the trained and critical mind was totally in sympathy with the innocent spirit in admiring the cartoon and, in fact, the uninstructed turned away from the ill-conceived later features of the Disney studio, not as decisively as the critics did, but in a substantial way. All the stale equations in which good and bad and popular and highbrow figure were exploded by Disney first and by UPA later. At the same time the influence of technology on the arts was made visible in the various phases of Disney's work—from simple black-and-white through color to lavish and superfluous use of color. In the next phase the economics of the business affected the techniques of UPA by forcing them to use fewer masterframes and flat backgrounds, restoring some of the original freshness. The whole progression is a warning to us never to despair and equally a warning never to be satisfied with the second-rate, for the first-rate can be at least as popular.

1956

JOE ADAMSON
SUSPENDED ANIMATION

I've just seen *Charlotte's Web*, and I want to say that any society which considers this a cute film and suitable to show to children is surely on the verge of collapse. This betrayal of the beautiful art form talented men labored decades to develop has generally been greeted as if it were a movie. "All the characters are delightful, as are the drawings, the colors, the songs, and, of course, the story itself," recommends *Good Housekeeping*. "The movie is beguiling. The children will love it," says *Time* Magazine. And *Newsweek* even goes so far as to gush, "This one leaves you with a warm afterglow."

Is there nowhere to turn? The kind of fraud Hanna and Barbera (the producers of *Charlotte's Web*) shamelessly palm off on innocent children every day (in TV series like *The Flintstones* and *The Jetsons*) is now brought to the neighborhood theater, and critics, charmed all to pieces by a film with no gratuitous violence in it, call it beguiling. It's like seeing "Hee Haw" gone filmic, and the newspapers applauding clean entertainment. Now Hanna-Barbera Productions has a new boom on, and *Charlotte* will spawn progeny, to outrage afresh every lover of real cartoons, and to leave *Newsweek* with a warm afterglow.

And the funny part of it is, there was a time when Hanna and Barbera made Tom & Jerry cartoons for MGM, and in all the beautiful animation that was turned out in the 40's and 50's, there was none to equal theirs. They have since discovered that it is easier to get rich by marketing quick-frozen imitations to somnam-

Above, Tex Avery's *Little Rural Riding Hood* (1949) and *below* Chuck Jones's *Robin Hood Daffy* (1958).

"Cartoon directors were always faced with . . . their own alternative to physical reality. The action in an animated cartoon is so completely under the director's control that it becomes a medium in which the film-maker's imagination not only *can* run absolutely riot, but *has* to . . ." (ADAMSON, page 611). "The one kind of movie which triumphantly asserts its non- or super-reality" (SELDES, page 594).

bulist pre-teeners who were not alive to see the great stuff come alive before them on the screen.

Charlotte's Web, see, is about this pig named Wilbur and his horror at the thought of being butchered when September comes. Most of the film concerns the plight of Wilbur and the efforts of the barnyard mammals, geese, and insects to save his life. Now, it's no secret to you or me that hundreds of pigs are slaughtered every day, and if we're going to watch an hour and a half of one pig's attempts to preserve himself, there ought to be something *pretty special* about that pig, to provide a willing suspension of disinterest. But there's nothing special about Wilbur, not the way Hanna and Barbera have pictured him. He's a mummy to start with. The complimentary adjectives which Charlotte the Spider weaves into her web may spook out the countryside, but there's no reason why they should fool anybody who's been watching the movie. A really good cartoon would get me all absorbed in Wilbur's personality, so that I couldn't bear the thought of anybody killing him. If it was, let's say, *Porky Pig* they were going to butcher, I'd be perfectly horrified.

But the funny part of that is: Porky Pig doesn't exist. (Sorry, Virginia.) Where did I ever get the unreal idea that this character who never lived could ever die? It was all in my imagination. Or, better still, in the imaginations of the Warner Brothers Cartoon Wizards who endowed him with life.

The great cartoons of that era managed to put powerful characters into funny situations and spice them up with dynamic visuals as a matter of *course*. They would throw in things like individual style, cinematic experimentation, and, most amorphous, that innate artistic sense by which one perceives the world and transforms it into a vision of itself—just as marginal, unpaid-for fringe benefits. A reliable assaying of gems like *Bad Luck Blackie*, *Baton Bunny*, *Kitty Kornered*, and *Back Alley Oproar* will reveal that Agee's famous "Comedy's Greatest Era" did not end with *The Bank Dick*, but instead transferred its domain from the literal to the fantastic.

At that time, Warner Brothers Cartoons were directed by clever men like Friz Freleng, Bob Clampett, Bob McKimson, and Chuck Jones. And especially Chuck Jones. *My Little Duckaroo* (1954) opens with one shot rich in the kind of witty detail Jones was good at: Daffy Duck sits proud and erect on horseback, his noble beak arching forward in grim determination, to meet his noble hat, sloping downward in sultry languor; his left hand elegantly twisted into a lampoon of a horsemanship display; his kerchief floating gauzily like an aftermath behind him; his steel eyes steeling themselves for the trouble his steely gaze is sure to invite; his demure horse, an equine peacock, high-stepping like a ballerina, blushing at the preposterous grandeur he is all too clearly a part of. Behind him, stuttering, Porky Pig (as a character named Comedy Relief) sings, "The Flower of Gower Gulch."

There was a time when this sort of thing was taken for granted. Only now is it beginning to dawn on people that beautiful effects like this don't just *happen* in a magical place called Hollywood. Daffy was a fascinatingly neurotic character in Jones' hands, forever shouldering one absurd costume after another and going out to try and convince the world that he really was Protector of the Weak, or The Scarlet Pumpernickel, or Duck Dodgers of the 24½th Century. It soon becomes clear that he is none of these things, or he wouldn't spend so much time announcing that he is. Daffy becomes one of those people who isn't satisfied just to live his life, and so must establish for himself an ideal existence in the remotest outposts of his head, and, in the act of acting out Dragnet parodies and Wild West take-offs *(Robin Hood Daffy, Dripalong Daffy, Rocket Squad)*, he fails to live up to his own self-image. He is ironically accompanied in his exploits by a serene Porky Pig, whom he holds in little esteem, and who, less clever but far wiser, is fully aware of the mammoth unimportance of the escapades in which they engage together.

A pig *stood* for something in those days. Poor old Wilbur just stands there.

The ability to create characters out of moving drawings, the ability to set up cats and jackrabbits who assume prior existences and have life after the fadeout, is not a gift God grants to just anybody. The alternating expressions of fear, wonder, terror, dismay, malevolence, bewilderment, withdrawal, determination, defeat, smugness, futility, and wounded pride that register on the physiognomy of the Roadrunner's potential nemesis, The Coyote, are enough to illustrate the point. Chuck Jones' characters are out to prove themselves to an often unconcerned universe. You can see it in their faces. Jones captures his characters in the act of reaching for something just beyond their grasp, of realizing that failure is inevitable, and of trying to tell themselves that it isn't so.

Look at the Coyote. Survival is not in question in his perpetual pursuit of that impossible bird. Most of us, having attempted to capture a roadrunner two or three times and failed, would give up and go chase a rabbit. But he is earnestly trying to prove to himself that such a thing is possible for him. And he has somehow gotten the idea that since simple schemes don't work, complicated ones must be the answer. Yet all he proves is that the more elaborate his preparations, the greater the chances of something going wrong, so that his obsession proves his undoing over and over. And secretly he knows it all the time: this we can tell from the heart-rending looks he gives us at the moment of failure, the haunted face of one who must live with the inevitability of disaster. There he is, staring at the dynamite, watching the impending onslaught of arrows, or, worst of all, sailing off one of those ubiquitous 5-mile cliffs, and nothing to do but submit to his fate—and then go on with the next scheme, momentarily restored by the fadeout, pretending none of this has happened.

The rest of Jones' menagerie display their hurts and fears just as graphically. There is a cat named Claude, who owns one half of a rivalry. Claude, the very picture of Mephistophelean cunning, never fails to get the best of himself by plotting remorseless torments for his chief rival in the household affection sweepstakes: a tiny terrier called Frisky who is too busy enjoying life to even realize there is a feud on, and is equally oblivious to the fact that the strongest, surest weapon is on his own side. All he has to do is bark, and the battle is won. He doesn't bark to be mean, he just barks because he's a dog, but it sends Claude straight to the ceiling every time, his claws stuck frantically into the plaster, his teeth clattering in panic. Two seconds later he is on the ground, mad as a hornet and scheming furiously, but Frisky is too good-natured even to fall for the schemes, and suddenly Claude is on the ceiling again, chattering like Morse Code. Justice, like the timing, is as swift, sure, and irrational as in the Roadrunner series. In cartoons like *No Barking* and *Two's a Crowd*, the action externalizes his internal tensions beautifully. His absolute, helpless fright at advances that so clearly bode no hostility make it painfully clear that

610

his insecurities are hardly going to be solved by plots against a terrier, and that his fate is sealed so long as he goes on viewing the world upside down.

But there was more than character to contend with. Cartoon directors were always faced with the problem of coming up with their own alternative to physical reality. The action in an animated cartoon is so completely under the director's control that it becomes a medium in which the film-maker's imagination not only *can* run absolutely riot, but *has* to, if his films are going to rise to the expectations of the art. The cartoon director is granted a level of freedom that extends in all directions, in every dimension: all the way from deciding what kinds of conflicts will be set up to determining the way the trees will be drawn. But, like any freedom, the freedom of animation brings with it its own responsibility. The stylization, the exaggeration, the free-wheeling disregard for earthly reality are liberating enough for a scene or two, but it's a thrill that can wear out pretty quickly, unless it's given guidance beyond the momentary. The liberation is inherent in the medium; the control is up to the individual director.

Most of them, of course, settle for the comfortable rut of talking cats and mice, and the casual walking on air that comes to a halt when the character realizes the ground is gone. But the better directors don't let unreality get off so easy. Each one of them, when he puts his mind to the task, manages to come up with a separate set of physical laws and behavioral properties that constitutes his own world. Chuck Jones' Coyote can fall five miles from a precipice and still be alive when he gets to the bottom. Tex Avery's wolf could probably endure such a fall, but he is more likely to develop brakes on the way down.

Tex Avery was a mild-mannered madman who directed cartoons at MGM contemporaneously with Hanna and Barbera. He is not famous for any specific character like the Roadrunner, or Tom & Jerry (though he did forge Bugs Bunny's character in his short stay at Warners), but has an underground reputation for isolated masterworks such as *Bad Luck Blackie*, *King Size Canary*, and *Little Rural Riding Hood*. Avery tends to express himself less through his characters than through the outrageous gags that make up his individual world. In *Slap-Happy Lion*, a kangaroo hops into its own pocket and vanishes. In *Billy Boy*, a goat is rocketed to the

611

moon and eats it. In *Northwest Hounded Police*, a fugitive wolf reaches his hideout in the wilderness, slams eight different doors into the same doorway, then turns around and, without uttering a gasp, drops his jaw to the floor with a thud.

Avery's world is the most Rabelaisian, the most fourth-dimensional in the cartoon universe, and his extra-terrestial lunacy is enormously funny and frighteningly vivid (the audience is "mesmerized with horror even as they laugh," says Raymond Durgnat). His comedy style consists of variations on Texas Tall Tales and on the kind of loose-knit panegyrics that used to pass for animation in the depressing days of the silent cartoon.

Once upon a time it was nothing for animated Mutt or Jeff to misplace his head and hardly notice. And Felix the Cat had a passion for detaching his tail and using it as a baseball bat matched only by his fondness for question marks and exclamation points as convenient props. But one is not surprised by such actions when they are carried on by spare little black and white drawings who speak in balloons and whose only audio impact is created by a convivial organist biding his time till the feature starts. One is simply not convinced of their presence. The animated cartoon never really caught on in the silent days, and Avery's cartoons are a good illustration of why: the creation of a specific universe was hardly even possible before the breaking of the soundtrack barrier. When Avery re-works in the 40's the rationale of the 20's we can see the degree to which sound and color (those twin Lucifers who earned the wrath of every God-fearing film aesthetician when they made their first appearance) were Heaven-sent for the particular needs of the cartoon. Avery can pull a gag that was meaningless on the silent screen, but is absolutely overwhelming with the full resources of the film medium behind it. The most unlikely events are suddenly so forceful and convincing that one daren't question them. In Avery's best cartoons, his animation has the power to make the most far-fetched event actually transpire before your very eyes, while his humor has the power to make the weightiest concern vanish in the light of its ridicule. Hallucinations assume the permanence of truths, and truth the shadowy form of hallucination.

One of Avery's favorite tricks is to hyperbolize out of all proportion some patent absurdity that is common to our mental makeup. *Bad Luck Blackie* (1949) ridicules the idea that a strolling black cat bodes trouble for some unwary pedestrian; this ancient superstition is one of those irrational notions we subconsciously accept, all the while knowing full well that it is perfectly senseless. Accompanied by a sprightly rendition of "Comin' Through the Rye," an angular, worldly-wise black cat dances methodically across the path of a treacherous bulldog, and forthwith the dog is beaned with a flowerpot. No source is even hinted at: it has come crashing down in perfect timing and that's that. As the film goes on, the villainous dog meets his various Dooms in the shape of a heavy trunk, a piano, a small bomb, a cash register, four horseshoes (and a horse, looking extremely puzzled), a fire hydrant, a safe, enough bricks to form a wall (which they do), an anvil, the kitchen sink, a bathtub, a steamroller, a passenger plane, a Greyhound bus, and, as a coup-de-grâce, the S.S. Arizona. We have been led in a logical progression from one common, well-accepted absurdity, on into the outward regions of an absurd universe. We can never look that superstition in the face again.

Another conjurer to conjure with is Walt Disney. When Disney set out to make a picture that was "beguiling," he generally succeeded. But it is important to realize that, especially in the 30's and early 40's, his art was not limited to the cuddlesome. At worst, his work was mere technical excellence in place of artistry, but often the artistry was undoubtedly there. In the carefully refined action you will find in a good Disney picture, the levels of subtlety and exaggeration, of exuberance and grace, of action and reaction, of reality and fantasy, merge so harmoniously into a Hymn to Movement that it bears repeated study in slow motion before it can all be absorbed. The "Plausible Impossible" was Disney's own articulation of what he was trying to accomplish by studying the physical principles of earthly movement (inertia, momentum, or the patterns of splashing raindrops) and inventing a stylized version for the cartoon world. The point was to make the fantasy come *alive* for an earth-bound audience, to connect the unreal actions with real human experience, so that the moving drawings up there on the screen had some meaning for the human people out there in their seats.

It was Disney who discovered, for all animators to follow, that establishing vivid characters was the surest means of effecting this

613

transposition. Cartoon characters in the silent days tended to be puppets. In 1933 Disney had the temerity to make a cartoon in which the three main characters looked exactly alike, but were readily distinguishable by their individual personalities, and *The Three Little Pigs* still stands as a milestone in animation. Where anybody else's version of *The Tortoise and the Hare* would have consisted of stale and convenient racing gags, Disney built the whole thing on a character contrast: the cocky hare, simultaneously impressive and annoying, and the pokey tortoise, both pathetic and sympathetic, are characterizations memorable enough to make the point of the story indelible. A mid-30s Disney cartoon like *The Band Concert* may make a clever comment on the self-absorption of musicians, but the great performances in the film belong to Mickey Mouse and Donald Duck, and their animators (Fred Moore and Dick Huemer, respectively) bring freshness and originality to the already-formulated principles of poetic movement and sharp characterization.

In the late 30's Disney began producing a succession of animated features, and sometimes was daring enough to have three in production at once. The whole concept of an animated feature is a touchy question. So long as film historians and critics restrict themselves to the feature film category it will be the only way an animator can attract any attention. But the incredible amount of patience, skill, and care that goes into every second of good animated motion renders the idea of dragging out the effort for a ninety-minute duration practically unthinkable. For this reason, many of Disney's features are more memorable in parts than as wholes, though, considering the peculiarities of the medium, this does not denigrate the level of achievement.

Bambi is probably the strongest and most consistently effective feature-length stretch of animation in existence, and deserves a place as one of the great films. Its naturalistic style of animation (a deer was kept on the studio lot for study throughout production, and stylization in the movement was subtly minimized) admirably suits its tone of devotion to the organic processes of Nature. *Bambi* is the story of innocence rising through adversity to an experienced maturity, and it alternates ingenuous humor with stark terror, its dramatic scenes (the death of Bambi's mother, the battle of the stags, the forest fire) presented with as much honesty and fervor as the "charming" scenes. The film also mixes naturalism with several powerful mythic elements: the human beings, who are treated as a mysterious, purposeless, unseen force, like a cancer on the face of the earth; and Bambi's father, a magnificent, god-like, superego personified, who materializes at moments of travail to summon the young deer's deepest resources and function as a Call to Destiny. In the same way, the rhapsodic texture of the film summons the deepest resources of the animation art, and in the carefully controlled visual exaltation (the opening track through the forest was done on the Multi-Plane camera and was reportedly a $40,000 single shot), every leaf of grass participates in the emotional effect.

Fantasia, another Disney hallmark, is one of those features more memorable in parts than as a whole. While "The Sorcerer's Apprentice" is a shining example of every one of the magical powers of this limitless art, "The Pastoral Symphony" is an encyclopedia of the mediocrities to which Hollywood often resigns itself.

But if *Fantasia* offers its delights piecemeal, no piece of the meal could be more enchanting than the "Night on Bald Mountain" segment, which (though hardly "delightful" in the *Good Housekeeping* sense), presents a phantasmagoria of grotesqueries that illuminates the dark side of human nature such as few demonic works have been able to do before or since. The images of evil in "Bald Mountain" are so uncompromised by any Mickey Mouse concept of cartooning (valkyries with bare breasts are even seen to populate the grimacing hillside) that you would think this sequence would have killed for Disney his cutey-pie stigma singlehanded. The awesome character of the Devil (designed by Albert Hurter and animated, with a respect for weight and power, by Bill Tytla), and the grisly visual distortions of the subsidiary demons (worked out by effects animators like Ub Iwerks and Joshua Meador) are demonstrative of the kind of visual magnificence Disney was able to achieve by organizing the work of many talented men in the direction of a single visual concept. When the subordinate ogres are coerced into hideous transmogrifications, and the Devil's eyes behind them burn *through* them, as if they were wisps of smoke, to glare directly at us, we are staring point blank at the awesome, barbarous underside of our own soul.

Fantasia points up, in its parallel of the twin art forms, the many ways in which animation, like music, strikes those chords that lie in the non-verbal realm, and deals with forces deeper within us than we sometimes care to admit. In the many dimensions of animation, the externalization of internal life proceeds in all directions. Ray Harryhausen's miracles with two-foot models in *The Seventh Voyage of Sinbad* and *Jason and the Argonauts* are filled with ingenious insights into such uncommon experiences as what it would be like to be a giant, one-eyed humanoid figure who has to walk on goat legs. Karel Zeman in *Baron Munchausen* and *The Fabulous World of Jules Verne* combines live action, pen and ink drawings, and model work with remorseless creativity that excites the eye and bends the mind. Norman McLaren animates human people in *Neighbors* and *A Chairy Tale* and combines abstraction with reality in unique and startling ways. Alexander Alexeieff moves pins on a pinboard to create the unearthly images in his own *Night on Bald Mountain*. And as far back as 1918, Winsor McCay, the first giant of animation, was turning a news item into a nightmare of Devastation and Despair in *The Sinking of the Lusitania*. In all these cases, flights of fantasy are emotionally charged, with whimsical character touches, whispers of true emotions, wisps of the world we know, to bridge the gulf to the world within, to excite in the mind of the spectator an atrophied spark, and transport him bodily into a new outpost of reality.

1973

ANNETTE MICHELSON
FILM AND
THE RADICAL ASPIRATION

The history of Cinema is, like that of Revolution in our time, a chronicle of hopes and expectations, aroused and suspended, tested and deceived. I came to know and care for film in a city which has traditionally sheltered and animated these hopes and expectations. It is not only the political and intellectual capital of its country, but that of filmmaking, as well. Quite simply, the distance between the Place de l'Opéra and the studios at Joinville is a matter of a subway ride, not of a transcontinental jet flight. I shall ask you to bear this elementary fact in mind because it has determined much of what I would ever have to say about most things. More than that it provides the terms of a general, if somewhat crude, metaphor for my concern today. To speak of Film and the Radical Aspiration is necessarily to evoke instances of convergence and dissociation.

Two statements, first, however: not mine, but drawn from the writings of men of quite dissimilar sensibilities and vocations, living and working at a distance of almost two generations. The first, Benjamin Fondane, a writer and critic, and man of the left, died, when still young, in a German concentration camp. Writing in 1933, he said,

> We are committed with all our strength to the denunciation of a
> world whose catastrophic end seems more than ever before inevi-

This essay, originally delivered as a talk at the New York Film Festival in 1966 and published in another version, has been rewritten specifically for this volume.

table. We demand its rightful liquidation, whether that liquidation produces an irremediable vacuum of nothingness or a sovereign renewal through revolutionary means. Such should be—and this regardless of the deep inner wounds inevitably involved in such an aspiration—the aims of will and consciousness today. . . . As for film, the curve of its development has rapidly ascended, only to sink into an immediate decline. Stuffed to bursting, tricked out with an absurd and meretricious pomp, with every kind of frill imaginable, it has hypertrophied into a monstrous industry. The attraction was merely potential, the magic contained . . . the seeds of an unpardonable decay until, with the abruptness of a volcanic eruption, the huge shambles collapsed beneath the weight of its own emptiness. And yet, the cinema continues to interest us for that which it is not, for that which it failed to become, for its ultimate possibilities. . . . It may be that film is the expression of a society unable to sustain a world . . . of the mind. It may be that this tardily conceived art, child of an aged continent, will perish in its infancy. It may be, too, that the Revolution is not utterly to be despaired of.

The second statement—just one sentence—was written by a Movie Star and published in *Film Culture* a year or two ago. The Movie Star in question, a performer of quite extraordinary charm and originality, is Taylor Mead, and I presume that some of you have seen him in independently produced films. Taylor Mead has said, "The movies are a Revolution."

Film, our most vivacious art, is young enough to remember its first dreams, its limitless promise, and it is haunted, scarred, by a central, ineradicable trauma of dissociation. The attendant guilt and ambivalence, their repressive effects, the manner above all, in which a dissociative principle has been alternately resisted or assumed, converted into an aesthetic principle, the manner in which this resistance or conversion modifies or re-defines cinematic aspirations are, like everything concerning film, unique in the history of western culture.

A dream, a presentiment of the medium, inhabits and traverses the 19th century. Almost every form of popular diversion characteristic of the era—the family album, the wax museum, the novel itself, the panopticon in all its forms—can be read as an obscure, wistful prefiguration of cinema. My own revelation of the wax museum as prefiguration came a year or so ago when I chose, as a

618

Christmas treat, to accompany a bright little American, French-educated boy to the Musée Grevin. It struck me, as we went slowly through the long, dark, labyrinthine corridors, punctuated by the rather grand and spectacular tableaux which chronicle the whole of French history, from early Gauls until the Gaullist regime, that the wax museum, in its very special, hallucinatory darkness, its spatial ambiguity, its forcing of movement upon the spectator, its mixture of diversion and didacticism, is a kind of proto-cinema. And of course the historical mode of discourse is, above all, that of the earliest films which celebrated state occasions, public festivities, followed monarchs to christenings and assassinations. The extraordinary rapidity of the cinema's growth seemed to confirm this vision of a century's wistful fantasy (only seventy years have passed since Méliès witnessed the Lumières' demonstration and produced his own first reel). So, too, did the general climate of anticipatory enthusiasm and accord which animated filmmaking and criticism in their early, heroic period. That climate seems, in retrospect, Edenic.

Consider the atmosphere surrounding the early theoretical discussions: the Eisenstein-Pudovkin debate on the nature of montage, involving the conception of images as "cells, not elements" engaged in dialectical conflicts, as opposed to the "linkage of chains." Or the discussion, somewhat less familiar to historians, of the function of the subtitle as it crystallized during the 1920's in France: Kirsanov's elimination of the title in the interest of visual explicitness, René Clair's reduction of the title's role to the strictest minimum, the stress placed by Desnos and Surrealists on its exclusively poetic use, on the subversion of "sense in the interests of poetry." While the controversy developed—and with the unique intensity and inventiveness which characterise critical discourse in France—technology was preparing to transcend the problem. The claim that the "shriek" or "grinding of brakes" was no less real or "present" for being understood rather than heard was rendered comically irrelevant; the problem was simply cancelled by the arrival of sound.

Generally speaking, however, discussion, fruitful or academic, took place within a context of broad agreement as to the probable or desirable directions of the medium. Styles, forms, inventions and theoretical preoccupations were largely complementary, not contradictory. A spectrum, rather than a polarity of possibilities was involved. The Surrealist's admiration of American silent comedy, reflected in the work of Artaud and Epstein among others, the universal excitement over the achievements of Russian film, Eisenstein's openly acknowledged debt to Griffith, testify to a certain community of aspiration. Eisenstein, in the very beautiful essay on "Griffith, Dickens and the Film Today" said that "what enthralled us was not only these films, it was also their possibilities." And speaking of montage: "Its foundation had been laid by American film-culture, but its full, completed, conscious use and world recognition was established by our films."

The excitement, the exhilaration of artists and intellectuals not directly involved in the medium was enormous. Indeed, a certain euphoria enveloped the early filmmaking and theory. For there was, ultimately, a very real sense in which the revolutionary aspirations of the modernist movement in literature and the arts, on the one hand, and of a Marxist or Utopian tradition, on the other, could converge in the hopes and promises, as yet undefined, of the new medium.

There was, among the intellectuals concerned with cinema's revolutionary potential, both social and formal, a general and touching reverence for an idea of its specificity. There was, above all, an immediate apprehension, cutting quite across theoretical differences, of its privileged status, its unique destiny.

In the celebrated essay on "The Work of Art in the Era of Reproduction Techniques,"* Walter Benjamin attacked as reactionaries, men such as Werfel, who, by relegating the movie to the articulation of fantasy and faery, were engaged in a reduction of its scope, a tactics of repression. The most intensely euphoric expression of the new passion, of the convergence of modernist aesthetics and an Utopian ideology is Elie Faure's "Art of Cineplastics," really an essay in aesthetics-as-science-fiction which predicts the cinema's radical transformation of the very nature of spatio-temporal perception, of historical consciousness and process.

Anticipations and speculations and, more significantly still, the inventions and achievements of the Americans, Russians, French,

---

* This essay appears as the final piece in the present collection under the title, "The Work of Art in the Age of Mechanical Reproduction" [eds.].

Germans and Scandinavians were predicated, then, upon complementary apprehensions of the morphological and syntactical possibilities of the medium evolving within a framework of concord and mutual recognition, shattered, ultimately, by the growing awareness of a principle of dissociation inherent in the art and its situation.

The point of shock is easily located in history: that moment, at the end of the 1920's in which the "hermaphroditic" nature of a craft which had already expanded and hardened into an industry, could no longer be ignored. The classical instrument of industrial revolution being division of labor, a generation of hardy adventurers, artist-entrepreneurs, director-producers, such as Griffith, were replaced by paid employees. The ultimate consequences involved something analogous to a dissociation of sensibility, which, in turn, rapidly engendered a register of limits and conventions that have acted to inhibit, displace, and reshape cinematic effort.

We are dealing with a Fall from Grace. For men like Griffith, Eisenstein, von Stroheim, Welles and many more of the most brilliant and radical talents, it created, as we know, in the gardens of California, an irrespirable atmosphere, a corruption which was to impair much of the best work done anywhere.

Intellectuals and filmmakers alike, here and abroad, reacted with an immediate tension of distrust and, in many instances, withdrawal. The widespread resistance to the introduction of the sound track, for example, could certainly be shown to mask or reflect an hostility to the prospect of the medium's accelerated development into an instrument of mass culture. A French philosopher of my acquaintance claims to have stopped going to the movies in 1929. For Fondane, "the sound film is good only in so far as it is dumb." And for Artaud, "cinematic truth lies within the image, not beyond it." The resistance to sound—and it was a resistance to the Word, not ever to music which had, from the beginning, found a place in cinematic convention—expressed a nostalgia for an era of mute innocence and untested hope. It was, in short, a pastoral attitude.

The disenchantment, the sense of moral and esthetic frustration expressed by Fondane, was general. The history of modern cinema is, nevertheless, to a large degree, that of its accommodation to those very repressive and corrupting forces of the post-1929 situation. A complex register of limits and conventions engendered by that situation has been *productively* used. Historical precedents abound, but few or none have attained a comparable degree of dialectical paradox, intricacy, and scandalousness.

It is the acceptance of the dissociative principle, its sublimation or conversion to aesthetic purposes, which characterise recent, advanced filmmaking in France and elsewhere in Europe. It is the almost categorical rejection of that principle and the aspiration to a radical organicity which animates the efforts of the "independent" filmmakers who compose something of an American *avant-garde*. All discussion of the nature and possibilities of advanced filmmaking today, of film aesthetics and of future possibilities must, I believe, take this divergence into account. It must also take into account the fact that the question is, as Walter Benjamin remarked, "not whether we are dealing with an art" (and some, apparently, still ask that question), "but whether or not the emergence of this medium has not transformed the nature of all art."

The general resistance in this country to the notion of this transformation assumes its most crucial aspect, not in circles unconcerned with film, but rather in those presumably animated by a commitment to its development. The discomfort and hostility of many, indeed most, film critics to those aspects of contemporary cinema which bypass, contradict or transcend the modes and values of psycho-social observation is familiar. The generally *rétardataire* character of our film criticism reflects a regressive anxiety about the manner in which postwar cinema, in Europe and America alike, has, at its best, transcended the conventions of a sensibility formed by the pre-modernist canon of a primarily literary 19th-century. One simply has to face the fact that a great part of a generation who came to maturity in the twenties, who were nourished by and committed to the formal radicalism of a Pound, a Stein or a Joyce, are these days concerned with, let us say, the novels of Saul Bellow and Norman Mailer! If the crux of cinematic development lies—as I think it largely does—in the evaluation and re-definition of the nature and role of narrative structure, we may say that the history of academicism in filmmaking and film criticism has been that of the substitution of novelistic forms and values for theatrical ones— and this in a century which saw a flowering of American poetry.

Critical malaise and contradictions, therefore, quite logically

622

focussed last season on two films of Jean-Luc Godard: *Le Petit Soldat* and *Alphaville*, first presented in New York within the context of the Lincoln Center Festival. I say "logically" because it is precisely in so far as *Alphaville* constitutes a really remarkable instance of a reconsideration of the nature and possibilities of certain narrative conventions that I wish to consider it ever so briefly at this point.

Alphaville is an anxious meditation, in the form of a suspense story, on the agony and death of love, liberty and language in a society which is trapped in the self-perpetuating dialectic of technical progress. It is about feeling in deep freeze. The violent rehearsal of the content-versus-style liturgies which greeted *Alphaville* testified, in negative fashion, to Godard's central importance. Together with a few of his European contemporaries he does dominate cinema now and much of what is done anywhere has to be situated in relation to the work of these men. Above all, however, the complex *statement* of the film in regard to the possibilities of narrative convention transcends, in interest and importance, the nature of its *discourse*, and the hostility displayed towards that *discourse*, I take to represent simply a displacement (or dislocation) of hostility to its formal, cinematic *statement*.

François Truffaut, reflecting somewhat casually on the history of film, once divided its protagonists into two sorts: the creators of *"spectacle"* or entertainment, such as Méliès, and the experimenters or inventors, such as Lumière. To this Godard replied that he had always tried to make "experimental" films in the guise of entertainments. *Alphaville* is such a film. Its conceptual and formal complexities fuse into an elaborate and precisely articulated metaphor of Immanence, of the ambiguity of location and dis-location, in both their spatial and temporal modes.

Paris now, her public buildings, offices, hotels, garages, corridors, staircases and escalators are revealed as invaded by the Future. Frontiers between past, present and future are—like the distinctions between invention and entertainment—abolished through a series of formal strategies: a *prise de conscience* secured through a *prise de vues*. This film, shot entirely on location, is the film of dis-location. And as narrative structure, lighting, cutting, produce a visual, temporal or situational transformation, so a continual play with language transforms things known and seen.

Thus, the low-income housing developments of post-1945 Paris, known as *Habitations à Loyers Modiques* are the clinics and insane asylums of the future: *les Hôpitaux des Longues Maladies*. The city's peripheral avenues, *les boulevards extérieurs*, shift and expand into an irrevocably disquieting suggestion of the routes of interplanetary space. Function and scale of object and place are continuously altered, as image and sound converge upon site and situation in the exploration of the cinematic figuration of dislocation, of the ambiguities of time and history. One thinks of Gertrude Stein: "Composition is not there, it is going to be there and we are here. *This is some time ago for us naturally.*" The shifting—within—simultaneity of sameness and difference, of being and going-to-be, while we *are*, "some time ago, naturally," structures the time-space within which the mind (and *Alphaville* is *"about"* the birth of mind and sensibility, the rebirth of language as a rebirth of love) is constrained to function: that of a dislocation with respect to time. The "past-future" tense of which Godard speaks is our *present situation*.

The progress or plot of *Alphaville*, is, therefore, the passage from one revelation to another; its peripeties are perceptions, structured by the pace and tension of a detective story, of "finding truth." In the face of this, the accusations of "triviality" or "pretentiousness" became embarrassingly irrelevant. The film "states" its concern with the creation of a morphology; the concentration is on pace, tension, weight and syntactic coherence through narration— narration being in this instance a form of "relating" in the fullest possible sense of the word: a manner of creating *relational* strategies through *telling*.

Alphaville constitutes a remarkable instance of a critical allegiance, shared by the major European filmmakers, to the conventions of Hollywood's commercial cinema, and of the conversion of those conventions to the uses of advanced cinema. For the allegiance has acted as context and pre-condition of formal radicalism. (And it is interesting to consider that Godard's attachment to the Monogram film, the "B series" production, is paralleled, or anticipated, by Eisenstein's life-long affection for the early films that began to come to Russia when he was a boy. He speaks with tenderness of films like *The House Of Hate* and *The Mark of Zorro*.) The importance of the suspense story, as refined by Hitchcock for the further use of men such as Resnais and Godard, lies in its paradigmatic character as narrative form, as a "vehicle" of dramatic and formal invention. Perfected in the Hollywood of an era following upon the Fall, it was adopted and refined, sublimated in the interests of a formal radicalism.

The earliest, and certainly the most sumptuous, anticipation of this strategy is Feuillade's *Vampires*, shown in its entirety here for the first time during last year's New York Film Festival. Together with *Alphaville*, it dominated the occasion. Made by a man of utterly intrepid imagination, its formal inventiveness is supported by a firm commitment to a notion of film as a technique of narrative for a mass public. I have discussed elsewhere the manner in which *Vampires* not only sets forth the themes developed in *Alphaville*, and the way in which the cinema of Méliès and Feuillade adumbrated, within the context of the medium's earliest stages, the principles and strategies of which Surrealist art and film provided a subsequent development.

"Please believe me," said Feuillade, "when I tell you that it is not the experimenters who will eventually obtain film's rightful recognition, but rather the makers of melodrama—and I count myself among the most devoted of their number. . . . I won't in the least attempt to excuse (this view). . . . I believe I come closer to the truth." It was strict adherence to the logic of this view which guaranteed, for Feuillade, a margin of improbability, of open-ness, of that oneiric intensity which gives *Vampires* its place among the masterworks of cinema.

Predicated on the development of a narrative convention both strict and elastic enough to accomodate a tension between dramatic probability and fantasy—between discourse and poetry—Feuillade's work opens out upon the future of film rather than upon its past. Which is to say, as Robbe-Grillet has said, that "Imagination, when really alive, is always of the present." And we might find a partial confirmation of this in Alain Resnais' fascination with Feuillade. Resnais' work, like that of his European contemporaries, perpetuates the commitment to the constraints and stimuli of a given form; above all, in its straining of the limits of that form, it exemplifies a commitment to the value of Form as such which animates the best of advanced European cinema today.

Now, if we assume, as I shall, that the revolutionary aspiration, *aesthetic and political*, achieved a moment of consummation in the Russian film of the twenties and early thirties, we know, too, that the paradigmatic fusion was dissolved by the counter-revolution of Stalinism. As this happened (and the installation of Stalinism in its more or less definitive form is contemporary with the introduction of sound into film), European cinema and European art as a whole abandoned a certain totality of aspiration. The process of dissociation, the split between formal and political aspects of radical or revolutionary efforts, was created, irremediably so—at least through our time. The result was either reaction, or a sublimation of the revolutionary aspiration into a purely formal radicalism. The vestiges of the politically revolutionary experience and tradition are henceforth expressed in the form of nostalgia and frustration. Politically oriented art at its best became a chronicle of absence, of negation, an analysis of dissociation, and, in the best modernist tradition, a *formal statement of the impossibility of discourse.*

The nostalgia and frustration are explicitly stated in Godard's *Le Petit Soldat*, by Michel, the hero: "In the early thirties, young people had the revolution. Malraux, for example, Drieu la Rochelle and Aragon. We don't have anything any more. They had the Spanish Civil War. We don't even have a war of our own." The formal articulation of this nostalgia for a revolutionary impulse and hope involves a succession of fascinating paradoxes and failures. The case of Resnais, who almost alone of his particular generation has attemped to articulate a strong personal political commitment, is particularly fascinating. I have in mind not only *Hiroshima* but *Muriel.* In both films he has visible difficulty in situating the commitment within the total structure of his work, in finding a visual trope that will not inflect the style, or distend the structure. The result is a rhythmical, dramatic, and visual caesura, the stylistic articulation of aphony.

The two explicitly political passages in these films are both distanced, bracketed as spectacles or diversions. In *Hiroshima* the anti-war demonstration is inserted as a film sequence enacted within the film, while in *Muriel*, the Algerian war is evoked, not shown, in an amateur movie, by an agonised verbal commentary (the account of a young girl's torture by French soldiers) in counterpoint to the series of innocuous amateur shots which parody the myth of barracks'-life hilarity.

This sequence constitutes the most brilliant, the definitive articulation of the disintegration of a cinematic arena for political discourse. The despair over that disintegration is the film's central political "statement." The "statement's" intensity, however, is further amplified through the further distancing of the bracketed statement from *itself* (the distance between image and commentary). Its isolation within the texture of the total work, its particular, stylistic disjunctiveness, its own colourless colour, are slightly at odds with the disjunctiveness and invented colour of the whole. Through a speculative and stylistic refraction Resnais proposes an image of the shameful scandal which generated the Fifth Republic. His trope is that of the caesura. The crack, the flaw, the rhythmic, visual gap or caesura created by this interlude or "diversion" is the *form* of Resnais' declaration of aphony. It declares his nostalgia for the film which could *not* be made; it renders the artist's struggle with the dissociative principle and its politics.

And it is fascinating, but distressing beyond telling, to see, in *La Guerre Est Finie*, Resnais' ultimate attempt to assume what he obviously regards as the discursive responsibility of his position, the diabolical logic of that principle in operation. Like *Alexander Nevsky*, *La Guerre Est Finie* is the chronicle of an artist's defeat; it represents a total inversion, the most concrete negation of a form and style. In this film, it is the erotic sequences which assume the aspect of interludes or diversions within the total structure, and the bracketing or distancing is achieved through a reversion to a hieraticism of style we have, of course, known and loved: that of *Hiroshima* and, above all, of *Marienbad*. These passages now produce the caesuras which arouse our nostalgia. Far more painfully, however, they declare Resnais' *own* nostalgia for his past achievements. *Vivement Harry Dickson!*

Lucien Goldmann, writing a few years ago in *Les Temps Modernes* of the supposed atrophy of historical and social consciousness in the New Wave directors, remarked with a sigh that political energy and vitality seemed concentrated in the Left, while cinematic talent was reserved for the Right. Goldmann's characteristically Lukacsian conservative taste and aesthetics aside, the problem needs to be restated—and far more explicitly than one can do here and now. Most briefly put, however, one might formulate it in the following manner: if, for the young Russians of the immediately post-Revolutionary period the problem was, as Eisenstein said, "to advance towards new and as yet unrealized qualities and means of expression, to raise form once more to the level of ideological content," the problem for Resnais and his peers is to accommodate ideological content to the formal exigencies of a modernist sensibility. Ultimately, ideology of any kind—whether that of Surrealism, Marxism, or the anti-humanism of the New Novel— provides, at best, a fruitful working hypothesis for the artist. Eisenstein's conception of montage as the triadic rehearsal of the Dialectic was aesthetically regenerative. The energy, courage and intellectual passion which sustained both theory and work were, of course, among the noblest of our century. Eisenstein is a model of the culture of our era—in his defeat as in his achievement, and down to the very fragmentary quality of his work!

There is a passage in his writings and it is the most tantalizing page he has bequeathed us—in which he describes a cinema of the mind, a film "capable of reconstructing all phases and all specifics of the course of thought."* He is shifting, at this point, from a pristine conception of "intellectual cinema" which had culminated in a projected film version of *Capital*, a rendering of analytic method, to another aspiration, more complex, even more problematic: the rendering of the movement of consciousness itself. He envisages the filmic "interior monologue" as the agent of the dissolution of "the distinction between subject and object," first undertaken in the novels of Eduard Dujardin, that "pioneer on the stream of consciousness," a dissolution completed in the work of Joyce. *Ulysses*, then, becomes the other prime Utopian project of the 1930's out of which Eisenstein's notion of "intellectual cinema" continues to be refined. He informs us, in his excitement, of a period of preliminary work upon his script for *An American Tragedy*, another project of that period which stimulated this sort of speculation, and of the "wonderful sketches" produced in the process.

> Like thought, they would sometimes proceed with visual images. With sound. Synchronized or non-synchronized. Then as sounds. Formless. Or with sound-images: with objectively representational sounds . . .
> Then suddenly, definite intellectually formulated words—as "in-

---

*Sergei Eisenstein, *Film Form, Essays in Film Theory*, ed. and trans. by Jay Leyda, New York: Harcourt, Brace and World, p. 105.

tellectual" and dispassionate as pronounced words. With a black screen, a rushing imageless visuality.

Then in passionate disconnected speech. Nothing but nouns. Or nothing but verbs. Then interjections. With zigzags of aimless shapes, whirling along with these in synchronization.

Then racing visual images over complete silence.

Then linked with polyphonic sounds. Then polyphonic images. Then both at once.

Then interpolated into the outer course of action, then interpolating elements of the outer action into the inner monologue.

As if presenting inside the characters the inner play, the conflict of doubts, the explosions of passion, the voice of reason, rapidly or in slow-motion, marking the differing rhythms of one and the other and, at the same time, contrasting with the almost complete absence of outer action: a feverish inner debate behind the stony mask of the face.

. . . The syntax of inner speech as distinct from outer speech. The quivering inner words that correspond with the visual images. Contrasts with outer circumstances. How they work reciprocally . . .

And Eisenstein ends by noting that "These notes for this 180° advance in sound film culture languished in a suitcase — and were eventually buried, Pompeii-like, beneath a mass of books. . . ." There they remained. Sound was to take Eisenstein in quite another direction, to the splendidly hieratic exacerbation of *Ivan the Terrible*.

This buried page, however, might figure as a blueprint for a cinema that was still to come. Its affirmation of disjunction, of abstraction, of the shifting relations of image and sound, its stress on polyphony, upon the use of silence and of the black screen as dynamic formal elements are familiar to us: Eisenstein, in a dazzling leap of the imagination, had invented on paper the essential tenor, the formal strategies of American Independent Cinema of our own last two decades.

It is exactly nineteen years — about the time we say we take to come of age — since "Cinema 16," a pioneer film society presenting work by artists of the independent persuasion to a New York audience, held a symposium on "Poetry and the Film." The proceedings, published in somewhat abridged form,* constitute a

---

The Film Culture Reader, P. Adams Sitney, ed., Praeger Publishers, New York, 1970.

document of enormous and multiple interest. Re-reading it now one is startled by an intensity and level of exchange to which we have grown unaccustomed in the present proliferation of such occasions; the text now stands as a major document of the period, a chapter in a polemical mode of the intellectual history of its time, its scene.

That time, that scene are the early '50's, and here are its players: Parker Tyler, a film critic already distinguished and actively involved, from the time of its wartime exile in New York, in the Surrealist tradition; Willard Maas, filmmaker; Arthur Miller, then the white hope of a certain native theatrical realism and Dylan Thomas, the visiting star performer of that period are there as "prose" and "poetry." With Maas acting as chairman or "moderator," as we've come to say, film and film-as-poetry are most strongly represented by Maya Deren, unquestionably one of the most gifted filmmakers and theoreticians of her generation.

The occasion fuses and opposes forces, notions about what such an occasion might be, its use, pre-suppositions about the conventions of a possible discourse on film. Inscribed within it, by the way, is the plain evidence of what it was to be both a woman and an independent filmmaker at that time—someone exposed to the lordly contempt affected by intellectuals for seriousness in film and seriousness in women. Thomas' wit and grandstanding joviality are thus directed against Deren's passionate attempt to define a subject about which they might profitably converse.

Miller, less narcissistic and more interesting, has obviously given more thought to the general matter at hand and there is, near the end, a remarkable moment, when he suddenly says, "I think that it would be profitable to speak about the special nature of any film, of the fact of images unwinding off a machine. Until that's understood, and I don't know that it's understood (I have some theories about it myself), we can't begin to create on a methodical basis, an aesthetic for that film. We don't understand the psychological meaning of images—any image—coming off a machine. There are basic problems, it seems to me, that could be discussed here." The remarks are offered, most likely, as antidote to what Miller obviously considers to be the questionable rhetoric of Deren's poetics, but the trajectory towards the assumption of that challenge is, of course, the history of our American filmic avant-garde and the re-examination of the materiality, the conditions and practical contingencies of filmmaking and projection have inflected an avant-garde which moves from the psychological to the epistemological mode of discourse.

Deren had proposed the poetic film as representing "an approach to experience in the sense that a poet is looking at the same experience that a dramatist may be looking at." Distinguishing it somewhat more specifically, she describes it as "vertical" in structure, "an investigation of a situation, in that it probes the ramifications of the moment, and is concerned with its qualities and its depth, so that you have poetry concerned, in a sense not with what is occurring but with what it feels like or what it means. A poem to my mind, creates visible or auditory form for something that is invisible, which is the feeling, or the emotion or the metaphysical content of the statement. Now it also may include action, but its attack is what I would call the vertical attack, and this may be a little bit clearer if you will contrast it to what I would call the horizontal attack to drama which is concerned with the development, let's say, within a very small situation from feeling to feeling. Perhaps it would be made most clear if you take a Shakespearean work that combines the two movements. In Shakespeare, you have the drama moving forward on a 'horizontal' plane of development of one circumstance—one action leading to another and this delineates the character. Every once in a while, however, he arrives at a point of action where he wants to illuminate the meaning to 'this' moment of drama and, at that moment, he builds a pyramid or investigates it 'vertically' if you will, so that you have a 'horizontal' development with periodic 'vertical' investigations which are the poems, which are the monologues. Now if you consider it this way, then you can think of any kind of combination being possible. You can have operas where the 'horizontal' development is virtually unimportant—the plots are very silly, but they serve as an excuse for stringing together a number of arias that are essentially lyric statements. Lieder are, in singing, comparable to the lyric poem, and you can see that all sorts of combinations would be possible."

One thing we note immediately: Deren is defining poetry in a manner quite natural, indeed endemic in her time, as being exclusively of the lyric mode. And referring to the tradition of the "lied," she assumes this as well to be quite unrelated to or disengaged from, the narrative. Though one might argue that view of "Gretchen am Spinnrade," one might dispute it for "Der Erlkonig." She is arguing, in any case, passionately and well for something one does sense as fundamental for her and her time. In positing her horizontal and vertical structures, she is positing disjunctiveness against linearity, claiming for film the strategic polarity of discourse which Jakobson, examining the structure of speech through its disorders in aphasia, proposed in the metonymic and metaphoric modes. Some questions, then: are such polarities valid, do they hold, do they concern us here and now?

We may now say, I think, "No, they are not and do not," but the last of these three questions is the one of major interest to us and demands our assent.

These polarisations serve to crystallize for their own time the thinking, feeling and, above all, the working impulse of a major film-maker initiating a tradition of criticism. Deren's concern with the lyric was essentially a step towards a radical revision of filmic temporality as a source of formal innovation. Reflecting 19 years later upon the best and most innovative of recent work in this country, one realizes that its common critical context is to be found not through definition of aspects of style or texture—not even that style and texture which have been called "structural"—but rather through the recognition that the best of recent work takes its place as an extended moment in a continuum of inquiry, constituting the most recent and most complete interplay of "verticality" and "horizontality" within that continuum.

Deren's own preoccupation with the "vertical" begins as an extension of that extraordinary intuition of film's temporal vistas which inserts within the literally split (spliced) second of a tower's crash, that odyssey of a "poet" whose "blood" had congealed, somehow, into a film. And that "Poet" had, indeed, spattered himself over that film's entire surface. Here is the model of his appearance: the narrator's voice, the signature, the plaster masks of hand and of face, the wire mask revolving in space, the autobiographical tableaux, the autobiographical incidents climaxing in a snowball fight which intensifies the referential dimension, recapitulating as it does the opening scene of an already celebrated work, *Les Enfants Terribles*. And then there is the opening dedication, the injunction to read, to decipher, the work as a coat of arms, the homage paid in the "Poet's" name, to the masters of Renaissance perspective from one who confesses his reluctance to "deform" space. Fearing no doubt the "Caligarism" which was the French film world's name for an expressionism more generally feared and detested, the Poet confines himself to a play, an assault upon the time of action while respecting its spatial integrity.

Deren, then, arguing for "her" "personal," "vertical," "poetic" film was to work in a direction which reversed Cocteau's. Rather than splice a moment through a moment of time in which she could insert the integrality of a film, she attempted to work with the moment, distending it into a structure of exquisite ambiguity, underwritten by the braver spatial strategies that came perhaps more easily to the developed kinetic sense of a dancer.

It then came to Stan Brakhage to radicalize the revision of filmic temporality in positing the sense of a continuous present, of a filmic time which devours memory and expectation in the presentation of presentness. To do this one had, of course, to destroy the spatio-temporal coordinates by which past and present events define themselves as against each other. The assault of Brakhage upon the space of representation, then, is the final and most radical break with that spatial integrity which Cocteau had been at pains, neo-classicist that he was, to preserve. It consummates the break with narrative structure, and Brakhage now moves into the climate of expressionism, pushing the abstractive process, contracting the depth of the visual field to the point where he destroys the spatiality of narrative, redefining time as purely that of vision, the time of appearance. In doing so he replaces the scene of action by the screen of eidetic imagery, projecting, as it were, the nature of vision itself as the subject of a new temporal mode. His editing style, at once assertive and uniquely fluid, creates that "convergence of a hundred spaces" which Klee had called for and which only a radically redefined cinematic temporality could provide. It is Utopian.

Doing this, Brakhage was to do more still—re-examining the photographic and projective processes themselves, opening them up as it were, reclaiming them for inclusion in the total work. Thus, in an unmailed proposal written for the Guggenheim Foundation:

> These films would be created not only with a sense of the projected experience but also (as in all my work recently) with an eye to their

speaking just as strips of celluloid held in the hand and to the light which can illuminate their multi-colored forms. They will be created out of the deepest possible conviction that such a viewing (or any other, such as a frame at a time through a slide projector) can and should be so integral with the projected experience as to add another dimension to that projected experience. Please understand that I arrive at such a conclusion from a working relationship with film and a realization that all my significant splices (adding moving image to moving image) are the result of viewing the film to be edited both through the editor at an approximate 24 frames a second and also as stilled strips of film. Similarly, out of an aesthetic understanding of time relativity, I have the sense that my finished films should be viewable either 16 frames a second or 24 frames a second. Very recently I have begun working toward a filmic realisation which will retain its integral form (considering the structure of the work of art as integral with all its emotional and intellectual statements) even when run backwards.*

The assault, then, upon the space of representation is accompanied by a reclamation of the elements and materials of the filmmaking and film-viewing experience, an extension of the ways in which light may be projected through the film, the creation of another surface through which the image is perceived, the painting, scratching or application of "foreign matter" to the surface of the film so that our heightened sense of a surface through which the image is viewed brings with it the heightened sense of the illusionism in which that apperception is grounded. All this, then, meant proposing—as Stein had done—that everything, including the materiality and contingencies of the making process, was food for poetry.

It is this proposal—and, though a curious prank of history— Arthur Miller's, that is accepted and developed in the best of recent work. The assertion of the still photographic frame composing the strip, the assertion, through the flicker, of the medium as projection of light, the assertion of the nature of projection through the use of sound, the assertion of the persistence of vision in the work of Jacobs, Sharits, Frampton, Gehr, Landow, Wieland and Snow, propose the terms of an epistemological concern with the nature of filmic process and experience which will require another space, another time, those of a new cinematic discourse.

---

*Stan Brakhage, "Metaphors on Vision," *Film Culture*, No. 30, Fall 1963.

For that discourse, then, spatio-temporal co-ordinates had to be re-invented and they quite naturally have been. In *Wavelength*, in the empty loft traversed by the zoom, Snow, voiding the film of the metaphoric proclivity of montage, re-creates a grand metaphor for narrative form. In the re-definition of "action" as the investigation of space through camera movement, Snow redefined the filmic form as the narrative of "one thing leading to another." *La Région Centrale* explores a landscape, pushes one's sense of space inward, obliterating the coordinates once again in the interests of an increasingly kinetic sense of seeing. Frampton plays in *Nostalgia* on the tension of past and present, of memory and expectation. Jacobs, distending the time and space of *Tom, Tom, the Piper's Son*, inscribes within a single work a history of film. Gehr, positing, in *Still* a space which we must interrogate, saying to ourselves, "Where is the surface in relation to which I am seeing what I see?" thereby poses the question of the time and space which might contain the multiple duration of superimposition. Landow, playing viewing against reading and reading against mis-reading, multiplies the modes of perception in time. Sharits substitutes or exchanges, as in *N.O.T.H.I.N.G.*, cause for effect. And Wieland prints and holds 1933, a static sign of time whose existence is made problematic by the continuous action in her loop film.

The cinema of *this* time, then, articulates an investigation of the terms of cinematic illusionism. It turns, from the fascinated consciousness of the eidetic, lyric mode, to precisely that "course of genuine investigation" which so preoccupied Eisenstein in his speculations upon the nature of "intellectual cinema" as instantiating the dynamics of analytic consciousness, recalling to us the view of Marx: "Not only the result, but the road to it also, is a part of the truth. The investigation of truth must itself be true; true investigation is unfolded truth, the disjunct members of which unite in the result."*

1966;   revised 1973

---

*Sergei Eisenstein, *The Film Sense*, ed. and trans. by Jay Leyda, New York: Harcourt Brace and World, p. 82.

VI

The Film Artist

Otis Ferguson's essay, "Before the Cameras Roll," vividly demonstrates the overwhelming variety of considerations, both commercial and personal, that influence the making of a Hollywood movie. When this *New Republic* critic of the late 1930s and early 40s traveled west to Hollywood, he was amazed by the number of workers who contributed to the final product—the producer, the writers, the director, the researchers, the costume designers, the musicians, the cinematographer, the cutters, and the special effects men. The question necessarily arises: How can a work of art result from such varied intentions and collective labor? Many argue that it could not possibly issue from such collective chaos, and they regard the products of Hollywood as mere commercial entertainments that cannot be compared to the "art films" of Europe or the "underground" works of the personal, experimental filmmaker.

One reply to this argument is to deny that a purely aesthetic intention or the vision of a single artist is necessary to create a work of art. Panofsky specifically compares the making of a film to the building of a cathedral, for the cathedral was built for the greater glory of God and was the result of the collective labor of as many specialists as a Hollywood film. François Truffaut, beginning in 1954 with his *Cahiers du cinéma* essay, "On Certain Tendencies in the French Cinema," developed an opposite response to the collective labor of filmmaking. His *"politique des auteurs"* defended the Hollywood studio film by maintaining that, although unappreciated or even unnoticed, the work of an author, an *auteur*, could be seen in many Hollywood films. This *auteur* was not the film's script writer, as many French film critics believed at the time, but the film's director, whose "signature" could be discerned by the sensitive critic who bothered to look for it. Truffaut's aim in this and succeeding articles was not to posit a general theory of film value; the pieces were polemics, specific reactions against contemporary French film critics and their valued style of French film-making, the "tradition of quality," which extolled the polished literary adaptations of such scenarists as Aurench and Bost *(La Symphonie Pastorale, The Red and the Black, The Idiot)* at the expense of the genuinely cinematic thinking of Jacques Tati, Jean Renoir, or Robert Bresson.

According to what has become known as the *"auteur* theory," the director's "style" or his "basic motifs," as the British critic Peter Wollen calls them, can be discerned by viewing his work as a whole—for these marks of directorial authorship will manifest themselves in all of a true *auteur's* films, even as he works with different writers, cinematographers, and stars. Andrew Sarris, the primary American spokesman for the *auteur* theory, suggests that not only is the distinguishable personality of the director a criterion of value, but that the "meaning" which he is able to impose on the material with which he must work is the "ultimate" glory of the cinema. This observation raises a problem, however, concerning Wollen's two key terms—"style" and "basic motifs." Does Sarris mean that the "ultimate" glory is a director's imposition of "style" (e.g., the use of deep-focus photography) on a film's given "basic motifs" (e.g., domestic melodrama) or does he mean that the glory is the director's imposition of a "style" that elicits new "basic motifs" (i.e., the meaning of love) from that melodrama? If the latter, does Sarris realize that the same can be said of any artist (say, Shakespeare in *King Lear* or *Othello*)? If the former, does Sarris mean that a director whose films deal with trash stylishly is an artist worthy of our attention?

Pauline Kael's reply to Sarris's "Notes on the Auteur Theory in 1962," is fiercely critical of Sarris's original version of the *auteur* theory— precisely because of the fuzziness about content and style. First, she finds it platitudinous to observe that one can find an artistic "signature" or "basic motifs" in the work of an artist. Critics in all the arts assume that the artist has such a "signature," otherwise they would not bother to study him at all. Besides, as she observes, the sheer distinguishability of an artistic personality has no bearing on the value of that personality or his work. What an artist's works have in common may simply be signs of his ineptitude or his limitations. Finally, she thinks, there is something perverse about admiring an artist for managing to make an artistic silk purse out of the sow's ear of Hollywood trash. Isn't the true artist responsible for the choice of his materials and for finding an appropriate form for his chosen subject?

Although Kael's refutation of Sarris is largely correct, it is worth remarking that those who proposed the *auteur* theory were not simply arguing that an artist's personality will manifest itself in his works. They were seeking to establish that there was, indeed, an artist at work where many had never seen one. In doing so, they unquestionably helped to establish or re-establish the reputations of certain directors who worked within the Hollywood system, directors who did not exert much more control over the total project than many studio hacks, but who managed to make the kind of personal, significant statement that John Ford or (as Peter Wollen shows) Howard Hawks did. But Sarris's insistence on the sheer value of an artist's triumphing over his material seems a mistake, even from Sarris's own point of view. This is a useful strategy for rescuing some Hollywood reputations, but it lays the wrong groundwork for demonstrating the merits of the directors that Sarris (and almost everyone else) most admires. Directors such as Lubitsch, Renoir, Chaplin, Welles, and Keaton in fact enjoyed a large measure of individual control over scripts, shooting, and cutting. One does not, as Kael puts it, admire these directors for "shoving bits of style up the crevasses of the plots." In extending Truffaut's defense of the effective Hollywood studio director to cinema in general, Sarris has betrayed its limitations. His more recent writings on the theory have realized these very limitations and have softened or modified many of his original contentions. Although these modified positions are more judicious critical statements, they seem less interesting as theoretical claims—and have certainly been less influential on critical thinking—than his original, most extreme ones.

There are other problems with a director-centered theory. If a director's signature can be discovered by a careful examination of all his works, this is equally true of certain screen writers, cinematographers, and stars. Often the mark they leave on a film will be greater than that of its director. Both Gerald Mast and Richard Corliss point out, for instance, that a film whose script is written by a Preston Sturges or a

Norman Krasna will more likely display their personality than that of its director, say a Mitchell Leisen. Similarly, Richard Koszarski argues that various studio styles and even the Hollywood style itself is better explained by the dominance of certain cinematographers than it is by reference to any directors or group of directors. In this same spirit, Pauline Kael's now famous essay, "Raising Kane," consciously attacks the *auteurist's auteur* and the *auteurist's auteur*-film by developing in detail the crucial contributions of *Citizen Kane*'s writer (Herman J. Mankiewicz), its cinematographer (Gregg Toland), and its leading actor (Welles the actor not the *auteur*).

Indeed, the most serious difficulty for any theory of the film *maker* as artist is the fact that many stars have made the most decisive contributions to the Hollywood films in which they have appeared, and that their unique "presence" can also be determined by viewing the totality of their works. In *The World Viewed* Stanley Cavell remarks how surprising he found the *auteur* theory, for it never previously occurred to him that anyone *made* a Hollywood film. For Cavell, the world of film revolved about, and was determined by, the star. When the European semiologist, Roland Barthes, writes of Garbo's "face," he implies that it is the main object of interest and the main conveyer of meaning in most of the films in which she appears. Kenneth Tynan, the British film and theatre critic, observes that "often during the decade in which [Garbo] talked to us, she gave signs that she was on the side of life against darkness: they seeped through a series of banal, barrel-scraping scripts like code-messages borne through enemy lines." And Charles Affron, the American professor of Romance Languages as well as the author of *Star Acting*, argues that Garbo's power and personality were such that her communicative face, body, and gestures triumphed over a series of different directors, indifferent scripts, an autocratic studio, and even over the Hollywood Production Code, which had been written to restrict the inherent sexual mystery that was the essence of her art. Affron claims that Garbo used the 1934 Hollywood Code in the same way that Racine used the seventeenth-century Code of Classical Decorum in *Phèdre*, to "provide a focus for artists whose techniques thrive on indirection, on restriction, on concentration."

It may be, as Sarris observes in *The American Cinema*, that the film will most likely fulfill the criterion of being a unified work of art when the director dominates. But even this claim, however plausible and pragmatic, has not been established either by the arguments of the *auteur* theorists or by the complex facts of the history of the American film. For every *Modern Times*, which is obviously the work of a single artistic vision, there is a *Casablanca*, whose success may be the result of its director, of the men who conceived the original script, of the writer who amended that original script and wrote much of the dialogue, of its male star, of the particular chemistry between its male and female stars, or of some mysterious compound of all those elements.

OTIS FERGUSON
BEFORE THE CAMERAS
ROLL

The worst things that happen in pictures happen previous to the
first day of actual shooting, usually. In many cases they happen
before the story is considered and bought. Yet these things are vital
in the art of making pictures, and though they may be improved,
I know of no happy state where they may be eliminated, just in the
nature of things.

In the book of How to Make a Picture, item one is, first get
an audience. To get and hold a body of followers large enough to
support this fabulous expense in production is the prime moving
force of the whole industry, however clumsy its lunges and however many times it cuts its own throat out of jealousy and mean-
ness. Audience support is the one reason for the emergence of men
with talent and push enough to go against the current (you'd never
have heard of them in a closed subsidy); it is responsible for both
the best and the worst, and I do not know how many thousands of
times someone has said, as I have heard them: I made that one so
I could make them give me this one. At the same time it has been a
powerful brake on the tendency of all art toward obscure faddism;
American writers and directors have had to learn to do it the hard
way, and it is the way they have learned to tell stories with a camera and a pair of cutting scissors which has come to lead the world,
to influence the technique of even the best filmmaking everywhere.

But that is all in the what-I-think-about-the-moon realm of pic-
turemaking. The audience is there. It is always there. It is there now
in such a steady multiple vigor that anybody with a brass voice and

craft enough to promote one or two thousand can make the world's worst picture and get away with it (the world's worst picture either will never be made or is made every second Monday after the first Tuesday). But to understand the relationship between those who pay their money to see, and those who make, buy, sell, distribute, and exhibit, you will have to be familiar with the subject or read some of the books in its endless library: this is not the class for beginners, and there is not space here for a subject so wide and intricate. The point is that any understanding of the making of any single picture demands this background of for-whom and to-what-end — as who in civilization would listen to his mouth clapping up and down on the subject of Shakespeare and think himself a critic if he had never so much as heard of the terms Elizabethan, Renaissance, Globe, Holinshed, buskin, blank verse? We must simply remember that when the act of creation involves a thousand people and a million dollars, and wonders of science too deep to see, there must be some kind of monumental and sometimes monstrous plant set up to manufacture and purvey this entertainment for millions.

The plant is Hollywood as a center with lines running out over the world, and the second chapter in the book is: To make a picture you have to have the backing *and* equipment. Now in most cases, the backing comes from one of the major or minor established companies. Not because it comes more readily, and certainly not because it will give you any scope to work in, but because these companies control the channels of distribution — you want to make a picture but you want it to be seen too, don't you? There is a long history of seesaw and confusion in this struggle for the upper hand as between the man who shows and the man who makes the shows. Great companies have swallowed up minor companies by buying up theater chains, *i.e.*, the means of their expansion and their competitors' dwindling revenue; great companies have then staggered under the load and gone down. Great chain owners have tried to dominate the companies, bought them or starved them out, and then failed because they had dried up the very thing they were selling at its source. Men like William Fox, not essentially a picture man, have grown to giant size in the field of build-and-buy-and-produce-for-it, and then been chivvied out by the bankers. The bankers have seen those billions lying around and got in to pick them up, only to discover that their brusque pirate's idea of how to run a picture studio left out the ingredient of how pictures could be made. In the long and varied contest, it is always the working producers who win out in the end. Individuals among them are constantly losing their shirts, but those who make pictures and know pictures must have the final say, as a whole. They are the geese who lay those golden eggs; bankers, exhibitors, distributors, operators, and the like can lay eggs only in the figurative sense. So helpless are they, one after the other, that you take as accepted such facts as that little Shirley Temple alone saved the farflung glory of Twentieth Century-Fox; that Deanna Durbin, also alone, kept Universal off the bread line.

The golden egg itself, of course, is the patents racket. So much costly and marvelous equipment is necessary in the processes of building cameras, making sound and color, that it was impossible the original small inventors or owners should not be bought or buried, until some powerful and unscrupulous monopoly like the American Telephone and Telegraph Company controlled or tied up all the patents being used in some important process or other, and naturally will never sell anything outright because the lease is so rich, beyond fable. Or that an outfit like Electrical Research Products Incorporated should not only control patents but own studios and lend money and generally be the people you have to see, always at your cost. There is du Pont too. There is Eastman. Names fill the sky like buzzards.

The best analysis of these financial, and all-powerful, ends of the business will probably be Leo Rosten's forthcoming book, though from what very little I know of it, it will not have understanding of the philosophy of showmanship, which has no philosopher. The best book on the movie man as operator is still *Upton Sinclair Presents William Fox*—an amazing book but again deficient in knowledge of movies, their cause and effect. For the strange rank growth of the industry in general through the early days, the book is Terry Ramsaye's *Million and One Nights*, if you can read it and remember that Ramsaye is on the whole a journalist whose feet hurt and that he works today as the right hand of the practically unspeakable Martin Quigley. Thousands have fussed and fumed, but I doubt anything else has been written with much pertinence to the forbidding factual mountain of make and sell, buy and beat the drum.

645

To go back to where we came from, you *can* go to one of the picture-loan promoters and prove to his satisfaction that you have an idea for a picture which will sell, and get financing. In that case you rent a studio and equipment at exorbitant cost, and make the picture, hiring your writers, directors, actors, and so forth. And then you get into the problem of what a picture is, what it takes.

The picture always starts at the beginning, which is (1) a writer's idea, (2) a successful book or play if you can buy it, (3) in some other studio. The toughest on the writer, and often on the public, is when the idea comes from a producer and is therefore not an idea —such not being his business—but an impulse. Budd Schulberg has written in these very pages how he and Scott Fitzgerald were sent by Walter Wanger to Hanover to cook up a story "around" Dartmouth simply because Walter Wanger went to Dartmouth and hasn't got out from under it yet. You didn't think that was an exception? Or the story I told last time about the producer who had an idea which boiled down to the title *Tomorrow's Generals*. Or the big-company executive who says, There's a lot of interest in the Lindbergh kidnaping, and it's safe by now, only it can't be Lindbergh and it can't be a kidnaping. Or the company which says, We are due for an ice-carnival picture, or a Colbert picture, or a non-gangster picture, or something like an Abbot and Costello, or something like what the hell is the name of that musical Fox is cleaning up on, or a period picture—everybody's still hot for the Civil War after *Gone with the Wind*.

On the whole it is the writer who takes the big rap. Stuff is shoved at him which should never even be considered for pictures, yet he must make a screenplay out of it because the company has money tied up in it and he is tied up with the company, just for the living. It will be done and will go out under his name, and I think it was Sidney Skolsky who broke the story about two writers coming home from work at Republic, one saying: "*You* take the credit title on this one; I had to take it last time." Or the writer shapes up a good screenplay and then has one to five expensive names called in to jigger it all out of true. Or he does some good work and everybody says that is really good work, and the picture is never made, and two months later the same everybodies are saying, Yes, I know, but I don't seem to remember the name.

Whatever the actual genesis, the picture has to start with a writer. If he has an idea of his own, fine, he will sell it as an original and maybe clean up by doing what is called the treatment on salary. But most of the time he has no time for ideas of his own. The company wants a Western, a South Sea Islands, a Hedy Lamarr, or some damn thing. It's a book or a play or a magazine series the company has on the shelf; it has to be done to write off a book loss that would worry the bankers; and it may have to be stretched to include a big deathbed sequence in the gutter at Tia Juana because Paramount has just finished with a whole Mexican street and square they built, and have it uneasy on their hands; or it may have to have a sea episode, to make use of the white-elephant tank and enormous ship models Korda has on his hands over at General Service.

You have a picture cooking, and you have a producer. You have to have a producer because that is the movies' middleman. He takes care of promoting the money, hiring the sound stages, the director, the actors; figuring costs and time elements, getting the thing cut and sound-tracked, ready and distributed. The producer may work in one of three ways. He may be a free-lance, completely free-lance, trusting in his own judgment to make a picture in the expectation that it will be good enough to force the big chains to buy and show it. He may be a semi-free-lance, a man who has got his own unit, and his own say in everything (the everything is a pipe dream) on a major lot. He may be just a yes-man to the executive in charge of production—and that is what he usually is. But in the present setup he is there, taking the responsibility for smash or flop; and the present setup is not considered all to the good by the men who make pictures, more and more of whom are taking over the producer's job themselves, demanding: Give the movies back to us, the moviemakers.

The independent producer is up against long odds. He may move in on, say, RKO. He has his own writers, director. But wait. It is very hard to tell where the equipment you are renting stops: you rent the carpenters, grips, gaffers, cameramen, sound men; why aren't you renting the chiefs of these departments? The director-producer either spends valuable days fighting it out with the front office or uses the company men. He may be somebody like Sam Goldwyn, who has a name that will strike anybody to silence, but even after his picture has been made, he has to fight United Artists on the way it is released, delayed, and generally hamstrung.

Or he may be a producer who is making a picture for one of the majors, and finds that although he has signed his director and stars, as of now, as of high salaries starting today, he has a rather weird time getting the stages and the general go-ahead from the company anxious to produce his production. What goes? After a while of negotiations he finds out. The producer has his own female lead signed up; the company does not mention her. After a few days of objecting to the story or the Toronto sequence, the company calls him up, surprise! With envy and with wonder it says, Why you lucky dog, you, we've *got* it. Are you lucky? Listén, get this: we just found we haven't a lead spot for May Bonnet, and, get this, you can have her! Jesus what a lucky guy. May Bonnet!

So he guessed it all along. May Bonnet is the cow this company signed a contract of $60,000 for two pictures and wants to pull out of making the second with, the first was so sad. They were stuck with her and they were doing the holdup on the producer who wanted to make a picture for them. And the final arrangement, the producer knowing necessity when he saw it, was that he bought the remainder of May Bonnet's contract for $30,000, tore it up, and told her to go back to her telephone and stay there, all alone, and found stages available for his picture with his own lead, and enough red ink to write the three-o into the budget.

But when a picture is started, many departments get to work, outside of the producer with his balances and arrangements, the writer and director dreaming up the story they are to tell (if the director is a fair name and not on the Metro or Warners' payroll — which is to say, lucky). The research department gets the script, and looks up the likeness with wonderful pertinacity and skill. The art department gets the green light and the art director delegates his draftsmen, painters, model builders, and curators to work up a rough draft, scene by scene, and then practically the whole picture in drawings, in miniatures, in paintings and models. These men build the thing you see, and change it as the camera requires; but it is always the art director himself who has laid it out, it is his department that has sketched out and painted in the things you see, from beautiful to bum. You have to have an art director, if only because he is the man who sees it in advance and starts the wheels moving for its realization.

Then there is sound, and with sound comes the musical director, who works after the picture has been made. He is a vital man in a picture's effect—at least he is when he is good enough and given any freedom; but like the cutters and special-effects men, he is not at work until after the cameras start rolling. You have to catch him later.

1941

ANDREW SARRIS
NOTES ON
THE AUTEUR THEORY IN
1962

I call these sketches Shadowgraphs, partly by the designation to remind you at once that they derive from the darker side of life, partly because, like other shadowgraphs, they are not directly visible. When I take a shadowgraph in my hand, it makes no impression on me, and gives me no clear conception of it. Only when I hold it up opposite the wall, and now look not directly at it, but at that which appears on the wall, am I able to see it. So also with the picture I wish to show here, an inward picture that does not become perceptible until I see it through the external. This external is perhaps not quite unobtrusive, but, not until I look through it, do I discover that inner picture that I desire to show you, an inner picture too delicately drawn to be outwardly visible, woven as it is of the tenderest moods of the soul.

SØREN KIERKEGAARD, in *Either/Or*

An exhibitor once asked me if an old film I had recommended was *really* good or good only according to the *auteur* theory. I appreciate the distinction. Like the alchemists of old, *auteur* critics are notorious for rationalizing leaden clinkers into golden nuggets. Their judgments are seldom vindicated, because few spectators are conditioned to perceive in individual works the organic unity of a director's career. On a given evening, a film by John Ford must take its chances as if it were a film by Henry King. Am I implying that the weakest Ford is superior to the strongest King? Yes! This kind of unqualified affirmation seems to reduce the *auteur* theory to a game of aesthetic solitaire with all the cards turned face up. By *auteur* rules, the Fords will come up aces as invariably as the Kings will come up deuces. Presumably, we can all go home as soon as the directorial signature is flashed on the screen. To those who linger, *The Gunfighter* (King 1950) may appear worthier than *Flesh* (Ford 1932). (And how deeply one must burrow to undermine Ford!) No matter. The *auteur* theory is unyielding. If, by definition, Ford is invariably superior to King, any evidence to the contrary is merely an optical illusion. Now what could be sillier than this inflexible attitude? Let us abandon the absurdities of the *auteur* theory so that we may return to the chaos of common sense.

My labored performance as devil's advocate notwithstanding, I intend to praise the *auteur* theory, not to bury it. At the very least, I would like to grant the condemned system a hearing before its execution. The trial has dragged on for years, I know, and everyone is now bored by the abstract reasoning involved. I have little in the way of new evidence or new arguments, but I would like to change some of my previous testimony. What follows is, consequently, less a manifesto than a credo, a somewhat disorganized credo, to be sure, expressed in formless notes rather than in formal brief.

I. AIMEZ-VOUS BRAHMS?

> *Goethe? Shakespeare? Everything signed with their names is considered good, and one wracks one's brains to find beauty in their stupidities and failures, thus distorting the general taste. All these great talents, the Goethes, the Shakespeares, the Beethovens, the Michelangelos, created, side by side with their masterpieces, works not merely mediocre, but quite simply frightful.*
>
> —LEO TOLSTOY, *Journal*, 1895–99

The preceding quotation prefaces the late André Bazin's famous critique of *"la politique des auteurs,"* which appeared in the *Cahiers du Cinéma* of April, 1957. Because no comparably lucid statement opposing the *politique* has appeared since that time, I would like to discuss some of Bazin's arguments with reference to the current situation. (I except, of course, Richard Roud's penetrating article "The French Line," which dealt mainly with the post-*Nou-*

velle Vague situation when the *politique* had degenerated into McMahonism.)

As Tolstoy's observation indicates, *la politique des auteurs* ante-dates the cinema. For centuries, the Elizabethan *politique* has decreed the reading of every Shakespearean play before any en-counter with the Jonsonian repertory. At some point between *Timon of Athens* and *Volpone*, this procedure is patently unfair to Jonson's reputation. But not really. On the most superficial level of artistic reputations, the *auteur* theory is merely a figure of speech. If the man in the street could not invoke Shakespeare's name as an identifiable cultural reference, he would probably have less contact with all things artistic. The Shakespearean scholar, by contrast, will always be driven to explore the surrounding terrain, with the result that all the Elizabethan dramatists gain more rather than less recognition through the pre-eminence of one of their number. Therefore, on balance, the *politique*, as a figure of speech, does more good than harm.

Occasionally, some iconoclast will attempt to demonstrate the fallacy of this figure of speech. We will be solemnly informed that *The Gambler* was a potboiler for Dostoyevsky in the most literal sense of the word. In Jacques Rivette's *Paris Nous Appartient*, Jean-Claude Brialy asks Betty Schneider if she would still admire *Pericles* if it were not signed by Shakespeare. Zealous musicologists have played *Wellington's Victory* so often as an example of inferior Beethoven that I have grown fond of the piece, atrocious as it is. The trouble with such iconoclasm is that it presupposes an ency-clopedic awareness of the *auteur* in question. If one is familiar with every Beethoven composition, *Wellington's Victory*, in itself, will hardly tip the scale toward Mozart, Bach, or Schubert. Yet that is the issue raised by the *auteur* theory. If not Beethoven, who? And why? Let us say that the *politique* for composers went Mozart, Beethoven, Bach, and Schubert. Each composer would represent a task force of compositions, arrayed by type and quality with the mighty battleships and aircraft carriers flanked by flotillas of cruisers, destroyers, and mine sweepers. When the Mozart task force collides with the Beethoven task force, symphonies roar against symphonies, quartets maneuver against quartets, and it is simply no contest with the operas. As a single force, Beethoven's nine symphonies, outgun any nine of Mozart's forty-one symphonies, both sets of quartets are almost on a par with Schubert's, but *The Magic Flute*, *The Marriage of Figaro*, and *Don Giovanni* will blow poor *Fidelio* out of the water. Then, of course, there is Bach with an entirely different deployment of composition and instrumentation. The Haydn and Handel cultists are moored in their inlets ready to join the fray, and the moderns with their nuclear noises are still mobilizing their forces.

It can be argued that any exact ranking of artists is arbitrary and pointless. Arbitrary up to a point, perhaps, but pointless, no. Even Bazin concedes the polemical value of the *politique*. Many film critics would rather not commit themselves to specific rankings ostensibly because every film should be judged on its own merits. In many instances, this reticence masks the critic's condescension to the medium. Because it has not been firmly established that the cinema is an art at all, it requires cultural audacity to establish a pantheon for film directors. Without such audacity, I see little point in being a film critic. Anyway, is it possible to honor a work of art without honoring the artist involved? I think not. Of course, any idiot can erect a pantheon out of hearsay and gossip. Without specifying any work, the Saganesque seducer will ask quite cynically, "Aimez-vous Brahms?" The fact that Brahms is included in the pantheon of high-brow pickups does not invalidate the industrious criticism that justifies the composer as a figure of speech.

Unfortunately, some critics have embraced the *auteur* theory as a short-cut to film scholarship. With a "you-see-it-or-you-don't" attitude toward the reader, the particularly lazy *auteur* critic can save himself the drudgery of communication and explanation. Indeed, at their worst, *auteur* critiques are less meaningful than the straight-forward plot reviews that pass for criticism in America. Without the necessary research and analysis, the *auteur* theory can degenerate into the kind of snobbish racket that is associated with the merchandising of paintings.

It was largely against the inadequate theoretical formulation of *la politique des auteurs* that Bazin was reacting in his friendly critique. (Henceforth, I will abbreviate *la politique des auteurs* as the *auteur* theory to avoid confusion.) Bazin introduces his arguments within the context of a family quarrel over the editorial policies of *Cahiers*. He fears that, by assigning reviews to admirers of given directors, notably Alfred Hitchcock, Jean Renoir, Roberto

653

Rossellini, Fritz Lang, Howard Hawks, and Nicholas Ray, every work, major and minor, of these exalted figures is made to radiate the same beauties of style and meaning. Specifically, Bazin notes a distortion when the kindly indulgence accorded the imperfect work of a Minnelli is coldly withheld from the imperfect work of Huston. The inherent bias of the *auteur* theory magnifies the gap between the two films.

I would make two points here. First, Bazin's greatness as a critic, (and I believe strongly that he was the greatest film critic who ever lived) rested in his disinterested conception of the cinema as a universal entity. It follows that he would react against a theory that cultivated what he felt were inaccurate judgments for the sake of dramatic paradoxes. He was, if anything, generous to a fault, seeking in every film some vestige of the cinematic art. That he would seek justice for Huston vis-à-vis Minnelli on even the secondary levels of creation indicates the scrupulousness of his critical personality.

However, my second point would seem to contradict my first. Bazin was wrong in this instance, insofar as any critic can be said to be wrong in retrospect. We are dealing here with Minnelli in his *Lust for Life* period and Huston in his *Moby Dick* period. Both films can be considered failures on almost any level. The miscasting alone is disastrous. The snarling force of Kirk Douglas as the tormented Van Gogh, the brutish insensibility of Anthony Quinn as Gauguin, and the nervously scraping tension between these two absurdly limited actors, deface Minnelli's meticulously objective decor, itself inappropriate for the mood of its subject. The director's presentation of the paintings themselves is singularly unperceptive in the repeated failure to maintain the proper optical distance from canvases that arouse the spectator less by their detailed draughtsmanship than by the shock of a *gestalt* wholeness. As for *Moby Dick*, Gregory Peck's Ahab deliberates long enough to let all the demons flee the Pequod, taking Melville's Lear-like fantasies with them. Huston's epic technique with its casually shifting camera viewpoint then drifts on an intellectually becalmed sea toward a fitting rendezvous with a rubber whale. These two films are neither the best nor the worst of their time. The question is: Which deserves the harder review? And there's the rub. At the time, Huston's stock in America was higher than Minnelli's. Most critics expected Huston to do "big" things, and, if they thought about it at all, expected

Minnelli to stick to "small" things like musicals. Although neither film was a critical failure, audiences stayed away in large enough numbers to make the cultural respectability of the projects suspect. On the whole, *Lust for Life* was more successful with the audiences it did reach than was *Moby Dick*.

In retrospect, *Moby Dick* represents the turning downward of Huston as a director to be taken seriously. By contrast, *Lust for Life* is simply an isolated episode in the erratic career of an interesting stylist. The exact size of Minnelli's talent may inspire controversy, but he does represent something in the cinema today. Huston is virtually a forgotten man with a few actors' classics behind him surviving as the ruins of a once-promising career. Both Eric Rohmer, who denigrated Huston in 1957, and Jean Domarchi, who was kind to Minnelli that same year, somehow saw the future more clearly on an *auteur* level than did Bazin. As Santayana has remarked: "It is a great advantage for a system of philosophy to be substantially true." If the *auteur* critics of the 1950's had not scored so many coups of clairvoyance, the *auteur* theory would not be worth discussing in the 1960's. I must add that, at the time, I would have agreed with Bazin on this and every other objection to the *auteur* theory, but subsequent history, that history about which Bazin was always so mystical, has substantially confirmed most of the principles of the *auteur* theory. Ironically, most of the original supporters of the *auteur* theory have now abandoned it. Some have discovered more useful *politiques* as directors and would-be directors. Others have succumbed to a European-oriented pragmatism where intention is now more nearly equal to talent in critical relevance. Luc Moullet's belated discovery that Samuel Fuller was, in fact, fifty years old, signaled a reorientation of *Cahiers* away from the American cinema. (The handwriting was already on the wall when Truffaut remarked recently that, whereas he and his colleagues had "discovered" *auteurs*, his successors have "invented" them.)

Bazin then explores the implications of Giraudoux's epigram: "There are no works; there are only authors." Truffaut has seized upon this paradox as the battle cry of *la politique des auteurs*. Bazin casually demonstrates how the contrary can be argued with equal probability of truth or error. He subsequently dredges up the equivalents of *Wellington's Victory* for Voltaire, Beaumarchais, Flaubert, and Gide to document his point. Bazin then yields some

655

ground to Rohmer's argument that the history of art does not con-firm the decline with age of authentic geniuses like Titian, Rem-brandt, Beethoven, or nearer to us, Bonnard, Matisse, and Stravin-sky. Bazin agrees with Rohmer that it is inconsistent to attribute senility only to aging film directors while, at the same time, honor-ing the gnarled austerity of Rembrandt's later style. This is one of the crucial propositions of the *auteur* theory, because it refutes the popular theory of decline for aging giants like Renoir and Chaplin and asserts, instead, that, as a director grows older, he is likely to become more profoundly personal than most audiences and critics can appreciate. However, Bazin immediately retrieves his lost ground by arguing that, whereas the senility of directors is no longer at issue, the evolution of an art form is. Where directors fail and fall is in the realm not of psychology but of history. If a director fails to keep pace with the development of his medium, his work will become obsolescent. What seems like senility is, in real-ity, a disharmony between the subjective inspiration of the director and the objective evolution of the medium. By making this distinc-tion between the subjective capability of an *auteur* and the objec-tive value of a work in film history, Bazin reinforces the popular impression that the Griffith of *Birth of a Nation* is superior to the Griffith of *Abraham Lincoln* in the perspective of timing, which similarly distinguishes the Eisenstein of *Potemkin* from the Eisen-stein of *Ivan the Terrible*, the Renoir of *La Grande Illusion* from the Renoir of *Picnic in the Grass*, and the Welles of *Citizen Kane* from the Welles of *Mr. Arkadin*.

I have embroidered Bazin's actual examples for the sake of greater contact with the American scene. In fact, Bazin implicitly denies a decline in the later works of Chaplin and Renoir and never mentions Griffith. He suggests circuitously that Hawks's *Scarface* is clearly superior to Hawks's *Gentlemen Prefer Blondes*, although the *auteur* critics would argue the contrary. Bazin is particularly critical of Rivette's circular reasoning on *Monkey Business* as the proof of Hawks's genius. "One sees the danger," Bazin warns, "which is an aesthetic cult of personality."

Bazin's taste, it should be noted, was far more discriminating than that of American film historians. Films Bazin cites as unques-tionable classics are still quite debatable here in America. After all, *Citizen Kane* was originally panned by James Agee, Richard Griffith, and Bosley Crowther, and *Scarface* has never been regarded as one of the landmarks of the American cinema by native critics. I would say that the American public has been ahead of its critics on both *Kane* and *Scarface*. Thus, to argue against the *auteur* theory in America is to assume that we have anyone of Bazin's sensibility and dedication to provide an alternative, and we simply don't.

Bazin, finally, concentrates on the American cinema, which invariably serves as the decisive battleground of the *auteur* theory, whether over *Monkey Business* or *Party Girl*. Unlike most "serious" American critics, Bazin likes Hollywood films, but not solely because of the talent of this or that director. For Bazin, the distinctively American comedy, western, and gangster genres have their own mystiques apart from the personalities of the directors concerned. How can one review an Anthony Mann western, Bazin asks, as if it were not an expression of the genre's conventions. Not that Bazin dislikes Anthony Mann's westerns. He is more concerned with otherwise admirable westerns that the *auteur* theory rejects because their directors happen to be unfashionable. Again, Bazin's critical generosity comes to the fore against the negative aspects of the *auteur* theory.

Some of Bazin's arguments tend to overlap each other as if to counter rebuttals from any direction. He argues, in turn, that the cinema is less individualistic an art than painting or literature, that Hollywood is less individualistic than other cinemas, and that, even so, the *auteur* theory never really applies anywhere. In upholding historical determinism, Bazin goes so far as to speculate that, if Racine had lived in Voltaire's century, it is unlikely that Racine's tragedies would have been any more inspired than Voltaire's. Presumably, the Age of Reason would have stifled Racine's neoclassical impulses. Perhaps. Perhaps not. Bazin's hypothesis can hardly be argued to a verifiable conclusion, but I suspect somewhat greater reciprocity between an artist and his *zeitgeist* than Bazin would allow. He mentions, more than once and in other contexts, capitalism's influence on the cinema. Without denying this influence, I still find it impossible to attribute X directors and Y films to any particular system or culture. Why should the Italian cinema be superior to the German cinema after one war, when the reverse was true after the previous one? As for artists conforming to the spirit of their age, that spirit is often expressed in contradictions, whether between Stravinsky and Sibelius, Fielding and Richardson, Picasso and Matisse, Chateaubriand and Stendhal. Even if the artist does not spring from the idealized head of Zeus, free of the embryonic stains of history, history itself is profoundly affected by his arrival. If we cannot imagine Griffith's *October* or Eisenstein's *Birth of a Nation* because we find it difficult to transpose one artist's unifying conceptions of Lee and Lincoln to the other's dialectical conceptions of Lenin and Kerensky, we are, nevertheless, compelled to recognize other differences in the personalities of these two pioneers beyond their respective cultural complexes. It is with these latter differences that the *auteur* theory is most deeply concerned. If directors and other artists cannot be wrenched from their historical environments, aesthetics is reduced to a subordinate branch of ethnography.

I have not done full justice to the subtlety of Bazin's reasoning and to the civilized skepticism with which he propounds his own arguments as slight probabilities rather than absolute certainties. Contemporary opponents of the *auteur* theory may feel that Bazin himself is suspect as a member of the *Cahiers* family. After all, Bazin does express qualified approval of the *auteur* theory as a relatively objective method of evaluating films apart from the subjective perils of impressionistic and ideological criticism. Better to analyze the director's personality than the critic's nerve centers or politics. Nevertheless, Bazin makes his stand clear by concluding: "This is not to deny the role of the author, but to restore to him the preposition without which the noun is only a limp concept. 'Author,' undoubtedly, but of what?"

Bazin's syntactical flourish raises an interesting problem in English usage. The French preposition "de" serves many functions, but among others, those of possession and authorship. In English, the preposition "by" once created a scandal in the American film industry when Otto Preminger had the temerity to advertise *The Man With the Golden Arm* as a film "by Otto Preminger." Novelist Nelson Algren and the Screenwriters' Guild raised such an outcry that the offending preposition was delected. Even the noun "author" (which I cunningly mask as *"auteur"*) has a literary connotation in English. In general conversation, an "author" is invariably taken to be a writer. Since "by" is a preposition of authorship and not of ownership like the ambiguous "de," the fact that Preminger both produced and directed *The Man with the Golden Arm* did not entitle him in America to the preposition "by." No one would have objected to the possessive form: "Otto Preminger's *The Man with the Golden Arm*." But, even in this case, a novelist of sufficient reputation is usually honored with the possessive designation. Now, this is hardly the case in France, where *The Red and the Black* is advertised as "un film de Claude Autant-Lara." In America, "directed by" is all the director can claim, when he is not also a well-known producer like Alfred Hitchcock or Cecil B. de Mille.

Since most American film critics are oriented toward literature or journalism, rather than toward future film-making, most American film criticism is directed toward the script instead of toward the screen. The writer-hero in *Sunset Boulevard* complains that people don't realize that someone "writes a picture; they think the actors make it up as they go along." It would never occur to this writer or most of his colleagues that people are even less aware of the director's function.

Of course, the much-abused man in the street has a good excuse not to be aware of the *auteur* theory even as a figure of speech. Even on the so-called classic level, he is not encouraged to ask "Aimez-vous Griffith?" or "Aimez-vous Eisenstein?" Instead, it is which Griffith or which Eisenstein? As for less acclaimed directors, he is lucky to find their names in the fourth paragraph of the typical review. I doubt that most American film critics really believe that an indifferently directed film is comparable to an indifferently written book. However, there is little point in wailing at the Philistines on this issue, particularly when some progress is being made in telling one director from another, at least when the film comes from abroad. The Fellini, Bergman, Kurosawa, and Antonioni promotions have helped push more directors up to the first paragraph of a review, even ahead of the plot synopsis. So, we mustn't complain.

Where I wish to redirect the argument is toward the relative position of the American cinema as opposed to the foreign cinema. Some critics have advised me that the *auteur* theory only applies to a small number of artists who make personal films, not to the run-of-the-mill Hollywood director who takes whatever assignment is available. Like most Americans who take films seriously, I have always felt a cultural inferiority complex about Hollywood.

659

Just a few years ago, I would have thought it unthinkable to speak in the same breath of a "commercial" director like Hitchcock and a "pure" director like Bresson. Even today, *Sight and Sound* uses different type sizes for Bresson and Hitchcock films. After years of tortured revaluation, I am now prepared to stake my critical reputation, such as it is, on the proposition that Alfred Hitchcock is artistically superior to Robert Bresson by every criterion of excellence and, further, that, film for film, director for director, the American cinema has been consistently superior to that of the rest of the world from 1915 through 1962. Consequently, I now regard the *auteur* theory primarily as a critical device for recording the history of the American cinema, the only cinema in the world worth exploring in depth beneath the frosting of a few great directors at the top.

These propositions remain to be proven and, I hope, debated. The proof will be difficult because direction in the cinema is a nebulous force in literary terms. In addition to its own jargon, the director's craft often pulls in the related jargon of music, painting, sculpture, dance, literature, theatre, architecture, all in a generally futile attempt to describe the indescribable. What is it the old jazz man says of his art? If you gotta ask what it is, it ain't? Well, the cinema is like that. Criticism can only attempt an approximation, a reasonable preponderance of accuracy over inaccuracy. I know the exceptions to the *auteur* theory as well as anyone. I can feel the human attraction of an audience going one way when I am going the other. The temptations of cynicism, common sense, and facile culture-mongering are always very strong, but, somehow, I feel that the *auteur* theory is the only hope for extending the appreciation of personal qualities in the cinema. By grouping and evaluating films according to directors, the critic can rescue individual achievements from an unjustifiable anonymity. If medieval architects and African sculptors are anonymous today, it is not because they deserved to be. When Ingmar Bergman bemoans the alienation of the modern artist from the collective spirit that rebuilt the cathedral at Chartres, he is only dramatizing his own individuality for an age that has rewarded him handsomely for the travail of his alienation. There is no justification for penalizing Hollywood directors for the sake of collective mythology. So, invective aside, "Aimez-vous Cukor?"

II. WHAT IS THE *AUTEUR* THEORY?

As far as I know, there is no definition of the *auteur* theory in the English language, that is, by any American or British critic. Truffaut has recently gone to great pains to emphasize that the *auteur* theory was merely a polemical weapon for a given time and a given place, and I am willing to take him at his word. But, lest I be accused of misappropriating a theory no one wants anymore, I will give the *Cahiers* critics full credit for the original formulation of an idea that reshaped my thinking on the cinema. First of all, how does the *auteur* theory differ from a straightforward theory of directors. Ian Cameron's article "Films, Directors, and Critics," in *Movie* of September, 1962, makes an interesting comment on this issue: "The assumption that underlies all the writing in *Movie* is that the director is the author of a film, the person who gives it any distinctive quality. There are quite large exceptions, with which I shall deal later." So far, so good, at least for the *auteur* theory, which even allows for exceptions. However, Cameron continues: "On the whole, we accept the cinema of directors, although without going to the farthest-out extremes of the *la politique des auteurs*, which makes it difficult to think of a bad director making a good film and almost impossible to think of a good director making a bad one." We are back to Bazin again, although Cameron naturally uses different examples. That three otherwise divergent critics like Bazin, Roud, and Cameron make essentially the same point about the *auteur* theory suggests a common fear of its abuses. I believe there is a misunderstanding here about what the *auteur* theory actually claims, particularly since the theory itself is so vague at the present time.

First of all, the *auteur* theory, at least as I understand it and now intend to express it, claims neither the gift of prophecy nor the option of extracinematic perception. Directors, even *auteurs*, do not always run true to form, and the critic can never assume that a bad director will always make a bad film. No, not always, but almost always, and that is the point. What is a bad director, but a director who has made many bad films? What is the problem then? Simply this: The badness of a director is not necessarily considered the badness of a film. If Joseph Pevney directed Garbo, Cherkassov, Olivier, Belmondo, and Harriet Andersson in *The Cherry Orchard*, the resulting spectacle might not be entirely devoid of merit with so many subsidiary *auteurs* to cover up for Joe. In fact, with this cast and this literary property, a Lumet might be safer than a Welles. The realities of casting apply to directors as well as to actors, but the *auteur* theory would demand the gamble with Welles, if he were willing.

Marlon Brando has shown us that a film can be made without a director. Indeed, *One-Eyed Jacks* is more entertaining than many films with directors. A director-conscious critic would find it difficult to say anything good or bad about direction that is nonexistent. One can talk here about photography, editing, acting, but not direction. The film even has personality, but, like *The Longest Day* and *Mutiny on the Bounty*, it is a cipher directorially. Obviously, the *auteur* theory cannot possibly cover every vagrant charm of the cinema. Nevertheless, the first premise of the *auteur* theory is the technical competence of a director as a criterion of value. A badly directed or an undirected film has no importance in a critical scale of values, but one can make interesting conversation about the subject, the script, the acting, the color, the photography, the editing, the music, the costumes, the decor, and so forth. That is the nature of the medium. You always get more for your money than mere art. Now, by the *auteur* theory, if a director has no technical competence, no elementary flair for the cinema, he is automatically cast out from the pantheon of directors. A great director has to be at least a good director. This is true in any art. What constitutes directorial talent is more difficult to define abstractly. There is less disagreement, however, on this first level of the *auteur* theory than there will be later.

The second premise of the *auteur* theory is the distinguishable personality of the director as a criterion of value. Over a group of films, a director must exhibit certain recurring characteristics of style, which serve as his signature. The way a film looks and moves should have some relationship to the way a director thinks and feels. This is an area where American directors are generally superior to foreign directors. Because so much of the American cinema is commissioned, a director is forced to express his personality through the visual treatment of material rather than through the literary content of the material. A Cukor, who works with all sorts of projects, has a more developed abstract style than a Bergman, who is free to develop his own scripts. Not that Bergman lacks personality, but his work has declined with the depletion of his ideas largely because his technique never equaled his sensibility. Joseph L. Mankiewicz and Billy Wilder are other examples of writer-directors without adequate technical mastery. By contrast, Douglas Sirk and Otto Preminger have moved up the scale because their miscellaneous projects reveal a stylistic consistency.

The third and ultimate premise of the *auteur* theory is concerned with interior meaning, the ultimate glory of the cinema as an art. Interior meaning is extrapolated from the tension between a director's personality and his material. This conception of interior meaning comes close to what Astruc defines as *mise en scène*, but not quite. It is not quite the vision of the world a director projects nor quite his attitude toward life. It is ambiguous, in any literary sense, because part of it is imbedded in the stuff of the cinema and cannot be rendered in noncinematic terms. Truffaut has called it the temperature of the director on the set, and that is a close approximation of its professional aspect. Dare I come out and say what I think it to be is an *élan* of the soul?

Lest I seem unduly mystical, let me hasten to add that all I mean by "soul" is that intangible difference between one personality and another, all other things being equal. Sometimes, this difference is expressed by no more than a beat's hesitation in the rhythm of a film. In one sequence of *La Règle du Jeu*, Renoir gallops up the stairs, turns to his right with a lurching movement, stops in hoplike uncertainty when his name is called by a coquettish maid, and, then, with marvelous postreflex continuity, resumes his bearishly shambling journey to the heroine's boudoir. If I could describe the musical grace note of that momentary suspension, and I can't, I might be able to provide a more precise definition of the *auteur* theory. As it is, all I can do is point at the specific beauties of interior meaning on the screen and, later, catalogue the moments of recognition.

The three premises of the *auteur* theory may be visualized as three concentric circles: the outer circle as technique; the middle circle, personal style; and the inner circle, interior meaning. The corresponding roles of the director may be designated as those of a technician, a stylist, and an *auteur*. There is no prescribed course by which a director passes through the three circles. Godard once remarked that Visconti had evolved from a *metteur en scène* to an *auteur*, whereas Rossellini had evolved from an *auteur* to a *metteur en scène*. From opposite directions, they emerged with comparable status. Minnelli began and remained in the second circle as a stylist; Buñuel was an *auteur* even before he had assembled the technique of the first circle. Technique is simply the ability to put a film together with some clarity and coherence. Nowadays, it is possible to become a director without knowing too much about the technical side, even the crucial functions of photography and editing. An expert production crew could probably cover up for a chimpanzee in the director's chair. How do you tell the genuine director from the quasichimpanzee? After a given number of films, a pattern is established.

In fact, the *auteur* theory itself is a pattern theory in constant flux. I would never endorse a Ptolemaic constellation of directors in a fixed orbit. At the moment, my list of *auteurs* runs something like this through the first twenty: Ophuls, Renoir, Mizoguchi, Hitchcock, Chaplin, Ford, Welles, Dreyer, Rossellini, Murnau, Griffith, Sternberg, Eisenstein, von Stroheim, Buñuel, Bresson, Hawks, Lang, Flaherty, Vigo. This list is somewhat weighted toward seniority and established reputations. In time, some of these *auteurs* will rise, some will fall, and some will be displaced either by new directors or rediscovered ancients. Again, the exact order is less important than the specific definitions of these and as many as two hundred other potential *auteurs*. I would hardly expect any other critic in the world fully to endorse this list, especially on faith. Only after thousands of films have been revaluated, will any personal pantheon have a reasonably objective validity. The task of validating the *auteur* theory is an enormous one, and the end will never be in sight. Meanwhile, the *auteur* habit of collecting random films in directorial bundles will serve posterity with at least a tentative classification.

Although the *auteur* theory emphasizes the body of a director's work rather than isolated masterpieces, it is expected of great directors that they make great films every so often. The only possible exception to his rule I can think of is Abel Gance, whose greatness is largely a function of his aspiration. Even with Gance, *La Roue* is as close to being a great film as any single work of Flaherty's. Not that single works matter that much. As Renoir has observed, a director spends his life on variations of the same film.

Two recent films—*Boccaccio '70* and *The Seven Capital Sins*—unwittingly reinforced the *auteur* theory by confirming the relative standing of the many directors involved. If I had not seen either film, I would have anticipated that the order of merit in *Boccaccio '70* would be Visconti, Fellini, and De Sica, and in *The Seven Capital Sins* Godard, Chabrol, Demy, Vadim, De Broca, Molinaro. (Dhomme, Ionesco's stage director and an unknown quantity in advance, turned out to be the worst of the lot.) There might be some argument about the relative badness of De Broca and Molinaro, but, otherwise, the directors ran true to form by almost any objective criterion of value. However, the main point here is that even in these frothy, ultracommercial servings of entertainment, the contribution of each director had less in common stylistically with the work of other directors on the project than with his own previous work.

Sometimes, a great deal of corn must be husked to yield a few kernels of internal meaning. I recently saw *Every Night at Eight*, one of the many maddeningly routine films Raoul Walsh has directed in his long career. This 1935 effort featured George Raft, Alice Faye, Frances Langford, and Patsy Kelly in one of those familiar plots about radio shows of the period. The film keeps moving along in the pleasantly unpretentious manner one would expect of Walsh until one incongruously intense scene with George Raft thrashing about in his sleep, revealing his inner fears in mumbling dream-talk. The girl he loves comes into the room in the midst of his unconscious avowals of feeling and listens sympathetically. This unusual scene was later amplified in *High Sierra* with Humphrey Bogart and Ida Lupino. The point is that one of the screen's most virile directors employed an essentially feminine narrative device to dramatize the emotional vulnerability of his heroes. If I had not been aware of Walsh in *Every Night at Eight*, the crucial link to *High Sierra* would have passed unnoticed. Such are the joys of the *auteur* theory.

1962

PAULINE KAEL
CIRCLES AND SQUARES

. . . the first premise of the auteur *theory is the technical compe-tence of a director as a criterion of value . . . The second premise of the* auteur *theory is the distinguishable personality of the direc-tor as a criterion of value. . . . The third and ultimate premise of the* auteur *theory is concerned with interior meaning, the ultimate glory of the cinema as an art. Interior meaning is extrapolated from the tension between a director's personality and his material. . . .*

Sometimes a great deal of corn must be husked to yield a few ker-nels of internal meaning. I recently saw Every Night at Eight, *one of the many maddeningly routine films Raoul Walsh has directed in his long career. This 1935 effort featured George Raft, Alice Faye, Frances Langford and Patsy Kelly in one of those familiar plots about radio shows of the period. The film keeps moving along in the pleasantly unpretentious manner one would expect of Walsh until one incongruously intense scene with George Raft thrashing about in his sleep, revealing his inner fears in mumbling dream talk. The girl he loves comes into the room in the midst of his un-conscious avowals of feeling, and listens sympathetically. This unusual scene was later amplified in* High Sierra *with Humphrey Bogart and Ida Lupino. The point is that one of the screen's most virile directors employed an essentially feminine narrative device to dramatize the emotional vulnerability of his heroes. If I had not been aware of Walsh in* Every Night at Eight, *the crucial link to*

666

High Sierra *would have passed unnoticed. Such are the joys of the* auteur *theory.*
— Andrew Sarris, "Notes on the Auteur Theory in 1962,"
Film Culture, Winter 1962–1963.

Perhaps a little more corn should be husked; perhaps, for example, we can husk away the word "internal" (is "internal meaning" any different from "meaning"?). We might ask why the link is "crucial"? Is it because the device was "incongruously intense" in *Every Night at Eight* and so demonstrated a try for something *deeper* on Walsh's part? But if his merit is his "pleasantly unpretentious manner" (which is to say, I suppose, that, recognizing the limitations of the script, he wasn't trying to do much) then the incongruous device was probably a misconceived attempt that disturbed the manner—like a bad playwright interrupting a comedy scene because he cannot resist the opportunity to tug at your heartstrings. We might also ask why this narrative device is "essentially feminine": is it more feminine than masculine to be asleep, or to talk in one's sleep, or to reveal feelings? Or, possibly, does Sarris regard the device as feminine because the listening woman becomes a sympathetic figure and emotional understanding is, in this "virile" context, assumed to be essentially feminine? Perhaps only if one accepts the narrow notions of virility so common in our action films can this sequence be seen as "essentially feminine," and it is amusing that a critic can both support these clichés of the male world and be so happy when they are violated.

This is how we might quibble with a different *kind* of critic but we would never get anywhere with Sarris if we tried to examine what he is saying sentence by sentence.

So let us ask, what is the meaning of the passage? Sarris has noticed that in *High Sierra* (not a very good movie) Raoul Walsh repeated an uninteresting and obvious device that he had earlier used in a worse movie. And for some inexplicable reason, Sarris concludes that he would not have had this joy of discovery without the *auteur* theory.

But in every art form, critics traditionally notice and point out the way the artists borrow from themselves (as well as from others) and how the same devices, techniques, and themes reappear in their work. This is obvious in listening to music, seeing plays, reading

667

novels, watching actors; we take it for granted that this is how we perceive the development or the decline of an artist (and it may be necessary to point out to *auteur* critics that repetition without development is decline). When you see Hitchcock's *Saboteur* there is no doubt that he drew heavily and clumsily from *The 39 Steps*, and when you see *North by Northwest* you can see that he is once again toying with the ingredients of *The 39 Steps*—and apparently having a good time with them. Would Sarris not notice the repetition in the Walsh films without the *auteur* theory? Or shall we take the more cynical view that without some commitment to Walsh as an *auteur*, he probably wouldn't be spending his time looking at these movies?

If we may be permitted a literary analogy, we can visualize Sarris researching in the archives of the *Saturday Evening Post*, tracing the development of Clarence Budington Kelland, who, by the application of something like the *auteur* theory, would emerge as a much more important writer than Dostoyevsky; for in Kelland's case Sarris's three circles, the three premises of the *auteur* theory, have been consistently congruent. Kelland is technically competent (even "pleasantly unpretentious"), no writer has a more "distinguishable personality," and if "interior meaning" is what can be extrapolated from, say, *Hatari!* or *Advise and Consent* or *What Ever Happened to Baby Jane?* then surely Kelland's stories with their attempts to force a bit of character and humor into the familiar plot outlines are loaded with it. Poor misguided Dostoyevsky, too full of what he has to say to bother with "technical competence," tackling important themes in each work (surely the worst crime in the *auteur* book) and with his almost incredible unity of personality and material leaving you nothing to extrapolate from, he'll never make it. If the editors of *Movie* ranked authors the way they do directors, Dostoyevsky would probably be in that almost untouchable category of the "ambitious."

It should be pointed out that Sarris's defense of the *auteur* theory is based not only on aesthetics but on a rather odd pragmatic statement: "Thus to argue against the *auteur* theory in America is to assume that we have anyone of Bazin's sensibility and dedication to provide an alternative, and we simply don't." Which I take to mean that the *auteur* theory is necessary in the absence of a critic who wouldn't need it. This is a new approach to aesthetics, and I hope

Sarris's humility does not camouflage his double-edged argument. If his aesthetics is based on expediency, then it may be expedient to point out that it takes extraordinary intelligence and discrimination and taste to *use* any theory in the arts, and that without those qualities, a theory becomes a rigid formula (which is indeed what is happening among *auteur* critics). The greatness of critics like Bazin in France and Agee in America may have something to do with their using their full range of intelligence and intuition, rather than relying on formulas. Criticism is an art, not a science, and a critic who follows rules will fail in one of his most important functions: perceiving what is original and important in *new* work and helping others to see.

THE OUTER CIRCLE

. . . the first premise of the auteur *theory is the technical competence of a director as a criterion of value.*

This seems less the premise of a theory than a commonplace of judgment, as Sarris himself indicates when he paraphrases it as, "A great director has to be at least a good director." But this commonplace, though it *sounds* reasonable and basic, is a shaky premise: sometimes the greatest artists in a medium bypass or violate the simple technical competence that is so necessary for hacks. For example, it is doubtful if Antonioni could handle a routine directorial assignment of the type at which John Struges is so proficient *(Escape from Fort Bravo* or *Bad Day at Black Rock),* but surely Antonioni's *L'Avventura* is the work of a great director. And the greatness of a director like Cocteau has nothing to do with mere technical competence: his greatness is in being able to achieve his own personal expression and style. And just as there were writers like Melville or Dreiser who triumphed over various kinds of technical incompetence, and who were, as artists, incomparably greater than the facile technicians of their day, a new great film director may appear whose very greatness is in his struggling toward grandeur or in massive accumulation of detail. An artist who is not a good technician can indeed create new standards, because standards of technical competence are based on comparisons with work already done.

Just as new work in other arts is often attacked because it violates the accepted standards and thus seems crude and ugly and incoherent, great new directors are very likely to be condemned precisely on the grounds that they're not even good directors, that they don't know their "business." Which, in some cases, is true, but does it matter when that "business" has little to do with what they want to express in films? It may even be a hindrance, leading them to banal slickness, instead of discovery of their own methods. For some, at least, Cocteau may be right: "The only technique worth having is the technique you invent for yourself." The director must be judged on the basis of what he produces—his films—and if he can make great films without knowing the standard methods, without the usual craftsmanship of the "good director," then that is the way he works. I would amend Sarris's premise to, "In works of a lesser rank, technical competence can help to redeem the weaknesses of the material." In fact it seems to be precisely this category that the *auteur* critics are most interested in—the routine material that a good craftsman can make into a fast and enjoyable movie. What, however, makes the *auteur* critics so incomprehensible, is not their *preference* for works of this category (in this they merely follow the lead of children who also prefer simple action films and westerns and horror films to works that make demands on their understanding) but their truly astonishing inability to exercise taste and judgment *within* their area of preference. Moviegoing kids are, I think, much more reliable guides to this kind of movie than the *auteur* critics: every kid I've talked to knows that Henry Hathaway's *North to Alaska* was a surprisingly funny, entertaining movie and *Hatari!* (classified as a "masterpiece" by half the *Cahiers* Conseil des Dix, Peter Bogdanovich, and others) was a terrible bore.

THE MIDDLE CIRCLE

. . . *the second premise of the* auteur *theory is the distinguishable personality of the director as a criterion of value.*

Up to this point there has really been no theory, and now, when Sarris begins to work on his foundation, the entire edifice of civilized standards of taste collapses while he's tacking down his floorboards. Traditionally, in any art, the personalities of all those involved in a production have been a factor in judgment, but that the *distinguishability* of personality should in itself be a criterion of value completely confuses *normal* judgment. The smell of a skunk is more distinguishable than the perfume of a rose; does that make it better? Hitchcock's personality is certainly more distinguishable in *Dial M for Murder, Rear Window, Vertigo,* than Carol Reed's in *The Stars Look Down, Odd Man Out, The Fallen Idol, The Third Man, An Outcast of the Islands,* if for no other reason than because Hitchcock repeats while Reed tackles new subject matter. But how does this distinguishable personality function as a criterion for judging the works? We recognize the hands of Carné and Prévert in *Le Jour se Lève,* but that is not what makes it a beautiful film; we can just as easily recognize their hands in *Quai des Brumes* —which is not such a good film. We can recognize that *Le Plaisir* and *The Earrings of Madame de . . .* are both the work of Ophuls, but *Le Plaisir* is not a great film, and *Madame de . . .* is.

Often the works in which we are most aware of the personality of the director are his worst films—when he falls back on the devices he has already done to death. When a famous director makes a good movie, we look at the movie, we don't think about the director's personality; when he makes a stinker we notice his familiar touches because there's not much else to watch. When Preminger makes an expert, entertaining whodunit like *Laura,* we don't look for his personality (it has become part of the texture of the film); when he makes an atrocity like *Whirlpool,* there's plenty of time to look for his "personality"—if that's your idea of a good time.

It could even be argued, I think, that Hitchcock's uniformity, his mastery of tricks, and his cleverness at getting audiences to respond according to his calculations—the feedback he wants and gets from them—reveal not so much a personal style as a personal theory of audience psychology, that his methods and approach are not those of an artist but a prestidigitator. The *auteur* critics respond just as Hitchcock expects the gullible to respond. This is not so surprising —often the works *auteur* critics call masterpieces are ones that seem to reveal the contempt of the director for the audience.

It's hard to believe that Sarris seriously attempts to apply "the distinguishable personality of the director as a criterion of value" because when this premise becomes troublesome, he just tries to brazen his way out of difficulties. For example, now that John

Huston's work has gone flat* Sarris casually dismisses him with: "Huston is virtually a forgotten man with a few actors' classics behind him . . ." If *The Maltese Falcon*, perhaps the most high-style thriller ever made in America, a film Huston both wrote and directed, is not a director's film, what is? And if the distinguishable personality of the director is a criterion of value, then how can Sarris dismiss the Huston who comes through so unmistakably in *The Treasure of Sierra Madre*, *The African Queen*, or *Beat the Devil*, or even in a muddled Huston film like *Key Largo*? If these are actors' movies, then what on earth is a director's movie?

Isn't the *auteur* theory a hindrance to clear judgment of Huston's movies and of his career? Disregarding the theory, we see some fine film achievements and we perceive a remarkably distinctive directorial talent; we also see intervals of weak, half-hearted assignments like *Across the Pacific* and *In This Our Life*. Then, after *Moulin Rouge*, except for the blessing of *Beat the Devil*, we see a career that splutters out in ambitious failures like *Moby Dick* and confused projects like *The Roots of Heaven* and *The Misfits*, and strictly commercial projects like *Heaven Knows, Mr. Allison*. And this kind of career seems more characteristic of film history, especially in the United States, than the ripening development and final mastery envisaged by the *auteur* theory—a theory that makes it almost de rigeur to regard Hitchcock's American films as superior to his early English films. Is Huston's career so different, say, from Fritz Lang's? How is it that Huston's early good—almost great— work, must be rejected along with his mediocre recent work, but Fritz Lang, being sanctified as an *auteur*, has his bad recent work praised along with his good? Employing more usual norms, if you respect the Fritz Lang who made *M* and *You Only Live Once*, if you enjoy the excesses of style and the magnificent absurdities of a film like *Metropolis*, then it is only good sense to reject the ugly stupidity of *Journey to the Lost City*. It is an insult to an artist to praise

---

* And, by the way, the turning point came, I think, not with *Moby Dick*, as Sarris indicates, but much earlier, with *Moulin Rouge*. This may not be so apparent to *auteur* critics concerned primarily with style and individual touches, because what was shocking about *Moulin Rouge* was that the content was sentimental mush. But critics who accept even the worst of Minnelli probably wouldn't have been bothered by the fact that *Moulin Rouge* was soft in the center, it had so many fancy touches at the edges.

his bad work along with his good; it indicates that you are incapable of judging either.

A few years ago, a friend who reviewed Jean Renoir's University of California production of his play *Carola*, hailed it as "a work of genius." When I asked my friend how he could so describe this very unfortunate play, he said, "Why, of course, it's a work of genius. Renoir's a genius, so anything he does is a work of genius." This could almost be a capsule version of the *auteur* theory (just substitute *Hatari!* for *Carola*) and in this reductio ad absurdum, viewing a work is superfluous, as the judgment is a priori. It's like buying clothes by the label: this is Dior, so it's good. (This is not so far from the way the *auteur* critics work, either.)

Sarris doesn't even play his own game with any decent attention to the rules: it is as absurd to praise Lang's recent bad work as to dismiss Huston's early good work; surely it would be more consistent if he also tried to make a case for Huston's bad pictures? That would be more consistent than devising a category called "actors' classics" to explain his good pictures away. If *The Maltese Falcon* and *The Treasure of Sierra Madre* are actors' classics, then what makes Hawks's *To Have and Have Not* and *The Big Sleep* (which were obviously tailored to the personalities of Bogart and Bacall) the work of an *auteur*?

Sarris believes that what makes an *auteur* is "an élan of the soul." (This critical language is barbarous. Where else should élan come from? It's like saying "a digestion of the stomach." A film critic need not be a theoretician, but it is necessary that he know how to use words. This might, indeed, be a first premise for a theory.) Those who have this élan presumably have it forever and their films reveal the "organic unity" of the directors' careers; and those who don't have it—well, they can only make "actors' classics." It's ironic that a critic trying to establish simple "objective" rules as a guide for critics who he thinks aren't gifted enough to use taste and intelligence, ends up—where, actually, he began—with a theory based on mystical insight. This might really make demands on the *auteur* critics if they did not simply take the easy way out by arbitrary decisions of who's got "it" and who hasn't. Their decisions are not merely not based on their theory; their decisions are *beyond* criticism. It's like a woman's telling us that she feels a certain dress *does* something for her: her feeling has about as much to do with

673

critical judgment as the *auteur* critics' feeling that Minnelli *has* "it," but Huston never had "it."

Even if a girl had plenty of "it," she wasn't expected to keep it forever. But this "élan" is not supposed to be affected by the vicissitudes of fortune, the industrial conditions of moviemaking, the turmoil of a country, or the health of a director. Indeed, Sarris says, "If directors and other artists cannot be wrenched from their historical environments, aesthetics is reduced to a subordinate branch of ethnography." May I suggest that if, in order to judge movies, the *auteur* critics must wrench the directors from their historical environments (which is, to put it mildly, impossible) so that they can concentrate on the detection of that "élan," they are reducing aesthetics to a form of idiocy. Élan as the permanent attribute Sarris posits can only be explained in terms of a cult of personality. May I suggest that a more meaningful description of élan is what a man feels when he is working at the height of his powers—and what we respond to in works of art with the excited cry of "This time, he's really done it" or "This shows what he could do when he got the chance" or "He's found his style" or "I never realized he had it in him to do anything so good," a response to his joy in creativity.

Sarris experiences "joy" when he recognizes a pathetic little link between two Raoul Walsh pictures (he never does explain whether the discovery makes him think the pictures are any better) but he wants to see artists in a pristine state—their essences, perhaps? —separated from all the life that has formed them and to which they try to give expression.

THE INNER CIRCLE

The third and ultimate premise of the auteur *theory is concerned with interior meaning, the ultimate glory of the cinema as an art. Interior meaning is extrapolated from the tension between a director's personality and his material.*

This is a remarkable formulation: it is the opposite of what we have always taken for granted in the arts, that the artist expresses himself in the unity of form and content. What Sarris believes to be "the ultimate glory of the cinema as an art" is what has generally been considered the frustrations of a man working against the given material. Fantastic as this formulation is, it does something that the first two premises didn't do: it clarifies the interests of the *auteur* critics. If we have been puzzled because the *auteur* critics seemed so deeply involved, even dedicated, in becoming connoisseurs of trash, now we can see by this theoretical formulation that trash is indeed their chosen province of film.

Their ideal *auteur* is the man who signs a long-term contract, directs any script that's handed to him, and expresses himself by shoving bits of style up the crevasses of the plots. If his "style" is in conflict with the story line or subject matter, so much the better —more chance for tension. Now we can see why there has been so much use of the term "personality" in this aesthetics (the term which seems so inadequate when discussing the art of Griffith or Renoir or Murnau or Dreyer)—a routine, commercial movie can sure use a little "personality."

Now that we have reached the inner circle (the bull's eye turns out to be an empty socket) we can see why the shoddiest films are often praised the most. Subject matter is irrelevant (so long as it isn't treated sensitively—which is bad) and will quickly be disposed of by *auteur* critics who know that the smart director isn't responsible for that anyway; they'll get on to the important subject—his *mise-en-scène:* The director who fights to do something he cares about is a square. Now we can at least begin to understand why there was such contempt toward Huston for what was, in its way, a rather extraordinary effort—the *Moby Dick* that failed; why *Movie* considers Roger Corman a better director than Fred Zinnemann and ranks Joseph Losey next to God, why Bogdanovich, Mekas, and Sarris give their highest critical ratings to *What Ever Happened to Baby Jane?* (mighty big crevasses there). If Carol Reed had made only movies like *The Man Between*—in which he obviously worked to try to make something out of a ragbag of worn-out bits of material—he might be considered "brilliant" too. (But this is doubtful: although even the worst Reed is superior to Aldrich's *Baby Jane*, Reed would probably be detected, and rejected, as a man interested in substance rather than sensationalism.)

I am angry, but am I unjust? Here's Sarris:

> A Cukor who works with all sorts of projects has a more developed abstract style than a Bergman who is free to develop his own scripts. Not that Bergman lacks personality, but his work has declined with

675

the depletion of his ideas largely because his technique never equaled his sensibility. Joseph L. Mankiewicz and Billy Wilder are other examples of writer-directors without adequate technical mastery. By contrast, Douglas Sirk and Otto Preminger have moved up the scale because their miscellaneous projects reveal a stylistic consistency.

How neat it all is—Bergman's "work has declined with the depletion of his ideas largely because his technique never equaled his sensibility." But what on earth does that mean? How did Sarris perceive Bergman's sensibility except through his technique? Is Sarris saying what he seems to be saying, that if Bergman had developed more "technique," his work wouldn't be dependent on his ideas? I'm afraid this *is* what he means, and that when he refers to Cukor's "more developed abstract style" he means by "abstract" something unrelated to ideas, a technique not dependent on the content of the films. This is curiously reminiscent of a view common enough in the business world, that it's better not to get too involved, too personally interested in business problems, or they take over your life; and besides, you don't function as well when you've lost your objectivity. But this is the *opposite* of how an artist works. His technique, his *style*, is determined by his range of involvements, and his preference for certain themes. Cukor's style is no more *abstract*(!) than Bergman's: Cukor has a range of subject matter that he can handle and when he gets a good script within his range (like *The Philadelphia Story* or *Pat and Mike*) he does a good job; but he is at an immense *artistic* disadvantage, compared with Bergman, because he is dependent on the ideas of so many (and often bad) scriptwriters and on material which is often alien to his talents. It's amusing (and/or depressing) to see the way *auteur* critics tend to downgrade writer-directors—who are in the *best* position to use the film medium for personal expression.

Sarris does some pretty fast shuffling with Huston and Bergman; why doesn't he just come out and admit that writer-directors are disqualified by his third premise? They can't arrive at that "interior meaning, the ultimate glory of the cinema" because a writer-director has no tension between his personality and his material, so there's nothing for the *auteur* critic to extrapolate from.

What is all this nonsense about extrapolating "interior" meaning from the tension between a director's personality and his material?

676

A competent commercial director generally does the best he can with what he's got to work with. Where is the "tension"? And if you can locate some, what kind of meaning could you draw out of it except that the director's having a bad time with lousy material or material he doesn't like? Or maybe he's trying to speed up the damned production so he can do something else that he has some *hopes* for? Are these critics honestly (and futilely) looking for "interior meanings" or is this just some form of intellectual diddling that helps to sustain their pride while they're viewing silly movies? Where is the tension in Howard Hawks's films? When he has good material, he's capable of better than good direction, as he demonstrates in films like *Twentieth Century, Bringing Up Baby, His Girl Friday*; and in *To Have and Have Not* and *The Big Sleep* he demonstrates that with help from the actors, he can jazz up ridiculous scripts. But what "interior meaning" can be extrapolated from an enjoyable, harmless, piece of kitsch like *Only Angels Have Wings*; what can the *auteur* critics see in it beyond the sex and glamor and fantasies of the high-school boys' universe—exactly what the mass audience liked it for? And when Hawks's material and/or cast is dull and when his heart isn't in the production—when by the *auteur* theory he should show his "personality," the result is something soggy like *The Big Sky*.

George Cukor's modest statement, "Give me a good script and I'll be a hundred times better as a director"* provides some notion of how a director may experience the problem of the given material. What can Cukor do with a script like *The Chapman Report* but try to kid it, to dress it up a bit, to show off the talents of Jane Fonda and Claire Bloom and Glynis Johns, and to give the total production a little flair and craftsmanship. At best, he can make an entertaining bad movie. A director with something like magical gifts *can* make a silk purse out of a sow's ear. But if he has it in him to do

---

*In another sense, it is perhaps immodest. I would say, give Cukor a clever script with light, witty dialogue, and he will know what to do with it. But I wouldn't expect more than glossy entertainment. (It seems almost too obvious to mention it, but can Sarris really discern the "distinguishable personality" of George Cukor and his "abstract" style in films like *Bhowani Junction, Les Girls, The Actress, A Life of Her Own, The Model and the Marriage Broker, Edward, My Son, A Woman's Face, Romeo and Juliet, A Double Life*? I wish I could put him to the test. I can only *suspect* that many *auteur* critics would have a hard time seeing those telltale traces of the beloved in their works.)

677

more in life than make silk purses, the triumph is minor—even if the purse is lined with gold. Only by the use of the *auteur* theory does this little victory become "ultimate glory." For some unexplained reason those traveling in *auteur* circles believe that making that purse out of a sow's ear is an infinitely greater accomplishment than making a solid carrying case out of a good piece of leather (as, for example, a Zinnemann does with *From Here to Eternity* or *The Nun's Story*).

I suppose we should be happy for Sirk and Preminger elevated up the glory "scale," but I suspect that the "stylistic consistency" of say, Preminger, could be a matter of his *limitations*, and that the only way you could tell he made some of his movies was that he used the same players so often (Linda Darnell, Jeanne Crain, Gene Tierney, Dana Andrews, et al., gave his movies the Preminger look). But the argument is ludicrous anyway, because if Preminger shows stylistic consistency with subject matter as varied as *Carmen Jones*, *Anatomy of a Murder*, and *Advise and Consent*, then by any rational standards he should be attacked rather than elevated. I don't think these films are stylistically consistent, nor do I think Preminger is a great director—for the very simple reason that his films are consistently superficial and facile. (*Advise and Consent*, an *auteur* "masterpiece"—Ian Cameron, Paul Mayersberg, and Mark Shivas of *Movie* and Jean Douchet of *Cahiers du Cinéma* rate it first on their ten best lists of 1962 and Sarris gives it his top rating—seems not so much Preminger-directed as other-directed. That is to say, it seems calculated to provide what as many different groups as possible want to see: there's something for the liberals, something for the conservatives, something for the homosexuals, something for the family.) An editorial in *Movie* states: "In order to enjoy Preminger's films the spectator must apply an unprejudiced intelligence; he is constantly required to examine the quality not only of the characters' decisions but also of his own reactions," and "He presupposes an intelligence active enough to allow the spectator to make connections, comparisons and judgments." May I suggest that this spectator would have better things to do than the editors of *Movie* who put out Preminger issues? They may have, of course, the joys of discovering links between *Centennial Summer*, *Forever Amber*, *That Lady in Ermine*, and *The Thirteenth Letter*, but I refuse to believe in these ever-so-intellectual protestations. The *auteur* critics aren't a very *convincing* group.

I assume that Sarris's theory is not based on his premises (the necessary causal relationships are absent), but rather that the premises were devised in a clumsy attempt to prop up the "theory." (It's a good thing he stopped at three: a few more circles and we'd really be in hell, which might turn out to be the last refinement of film tastes—Abbott and Costello comedies, perhaps?) These critics work embarrassingly hard trying to give some semblance of intellectual respectability to a preoccupation with mindless, repetitious commercial products—the kind of action movies that the restless, rootless men who wander on Forty-Second Street and in the Tenderloin of all our big cities have always preferred just because they could respond to them without thought. These movies soak up your time. I would suggest that they don't serve a very different function for Sarris or Bogdanovich or the young men of *Movie*—even though they devise elaborate theories to justify soaking up their time. An educated man must have to work pretty hard to set his intellectual horizons at the level of *I Was a Male War Bride* (which, incidentally, wasn't even a good *commercial* movie).

"Interior meaning" seems to be what those in the know know. It's a mystique—and a mistake. The *auteur* critics never tell us by what divining rods they have discovered the élan of a Minnelli or a Nicholas Ray or a Leo McCarey. They're not critics; they're inside dopesters. There must be another circle that Sarris forgot to get to —the one where the secrets are kept. . . .

1963

PETER WOLLEN
FROM SIGNS AND MEANING IN THE CINEMA

THE AUTEUR THEORY

The *politique des auteurs*—the *auteur* theory, as Andrew Sarris calls it—was developed by the loosely knit group of critics who wrote for *Cahiers du Cinéma* and made it the leading film magazine in the world. It sprang from the conviction that the American cinema was worth studying in depth, that masterpieces were made not only by a small upper crust of directors, the cultured gilt on the commercial gingerbread, but by a whole range of authors, whose work had previously been dismissed and consigned to oblivion. There were special conditions in Paris which made this conviction possible. Firstly, there was the fact that American films were banned from France under the Vichy government and the German Occupation. Consequently, when they reappeared after the Liberation they came with a force—and an emotional impact—which was necessarily missing in the Anglo-Saxon countries themselves. And, secondly, there was a thriving ciné-club movement, due in part to the close connections there had always been in France between the cinema and the intelligentsia: witness the example of Jean Cocteau or André Malraux. Connected with this ciné-club movement was the magnificent Paris *Cinémathèque*, the work of Henri Langlois, a great *auteur*, as Jean-Luc Godard described him. The policy of the *Cinémathèque* was to show the maximum number of films, to plough back the production of the past in order to produce the culture in which the cinema of the future could thrive. It gave French *cinéphiles* an unmatched perception of the historical dimensions of Hollywood and the careers of individual directors.

THE AUTEUR THEORY

The *auteur* theory grew up rather haphazardly; it was never elaborated in programmatic terms, in a manifesto or collective statement. As a result, it could be interpreted and applied on rather broad lines; different critics developed somewhat different methods within a loose framework of common attitudes. This looseness and diffuseness of the theory has allowed flagrant misunderstandings to take root, particularly among critics in Britain and the United States. Ignorance has been compounded by a vein of hostility to foreign ideas and a taste for travesty and caricature. However, the fruitfulness of the *auteur* approach has been such that it has made headway even on the most unfavorable terrain. For instance, a recent straw poll of British critics, conducted in conjunction with a Don Siegel Retrospective at the National Film Theatre, revealed that, among American directors most admired, a group consisting of Budd Boetticher, Samuel Fuller and Howard Hawks ran immediately behind Ford, Hitchcock and Welles, who topped the poll, but ahead of Billy Wilder, Josef Von Sternberg and Preston Sturges.

Of course, some individual directors have always been recognised as outstanding: Charles Chaplin, John Ford, Orson Welles. The *auteur* theory does not limit itself to acclaiming the director as the main author of a film. It implies an operation of decipherment; it reveals authors where none had been seen before. For years, the model of an author in the cinema was that of the European director, with open artistic aspirations and full control over his films. This model still lingers on; it lies behind the existential distinction between art films and popular films. Directors who built their reputations in Europe were dismissed after they crossed the Atlantic, reduced to anonymity. American Hitchcock was contrasted unfavourably with English Hitchcock, American Renoir with French Renoir, American Fritz Lang with German Fritz Lang. The *auteur* theory has led to the revaluation of the second, Hollywood careers of these and other European directors; without it, masterpieces such as *Scarlet Street* or *Vertigo* would never have been perceived. Conversely, the *auteur* theory has been sceptical when offered an American director whose salvation has been exile to Europe. It is difficult now to argue that *Brute Force* has ever been excelled by Jules Dassin or that Joseph Losey's recent work is markedly superior to, say, *The Prowler*.

681

In time, owing to the diffuseness of the original theory, two main schools of *auteur* critics grew up: those who insisted on revealing a core of meanings, of thematic motifs, and those who stressed style and *mise en scène*. There is an important distinction here, which I shall return to later. The work of the *auteur* has a semantic dimension, it is not purely formal; the work of the *metteur en scène*, on the other hand, does not go beyond the realm of performance, of transposing into the special complex of cinematic codes and channels a pre-existing text: a scenario, a book or a play. As we shall see, the meaning of the films of an *auteur* is constructed *a posteriori*; the meaning — semantic, rather than stylistic or expressive — of the films of a *metteur en scène* exists *a priori*. In concrete cases, of course, this distinction is not always clear-cut. There is controversy over whether some directors should be seen as *auteurs* or *metteurs en scène*. For example, though it is possible to make intuitive ascriptions, there have been no really persuasive accounts as yet of Raoul Walsh or William Wyler as *auteurs*, to take two very different directors. Opinions might differ about Don Siegel or George Cukor. Because of the difficulty of fixing the distinction in these concrete cases, it has often become blurred; indeed, some French critics have tended to value the *metteur en scène* above the *auteur*. MacMahonism sprang up, with its cult of Walsh, Lang, Losey and Preminger, its fascination with violence and its notorious text: "Charlton Heston is an axiom of the cinema." What André Bazin called "aesthetic cults of personality" began to be formed. Minor directors were acclaimed before they had, in any real sense, been identified and defined.

Yet the *auteur* theory has survived despite all the hallucinating critical extravaganzas which it has fathered. It has survived because it is indispensable. Geoffrey Nowell-Smith has summed up the *auteur* theory as it is normally presented today:

> One essential corollary of the theory as it has been developed is the discovery that the defining characteristics of an author's work are not necessarily those which are most readily apparent. The purpose of criticism thus becomes to uncover behind the superficial contrasts of subject and treatment a hard core of basic and often recondite motifs. The pattern formed by these motifs . . . is what gives an author's work its particular structure, both defining it internally and distinguishing one body of work from another.

682

It is this "structural approach," as Nowell-Smith calls it, which is indispensable for the critic.

The test case for the *auteur* theory is provided by the work of Howard Hawks. Why Hawks, rather than, say, Frank Borzage or King Vidor? Firstly, Hawks is a director who has worked for years within the Hollywood system. His first film, *Road to Glory*, was made in 1926. Yet throughout his long career he has only once received general critical acclaim, for his wartime film, *Sergeant York*, which closer inspection reveals to be eccentric and atypical of the main *corpus* of Hawks's films. Secondly, Hawks has worked in almost every genre. He has made westerns *(Rio Bravo)*, gangsters *(Scarface)*, war films *(Air Force)*, thrillers *(The Big Sleep)*, science fiction *(The Thing from Another World)*, musicals *(Gentlemen Prefer Blondes)*, comedies *(Bringing up Baby)*, even a Biblical epic *(Land of the Pharaohs)*. Yet all of these films (except perhaps *Land of the Pharaohs*, which he himself was not happy about) exhibit the same thematic preoccupations, the same recurring motifs and incidents, the same visual style and tempo. In the same way that Roland Barthes constructed a species of *homo racinianus*, the critic can construct a *homo hawksianus*, the protagonist of Hawksian values in the problematic Hawksian world.

Hawks achieved this by reducing the genres to two basic types: the adventure drama and the crazy comedy. These two types express inverse views of the world, the positive and negative poles of the Hawksian vision. Hawks stands opposed, on the one hand, to John Ford and, on the other hand, to Budd Boetticher. All these directors are concerned with the problem of heroism. For the hero, as an individual, death is an absolute limit which cannot be transcended: it renders the life which preceded it meaningless, absurd. How then can there be any meaningful individual action during life? How can individual action have any value — be heroic — if it cannot have transcendent value, because of the absolutely devaluing limit of death? John Ford finds the answer to this question by placing and situating the individual within society and within history, specifically within American history. Ford finds transcendent values in the historic vocation of America as a nation, to bring civilisation to a savage land, the garden to the wilderness. At the same time, Ford also sees these values themselves as problematic; he begins to question the movement of American history itself. Boetticher, on the contrary, insists on a radical individualism.

"I am not interested in making films about mass feelings. I am for the individual." He looks for values in the encounter with death itself: the underlying metaphor is always that of the bull-fighter in the arena. The hero enters a group of companions, but there is no possibility of group solidarity. Boetticher's hero acts by dissolving groups and collectives of any kind into their constituent individuals, so that he confronts each person face-to-face; the films develop, in Andrew Sarris's words, into "floating poker games, where every character takes turns at bluffing about his hand until the final showdown." Hawks, unlike Boetticher, seeks transcendent values beyond the individual, in solidarity with others. But, unlike Ford, he does not give his heroes any historical dimension, any destiny in time.

For Hawks the highest human emotion is the camaraderie of the exclusive, self-sufficient, all-male group. Hawk's heroes are cattlemen, marlin-fishermen, racing-drivers, pilots, big-game hunters, habituated to danger and living apart from society, actually cut off from it physically by dense forest, sea, snow or desert. Their aerodromes are fog-bound; the radio has cracked up; the next mail-coach or packet-boat does not leave for a week. The *élite* group strictly preserves its exclusivity. It is necessary to pass a test of ability and courage to win admittance. The group's only internal tensions come when one member lets the other down (the drunk deputy in *Rio Bravo*, the panicky pilot in *Only Angels Have Wings*) and must redeem himself by some act of exceptional bravery, or occasionally when too much 'individualism' threatens to disrupt the close-knit circle (the rivalry between drivers in *Red Line 7000*, the fighter pilot among the bomber crew in *Air Force*). The group's security is the first commandment: "You get a stunt team in acrobatics in the air—if one of them is no good, then they're all in trouble. If someone loses his nerve catching animals, then the whole bunch can be in trouble." The group members are bound together by rituals (in *Hatari!* blood is exchanged by transfusion) and express themselves univocally in communal sing-songs. There is a famous example of this in *Rio Bravo*. In *Dawn Patrol* the camaraderie of the pilots stretches even across the enemy lines: a captured German ace is immediately drafted into the group and joins in the sing-song; in *Hatari!* hunters of different nationality and in different places join together in a song over an intercom radio system.

684

Hawks's heroes pride themselves on their professionalism. They ask: "How good is he? He'd better be good." They expect no praise for doing their job well. Indeed, none is given except: 'The boys did all right.' When they die, they leave behind them only the most meagre personal belongings, perhaps a handful of medals. Hawks himself has summed up this desolate and barren view of life:

> It's just a calm acceptance of a fact. In *Only Angels Have Wings*, after Joe dies, Cary Grant says: "He just wasn't good enough." Well, that's the only thing that keeps people going. They just have to say: "Joe wasn't good enough, and I'm better than Joe, so I go ahead and do it." And they find out they're not any better than Joe, but then it's too late, you see.

In Ford films, death is celebrated by funeral services, an impromptu prayer, a few staves of "Shall we gather at the river?"—it is inserted into an ongoing system of ritual institutions, along with the wedding, the dance, the parade. But for Hawks it is enough that the routine of the group's life goes on, a routine whose only relieving features are "danger" *(Hatari!)* and "fun." Danger gives existence pungency: "Every time you get real action, then you have danger. And the question, 'Are you living or not living?' is probably the biggest drama we have." This nihilism, in which 'living' means no more than being in danger of losing your life—a danger entered into quite gratuitously—is augmented by the Hawksian concept of having "fun." The word "fun" crops up constantly in Hawks's interviews and scripts. It masks his despair.

When one of Hawks's *élite* is asked, usually by a woman, why he risks his life, he replies: "No reason I can think of makes any sense. I guess we're just crazy." Or Feathers, sardonically, to Colorado in *Rio Bravo*: "You haven't even the excuse I have. We're all fools." By "crazy" Hawks does not mean psychopathic: none of his characters are like Turkey in Peckinpah's *The Deadly Companions* or Billy the Kid in Penn's *The Left-Handed Gun*. Nor is there the sense of the absurdity of life which we sometimes find in Boetticher's films: death, as we have seen, is for Hawks simply a routine occurrence, not a *grotesquerie*, as in *The Tall T* ('Pretty soon that well's going to be chock-a-block') or *The Rise and Fall of Legs Diamond*. For Hawks "craziness" implies difference, a sense of apartness from the ordinary, everyday, social world. At the same time, Hawks sees the ordinary world as being "crazy" in a much more fundamental sense, because devoid of any meaning or values. "I mean crazy reactions—I don't think they're crazy, I think they're normal—but according to bad habits we've fallen into they seemed crazy." Which is the normal, which the abnormal? Hawks recognises, inchoately, that to most people his heroes, far from embodying rational values, are only a dwindling band of eccentrics. Hawks's 'kind of men' have no place in the world.

The Hawksian heroes, who exclude others from their own *élite* group, are themselves excluded from society, exiled to the African bush or to the Arctic. Outsiders, other people in general, are perceived by the group as an undifferentiated crowd. Their role is to gape at the deeds of the heroes whom, at the same time, they hate. The crowd assembles to watch the showdown in *Rio Bravo*, to see the cars spin off the track in *The Crowd Roars*. The gulf between the outsider and the heroes transcends enmities among the *élite:* witness *Dawn Patrol* or Nelse in *El Dorado*. Most dehumanised of all is the crowd in *Land of the Pharaohs*, employed in building the Pyramids. Originally the film was to have been about Chinese labourers building a "magnificent airfield" for the American army, but the victory of the Chinese Revolution forced Hawks to change his plans. ("Then I thought of the building of the Pyramids; I thought it was the same kind of story.") But the presence of the crowd, of external society, is a constant covert threat to the Hawksian *élite*, who retaliate by having "fun." In the crazy comedies ordinary citizens are turned into comic butts, lampooned and tormented: the most obvious target is the insurance salesman in *His Girl Friday*. Often Hawks's revenge becomes grim and macabre. In *Sergeant York* it is "fun" to shoot Germans "like turkeys"; in *Air Force* it is "fun" to blow up the Japanese fleet. In *Rio Bravo* the geligniting of the badmen "was very funny." It is at these moments that the *élite* turns against the world outside and takes the opportunity to be brutal and destructive.

Besides the covert pressure of the crowd outside, there is also an overt force which threatens: woman. Man is woman's "prey." Women are admitted to the male group only after much disquiet

Howard Hawks's battle between the sexes. Carole Lombard and John Barrymore in *Twentieth Century* (1934), Cary Grant and Katharine Hepburn in *Bringing Up Baby* (1938). "Besides the covert pressure of the crowd outside, there is also an overt force which threatens: woman. Man is woman's 'prey'" (WOLLEN, page 686).

and a long ritual courtship, phased round the offering, lighting and exchange of cigarettes, during which they prove themselves worthy of entry. Often they perform minor feats of valour. Even then though they are never really full members. A typical dialogue sums up their position:

Woman: You love him, don't you?
Man (embarrassed): Yes . . . I guess so. . . .
Woman: How can I love him like you?
Man: Just stick around.

The undercurrent of homosexuality in Hawks's films is never crystallised, though in *The Big Sky*, for example, it runs very close to the surface. And he himself described *A Girl in Every Port* as "really a love story between two men." For Hawks men are equals, within the group at least, whereas there is a clear identification between women and the animal world, most explicit in *Bringing Up Baby*, *Gentlemen Prefer Blondes* and *Hatari!* Man must strive to maintain his mastery. It is also worth noting that, in Hawks's adventure dramas and even in many of his comedies, there is no married life. Often the heroes were married or at least intimately committed, to a woman at some time in the distant past but have suffered an unspecified trauma, with the result that they have been suspicious of women ever since. Their attitude is "Once bitten, twice shy." This is in contrast to the films of Ford, which almost always include domestic scenes. Woman is not a threat to Ford's heroes; she falls into her allotted social place as wife and mother, bringing up the children, cooking, sewing, a life of service, drudgery and subordination. She is repaid for this by being sentimentalised. Boetticher, on the other hand, has no obvious place for women at all; they are phantoms, who provoke action, are pretexts for male modes of conduct, but have no authentic significance in themselves. "In herself, the woman has not the slightest importance."

Hawks sees the all-male community as an ultimate; obviously it is very retrograde. His Spartan heroes are, in fact, cruelly stunted. Hawks would be a lesser director if he was unaffected by this, if his adventure dramas were the sum total of his work. His real claim as an author lies in the presence, together with the dramas, of their inverse, the crazy comedies. They are the agonised exposure of the underlying tensions of the heroic dramas. There are two principal themes, zones of tension. The first is the theme of regression: of regression to childhood, infantilism, as in *Monkey Business*, or regression to savagery: witness the repeated scene of the adult about to be scalped by painted children, in *Monkey Business* and in *The Ransom of Red Chief*. With brilliant insight, Robin Wood has shown how *Scarface* should be categorised among the comedies rather than the dramas: Camonte is perceived as savage, child-like, subhuman. The second principal comedy theme is that of sex-reversal and role-reversal. *I Was A Male War Bride* is the most extreme example. Many of Hawks's comedies are centred round domineering women and timid, pliable men: *Bringing Up Baby* and *Man's Favourite Sport*, for example. There are often scenes of male sexual humiliation, such as the trousers being pulled off the hapless private eye in *Gentlemen Prefer Blondes*. In the same film, the Olympic Team of athletes are reduced to passive objects in an extraordinary Jane Russell song number; big-game hunting is lampooned, like fishing in *Man's Favourite Sport*; the theme of infantilism crops up again: "The child was the most mature one on board the ship, and I think he was a lot of fun."

Whereas the dramas show the mastery of man over nature, over woman, over the animal and childish; the comedies show his humiliation, his regression. The heroes become victims; society, instead of being excluded and despised, breaks in with irruptions of monstrous farce. It could well be argued that Hawks's outlook, the alternative world which he constructs in the cinema, the Hawksian heterocosm, is not one imbued with particular intellectual subtlety or sophistication. This does not detract from its force. Hawks first attracted attention because he was regarded naïvely as an action director. Later, the thematic content which I have outlined was detected and revealed. Beyond the stylemes, semantemes were found to exist; the films were anchored in an objective stratum of meaning, a plerematic stratum, as the Danish linguist Hjelmslev would put it. Thus the stylistic expressiveness of Hawks's films was shown to be not purely contingent, but grounded in significance.

Something further needs to be said about the theoretical basis of the kind of schematic exposition of Hawks's work which I have outlined. The 'structural approach' which underlies it, the definition of a core of repeated motifs, has evident affinities with methods

689

which have been developed for the study of folklore and mythology. In the work of Olrik and others, it was noted that in different folk-tales the same motifs reappeared time and time again. It became possible to build up a lexicon of these motifs. Eventually Propp showed how a whole cycle of Russian fairy-tales could be analysed into variations of a very limited set of basic motifs (or moves, as he called them). Underlying the different, individual tales was an archi-tale, of which they were all variants. One important point needs to be made about this type of structural analysis. There is a danger, as Lévi-Strauss has pointed out, that by simply noting and mapping resemblances, all the texts which are studied (whether Russian fairy-tales or American movies) will be reduced to one, abstract and impoverished. There must be a moment of synthesis as well as a moment of analysis: otherwise, the method is formalist, rather than truly structuralist. Structuralist criticism cannot rest at the perception of resemblances or repetitions (redundancies, in fact), but must also comprehend a system of differences and oppositions. In this way, texts can be studied not only in their universality (what they all have in common) but also in their singularity (what differentiates them from each other). This means of course that the test of a structural analysis lies not in the orthodox canon of a director's work, where resemblances are clustered, but in films which at first sight may seem eccentricities.

In the films of Howard Hawks a systematic series of oppositions can be seen very near the surface, in the contrast between the adventure dramas and the crazy comedies. If we take the adventure dramas alone it would seem that Hawks's work is flaccid, lacking in dynamism; it is only when we consider the crazy comedies that it becomes rich, begins to ferment: alongside every dramatic hero we are aware of a phantom, stripped of mastery, humiliated, inverted. With other directors, the system of oppositions is much more complex: instead of there being two broad strata of films there are a whole series of shifting variations. In these cases, we need to analyse the roles of the protagonists themselves, rather than simply the worlds in which they operate. The protagonists of fairy-tales or myths, as Lévi-Strauss has pointed out, can be dissolved into bundles of differential elements, pairs of opposites. Thus the difference between the prince and the goose-girl can be reduced to two antinomic pairs: one natural, male versus female, and the other cultural, high versus low. We can proceed with the same kind of operation in the study of films, though, as we shall see, we shall find them more complex than fairy-tales. . . .

1969

RICHARD CORLISS
THE HOLLYWOOD
SCREENWRITER

Eight years ago, when popular movie criticism consisted mainly
of plot summaries and star-gazing, and Bosley Crowther of *The
New York Times* was scorning Godard and ignoring Ford and
Hawks, *Film Culture* magazine published two articles by Andrew
Sarris that were to revolutionize film criticism in the United
States. In the first article, "Notes on the Auteur Theory in 1962,"
Sarris proposed an Americanization of the *politique des auteurs*,
which held that the director is the author of a film and that visual
style is the key to assessing a director's standing as an *auteur*. In
The American Cinema, he evaluated—indeed, he rated—106 Amer-
ican directors (and seven foreigners) in categories ranging from the
"Pantheon" to "Oddities and One Shots."

It took some time for the importance of Sarris' work to become
evident to the community of film scholars. Hadn't Pauline Kael
demolished his stratified silliness for good in a *Film Quarterly*
polemic read by far more people than Sarris' original articles?
Hadn't Dwight Macdonald resigned his regular column in *Film
Quarterly* because Sarris was invited to contribute, and hadn't
he done so with a venom that suggested an angry redneck burning
a cross on the lawn of his new Negro neighbor's house? Hadn't
Richard Dyer MacCann conspicuously omitted Sarris' writing
(or any *auteur* criticism) from his anthology, *Film: A Montage of
Theories*, which did include a piece by Kael the theory-baiter?

It's a pity that Academia didn't notice what Sarris had going for
him: an engaging prose style that ranged from entertainingly analytical to deliriously lyrical; a popular, hip publication *(The Village*

Voice) just right for reaching the young intellectuals for whom film was the most exciting art; a subject matter (the Hollywood sound film) that he knew almost viscerally, and whose product was bound to interest his readers more than the "serious" European films praised by his detractors; and a burgeoning group of articulate acolytes (like Roger Greenspun and James Stoller) who could spread the faith without his losing face.

Came the Revolution, which coincided with the growing number of film courses and monographs. Sarris' thoughtful and well-timed challenge to the near-monopoly of social-realist criticism was adopted by most of the younger critics, and even adapted by some of the less secure older ones. It was refreshing to examine films as the creations of artists rather than of social forces, and to be able to do so in a manner that was serious without being solemn. Americans could finally admit that their movies weren't sinful just because they were entertaining, and that the films deserved to be judged by the same artistic standards applicable to any film.

By 1969, when Sarris expanded *The American Cinema* to book length, the critical attitude that had begun as a reaction to the party line was in serious danger of hardening into the Gospel According to St. Andrew. *The New York Times* had been converted into a veritable *auteur* shrine; its first- and second-string critics adhered closely to Sarris' tastes and standards, and its Almanac welcomed the word *auteur* into the English language, along with *acid*, *activist* and *Afro*. Film societies mounted ambitious retrospectives of directors, from John Ford and Jean Renoir to Sam Fuller and Russ Meyer. Publishers commissioned extended studies of Fritz Lang (who has made forty-three films) and Roman Polanski (who has made five). The Revolution was victorious.

In some respects, however, the anarchists show tendencies of close-minded classicism. They put the spotlight on the once-despised Hollywood movie system and sprinkled a little cultural respectability on the industry's "hack" directors—fine. But in doing so they retarded investigation of other, equally vital film crafts, especially that of the screenwriter, who creates (or creatively adapts) a film's plot, characters, dialogue and theme.

The director *is* right in the middle of things. At the very least, he's on the sound stage while the director of photography is lighting the set that the art director has designed and, later, while the actors are speaking the lines that the screenwriter wrote. Quite

693

often, he steers all these factors—story, actors, camera—in the right *direction*. So why not just say it's his film, that he is the author? Simply because the director is almost always an interpretive artist, not a creative one, and because the Hollywood film is a corporate art, not an individual one. This doesn't diminish the importance of the director, or the validity of the Hollywood film as an art. Both Chartres and *Charade* were the work of a number of individuals who contributed their unique talents to a corporate enterprise, but this fact doesn't necessarily make either work less appropriate for serious study than, say, the Mona Lisa or *Mothlight*. It just makes it more difficult for the critic to assign sole authorship to the work—and why should he waste time on a Name Game like this?

In the same way, both Stanley Donen and Stan Brakhage may be called film artists, but Donen is an interpretive artist while Brakhage is a creative one; Donen is a conductor and Brakhage is a composer. Donen is a film *director* who collaborates with his writers, actors and technicians in a completely different way than Brakhage, the film*maker*, collaborates with his film strips and viewer. The case can be made that Donen is a better film director than Brakhage is a filmmaker; they work in separate but equal film traditions, and it is possible that Donen succeeds in his genre, whereas Brakhage may fail in his. The theory used to be that the solitary, creative artist produced Art, and the corporate, interpretive craftsman produced Entertainment—a prejudice that kept people from examining the Hollywood movie. The *auteur* theory says, in effect, "What you thought was just Entertainment is really Art, because it is the work of an individual creator—an *auteur*. Therefore the Hollywood movie is worthy to be examined."

Many films are indeed dominated by the personality of the director, although not, perhaps, in the way the auteurists mean. The phrase "directorial personality" makes more sense if taken quite literally. The good director is usually a man with a strong, persuasive personality. He has to be a combination of tough guy, to make the technicians respond to his commands, and best friend, to coax a good performance out of a sensitive actress. Whether he directs with a riding crop (Stroheim), an icy stare (Sternberg), or a few soft-spoken words (Cukor), his personality is often crucial to the success of a film. The importance of a director's personal—or even visual—style is not questioned here, only the assumption that he creates a style out of thin air (with his collaborating craftsmen acting merely as paint, canvas, bowl of fruit, and patron), instead of adapting it to the equally important styles of the story and performers. The same literal meaning can apply to a director's "authority," which accurately describes his function on the set.

But the director need not be the only dominant force in a successful film. Often the actor is the *auteur*. Keaton and Chaplin may be fine directors, but it is their screen personalities that we especially cherish. Who would trade Keaton the actor for Keaton the director? And who would prefer analyzing the directorial styles of James W. Horne, Donald Crisp, Edward Sedgwick or Charles F. Reisner to savoring that sublime bodily mechanism that Buster controls so beautifully? The unique cinema personae of W. C. Fields, Mae West and Laurel and Hardy also flourished with little regard to the director of record, and can be defined without much reference to him — although, quite naturally, the combination of the comedians with different scripts and directors produced varying results. The same can be said of such incandescent performers as Greta Garbo, Katharine Hepburn and Cary Grant. Just as one can be drawn to an exercise in visual style like Blake Edwards' *Darling Lili* without finding it a completely successful film, so can one delight in the way Garbo dignifies and illuminates a rickety melodrama like *Mata Hari* with her beauty, her passion, and her ironic acceptance of an innate and tragic superiority.

It's instructive — indeed, it's often fun — to see a great actor transcend a ridiculous script and unfeeling direction; it's interesting to watch a fine director play around with an incredible story and poor performers. But the real joy in movies comes from seeing the fortuitous communion of forces (story, script, direction, acting, lighting, editing, design, scoring) that results in a great Hollywood film. *Frankenstein, Scarface, Love Me Tonight, Camille, Holiday, Mr. Smith Goes to Washington, His Girl Friday, Citizen Kane, Penny Serenade, Casablanca, Double Indemnity, Body and Soul, Rachel and the Stranger, Born Yesterday, Seven Brides for Seven Brothers, The Searchers, Invasion of the Body Snatchers, Psycho, The Manchurian Candidate, Charade* and *Planet of the Apes* are just a few examples of collaborative movie-making at its best. Intelligent appreciation of films like these, and not scholastic disputes over the validity of individual signatures, should be our first critical concern.

The cry *"cherchez l' auteur"* can lead unwary film scholars astray when the *auteur* happens to be the author—or rather, when the script is the basis for a film's success. More often than not, when a fine film is signed by a mediocre director, the film's distinctive qualities can be traced to the screenwriter. There's no need to rescue Mitchell Leisen, Garson Kanin, Sam Wood and William D. Russell from the underworld of neglected directors simply because they were each fortunate enough to direct a comedy written by Norman Krasna (*Hands Across the Table, Bachelor Mother, The Devil and Miss Jones*, and *Dear Ruth*, respectively). The direction of these films is usually adroit and sensitive, and the presence of charming comediennes enhances them even further; but the delightfully dominant personality behind the screen is undoubtedly Krasna's. Similarly, the team of Sydney Gilliatt and Frank Launder constructed the frame—and contributed most of the furnishings— for two witty thrillers of the Thirties, Alfred Hitchcock's *The Lady Vanishes* and Carol Reed's *Night Train*. With the credits and Hitchcock's cameo cut from the films (but with the Gilliatt and Launder figures, in the puckish persons of Naunton Wayne and Basil Radford, left in), even an auteurist might have trouble determining which director was responsible for which film. That is because the authorship, and thus the responsibility, belonged to the two writers.

Body and Soul, written by Abraham Polonsky and directed by Robert Rossen, fits securely into Polonsky's very personal urban Hellmouth, with its Breughelesque, subway-at-rush-hour density, its stylized but fiercely realistic dialogue, and its cheeky characters who seem to carry both a chip and an albatross on their shoulders. His authorship of *Body and Soul* can be certified, if need be, by a look at his next film, the malignant *Force of Evil*, which he also directed, and which extends and enriches the penny-ante pessimism of *Body and Soul*. Waldo Salt's adaptations of *Rachel and the Stranger* (1948) and *Midnight Cowboy* (1969) are both graced by intelligent empathy for some very unusual characters, and by the gentle humor he evokes from the most improbable situations. Ring Lardner Jr.'s penchant for bantering, overlapping dialogue distinguishes *Woman of the Year* (1942) and *M*a*s*h* (1970), although most of his other assignments during those three decades offered him little chance to display his talent. Paul Mazursky and

Larry Tucker, not director Hy Averback, are surely the authors of *I Love You, Alice B. Toklas;* its successor, *Bob & Carol & Ted & Alice*, evinced the same social concerns and behavioral absurdities, while Averback has loped further into obscurity with each new film. (Significantly, now that Mazursky is a director, he tends to ignore the contribution of his writing partner.)

It's clear that some method of classification and evaluation is necessary, both to identify and to assess the contributions of the over-paid but underrated *genus* known as the screenwriter. But that is a game that conceals even more perils than Sarris' Hit Parade of Directors. Once the *auteur* scholar accepts the myth of the omnipotent director, his game is won: he can Pass Kael and Collect $200. Indeed, even an adherent of the *politique des collaborateurs* can be fairly sure that the director of record is the man who hollered "Action!" and "Cut!"—though his importance in controlling what went on between those two commands may be disputed. But the size of a screenwriter's contribution to any given film is often far more difficult to ascertain. A writer may have received screen credit for work he didn't do (such as Sidney Buchman on *Holiday*) or for a few minor suggestions (Orson Welles on *Citizen Kane*). More likely, his name may not appear on the screen even if he has written virtually the entire script. Ben Hecht was responsible for far more of *Gone with the Wind*'s dialogue than Sidney Howard, who had merely written a treatment of the Margaret Mitchell novel for producer David O. Selznick. But it was Howard who received sole screen credit, as well as a posthumous Oscar— for Hecht's work. Michael Wilson wrote the screenplay for *Friendly Persuasion* and co-scripted *The Bridge on the River Kwai*. But the Hollywood Blacklist kept his name off both films, and the writing Oscar for *Kwai* was awarded to Pierre Boulle, who had nothing to do with the film adapted from his novel.

A more subtle problem is appraising the work of a screenwriter who specializes in adaptations. Few screenwriters can boast a more impressive list of credits than Donald Ogden Stewart. As with George Cukor, the director for whom he produced his finest scripts, Stewart's "filmography is his most eloquent defense." Both Stewart and Cukor, however, had the good luck to be assigned adaptations of some of the wittiest and most actable theatre pieces of their time —*Holiday*, *The Women* (for which Stewart received no screen credit), *The Philadelphia Story*, and *Edward, My Son*, among others—and Stewart adhered closely to both in spirit and letter. Stewart's achievement should not be degraded; many screenwriters failed at the delicate craft he mastered. But, as with directors, one can distinguish several levels of screenwriting: the indifferent work of a mediocre writer, whether an original script or an adaptation (which we may call procrustean); the gem polishing of a gifted adaptor like Stewart (protean); and the creation of a superior original script, like Herman J. Mankiewicz's *Citizen Kane* or Polonsky's *Body and Soul* (promethean). When faced with the career of a Stewart, the critic who has discarded the convenience of the *auteur* theory must compare Stewart's adaptation with the source work, in hopes of detecting such changes as plot compression or expansion, bowdlerization, addition or deletion of dialogue, and differences in theme and tone. At worst, this research will exhaust and discourage the critic; at best, it will convince him that the creation of a Hollywood movie involves a complex weave of talents, properties, and personalities.

When a screenwriter, like Preston Sturges or George Axelrod, has a distinctive style, his contributions to films with multiple script credits can usually be discerned. But the hallmark of many of the best screenwriters is versatility, not consistency. Subject matter dictates style. Given the chameleon-like quality of these writers, how are we to know which part of the *Casablanca* script is the work of the sophisticated but self-effacing Howard Koch, and which part was written by Warners' prolific Epstein brothers? Luckily, Koch himself has told the *Casablanca* production story, and revealed that the Epsteins fabricated a plot around the name of a saloon—Rick's—they had found in an unproduced play, and that, when the brothers moved on to another assignment, Koch developed the strands of their story into a full-blooded screenplay that reads as well as it plays. We don't have many of these memoirs, though, and since most Hollywood egos are about as large as the Graf Zeppelin, the accounts of screenwriters may be taken with the same pillar of salt we keep handy for directors' interviews and actors' autobiographies.

Nevertheless, a screenwriter's work should, and can, be judged by considering his entire career, as is done with a director. If a writer has been associated with a number of favorite films, if we can distinguish a common style in films with different directors and actors, and if he has received sole writing credit on several films, an authorial personality begins to appear. The high polish and excitement of Koch's other work, for example (he wrote *Invasion from Mars*, better known as *War of the Worlds*, for the Orson Welles Mercury Theatre, and his film scripts include *The Letter, Sergeant York, Three Strangers, Letter from an Unknown Woman,* and *The Thirteenth Letter*), and his fulfillment of the three conditions mentioned above, give credence to his account of the writing of *Casablanca*. In fact, most of the best screenwriters were the sole authors of a substantial number of scripts.

The paucity of critical and historical literature makes all screenwriters "Subjects for Further Research." The cavalier groupheadings on the following lists are meant only to emphasize the tentative nature of the classifications. As more films are seen from a screenwriter's point of view, names will be shuffled from one list to another. Ultimately, each of these fine screenwriters, and a hundred more, should have an artistic identity clear enough so that such capricious classifications will be unnecessary. Until that enlightened time comes to pass, we must make do with an Acropolis of Screenwriters something like the one which follows. (To make matters even more delphic, the screenwriter's work is defined simply by three of his finest films.)

The men and women so honored, by adapting their conspicuous talents to the byzantine demands of the trade, developed the most successful screenwriting techniques. Success usually begat power, and power begat authority. By authority is meant the right to complete your own script without being forced to surrender it to the next fellow on the assembly line, the right to consult with any actor or director who wants changes, and the right to fight for your film through the taffy pull of front-office politics, pressure groups, and publicists. The power of the most important screenwriters often resulted in superior films, in which the distinctive contributions of writer and director can be analyzed with greater assurance. Inevitably, some writers had literary pretensions, not only for themselves but for the cinemah, and when these men achieved some measure of autonomy, the cheerful cynicism of their earlier, more successful scripts was replaced by sesquipedalian platitudes on The Brotherhood of Man Through World Government. Thus, the most famous screenwriters, such as Dudley Nichols, Dalton Trumbo and, of late, Buck Henry, are not necessarily the best. Nichols' thought-

699

ful articles on the need for sparse, realistic dialogue were not often matched by his actual scripts, which tend to talk the characters into the ground with palaver and pontification. Dalton Trumbo's private letters (now published in book form) reveal an easy-going but pungent wit that was concealed by his attempts to radicalize bourgeois movie melodrama. The pomp currently surrounding Buck Henry derives largely from the fortuitous circumstance of his visible connection with Mike Nichols and *The Graduate*, a film whose dialogue was lifted, almost word for word, from Charles Webb's novel. When on his own (in *The Troublemaker* and *Candy*), Henry's humor is decidedly undergraduate, even sophomoric.

Unfortunately, the best screenwriters are likely to be ignored by film critics and historians. It's a minor scandal that film students are aware of Don Siegel's montages for *Casablanca* but not of Howard Koch's script; that Jules Furthman is trampled under foot in the mad rush to canonize Hawks and Sternberg; that film buffs, who can trace Gregg Toland's deep-focus work from *Wuthering Heights* through *Citizen Kane*, don't know, and probably don't care, that Herman Mankiewicz wrote *Citizen Kane* with only nominal assistance from Orson Welles. "In my opinion," Welles said twenty years ago, "the writer should have the first and last word in filmmaking, the only better alternative being the writer-director, but with the stress on the first word."

Perhaps the day of the hyphenate, the writer-director, has already dawned, and the screenwriter will become just another high-priced artifact in that great Hollywood auction in the sky. Perhaps not. Some of the most successful and popular films of the Right-Now Generation have been close adaptations of novels, with tight, efficient scripts (such as *The Graduate*, *Rosemary's Baby* and *Midnight Cowboy*). It's also encouraging to note the return to prominence of veteran screenwriters who have learned to meet the demands of a youth market while doing work that an adult can be proud of: Waldo Salt with *Midnight Cowboy*, Ring Lardner Jr. with *M*a*s*h*, Abraham Polonsky with *Tell Them Willie Boy is Here*, and Albert Maltz with *Two Mules for Sister Sara*. But whether these trends are heralding the screenwriter's second wind or portending his last gasp, the first forty years of the American commercial sound film cannot be evaluated without considering the crucial role he has played. The best screenwriters were talented and tenacious enough to assure that their visions and countless revisions would be realized on the screen. Now it is time for them to be remembered in film history.

ACROPOLIS

PARTHENON	ERECHTHEION	BRAURONION	PANDROSEION
Sidney Buchman	**George Axelrod**	**W. R. Burnett**	**Charles Brackett**
Mr. Smith Goes	The Manchurian Candidate	High Sierra	Midnight
to Washington	How to Murder Your Wife	The Asphalt Jungle	To Each His Own
Theodora Goes Wild	Lord Love a Duck	The Great Escape	The Model and the Marriage
Here Comes Mr. Jordan	**Borden Chase**	**John Huston**	Broker
Jules Furthman	Red River	The African Queen	**Delmer Daves**
Rio Bravo	Winchester 73	Jezebel	An Affair to Remember
The Big Sleep	The Far Country	The Maltese Falcon	Dark Passage
Shanghai Express	**Garson Kanin**	**Nunnally Johnson**	Professor Beware
Ben Hecht	Born Yesterday	Jesse James	**Philip Dunne**
Scarface	Pat and Mike	Prisoner of Shark Island	How Green Was My Valley
Gone With the Wind	Adam's Rib	The Dirty Dozen	The Ghost and Mrs. Muir
The Scoundrel	**Charles Lederer**	**John Lee Mahin**	Hilda Crane
Howard Koch	His Girl Friday	North to Alaska	**Frances Goodrich and**
Casablanca	The Thing	Red Dust	**Albert Hackett**
Letter from	The Front Page	The Horse Soldiers	The Thin Man
an Unknown Woman	**Anita Loos**	**Joseph L. Mankiewicz**	Seven Brides
The Letter	Reaching for the Moon	All About Eve	for Seven Brothers
Norman Krasna	Hold Your Man	A Letter to Three Wives	It's a Wonderful Life
Bachelor Mother	Down to Earth	Million Dollar Legs	**Casey Robinson**
Hands Across the Table	**Daniel Mainwaring**	**Seton I. Miller**	Now Voyager
The Devil and Miss Jones	Invasion of the	The Criminal Code	Dark Victory
Frances Marion	Body Snatchers	Ministry of Fear	Captain Blood
Camille [1936]	Out of the Past	The Dawn Patrol [1930]	**Charles Schnee**
Stella Maris	The Tall Target	**Dudley Nichols**	The Bad and The Beautiful
The Scarlet Letter	**Herman J. Mankiewicz**	Judge Priest	They Live By Night
Frank S. Nugent	Citizen Kane	Sister Kenny	I Walk Alone
The Searchers	Citizen Kane	Swamp Water	**R. C. Sheriff**
Wagonmaster	Citizen Kane	**Abraham Polonsky**	The Invisible Man
Two Rode Together	**Robert Riskin**	Force of Evil	Odd Man Out
Samson Raphaelson	It Happened One Night	Body and Soul	The Old Dark House
Trouble in Paradise	Platinum Blonde	Madigan	**Frank Tashlin**
Suspicion	The Whole Town's Talking	**Morrie Ryskind**	Will Success Spoil
The Shop Around	**Donald Ogden Stewart**	Penny Serenade	Rock Hunter?
the Corner	Holiday	A Night at the Opera	The Paleface
Preston Sturges	Love Affair	Stage Door	Bachelor Flat
The Lady Eve	Edward My Son	**Jo Swerling**	**Anthony Veiller**
Sullivan's Travels	**Michael Wilson**	Leave Her to Heaven	The Killers
Easy Living	Five Fingers	Lifeboat	The List of
Billy Wilder	Lawrence of Arabia	Man's Castle	Adrian Messenger
Ninotchka	A Place in the Sun		The Stranger
Sunset Boulevard			**Phillip Yordan**
Some Like It Hot			The Man From Laramie
			The Fall of the
			Roman Empire
			Johnny Guitar [disputed by
			the authors of *Trente Ans*
			du Cinema Americain who
			contend that Ben Maddow
			is the film's
			sole screenwriter.]

1970

GERALD MAST
FROM THE COMIC MIND: COMEDY AND THE MOVIES

PRESTON STURGES
AND THE DIALOGUE TRADITION

One of the major traditions of sound comedy is the American film that generates its comedy through talk. Creating within the confines of the Hollywood studio system, several directors made distinctive, clever, and intelligent comedies that, like most American films of the 1930s and 1940s, were dialogue films in which pictures primarily supported the talk. But if the talk was good, the pictures pleasant and functional, the performances energetic and compelling, and the structural conception careful and clever, the comedy could be very entertaining indeed.

Because the dialogue comedy was so dependent on talk and structure, it was equally dependent on the scriptwriter who devised the talk and structure. The dialogue comedies were *written* comedies, and the writer played almost as great a role in shaping the film as its director. The scripts of Ben Hecht, Preston Sturges, Robert Riskin, Dudley ·Nichols, Herman J. Mankiewicz, Charles Lederer, Garson Kanin, and Ruth Gordon frequently overwhelmed the weak director, exerting far more influence over the film than the director's "auteurial" style. If that fact seems to contradict the assumption that the director is a film's prime mover, it is equally true that in the best dialogue comedies the insight of the writers fused perfectly with the style and attitudes of the director, who expanded the sharp script into the full and final comic conception.

Underlying the best of the dialogue comedies was usually a subtle and silent rebellion against the very studio system and values that produced them. Most of these films slyly bit the hand that fed them, but the bite was very coy and the teeth were often capped with the same tinsel and rhinestones that Hollywood so adored. The comedies developed a unique aesthetic for destroying Hollywood assumptions and conventions while appearing to subscribe to them. Their primary targets were the familiar movie definitions of love, sex, success, and propriety. And by shredding the Hollywood clichés, the comedies frequently implied a more human, sensible, and sensitive system of emotional relationships and moral values. As in the earliest American comedies, the sting of raucous, vulgar sincerity popped the balloon of pretentious gentility. . . .

No one made better dialogue comedies than Preston Sturges, primarily because no one wrote better dialogue. Sturges is one of those filmmakers whose one-liners are often as memorable as his whole films. In *Easy Living* (a Sturges screenplay that completely dominates its director, Mitchell Leisen), Jean Arthur is sitting on a Fifth Avenue bus when a sable coat descends from the skies to land on her head. She angrily turns to the man behind her, a Hindu wearing a turban, and snaps, "What's the big idea, anyway?" His answer, "Kismet." Ironically, the joke also functions in the film, for Kismet, fate, is the driving force in the film's plot.

In *The Great McGinty*, a crooked politician remarks, "If it wasn't for graft, you'd get a very low type of people in politics." When McGinty subsequently runs out on his wife, he tells her about the money he stashed away "to send the kids through college—without selling magazines." And the most brilliant collection of Sturgesisms opens *Sullivan's Travels*, as an idealistic director discusses a socially conscious film with his money-minded producers:

"You see the symbolism of it? Capital and Labor destroying each other."
"It gives me the creeps."

"It was held over a fifth week at the Music Hall."
"Who goes to the Music Hall? Communists."

"It died in Pittsburgh."
"What do they know in Pittsburgh?"
"They know what they like."
"Then why do they live in Pittsburgh?"

The Sturges emphasis on dialogue determines his film technique, which relies on the conventional American two-shot to capture the faces and features while the characters talk, talk, talk. But it is such good talk—incredibly rapid, crackling, brittle—that the film has plenty of life. Like Hawks, Sturges was a master of the lightning pace. When Sturges uses special, cinematic devices, he inevitably turns them into self-conscious bits of trickery and gimmickry that harmonize well with the parodic spirit of the film. His favorite game with the sound track is to use musical backgrounds that comment parodically on the action in the scene. The opening of *Sullivan's Travels* uses melodramatic "movie music" that underscores a stagey, predictable gunfight on top of a speeding train. We later discover the scene was indeed part of a melodramatic movie within the movie. *The Palm Beach Story* opens with the William Tell Overture to underscore a breathtakingly funny pseudo-melodramatic montage sequence that finally brings a future husband and wife to the altar. The film's final use of music is just as clever. While Rudy Vallee serenades Claudette Colbert with "Goodnight, Sweetheart" (complete with full orchestra) outside her window, the sweetheart takes refuge in the arms (and, by implication, bed) of her husband inside the room. Rudy's romantic singing drives her into the arms of his rival. And perhaps Sturges uses music most effectively and wittily in *Unfaithfully Yours* (1948) when an orchestra conductor imagines three separate strategies for handling his adulterous wife, each perfectly correlated with the musical feeling of the piece he is conducting.

Sturges also reserves his manipulation of editing and the camera for the occasional tricky effect. *Christmas in July* uses a comically obtrusive zoom shot accompanied by a whistling kazoo to achieve its final miraculous solution. *The Lady Eve* combines jarring shock-cuts and screaming train whistles as comic punctuation for each of Eve's "revelations" of her previous affairs to her innocent husband. The opening sequence of *The Palm Beach Story* is a dizzying, almost illogical montage that parallels a melodramatic murder in a closet with a wedding (breaking out of the closet?). Sturges similarly punctuates his scenes of talk with an occasional bit of physical, slapstick comedy (the automat scene in *Easy Living*, the racing land yacht in *Sullivan's Travels*, the escape from prison in *McGinty*, the rifle-shooting sequence aboard the train in *Palm*

Beach) that cunningly—sometimes too cunningly—injects motion into his motion pictures.

Sturges' cleverness also shows itself in the unconventional, unexpected people and situations with which he filled his films. His crazy foreigners—Louis Louis in *Easy Living*, the Boss in *McGinty*, Toto in *Palm Beach*—are burlesques of the Hollywood cliché. Where most of Sturges' contemporaries contrasted the pure, natural American with the corrupt, suave European (Henry James in Hollywood terms), Sturges' foreigners parody American ideals by trying to imitate them. Louis tries to open a huge, grotesque hotel rather than remain a brilliant French chef. His aspirations to gentility and class are undercut by his vulgarity and pronunciation—the Imperial "Suit" (suite), "phenonemom," "inwisibles." The Boss explains his American success by referring to the romantic tradition of the robber baron and by pointing out that, if it weren't for him, "everyone would be at the mercy" (but he never says at the mercy of what). Toto is the looniest foreigner of all, a slimy gigolo, ugly and wormlike, whose sole functions seem to be to parade around in a series of different costumes, to intrude into conversations with his single coherent word, "Greetings" ("His English is a little elementary"), and to chatter in some stew of languages that makes it impossible to tell to which tongue he owes his original allegiance.

Among the other wonderful Sturges caprices is "the Wienie King" in *Palm Beach*, a gruff, testy, deaf old gentleman who still loves the ladies and who can carry on whole conversations without understanding a single word. To Sturges we owe the comic and rare opportunity to hear Eugene Pallette, the human bullfrog, sing "For Tonight We'll Merry Merry Be" in *The Lady Eve*. *Easy Living* features a youth magazine called *The Boys' Constant Companion*. Ironically, this magazine is staffed entirely by prune-faced, moralistic old maids and misters. And about this magazine Sturges sneaks in a wonderfully sly bit of obscenity (Sturges, like Lubitsch, was a master at ducking the censor) when the rich businessman mistakenly refers to the publication as *The Boys' Constant Reminder*.

Sturges also delighted in showing apparently conventional Hollywood characters and scenes in a very unconventional light. The conventional boy and girl in *Christmas in July* engage in verbal battles that no Hollywood juvenile and ingenue ought to have. (He even tells her to shut up.) *The Lady Eve* contains two seduction scenes in which the lady throws herself at the recalcitrant gentleman, who insists on protecting both her and his virtue. The idyllic, conventional life of the rich receives rough treatment in the opening scene of *Easy Living*, when the wealthy husband and wife fight (almost to the death) over her newest sable coat. The Hollywood clichés of loving father and daughter get a tough beating from the continual violent arguments between Diana Lynn and William Demarest in *The Miracle of Morgan's Creek*. *Sullivan's Travels* reverses the clichés of city sensuality and country purity as a fat, lecherous farm widow does her utmost to enjoy the physical pleasures of Sullivan's young, firm body. The best things in the Sturges films are these surprising pieces of reversal and burlesque.

As for their wholes, each of the Sturges films begins with a parodic premise. *The Great McGinty* (1940) parodies both Hollywood "flashback" stories and the American ideal that anyone can rise to greatness; *Sullivan's Travels* (1941), Hollywood production values and the Hollywood iconoclast's urge to say something significant; *The Lady Eve* (1941), shipboard romance and virginal innocence; *The Miracle of Morgan's Creek* (1943), small-town Americana, the sanctity of motherhood, and patriotism; *The Palm Beach Story* (1942), marital tensions; *Unfaithfully Yours* (1948), marital infidelity; and so forth. The best Sturges films never desert delicate, fast-paced parody for moralistic, sentimental conclusions.

The Great McGinty is unrelentingly ironic. It begins with a delicious red herring, a framework story that seems to promise the tale of an erring bank clerk in a South American "banana republic." But the film couldn't care less about this bank clerk. The real story turns out to be about the bartender (Brian Donlevy), the man who stops the clerk from shooting himself. The bartender (only several reels later do we discover his name is McGinty) tells of his rise from hobo to governor. He begins his political career as a two-dollar voter for the political machine of some big city, substituting for those registered voters who are no longer alive to vote for the machine candidates. In his zeal, an ironic burlesque of "get out and vote," the hobo votes 37 times, earning himself $74. That is American ingenuity and gumption doubled and redoubled.

From this auspicious beginning the hobo rises through the machine's ranks. He first shakes down the shady businessmen (and women) who don't want to pay protection; for example, Madame LaJolla (pronounced "Hoya"), a "fortune-teller," must come up with $250 or "Madame LaJolla doesn't jolla any more." Then Dan McGinty wins his first office—alderman. He develops more refined methods for plucking higher sums. Finally, after acquiring a wife and kids, McGinty becomes "reform" mayor. (The Boss ironically runs the "Reform Party" as well as the machine.) In each of McGinty's steps up the political ladder, his style gets smoother (he even grows a mustache), his clothes get slicker (from hobo rags to a ridiculous plaid suit referred to as a "horse blanket" to a dapper three-piece business suit to a top hat and tails).

But McGinty gets into trouble when he falls in love with the woman he married for political convenience. She suddenly feels qualms about McGinty's "municipal improvements" (euphemism for graft) and the grafters who support him—slum landlords, owners of sweatshops. She urges McGinty to institute genuine reform, to buck the party, to make the world safe for the children. McGinty has his doubts. To his wife's sentimentalities about the "dark, airless factories," McGinty retorts with his own sentimentalities: the factory where he worked as a kid was clean and neat, a place where he labored profitably "instead of playing on the streets learning a lot of dirty words." But the wife's sentimentalities triumph—and Sturges clearly parodies yet another political cliché, the woman behind the man. (These were, after all, the years of Franklin D. and Eleanor.) Ironically, McGinty's one honest moment costs him his family, his power, his wife, and his fortune. When he bucks the Boss, the Boss bucks back, and the two of them end up in the "banana republic," continuing their long feud over who exactly is boss.

The unadulterated cynicism of *The Great McGinty*, its burlesque of the democratic political process and its reduction of an ideal—America as "the land of opportunity"—to the absurd would never have been accepted by audiences one year later. During the war years Sturges had to worry not only about the censor but also about stepping on the sensitive moral toes of a country sacrificing its young men to preserve the very ideals that *McGinty* burlesques. Sturges' greater consciousness of audience values is clear in *Sullivan's Travels*, in which the cynicism is tempered by an uplifting moral affirmation. The plot of this film springs from the tension between an intellectual film director who wants to make a "significant," socially conscious film, *Oh Brother, Where Art Thou?* and the producers who want him to keep making the escapist fluff at which he excels, *Ants in Your Pants of 1941*. The first part of the film convincingly demonstrates that a man with a college educa- tion, swimming pool, alimony payments, butler, and a troop of publicity men on his tail is incapable of capturing the desperation and misery of the poor and suffering. (There is perhaps a conscious reference to Ford's *The Grapes of Wrath* and the Pare Lorenz docu- mentaries in the film's depiction of starving tramps and govern- ment camps.)

But the second half of the film takes Sullivan and the audience in a very different direction and toward a very different conclusion. Through a series of bizarre accidents, Sullivan winds up truly wretched and helpless, an inmate of a brutal Southern prison (evok- ing the Hollywood chain-gang genre). In the midst of his misery, Sullivan goes to the movies; the prisoners are guests of a black congregation on its movie night. Sturges shows the parallel misery of both blacks and prisoners; as the convicts shuffle into the humble chapel wearing chains, the blacks sing, "Let My People Go." After this rather idealized display of social misery, the movie flashes on the screen (the third film within this film about films), a Walt Dis- ney cartoon with Mickey Mouse and Pluto. And all the down- trodden members of the audience respond in unison to the funny film—with laughter. From this demonstration, Sullivan concludes (after he gets out of prison as bizarrely as he got in) that *Oh Brother, Where Art Thou?* is not worth making. He directly pro- claims, "There's a lot to be said for making people laugh. That's all some people have. It isn't much, but it's better than nothing in this cockeyed caravan." After the explicit proclamation, only slightly softened by the fancy metaphor, Sturges ends the film with an equally explicit montage of laughing faces.

Christmas in July also insists on a moralistic ending, for the young man learns that his own ability is a stronger asset than any windfall (after which Sturges gives him the windfall). *Hail the Con- quering Hero* ends with the young man's confession of his dishon- esty to the whole town, a greater act of personal heroism than the very clichés that forced the man into his initial lie (after which the town elects him mayor). *Mad Wednesday* ends with the implication that it is better to be "mad," spontaneous, and free than to be chained to a stifling, deadening routine (and after Harold Diddle-bock's lesson in spontaneity, he discovers he has miraculously won both riches and the hand of the woman he loves).

So many of the Sturges films end with these "miracles"—like those sextuplets which are the miracle of Morgan's Creek. Such miracles are cop-outs. Despite their obvious parodies of Hollywood success stories and the Hollywood homily that the rewards go to the virtuous, Sturges' endings, like René Clair's, are incapable of tracing the implications of the issues that he himself has introduced. Either Sturges sells out to Hollywood's commercial necessities, or he is a lazy, sloppy thinker who cannot refuse the easy road (as James Agee suggests), or, like René Clair, he simply "likes happy endings"—whether they make intellectual sense or not.

The absence of these moralizing and miraculous solutions in Sturges' domestic films perhaps accounts for their greater unity and consistency. *Easy Living*, *The Lady Eve*, and *The Palm Beach Story* do not desert irony and satire to give the audience an obligatory piece of optimistic inspiration. In its own way *Easy Living* is a much better film about the Depression than *Sullivan's Travels*, simply because it plays on the irony that for some people a $58,000 sable coat is so valueless that it can be thrown away like a piece of trash, and for others a $58,000 sable coat is so valueless that it can't provide a nourishing meal or a necessary job.

Despite the Sturges toughness, his scorn for fakery and poses, his ridiculing of false ideals, it is more difficult to see what he accepts than what he rejects. If there is a positive Sturges ideal, it can be seen more easily in his people than in the moral summaries that conclude so many of his films. The members of the Sturges troupe —the character actors he uses over and over again—say much about Sturges' values. William Demarest is Sturges' alter ego; tough, cynical, anti-sentimental, he owes no allegiance to abstractions, but is always loyal to his friends. Jimmy Conlin—the owlish flea, nervous, squeaky-voiced—usually comforts those in trouble. Eric Blore, a man of words and poses, knows how to twist appearances to make people accept the fake as real. Robert Greig, the inevitable butler, enjoys the luxury of being a butler and is a loyal cynic who refuses to romanticize the class question. Edgar Kennedy —bartender, private detective—never lets his gruff voice and appearance interfere with his human compassion. And so forth. Most of the Sturges players are mixtures of toughness and softness (even the mincing Franklin Pangborn), scornful of idealistic clichés, usually responsive to each other as people.

In his attack on sentimental and pretentious clichés, Sturges is clearly part of the great American comic tradition that stretches back to the earliest comic jests. Like Lubitsch, Hawks, and Ben Hecht, Sturges disguised his contempt for the Hollywood beatitudes with cinematic conventions that looked very much like the usual Hollywood product. For most members of the audience, *Easy Living* was a wonderful chance to indulge fantasies about incredible luxuries dropping from the skies. The ornate, lavish sets—particularly the Imperial "Suit"—looked exactly like the gaudy settings of their favorite M-G-M films. But for a few members of the audience, the film was a chance to see the grotesque excesses of wealth, the immense gap between rich and poor, and the instability of a stock market that could rise and fall crazily on the whims of a dizzy lady. Further, the film coyly exposes the importance of sex in our supposedly puritanical society; Mary Smith derives all her power from everyone else's assumption that she is sleeping with the powerful financier. In his delightful games with Hollywood expectations, Sturges' cleverness and iconoclasm are more impressive than the depth and complexity of his vision. Sturges very quickly ran out of that iconoclastic energy in the years following the war.

1973

RICHARD KOSZARSKI
THE MEN WITH
THE MOVIE CAMERAS

When applying the spotlight theory of film history, attention is directed from one "golden age" to another, flitting back and forth across Europe, back and forth across the Atlantic, following the cinematic muse as it settles first with one national cinema and then another. This theory is quite serviceable in the writing of cursory film histories, but always raises the problem of specifically delineating each national cinema to which the author seeks to attribute greatness. Those who apply this technique most strictly tend to choose movements that are easy to talk about in terms commonly employed in literary analysis. It is a strong thematic quality which unites the Soviet, German, or post-war Italian schools for these writers, and any utilization of editing, design or camerawork is shuffled uncomfortably to a far corner and discussed as ancillary technique. This is only to be expected, given the state of film historical study and the predilections of many film historians. Occasionally the more daring among them will try to relate the "style" of a particular movement to the "content" of that movement, but seldom will you find any admission that the style *is* the movement, and the way a story is told *is* the story. Our conditioned vocabularies resist defining a movement in terms of juxtaposition or spacial relationships, and consequently, the only film movements that get generally discussed *as* movements are those who have a strong and unifying thematic core susceptible to analysis in literary fashion.

When film criticism grew into a more artist-centered format, it was still these thematic values that dominated the conversation.

Directors, even such obvious visual stylists as Ophuls or Dreyer, were discussed primarily in terms of the story content of their work, certainly a strange approach for criticism of this most modern of art forms. Recently the grip of director-as-auteur criticism has loosened, and fleeting spotlights of attention have been directed to other participants in the filmmaking process. Last year *Film Comment* devoted a whole issue to the work of the screenwriter, certainly a fresh approach in the welter of director-centered criticism that has appeared in the past decade, but predictably devoted to a type of filmmaker intimately bound up with story and narrative elements, and thus susceptible to the standard forms of literary/thematic analysis employed previously.

Written criticism necessarily tends towards what can be verbalized most satisfactorily, and so film criticism has always centered on those elements of this variegated art form which are most manageable in literary terms. But the form demands critics equipped to discuss it not only in the terms of written literature, but with a critical vocabulary conscious of developments in post-war music and art as well, prepared to discuss the *moving picture* in terms of the questions raised by these related disciplines. Only then can we successfully appreciate the work of those whose creative contribution is involved most directly with the more plastic and rhythmic elements of the medium, those who lend form and movement to the structure of the moving image. At this state in film history a monograph on Margaret Booth would be most welcome. Or on the other hand, a study of those who put the images on the film in the first place. It is simply preposterous that there is not a *sentence* on the art of Lee Garmes or Gregg Toland, not any proper critical evaluation. What were these men doing? It is a very hopeful sign that the American Film Institute has been spending more attention lately in compiling oral histories of cinematographers, and that several books have appeared recently with similar information. But these are only tools for scholars and critics, with little value as ends in themselves.

They are only starting points in analysis. They do, however, represent new material not previously collected and absolutely crucial to any understanding of the work of the film artists involved. Even more importantly, they illuminate still another "golden age," which unlike that of Germany or Italy or Great Britain was not one defined so easily by its content as by its style—the Hollywood golden age, the classic period of the American studios, from 1915 up to the Fifties. It becomes clear that here was the key unifying element of the Hollywood style, a visual hallmark which effectively evaded the attentions of most previous historians.

The process of absorption, synthesis and change is what marks Hollywood photography throughout, the idea of building on earlier models, foreign models, contemporary models, taking everything of quality in sight and putting it to use for their own particular ends. This eclecticism was developed into an unmistakeably fluid and dynamic style by Hollywood cameramen over the four or five decades of Hollywood's ascendance, and its roots may be traced back to the very beginnings of American production. When G. W. Bitzer began work at Biograph in 1898 the motion picture had just left the laboratories of its inventors. Lumière, Dickson—Friese-Greene if you insist—had demonstrated just before the turn of the century the success of their mechanical contrivances in catching and reduplicating action in movement. But after perfecting the device they left its development to other hands, and the motion picture passed from inventors and mechanics fascinated by the problem of movement to businessmen and artists enthralled by the fact of movement itself. To Méliès and Porter, to Smith and Selig and Lubin and dozens of other vague figures of this transitional period, the fate of this latest Victorian marvel was entrusted. The manner of their success is still something that awaits the proper Gordon Hendricks treatment, but one factor which unified all of their work was an intense personal contact with all the elements of the film-making process.

This was the scene into which Bitzer wandered in 1898. A film was generally conceived, shot, developed and printed by one man —a not infelicitous situation for 50- or 100-foot productions. This is the way Bitzer himself learned filmmaking, and his early work preserved on Library of Congress paper prints casts an interesting light on the nature of his collaboration with Griffith years later. But of all these functions, by far the chief was photography. "Making a moving picture" meant turning the crank; thinking up a story, handling the actors and cutting the material together was just icing on the cake. Soon a primitive division of labor was introduced for

713

the more complicated productions, and specialized film "directors" like Wallace McCutcheon began to restrict themselves to working solely with the stories and actors of the increasingly complicated narrative films. But the mechanical portion of the machine art was left to the cameramen, and when the time came this is what Bitzer and many others chose to specialize in. The responsibility of this position was such that when Griffith arrived in 1908 he found his cameramen were often slow to implement the suggestions and improvements he thought of for his films. They reasoned that if anything went wrong with the film, if an image failed to register, it was the cameraman and not the director who was in trouble. The camera was still the whole show.

But the growth of the modern cinema restructured all of this again. The Hollywood studio tradition grew up around the idea of division of labor, of departmentalization, of a specialist for every aspect of the production—literary, scenic, photographic, or whatever. Screenwriters decided what Hollywood films had to say, and directors how it would be said. But putting the image on film—"making the moving picture"—was still the responsibility of the cameraman. And in the pre-war years this was no mean accomplishment. Lethargic emulsions, sputtering or non-existent lighting, crotchety camera mechanisms and super-slow lenses made great cameramen out of anyone who could succeed in getting a clearly focussed image on the film—yet those troublesome days were certainly a fruitful training ground. By 1915 mechanical difficulties had been swept away and expression in terms of light was made possible on a major scale.

Three films of that year, fortunately all extant in fine quality prints, offer good examples: De Mille's *The Cheat*, shot by Alvin Wyckoff; Dwan's *David Harum*, shot by Hal Rosson; and Griffith's *The Birth of a Nation*, shot by Billy Bitzer. In these three films one can see already formed the basis of the whole tradition of American cinematography. Wyckoff's use of shadows for psychological effect, of superb figure molding, of intricately accomplished trick work, points to the whole romantic-expressionist tradition of Lee Garmes, John Seitz and Bert Glennon. Rosson's warm and documentary-like examination of the countryside (complete with precocious deep focus and tracking movements) prefigures the deceptively uncomplicated styles of George Schneiderman or William

714

Clothier. And Bitzer's bravura camerawork, which can encompass intimate human drama and grandscale panorama in the same shot (as in Sherman's march to the sea), has been carried on by such men as Leon Shamroy and Robert Surtees.

Over the intervening years the continuity of this visual style was fostered by a number of methods which enabled younger cameramen to work under more experienced veterans in a direct way, either as operators, second cameramen, or assistants. Thus, an informal "school" of one particular visual style can be traced in a reasonably clear manner (something which can't be done with directors, for example, whose assistants were usually busy rounding up extras). Many cameramen were under contract to studios for years, and such cross-pollination no doubt resulted in one particular style heavily influencing a wide variety of younger assistants who were also under contract at the time. One can discuss an Ernest Palmer or Arthur Miller or Leon Shamroy style at Fox, for example, which would exist outside of any particular trend in studio production. Of course, when such a studio style was definitely promoted, it was the cameraman who carried it along. Warner Brothers films of the Thirties are probably visualized more clearly in terms of Sol Polito, Tony Gaudio and Barney McGill, than through Wellman, LeRoy or even Curtiz. Paramount's glossiest period was the result of Victor Milner and Lee Garmes as much as Lubitsch, Sternberg or Mamoulian. William Daniels, Oliver Marsh and Harry Stradling Sr. went a long way toward producing the MGM look. And Joe Walker was Columbia all by himself.

Once such a studio style had been fixed it seemed to pervade the rafters of the studio itself. George Folsey moved from Paramount *(Applause, The Smiling Lieutenant)* to Metro *(Meet Me in St. Louis, The White Cliffs of Dover)* but his style didn't move with him. Only those cameramen with the strongest personal styles were able to cross studio boundaries with impunity and imprint their own vision on everything. Hal Rosson could make a Metro Fleming *(Red Dust)* look like a Paramount Sternberg *(The Docks of New York)*, and Bert Glennon, Joe August or Gregg Toland could do the same thing.

Just as many of the great cameramen were associated most strongly with individual studios, another group was so linked to individual directors that their work together created a fusion of per-

715

Three films photographed by Gregg Toland—*Citizen Kane* (directed by Orson Welles), *Wuthering Heights* (directed by William Wyler), and *The Best Years of Our Lives* (also directed by Wyler). Note the triangular composition of all three and the use of screen depth. "Only those cameramen with the strongest personal styles were able to cross studio boundaries with impunity and imprint their own vision on everything" (KOSZARSKI, page 715).

Citizen Kane (1941): Joseph Cotton, Orson Welles, and Everett Sloan.

Wuthering Heights (1939): Geraldine Fitzgerald, Laurence Olivier, Leo G. Carroll, and Flora Robson.

The Best Years of Our Lives (1946): Dana Andrews, Teresa Wright, Myrna Loy, Fredric March, Harold Russell, and Cathy O'Donnell.

sonal styles similar to some of the studio/cameraman associations. Bitzer and Griffith are the chief examples, but John Seitz and Rex Ingram (and later Billy Wilder), Karl Brown and James Cruze, and Robert Burks and Alfred Hitchcock are also notable pairings and, when these associations broke up, the effect on the visual style of both partners was often quite noticeable (Hitchcock's work after Burks' death, for example).

But Hollywood's visual style was not a purely inbred tradition. As with everything else, the studios could appropriate a pictorial style from overseas and make it their own. In the late Twenties and early Thirties a "German look" was highly cultivated, but there was no mistaking *Flesh and The Devil* or *Svengali* as anything but pure Hollywood, no matter how hard they tried. The finest Hollywood cameramen always added to the techniques they adopted from overseas, and to see this most clearly look at *Sunrise* against the context of Murnau's earlier films. The German cameramen had retained their primary interest in engineering; creative photography was concerned with the designing of tracking and dollying equipment. But Struss and Rosher quickly adapted to the moving style called for by Murnau and combined with this their own backgrounds in portrait photography. The visual difference between *Sunrise* and *The Last Laugh* can be seen in the figure molding on the faces of George O'Brien and Janet Gaynor, a lighting sophistication undreamed of in Germany at the time, but well grounded in American camerawork throughout the Twenties. Karl Freund and the other German cameramen who successfully worked in America quickly adapted themselves to these new complexities of shading, and we can trace this change by watching their earliest American work.

The post-World War II period brought the influence of the documentarists and Italian neo-realists, but here again it was digested and made part of the evolving tradition. Look at James Wong Howe's *The Rose Tattoo*, which echoes the grim texture of Magnani's Italian films—an amazing hybrid, but still a most polished piece of Hollywood craftsmanship underneath. And when the studios weren't borrowing stylistic touches from overseas they were often borrowing the cameramen themselves: Freund, Maté, Planer and others came over and brought part of the European tradition with them. Karl Freund made *Murders in the Rue Morgue* a sequel to *Caligari* and *The Golem*. One can see Dreyer's wall-eyed lighting effects behind Rita Hayworth in Rudolph Maté's photography of *Gilda*. As for Franz Planer, his work with Ophuls on both sides of the Atlantic is reflected in the elegance of such diverse work as *Holiday* and *Breakfast at Tiffany's*. The list could go on and on.

In the flow of these influences, as well as their absorption into the general fabric of Hollywood style, . . . one not only sees the growth of the individual artist, but the historical context that prompted certain developments and his reactions and contributions to them. . . . Taken together these form the fabric of Hollywood's visual style with all the individual strands showing through. Combined with the work of directors, writers, designers and others, they form a picture of classic Hollywood as the Florence of the West, bringing together creative ideas and creative talents from all over the world, then blending them into a new and dynamic synthesis.

This fabled mixture held so long as there was a framework to support it all. When that dropped out it meant more than the collapse of the studio method of filmmaking. Without this structure to support growth and change, American cinematography turned from inspired eclecticism to fragmented inspiration. It came full circle again to the days of Billy Bitzer, as today's pioneers roam the streets with portable equipment and Angenieux lenses, starting their own traditions.

1972

ROLAND BARTHES
THE FACE OF GARBO

Garbo still belongs to that moment in cinema when capturing the human face still plunged audiences into the deepest ecstasy, when one literally lost oneself in a human image as one would in a philtre, when the face represented a kind of absolute state of the flesh, which could be neither reached nor renounced. A few years earlier the face of Valentino was causing suicides; that of Garbo still partakes of the same rule of Courtly Love, where the flesh gives rise to mystical feelings of perdition.

It is indeed an admirable face-object. In *Queen Christina*, a film which has again been shown in Paris in the last few years, the make-up has the snowy thickness of a mask: it is not a painted face, but one set in plaster, protected by the surface of the colour, not by its lineaments. Amid all this snow at once fragile and compact, the eyes alone, black like strange soft flesh, but not in the least expressive, are two faintly tremulous wounds. In spite of its extreme beauty, this face, not drawn but sculpted in something smooth and friable, that is, at once perfect and ephemeral, comes to resemble the flour-white complexion of Charlie Chaplin, the dark vegetation of his eyes, his totem-like countenance.

Now the temptation of the absolute mask (the mask of antiquity, for instance) perhaps implies less the theme of the secret (as is the case with Italian half mask) than that of an archetype of the human face. Garbo offered to one's gaze a sort of Platonic Idea of the human creature, which explains why her face is almost sexually undefined, without however leaving one in doubt. It is true that this film (in which Queen Christina is by turns a woman and a young cavalier) lends itself to this lack of differentiation; but Garbo does not perform in it any feat of transvestism; she is always herself, and carries without pretence, under her crown or her wide-brimmed hats, the same snowy solitary face. The name given to her, *the Divine*, probably aimed to convey less a superlative state of beauty than the essence of her corporeal person, descended from a heaven where all things are formed and perfected in the clearest light. She herself knew this: how many actresses have consented to let the crowd see the ominous maturing of their beauty. Not she, however; the essence was not to be degraded, her face was not to have any reality except that of its perfection, which was intellectual even more than formal. The Essence became gradually obscured, progressively veiled with dark glasses, broad hats and exiles: but it never deteriorated.

And yet, in this deified face, something sharper than a mask is looming: a kind of voluntary and therefore human relation between the curve of the nostrils and the arch of the eyebrows; a rare, individual function relating two regions of the face. A mask is but a sum of lines; a face, on the contrary, is above all their thematic harmony. Garbo's face represents this fragile moment when the cinema is about to draw an existential from an essential beauty, when the archetype leans towards the fascination of mortal faces, when the clarity of the flesh as essence yields its place to a lyricism of Woman.

Viewed as a transition the face of Garbo reconciles two iconographic ages, it assures the passage from awe to charm. As is well known, we are today at the other pole of this evolution: the face of Audrey Hepburn, for instance, is individualized, not only because of its peculiar thematics (woman as child, woman as kitten) but also because of her person, of an almost unique specification of the face, which has nothing of the essence left in it, but is constituted by an infinite complexity of morphological functions. As a language, Garbo's singularity was of the order of the concept, that of Audrey Hepburn is of the order of the substance. The face of Garbo is an Idea, that of Hepburn, an Event.

1957

721

KENNETH TYNAN
GARBO

What, when drunk, one sees in other women, one sees in Garbo sober. She is woman apprehended with all the pulsating clarity of one of Aldous Huxley's mescalin jags. To watch her is to achieve direct, cleansed perception of something which, like a flower or a fold of silk, is raptly, unassertively, and beautifully itself. Nothing intrudes between her and the observer except the observer's neuroses: her contribution is calm and receptiveness, an absorbent repose which normally, in women, coexists only with the utmost vanity. Tranced by the ecstasy of existing, she gives to each onlooker what he needs: her largesse is intarissable. Most actresses in action live only to look at men, but Garbo looks at flowers, clouds, and furniture with the same admiring compassion, like Eve on the morning of creation, and better cast than Mr. Huxley as Adam. Fame, by insulating her against a multitude of experiences which we take for granted, has increased rather than diminished her capacity for wonder. In England two years ago she visited Westminster Abbey, early one morning when no one was about, and in this most public of places found a source of enormous private enchantment. A walk along a busy street is for her a semi-mystical adventure. Like a Martian guest, she questions you about your everyday life, infecting you with her eagerness, shaming you into a heightened sensitivity. Conversing with her, you feel like Ramon Novarro, blinded in *Mata Hari*, to whom she said: "Here are your eyes," and touched her own.

I half-believed, until I met her, the old hilarious slander which whispered that she was a brilliant Swedish female impersonator who had kept up the pretence too long; behind the dark glasses, it was hinted, beneath the wild brown hair, there lurked the features of a proud Scandinavian diplomat, now proclaiming their masculinity so stridently that exposure to cameras was out of the question. This idle fabrication was demolished within seconds of her entering the room; sidelong, a little tentative, like an animal thrust under a searchlight, she advanced, put out a hand in greeting, murmured something muted and sibilant to express her pleasure, and then, gashing her mouth into a grin, expunged all doubt. This was a girl, all right. It is an indication of the mystery which surrounds her that I felt pleased even to have ascertained her sex.

"Are you all things to all men?" someone asks her in *Two-Faced Woman;* to which the honest reply (I forget the scripted one) would be: "To all men, women, and children." Garbo, Hepburn, and Dietrich are perhaps the only screen personalities for whom such a claim could seriously be made. "She has sex, but no particular gender," I once wrote of Dietrich, "her masculinity appeals to women, and her sexuality to men"; which is also true of Hepburn. Yet Garbo transcends both of them. Neither Hepburn nor Dietrich could have played Garbo's scenes with her son in *Anna Karenina;* something predatory in them would have forbidden such selfless maternal raptures. Garbo alone can be intoxicated by innocence. She turns her coevals into her children, taking them under her wing like a great, sailing swan. Her love is thus larger than Hepburn's or Dietrich's, which does not extend beyond the immediately desired object. It was Alistair Cooke who pointed out that in her films she seemed to see life in reverse and, because she was aware of the fate in store for them, offered the shelter of her sympathy to all around her. Through the cellophane *Kitsch* (how it dates!) of the Lubitsch touch she pierced, in *Ninotchka*, to affirm her pity for the human condition. The words were addressed to Melvyn Douglas, but we all knew for whom they were really intended, and glowed in the knowledge: "Bomps will fall, civilizations will crumble—but *not yet. . . . Give us our moment!*" She seemed to be pleading the world's cause, and to be winning, too. Often, during the decade in which she talked to us, she gave signs that she was on the side of life against darkness: they seeped through a series of banal, barrel-scraping scripts like code messages borne through enemy lines. Sometimes, uttering sentences that were plainly designed to speed the end of literature, she could convey her universal charity only in glimpses, such as, for instance, a half-mocking, half-despairing catch in the wine-dark voice. Round the militant bluster of M-G-M dialogue she wrapped a Red Cross bandage of humanity.

It is likely that too many volumes have been read into and written about her, and that every additional adulatory word reinforces the terror I am sure she feels at the thought of having to face us again and measure up to the legend. Possibly we exaggerated her intelligence from the beginning; perhaps she was perfectly happy with the velvet-lung, musk-scented tin lizzies that Salka Viertel and S. N. Behrman (among others) turned out as vehicles for her. Perhaps association with Lewis Stone and Reginald Owen, a stout pair of uncle-substitutes who crop up, variously bewigged, in many of her films, was vitally necessary to inspire her. Recall, too, that Carl Brisson and John Gilbert are known to have been high on her list of ideal men; and that we have no evidence that she has ever read a book. Except physically, we know little more about Garbo than we know about Shakespeare. She looks, in fact, about thirty-four, but her date of birth is disputable; the textbooks oscillate between 1905 and 1906, and one biography ungallantly plumps for 1903, which may, of course, be a wound left by an embittered typesetter. Stockholm cradled her, and like Anna Christie, she was the daughter of an impoverished sailor. She had a brother and two sisters, left school at fourteen, entered the newly expanding Swedish film industry, and was discovered by Mauritz Stiller. After the completion of *Gösta Berling* in 1924, her life is a list of movies, twelve silent, fourteen talking, and a file of newspaper pictures catching her aghast and rain-coated, grey-faced and weirdly hatted, on the gangplanks of ships or the stairways to planes. We often know where she is going, but never why. Occasionally a man is with her, a sort of Kafkaesque guard, employed to escort her to her next inscrutable rendezvous. Baffled, we consult the astrologers, who tell us that those born, as she was, between the end of August and the end of September are almost bound to be perfectionists; but what, we are left sighing, is she perfecting?

She changed her name from Gustaffson to Garbo, the Swedish word for a sprite. I used to think the Spanish "garbo" an insult to her, having heard it applied to matadors whose work seemed to me no more than pretty or neat. A Hispanophile friend has lately corrected me: "garbo," he writes, "is animal grace sublimated—the

724

flaunting of an assured natural charm, poise infected by *joie de vivre*, innate, high-spirited, controlled, the essentially female attribute (even in bullfighters). . . ." In short, "garbo" is Garbo without the melancholy, with no intimations of mortality. The word describes the embryo, the capital letter invests it with a soul. It is the difference between *Gösta Berling* and *Anna Karenina*.

But here again I am acquiescing in the myth of gloom. Long before the fit of hoarse hysterics that convulsed her when Melvyn Douglas fell off his chair, Garbo had laughed, even if it was only "wild laughter in the throat of death," and made us laugh too. She was never wholly austere. Posing as a man in the tavern scene of *Queen Christina*, how blithely she made us smile at her awkwardness when asked to share a bedroom with the Spanish ambassador! A secret half-smile, with the lips drawn back as if bobbing for apples, was always her least resistible weapon. Her gaiety coalesced, to the dismay of academic distinctions, with plangency. Her retirement is unforgivable if only because it means that now we shall never see her as Masha in *The Three Sisters*, a part Chekhov might have written for her. It takes lesser actresses to express a single emotion, mirth or mirthlessness. Garbo's most radiant grins were belied always by the anxiety in the antennae-like eyebrows; and by the angle of her head she could effect a transition, not alone of mood, but of age. When it was tilted back, with the mouth sagging open, she was a child joyously anticipating a sweet; when it was tipped forward, the mouth still agape, she became a parent wide-eyed at her child's newest exploit.

Some of her impact, certainly, was derived from the exoticism of her accent; hers was probably the first Swedish voice that many a million filmgoers had ever heard. Anglo-Saxons are notoriously prone to ascribe messianic characteristics to any stranger with a Slavic, Teutonic, or Nordic intonation; Bergner and Bergman are examples that come to mind, and the history of the London stage is punctuated with shrieks of exultation over long-forgotten soubrettes with names like Marta Kling, Svenda Stellmar, on Ljuba Van Strusi. Garbo was unquestionably assisted by the fact that she had to be cast, more often than not, as an exile: how often, to go about her business of home-wrecking, she arrives by train from afar! The smoke clears, revealing the emissary of fate, hungrily licking her lips. The displaced person always inspires curiosity: who displaced her, what forces drove her from her native land? If it was

Garbo's luck to provoke these inquiries, it was her gift which answered them. The impulse behind her voyages was romantic passion. Bergner might have left home to collect Pekes, Bergman to go
on a hiking tour: Garbo could only have journeyed to escape or to
seek a lover. Which is, as a line in *Ninotchka* has it, "a netchul impulse common to all."

Superficially, she changed very little in the course of her career;
a certain solidity in her aspect suggested, at the very end, a spiritualized reworking of Irene Dunne, but that was all. She could still (and
often did) fling her head flexibly back at right-angles to her spine,
and she kissed as thirstily as ever, cupping her man's head in both
hands and seeming very nearly to drink from it. And her appeal
never lost its ambiguity. The after-dinner cooch-dance which drives
Lionel Barrymore to hit the bottle in *Mata Hari* reveals an oddly
androgynous physique, with strong-kneed legs as "capable," in
their way, as the spatulate fingers: nothing is here of Herrick's
"fleshie Principalities." Pectorally, the eye notes a subsidence hardly
distinguishable from concavity: the art that conceals art could
scarcely go further. If this undenominational temple-dance is seductive (and, like the swimming-pool sequence in *Two-Faced Woman*,
it is), the explanation lies in our awareness that we are watching a
real, imperfectly shaped human being, and not a market-fattened
glamour-symbol.

I dwell on Garbo's physical attributes because I think the sensual
side of acting is too often under-rated: too much is written about
how actors feel, too little about how they look. Garbo's looks,
and especially her carriage, always set up a marvellous dissonance
with what she was saying. The broad ivory yoke of her shoulders
belonged to a javelin-thrower; she walked obliquely, seeming to
sidle even when she strode, like a middle-weight boxer approaching
an opponent: how could this athletic port enshrine so frail and
suppliant a spirit? Queen Christina, reputedly her favourite character, is encased for several reels in masculine garb, and when besought by her counsellors to marry, she replies: "I shall die a
bachelor!" And think of: "I am Mata Hari—I am my own master!"
To lines like these Garbo could impart an enigmatic wit which
nobody else could have carried off. Deficient in all the surface
frills of femininity, she replaced them with a male directness. Her
Marie Walewska was as lion-hearted as Napoleon himself, and I

726

have heard her described as "Charlemagne's Aunt." Her independence (in the last analysis) of either sex is responsible for the cryp-
tic amorality of her performances. In most of the characters she
played the only discernible moral imperative is loyalty, an animal
rather than a human virtue—that "natural sense of honour" which,
as Shaw says, "is nowhere mentioned in the Bible."

"Animal grace sublimated": I return to my correspondent's
phrase. If it is true (as I think it is) that none of Garbo's clothes ever
appear to be meant for her, much less to fit her, that is because her
real state is not in clothes at all. Her costumes hamper her, whether
they are stoles or redingotes or (as on one occasion) moiré, sè-
quinned, principal-boy tights. She implies a nakedness which is
bodily as well as spiritual. It is foolish to complain that, basically,
she gave but one performance throughout her life. She has only
one body, and in this incarnation that is all we can expect.

Through what hoops, when all is said and done, she has been
put by Seastrom, Cukor, Clarence Brown, and the rest of her
mentors! She has gone blonde for them, danced "La Chica-Choca"
for them, played a travesty of Sarah Bernhardt for them, stood
straight-faced by for them as Lewis Stone warned her of "a new
weapon called The Tank." Can we ask for more self-abnegation?
A life of Duse was once mooted for her—what an *éducation senti-
mentale*, one guesses, she would have supplied for D'Annunzio!
Later she hovered over, but did not settle on, a mimed role in
Lifar's ballet version of *Phèdre*. And at the last moment, when all
seemed fixed, she sidestepped the leading part in Balzac's *La
Duchesse de Langeais*. The most recent, least plausible rumour of
all insisted that she would film *La Folle de Chaillot*, with Chaplin
as the Rag-Picker. . . .

So it looks as if we were never to know whether or not she was
a great actress. Do I not find the death scene of *Camille* or the bed-
room-stroking scene of *Queen Christina* commensurate with the
demands of great acting? On balance, no. The great actress, as G. H.
Lewes declared, must show her greatness in the highest reaches of
her art; and it must strictly be counted against Garbo that she never
attempted Hedda, or Masha, or St Joan, or Medea. We must acclaim a glorious woman who exhibited herself more profoundly
to the camera than any of her contemporaries; but the final ac-
colade must, if we are honest, be withheld.

1953

Greta Garbo in *Love* (1927) and *Anna Christie* (1930). "Garbo still belongs to that moment in cinema when capturing the human face still plunged audiences into the deepest ecstasy . . ." (BARTHES, page 720). "*Anna Christie*, where she could ensconce herself, most of the time, in mute or monosyllabic sullenness . . ." (PANOFSKY, page 256).

CHARLES AFFRON
UNCENSORED GARBO

When a monarch caresses a bedpost it's not only "pornographic," it's downright "dangerous." Martin Quigley signals *Queen Christina* (1933) among the "Pictures Typical of Wrong Standards."[1] Queens, you see, have "authority, acceptance." Perhaps he feared a nationwide epidemic of bedroom fetishism. Women who had already plucked their eyebrows and bobbed their hair à la Garbo would henceforth spend their time fondling boudoir furniture rather than silently and invisibly indulging in the "pure love" sanctioned by the Production Code.

Garbo and her films transgress. She made fifteen talkies. In thirteen of them she portrays what used to be called a "bad woman," her badness ranging from sexual dalliance to genteel mistressdom to prostitution. Sex and marriage are compatible in only two of these films, and there the tandem is qualified by the shadiest of pasts (*As You Desire Me*, 1932) and a ploy that invoked the censors' wrath (*Two-Faced Woman*, 1941). Garbo is no naughtier than her rivals, at least according to the Production Code. Aside from Marie Dressler, female stars at MGM and elsewhere shone in sexuality. Even the pre-pubescent Shirley Temple and the virginal Janet Gaynor tease us to a heightened sexual awareness. We often scorn the vulgar "good" taste and manners of Irving Thalberg's hegemony at

[1]Martin Quigley, *Decency in Motion Pictures* (New York City, 1937), pp. 31–40.

MGM, but during his most active years, the studio's output can be characterized as positively dirty-minded. Norma Shearer played a modern "divorcée" (1930) and an exceedingly "free soul" (1931). In fact, two of Mrs. Thalberg's films, *Strangers May Kiss* (1931) and *Riptide* (1934), rate inclusion in Quigley's list of infamy. Joan Crawford was both "possessed" (1931) and "chained" (1934) prior to 1935. Even brave Jeanette was Lubitsch's "merry widow" (1934) and a singing Mata Hari-like spy in *The Firefly* (1937) before sprouting wings in *I Married an Angel* (1942). MGM was to become home to Judge Hardy (in *A Family Affair*, 1937) and Mrs. Miniver (1942), but only after Harlow had disported herself in its bathtubs and bedrooms, censorably "reckless" (1935).

If we use the obvious norms, Garbo's conduct seems considerably more decorous than that of many other leading ladies in the 30's. In *Grand Hotel* (1932) a flimsy negligée, an exposed knee, in *Mata Hari* (1932) her peek-a-boo dancing regalia— these are exceptions in a cinema wardrobe that consistently drapes every inch of her uncurvacious body. The most damaging effects of censorship on her career had little or nothing to do with the abolition of provocative gestures or risqué attires. The Code seemed more interested in the scripts, in the supposed "ideas" of films, than their potent and not-so subtexts. Censors fussed over the adulterous affair of Marie Walewska and Napoleon, enfeebling whatever spirit there might have been in *Conquest* (1937), and between Garbo and Boyer, a pair of screen lovers whose rhythms ought to have been perfectly matched. In other films Clarence Brown failed to solve easier problems than those presented by an evasive script, a welter of dull, lavish sets, and a heroine whose role was so lacking in definition. *Two-Faced Woman* is notorious in the history of film censorship. It elicited from a particularly enraged Legion of Decency the first blanket condemnation against a major studio film in several years. It was banned in Australia and Providence, R. I.[2] Cardinal Spellman labelled it as "the occasion of sin and as dangerous to public morals."[3] The Catholic Interest

---

[2]*New York Times*, Nov. 26, 1941, p. 29.
[3]*Ibid*, Nov. 27, 1941, p. 25.

Committee of the Knights of Columbus of Manhattan and the Bronx called it "a challenge to every decent man and woman."[4] Today we need a lively imagination to perceive such resonances in the film. The short scene inserted in the revised version may have cleared up Melvyn Douglas's confusion about which of Garbo's two faces he was looking at, but makes the film neither more or less innocuous, nor more or less boring. (Oh that Garbo had worn one scarred face in another 1941 film of Cukor, rather than the two silly ones that here end her career!)

The paradox of *Two-Faced Woman* is that it stirred such an uproar, and that Garbo was punished for a performance in which the quality of her sexuality was muted, lacking in intensity, almost without suggestive power. I suppose we should be thankful that the guardians of the Code were so busy being alert to white slavery, VD and children's sex organs that they remained blissfully insensitive to the more disquieting reverberations in Garbo's other films. Perhaps they assumed the public was insensitive as well. It seemed more important to protect the sanctity of marriage, so foully menaced by the polemic of a film as engagé as *Two-Faced Woman*, featuring the radical Constance Bennett and Roland Young, and the inflammatory tribal dance, the "Chica-Choca," led by Garbo herself.

The true perversion of *Two-Faced Woman* is that it vitiates Garbo's sexuality. Everyone knew Garbo was a sex-goddess, perhaps even a love-goddess. The rites befitting a goddess are practised in mystery. Those films that acknowledge the mystery and abet Garbo in visualizing her secret ceremonies, release her from the purview of the Production Code and detach her from its expectations, its moral standards. There is no provision for a sexuality as personal, as inner-directed, as unrelated to recognizable contexts as Garbo's. Indeed, the Code makes little sense when applied to the individuality of even more obviously "sexy" leading ladies. How do you apply standards to that which, by definition, is unstandard? If Garbo, Harlow, West, Dietrich are stars, they are beyond our poor measure.

---

[4]*Ibid*, Nov. 30, 1941, p. 71.

But our poor measure is not without value. It functions as an optic, focusing on the star a set of powers that magnify her anomalous aspects, foreign to our experience, and so desirable. Like any strong magnifier not dexterously oriented, it distorts, perhaps obliterates the image under scrutiny. The Code, with its prohibition of sexual explicitness, with its written and unwritten set of strictures, is analogous to the Classical unities and the conventions of *bienséance* that operate in French tragedy of the 17th century. The Classical Doctrine and its accompanying rules guarantee the intensity of Phèdre's passion; the Production Code, heavy with the trappings of bourgeois prudery and decorum, unleashes Garbo's longing, her belief that sex is a matter of life and death. Yet the degree of stylization demanded by both codes, Classical and Production, is not without its dangers. The relationship between style and experience has a breathtaking delicacy. The intimacy to which Phèdre draws us is perfectly strung on conventions of dramaturgy and versification that lose much of their potency after Racine's last plays. Garbo is sublimely served by the obliquity of representation that is the studio's response to the Code, but with only frustrating intermittency, and ultimately, not at all.

Her silent films offer a field of useful comparison. At first, the sexuality of Garbo's pre-Code work is ill-defined, almost caricatural, in the vamping of *The Torrent* (1926), *The Temptress* (1926) and *Flesh and the Devil* (1927). Her pervasive orality, aggressively open-mouthed kissing and interminable puckering over a cigarette and a communion cup are like pale-blue illustrations, ones we've seen too often before. The cigarette sequence in *Flesh and the Devil* survives for its historical importance in the Garbo canon, and for its fancy chiaroscuro photography. She is, however, much more provocative in her remaining films prior to her sound debut in *Anna Christie* (1930). Edmund Goulding, Fred Niblo and Sidney Franklin deck her out in varieties of erotically visual paraphernalia, and their inventions help us distinguish between Garbo, Negri and other two-syllabled sirens. The shadows, the exotic framing and dressing up in *Wild Orchids* (1929) play a baroque hide-and-seek with Garbo's image. *The Mysterious Lady* (1928) prefigures Sternberg's *Dishonored* (1931) in ways too obvious to mention, and show Garbo every bit as comic a tease as Dietrich will soon be. Yet titillation is peripheral to Garbo's erotic presence. It's a comfort to discover her expertise in ironic modes, but it's a greater comfort to watch as she liberates sensation from irony, clasping it to the core of her imagination.

Garbo's self-centered eroticism emerges clearly in Goulding's version of *Anna Karenina, Love* (1927), where the director exploits her refractive presence. She gazes thoughtfully, longingly at an Italian child, caresses his hair, seems to recreate his face, transforming it into that of the son she abandoned in Russia. The child leaves, the actress draws within herself, and with an ineffable cadence transfers this concentration to her love for Vronsky. The time of this configuration gives Garbo's face the span needed to juxtapose its aspects, to space them for our perusal, and to sum them in her love-filled eyes.

The most extended projection of the star's *innigkeit* occurs in Clarence Brown's pre-Code *A Woman of Affairs* (1929), a cleaned and blocked version of Michael Arlen's *The Green Hat*. Even before the official rules of censorship were formulated, the studio felt obliged to change the heroine's name from that veritable sound of dissipation, Iris March, to Diana Manners. The politely chaste goddess of the chase? Other equally risqué details were modified. The film is not at its most sensational during the several gropings of Gilbert and Garbo. It is the hospital sequence we all remember, and do so, in part, because Garbo so highly eroticizes a context full of non-erotic elements: the corridor, the severe hospital gown, the nuns. Garbo refracts her desire through these elements, isolating it in a space initially alien but eventually hers. Desire is finally lodged in the enormous bouquet of flowers that envelops her face. She fondles and devours this proxy-lover, losing herself in it as neither the conventions of love-making nor the laws of physics would permit with the lover himself. Her co-star excluded, she appropriates object-referents and exhibits a sexuality basic to art in its obsessive metaphorization—its fetishism. Garbo creates an intimate metaphoric relationship between being and object. This relationship is indeed more intimate than one established between two people, unless one

734

of them is objectified. Oblivious to the other characters during this part of the sequence (her progressive discovery of them is a remarkable transition from the register of poetry to the register of drama), Garbo allows us to share her greatest privacy, to enter that secret place where gesture and face and object configure the fullness of passion. Garbo shows us things we were never meant to see. As Phèdre opens herself to the gaze and the metaphoric sword of Hippolyte, so Garbo thrusts herself on us, staggering down the corridor, rapt in longing, and sharing it with her audience on this bridge of flowers. Her screen lover, John Gilbert, is denied the privileged point of view of camera and movie-goer.

In her Code-bound vehicles Garbo transmits similar bounty. In fact, since Garbo never thrived on explicit forms of transmission, it is logical to expect her to flourish in the indirectness of sexual referentiality developed during the 30's.

One immediate benefit of the Code, even in its pre-1934 application, is Garbo's almost complete devampification. Outside of a moment or two in *Mata Hari* and *As You Desire Me*, she doesn't have to indulge in eye-rolling and hip-swinging until *Two-Faced Woman*. Without benefit of the usual signals—winks, leers, funny dialogue, a voluptuous body—Garbo appears to be a woman who enjoys sex, who is eager to make love. Even in *Romance* (1930), one of her emptiest films, Garbo conveys sexual joy, no small feat considering the excessive chastity of her leading man, Gavin Gordon, and the rest of the furniture.

Responding to inventive and sympathetic directors, Edmund Goulding and Rouben Mamoulian, Garbo gives what are arguably her most erotic performances in *Grand Hotel* and *Queen Christina*. A stronger case must be made for Goulding than has been in the past. He is often relegated to the Faith Baldwin-Frances Parkinson Keyes school of directors, yet the visual arabesques of *Grand Hotel*, the interlocking sweep of shots and plot, seem to be more and more his responsibility as we become increasingly familiar with the directorial grace of *Dark Victory* (1939) and *The Constant Nymph* (1943). It is precisely this grace that matches Garbo's *rubato*, her phrasing of expression and posture. Goulding measures many of the shots

735

to Garbo's extended span of concentration, allowing her to bring together ambiguities of mood and plastique in unfragmented coherence. And it is in these shots, after the ballerina attitudinizing has been gotten out of the way, that Garbo is at her most erotic.

The duration of one brief shot is sufficient for Garbo and Goulding to explore the kind of desire Mr. Quigley would label "impure." After a night of love, the ballerina discovers that the stranger who prevented her suicide is a hotel thief. Despite her full gallery of kept women, for Garbo the essence of sex is not saleable. Her disappointment over Barrymore's confession in *Grand Hotel* gives way almost immediately to belief in the sincerity of his love. The shot in question charts her passage from incredulity to joy. At first withheld, her face, her eyes cross the frame's field, accompanied by a hand caressing the Great Profile and lips sensually exaggerating the nickname, "Flix." A word becomes a kiss, a sexual metaphor if there ever was one. We don't see the kiss she implants on Barrymore—the back of his head is in the way. After the one she has bestowed on us it would be redundant. The back of Barrymore's head is, in fact, an essential element in the shot's dynamics. It sweeps across Garbo's face, and she reappears at the other side of the frame, enraptured, her smile a sign of utter satisfaction. The shot ends when she almost imperceptibly blows on her lover's neck, gently kisses it, and finally nestles her own face there in ecstasy. We were denied the love scene of the previous night. Garbo here gives us a version of her arousal and fulfillment, and in the duration of the shot shows it all, locked in a rhythm that is hers alone.

One of Garbo's telephone scenes offers a variant of this erotic shorthand as well as a reminder of the sexual metaphors of *A Woman of Affairs*. The phone becomes a surrogate lover she addresses in a wide range of tones and fondles with a passion she would be loath to exhibit if the phone were indeed her lover.

Near the film's end she emerges from the door of the Grand Hotel, greets the sun, and, trembling with anticipation, traverses the frame with a movement so sinuous that she seems to be arriving and departing at once, reluctant to leave the sun

736

of Berlin, anxious to be on her way to the sun of Tremezzo and the arms of her lover. It is the ambiguity of this movement, executed in front of a revolving door, that conveys Garbo's eagerness for love, an eagerness that dispels absence, that animates the world around her with the delight of this refracted, stylized sexuality. The obliquity of the referents and the obliquity of her response isolate the thrill of her feeling to such a degree that her lovers often seem in the way, distracting and unnecessary to the erotic design.

This is precisely the case in the *Queen Christina* sequence to which Quigley took such heated exception, although I suspect he reacted to its more explicit yet less erotic aspects. The two-shots are disappointing, and not only because John Gilbert looks so absurd in a caricatural coiffure, moustache and chin piece. The best parts of the sequence expose Garbo in the solitude of her imagination. The relationship between the cadence of her body and a series of textures creates a pattern more deeply challenging to middle-class morality than the obligatory clinches. Fetishism is not singled out in the Code, but the degree to which it is here displayed would seem threatening indeed.

Garbo has already refined our apprehension of sexuality during the sex-role game she plays with Gilbert. The passage from a lightly worn masculinity to her own version of womanliness is accomplished with signs so faint and tantalizing as to leave us hovering over her identity. The removal of a jacket discloses a shirt less bulging than Gilbert's, a slightly bent knee, a barely tilted head, and a sexuality so rich in variety as to prohibit our most inventive attempts at classification.

After what seem like uninterrupted days and nights of love-making, Garbo literally draws the images of love from the textures of the room and reciprocally animates the furniture and shapes with her self-absorption. This appropriation of place and feeling begins with an unusually angled two-shot of Garbo alone, her profile and her reflection in a mirror. She eventually finds Gilbert in that mirror, but not until she has offered us this privileged view of her face, reorganized and newly possessed.

The sequence proceeds with variants of reflection, Garbo

impressing herself on surfaces whose degrees of tensility constantly modify her presence. The geometry of the spinning wheel tunes us to formality; the wool and the bed yield readily to the touch. At the center of the pattern is another shot analogous to the flower sequence in *A Woman of Affairs,* an extreme closeup of Garbo's face sinking into a pillow, receiving from it and transmitting to it versions of love recollected, present and anticipated. The final object, the bedpost, is touched by the magic of her face and hand, the wood endowed with the receptivity of the preceding surfaces, and relieved of its banal sexual symbolism. It shares in the richness of sexuality Garbo has imparted to a situation whose introduction was ripe for farce and whose resolution risked being as treacly as its accompanying music. Garbo's love-making is projected through filters that organize the experience in a perceptible style while enhancing sensation and presence. It never occurs to us to wonder if sex is simulated. We see Garbo more fully than we ever see Marilyn Chambers or Georgina Spelvin.

If this is perhaps the most fully developed rendition of Garbo's passions, it is happily not the last. In *The Painted Veil* (1934) the baroque orientalia of her liaison with George Brent, again preceded by a moment of literal self-reflection, is properly subsumed by the mosquito-netted, becowled sublimation of her love for Herbert Marshall, her worthiest partner since Nils Asther. *Anna Karenina* (1935) has an unhappy affair with Clarence Brown, who has predictibly increased difficulty in coping with the Code's stricter application. However Cukor's *Camille* (1937) is proof that neither actress nor director need feel prohibited by the Code, or more accurately, that prohibitions can be made to work to passion's advantage. In the atmosphere provided by Cukor, Garbo's breathlessness neatly links a consumptive chest and an avidity for sex.

The film and the star function on two levels of sexuality. The first is a luxurious and forthright depiction of the demi-monde that the censors must have excused in deference to the Dumas play's "light classical" reputation. The production values we often find so stultifying in M-G-M films of this period are positive elements in *Camille,* their sumptuousness exciting in radically sensational ways. Garbo on the prowl at the film's opening, suitably displaying her public sexuality in a theatre, reminds us of the way she picked up Robert Montgomery in *Inspiration* (1931); Laura Hope Crews and Lenore Ulric perform with a bawdiness quite remarkable in 1937; an unheard but pointedly laughed at dirty joke is the basis for an extended sequence. The humor and panache, the expensiveness of *Camille* are thresholds for the second level of sexuality, Garbo's hysteria, a highly pitched emotional vibrato scarcely muffled by her worldliness. It breaks through sophistication just as desire breaks through wisdom. She and Henry Daniell collaborate on a laughing duet (he is playing Chopin, *prestissimo*, at the time), during which Garbo's voice, ranging from brittleness to desperation, sings her frustration over her thwarted tryst with Robert Taylor. Wonderfully paradoxical, just before this episode, her gentle laugh at Taylor's ingenuous protestations of love becomes a hysteria made of near-silence, a breathy, whispering voice, her neck extravagantly arched in abandon. This pattern is amplified when she sacrifices Taylor, feigning boredom with her country life and her callow lover. Mercilessly coiffed in corkscrew curls, she mocks Taylor's seriousness, and then, in an anguished embrace, her face visible over his shoulder, she reveals to the camera alone the depths of her longing. We are tempted to forget the sexual core of a film so redolent of bourgeois morality and bourgeois notions of nobility, a film whose decor is so decorous and whose heroine suffers so grandly for her sins. Yet Garbo and Cukor keep the pulse of desire rapidly beating and consistently challenge us with the daring of their gestures. The plot and the dialogue are for the censors; the face, Garbo's ultimate field of sexuality, is for us.

Its suggestive power is never greater than in the shot preceding Taylor's return, near the film's end. A duration of forty-five seconds contains Garbo's joy, her anxiety, her frustration, and above all, her longing. There is something cruelly intimate about the way the camera hovers above, almost pinning her to the pillow, allowing her no area for escape. Her rapidly changing expressions constantly recompose a face the years have taught us to cherish in tranquillity. The activity contained in this closeup is rare, and denies the potential of off-frame space. Garbo's face is posited as the locus of all meaning in closeups ranging from *The Saga of Gosta Berling* (1924) to *Two-Faced Woman*, yet never with this degree of exertion. The dynamics of this frame bind us just as tightly as Garbo. Trapped, she shows all, just as Phèdre did, truest in the fullness of desire. She even has her Nanine, a faithful confidante, as befits a tragic heroine. The severity of this shot is emblematic of Garbo at her most effective, opening her being to scrutiny in inverse proportion to her real-life need for privacy. An actress, timid to the degree of banning all visitors from the set, of having the shooting area surrounded by screens, excluding even the director, has no shame in front of the camera. Her superficial reticence is akin to those heroic couplets, and it constitutes a style that leads to equally complete revelations. The rules upheld by the Académie Française and the Hays-Breen offices provide a focus for artists whose techniques thrive on indirection, on restriction, on concentration. The Code fails to inhibit an actress whose most cherished fetish is a movie camera, and who gladly shares her obsession with an audience that is figuratively peering through its lens.

1975

VII

Film and Society

Theorists have compared viewing a film both with reading a novel and with watching a play. Like the reader of a novel, the viewer of a film, sitting in a darkened hall, enjoys a degree of solitude. Like the viewer of a play, the movie-goer sits in a public place and reacts to humanly significant events in the company of other human beings. André Bazin, who distinguished between the "community" that views a play and the "mass" that watches a film, tries to hold both of these features in balance. But most theorists emphasize one or the other.

As we have seen, for Stanley Cavell, watching a film preserves the modern sense of privacy, offering the viewer both invisibility and an absence of responsibility. The experience is essentially voyeuristic and even pornographic. Parker Tyler's view of the film experience is even more explicitly sexual and psychological. For him, the "dark-enshrouded" passivity of the movie house encourages "the daylight dream." In this state the movie screen transcends its role as a mirror of nature, and the viewer's unconscious mind can read the film's images symbolically. Tyler realizes that the Hollywood film (as opposed to the European film) cannot meet the standards of high art. But the resonant images of a Hollywood film mirror mythic cultural values and evoke primitive responses in the mass audience. Modern movie stars, "the gods and goddesses of Hollywood," are vestiges of the old Greek divinities and they gratify our deepest sexual fantasies. Comparative mythology and psychoanalysis have made us aware of the persistence of deep psychic needs, and the Hollywood film responds to these needs in a way that contemporary popular religions fail to do.

Gene Youngblood, the young American critic and disciple of Buckminster Fuller, doesn't think that we daydream at Hollywood movies, but he does think that they put us to sleep. He sympathizes with Ken Kelman's observation that "the spectator is reduced to a *voyeur*—which is, increasingly, the individual's role in society at large." Youngblood believes that films ought to expand the audience's consciousness, as "experimental" films do. Narrative films, and especially the "genre" films of commercial cinema, are "redundant" and tell audiences what they already know. All narratives tell stories based on certain assumptions about human nature and personality that are themselves the opinions of unexpanded men. For Youngblood there is no human nature, no essential human condition (as there is for Parker Tyler). Unexpanded man has simply invented such comforting concepts to mask his ignorance. The only value in even the best narrative films is their "design science" (personal style and technique). They say nothing new, but they say it well.

Youngblood wants to free the audience to create along with the film. Art is "research"; the more information the artist provides the more energy we then have to modify ourselves and to grow, to accept just those responsibilities that Cavell's movie *voyeur* wishes to avoid. Youngblood's view raises many difficult issues about the ends of art and the nature of man, but it is worth observing briefly that he does very little to show that all the films and kinds of film that he classifies as non-commercial (indeed, is *2001: A Space Odyssey* non-commercial?) are actually capable of expanding consciousness. After all, Andy Warhol's audiences probably find most of his "information" about "polymorphous perversity" as redundant as their parents find Frank Capra's or John Ford's "information" about traditional American values. The nature of that "information" and the representation of those values are the subjects of the next three essays.

Andrew Bergman, the young American historian, argues that

the relations between the Hollywood film and the society that receives it are complex. For him, Frank Capra's films of the mid-thirties projected a social fantasy that had a special appeal for Americans during the depression years. These films reconciled the irreconcilable and suggested that Americans were all the same, that what appeared to be class conflicts were really only conflicts of personality. By the late thirties, however, the external threat of totalitarianism had succeeded the depression as America's main social problem, and Capra's films now suggested that the common decency of Americans could prevail over the forces that brought about World War II. But Bergman does not think that Capra's films simply reflected social moods and the nation's self-image. As Bergman says, "By the time he started the *Why We Fight* series, Capra could know that Americans were fighting for, among other things, Frank Capra films."

The Editors of *Cahiers du Cinéma* employ the language of semiotics, and the insights of Freud and Marx, in their analysis of John Ford's *Young Mr. Lincoln*. In their view, every film is part of the ideological superstructure which reflects a society's economic base. Inevitably, therefore, a Hollywood film will reflect the ideology of American capitalism. This ideological undertaking will, among other things, require the repression of politics and of eroticism. Thus, *Young Mr. Lincoln* attempts to suppress the realities of politics by presenting Lincoln's career as one based on an idealist morality superior to mere politics. "The enterprise consisting of the concealment of politics (of social relations in America, of Lincoln's career) under the idealist mask of Morality has the effect of regilding the cause of Capital with the gold of myth, by manifesting the 'spirituality' in which American Capitalism believes it finds its origins and sees its eternal justification. The seeds of Lincoln's future were already sown in his youth—the future of America (its eternal values) is already written into Lincoln's moral virtues, which include the Republican Party and Capitalism." Although films inevitably reflect the ideology of the society that produces them, they do not necessarily give that ideology a full and unhampered passage. A "reading" of the film may turn up internal tensions, features of the film text that consti-

743

tute an internal criticism of its ideology. This may be true even of a director like Ford who is consciously sympathetic to that ideology. Indeed, the editors of *Cahiers* find that Ford's Lincoln is characterized by a violence which displays his truly repressive character and which, according to J. P. Oudry, shows the distance that Ford, or his "writing," keeps between himself and the idealist propositions that he uses.

Brian Henderson, a Marxist-oriented American critic, studies the camera style of Godard's late films, especially of *Weekend*. He finds that the long, slow tracking shot which characterizes Godard's late style achieves a kind of "flatness" that distinguishes Godard from both the montage school of Eisenstein and the composition-in-depth aesthetic advocated by Bazin. Henderson offers an ideological interpretation of this style. Composition-in-depth projects a bourgeois world, infinitely deep, rich, complex, ambiguous and mysterious. Godard's flat frames by contrast collapse this world into a two-dimensional actuality. This reversion to a cinema of one plane is a demystification, an assault on the bourgeois world and its self-image. Composition-in-depth encourages the viewer to pick and choose within the bourgeois world, but Godard's flattened space requires him to view that world as a totality, and to accept or reject it. Godard's own camera style does much of the Marxist work that the editors of *Cahiers du Cinéma* must do for a bourgeois filmmaker like Ford.

Walter Benjamin, the pre-war Marxist critic, reflects on the alterations in the artistic superstructure that the capitalist mode of production produces. In the past, art works have been unique objects, possessing "aura" and traditional "authority." They played a ritual role, contemplated by men who kept a "natural" distance from them. But the contemporary masses want to see things closer, spatially and humanly. They overcome the uniqueness of the work of art by accepting a mechanical reproduction of it as an equivalent. These reproductions are no longer hallowed cult objects but consumer goods sold on the market; rather than absorbing their beholders they are absorbed by them. Reactions to these "works of art" are rarely personal and are almost completely determined by the mass audience to which the individual is subordinated. Indeed, films have now become one of the most powerful agents of mass political movements—in them the mass has for the first time come face to face with itself. In Benjamin's view, the film and the audience's relation to it is so different from all that has gone before that he is inclined to think that photography has transformed the very nature of art.

PARKER TYLER
FROM MAGIC AND MYTH
OF THE MOVIES

PREFACE

That the movies offer nothing but entertainment is a myth in a sense never used or implied in the following pages. I am not denying that millions of America's movie fans succeed in finding only entertainment in the nation's theaters. Aside from the newsreels and the documentaries given impetus by the war, entertainment remains all that is consciously demanded by those paying rising prices at movie box offices. . . . Patrons of all art media may get more than they demand as well as less, and since the surplus is not precisely expected, it may register vaguely, obliquely, unconsciously. Especially is this true of the movie audience, if only because as a large mass it is critically inarticulate. I hope that my efforts may succeed in giving it some voice on the positive side— movie reviewers take care of its voice on the negative side—and I hope also that for the benefit of students and those hitherto indifferent to the "folk" art of cinema I may further demonstrate that Hollywood is a vital, interesting phenomenon, at least as important to the spiritual climate as daily weather to the physical climate. A myth foisted specifically on the movies proper rather than on the reaction of audiences is furnished by devotees of both stage and novel who scorn movies as below the serious level—as standing in relation to true art somewhat as the circus does to the legitimate stage. But unfortunately these judges, unaware of the ritual importance of the screen, its baroque energy and protean symbolism, are unwarrantably summary, basically uneducated in the movie medium.

... The true field of the movies is not *art* but *myth*, between which—in the sense "myth" is invariably used here—there is a perhaps unsuspectedly wide difference. Assuredly a myth is a fiction, and this is its bare link with art, but a myth is specifically a free, unharnessed fiction, a basic, prototypic pattern capable of many variations and distortions, many betrayals and disguises, even though it remains *imaginative* truth. It has one degraded function connected with the idea of entertainment I discussed above, as when the word itself becomes adjectival and is deliberately attached to that pseudonymous Baltic kingdom having no existence saving in fifth-rate novels and in the movies. It is unsound to make a fact such as the existence of the very nation where a story occurs into a fiction, for it is like taking the props out from under a building and assuming it will still stand. No matter how fantastic an action, its background must be firm. It is the status of background that determines the strength of a myth, the status of its perspective in human history.

Essentially the *scene* of imaginative truth, or art, is the mind itself, but in some manner this truth must be objective, capable of projection onto the screen of the world. In a sense man *is* his past, the past of his race, and all the beliefs he ever held. Reality cannot be made up from the material facts of his existence, his immediate sensory reactions; nor can it be fundamentally a world that never was. Certainly man has ceased to believe much he used to believe. "Oh, that is a myth," we say, meaning that even if significant, it is an ideal or an illusion, a thing that has no substance. But psychology has taught us the strange reality of chimeras, their symbolic validity; and comparative mythology has revealed the great persistence of psychic patterns, with special reference to the supernatural, whose continuity in human belief is sometimes surprisingly self-evident. At one time men believed the earth was flat. Today this is a purely ornamental myth; it has died because imagining the earth is flat has no relation to our desires or employments. At one time the pagans believed in Diana as goddess of the moon and the hunt. Today this also might be considered a decorative myth, something in the fairy-tale class. Yet like so many legends it holds a mesmeric appeal for the mind; Diana represents, as a matter of fact, a certain sexual type—the vigorous virgin, the woman resistant to love; and yet according

748

to the legend Endymion made her lose her heart; that is, the man lived who could break down her defenses merely through his physical image. Obviously this sexual pattern is repeated today. The modern belief that the earth is round corresponds to the conditions of our planetary existence insofar as, proceeding on this premise, our astronomical calculations work out. The belief is consistent with *all the facts*. Today the fact that Diana once had for the pagans a reality she does not have for us means merely that the myth lives in another form. It is an ideal archetype, a part of human experience that has its home in the imagination. And yet . . . that which was true once may become true again. What was symbolized by the Diana myth in actual human experience is a permanent legacy of the race. So the essence of myth also has the status of permanent possibility . . . in short, *desires* may have the same power over the mind and behavior, indeed a much greater power, than *facts*.

In the following pages I have occasion to refer specifically to the great researches made in ancient magic by Sir James Frazer. That there are anthropological assumptions contradictory to various of Frazer's own premises is of no importance to the point I am making. In order to explain a single phenomenon, the priest cult of the King of the Wood at Nemi, Frazer accumulated into one work a prodigious array of ancient primitive beliefs and customs suggesting the limitless lineage of the relatively recent cult at Nemi. At this moment, as when his book was written, nobody is a devotee of this cult; nobody believes in the magic of the golden bough that had to be plucked by the aspirant to Diana's priesthood before he was empowered to kill in single combat the incumbent priest. And yet those who do not profoundly know anthropology might be astonished to learn how much of our personal lives is influenced by all the ancient magical and religious beliefs connected with this one cult. The whole history of the decay and fall of gods, the extermination of divine hierarchies, could be told with just the Nemian cult as basis. In discussing in later pages the male comics of the screen who entertained troops all over the world during the war, I show how they may be considered modern medicine men or primitive priests, scapegoats who transferred to themselves the inner fears of the soldier striving to be brave and made cowardice and bravery alike into a kind of joke. Consequently in relation to my argument the myth is not, as a psychological or historical nucleus of fact, necessarily to be judged as true or false, illusory or real, according to its specific labels, its historic status, its literal beliefs. Essentially myths are not factual but symbolic. I assume that movies are essentially likewise.

. . . Briefly movies, similar to much else in life, are seldom what they seem. In this sense—being, to begin with, fiction—movies are dreamlike and fantastic, their fantasy and examples of this are the folk myths of the absent-minded professor, of the efficiency expert, and of the eccentricity of genius. . . .

Naturally when I ally myth with superstition I am taking not only Frazer's view of the profound interrelatedness of myths but also Freud's view that beneath the upper levels of the mind lies a vast human capacity to think in terms of frantic passions and above all in terms of symbols. Even ten years ago it would have been thought impossible by movie moguls that a surrealist artist, Salvador Dali, should be employed to devise images to portray movie dreams, which in turn are subjected to psychoanalysis, a clinical process that provides the solution of the plot. . . .

The fundamental eye trickery that is a genius of the camera—you see the object, yet it isn't there—came to the fore in the movies and ever since then has mocked with its dynamic plasticity the very form from which it developed, the still camera. Today the movie has all the flexibility of the novel as well as the vision and speech of the stage. In striving through imaginative works to create the illusion of reality the movie screen must constantly transcend its own mirror nature of literal reflection. Camera trickery is really camera magic, for illusion can be freely created by the movie camera with more mathematical accuracy and shock value than by sleight-of-hand magic or stage illusion. The very homogeneity of cinema illusion—the images of the actors themselves are illusive, their corporal bodies absent—creates a throwback in the mood of the spectator to the vestiges of those ancient beliefs that I discuss in detail later in the chapter on supernaturalism, such as beliefs in ghosts, secret forces, telepathy, etc.

Moreover, the movie-theater rite corresponds directly to the profoundly primitive responses of the audience; the auditorium is dark, the spectator is relaxed, the movie in front of him requires less sheer mental attention than would a novel or stage play—less attention because all movement seems to exist on the screen; even the background changes easily, quickly; the whole world moves around the spectator, who is a still point. From the capacity of the screen for trick illusion, plus the dark-enshrouded passivity of the spectator, issues a state of daydream, which I termed in my previous book "the daylight dream" because it occurs in the dark: the screen is the focus of light, while the spectator is conscious in a darkness of the bedroom. It is in daydreams that magic seems to operate, in daydreams that things begin to seem rather than to be. "The movie theater," to quote directly from my previous book, "is the psychoanalytic clinic of the average worker's daylight dream." It is likewise in the process of psychoanalysis, where the *part*, truly recognized as symbol, transforms the meaning of the whole. The movie process is a complex myth of sheer synecdoche. People go to the movies merely to see a favorite player, or for the locale or period, or for the genre, or because they are bored almost to death. How, under these conditions, can anyone hope to appreciate the *whole* movie, especially since, to begin with, the movie can hardly be considered a whole?

No longer does man believe in myth or magic. No! For magic has been sifted and reorganized into science and governs only his material world, not the realm of his spirit, while comparative mythology and anthropology merely comprise school subjects. The sects of Christian religion have organized Western man's spiritual beliefs under one heading: the myth of Christ. Yet Christ's myth too can be related to pagan myths. The very fact that for children the Bible itself is but another series of fairy tales, weighted but little by a sense of historical fact, alone demonstrates my point as to the basic importance of myth with regard to popular or folk art. Our imaginary lives as children survive in us as adults and enrich our subsequent natures. So the fairy-tale lives of primitive races, our ancient antecedents, survive in the religions we formally believe in today as well as among those tribes still unassimilated to modern civilization. I do not claim any absolute value for the myth and magic of Hollywood or for those modern vestiges of the old Greek divinities I have dubbed "the gods and goddesses of Hollywood." On the contrary the principle I mean is one of relativity and metamorphosis rather than absolutism and changelessness: just as a word has synonyms and antonyms—so has a myth. In

751

psychoanalytical symbolism, the deepest symbolism of the mind, the identity of objects is established by a complex frame of reference in which an image may represent one of three objects or all three objects at once. If, then, I say that the actors of Hollywood are an enlarged personnel of the realistically anthropomorphic deities of ancient Greece, I do not indulge in a mere bit of verbal humor, satiric or otherwise; on the other hand neither am I proposing or assuming the existence of an unconscious cult of supernatural worship. I feel I am but calling attention to the fact that the glamour actors and actresses of the movie realm are fulfilling an ancient need, unsatisfied by popular religions of contemporary times. Those men and women who perform for us are human, as we are; they have homes, children, love affairs; they suffer and die. And yet a magic barrier cuts across the texture of our mutual humanity; somehow their wealth, fame, and beauty, their apparently un-limited field of worldy pleasure—these conditions tinge them with the supernatural, render them immune to the bitterness of ordinary frustrations. It does not matter if this thought is a mythological exaggeration. It is a *tendency* of the popular imagination. The secret of the power of Hollywood gods and goddesses is that they seem to do everything anyone else does except that when they die—in movies—they die over and over; when they love, they love over and over. Even as the gods do, they undergo continual metamor-phoses, never losing their identities, being Rita Hayworth or Glenn Ford no matter what their movie aliases. And like Jupiter in the modern comedy, *Amphitryon 38*, they can condescend, even be ridiculous. All that the public demands is what it always gets— the power to make and break stars—but gods have always led basically mortal lives.

Lastly, in this and my previous book, do I have *a method*? Not in the sense that I am selling ideas, nor above all, is mine a method by which one can test the high or low esthetic content of a given movie. . . . If my method is worthy of a label, it is "psychoanalytic-mythological," often socially angled. I have invented little or nothing. I have merely applied it to new material and formulated in accordance with the reapplication. That I speak metaphorically, in dream symbols, and . . . in terms of my own "hallucination," is a fact I wish not only to admit but to proclaim. Yes, I have made up a collective myth of my own, and I confess that in so doing I have plagiarized Hollywood exhaustively. If I have interpreted many things as dreams are interpreted, I cite as belated authorities recent movies of psychoanalytical themes and dream-symbol material. Indirectly, however, I have only been obeying Hollywood's own law of fluidity, of open and ingenious invention. If I have formulated an element of moviedom to be known as "the supernatural hush" and interpreted it as applicable at once to the hush of a cathedral, the hush of a psychiatrist's clinic, the hush of an isolated lovers' session on Riverside Drive, and the hush of the studio while Jennifer Jones does a scene in *The Song of Bernadette*, I feel that I am defining a quality of the movies as one would classify an acidic combination in the laboratory. And if in one of the magic-lantern metamorphoses internal movie meanings are discussed in terms of doubting the evidence of the senses, I am merely following the technique of psychoanalysis as well as paralleling legal criticism of circumstantial evidence of crimes: *things are not always what they seem*. I hope to have revealed a deeper sort of truth than that to be found on surfaces and at the same time to have assembled here a little mythology, a kind of concordance, showing the frequently unconscious magic employed by Hollywood—a magic of dream creation that far transcends its literal messages.

1947

GENE YOUNGBLOOD
FROM EXPANDED CINEMA

ART, ENTERTAINMENT, ENTROPY

"It is easier to copy than to think, hence fashion. Besides, a community of originals is not a community."

WALLACE STEVENS

The current generation is engaged in an unprecedented questioning of all that has been held essential. We question traditional concepts of authority, ownership, justice, love, sex, freedom, politics, even tradition itself. But it's significant that we don't question our entertainment. The disenfranchised young man who dropped out of college, burned his draft card, braids his hair, smokes pot, and digs Dylan is standing in line with his girl, who takes the pill, waiting to see *The Graduate* or *Bonnie and Clyde* or *Easy Rider*—and they're reacting to the same formulas of conditioned response that lulled their parents to sleep in the 1930s.

We've seen the urgent need for an expanded cinematic language. I hope to illustrate that profit-motivated commercial entertainment, by its very nature, cannot supply this new vision. Commercial entertainment works against art, exploits the alienation and boredom of the public, by perpetuating a system of conditioned response to formulas. Commercial entertainment not only isn't creative, it actually destroys the audience's ability to appreciate and participate in the creative process. The implications become apparent when we realize that, as leisure time increases, each human will be forced to become a creative, self-sufficient, empirical energy laboratory.

754

D. H. Lawrence has written: "The business of art is to reveal the relation between man and his circumambient universe at this living moment. As mankind is always struggling in the toil of old relationships, art is always ahead of its 'times,' which themselves are always far in the rear of the living present." Jean-Jacques Lebel stated the same idea in different terms when he described art as "the creation of a new world, never seen before, imperceptibly gaining on reality."

We've seen that man is conditioned by, and reacts to, certain stimuli in the man-made environment. The commercial entertainer is a manipulator of these stimuli. If he employs a certain trigger mechanism, we're guaranteed to react accordingly, like puppets, providing he manipulates the trigger properly. I'm not saying the artist doesn't resort to audience manipulation; we know he often does. The point, however, is the motivation in doing so. If the artist must resort to trigger mechanisms to make himself clear, he will; but it's only a means to his end. In the case of the commercial entertainer, however, it's the end in itself.

Plot, story, and what commonly is known as "drama" are the devices that enable the commercial entertainer to manipulate his audience. The very act of this manipulation, gratifying conditioned needs, is what the films actually are about. The viewer purchases it with his ticket and is understandably annoyed if the film asks him to manipulate himself, to engage in the creative process along with the artist. Our word poetry derives from the Greek root *poiein* meaning "to make" or "to work." The viewer of commercial entertainment cinema does not want to work; he wants to be an object, to be acted upon, to be manipulated. The true subject of commercial entertainment is this little game it plays with its audience.

By perpetuating a destructive habit of unthinking response to formulas, by forcing us to rely ever more frequently on memory, the commercial entertainer encourages an unthinking response to daily life, inhibiting self-awareness. Driven by the profit motive, the commercial entertainer dares not risk alienating us by attempting new language even if he were capable of it. He seeks only to gratify preconditioned needs for formula stimulus. He offers nothing we haven't already conceived, nothing we don't already expect. Art explains; entertainment exploits. Art is freedom from the conditions of memory; entertainment is conditional on a present that is conditioned by the past. Entertainment gives us what we want; art gives us what we don't know we want. To confront a work of art is to confront oneself—but aspects of oneself previously unrecognized.

The extent to which blatant audience manipulation not only is tolerated but extolled is alarming. Alfred Hitchcock, for example, in his interview with François Truffaut, finds merit in his ability to manipulate preconditioned needs for formula stimulus. Speaking of *Psycho*, Hitchcock frankly admits: "It wasn't a message that stirred them, nor was it a great performance, or their enjoyment of the novel . . . they were aroused by the construction of the story, and the way in which it was told caused audiences all over the world to react and become emotional."

It is essential to understand that Hitchcock openly admits that he didn't even try to expand awareness or to communicate some significant message, but only exploited a universal tradition of dramatic manipulation in order to supply his audience with the gratification it paid for. The audience sees itself and its dreams reflected in the film and reacts according to memory, which Krishnamurti has characterized as being always conditioned. "Memory," says Krishnamurti, "is always in the past and is given life in the present by a challenge. Memory has no life in itself; it comes to life in the challenge [preconditioned formula stimulus]. And all memory, whether dormant or active, is conditioned. It is this process that the entertainment industry calls audience identification.

To a healthy mind, anything that is primarily art is also immensely entertaining. It seems obvious that the most important things should be the most entertaining. Where there's a difference between what we "like" and what we know to be vital, we have a condition of schizophrenia, an unnatural and destructive situation. I speak deliberately of a "healthy" mind as one capable of creative thinking. Filmmaker Ken Kelman: "The old cinema removes experience, making us see things along with (or through) a protagonist with whom we identify, and a plot in which we are caught. Such an approach tends toward not only a lack of viewpoint, of definition of *whose* experience it is, but also filters the power of sight into mere habit, dissolves insight into vicariousness. The spectator is reduced to a voyeur—which is, increasingly, the individual's role in society at large."

Minimalist painter David Lee: "When people do not trust their senses they lack confidence in themselves. For the last few centuries people have lacked confidence. They have not trusted their experience to provide a standard for knowing how to act." It is quite obvious that most of us not only don't know much about art, we don't even know what we like. Krishnamurti: "One of the fundamental causes of the disintegration of society is copying, which is the worship of authority."

Imitation is the result of inadequate information. Information results in change. Change requires energy. Energy is the result of adequate information. Energy is directly proportional to the amount of information about the structure of a system. Norbert Wiener: "Information is a name for the content of what is exchanged with the outer world as we adjust to it and make our adjustment felt upon it . . . to live effectively is to live with adequate information." From the cinema we receive conceptual information (ideas) and design information (experiences). In concert they become one phenomenon, which I've described as the experiential information of aesthetic conceptual design. This information is either useful (additive) or redundant. Useful information accelerates change. Redundant information restricts change. If sustained long enough redundant information finally becomes misinformation, which results in negative change.

In communication theory and the laws of thermodynamics the quantity called entropy is the amount of energy reversibly exchanged from one system in the universe to another. Entropy also is the measure of disorder within those systems. It measures the lack of information about the structure of the system. For our purposes "structure of the system" should be taken to mean "the human condition," the universal subject of aesthetic activity. Entropy should be understood as the degree of our ignorance about that condition. Ignorance always increases when a system's messages are redundant. Ignorance is not a state of limbo in which no information exists, but rather a state of increasing chaos due to *mis*information about the structure of the system.

The First Law of Thermodynamics states that energy is constant: it cannot be created or destroyed; its form can change, but not its quantity. The Second Law states that the amount of energy within a local system is naturally entropic—it tends toward disorder, dissipation, incoherence. And since energy is defined as "a capacity to rearrange elemental order," entropy, which runs counter to that capacity, means less potential for change. We've learned from physics that the only anti-entropic force in the universe, or what is called negentropy (negative entropy), results from the process of feedback. Feedback exists between systems that are not closed but rather open and contingent upon other systems. In the strictest sense there are no truly "closed" systems anywhere in the universe; all processes impinge upon and are affected by other processes in some way. However, for most practical purposes, it is enough to say that a system is "closed" when entropy dominates the feedback process, that is, when the measure of energy lost is greater than the measure of energy gained.

The phenomenon of man, or of biological life on earth taken as a process, is negentropic because its subsystems feed energy back into one another and thus are self-enriching, regenerative. Thus energy is wealth, and wealth according to Buckminster Fuller is "the number of forward days a given system is sustainable." Biologist John Bleibtreu arrived at a similar conclusion when he noted that the concept of time can best be viewed as a function of the Second Law of Thermodynamics—that the measure of entropy in a system is a measure of its age, or the passage of time since the system originated. In other words the degree of a system's entropy is equal to redundancy or stasis whereas its negentropy is equal to kinesis or change. So information becomes energy when it contributes to the self-enriching omni-regenerative wealth of the system. When it's not contributing (i.e., redundant) it is allowing the natural entropy to increase.

"It is possible to treat sets of messages as having an entropy like sets of states of the external world . . . in fact, it is possible to interpret the information carried by a message as essentially the negative of its entropy . . . that is, the more probable the message the less information it gives. Clichés, for example, are less illuminating than great poems." Thus the more information concerning the human condition that the artist is able to give us, the more energy we have with which to modify ourselves and grow in accord with the accelerating accelerations of the living present.

Commercial entertainment may be considered a closed system since entropy dominates the feedback process. To satisfy the profit motive the commercial entertainer must give the audience what it expects, which is conditional on what it has been getting, which is conditional on what it previously received, ad infinitum. Inherent in the term "genre," which applies to all entertainment, is that it must be probable. The content of westerns, gangster movies, romances, etc., is probable in that it can be identified and comprehended simply by classification. The phenomenon of drama itself usually is not considered a genre, but is in fact the most universal and archetypical of all genres. Drama, by definition, means conflict, which in turn means suspense. Suspense is requisite on the expectation of known alternatives. One cannot expect the unknown. Therefore expectation, suspense, and drama are all redundant probable qualities and thus are noninformative.

Drama requires a plot that forces the viewer to move from point A to point B to point C along predetermined lines. Plot does not mean "story" (beginning-middle-end). It simply indicates a relatively closed structure in which free association and conscious participation are restricted. Since the viewer remains passive and is acted upon by the experience rather than participating in it with volition, there's no feedback, that vital source of negentropy. Norbert Wiener: "Feedback is a method of controlling a system by reinserting into it the results of its past performance . . . if the information which proceeds backward from the performance is able to change the general method and pattern of performance, we have a process which may well be called learning." Fuller: "Every time man makes a new experiment he always learns more. He cannot learn less."

In the cinema, feedback is possible almost exclusively in what I call the synaesthetic mode, which we'll discuss presently. Because it is entirely personal it rests on no identifiable plot and is not probable. The viewer is forced to create along with the film, to interpret for himself what he is experiencing. If the information (either concept or design) reveals some previously unrecognized aspect of the viewer's relation to the circumambient universe—or provides language with which to conceptualize old realities more effectively—the viewer re-creates that discovery along with the artist, thus feeding back into the environment the existence of more creative potential, which may in turn be used by the artist for messages of still greater eloquence and perception. If the information is redundant, as it must be in commercial entertainment, nothing is learned and change becomes unlikely. The noted authority on communication theory, J. R. Pierce, has demonstrated that an increase in entropy means a decrease in the ability to change. And we have seen that the ability to change is the most urgent need facing twentieth-century man.

The notion of experimental art, therefore, is meaningless. All art is experimental or it isn't art. Art is research, whereas entertainment is a game or conflict. We have learned from cybernetics that in research one's work is governed by one's strongest points, whereas in conflicts or games one's work is governed by its weakest moments. We have defined the difference between art and entertainment in scientific terms and have found entertainment to be inherently entropic, opposed to change, and art to be inherently negentropic, a catalyst to change. The artist is always an anarchist, a revolutionary, a creator of new worlds imperceptibly gaining on reality. He can do this because we live in a cosmos in which there's always something more to be seen. When finally we erase the difference between art and entertainment—as we must to survive—we shall find that our community is no longer a community, and we shall begin to understand radical evolution.

1970

ANDREW BERGMAN
FROM WE'RE IN THE MONEY

FRANK CAPRA AND SCREWBALL
COMEDY, 1931—1941

Film comedy in the early thirties had blown things apart. Destructive and corrosive, the Marxes and Fields and Lubitsch had been of a piece with the cold-eyed, suspicious and edgy spirit of 1930–1933. In the mid-thirties, something new emerged: a comedy at once warm and healing, yet off-beat and airy. Film historians would label this phenomenon "screwball" comedy. The titles are familiar: *It Happened One Night, Mr. Deeds Goes To Town, My Man Godfrey, You Can't Take It With You, Easy Living, Nothing Sacred,* and *The Awful Truth* have endured the years with grace and verve. And for good reason. They were (and remain) very funny, perfectly paced, and alive with good humor and terrific people. They left one with what Frank Capra, the most notable of the "screwball" directors, called "a glow of satisfaction."

The glow was genuine: screwball comedies were received with love and are to this day. (One has only to attend a screening of *Mr. Deeds* or *It Happened One Night* to see the hold these films still have over their audience, especially those who remember them from the thirties.) They were special films, for a number of reasons.

First, they brought out the best in a number of incredibly attractive and talented actors and actresses. In Capra's *It Happened One Night,* Clark Gable came into his own as an ironic masculine presence, played off against Claudette Colbert's uncertainty and dewiness. Jean Arthur (*Deeds, You Can't Take It*

With You, Easy Living, and *Mr. Smith Goes To Washington*) had the most wonderful speaking voice anyone had ever heard: she was the one movie star men could actually visualize marrying. Carole Lombard quivered with easily cured neuroses in *My Man Godfrey* and *Nothing Sacred* and was a beautiful comedienne. Capra turned Gary Cooper, in *Deeds* and *Meet John Doe,* into the off-beat embodiment of small-town simplicity, honesty and common sense.

But the overwhelming attractiveness of the screwball comedies involved more than the wonderful personnel. It had to do with the effort they made at reconciling the irreconcilable. They created an America of perfect unity: all classes as one, the rural-urban divide breached, love and decency and neighborliness ascendant. It was an American self-portrait that proved a bonanza in the mid-thirties.

Lewis Jacobs has stated the conventional view: "If 'screwball' comedies successfully turned the world on its ear, that was perhaps the way it already looked to a depression generation which felt cheated of its birthright." The "screwball" quality is taken as a kind of veneer, a desperate cover for Depression-bred alienation. Arthur Knight soberly notes that these comedies had "as their points of departure the terrible realities of the period—unemployment, hunger and fear." Neither perspective really seems to work. The screwball comedies were very much a response to the Depression, but not in the tradition of alienation implied by Jacobs and certainly not as the socially aware documents Knight attempts to make of them. Simply stated, the comic technique of these comedies became a means of unifying what had been splintered and divided. The "whackiness" cemented social classes and broken marriages; personal relations were smoothed and social discontent quieted. If early thirties comedy was explosive, screwball comedy was implosive: it worked to pull things together.

Frank Capra's America

Frank Capra's early years could be textbook assignments on the humble beginnings of great men. The Capras arrived in California from Sicily in 1903, and young Frank started hawking newspapers to help keep the poor family solvent. Graduating from high school at a precocious fifteen, he entered the California Institute of Technology and worked his way through school, waiting on tables and running a student laundry. He graduated in 1918, entered the service, and emerged from his hitch into a career crisis. Dropping chemical engineering, Capra drifted, did farm work, was an extra in some westerns, and sold dubious mining stock to gullible farmers and farmers' wives. Going from door to door, he became a "tinhorn gambler and petty financial pirate."

Capra's movie-making vocation began as part of his quest for some easy money. Arriving in San Francisco, he told a local producer, "I'm from Hollywood," and was hired to direct "cine-poems" for seventy-five dollars per week. From that point in the mid-twenties, Capra was set in pictures, blossoming into a major director in the early thirties, and becoming a star director with *Lady For A Day* in 1933. In 1934, Capra got Columbia Pictures to purchase, for five thousand dollars, the rights to a Samuel Hopkins Adams story entitled "Night Bus." MGM lent the services of a second-rank star named Clark Gable, and Capra borrowed Claudette Colbert from Paramount. Neither star was enthused by the prospect of working at Columbia, at that time a decidedly second-class studio. The budget was minimal. Nevertheless, *It Happened One Night* became *the* picture of 1934, stirring a genuinely spontaneous wave of affection throughout the country, playing return engagements and making the fortunes of Columbia, Colbert, Gable, and Frank Capra. Screwball comedy dominated the rest of the decade.

Capra's erratic background was reflected in his best films. The seemingly wide-eyed immigrant boy who travelled the traditional path to success in college (carrying trays in the commons, pen and slide rule concealed beneath the white jacket) was obviously one with faith in the classic American route to opportunity and fulfillment. But the Capra who hustled farmers and sold coupons to their wives, the Capra who turned from chemical engineering to the glib sales pitch and "I'm from Hollywood," was more cold-eyed than wide-eyed. Those two Capras—immigrant dreamer and con man—gave a peculiarly attractive and beguiling quality to his best work. He had a perfect pitch for Americana, for depicting what he passed over as American types, and a sheer genius for manipulating those types. Capra's comedy was a wide-eyed and affectionate hustle—the masterwork of an idealist and door-to-door salesman.

Capra's Films, 1934–1941

It Happened One Night (Columbia, 1934)
Mr. Deeds Goes To Town (Columbia, 1936)
Lost Horizon (Columbia, 1937)
You Can't Take It With You (Columbia, 1938)
Mr. Smith Goes To Washington (Columbia, 1939)
Meet John Doe (Warner, 1941)

Before creating the screwball comedy, Capra seemed comfortable with the shyster mania that prevailed between 1931 and 1933. *Platinum Blonde* (Columbia, 1931) showed his initial sympathy with, and attraction to, newspapermen and their racy urban milieu. His hero was an urban Mr. Deeds, an individualist ace reporter with disdain for a world of "phonies." By 1936, the "phonies" would include those very newspapermen. In 1932, Capra directed a movie about bank failures entitled *American Madness,* with Walter Huston the beleaguered and incorruptible banker, kept afloat during the panic by the faith of his depositors. That kind of faith was typical of Capra.

His next vehicle, *Lady For A Day,* was taken from a Damon Runyon story ("Madam La Guimp"), and the choice of material indicated Capra's continued affection for the shyster city. Runyon's world was peopled by the breezy and the sleazy of a Broadway long since gone. Capra revelled in the efforts of various blondes, race touts, and gamblers to pass off "Apple Annie" as a lady of wealth to secure her daughter's marriage to royalty. Eventually, the police and Mayor and Governor of New York pitch in to bring off the deception. It was all urban, this unity—a cheerful combine of all the types Capra would turn against in *Deeds.* A different city—cynical and destructive—appeared in his work from 1934 on.

In the late thirties, Capra evolved the shyster into a vaguely fascistic threat. The urban sharper became the Wall Street giant, communications mogul, munitions kingpin, and reactionary political force embodied in the corpulent and bespectacled figure of Edward Arnold. Capra's emphasis upon the melting of class tensions changed as the decade ended. Class amiability, the end of *It Happened One Night* and *You Can't Take It With You* (and non-Capra works like *My Man Godfrey* and *Easy Living*), became a means. If the mid-thirties witnessed a stress on the resolution of social tensions, Capra, by 1939, fancied that resolution to be an accomplished fact. And so the common decency of all Americans, rich and poor, got turned, in *Mr. Smith* and *Meet John Doe*, against threats to our most sacred national institutions. Capra was exchanging the symbols and dynamics of the thirties for those of the forties.

With *It Happened One Night*, the first of the screwball comedies, Capra began to turn against the city. His central character, Peter Warne (Gable), was a newspaper reporter and had all the qualities the early thirties had bestowed upon that role: brash, resilient, more interested in sensation than in personal financial gain. He was a man of the city. Yet Capra added dimensions to his character that pointed toward liberation from the iron-clad cynicism of the New York reporter: a vague idealism and dreaminess that aimed at escape, an offbeat cockiness that could effect that escape. Capra's two greatest films—*It Happened One Night* and *Deeds*—both involved the liberation of newspaper reporters. In *Deeds*, the reporter would stand for a whole range of debased urban values, but Gable's role is more complex. He was part hack reporter, part Longfellow Deeds, the small-town idealist.

He hates the newspaper world and vaguely yearns to get out. "I saw an island in the Pacific once," he tells millionairess Ellen Andrews (Colbert). "Never been able to forget it." But he is still the wise-cracking news hawk, feuding with his editor and hot for scoops. And adjusting that great thirties hat (brim down), Gable looked the perfect reporter. When he comes across the heiress Ellen Andrews, she is attempting to escape from her father (Walter Connolly) by bus. She remains at his side, at first out of fear that he will reveal her whereabouts and then, inevitably, out of love. From the process by which mutual cynicism melted before romance evolved screwball comedy.

The "screwball" act was individualistic, idiosyncratic, and, above all, disarmingly open. Capra said that his films insisted upon characters who "are human and do the things human beings do—or would do if they had the courage and the opportunity." His central characters had both. When their night bus is halted by a torrential rain, Warne unhesitatingly takes a single room for himself and the skittish millionairess—and then proceeds to hang a blanket between their beds, calling it the "wall of Jericho." The blanket separates, but the offbeat act of putting it up brings them closer together. They wisecrack over it, get comfortable with each other. The fact that Ellen is short of funds and dependent on Warne's lower middle-class street wit just to survive foreshadows the ultimate melting of class barriers between them.

In a famous hitch-hiking episode, Gable nailed down his stardom when he claimed to have perfected all the nuances of the thumb. He completely fails. Colbert demonstrates her own resourcefulness by stepping to the road, raising her skirt, and bringing the first car to a screeching halt. Both having demonstrated their "screwballness," their class differences disappear. Audiences loved them and loved Capra—for their daring, and his.

When her father's private detectives come pounding on their motel door, the couple inventively phases into a comic, mock married squabble: he the exasperated slob of a husband, she the shrill and hysterical plumber's daughter. The detectives exit in confusion, mumbling about "wrong room"—and Peter and Ellen draw even closer. It set the pattern for all screwball comedy: each act of inventive fancy resulted in greater unity. And in *It Happened One Night,* as in most screwball comedy, that invention broke down walls rooted invariably in class. Peter and Ellen—he a working stiff, she with millions—come to each other with strong initial antagonisms. At the film's beginning, he is full of loathing for her world of wealth and society parties, full of contempt for her flight to marry a playboy named King Westley. Peter calls her a "spoiled rich kid. . . . Haven't you ever heard of humility? You, King Westley, your father are all a lot of hooey to me." She is put off by his brashness, appalled and secretly thrilled by his world.

But Capra, Colbert, and Gable were hardly about to lead us to class warfare. The director discovers rich stores of "screwballness" and good humor not only in the young couple but in Ellen's wealthy father as well. Having made his fortune by tough initiative, not sloth, he greatly prefers Peter's individualistic strength to the idle, polo-playing wealth of Westley. He therefore helps effect his daughter's marriage to Peter. Walking down the aisle on the day of her scheduled wedding to Westley, he turns to Ellen and whispers "You're a sucker to go through with this" and informs her that a car waits. Clad in white, the bride dashes away from the elaborate ceremony, as the assembled guests stand in horror, to the arms of Clark Gable.

The good sense of the wealthy father should perhaps be no surprise; one acute analysis of Hollywood's attitudes toward the rich noted that the "rich household itself is fumed against, but the kingpin of the household is not." The leftist *New Theatre* was appalled at the "wish-fulfillment" involved in the portrait of "a grumpy plutocrat who, of course, had a heart of gold. *It Happened One Night* took place in a social and economic vacuum." It was not so much a vacuum as a fantasy. For Capra, Americans were all the same—social class served as a character, rather than an economic, definition. Beneath the silk hats were common men who had ridden their initiative all the way. "Class" conflicts, in mid-thirties comedy, were really personality conflicts, and hence easily resolved by a good chat. So at the unifying conclusion of Capra's *You Can't Take It With You*, super-plutocrat Edward Arnold whips out his harmonica and plays along with the "whacky" Vanderhof family, immediately embracing their values.

With the wealthy father simply John Doe writ large, carrying a contract-filled briefcase rather than a lunch bucket, Capra helped reinforce an important myth in America. And the myth was rarely as important as in the mid-thirties, when the pieces of the old success formula were being carefully glued back together. Robert and Helen Lynd quote a 1936, Muncie, Indiana, editorial on the subject:

Nearly All Are in "Working Class"

In the United States . . . every man has worked who had the ambition and the opportunity to do so. There has been no class of idle rich. The average industrialist has put in as many hours as the salaried man or wage earner, and he often points with pride to the number of jobs he has been able to afford for others through the effort of his own thrift, intelligence and industry.

. . . The great danger is that an attempt at redistribution of wealth, through increasingly high taxes, will end in poverty and misery for all, as has been the case in Russia. But there is another danger which is just as great—a danger that the United States will become a nation of class-conscious haters. Such a condition will spell the end of American prosperity and progress.

The Alexander Andrews type was by no means limited to Capra. As Barbara Deming observed:

. . . film after film is obedient to a compulsion to clear of any serious censure the big money man, the big breadwinner. . . . Censure of the idle rich but not of the rich who work for their money is of course in the Puritan tradition. And it is in that tradition for a millionaire to be identified with . . . the common man. For is he not just that—the common man who has fulfilled himself?

Other successful screwball comedies picked up on this trend. *My Man Godfrey* (Universal, 1936. Director, Gregory LaCava) set "hobo" William Powell (really a Boston blueblood) as a butler in the bizarre household of the fabulously wealthy Bullock family. Carole Lombard floats about in a starry stupor, her mother exists in total befuddlement, but the head of the house, Eugene Pallette, is rock solid, a wealthy common man attempting to cope with his "zany" women. Powell finds no trouble in convincing him of a scheme to get the jobless back to work and builds a night club called The Dump on the site of a former shantytown. The hobos get token employment—with vague plans for relief and housing projects come winter.

The *New Theatre* complained of "the familiar condescending

paternalism of the upper classes toward their charges—the masses." F. Scott Fitzgerald had seen it even more clearly. "Let me tell you about the very rich," he wrote in 1926. "They are different from you and me. Even when they enter deep into our world or sink below us, they still think they are better than we are." The blueblood turned "hobo" certainly thought so and Pallette, the wealthy common man, winds up with nothing but *noblesse oblige* toward bums.

Having opened a hobo camp with Powell, like Henry V, mingling with the masses, *My Man Godfrey* ended with rich and poor together. At The Dump, the rich walk through the doors. The poor hold them open. Thus "the terrible realities of the period" Arthur Knight saw as points of departure. Screwball directors handled depression milieus as if with tongs: their vision depended on it. *My Man Godfrey* placed its faith with the good-natured rich.

So did *Easy Living* (Paramount, 1937). Director Mitchell Leisen presented a soft-hearted Wall Streeter (Edward Arnold) and a plain Jane working girl (Jean Arthur) and left no doubt that some kind of union lay ahead. That Arnold would be delighted to have son Ray Milland marry Jean was preordained. Domestic tranquillity was assured. Maybe Edward Arnold would let your daughter marry his son. Maybe Eugene Pallette would lend you money.

"Mr. Deeds Goes To Town"

In 1936, Frank Capra was surely encouraged to extend his "screwball" perspective. *It Happened One Night* had become one of the great triumphs of American film, both financially and in winning all major Academy Awards for 1934: best film, screenplay, director, actor, and actress, the only film ever to achieve such a sweep. *The Nation* noted the "wholly spontaneous response with which the picture was received."

Confident of his audience, Capra turned to the small-town hero and away from the city, Longfellow Deeds (Gary Cooper) is set against the slick morality, fortune-hunting and cynicism of the shyster city, neutralizes its debasing influences, and emerges ascendant. If he had felt at home with newspapermen and Broadway sharpers between 1931 and 1933, Capra now turned against them and made them stand for the decline of the nation's traditional verities—rooted in village virtues.

Through *Mr. Deeds Goes To Town* parade all the sleek, compromised figures of the early thirties, all those men with the little mustaches: headline-crazy newsmen, society swells, corrupt lawyers, and a jeering public. In a series of encounters with Deeds, their cynicism gets blunted and turned against them.

The plot line bestowed upon Deeds an inheritance of twenty million dollars. He responds, "Twenty million! That's a lot, isn't it?" and turns to play his tuba. A screwball. Brought unwillingly to New York from his little home in Mandrake Falls, Deeds gets housed in a mansion complete with butlers, bodyguards, and a rasping, jaded press agent played by Lionel Stander, the incarnation of Broadway cynicism. Besieged by the city's jackals, Deeds refuses to be taken in and begins showing up New York's corrupted value system.

He withholds his power of attorney from the shysters who seek it. He dismisses fortune-hunters: a lawyer with a competing claim, a society belle named Madame Pomponi (the comic strip name indicating the quality of Capra's urban demonology) and the "opera board." This board requests $100,000 to cover its losses: Deeds, the practical Yankee, rebels. If the opera is losing money, "there must be something wrong." It must give "the wrong kind of show." Profit is the practical, small-town yardstick here, and his screwball individuality in rejecting the request works a unity. Press agent Stander delights in the rebuff to the snobs and starts warming toward his yokel boss.

Deeds wins over the newspaper crowd by melting the tough exterior of reporter Babe Bennett. Assigned to keep Deeds on the front page, she insinuates herself into his guileless affections and relays his exploits (slugging arrogant New York literati, drunkenly feeding doughnuts to a horse), to laughing, heartless New York. But when Babe hears his raptures in front of Grant's Tomb ("I see an Ohio farm boy becoming a great general . . . becoming President"—the first touches of the patriotic sentimentality which would engulf *Mr. Smith Goes to Washington* and which Capra did so brilliantly), she comes to

770

his side, loving the innocence she fears she has lost. And the fact of her small-town origins only solidifies her unity with Mr. Deeds. Soon her editor is likewise protecting him from the urban predators.

Capra shrewdly added some topicality to *Deeds*, and made his hero virtually untouchable, except by those who advocated corruption and starvation. A hungry farmer breaks into Deeds' mansion, waves a pistol about, and breaks down in despairing sobs. Deeds, to the horror of all the shysters, decides to sink his entire twenty million into small farms to be distributed to the needy poor. What was called Capra's *"Saturday Evening Post* socialism" was simply benevolence from above. What made it seem like more was Deeds' small-town, tuba-playing character, his "screwballness." His idiosyncracies were simply small-town virtues disdained by Shyster City. Deeds the village democrat forbids his butler from getting down on his knees; Deeds the village prankster slides down the bannister of his mansion; the fair-minded Deeds realizes he must share his wealth. Importantly, the wealth is a fluke to begin with. Not earned by initiative or wisely invested or saved—just given. There was nothing to do but give it away: the objects of the philanthropy—small farmers and land rather than libraries—made it seem more daring than it really was. Such was Capra's skill that he used this last "screwball" act to unify virtually everybody.

When corrupt lawyers, in a desperate attempt to prevent the hero from distributing his fortune, claim him insane and have him institutionalized, city and country join to vindicate Deeds. Deeds wins over the judge, who calls him, as the poor farmers and newspapermen cheer him on, "the sanest man in the courtroom." Yokels and city slickers, city and country, rejoice; Deeds and Babe embrace, in love. All is reconciliation. "Goodness, simplicity, disinterestedness," wrote Graham Greene, "these in his hands become fighting qualities." The Broadway crowd, observed Richard Griffith, "end by applauding his rejection of the metropolis and all that it stands for."

Deeds stayed near the top in the box office sales in April and May of 1936. "One of those pictures," said a theatre owner in Eminence, Kentucky, "that people tell their friends about." A theatre manager in Fort Worth was "flabbergasted," and a truly captive audience in Trenton, New Jersey's State Prison told the institution's recreational director "how much they enjoyed it, which is rather unusual, our audience being much more prompt to voice disapproval than approval of films."

Richard Griffith attempted to assess *Deeds'* popularity and concluded that behind Capra the Humanitarian lay Capra the Coupon Salesman:

> The thesis of this sentimental comedy was welcomed by huge sections of the American public. What need for the social reorganization proposed by the New Deal if prosperity and peace could be recovered by redemption of the individual? This idea, absolving the middle-class from realistic thinking about the forces which governed their lives, has proved perennially popular.

But faith in the easy melting of social tension and appreciation of the New Deal were certainly not contradictory impulses. In 1936, Franklin Roosevelt proved at least as popular as Longfellow Deeds. Farm belt and city, middle class and poor voted for the buoyant, endlessly resourceful President. An illusory electoral unity reigned.

Capra would not concern himself with national politics until *Mr. Smith Goes To Washington* and *Meet John Doe*. In *Deeds*, he was concerned with constructing a nearly all-embracing unity by having his village type force the urbanites to accept his values. The film ran the "back to the earth" formula in reverse; rather than advocating return to the land, Capra attempted to bring the values of the country back to the city. Alistair Cooke observed that the director was "starting to make movies about themes instead of people" and Robert Stebbins told *New Theatre* readers of Capra's "underlying . . . implication, if not recognition, that the world is a place of sorrows, where the great multitude of men suffered for the excesses of a few."

But socially conscious *Weltschmerz* was scarcely Capra's stock in trade; his optimism was infectious, his contrivance of unity stunning, and his manipulation of the old symbols of shysterism the work of a Hollywood virtuoso. He was steeped in Hollywood's character types. The wide-eyed immigrant boy could effortlessly pull social synthesis out of the America which existed in his imagination; the coupon salesman sensed friendly territory in 1936.

1937–1941

Where could Capra go from the social unity of *Deeds?* Into the ethos of World War Two. In 1937, he took James Hilton's tale of Shangri-La and filmed *Lost Horizon.* The social togetherness wrought on Broadway was assumed to exist in the Himalayas. Perfect peace reigned in Shangri-La: inner and outer tranquillity kept men from aging. Because no social conflict existed to begin with, Capra found himself with nothing to work toward. He repeated himself, was talkier than usual and, seen today, *Lost Horizon* suffers, despite many beautiful touches. Its static quality was inevitable once unity was assured.

Capra returned to more familiar ground in filming the Moss Hart-George S. Kaufman play, *You Can't Take It With You,* but began changing his villains, once he had disposed of the shysters. The heroes are individualists: a carefree, zany family and its satellites living in a house scheduled to be demolished in the construction of a giant munitions plant. Grandpa Vanderhof (Lionel Barrymore) has not worked in years, but contentedly maintains his stamp collection; his daughter (Spring Byington) writes plays in order to make use of a typewriter; a son-in-law makes fireworks; one granddaughter studies ballet and pirouettes about the house, and the other granddaughter is Jean Arthur. Capra set this crew against the banker and munitions king Kirby (Edward Arnold), linked Jean Arthur romantically with Kirby's son (James Stewart), and laid the groundwork for a final unity. This involved Kirby's seeing the wisdom of Grandpa's crackerbarrel bohemianism and giving up his cartel. Kirby whips out his harmonica and plays along with Grandpa as the film closes, having totally accepted a subversive philosophy of absolute freedom and tolerance for everybody's foibles.

While the unity was an absurdity, Kirby's character indicated the shift in Capra's demonology. While he is surrounded by shyster lawyers, Kirby is no early thirties crook. He seems very much the cold-blooded monopolist, building a munitions

773

empire to capitalize on the day of conflict. As noted in a profile in *The New Yorker,* Capra was very conscious of how he
was developing his characters:

> Realizing that Messrs. Kaufman and Hart had somehow over-
> looked the true implications of their major characters, Capra
> . . . changed Grandpa Vanderhof from a whimsical old madcap
> to a serious denouncer of those who prefer gold to friends, and
> the mild and inoffensive Mr. Kirby, who had been a rich boy's
> father, to a sinister munitions man who causes at least one
> suicide.

Capra's ending broke him down, but how much longer could
the Kirbys of the world be contained?

In *Mr. Smith* and *Meet John Doe,* the comic mode would take
second place to Capra's exploration of the evils larger than
simple shysterism which seemed to be enveloping the world.
Europe's crumbling made simple portrayals of unity impossible. Even Capra coundn't end a movie with Hitler playing
the harmonica.

Jefferson Smith and John Doe

Capra's Jefferson Smith, U.S. Senator, was a variation of the
character of Deeds placed in Washington. Played by James
Stewart with a genuinely felt conviction, Mr. Smith discovers
that the institutions and personalities he revered as the head
"Boy Ranger" of his state are rotted from within. After he has
been named junior senator of his state, Smith is shocked to see
that his state's revered senior senator, Joseph Paine (Claude
Rains), is the puppet of Edward Arnold. His power escalating
with each film, Arnold now controls the state's newspapers,
industries, and politics. Smith decides to buck this near-totali-
tarian grip, drawing inspiration from the Lincoln Memorial
and Capitol Dome (Capra evoking patriotic spirit from these
symbols with the clarity and fervor of the successful immigrant, like no one has before or since). Smith learns the consequences: the Arnold-controlled press and radio are turned
against him. The one paper that supports his position (the
"Boy Ranger" weekly) is seized by Arnold's thugs and, getting
even uglier, his supporters are hosed and beaten. Senator

774

Paine erects an elaborate lie to wreck Smith's career, but the young idealist embarks on a filibuster, refusing to stop talking until he, and his nation, have been vindicated.

Why Capra was doing all this, in 1939, suddenly becomes very clear. As Smith held the Senate floor, the director brought in the veteran radio newsman H. V. Kaltenborn to spout breathlessly into a large, round CBS microphone, "democracy in action," and to announce that German and Italian diplomats were in the gallery to see how the process worked. The relationship between the Arnold machine and the politics of these diplomats was far from esoteric.

As Smith held out against everything that was rotten in the world, Capra really began orchestrating the symbols of the 1940s. A simple American like Jefferson Smith, with plenty of idealism and gumption (and the urgings of Jean Arthur, again in the role of cynic turned believer), could fight the complex, shadowy, and undemocratic forces that were darkening the globe. Capra managed the situation like the virtuoso he was: Smith on the Senate floor, sapling-straight and eyes teary; Smith going to the Lincoln Memorial for a chat with the Great Emancipator; fat Edward Arnold screaming orders into telephones. A nation in its movie theatres was being girded for war, by the old master of belief. When Senator Paine admits the truth, Smith is vindicated, but the end was not unity, rather it was a reinforcement of faith in the emblems of democracy.

In *Meet John Doe*, Capra expressed his faith in common Americans ("I have a definite feeling," he told *The New Yorker*, "that the people are right. People's instincts are good, never bad.") in the face of the kind of threat raised in *Mr. Smith Goes To Washington*. Edward Arnold repeats his role, except that by 1941 Capra made even more explicit the kind of danger he was talking about: Arnold, the wealthy publisher, industrialist, and politician, now has a private police force. He sets up "John Doe" clubs all over the country—clubs of average citizens rallied to the "cause" of common decency and neighborliness—to establish his own political base independent of the two parties. He seems to have absolute control over big business and big labor, leaders of both kowtowing to him

775

throughout the film. But the spirit of John Doe (Gary Cooper—a washed-up baseball player picked to be the public symbol of John Doe) was the spirit Capra brought to the approaching war: "We're the people and we're tough. A free people can beat the world at anything . . . if we all pulled the oars in the same direction." Recognizing their common interests (the defeat of antidemocratic evil), Americans could rejoice in their classlessness and vanquish the Nazis.

Cooper had beaten back the "threats" of the early thirties in *Deeds;* now he confronted the steely menace of the forties. Instead of being a stooge, Cooper turns against Arnold at a huge ballpark rally and reveals the plans for political power. He is chased by Arnold's private police force, but his decent voice, like Smith's, like Deeds', could not be stilled. After *Meet John Doe,* Capra would direct the *Why We Fight* series for the United States Government, shoring up the home front. But he had, in fact, begun showing why we would fight with *Mr. Smith.*

To see the Capra films from 1934 to 1941 is to learn more about a nation's image of itself than one has any right to expect. How much did Capra create, and how much did he respond to? His classlessness was an obvious fantasy, but the myth obviously was dear to Americans. He created a tradition in effecting the screwball social peace of *It Happened One Night* and responded to tradition in *Deeds* by neutralizing the shyster world, a world very much Hollywood's creation. Once the thirties had been crossed with the nation's basic institutions intact and relatively unscathed, Capra was free to argue from greater strength; fascism was neither his nor Hollywood's creation.

The way in which Capra manipulated images—city, small town, village hero, profiteer, little man, government, radio—represented genius. He understood enough of what people wanted, after the revelation of the screwball comedies' gigantic success, to help create a consciousness, and to build himself into the system. His fantasy of a social unity entered into the quasi-reality of all mass media. Robert Warshow's remarkable insight that, although Americans rarely experienced gangsterism in their lives, "the experience of the gangster *as an experience of art* is universal to Americans," is extremely relevant to Capra. His America was an experience of art.

That world of Deeds and Smith and Doe had become part of the nation's self-image. No one knew that better than Frank Capra. "I never cease to thrill at an audience seeing a picture," he said. "For two hours you've got 'em. Hitler can't keep 'em that long. You eventually reach more people than Roosevelt does on the radio." By the time he started the *Why We Fight* series, Capra could know that Americans were fighting for, among other things, Frank Capra films.

1971

A COLLECTIVE TEXT
BY THE EDITORS
OF *CAHIERS DU CINÉMA*
JOHN FORD'S
YOUNG MR. LINCOLN

Lincoln is not the product of popular revolution: the banal game of universal suffrage, ignorant of the great historical tasks that must be achieved, has raised him to the top, him, a plebeian, a self-made man who rose from being a stone breaker to being the Senator for Illinois, a man lacking intellectual brilliance, without any greatness of character, with no exceptional value, because he is an average, well-meaning man. (Friedrich Engels and Karl Marx, Die Presse, *12-10-1862.)*

At one point in our interview. Mr. Ford was talking about a cut sequence from Young Mr. Lincoln: *and he described Lincoln as a shabby figure, riding into town on a mule, stopping to gaze at a theatre poster. "This poor ape," he said, "wishing he had enough money to see Hamlet." Reading over the edited version of the interview it was one of the few things Ford asked me to change; he said he didn't much like "the idea of calling Mr. Lincoln a poor ape." (Peter Bogdanovich*, John Ford, Studio Vista, *London, 1967.)*

Young Mr. Lincoln: American film by John Ford. *Script:* Lamar Trotti. *Photography:* Bert Glennon. *Music:* Alfred Newman. *Art director:* Richard Day, Mark Lee Kirk. *Set decorations:* Thomas Little. *Editor:* Walter Thompson. *Costume:* Royer. *Sound assistant:* Robert Parrish. *Cast:* Henry Fonda (Abraham Lincoln), Alice Brady (Abigail Clay), Arleen Wheelan (Hannah Clay), Marjorie Weaver (Mary Todd), Eddie Collins (Efe Turner), Pauline Moore (Ann Rutledge), Ward Bond (J. Palmer Cass), Richard Cromwell (Matt Clay), Donald Meek (John Felder),

Judith Dickens (Carrie Sue), Eddie Quillan (Adam Clay), Spencer Charters (Judge Herbert A. Bell), Milburn Stone (Stephen A. Douglas), Cliff Clark (Sheriff Billings), Robert Lowery (juror), Charles Tannen (Ninian Edwards), Francis Ford (Sam Boone), Fred Kohler, Jr. (Scrub White), Kay Linaker (Mrs. Edwards), Russel Simpson (Woolridge), Charles Halton (Hawthorne), Clarence Wilson (Dr. Mason), Edwin Maxwell (John T. Stuart), Robert Homans (Mr. Clay), Jack Kelly (Matt Clay boy), Dickie Jones (Adam Clay boy), Harry Tyler (barber), Louis Mason (clerk), Jack Pennick (Big Buck), Steven Randall (juror), Paul Burns, Frank Orth, George Chandler, Dave Morris, Dorothy Vaughan, Virginia Brissac, Elizabeth Jones. *Producer:* Kenneth Macgowan. *Executive producer:* Darryl F. Zanuck. *Production:* Cosmopolitan/Twentieth Century Fox, 1939. *Distribution:* Associated Cinemas. Length: 101mn.

1

This text inaugurates a series of studies the need for which was indicated in the editorial of issue No. 218 [*Cahiers du Cinéma*]. We must now specify the objects and method of this work, and the origin of its necessity which has hitherto been merely affirmed.

1. Object: a certain number of "classic" films, which today are *readable* (and, therefore, anticipating our definition of method, we will designate this work as one of reading) insofar as we can distinguish the historicity of their inscription:* the relation of these films to the codes (social, cultural . . .) for which they are a site of intersection, and to other films, themselves held in an intertextual space; therefore, the relation of these films to the ideology which they convey, a particular

---

*This usage of inscription (*l'inscription*) refers to work done by Jacques Derrida on the concept of *écriture* in *Theorie d'ensemble* (Collection Tel Quel, 1968) which will be taken up in a future issue of *Screen*. *Cahiers'* point here is that all individual texts are part of and inscribe themselves into one historically determined "text" (*l'histoire textuelle*) within which they are produced; a reading of the individual text therefore requires examining both its dynamic relationship with this general text and the relationship between the general text and specific historical events.—ED. *Screen*.

"phase" which they represent, and to the events (present, past, historical, mythical, fictional) which they aimed to represent.

For convenience we will retain the term "classic" (though obviously in the course of these studies we will have to examine, and perhaps even challenge it, in order finally to construct its theory). The term is convenient in that it roughly designates a cinema which has been described as based on analogical representation and linear narrative ("transparence" and "presence") and is therefore apparently completely held within the "system" which subtends and unifies these concepts. It has obviously been possible to consider the Hollywood cinema as a model of such "classicism" insofar as its reception has been totally dictated by this system—and limited to a kind of non-reading of the films assured by their apparent non-writing, which was seen as the very essence of their mastery.

2. Our work will therefore be a *reading* in the sense of a *rescanning* of these films. That is, to define it negatively first: (a) it will not be (yet another) commentary. The function of the commentary is to distill an ideally constituted sense presented as the object's ultimate meaning (which however remains elusive indefinitely, given the infinite possibilities of talking about film): a wandering and prolific pseudo-reading which misses the reality of the inscription, and substitutes for it a discourse consisting of a simple ideological delineation of what appear(s) to be the main statement(s) of the film at a given moment.

(b) Nor will it be a new *interpretation,* i.e., the translation of what is supposed to be already in the film into a critical system (meta-language) where the interpreter has the kind of absolute knowledge of the exegetist blind to the (historical) ideological determination of his practice and his object-pretext, when he is not a hermeneute à la Viridiana slotting things into a pre-ordained structure.

(c) Nor will this be a dissection of an object conceived of as a closed structure, the cataloguing of progressively smaller and more "discrete" units: in other words, an inventory of the elements which ignores their predestination for the filmmaker's writing project and, having added a portion of intelligibility to the initial object, claims to deconstruct, then reconstruct that object, without taking any account of the dynamic of the inscription. Not, therefore, a mechanistic structural reading.

(d) Nor finally will it be a demystification in the sense where it is enough to re-locate the film within its historical determinations, "reveal" its assumptions, declare its problematic and its aesthetic prejudices and criticise its statement in the name of a mechanically applied materialist knowledge, in order to see it collapse and feel no more needs to be said. This amounts to throwing the baby out with the bathwater without getting wet. To be more precise, it would be disposing of the film in a moralist way, with an argument which separates the "good" from the "bad," and evading any effective reading of it. (An effective reading can only be such by returning on its own deciphering operation and by integrating its functioning into the text it produces, which is something quite different from brandishing a method—even if it is Marxist-Leninist— and leaving it at that.)

It is worth recalling that the external and mechanistic application of possibly even rigorously constructed concepts has always tried to pass for the exercise of a theoretical practice: and—though this has long been established—that an artistic product cannot be linked to its socio-historical context according to a linear, expressive, direct causality (unless one falls into a reductionist historical determinism), but that it has a complex, mediated and *decentred* relationship with this context, which has to be rigorously specified (which is why it is simplistic to discard "classic" Hollywood cinema on the pretext that since it is part of the capitalist system it can only reflect it). Walter Benjamin has insisted strongly on the necessity to consider literary work (but similarly any art product) not as a reflection of the relations of production, but as having a place *within* these relations. (Obviously he was talking of progressive works, past, present, and to come: but a materialist reading of art products which appear to lack any intentional critical dimension concerning capitalist relations of production must do the same thing. We will return later at greater length to this basic notion of "the author as producer.") In this respect we must once again quote Macherey's theses on literary production (in particular those concerning the Leninist corrections to Trotsky and Plekhanov's simplistic positions on Tolstoy) and Badiou's concerning the autonomy of the aesthetic process and the complex relation historical truth/ideologies/author (as place and not as "internalisation")/work.

And that, given this, denouncing ideological assumptions and ideological production, and designating them as falsification and error, has never sufficed to ensure that those who operated the critique themselves produced truth. Nor what's more has it sufficed to bring out the truth about the very things they are opposing. It is therefore absurd to demand that a film account for what it doesn't say about the positions and the knowledge which form the basis from which it is being questioned; and it is too easy (but of what use?) to "deconstruct" it in the name of this same knowledge (in this case, the science of historical materialism which has to be practised as an active method and not used as a guarantee). Lest we be accused of dishonesty, let us make it clear that the points made in paragraph (d) refer to the most extreme positions within *Cinethique.*

3. At this point we seem to have come up against a contradiction: we are not content to demand that a film justify itself vis à vis its context, and at the same time we refuse to look for "depth," to go from the "literal meaning" to some "secret meaning"; we are not content with what it says (what it intends to say). This is only an apparent contradiction. What will be attempted here through a re-scansion of these films in a process of active reading, is to make them say what they have to say *within* what they leave unsaid, to reveal their constituent lacks; these are neither faults in the work (since these films, as Jean-Pierre Oudart has clearly demonstrated—see the preceding issue [No. 222]—are the work of extremely skilled filmmakers) nor a deception on the part of the author (for why should he practice deception?); they are *structuring absences,* always displaced—an overdetermination which is the only possible basis from which these discourses could be realised, the unsaid included in the said and necessary to its constitution. In short, to use Althusser's expression—"the internal shadows of exclusion."

The films we will be studying do not need filling out, they do not demand a teleological reading, nor do we require them to account for their *external* shadows (except purely and simply to dismiss them); all that is involved is traversing their statement to locate what sets it in place, to double their writing with an active reading to reveal what is already there, but silent, to make them say not only "what this says, but what it doesn't say because it doesn't want to say it" (J. A. Miller, and we would add: what, while intending to leave unsaid, it is nevertheless obliged to say).

4. What is the use of such a work? We would be obliged if the reader didn't envisage this as a "Hollywood revisited." Anyone so tempted is advised to give up the reading with the very next paragraph. To the rest we say: that the structuring absences mentioned above and the establishment of an ersatz which this dictates have some connection with the sexual *other scene*, and that "other scene" which is politics; that the double repression—politics and eroticism—which our reading will bring out (a repression which cannot be indicated once and for all and left at that but rather has to be written into the constantly renewed process of its repression) allows the answer to be deduced; and this is an answer whose very question would not have been possible without the two discourses of overdetermination, the Marxist and the Freudian. This is why we will not choose films for their value as "external masterpieces" but rather because the negatory force of their writing provides enough *scope* for a reading—because they can be re-written.

2. HOLLYWOOD IN 1938–39

One of the consequences of the 1929 economic crisis was that the major banking groups (Morgan, Rockefeller, DuPont, Hearst, General Motors, etc.) strengthened their grip on the Hollywood firms which were having problems (weakened by the talkies' "new patents war").

As early as 1935, the five Major Companies (Paramount, Warner, MGM, Fox, RKO) and the three Minor (Universal, Columbia, United Artists) were totally controlled by bankers and financiers, often directly linked to one company or another. Big Business's grip on Hollywood had already translated itself (aside from economic management and the ideological orientation of the American Cinema) into the regrouping of the eight companies in the MPPA (Motion Pictures Producers Association) and the creation of a central system of self-censorship (the Hays code—the American bank is known to be puritanical: the major shareholder of the Metropolitan in New York, Morgan, exercised a real censorship on its programmes).

It was precisely in 1935 that, under the aegis of the Chase National Bank, William Fox's Fox (founded in 1914) merged with Darryl F. Zanuck's 20th Century Productions, to form 20th Century Fox, where Zanuck became vice-president and took control.

During the same period, and mainly in 1937–38 the American cinemas suffered from a very serious drop in box-office receipts (this is first attributed to the consequences of the recession, then, with the situation getting worse, to lack of regeneration of Hollywood's stock of stars); the bank's boards, very worried, ordered a *maximum reduction in costs of production*. This national marketing crisis (in a field in which Hollywood films previously covered their entire costs, foreign sales being mainly a source of profits) was made even worse by the reduced income from foreign sales; this was due to the political situation in Europe, the gradual closure of the German and Italian markets to American films, and the currency blockade set up by these two countries.

3. THE USA IN 1938–39

In 1932, in the middle of the economic crisis, the Democrat Roosevelt became President, succeeding the Republican Hoover whose policies, both economic (favourable to the trusts, deflationist) and social (leaving local groups and charitable organisations to deal with unemployment: cf. *Mr. Deeds Goes to Town*, Capra) had been incapable of avoiding the crisis and also of suppressing its effects. Roosevelt's policies were the opposite; federal intervention in the whole country's economic and social life, States as private powers (New Deal); establishment of federal intervention and public works agencies,

784

impinging on the rights and areas previously reserved to State legislature and private companies (a controlled economy, social budget etc.): so many measures which encountered violent opposition from the Republicans and Big Business. In 1935 they succeeded: the Supreme Court declares Roosevelt's federal economic intervention agencies to be unconstitutional (because they interfere with the rights of the States). But Roosevelt's second victory in 1936 smashed these manoeuvres, and the Supreme Court, threatened with reform, ended up by recognising the New Deal's social policies and (among others) the right to unionise.

At the level of the structures of American society, the crisis and its remedies have caused the strengthening of the federal State and increased its control over the individual States and the Trust's policies: by its "conditional subsidies," its nationwide economic programmes, its social regulations, the federal government took control of vast areas which had previously depended only on the authority of the States and on the interests of free enterprise. In 1937, "the dualist" interpretation of the 10th amendment of the Constitution—which forbade any federal intervention in the economic and social policies of the States (their private domain)—was abrogated by the Supreme Court from its judgments. This strengthening of federal power at all levels had the effect of *increasing the President's power.*

But, as early as 1937, a new economic crisis emerged: economic activity dropped by 37% compared to 1929, the number of unemployed was again over 10 million in 1938, and despite the refloating of major public works, stayed at 9 million in 1939 (cf. *The Grapes of Wrath*). The war (arms industries becoming predominant in the economy) was to help end the new crisis by allowing full employment. . . .

Federal centralism, isolationism, economic reorganisation (including Hollywood), strengthening of the Democrat-Republican opposition, new threats of internal and international crisis, crisis and restrictions in Hollywood itself; such is the fairly gloomy context of the *Young Mr. Lincoln* (1939) undertaking.

It is no doubt difficult, but necessary to attempt to estimate

785

the total and respective importance of these factors to the project and the ideological "message" of the film. In Hollywood, more than anywhere else the cinema is not "innocent." Creditor of the capitalist system, subject to its constraints, its crises, its contradictions, the American cinema, the main instrument of the ideological super-structure, is heavily determined at every level of its existence. As a product of the capitalist system and of its ideology, its role is in turn to reproduce the one and thereby to help the survival of the other. Each film, however, is inserted into this circuit according to its specificity, and there has been no analysis if one is content to say that each Hollywood film confirms and spreads the ideology of American capitalism: it is the precise articulations (rarely the same from one film to the next) of the film and of the ideology which must be studied (see 1).

4. FOX AND ZANUCK

20th Century Fox (which produced *Young Mr. Lincoln*), because of its links with Big Business, also supports the Republican Party. From its inception the Republican Party has been the party of the "Great Families." Associated with (and an instrument of) industrial development, it rapidly became the "party of Big Business" and follows its social and economic directives: protectionism to assist industry, anti-unionist struggle, moral reaction and racism (directed against immigrants and Blacks—whom the party had fleetingly championed in Lincoln's time: but it is common knowledge that this was due once again to economic reasons and to pressures from religious groups, groups which fifty years later, were to lead a campaign against everything that is "unamerican").

In power from 1928 to 1932 with Hoover as president, the Republican Party is financed by some of Hollywood's masters (Rockefeller, DuPont de Nemours, General Motors, etc.). At the elections in 1928, 87% of the people listed in *Who's Who in America* supported Hoover. He has put the underwriters of Capital at key posts in the administration: the Secretary to the Treasury is none other than Mellon, the richest man in the world (take an example of his policies: he brings down the income tax ceiling from 65% in 1919 to 50% in 1921, and 26% in 1929).

Forced by Roosevelt to make a number of concessions, American Big Business goes to war against the New Deal as soon as the immediate effects of the depression decrease (for example, the private electricity companies withdraw their advertising—which, in the USA, is equivalent to a death sentence—from the newspapers which support Roosevelt and his Tennessee Valley Authority) and they do everything in their power to win the 1940 election.

All this allows us to assume that in 1938–39, Fox, managed by the (also) Republican Zanuck, participated in its own way in the Republican offensive by producing a film on the legendary character Lincoln. Of all the Republican Presidents, he is not only the most famous, but on the whole the only one capable of attracting mass support, because of his humble origins, his simplicity, his righteousness, his historical role, and the legendary aspects of his career and his death.

This choice is, no doubt, all the less fortuitous on the part of Fox (which—through Zanuck and the contracted producer Kenneth Macgowan—is as usual responsible for taking the initiative in the project, and not Ford) that during the preceding season, the Democrat Sherwood's play "Abe Lincoln in Illinois" had been a great success on Broadway. With very likely the simultaneous concern to anticipate the adaptations planned in Hollywood of Sherwood's play (John Cromwell's film with Raymond Massey came out the same year and, unlike Ford's, was very successful), and to reverse the impact of the play and of Lincoln's myth in favour of the Republicans, Zanuck immediately put *Young Mr. Lincoln* into production— it would, however, be wrong to exaggerate the film's political determinism which cannot, under any circumstances, be seen, in contrast, for example, to Zanuck's personal productions, *The Grapes of Wrath*, or *Wilson*, as promoting the company's line.

Producer Kenneth Macgowan's past is that of a famous theatre man. Along with Robert Edmund Jones and Eugene O'Neill, he has been manager of the Provincetown Playhouse; they had had a considerable influence on American theatre. A friend of Ford's, whom he met at RKO during the period of *The Informer,* he moved over to Fox in 1935 (there he produced *Four Men and a Prayer* among others) and became the man responsible for historical biographies which constitute the core of the company's productions.

Young Mr. Lincoln is far from being one of Fox's most important productions in 1939, but this film was shot in particularly favourable conditions; it is one of the few cases in which the original undertaking was least distorted, at least at the production stage: of thirty films produced by Macgowan in the eight years he spent at Fox (1935–43) this is one of the only two which were written by only one scriptwriter (Lamar Trotti) (the other being *The Return of Frank James,* written by S. M. Hellman). Another thing to remark on: these two scripts were written in close collaboration with the directors, who were, therefore, involved at a very early stage instead of being chosen at the last minute, as is the custom, even at Fox (the "directors studio"). Ford even says of the script: "We wrote it together" (with L. Trotti) a rare if not exceptional statement coming from him.

Lamar Trotti had already written two comedies on old America for Ford (of the species known as "Americana"), *Judge Priest* and *Steamboat Round the Bend,* before specialising in historical films with Fox (such as *Drums Along the Mohawk,* directed by Ford after *Young Mr. Lincoln*).

The background to a whole section of the script is the obsession with lynching and legality which is so strong in the thirties' cinema, because of the increase in expeditive justice (lynching), the consequences of gangsterism, the rebirth of terrorist organsations such as the KKK (cf. Lang's *Fury,* Mervyn LeRoy's *They Won't Forget,* Archie Mayo's *Black Legion*). Trotti, a southerner (he was born in Atlanta and had been a crime reporter before editing a local Hearst paper), combined one of Lincoln's most famous anecdotes with a memory from his youth. "When Trotti was a reporter in Georgia he had covered the trial of two young men accused of murder at which their mother, the only witness, would not tell which son had committed the crime. Both were hanged" (Robert G. Dickson, "Kenneth Macgowan" in *Films in Review,* October 1963). In

Lincoln's story, a witness stated having seen, in the moonlight an acquaintance of Lincoln's (Duff Armstrong) participate in a murder. Using an almanac as evidence, Lincoln argued that the night was too dark for the witness to have seen anything and thus obtained Armstrong's acquittal with this plea.

5. FORD AND LINCOLN

Ford had already spent the greater part of his career with Fox: he made thirty-eight movies between 1920 and 1935! Since Zanuck's take over, he had made four movies in two years, the first, in 1936, *The Prisoner of Shark Island* ("I haven't killed Lincoln"). Thus it was to one of the company's older and more trustworthy directors that the project was entrusted. The same year, again with Zanuck, Ford shot *Drums Along the Mohawk* (whose ideological orientation is glaringly obvious: the struggle of the pioneers, side by side with Washington and the Whigs against the English in alliance with the Indians) and, in 1940, *The Grapes of Wrath*, which paints a very gloomy portrait of the America of 1938–39. Despite the fact that he calls himself a-political we know that Ford in any case greatly admires Lincoln as a historical figure and as a person: Ford, too, claims humble peasant origins—but this closeness with Lincoln as a man is, however, moderated by the fact that Ford is also, if not primarily, Irish and Catholic.

In 1924 already, in *The Iron Horse*, Lincoln appears as favouring the construction of the intercontinental railway (industry and unification); at the beginning of *The Prisoner of Shark Island*, we see Lincoln requesting "Dixie" from an orchestra after the Civil War (this is the tune which he "already" plays in *Young Mr. Lincoln*): symbolically, the emphasis is put on Lincoln's unifying, nonvindictive side and his deep southern sympathies by means of the hymn of the Confederation; in *Sergeant Rutledge* (1960) he is evoked by the Blacks as their Saviour; the anti-slavery aspect; in *How the West Was Won* (1962) the strategist is presented; finally in *Cheyenne Autumn* (1964), a cornered politician turns to a portrait of Lincoln, presented as the model for the resolution of any crisis.

Each of these films thus concentrates on a particular aspect

789

either of Lincoln's synthetic personality or of his complex historical role; he thus appears to be a sort of universal referent which can be activated in all situations. As long as Lincoln appears in Ford's fiction as a myth, a figure of reference, a symbol of America, his intervention is natural, apparently in complete harmony with Ford's morality and ideology; the situation is different in a film like *Young Mr. Lincoln* where he becomes the protagonist of the fiction. We will see that he can only be inscribed as a Fordian character at the expense of a number of distortions and reciprocal assaults (by him on the course of fiction and by fiction on his historical truth).

6. IDEOLOGICAL UNDERTAKING

What is the subject of *Young Mr. Lincoln?* Ostensibly and textually it is "Lincoln's youth" (on the classic cultural model—"Apprenticeship and Travels"). In fact—through the expedient of a simple chronicle of events presented (through the presence and actualisation effect specific to classic cinema) as if they were taking place for the first time under our eyes, it is the *reformulation* of the historical figure of Lincoln on the level of the myth and the eternal.

This ideological project may appear to be clear and simple—of the edifying and apologetic type. Of course, if one considers its statements alone, extracting it as a *separable ideological statement* disconnected from the complex network of determinations through which it is realised and inscribed —through which it possibly even criticises itself—then it is easy to operate an illusory deconstruction of the film through a reading of the demystificatory type (see 1). Our work, on the contrary, will consist in activating this network in its complexity, where philosophical assumptions (idealism, theologism), political determinations (republicanism, capitalism) and the relatively autonomous aesthetic process (characters, cinematic *signifiers*, narrative mode) specific to Ford's writing, intervene simultaneously. If our work, which will necessarily be held to the linear sequentiality of the discourse, should isolate the orders of determination interlocking in the film, it will always be in the perspective of their relations: it therefore demands a recurrent reading, on all levels.

7. METHODOLOGY

Young Mr. Lincoln, like the vast majority of Hollywood films, follows linear and chronological narrative, in which events appear to follow each other according to a certain "natural" sequence and logic. Thus two options were open to us: either, in discussing each of the determining moments, to simultaneously refer to all the scenes involved; or to present each scene in its fictional chronological *order* and discuss the different determining moments, emphasising in each case what we believe to be the main determinant (the key signification), and indicating the secondary determinants, which may in turn become the main determinant in other scenes. That first method thus sets up the film as the object of a reading (a text) and then supposedly takes up the totality of its overdetermination networks simultaneously, *without taking account of the repressive operation* which, in each scene, determines the realisation of a key signification; while the second method *bases itself on the key signification of each scene,* in order to understand the scriptural operation (overdetermination and repression) which has set it up.

The first method has the drawback of turning the film into a text which is *readable a priori;* the second has the advantage of making the reading itself participate in the *film's process of becoming-a-text,* and of authorising such a reading only by what authorises it in each successive moment of the film. We have therefore chosen the latter method. The fact that the course of our reading will be modelled on the "cutting" of the film into sequences is absolutely intentional, but the work will involve breaking down the closures of the individual scenes by setting them in action with each other and *in* each other.

8. THE POEM

After the credits (and in the same graphic style: i.e., engraved in marble) there is a poem which consists of a number of questions which "if she were to come back on earth," Lincoln's mother would ask, concerning the destiny of her son.

(a) Let us simply observe for the moment that the figure of the mother is inscribed from the start, and that it is an absent

Mother, already dead, a symbolic figure who will only later make her full impact.

(b) The enumeration of questions on the other hand programmes the development of the film by designating Lincoln's problematic as being that of a choice: the interrogative form of this poem, like a matrix, generates the binary system (the necessity to choose between two careers, two pies, two plaintiffs, two defendants, etc.) according to which the fiction is organised (see 14).

(c) In fact, the main function of the poem, which pretends that the questions posed therein haven't yet been answered (whereas they are only the simulation of questions since they presume the spectator's knowledge of Lincoln's *historical character*), is to set up the dualist nature of film and to initiate the process of a double reading. By inviting the spectator to ask himself "questions" to which he already has the answers, the poem induces him to look at history—something which, for him, has already happened—as if it were "still to happen." Similarly, by on the one hand playing on a fictional structure of the "chronicle" type ("natural" juxtaposition and succession of events, as if they were not dictated by any determinism or directed towards a necessary end), and on the other hand by contriving, in the scenes where a crucial choice must be made by the character, a margin of *feigned indecisiveness* (as if the game had not already been played, Lincoln had not entered history, and as if he was taking every one of his decisions on the spot, in the present), the film thus effects a *naturalisation* of the Lincolnian myth (which already exists as such in the mind of the spectator).

The retroactive action of the spectator's knowledge of the myth on the chronicle of events and the naturalist rewriting of the myth in the divisions of this chronicle thus impose a reading in the future perfect. "What is realised in my story is not the past definite of what once was since it is no more, nor the perfect of what has been in what I am, but the future perfect of what I will have been for what I am in the process of becoming" (Lacan).

A classic *ideological* operation manifests itself here, normally, through questions asked after the event whose answer, which has already been given, is the very condition for the existence of the question.

9. THE ELECTORAL SPEECH

First scene. A politician dressed in townclothes (John T. Stuart, later to become Lincoln's associate in Springfield) addresses a few farmers. He denounces the corrupt politicians, who are in power, and Andrew Jackson, President of the USA; he then introduces the local candidate whom he is sponsoring: young Lincoln. The first shot, in which we see Lincoln, shows him sitting on a barrel leaning backwards, in shirtsleeves, wearing heavy boots (one recognises the classic casualness of Ford's hero, who has returned and/or is above everything). In the next shot, addressing the audience of farmers, Lincoln in a friendly tone (but not without a hint of nervousness) declares: "My politics are short and sweet like your ladies' dances; I am in favour of a National Bank and for everybody's participation in wealth." His first words are "You all know who I am, plain Abraham Lincoln"—this is meant not only for the spectators in the film, who are anyway absent from the screen, but also to involve the spectator of the movie, brought into the cinematic space; thus this treatment in the future perfect is immediately confirmed (see 8).

This programme is that of the Whig party, at that time in opposition. It is in essence the programme of nascent American capitalism: protectionism to favour national industrial production, National Bank to favour the circulation of capital in all the states. The first point traditionally has a place in the programme of the Republican Party (it is thus easily recognisable to the spectator of 1939); the second calls to mind a point in history: while in power before 1830, the Whigs had created a National Bank (helping industrial development in the North) whose powers Jackson, who succeeded them, attempted to weaken: the defence of this bank was thus one of the demands of the Whigs, who later became Republicans.

(a) The specifically *political* notations which introduce the film, have the obvious function of presenting Lincoln as the candidate (that is, in the future perfect, the President, the champion) of the Republicans.

(b) But the scorn which is immediately shown towards the "corrupt politicians" and the strength in the contrast of Lincoln's programme which is simple as "a dance," have the effect of introducing him (and the Republicans in his wake) as the opposition and the remedy to such "politics." Furthermore we will see later that it is not only his opponents' politics which are "corrupt," but all politics, condemned in the name of morality (the figure of Lincoln will be contrasted, with that of his opponent Douglas, with that of the prosecutor, as the defender of Justice versus the politicians, the Uncompromising versus the manipulators).

This disparagement of politics carries and confirms the *idealist* project of the film (see 4 and 6): moral virtues are worth more than political guile, the Spirit more than the Word (cf. 4, 6, 8). (Likewise, politics appears again, later, as the object of discussion among drunks—quarrel between J. P. Cass and his acolyte—or of socialite conversation: carriage scene between Mary Todd and Douglas).

But what is most significant here is that the points of the electoral programme are *the only indications* of a *positive relation* between Lincoln and politics, all others being negative (separating Lincoln from the mass of "politicians").

(c) We may be surprised that a film on Lincoln's youth could thus empty out the truly political dimension from the career of the future President. This massive omission is too useful to the film's ideological purpose to be fortuitous. By playing once again on the spectator's knowledge of Lincoln's political and historical role, it is possible to establish the idea that these were founded on and validated by a Morality superior to all politics (and could thus be neglected in favour of their Cause) and that Lincoln always draws his prestige and his strength from an intimate relationship with Law, from a (natural and/or divine) knowledge of Good and Evil. Lincoln *starts* with politics but soon rises to the moral level, divine right, which for an idealist discourse—originates and valorises all politics. Indeed, the first scene of the film already shows Lincoln as a political candidate without providing any information either on what may have brought him to this stage: *concealment of origins* (both his personal—family—origins and those of his political knowledge, however basic: that is "his education") which establishes the mythical nature of the character; or on the results of this electoral campaign (we know that he was defeated, and that the Republicans' failure resulted in the shelving of the National Bank, among other things): as if they were in fact of no importance in the light of the already evident significance of fate and the myth. Lincoln's character makes all politics appear trivial.

But this very *repression* of politics, on which the ideological undertaking of the film is based, is itself a *direct result* of political assumptions (the eternal false idealist debate between morality and politics: Descartes versus Machiavelli) and at the level of its reception by the spectator, this repression is not without consequences of an equally political nature. We know that the ideology of American Capitalism (and the Republican Party which traditionally represents it) is to assert its divine right, to conceptualise it in terms of permanence, naturalism and even biology (cf. Benjamin Franklin's famous formula: "Remember that money has genital potency and fecundity") and to extol it as a universal Good and Power. The enterprise consisting of the concealment of politics (of social relations in America, of Lincoln's career) under the idealist mask of Morality has the effect of regilding the cause of Capital with the gold of myth, by manifesting the "spirituality" in which American Capitalism believes it finds its origins and sees its eternal justification. The seeds of Lincoln's future were already sown in his youth—the future of America (its eternal values) is already written into Lincoln's moral virtues, which include the Republican Party and Capitalism.

(d) Finally, with the total suppression of Lincoln's political dimension, his main historico-political characteristic disappears from the scene of the film: i.e., his struggle against the Slave States. Indeed, neither in the initial political sequence, nor in the rest of the film is this dominant characteristic of his history, of his legend even, indicated, whereas it is mainly to it that Lincoln owes his being inscribed into American history more than any other President (Republican or otherwise).

Strangely enough, only one allusion is made to slavery (this exception has the value of a signal): Lincoln explains to the defendants' family that he had to leave his native state since "with all the slaves coming in, white folks just had a hard time making a living." The fact that this comment emphasises the economic aspects of the problem at the expense of its moral and humantarian aspects would appear to contradict the points outlined above (primacy of morality over politics) if Lincoln had not spoken these words in a scene (see 19) where he puts himself in the imaginary role of the son of the poor farmer family. He recalls his own origins as a poor white who, like everyone else, suffered from unemployment. The accent is thus put on the economic problem, i.e., the problem of the whites, not the blacks.

The *not-said* here, this exclusion from the scene of the film of Lincoln's most notable political dimension, can also not be fortuitious (the "omission" would be enormous!), it too must have *political significance*.

On the one hand, it was indeed necessary to present Lincoln as the unifier, the harmoniser, and not the divider of America (this is why he likes playing "Dixie": he is a Southerner). On the other hand, we know that the Republican Party, abolitionist by economic opportunism, after the Civil War rapidly reappeared as more or less racist and segregationist. (Already, Lincoln was in favour of a progressive emancipation of the blacks, which would only slowly give them equal rights with the whites). He never concealed the restrictions he asked for concerning the integration of blacks. Considering the political impact that the film could have in the context described above (see 3, 4) it would have been in bad taste on both these accounts to insist on Lincoln's liberating role.

This feature is thus silenced, excluded from the hero's youth, as if it had not appeared until later, when all the legendary figure's other features are given by the film as present from the outset and are given value by this predestination.

The shelving of this dimension (the Civil War) which is directly responsible for the Lincolnian Legend thus allows a political use of this legend and, at the same time, by castrating Lincoln of his historico-political dimension, reinforces the idealisation of the myth.

796

But the exclusion of this dominant sign from Lincoln's politics is also possible because *all the others* are rapidly pushed out (except for the brief positive and negative notations mentioned above which in any case are in play as *indicators* — of the general repression of politics — and of stamping of the Republican cause by the seal of the Myth) and because this fact places the film immediately on the purely ideological plane (Lincoln's a-historical dimension, his symbolic value).

Thus what *projects the political meaning* of a film is not a directly political discourse: it is *a moralising discourse.* History, almost totally reduced to the time scale of the myth with neither past nor future can thus, at best, only survive in the film in the form of a *specific repetition:* on the teleological model of history as a continuous and linear development of a pre-existing *seed,* of the future contained in the past (anticipation, predestination). Everything is there, all the features and characters of the historical scene are in their place (Mary Todd who will become Lincoln's wife, Douglas whom he will beat at the presidential elections, etc., right up to Lincoln's death: in a scene which Fox cut, before the film was first released, one could see Lincoln stop in front of a theatre presenting Hamlet and facing one of the (Booth family) troupe of actors — (his future murderer), the problematic of deciding (see 14) and of unifying is already posed. . . . The only missing thing is the main historical feature, this being the one on which the myth was first constructed.

But such repression is possible (acceptable by the spectator) only inasmuch as the film plays on what is *already known* about Lincoln, treating it as if it were a factor of *non-recognition* and at the limit, a not-known (at least, something that nobody wants to know any more, which for having been known is all the more easily forgotten): it is the already constituted force of the myth which allows not only its reproduction, but also its reorientation. It is the universal knowledge of Lincoln's fate which allows, while restating it, the omission of parts of it. For the problem here is not to build a myth, but to negotiate its realisation and even more to rid it of its historical roots in order to liberate its universal and eternal meaning. "Told," Lincoln's youth is in fact *rewritten* by what has to filter through the Lincolnian myth. The film establishes not only

Lincoln's total predestination (teleological axis) but also that *only that to which he has been shown to be predestined* deserves immortality (theological axis). A double operation of addition and subtraction at the end of which the historical axis, having been abolished and mythified, returns cleansed of all impurities and thus recuperable to the service not just of Morality but of the morality re-asserted by capitalist ideology. Morality not only rejects politics and surpasses history, it also rewrites them.

10. THE BOOK

Lincoln's electoral speech seems to open up a fiction: electoral campaign, elections. . . . A problem is presented, which we have the right to expect to see solved, but which in fact will not be solved. To use the Barthesian formula, we have the elements of a hermeneutic chain: enigma (will he or won't he be elected?) and non-resolution. This chain is abandoned by the use of an abrupt fictional displacement: the arrival of the family of farmers. Lincoln is called away to help them. This family comprises the father, the mother and two twelve year old boys. They want to buy some material from Lincoln thus informing us of his occupation: he is a shopkeeper. But the family has no money: Lincoln offers them credit, and confronted by the mother's embarassment, argues that he himself has acquired his shop on credit. The situation is resolved by the use of barter: the family owns a barrel full of old books (left behind by the grandfather). Delighted at the mere mention of a book (legendary thirst for reading) Lincoln respectfully takes one out of the barrel: *as if by chance*, it is Blackstone's "Commentaries." He dusts the book, opens it, reads, realises that it is about Law (he says: "Law") and is delighted that the book is in good condition (the Law is indestructible).

(a) It's a *family* (see 19) of pioneers who are *passing through* that give Lincoln the opportunity of coming in contact with Law: emphasis on the luck-predestination connection as well as on the fact that *even without knowing it* it is the humble who transmit Law (religiously kept by the family as a legacy from the ancestor). On the other hand we have here a classic Fordian fictional feature (apart from the family as a displaced

Henry Fonda, in *Young Mr. Lincoln* (1939), "dusts the book, opens it, reads, realizes that it is about Law (he says: 'Law') and is delighted that the book is in good condition (the law is indestructible). . . . It's a *family* . . . of pioneers who are *passing through* that give Lincoln the opportunity of coming in contact with Law . . ." (EDITORS, page 798). Henry Fonda and Pauline Moore in *Young Mr. Lincoln*. "It is in nature that Lincoln communes with Law: It is at the moment of this communion that he meets Woman . . ." (EDITORS, page 801).

centre): meeting and exchange between two groups whose paths need not have crossed (a new fictional sequence is born from this very meeting; it is first presented as a suspension and simple digressive delay of the main narrative axis, later it constitutes itself as being central, until another sequence arises, functioning in the same mode, Ford's total fiction existing finally only as an articulation of successive digressions).

(b) Lincoln makes a brief but precise speech in praise of credit: "I give you credit"—"I don't like credit" (says the farmer-woman incarnating the dignity of the poor)—"I myself bought my shop on credit": when one is aware of the role played by the extension of credit in the 1929 crisis, this kind of publicity slogan uttered by an American hero (who later, with ever increasing emphasis, will be the Righteous man) tends to appear as a form of exorcism: without credit, the development of capital is impossible; in a period of recession (1935–40), when unemployment is high, and wages have gone down, the maintenance of the level of consumption is the only thing which allows industry to carry on.

(c) The fact that Law is acquired by barter introduces a circuit of debt and repayments which is to run through the film (see 23).

d) The principle function of this sequence is to introduce a number of constituent elements of the symbolic scene from which the film is to proceed by *varying* and activating it (in this sense it is the true expository scene of the fiction, the first scene becoming pretextual and possibly even *extra-textual*): The Book and the Law, the Family and the Son, exchange and debt, predestination. . . . This *setting up* of the fictional matrix means *putting aside* the first sequence (political speech): a simple digression, first believed to be temporary, but then seen to be in fact the first step in the operation of the repression of politics by morality which will continue through the whole film (see 9).

11. NATURE, LAW, WOMAN

Third sequence: lying in the grass under a tree, near a river, Lincoln is reading Blackstone's "Commentaries." He summarises its theories in a few sentences: "The right to acquire and hold property . . . the right to life and reputation . . . and wrongs are a violation of those rights . . . that's all there is to it: right and wrong. . . ." A young woman appears and expresses surprise that he should lie down while reading. He gets up and answers: "When I'm lying down, my mind's standing up, when I'm standing up, my mind lies down." They walk along the river discussing Lincoln's ambitions and culture (poets, Shakespeare, and now Law). They stop and while she is talking he starts to stare at her and tells her that he thinks she is beautiful. This declaration of love continues for a few moments, centered on the question of those who do and those who don't like redheads, then the young girl leaves the scene (the frame, the shot). Alone, Lincoln approaches the river and throws a stone into it. Close up of the ripples on the water.

(a) The first anecdotic *signifié* of the scene refers to Lincoln's legend: like any layman in law in the States at that time, Lincoln discovers Law in Blackstone. His "Commentaries" were young America's legal Bible and they largely inspired the 1787 constitution. They are, in fact, no more than a summary and a confused vulgarisation of 18th Century English Law. The second anecdotic *signifié* (again made explicit in the following scene) is Lincoln's first acknowledged love affair, his relationship with Ann Rutledge—presented in the legend and the film as the ideal wife (who shares similar tastes) whom he will never meet again.

(b) Centred on Lincoln, the scene presents the relationship Law-Woman-Nature which will be articulated according to a system of complementarity and of substitution-replacement.

It is in nature that Lincoln communes with Law:

It is at the moment of this communion that he meets Woman: the relationship Lincoln-Woman replaces the relationship Lincoln-Law since Woman simultaneously interrupts Lincoln's reading of the book by her arrival and marks her appreciation of Lincoln's knowledge and encourages him in his vocation as man of knowledge and Law.

The declaration of love is made according to the classic (banal) cultural analogy Nature-Woman, in Nature (on the bank of a river). But above all the promotion of the river to the status of the woman corresponds to the Woman's (the wife's) disappearance from the sequence (which in the fiction turns out to be definitive); this promotion is signalled by the throwing of the stone (see 18).

Just as culturally determined and codified as the relationship Nature-Woman, the equivalence Nature-Law is here underlined precisely by the fact that the Law book is Blackstone, for whom all forms of Law (the laws of gravitation as well as those which regulate society) grow from a natural Law which is none other than God's law. In the final analysis, this supreme law separates Good from Evil, and is indeed called upon to legislate on the soundness of other human laws (the spirit against the word, see 6, 7, 9). Consequence: the acquisition and the defence of property are here presented as being based on the natural, indeed, on the divine (cf. the ideology of capitalism, 4, 9).

12. THE TOMB, THE BET

The ripples caused by the stone falling in the river dissolve into ice breaking up on the same river, as a transition between the scenes. A "dramatic" music underlines this passage. Lincoln arrives near a tomb covered in snow, near the river, at the spot where the preceding scene took place. Ann Rutledge's name can be read on the marble stone. Lincoln places a bunch of flowers on the tomb, while soliloquising on the return of spring ("the woods are already full of them too, the snow when it's drifting . . . ice breaking up . . . coming of the spring"). He says he is still hesitant on the path to follow: whether to stay in the village or to follow Ann's advice, go to town and choose a legal career. He picks up a twig of dead wood: if it falls towards Ann, he will choose law, if not, he will stay in the village. The twig falls on Ann's side. Lincoln, kneeling down, says: "Well Ann, you win, it's the Law" and after a moment of silence "I wonder if I could have tipped it your way just a little."

(a) The dissolve, which links the scene of the declaration of love (see 11) to that of the loved one's tomb, gives the impression that the transition from one to the other follows the same time-scale as the transition from summer to spring (the breaking ice) according to a symbolic (classic) opposition of the seasons: life/death (and resurrection). There is at the same time a smooth (continuous) succession from one season to the other, and a brutal contrast (Ann alive in one shot, dead in the next) between the two scenes. The effect of temporal continuity reinforces the violence of the contrast (the fictional shock) between life and death.

This process of temporal sequence and continuity (which is specific to great classical cinema) has in fact the function of absorbing referential time by juxtaposing and connecting two events (romance, death) separated by what will appear only later (at his arrival in Springfield) to be an interval of many years. This elimination has the effect of presenting Lincoln's first decisive choice (to become a lawyer) as if it had been neither thought out nor elaborated, nor rational: it *denies him the time of reflection*, it abolishes all *work*. Thus, once again, following the film's general strategy, it submits the hero to predestination, by reducing referential time to cinematic time: new *coup de force* by the film.

(b) Lincoln's definitive acceptance of Law is thus, once again, made under Woman's direct influence (we have seen in 11 the nature of her relationship with Law and Nature) and is in phase with the awakening of nature. But despite the fact that this decision is inevitable, both because of the logic of the symbolic axis Woman-Nature-Law, and because of the spectator's knowledge of Lincoln's fate, the film skilfully creates suspense, pretending that luck could change the course of events. As with Hitchcock with whom suspense, far from being weakened by our knowledge of the outcome, is increased at each viewing by this knowledge, the tension built up in the scene, far from being compromised by our knowledge of Lincoln's future (perfect), is increased by it. The film's supreme guile then consists in reintroducing—deceptively—at the very end of the scene the indication of intention, a voluntary choice on Lincoln's part ("I wonder if I could have tipped it your way just a little") which is, in fact, no more than a feigned delegation of power: as if Lincoln's already-accomplished destiny

803

were referring to him to decide its path, following Spinoza's principle of "verum index sui," of truth as indicator of itself, *the self-determination of an already determined figure.*

13. THE PLAINTIFFS

Lincoln's arrival in Springfield. He sets himself up as a solicitor. Two Mormon farmers consult him, intending to take legal action. One owes the other money and the second has satisfied himself by violently beating up the first; therefore the first is claiming damages of an amount roughly equivalent to his debt. Having read the two plaintiffs' statements, Lincoln informs them of the quasi equivalence of their respective debts, the difference being equal to his bill; faced with their hesitation he threatens the use of force, if they don't accept his compromise. The farmers agree to pay him, and one of them tries to give him a fake coin. Lincoln first notices this by the sound it produces, then by biting the coin, and the scene ends on Lincoln's very insistent stare fixed on the forger.

(a) Lincoln's first legal act in the film is the solution of an extremely commonplace case. In fact, this anecdote which introduces the viewer to the violence of social relations in Lincoln's period, indicates his legal function which throughout the film is to repress violence even, as a final resort, by the use of a specifically legal violence (incarnated in Lincoln's physical strength but, most of the time, simply manifested by a verbal threat).

(b) The scene insists on Lincoln's supreme *cleverness*, in resolving any situation, the Law being able to decide either by taking one side against the other, or like here, by craftily restoring the balance between the two sides of the scales. This second solution is obviously preferred by the film because it emphasises Lincoln's legendary unifying role.

(c) Lincoln knows about money: he is not interested in its origin (credit, exchange, debt form, a circle) but it has a ring, a consistency, a value. It is precisely about a money-swindle that Lincoln's *castrating power* (see 16 and 22) is manifested for the first time, as an empty, icy, terrifying stare and his speed at hitting his opponents where it hurts, characteristics which will constitute the terrifying dimension of Lincoln's figure accentuated from scene to scene. Here for the first time the supreme process of Law eclipses the anecdotal character of Lincoln.

It will be observed that this terrifying dimension widely exceeds all the connotative *signifiés* (whether psychological—"I'm a farmer too, you can't fool me," or moral—reprobation, or situational, etc.) which could be applied to it. The irreducible character of Lincoln's castrating figure will persist throughout the film, transcending, altering the ideological discourse.

14. THE CELEBRATIONS

It is in order to take part in the Independence Day celebrations that Lincoln is in such a hurry to conclude the quarrel between the farmers. This celebration is made up of a number of episodes, announced in a programme, the order of which we will follow: (a) a parade (in which Lincoln meets Douglas, his opponent, and Mary Todd, his future wife); (b) a pie judging contest in which Lincoln is the judge (and during which the family from the first scene reappear); (c) a Tug of War (across a pond) in which Lincoln takes part (and in the course of which there is an incident between the family and two roughnecks); (d) a rail splitting contest (longitudinal section of a tree trunk) which Lincoln wins; (e) the burning of tar barrels.

(a) Lincoln is confronted by a historical evocation of America: the local militias parade past him, followed by the veterans of the war against Spain, and finally the survivors of the War of Independence, whom Lincoln salutes by removing his top hat. But Lincoln's slightly ridiculous solemnity is underlined on the one hand by the other spectators' joyful exuberance, and on the other by a succession of grotesque incidents, coupled with the veterans' shabby appearance, very much in the Fordian tradition.

(b) The principle of Justice (whether or not to choose) is here realised through a series of derivatives which exhaust all its modalities: either Lincoln literally splits a rail in two, and thus separates himself from, places himself above his opponents (adventitious meaning: affirmation of the physical strength of literally his cutting edge): or he doesn't hesitate to give *his* side, that is the right side, a helping hand, to help it win (by tying the rope to a horse-drawn cart): Law represented by its ideal figure has every right: just as it doesn't hesitate to use force (see 13, 16) so it doesn't shrink before the use of cunning and deception; a deception whose scandalous aspect is masked by the triviality of the stake; and the "Fordian gag" aspect of the action. Finally, more subtly, faced with the undecidable character of a situation (the ethic, or gastronomic, impossibility of preferring the product of one cook to that of another) the fiction itself must, by abandoning the scene, censor the moment of choice and not show Lincoln making an impossible choice, both for the sake of the scene and for that of the myth.

(c) The celebration sequence is made up of a series of fictionally autonomous *sketches* which are in fact determined by the necessity of presenting a certain number of Lincoln's features. This mode of narration continues and stresses that of the preceding scenes: namely a succession of sequences whose length can vary but which are all subject to the *unity of action*. Indeed each of them establishes a situation, presents, develops and syntagmatically encloses an action (whether this latter is resolved in terms of the diegesis or not: nothing said of the consequences of the electoral speech, no decision about the pies). (Insofar as it closes a scene only, the closure does not preclude the later reinvestment of any one of the elements which the scene has elevated to the status of a signifier: for example, the Law book or the Mother).

In fact it is at the moment of its greatest systematisation (a series of headings) that this mode of narration is *infiltrated by the first elements of a new narrative principle* (that of the detective story enigma and its solution: a hermeneutic chain which articulates all the following sequences). Indeed, during the different episodes of the celebration, characters who will all play a more or less important role in the problem are present: Douglas and Mary Todd, the Clay family, the two bad boys, and a few extras who will reappear at the lynching and the trial. This new narrative device is reinforced (at the end of the celebration) by a scene (between Carrie Sue and her fiancé, Matt, the younger Clay son) which seems to reproduce Hollywood's most banal clichés (chatter of lovers, discussion of the future: how many children); in fact it is important insofar as it is the first scene from which Lincoln is physically absent. He is, however, constantly mentioned: first, indirectly, by Carrie Sue, who is very excited by the celebration and makes her fiancé promise to bring her back every year (what can be here taken as a simple whim, the manifestation of innocent joy and desire—the innocence briefly unmasked when she tells Matt she wishes "we was married right now. . ."—will be revealed and accentuated in all the scenes where Carrie Sue is present as the systematic denial of the violent erotic attraction provoked—not in her alone—by Lincoln of the direction indicated by the film in 19 where Lincoln identifies her with Ann Rutledge); then, directly, by the fiancé who says: "I wish it was going to be that fella's splitting them rails again," taking it on himself to formulate on her behalf *what she cannot say*.

15. THE MURDER

The new plot, which this scene develops and which is to dominate the rest of the film, started, as we noted, with the appearance of a number of elements which disturb the course of the celebration and its narrative presentation; the deputy sheriff (Scrub White) and his friend (J. Palmer Cass) somewhat worked up and high, pester Adam's (one of the Clay sons) wife. A fight breaks out, and is stopped by the mother's (Abigail Clay) intervention. This forgotten quarrel brutally reemerges during the final act of the celebration: the burning of the tar barrels. The two brothers and Scrub White start fighting again; this results in the death of the latter.

We have purposely not described the scene here; it is literally *indescribable*, insofar as it is the realisation—through the succession and length of the shots, abrupt changes of angle, play on distance, the reactions, and the behaviour of the participants, the successive arrival of witnesses—of an amazing system of *deception* which affects all the characters implicated

in the event, and blinds them as well as the spectator. The radical difference between Ford's procedure here, and other films
of the enigma, must at first give the spectator only scraps of
knowledge and deprive him of a number of clues, the revelation of which, after the event, will provide the solution to the
plot; whereas here, on the contrary, everything is given,
present, but undecipherable, and it can only be deciphered at
the second, *informed*, look.

The system of deception here set up is effective because *it
develops as the scene progresses:* all the characters are caught up
in it and duped, thus making it more powerful; and the spectator, witnessing these successive mystifications and called
upon to agree with all, is thus the most deceived.

But we must also note that the effect of the deception continues and is *legitimised* by the substitution of a deceptive
question: *which of the two brothers killed him?* for the real question: who killed him? The former question implies that the latter has already been answered, thus (successfully) suppressing
the first: it will only be brought back by Lincoln (see 22).

All the different characters of the scene—*among them the
spectator*—have either an active or a passive relationship to
the deception—either way strengthening its influence. The
spectator, who will be completely duped, is the initial witness
of the fight: for him a perfectly plausible causal chain is constituted (except for one thing which we will specify): a cause of
death: the shot; an effect: the wounded man's moans as he lies
on the ground; reactions of the guilty: the two brothers, frightened, take refuge near their mother who has just arrived.
There is only one element to contradict this causal chain: before hearing the shot, we see Scrub White's arm, which holds
the weapon, turned away. But this element of confusion
(Scrub White appearing to be seriously wounded by his own
weapon when it was pointed elsewhere) far from invalidates
this first setting up of the deception; on the contrary, it pro-
vokes distraction, thus permitting the intervention of a new
factor (Cass's arrival) to pass almost unnoticed: the wounded
man's death throes at this point can easily be accommodated
by a classic typology: dying-in-one's-best-friend's-arms.

Cass, arriving during this break in attention, kneels down

by his friend, placing himself *between him and the spectator* (long shot). He gets up in a *close up* shot, holding a bloody knife (a weapon which had not previously been seen): a shot which *independently of his drama* (as in Kuleshov's experiment) *is classically a shot of the guilty* (which is indeed what Cass is, since it is he who gave his friend this fatal knife wound but we will only learn this at the end of the movie, *even though all this has already been shown but rendered not-readable*).

The two sons Adam and Matt behave, even before Cass's arrival (ever since the shot was fired), like guilty men. Cass saying "He's dead" confirms them in this guilt; each one believes the other to be guilty but takes responsibility for the crime to protect his brother.

The mother intervenes when the shot is fired, and, seeing a man aground and her two sons alive but frightened, enters into the system of deception in her turn, believing them to be guilty. This feeling is strengthened when Cass gets up showing the knife, a knife which she recognises, believing then that she knows which of her two sons is guilty. But since they both accuse themselves, she plays the game and refuses to say which one she believes to be guilty (refusing to sacrifice one for the sake of the other). This refusal reinforces the deception because it accepts the displacement of the question: the mother thinks she keeps a secret, but it is the wrong one.

The spectator in his turn accepts this second causal chain: since the victim has been murdered with a knife by one of the two brothers, the gun shot from now on appears to him as a trivial episode, even a digression.

Thus what is happening here is precisely the cinematic questioning of direct vision, of perception insofar as it conceals the structure. The work that needs to be done to make the scene legible is not a search for hidden meanings, but the bringing to light of the *meaning which is already there:* which is why, paradoxically, it is our type of reading (see 1) of the film *in its entirety* which is called for and justified by this central scene.

This sequence and the preceding one (dialogue between the lovers) constitute, as we have already said, *a new fiction, from which Lincoln is absent.* He only comes into it when everything is decided (the crime committed, the accused taken away by the sheriff): neither actor, nor witness, *a priori* uninvolved in the problem, he *has no knowledge of it*. This is a necessary condition, in terms of Lincoln's mythical role, for the truth to emerge by magical rather than scientific means: to solve this crime story situation Lincoln will use means very different from those of an enquiry along ordinary thriller lines.

16. THE LYNCHING

(a) Introduced at the end of the celebration by the burning of the barrels (a commonplace episode in American celebrations, but here dramatically emphasised by the double fictional and historical context: KKK/fascist *auto-da-fés*), the cycle of violence (fight, crime) will culminate with the lynching. (The scene thereby acquires extra political significance because in the years 1925–35 a large number of lynchings took place in the USA—see films from that period, e.g., *Fury*.) This violence carries with it an acceleration of the narrative: between the moment when the defendants are taken away and the one when the lynching starts, there are only a few seconds, the time of a reframing; during this time Lincoln offers his legal services to the mother. She asks who he is, since she doesn't recognise him as the man who once gave her credit (this is not without importance, see the circulation of the debts 19) whereas he has just recognised her as the woman who gave him the Book. He answers, after a pause, "I'm your lawyer, ma'am."

(b) Inside the prison, under attack from the lynchers, there is a violent contrast between the understandable nervousness of the defendants and the sheriff and the unjustifiable panic of Cass (who has just been promoted deputy sheriff); for the second time—and here again in a non-readable way—the film exposes Cass as the culprit, i.e., as the man who is afraid of being lynched.

(c) Lincoln's action, insofar as he represents Law, can only be the, if necessary, violent, prohibition of any non-legal violence. Since the whole film is meant to manifest Lincoln's absolute superiority to all those who surround him, the scene of

the lynching provides the opportunity for a masterly demonstration of it in a number of set scenes, each new stage of his
victory increasing his castrating violence; this is inversely proportional to the expenditure of physical violence (since, in the
ideological discourse, Law must have power insofar as it is
legitimised by its own statement, not through physical
strength, which is used as a last resort and often simply as a
verbal threat). Here the escalation of legal repression is effected in many stages: 1. alone, Lincoln physically repels the
lynchers' assault (courage and physical strength), 2. he incites
one of the leaders to single combat, this the man evades (verbal threat based on knowledge of the opponent's weakness), 3.
he defuses the crowd's anger by a cunning speech (so cunning, that the mother, not knowing *who he is*—i.e., in the fiction a good man, and in the myth President Lincoln—takes
his speech literally and is very disturbed, before *believing* in
him); he is also humorous (shifting to another level: complici-
ty/familiarity with the crowd), 4. he throws back on the crowd
the threat of its own violence by showing it that each one of
them one way or the other, could be lynched (intimidation
producing terror), 5. addressing one individual amongst the
lynchers, whom he knows to be a religious man, he threatens
him with retribution in the name of the Bible (ultimate recourse to divine writing as an instance of the Law). Lincoln's
castrating triumph is sanctioned in the film itself not only by
the subsiding of the crowd's anger, but very precisely by the
lowering of the tree trunk, which on Lincoln's order is
dropped by the lynchers—who are dispersing. (Note that it is
with this same tree trunk that the lynchers attempted to break
open the prison door, protected by Lincoln's body.)

17. THE DANCE

Invited by Mary Todd to a dance (the invitation card, con-
gratulating him on his attitude in this "recent deplorable uprising" says, "My sister invites you . . .": here again, denial
of desire), Lincoln abandoning his boots, vigorously shines
his black high button shoes, and with the same unusual concern to be smart cuts his hair (see the anecdote told by Eisen-

stein about the new President moving to Washington: "he went as far as cleaning his own boots. Somebody said: *Gentlemen never clean their boots—And whose boots do real gentlemen clean?"*). The dance is in full swing, elegant and very genteel. Lincoln enters the lobby and is immediately surrounded by elderly gentlemen whom he entertains with funny stories (which we cannot hear). He is asked about his family ("Are you by any chance a member of the well-known Lincoln family from Massachusetts?"—"I'd say the evidence is against it if they own land"). Mary Todd responds absentmindedly to Douglas's advances, she is only interested in Lincoln. She goes to him and demands that he ask her to dance. He replies that he would very much like to dance with her, but warns her that he is a very poor dancer. He follows her to the middle of the dance floor, they start to dance a kind of waltz, then a polka, which Mary Todd suddenly interrupts and drags Lincoln to the balcony.

(a) The dance sequence is more or less compulsory in Ford's films. These dances almost always have the function first of setting up and ordering a ritual *miming ideal harmony*, which in fact is far from regulating the relations of the social group; then later, to disturb, unmask and destroy this simulation of harmony by the intervention of a foreign element. Here Lincoln's social heterogeneity gives place to the realisation of his symbolic otherness (figure of the Law): this involves him (socially and sexually) in a seduction relationship which simultaneously *integrates and excludes him;* this causes a confusion which is not resolved dramatically, unlike what takes place in other Ford films (cf. the dance in *Two Rode Together, Fort Apache* for example).

(b) The scandal of Lincoln's difference is even more noticeable to the spectators than to the characters of the scene. First it is apparent at the *physical* level, his shape, size, gait, rigidity, his undertaker look (Lincoln's mythical costume), then, while he is dancing, in the lack of co-ordination and rhythm in his movements. On the other hand, the social difference (made clear in the scene where Lincoln is dressing for the dance), emphasised by the question about his family, is immediately defused of any political significance and deflected into an amiable originality (it is out of the question according to the film's ideological system, that his class origins should play anything but a positive role).

(c) But it is at the symbolic level that the scandal is most apparent. In terms of the logic of castration, Lincoln's status, whereas it is realised in the lynching scene in its active form (castrating action), figures here in the passive form: that of *inversion* (the fact that these two dimensions—the action of castrating/being castrated—belong together will be made obvious in the balcony scene). Indeed, Mary Todd fully takes the initiative. First she expresses her resentment at Lincoln's coldness (in her conversation with Douglas); then she accuses Lincoln of not making the first move, and demands that he dance with her; finally she brings the dance to a sudden halt and drags him out to the balcony. Thus if the dance scene signifies the hero's social recognition (reward), the dance with Mary Todd puts him into a real castration, the retroactive effect of the lynching scene (which already implied it logically, writing it into the unconscious of Ford's text). There the castrating action was made on the basis of a castration which becomes effective in the dance scene and particularly in the balcony scene.

18. THE BALCONY

As soon as he is on the balcony, Lincoln is enchanted by the river. Mary Todd waits for a moment for Lincoln to speak or show some interest in her. Then she draws aside, leaving him alone in front of the river.

(a) Dance, balcony, river, moonlight, couple: all these elements create a romantic, intimate, sentimental atmosphere. The scene, however, mercilessly destroys this atmosphere (whose physical signifieds could be already read as more fantastic than romantic) to introduce the dimension of the Sacred.

(b) The transfer from one dimension to the other is effected by Lincoln's enchantment with the river: the commonplace accessory of the "romantic scene" is shifted to another scene and is at the same time the agent of this shift: another scene (from which Mary Todd, having no place, withdraws) in which a process of displacement-condensation takes place so that the river simultaneously evokes the first woman Lincoln loved (Ann Rutledge)—an evocation here emptied of any nostalgic or sentimental character—and (see 11) the relationship Nature-Woman-Law. The river is here the ratification of Lincoln's contract with Law. Lincoln, faced with his fate, accepts it; the classic moment of any mythological story. Here the hero sees his future written and accepts its revelation (the balcony, also a typical accessory of romantic love scenes, is here promoted, by Lincoln's gesture and the camera angle, to the anticipated role of the presidential balcony). Correlatively, Lincoln's renunciation of pleasure is written here: from now on Ann Rutledge's death must be read as the real origin both of his castration and of his identification with the Law; and the "inversion" of the dance scene as well as its relation to the lynching scene take on their true meaning: Lincoln does not have the phallus, he is the phallus (see Lacan, *"La signification du phallus"*).

19. THE FAMILY

Immediately after the lynching Lincoln accompanies the mother (Mrs. Clay) and her two daughters-in-law back to their wagon. He tells her, "My mother would be just about your age if she were alive, you know she used to look a lot like you." After the scene of the balcony and before the opening of the trial, he goes to visit the family. On his way to the Clay farm, as he passes the river again, his companion tells him, "I've never known a fella look at a river like you do; fella would think it was a pretty girl the way you carry on" (see 11, 18).

(a) The scene in the farm yard acts as a reminder: Lincoln fantasises himself in the role of son of the family. First, by chopping wood (see 14), he evokes the time when this was his daily task—and compares himself to the son of the family. Then, one by one all the elements of the scene remind him of his house, his garden, his trees, the members of his family; he himself asserts the sequence of these equivalences: Mrs. Clay = his mother, Sarah = his dead sister, whose name was also Sarah, Carrie Sue = Ann Rutledge; and even the dish which is being cooked is his favourite dish: turnips. This insistent parallelism between the Lincoln family and the Clay family is carried through to the *absence* of the father: total exclusion in the case of Lincoln's father who is not even mentioned; the disappearance from the fiction of Mr. Clay (present in the first scene) is explained by an "accident." The rejection of the Name of the Father logically corresponds to Lincoln's identification with the Law (his installation in the place of the great Other) which can neither guarantee itself nor originate itself through any other law than itself. We can here diagnose the *paranoia* which governs the symbolics of the film.

This reliving of memories also has the function of stressing Lincoln's social origins (see 9).

(b) This climate of nostalgic effusion—unique in the film—is brutally interrupted by one of Lincoln's fixed stares which can from now on be understood as the mark of his possession by Law. Giving up the role of son, he becomes inquisitor, interrupts the mother by asking her persistently which of her two sons is guilty. Terrified she refuses to answer (as she had done earlier in front of the sheriff, and will do later in front of the prosecutor). Her consternation affects Lincoln and makes him immediately cast off his attitude of investigator; he gives up both trying to discover the mother's secret (but it is a useless secret) and separate the two sons (for the problematic of one or the other, he substitutes that of all or nothing) and once again symbolically takes their place beside the mother. Let us add that the film firmly avoids a possibility which could have been exploited: namely that the question of the choice between the two sons might upset Lincoln himself, make him doubt or worry for a moment: Lincoln is totally ignorant of the *lamma sabbachtani.*

(c) But this scene has the simultaneous function of continuing the circuit of debt and gift which links and will continue to link Lincoln and the mother, and of providing it with an *origin:* fictionally introduced by the exchange—unequal in Lincoln's favour—of the material for the Book (see 10), it seems at the symbolic level to go back to the time when the child "used to stretch out while my mother read to me"; the situation is here reversed since Mrs. Clay can't read and it is Lincoln—

still paying off this debt of which Mrs. Clay is unaware—who reads her the letter from her sons (note the way in which he pronounces the first words of this letter: "Dear Ma").

The origin of Lincoln's knowledge is here given for the second time (see 11) as being feminine-maternal; the same equivalence Woman-Nature-(Mother)-Law is once again posed, the identification of Lincoln to the Law being related to the preliminary identification of the Law with Nature and Woman-Wife-Mother; the debt contracted by Lincoln towards his mother (she teaches him to read) as well as Mrs. Clay (she gives the Book) and Ann Rutledge (she pushes him towards knowledge) can only be "paid back" by his assumption of this mission, and his incarnation of the Law. Let us not insist on the assumptions behind this series (see 6), but notice that the circulation of the debt and its resolution are here enriched with an extra indicator: to answer, under the mother's dictation, the sons' letter, Lincoln asks Sarah for some paper; she gives him an almanac. Thus it is from the same family that Law and Truth originate: through the Book (the carrier of the Law) and the almanac: first used as a support for writing (letter from the mother to the imprisoned sons), it will reveal the truth when *exhibited by Lincoln* (see 22); it carries the solution to the enigma, it is the sign of Truth.

20. THE TRIAL

(a) The trial, a classic feature of Hollywood cinema, represents the staging of American legalist ideology and constitutes a microcosm of the social whole (sample of the different social strata represented by this or that type, this or that "silhouette"); confidence in the forms of legality is based precisely on this representativeness of the trial: it is America itself which constitutes the Jury, and who cannot be wrong, so that the Truth cannot fail to manifest itself by the end of the proceedings (carried out according to an almost ritualised alternation of comic and tragic moments). We have here a slight departure from this traditional trial, since the question is not to prove the culpability or the innocence of a defendant, but to *choose* (according to the principle of alternatives which has

816

regulated the whole film) between two defendants. But here, as everywhere else, the constraints of the film's ideological strategy will compel Lincoln to *choose not to choose*, either (see 13) by deciding to re-establish the balance between the two parties, or (see 14) by indefinitely postponing the choice, or even, in the trial, by positively refusing to decide, thus trying to save both brothers, be it at the risk of losing both; all things which label and confirm Lincoln as a unifier and not a divider.

(b) During the different stages of the trial, Lincoln appears successively 1. As the weigher of souls: he quickly estimates the moral value of the members of the jury (and he does this according to norms which escape common understanding, even conventional morality: he accepts a man who drinks, lynches, loafs about, because by admitting to these faults, he manifests his deeper honesty). 2. As entertainer of the crowd (jokes, little stories, etc . . .) which put him in contrast with the prosecutor, a starchy man of mean appearance. 3. As manifesting his castrating power over Cass, whom he immediately attacks without apparent reasons: intimidation, vicious inter-rogation, and totally displaced onomastic play on words, thun-dering looks: all these things imply a premonition of Cass's guilt on Lincoln's part, which is not backed up by any knowl-edge but is nonetheless the Truth. For throughout the film Lincoln relates not to knowledge, but to Truth (= Law). 4. As the spirit opposed to the word, the natural and/or divine Law to social Laws which are their more or less perfect transcrip-tion (he interrupts the prosecutor's cross-examination of the mother by telling him, "I may not know so much of Law, Mr. Prosecutor, but I know what's right and what's wrong"). 5. As the righteous against the corridor filibusterer, morality against politics (i.e., his political opponent Douglas's asides with the prosecutor and with Cass).

(c) But this first day of the trial ends in a defeat for Lincoln, brought about by a sensational development: Cass's second testimony. From humanitarian concern, to save at least one of the two defendants, he goes back on the first evidence he gave, and claims to have been an eye-witness of the murder (thanks to the moonlight) and points out the murderer: the elder of the two brothers. In the hermeneutic chain ("which one has kil-

led?'') this reversal of the situation introduces a deceptive answer. A new question is thus posed: how will Lincoln sort this
one out, not only to win the trial, but also to remain faithful to
his refusal to choose?

21. THE NIGHT

(a) As before any "great crisis" in Hollywood cinema, there
is a pause: the scene of the family vigil in the prison—whose
function, in very classically codified form, is to instil a sense of
expectancy allowing a dramatic resurgence. Here the demands
of this code (tension-relaxation-tension) are precisely fulfilled:
no information is given which makes the drama progress (the
family's communion in song replacing/forbidding all explanatory dialogue); it is a "precarious situation lived through with
serenity." But the lack of any allusion on the part of the other
members of the family to the guilt of the elder brother is itself
sufficient to ratify Cass's accusations against him; the fact that
it is not questioned—as if it presented no problem—seems to
authenticate it.

In the duration of the scene, its adherence to the code seems
perfect and even excessive: the convention is accepted and
pushed to its extreme by the Fordian inscription (for everything which delineates the family group in Ford is grafted
here), even to bestowing its character of strangeness on the
scene (static frame, scenes shot from the front, strong light-
dark contrasts, position of the characters, choir). But this adherence on repeated reading is revealed to be a deception.
When we know that the real culprit is neither of the brothers,
the absence of any discussion between them or with their family has the effect of a real *coup de force* at the price of which the
miraculous dimension of Lincoln's revelation of the Truth is
made possible. The scene is thus regulated—with great skill—
by *the necessity of making the code* (the waiting period in which
the group communes in silence or song—when words are useless, even improper) *responsible for the censorship of any information* about the defendants' innocence. If the scene is silent,
it is because anything that might be intimated would inevita-

bly have lifted the deception from the enigma and ruined the magic of Lincoln's act.

(b) The second part of this night of vigil starts, concerning Lincoln, on the same model: the hero's solitude and meditation before the decisive test. Lincoln is in his rocking chair by his office window, playing the Jew's harp. This isolation signifying his defeat is strengthened by two events: 1. Douglas and Mary Todd go past his window in a carriage; they both look at him condescendingly; Mary Todd turns away and says to Douglas: "You were discussing your political plans Mr. Douglas, please go on." 2. The judge appears in Lincoln's office and, arguing from his long experience, suggests a double compromise: to get help the next day from a more experienced lawyer (he suggests Douglas) and to agree to plead guilty to save the other brother. Lincoln categorically refuses: "I'm not the sort of fella who can just swap horses in the middle of the stream."

In 1. the change in size between the first long shot of the carriage and the close up when Mary Todd speaks, a trick of the direction which eliminates the "real" distance by changing the axis (high angle shot) and the width of the shot so that Lincoln appears to be right above the carriage, and Mary Todd's words cannot then fail to reach him, thanks to this unrealistic-proximity—compel the viewer to interpret them as being addressed not to Douglas (Lincoln's eternal contrast) but to Lincoln, and their political contents *standing* for an erotic content. "You were discussing your political plans Mr. Douglas, please go on" can be read as, "I couldn't possibly do so with you Lincoln, *nor make love*" at a time when everything in Mary Todd's behaviour, look, and gestures points to her obvious spite, and to her speech as a denial of her desire. In the film's other scenes the repression taking place alternately between the erotic and the political (Law as repressed desire and as natural/divine morality) becomes here, in a single sentence, the repression of the erotic by the political.

In 2. Lincoln's paranoid features are confirmed: his refusal of all help, of any compromise, his hallucinatory faith in his own power, his certainty of being Chosen, his rigidity, the holding out to the bitter end.

22. VICTORY

Second day of the trial. Lincoln calls the main prosecution witness, Cass, back to the witness box, and by his questions makes him *repeat* his statement of the previous day point by point: it was in fact thanks to the full moon that he was able to witness the scene; it is to save one of the two brothers that he has gone back on his first statement. Mary Todd, like the rest of the public doesn't see the point of Lincoln's insistence to have things which are already known repeated. Lincoln pretends to let Cass go again, and just as he is about to leave the well of the Court, he suddenly asks him, "What d'you have against Scrub White, what did you kill him for?" Pulling the almanac out of his hat he thrusts it forward, saying: "Look at page 12: see what it says about the moon; it says it was in it's first quarter and set at 10.21 p.m., forty minutes before the murder" and, addressing Cass, "You lied about this point, you lied about the rest." From this point onwards Lincoln harasses Cass with questions until, collapsing, in a broken, shrill voice, he confesses: "I didn't mean to kill him. . . ." The confession obtained, Lincoln casually turns away from his victim and, addressing the prosecutor: "Your witness," while Cass's former supporters surround him threateningly.

(a) The almanac: a *signifier* first present in the scenes where the mother asks Lincoln to write to her imprisoned sons for her (see 19) as a simple support for writing, reappears on the first day of the trial (where it is on Lincoln's table, near his hat), then in the night scene where Lincoln is fingering it with apparent casualness. It is finally produced as *sign* of the Truth at the end of the second day of the trial, when Lincoln pulls it out of his hat like a conjuror.

We have here the typical example of a signifier running through the film without a signified, representing nothing, acquiring the status of a sign under Lincoln's revelation (the almanac representing proof of the truth for everyone) *but without ever having been an indicator.* Thus the thriller process of deduction is *completely eliminated* in favour of a scriptural logic which demands that such a signifier be produced as a veiled

820

term whose very concealment and sudden final revelation would constitute a *mise en scene* inseparable from the meaning it induces, the mark of the unconscious determination of its writing into Ford's text. Veiled, 1, in the extent to which it realises the operation of repression of (erotic/criminal) violence in the fiction, whose return is effected according to a rhetoric of negation, and, 2, because its only *place* is that of a term whose sole function is to effect a mediation (between the criminal and the crime, between the mother and the sons), it is thereby doomed to disappearance as it is produced and to be included/excluded from the propositions in which it is actualised, by the very fact that it determines the production of their meaning; this is so to the extent to which the *signifier* of truth must remain veiled as long as truth is not stated, since at no moment is it presented as a clue (which would imply a work, the exercise of a knowledge, even a manipulation, which is not the case here). Lincoln's powers are thus not presented as the exercise of the art of detective deduction, but as a paranoid interpretation which short-circuits its process. Thus the proof of the crime seems to be materialised by the mere faculty which Lincoln has of producing the signifier as the concrete result of his omnipotent powers of Revelation.

But the manifestation of this omnipotence at the end of the film, made necessary by the ideological project (Lincoln, a mythical hero representing Law and guarantor of Truth), takes place at the end of the series of relations of co-presence between Lincoln and the almanac (three scenes where it is present without Lincoln knowing what to do with it in terms of the truth) and in such an unlikely and arbitrary (magical) way that it can be read in the following ways: 1, effectively as omnipotence, 2, as a pure fictional *coup de force* implying an imposition of Ford's writing on Lincoln's character (Lincoln's omnipotence is then *controlled and limited* by Ford's omnipotence, the latter not adopting the best possible viewpoint on his character, which would have been to show him as himself having the revelation of the Truth, and not merely as its agent) and 3, as Lincoln's *impotence* insofar as he appears subject to the power of the signifier (the almanac) and in a position of radical non-recognition regarding it, such that one can just as well say that the truth revolves around Lincoln (and not Lincoln around the truth) and that it is not Lincoln who uses the signifier to manifest the truth, but the signifier which uses Lincoln as mediator to accede to the status of the sign of truth. 2 and 3 (one specific to the film's writing, the other to its reading: but as we have stated in the introduction, we do not hesitate to force the text, even to rewrite it, insofar as the film only constitutes itself as a text by integration of the reader's knowledge) *manifest a distortion of the ideological project by the writing of the film.*

(b) Once the truth is revealed, Lincoln harasses Cass with brutal questions until he obtains his confession. 1. Lincoln must obtain from the culprit the confirmation of what he has just stated to be truth; on the one hand to finalise the fiction (save the two brothers, solve the mystery: but at the same time, this solution is the admission that the enigma was, in fact, a mere deception set up by the film); and on the other hand to be confirmed in the eyes of the other characters as possessor of the truth (if it is in fact enough for the spectator—who knows who Lincoln is—to see him reveal the truth to believe it, the characters of the fiction, his enemies, those who have witnessed his failure of the previous day, etc . . . cannot be so easily satisfied with his word). 2. Lincoln's insistence and violence at this moment can be read, first, as the classic harshness of rampant Justice, but mainly as the culmination of Lincoln's castrating power (see 16), which is attested by the fact that Cass, around whom the whole film has accumulated the clichés of hypervirility, collapses in tears when he confesses, crying like a child. 3. This excessive violence of the characterisation of Lincoln in the writing of the film, which is motivated neither by the needs of Lincoln's cause (he could triumph without terror) nor by those of the fiction (Cass could confess without resisting) shows an imbalance with the idealised figure of Lincoln: even if this violence in the writing implies no intentional criticism of the character Lincoln, it makes visible—by its own scriptural excesses—the truly repressive dimension of the figure which this writing dictates, and deroutes what could have been edifying or hagiographic in the ideological project of the film.

23. "TOWARDS HIS DESTINY"

After his victory, Lincoln leaves the court alone. Four people are waiting for him, among them Mary Todd and Douglas. She congratulates him, looking at him seductively. Douglas then comes to shake his hand: "I give you my sincere promise never to make the mistake of underrating you again." Lincoln replies, "Neither of us will underrate each other again." He is about to go but is called back, "The town's waiting." He moves towards the door, fully lit, and the crowd can be heard applauding off-set.

(a) Victorious, Lincoln is *recognised* by those who doubted him: this type of scene (recognition of the hero) belongs to a very classic register. But the way in which the scene is filmed, the camera at a slightly low angle shot, disposition of the groups, Lincoln's rather weary solemnity, the tone in which he is called ("the town's waiting") and, chiefly, when he goes to the threshold, his entry into a beam of violent light, the frontal low angle shot when he faces the crowd whom he greets by removing his hat, the very harsh lighting of the end of this scene, all set this sequence in a very specifically theatrical dimension: congratulations backstage after the performance, recall to the stage of the primadonna. But the fact that, by spatial displacement, this *encore* takes place not in the court in front of the spectators of the trial, but on another stage (the street, the town, the country) and in front of a crowd *which is not shown* (which is no longer only the inhabitants of Springfield but of America) retroactively shows the performance of the trial (definitely given as theatrical by the entrances, the recalls, the repeats, the attitude of the spectators, the wings, etc.) to be a simple rehearsal (provincial tour) and what is to follow on the other stage (which the whole film has played on as something having already happened which no one could be ignorant of) will be the real performance (national tour); and the *encore* is, in fact, the true entrance on the stage of the legend. At the moment when he is *discovered* (intercepted) by the others as Lincoln, and stripped of his character, he can only act it out, play his own role. This interception is very precisely indicated in the film by the violent call of the brilliant light: the reference to German expressionism (even to horror films: *Nosferatu*)—much admired by Ford, as we well know— is therefore compulsory at this point.

(b) Preceding the film's last shots which will only serve to heighten this tragic dimension, we have the scene of farewell to the Clays; like all other scenes with the family (as a function of its status in relation to Lincoln) it is treated in an intimate, familiar way, without solemnity. A scene in which the fiction will terminate the double circuit of the symbolic debt linking Lincoln to Mrs. Clay and of the desire which drives Carrie Sue (as we have seen she is a substitute for Ann Rutledge) towards a Lincoln who can no longer love her; first the mother insists on paying Lincoln and gives him a few coins which he accepts, saying: "Thank you ma'am its mighty generous of you"; then Carrie Sue leaps to his neck and kisses him, saying: "I reckon I'd just about die if I didn't kiss you Mr. Lincoln." This confirms everything in Carrie Sue's attitude, which already exceeded the simple feeling of gratitude towards Lincoln, showing her to be driven by the desire, which, throughout the film, makes her "play" around him, thus allowing her kiss to be read as a form of "acting out," a substitute for orgasm.

(c) Final scene: Lincoln takes leave of his companion (who is simultaneously a classic theatrical confidant and a sort of Sancho Panza, who is at his side in a number of scenes in the film) by telling him, "I think I might go on apiece . . . maybe to the top of that hill." The confidant goes out of frame. A storm threatens. Lincoln is slowly climbing the hill. A last shot shows him facing the camera, with a vacant look, while threatening clouds cross the background and the "Battle Hymn of the Republic" begins to be heard. Lincoln leaves the frame. Rain begins to fall violently and continues into the final shot of the film (his statue at the Capitol) while music intensifies.

Here again, it is the excesses of Ford's writing (accumulation of signs of the tragic, of ascent: hill—mythical reference—storm, lightning, rain, wind, thunder, etc.) which, by overlaying all the clichés, underlines the monstrous character of the figure of Lincoln: he leaves the frame and the film (like *Nosferatu*) as if it had become impossible for him to be filmed any longer; *he is an intolerable figure*, not because he has become too big for any film on account of the ideological project but rather because the constraints and violences of Ford's writing have exploited this figure for their own ends and manifested its excessive and monstrous dimensions, have no further use for it and so return it to the museum.

24. WORK OF THE FILM

With the fiction reaching saturation point here, what culminates in the final sequence is nothing other than the effects of meaning, re-scanned by our reading through the film as a whole, taken to their extreme. That is: the unexpected results (which are also contrary in relation to the ideological project) produced by the inscription—rather than flat illustration—of this project within a cinematic texture and its treatment by a writing which, in order to carry through the project successfully, maximising its value *and only that* (it's obvious that Ford takes practically no distance in relation to the figure and the ideology of Lincoln), is led to: such distortions (the setting up of a system of deception); such omissions (all those scenes, necessary in the logic of the crime thriller but whose presence could have lessened the miraculous dimension of Lincoln's omnipotence: the confrontation with the accused, the least one could expect of a lawyer); such accentuations (the dramatisation of the final scenes); such scriptural violence (be it for the repression of violence—the lynching, the trial); such a systemisation of determination and election (throughout a film which, at the same time, wants to play on a certain suspense and free choice without which the fiction could neither develop nor capture interest); in short to such a *work* that, today, simply delimiting its operation and the series of means it puts into action allows us to see the price at which such a film could be made, the effort and detours demanded to carry the project through.

And which Jean-Pierre Oudart in the following conclusion, the point of departure of our study, cannot but repeat.

25. VIOLENCE AND LAW

I. A discourse on the Law produced in a society which can only represent it as the statement and practice of a moralist prohibition of all violence, Ford's film could only reassert all the idealist representations which have been given it. Thus it is not very difficult to extract from it an ideological statement which seems to valorise in all innocence the ascetic rigour of its agent, making it into the unalterable value which circulates throughout the film from scene to scene; it is also easy to observe that this cliché, presented as such in the film and systematically accentuated, is not there merely to ensure the acceptability of the Fordian inscription. Without this cliché which provides the fiction with a kind of metonymic continuity (the same constantly re-asserted figure)—whose necessity is moreover overdetermined, its function being more than simply setting up a character whose "idealism" can most conveniently be signified by the external signs of the very puritan sense of election—the film would appear, in fact does appear in spite of it, to be a text of disquieting unintelligibility; through its constant disconnections, it places us in a forced position for the reading and in fact its comprehension demands:

(1) That one first take no account of this at once insistent and fixed statement;

(2) That one listens carefully to what is stated in the succession of so obviously "Fordian" scenes which support this statement, and in the relations between the figures, all more or less part of the Fordian fiction, which constitute these scenes;

(3) That one tries to determine how all these are involved; i.e., to discover what the operation by which Ford inscribes this character into his fiction consists of, insofar as, despite appearances, it is not superimposed on Ford's "world," does not traverse it like a foreign body, but finds through this inscription into his fiction a designated place as representative of his Law; for the filmmaker promotes the character to the role to which his (legendary) historical referent destines him only at the price of his subjection to the (Fordian) fictional

logic. This determined his entry there in advance, insofar as his role was already written and his place already set out in Ford's fiction. The work of Ford's écriture only becomes apparent in this film through the problem involved in producing the character in this role, in that he took a place which was already occupied.

II. It is the character of the mother that incarnates the idealised figure of Ideal Law in Ford's fiction. Moreover, it is often, as in *Young Mr. Lincoln,* the widowed mother, guardian of the deceased father's law. It is for her that the men (the regiment) sacrifice the cause of their desire, and under her presidency that the Fordian celebration takes place; this in fact consists in a simulacrum of sexual relations from which all effective desire is banned. But it is in the constantly renewed relationship of this group with another (the Indians), in the dualism of Ford's universe that the inscription of the structural imperative of Law which dictates the deferment of desire and imposes exchange and alliance is realised, in violence, guided by the mediating action of the hero (often a bastard) who is placed at its intersection.

III. In *Young Mr. Lincoln* one of the results of using a single character for both roles is that he will have both their functions, which will inevitably create, by their interference and their incompatibility (insofar as one secures the taboo on the violence of desire, the other is agent of its inscription), disturbances, actions which oppose the order of Ford's world, and it is remarkable that each comical effect always shows them up (there is no film in which laughter is so precisely a sign of a constant disorder of the universe). The compression of their functions will in fact be used only on the one level of the castration of the character (signified at the ideological level by its puritan cliché, and at the same time written, in the unconscious of the text, as the effect of the fictional logic on the structural determination of the character) and of his castrating action, in a fiction ruled by Ideal Law alone since the dualism of Ford's world is abandoned in favour of the mass-individual opposition. (In fact the political conflict intervenes only as a secondary determination of the fiction and literally only acts backstage.) In fact, we see that:

(1). The character's calling originates in his renouncing the pleasures of love; it is strengthened because he resists its attraction: Lincoln becomes so well integrated in the fiction and so vigilant against the violences and plots which take place there only because he refuses to give in to the advances constantly made to him by women, affected by a charm which is due only to the prestige of his castration.

(2). This extreme postponement of the hero's desire soon becomes meaningful since it permits him to become the restorer of Ideal Law, whose order has been perturbed by a crime which the Mother has not been able to prevent but which she will attempt to stifle.

This shows that:

(1). The puritan cliché which Ford emphasises has the very precise function of promoting the character to his role as mediator, insofar as the pleasure which he rejects allows him to thwart any attempt at sexual and political corruption; it thus simultaneously guarantees the credibility of the figure of Lincoln and the position of the character as the figure of Ideal Law in Ford's fiction. At the obvious price of installing him within a castration, whose comical aspects Ford uses sufficiently to indicate how indifferent he is to producing an edifying figure, and how much more attentive he is to the disturbing results of its presence in the fiction: for example, in the dance scene in which his character perturbs the harmony, where the agent of Law behaves like a kill-joy, thus making visible what the harmony of the Fordian celebration would conceal.

(2). The fact that the character literally takes the place of the Mother, i.e., takes on simultaneously her ideal position and her function (since he assumes responsibility for her children, and promises to feed them well in the new home which the prison becomes), gives rise to a curious transformation of the figure, as this repetition of roles is effected under the sign of a secret which the Mother must (believes she does) keep to try to prevent any violence—even, inconceivably, that of the Ideal Law which she incarnates—against her children; and by thus incubating the crime she projects her role into a quasi erotic (almost Hitchcockian) dimension never presented as such by Ford, since usually the fiction protects her from any relationship with the crime (since it is part of her function to be ignorant of violence). This is comically reintroduced in the final scene of the trial, when the real proof (an almanac on a sheet of which should have been written the letter of love which Lincoln was planning to write for her, only to lull her attention and extract confessions from her) is pulled out of Lincoln's hat; it was necessary for the re-establishment of Law that by the end of the trial a signifier (the proof of the crime) be produced whose very occultation renders it erotic; and that it must necessarily be produced by the figure of Law to fit into the fictional logic since it is from this ideal Law that originated the cancellation of the criminal act in the fiction, the statement of the taboo on violence (on pleasure), the position of the Mother as the figure of forbidden violence (pleasure), the possession of the phallus by this figure (as a signifier of this pleasure) and the production of the proof of the crime as if it were a phallic signifier obviously proceeding from the same statement. In such fictions this usually means, either that the weapon, the trace of the crime, acts like a letter which Law must decipher, since its very proscription has written it, or that the confession be produced by the criminal as a return of the repressed in an erotic form. The two results are here compressed, Law producing the proof of the crime (the writing which reveals the murderer) as if it were a phallic object which Ford's comedy presents like the rabbit pulled out of the conjuror's hat; the improbable levity with which Ford brings the trial to its close really can only be read as a masking effect which conceals to the end the "human" context, thus allowing the logic of the inscription to produce this gag as its ultimate effect, a final consequence of Lincoln's re-enactment of the Mother's role, a fantastic return of the mask.

IV. The fact that the overdetermination of this inscription of the Lincoln figure, as agent of the Law, in Ford's fiction by all the idealised representations of Law and its effects produced by the bourgeoisie, far from having been erased by Ford, has been declared by his writing and emphasised by his comedy, shows what a strange ideological balancing act the filmmaker has insisted on performing, and what strange scriptural incongruities he has insisted on exploiting; to the extent that by the fictional constraints he gave himself, by giving up the usual bisection of his fiction and the sometimes truly epic inscription of Law thereby articulated (which recalls Eisenstein in *The General Line*) he could only produce the Law as a pure prohibition of violence, whose result is only a permanent indictment of the castrating effects of its discourse. Indeed to what is the action of his character reduced if not hitting his opponents at their weakest point—weaknesses which Ford always perversely presents as being capable of provoking a deadly laughter? So that the sole but extreme violence of the film consists of verbal repression of violence which, in certain scenes (the unsuccessful lynching) is indicated as really being a death sentence, a mortal interdict which has no equivalent except maybe in Lang, and which shows the distance Ford, or rather his writing, keeps between himself and the idealist propositions which he uses.

V. For, with a kind of absolute indifference to the reception given to his stylistic effects, the filmmaker ends by practising stubbornly a scriptural perversion, which is implied by the fact that, paradoxically, in a film meant to be the Apology of the Word, the last word is always given to the iconic signifier, entrusted by Ford with the production of the determining effects of meaning. And as in this film what is to be signified is always either the (erotic, social, ideological) separation of the hero relative to his surroundings, or the immeasurable distance between him and his actions, or the absence of any common denominator between the results he obtains and the means he uses, and those obtained by his opponents (insofar as he holds the privilege of the castrating speech), Ford succeeds, by the economy of means which he uses to that effect—his style forbidding him the use of effects of implicit valorisation of the character, which he could have drawn from an "interiorised" writing—in simultaneously producing the same signifier in completely different statements: (for example, in the moonlight scene, where the moonlight on the river indicates, at the same time, the attempted seduction, the past idyll, and the hero's "idealist" vocation); or even in renewing the same effect of meaning in totally different contexts (the same spatial disconnections of the character used in the dance

830

scene and the murder scene). So that the intention of always making sense, of closing the door to any implicit effect of meaning, of constantly re-asserting these same meanings, in fact results—since to produce them the filmmaker always actualises the same signifiers, sets up the same stylistic effects— in constantly undermining them, turning them into parodies of themselves. (With Ford parody always proceeds from a denunciation of the writing by its own effects.) The film's ideological project thus finds itself led astray by the worst means it could have been given to realise itself (Ford's style, the inflexible logic of his fiction), mainly to the benefit of a properly scriptural projection (obtained not by the valorisation after the event of previously constituted effects of meaning, but proceeding directly from the inscription, produced anew and resolved in each scene, of the character in Ford's fiction), of the effects of the repression of violence: a violence whose repression, written thus, turns into exorcism and gives to its signifiers, in the murder and the lynching scenes, a fantastic contrast which contributes considerably to the subversion of the deceptively calm surface of the text.

1970

BRIAN HENDERSON
TOWARD A NON-BOURGEOIS
CAMERA STYLE

Godard has developed a new camera style in his later period.[1] Its prime element is a long, slow tracking shot that moves purely laterally—usually in one direction only (left to right or right to left), sometimes doubling back (left to right then right to left, right to left then left to right)—over a scene that does not itself move, or strictly speaking, that does not move in any relation to the camera's movement. Examples of this shot are the automobile trilogy or triptych: the backed-up highway of cars in *Weekend*, the wrecked cars piled up in *One Plus One*, and the auto assembly line in *British Sounds*; most of the studio scenes with the Stones in *One Plus One*; several of the guerilla scenes in *Weekend* ("I salute you, old ocean"); and the shot of the University of Nanterre and environs in *La Chinoise*. Before we consider this shot as part of a stylistic complex and in the various contexts in which it appears, we must consider the shot in itself—its structure and implications as shot.

First we must distinguish Godard's tracking shot from other such shots in the history of cinema. It is not, first of all, forward camera movement, proving the depth of space, as in Murnau. Godard's tracking shot moves neither forward nor backward in space, nor in any diagonal or arc, nor at any angle

---

[1] This article is part of a longer critical study, *"Weekend* and History," which considers that film in its various historical contexts—cinema and dramatic history, history of the bourgeoisie, human history.

but 90° to the scene it is shooting. That is, Godard's track lies exactly along the 0°/180° line. The scenes or subjects which these shots address lie also along a 0°/180° line, which, furthermore, is exactly parallel to the camera line. This extreme stylization, wherein a plane or planes of subject are paralleled exactly by the plane of art, is unusual in cinema and gives the shot very much the form of a planimetric painting. A partial exception to the rule is the camera's sinuosity in the traffic jam shot in *Weekend,* its slight "angling" to left and right as it moves laterally, getting slightly behind or ahead of the scene it is filming, a kind of warp in the shot's even, continuous space-time. The base line of the camera's movement remains exactly straight, however, and exactly parallel to the scene. More fundamental departures from the lateral track are the Action Musicale sequence-shot in *Weekend,* in which the camera remains in the center of the scene and *turns* 360°, and the shot in *One Plus One,* in which the camera *tracks* 360° around the studio in which the Stones are playing. In the first the camera is at the center of a circle, in the second at the periphery, but in both there is the sense of a circular subject rendered flat and linear: these shots look like the lateral tracking shot and fit easily into formats which align them end-to-end with such shots.

The shot, secondly, is not like Ophuls's tracking shots which—though often lateral and hence formally like Godard's—are essentially following shots. Ophuls tracks in order to follow his characters, to give them movement or to attend their movement. His tracks center on, are filled with, derive life and motion from his characters, that is, from individuals. Godard, like Eisenstein, repudiates "the individualist conception of the bourgeois hero" and his tracking shots reflect this. His camera serves no individual and prefers none to another. It never initiates movement to follow a character and if it picks one up as it moves it leaves him behind as haphazardly (the workers and Wiazemsky in the Action Musicale and the shot with Juliet Berto in and out, in *Weekend*). Also—though some may dispute this—Ophuls's tracks are essentially uncritical of their subjects, whereas the essence of Godard's tracking shot is its critical distance from what it surveys. Also, Ophuls frequently uses the composition-in-depth technique of interposing objects in the foreground, between character and camera. Godard never does this.

Thirdly, the shot is not like Fellini's pans and short tracks, though the latter also survey persons fixed in space rather than moving ones, that is, "discover" them in place as the camera moves. There are two chief differences. First, Fellini's camera *affects* his characters, calls them into life or bestows life upon them. Godard's camera does not affect the reality it unfolds and is not affected by it. There is a different camera dialectic in each: Fellini's camera interacts with reality, touches and is touched, causes as well as registers effects; Godard's camera assumes a position over against reality, outside, detached. Secondly, Fellini's tracks are frequently subjective—in the sense that the camera eye is a character's eye. In "8½" the reactions of characters to the camera are their reaction to Guido; the pain we feel when we see them is Guido's pain. Because subjective, Fellini's tracks are most often in medium close or close-up range, sometimes with only faces coming into view; Godard's tracks, which are never subjective, are usually in long shot, taking in as much of an event and its context as possible. Also, Fellini introduces depth by arraying characters and objects in multiple planes, some very close to the camera, others at a distance, making for surprise and variety as the camera moves over them. Godard avoids depth: he arranges his characters in a single plane only—none is ever closer to the camera than another. The resulting flatness of Godard's shots, particularly in *Weekend,* is discussed below.

Godard's tracking shot is a species of long take,[2] very often of sequence shot,[3] but it has few or none of the characteristics in terms of which André Bazin discussed and defended the

---

[2] A single piece of unedited film; of course "long" is relative to "short"—the cut-off would seem to be a shot used for wholly independent effect rather than as part of a montage pattern. None of Eisenstein's early films contains a single long take—such was the theoretical purity of his practice; no Godard film is without several long takes.

[3] A sequence filmed in one take; a one-shot sequence. A sequence is a series of closely related scenes; a scene is a shot or shots that cover a single and continuous dramatic action. We must bear in mind that Godard's "sequences" are not those of conventional narrative cinema, hence the concepts "sequence"

shot and cinematic styles based upon it. In Godard's shot there is continuity of dramatic space and time, the irreducibles of the long take (indeed its very definition); but there is strict avoidance of composition-in-depth, for Bazin the essence of the shot—or that of greatest value in its use. As mentioned, Godard's frames are flat, composed in relation to the plane occupied by his characters. Other planes, where present, are used merely as backdrop to this one. Not only composition-in-depth but the *values* which Bazin found in composition-in-depth are missing in Godard's version of the long take (and in late Godard generally): greater realism, greater participation on the part of the viewer, and a reintroduction of ambiguity into the structure of the film image. It is clear that Godard is no realist; in *La Chinoise* he specifically repudiates the realist aesthetic (of Bazin and others): "Art is not the reflection of a reality; it is the reality of that reflection." Godard's later style does require the active participation of the viewer, but not in Bazin's sense of choosing what to see within a multi-layered image and, presumably, making his own moral connections within it also. Godard presents instead an admittedly synthetic, single-layered construct, which the viewer must examine critically, accept or reject. The viewer is not drawn *into* the image, nor does he make choices within it; he stands outside the image and judges it *as a whole*. It is clear also that Godard of the later films is not interested in ambiguity—through flatness of frame and transparency of action, he seeks to eliminate ambiguity. Thus Godard uses the long take for none of the traditional reasons; in fact he reinvents the long take, and the tracking shot, for his own purposes.

A camera moves slowly, sideways to the scene it is filming. It tracks. But what is the result when its contents are projected on a screen? It is a band or ribbon of reality that slowly unfolds itself. It is a mural or scroll that unrolls before the viewer

---

and "sequence shot" lose the reasonably clear meaning they had for Bazin. What meanings will take their place, we do not yet know. See André Bazin, "The Evolution of the Language of Cinema" (tr. by Hugh Gray), in *What Is Cinema?* (Berkeley, 1967), at 23; also contained in *The New Wave*, ed. by Peter Graham (New York, 1968), at 25. [And reprinted here, pp. 123–39.]

and rolls up after him. To understand the nature of this visual band we must go beyond the tracking shot itself. We encounter here the aesthetic problem of parts and wholes: Godard's tracking shot is but one element in a remarkably rich and complete stylistic complex or repertoire. It appears not in isolation, but in formal combinations with other kinds of shots, and with sounds. In short, the tracking shot cannot be understood apart from the varying contexts in which it appears—it has a different meaning and formal function in *La Chinoise*, in *Weekend*, in *One Plus One*, and in *British Sounds*, and even at different places within the same film. Moreover, the matter of "context" is not as simple as it might appear. Each of the latter films is built upon a complex camera/sound conception or donnée, and no two of these are alike. Our principal concern is the formal construction of *Weekend* and the specific role of the tracking shot in that construction; that is, the relation of formal part and whole. We will not understand either aspect of *Weekend*, however, until we see that film's characteristic shot in the alternative contexts of the other late films and understand the formal principles of those works themselves. The use of the tracking shot in the other films clarifies its use in *Weekend* and the formal principles of the other films put into perspective the formal principle of *Weekend* itself.

La Chinoise contains some interesting instances of the tracking shot even though the film is in no sense built upon this shot, as both *Weekend* and *One Plus One* are. (In the latter films, the whole is chiefly a relation among tracking shots; in *La Chinoise* the whole is a relation among many kinds of shots, relatively few of which are tracking shots.) There are, first of all, the remarkable shots from the balcony, in which the action within the apartment is carefully orchestrated in relation to the camera's passage, in various mathematical variations, along the apartment's three windows and two walls, and back. There is, secondly, a usage of the shot as a special kind of documentation. As Véronique describes her awakening to social contradictions at Nanterre, the camera tracks slowly (from right to left) across the shabby, overcrowded dwellings of the Algerian workers who live near the university, coming to rest at last on the modern, efficient buildings of the university complex. The workers' shacks are flat and horizontal, the university buildings high and vertical, but the shot is set up so that the camera does not have to move back to take in the tall, commanding structures—it takes in everything within a single perspective. Eisenstein would have cut from a shot of the one to a shot of the other, making the juxtaposition for the viewer, obliterating time and space relations to make a clearcut social relation. Godard observes the time and space relations and lets the viewer make the social relation. His shot establishes the true proportions of extreme contrast and close proximity. He does this by virtue of the long take's continuity of dramatic space and time, which this usage reveals as itself a form of argumentation or demonstration; the shot has its own internal relations, its own logic. This instance of the shot seems Bazinian but, far from fidelity to the real, Godard rips this bit of footage from its grounding in the real and puts it down in the midst of a highly abstract film essay. Godard impresses the real into his own service—ignoring the form of the real itself, he subjects it firmly to his own formal construct. Besides the tracking shots, *La Chinoise* also includes several static long takes—the two dialogues between Véronique and Guillaume, the assassination scene—as well as montage (or collage) constructions. (It has become a commonplace that modern film-makers fall between Eisenstein and Bazin, that they combine editing techniques and long takes in various, distinctive styles.) The overall formal principle of *La Chinoise* would seem to be collage, which is also the formal principle of *The Married Woman*, portions of *Le Gai Savoir*, and, in certain senses, of *Pravda*.

The difference between montage and collage is a complex question. Film critics generally use the term collage without elucidating its meaning nor even its difference from montage. There is sometimes the suggestion that the pieces of a collage are shorter or more fragmented than those of a montage, but this does not hold up. Modern film-makers rarely use any shorter than Eisenstein's average shot in *Potemkin*. Moreover, collage as practiced by moderns allows long takes and tracking shots; montage as practiced by Eisenstein did not. It seems clear that the difference between montage and collage is to be found in the divergent ways in which they associate and order images, not in the length or nature of the images themselves. Montage fragments reality in order to reconstitute it in highly organized, synthetic emotional and intellectual patterns. Collage does not do this; it collects or sticks its fragments together in a way that does not entirely overcome their fragmentation. It seeks to recover its fragments *as fragments*. In regard to overall form, it seeks to bring out the internal relations of its pieces, whereas montage imposes a set of relations upon them and indeed collects or creates its pieces to fill out a pre-existent plan. (This point is discussed further in the comparison of the collage principle to the visual organization of *Weekend* and *One Plus One* below.)

In *Weekend* the collage principle all but disappears. Intercut titles—showing the day and the hour, the car speedometer, names of sequences such as "Action Musicale," "Scenes from Provincial Life"—serve as breaks within takes and between scenes, but all within the film's single-image continuum. They do not interact with the pictorial images to form montage patterns, as in *La Chinoise*. Conversely: whereas in *La Chinoise* the tracking shot is incidental, in *Weekend* it is the master shot: the entire film aspires to the condition of this shot. The cuts are merely connective; once outside the Paris apartment, the film might as well be a single, fixed-distance travelling shot along the highway and across the provincial landscape. *Weekend* indeed approximates this ideal form by its remarkable adherence to a single camera range—it is filmed almost entirely in long shot. Thus *Weekend* is the film in which the structure of the tracking shot and the formal principle of the whole very nearly coincide. Not just its characteristic shot but the whole of *Weekend* itself is a continuous visual band that unfolds itself along a linear axis.*

We have found that *Weekend* is the one film among the later

---

*Omitted from this reprinting is a passage that extends the discussion of the tracking shot and of part-whole relations to the films that Godard made after *Weekend*—*One Plus One, British Sounds, Le Gai Savoir, Pravda,* and *Wind From the East.* In these films, more than in *Weekend* and *La Chinoise,* the organization of sound-image relation (at levels of part and whole) is fundamental.
—B.H.

838

works in which the structure of the tracking shot and the formal principle of the whole are nearly identical. Because the shots of *Weekend* deal with a single situation (rather than two or more), they are not juxtaposed (as in *One Plus One*), but merely linked—as though to form one long composite tracking shot. This continuity is emphasized by the near-constant camera range of long shot, which renders the entire film, even static shots, into a single band of reality. In our discussion of the tracking shot as long take we distinguished it from composition-in-depth shots and thereby characterized the tracking shot in terms of a certain kind of flatness. If the overall structure of *Weekend* parallels that of the tracking shot, then the film as a whole must exhibit flatness also. In light of our distinction between parts and wholes, it must also be that flatness of the whole is something different from flatness of the part; and in *Weekend* this is found to be true. Nevertheless—flatness seems an odd category in which to discuss the formal organization of a work, partly because it seems a negative concept, partly because "flatness" has no meaning except in relation to "depth." In fact, however, *Weekend* itself is negative—regarding its subject, the bourgeoisie—in several important respects. And, as we shall see also, the "flatness" of *Weekend* has specific relation to a previous "depth"—composition-in-depth, the principal mode of bourgeois self-presentment in cinema.

If we now propose to discuss the formal organization of *Weekend*, part and whole, in terms of flatness, the effect may well be one of anti-climax and disappointment. If this is so, it is due in large measure to the imprecision that such terms, and especially this term, carry in film analysis. What this means, since the category of flatness comes up inescapably here and elsewhere, is that some theoretical clarification needs to be done. This task cannot be undertaken here but minimal clarification must be done to permit our analysis of *Weekend*. There is no single sense of flatness in cinema but in fact several senses, not only in regard to different films but often in regard to the same film. A single work may be flat in several senses, or now in one sense and now in another; so we must ask not simply which films and scenes are "more flat" than others but in precisely which senses they are flat. An equally great problem area is how critics use the judgment of flatness—the correlations they make between flatness and other matters, particularly those of subject and meaning. Clearly an undifferentiated judgment of flatness cannot be the basis for an adequate interpretation or discussion of subject. A correlation between the "flatness" of *Made in USA* or *Weekend* and Herbert Marcuse's theory of a One Dimensional society is too general—in regard to both elements—to be of much use. Criticism must cut finer than this or it is not helpful. Rather we must ask in each case which of several kinds of flatness has/have been achieved and what is its/their specific relation to the subject of the part and/or whole to which it relates.

Cinema, like painting, is a two-dimensional art which creates the illusion of a third dimension. Painting is limited to its two dimensions; cinema is not. Cinema escapes the limits of two dimensions through its own third dimension, time. It does this by varying its range and perspective, by taking different views of its subject (through montage and/or camera movement). Cinema overcomes two-dimensionality through its "walk-around" capability, which is also a prime feature of ordinary human perception. E. H. Gombrich says: "While (one) turns, in other words, he is aware of a succession of aspects which swing round with him. What we call 'appearance' is always composed of such a succession of aspects, a melody, as it were, which allows us to estimate distance and size; it is obvious that this melody can be imitated by the movie camera but not by the painter with his easel." (*Art and Illusion*, pp. 256–7). Cinema can take several views of a subject, go from one camera angle to a reverse angle or other angle, from long shot to close-up, etc. It can take the measure of a character or object from many sides, in short, in three dimensions. Both montage and composition-in-depth accomplish this walk-around project, both create and explore three dimensions, though in two-dimensional steps or segments, so to speak. It is obvious how montage accomplishes this—through a succession of shots from different angles and at different ranges. It is equally clear that a moving camera can accomplish the same succession of aspects within a single shot. Even in those long takes which do not involve a moving camera, the actors themselves may move with respect to the camera; that is, they walk back-and-forth, or at diagonals, changing in relative size, etc. In short, the actors *turn themselves* around for us, creating different angles and perspectives on themselves. Instead of the camera's walking around, they walk around in relation to the camera. This also is well beyond the two dimensions of painting, whereby we see only one side of a figure, which must stand for and suggest his entirety.

It is precisely cinema's capacity for depth which Godard excludes in *Weekend*. His moving camera, by adhering rigidly to the single-perspective, one-sided view of painting, eliminates the succession of aspects. The tracking shot's lateral motion *extends* this single perspective rather than alters it, very much as a mural does. The movement of Godard's camera creates not a succession of aspects, but a single aspect upon an unfolding subject matter. Both montage and the usual moving camera multiply aspects or perspectives *in regard to a single subject*. To borrow a term from music, the succession of aspects is a kind of *elaboration*. The subject in question is put through multiple variations (or views), toward some *exhaustion* of its nature, meaning, or appearance. Godard's tracking shot does not elaborate in this sense. Its variations through time open up ever new subject matter; they do not elaborate or take multiple views of the same subject, as both montage and composition-in-depth (nearly) always do. Throughout the duration of a tracking shot, a one-to-one relation is maintained: a single perspective per stretch or segment of subject matter, with never a doubling or curving of perspective on a single subject.

It should be emphasized that this flatness of the single aspect is a formal quality of the whole, not of the part. We cannot judge aspect succession or constancy on the basis of the part alone since the succession of aspects is often a succession *of shots*. It is true that each tracking shot in *Weekend* is flat in this sense of singleness of perspective, but what is done in one shot may be undone, or complemented, by another. This is the method of montage, whereby the angle and range of one shot give way to those of another and another, until a totality

841

of aspects is accumulated. Even with lateral long takes, a subsequent tracking shot may provide a different view of the subject of a previous tracking shot. Thus we do not know until a film is over whether a given subject is elaborated multiply or not. We must look at *all* the shots of a sequence or film before we can say whether they present a succession of aspects on a single subject or, as in *Weekend,* a single aspect on a single, unfolding subject. Thus the flatness of the mural effect is an attribute or quality of the whole.

We have argued that *Weekend* is flat in an overall or structural sense in that it eliminates the succession of aspects, by which cinema approximates the third dimension. This is an absolute flatness—a sequence, a film either varies aspects or it does not. Generally speaking, the frames of *Weekend* are also relatively flat in several painterly respects, and this is always a relative flatness, a question of more or less. The clearest case of this kind of flatness is achieved by posing a character or characters against a short wall or background, as Godard does in *Masculin Feminin, Made in USA,* and other films, and as Skolimowski does in all his films. *Weekend* has certain of these shots, but it also has others with considerable depth—the camera follows its subject, the bourgeois couple, across a continuous background/landscape that is sometimes flat (thick foliage behind the pair), sometimes deep (the highway backup).

But there are other kinds of flatness. The shallow wall shot achieves flatness simply by eliminating the long shot range, and perhaps also the medium-shot range. Godard's tracking shot achieves a converse flatness by eliminating the close-up, medium-close, and often medium shot ranges—by arranging his subject(s) and background all within the long shot range. The point may be clarified by a comparison with composition-in-depth, which aims for maximum visual and expressive use of depth, in that both a close-up and a long shot can be included within the same shot. Composition-in-depth achieves its illusion of great depth by arranging its subject through all possible ranges of the deep-focus shot and, of course, by making dramatic relations among these subject ranges. Godard achieves flatness using only a portion of the depth which deep-focus lenses permit—he uses the long-shot range and leaves the shorter ranges "blank," so to speak. Thus, even where there are several planes in a *Weekend* shot—highway, countryside, tree-line, etc.—they are all relatively flattened together, because all lie within the long-shot range. (Moreover, Godard does not achieve this flattening by using telephoto lenses, as Kurosawa did in *Red Beard*.)

Secondly, Godard's planes, even where multiple, are strictly parallel—they do not intersect or interrelate. Consequently the eye is not led back into the depth of the frame nor forward to its surfaces. How we have to "read" a painting or frame is one aspect of its depth; to read the frames of *Weekend*, the eye moves strictly from left to right (sometimes from right to left), never from front to back or back to front. What is true in a compositional sense is also true of the subject of these frames: the film's action. The characters, their movements and activities, never take us into or out of the frame but always from side to side. Neither in a compositional sense nor a narrative sense are we ever required to relate foreground and background in *Weekend*. Strictly speaking, there is no foreground and background, only background, just as in the shallow wall shot there is only foreground. In another sense, foreground and background are here merged into a single plane. Again, composition-in-depth provides a definitive contrast. Like the baroque in painting, composition-in-depth makes a great deal of foreground/background relations, of foreshortening, of huge objects in the foreground, etc. It is not too much to say that foreground/background relation is the axis of composition-in-depth expressivity. As we have seen, it is its moral base also.

Thirdly, the non-intersection of planes in *Weekend* is the result not only of their strict parallelism but also of the fixed, 90° camera angle, which arranges all planes in parallel to the borders of the frame itself. Of these planes, all are inert or non-operative in both a narrative and a compositional sense, except that occupied by the characters. All interest and movement reside in the characters and they occupy (or constitute) always the same plane; they do not move between planes. *Weekend* is single-planed in the sense that the camera and the viewer's eye fix upon only one plane, that occupied by the

843

characters, and follow it out, in one direction only, at infinite length. The frame may contain several planes, but the film as a whole is constructed in relation to only one of these.

Weekend's single-plane construction sets it apart from either school of film aesthetics, montage or composition-in-depth; comparing *Weekend* to them will help us understand the various senses of the film's flatness historically. It is clear that montage editing (and overall film construction) involves or results in a series of planes or planar perspectives. Cutting among close-ups, medium close-ups, medium shots, and long shots, in any order or combination, is obviously an alternation of the planes of a scene, and the result when assembled a sequence of planes.[4] The scene or event is broken into its component parts or planes, then these are reconstructed in various patterns, in accord with a structural montage principle— rhythmic, emotional, or intellectual. Besides changes of camera range, there are also changes of angle, which can alternate planar perspectives rather than particular planes. Cutting to a different angle on the same scene, however, is also a rearrangement or reordering of the planes bearing upon the action. This ordering or sequence of planes is the very texture of Eisenstein's art. Composition-in-depth is not fundamentally different in principle and overall purpose. Composition-in-depth internalizes the sequence of planes within the shot; its ideal, as Bazin presents it, is the inclusion of all planes bearing upon an action within a single camera set-up. With all the planes of a situation before or available to the camera, the en-

---

[4] As it happens, this phrase also appears in Stuart Gilbert's translation of André Malraux's *Museum Without Walls* (Garden City, 1967, page 75): "The means of reproduction in the cinema is the moving photograph, but its means of expression is the sequence of planes. (The planes change when the camera is moved; it is their sequence that constitutes cutting.)." A similar mistranslation of the French *plan* (shot) as plane occurs in Gilbert's translations of Malraux's variants of this passage in *The Psychology of Art: I: Museum Without Walls* (New York, 1949–51, page 112) and in *The Voices of Silence* (New York, 1953, page 122), in which Malraux is made to assert that "the average duration of each [plane] is ten seconds." But Malraux was simply expounding the classical view that cutting, the sequence of shots, is the source of expressivity in cinema.

844

tire action of the scene may be worked out within a single shot. As with montage cinema, dramatic action is advanced by way of the alternation and interaction of planes, but now this is done by camera movement and/or by the movement of actors, themselves planes or parts of planes, through or in relation to the planes of the scene. At the same time the camera must organize these planes in terms of importance, dramatic interest, etc. By composition-in-depth the succession of planes is greatly fluidized, proceeding in a smooth flow rather than in jumps, but the right solution to a given scene becomes more difficult and complex. Implicit in the shot's first image, or accessible to it, must be all the scene's action and the full exploitability of its planes. Shots must be worked out carefully and carefully rehearsed. An example of the way that composition-in-depth orders planes within the frame is given by Bazin— the scene in *The Little Foxes* in which the steel box sought by several characters occupies the extreme foreground of the frame while its seekers are arrayed in multiple planes behind it. A more extreme case is the scene in *Citizen Kane* in which Mrs. Kane learns about her son's inheritance. Shot with a static camera, the shot is very narrow and very deep, virtually a visual corridor. Within the squeezed cabin room we see the mother huge in the foreground, the banker from the East behind her, the window in the wall of the cabin behind them, and in the far distance, young Kane playing with his sled. Not only the composition of the shot but its dramatic action requires the eye to move continually back and forth. It is clear that Godard's treatment of planes in *Weekend* is directly opposed to that of this shot, an extreme in the opposite direction. Godard's visual field has little or no depth and has—or aspires to—infinite length; that is, it exists in a single lateral plane.

Consideration of *Weekend* points up underlying similarities between montage and composition-in-depth and serves to set Godard's film apart from either school of film aesthetics: both montage and composition-in-depth define cinema in terms of a multiplicity of planes and both see the problem of form or technique as the inclusion or relation of planes in a meaningful format. Godard in *Weekend* renounces the multiplicity of

845

planes as a project of cinema and hence rejects both schools.

What are the implications of these shifts from three dimensions to two, from depth to flatness? An ideological interpretation suggests itself—composition-in-depth projects a bourgeois world infinitely deep, rich, complex, ambiguous, mysterious. Godard's flat frames collapse this world into two-dimensional actuality; thus reversion to a cinema of one plane is a demystification, an assault on the bourgeois world-view and self-image.[5] Weekend's bourgeois figures scurry along without mystery toward mundane goals of money and pornographic fulfillment. There is no ambiguity and no moral complexity. That space in which the viewer could lose himself, make distinctions and alliances, comparisons and judgments, has been abrogated—the viewer is presented with a single flat picture of the world that he must examine, criticize, accept or reject. Thus the flatness of Weekend must not be analyzed only in itself but in regard to the previous modes of bourgeois self-presentment, particularly of composition-in-depth. The subject of Weekend is the historical bourgeoisie, the bourgeoisie in history; the film's flatness must not be seen statistically, as a single moment, but dialectically, as a flattening. Given this overall correlation, the specific correlations of the several senses of flatness fall into place. The succession of aspects not only multiplies viewpoints on the bourgeois world so that final judgment and any kind of certainty become impossible, it projects a bourgeois world infinitely inexhaustible and ela-

---

[5] This transition is more than a formal one. The practitioners and advocates of composition-in-depth genuinely believed in this moral depth and ambiguity. Bazin points out that the conception and interpretation of Citizen Kane depend on the composition of the image. It could hardly be otherwise in a great masterpiece. William Wyler's composition-in-depth films, which (as Bazin says) have little or no ambiguity, are not masterpieces. In such a case composition-in-depth becomes merely an imposed format, a style without internal correlates. (Wyler's better films, such as The Letter, are not structured around composition-in-depth). Welles, the greatest composition-in-depth director, is also the director who has made the most of the theme of inexhaustible mystery. Not only Kane but many or most of Welles's other films center on impenetrable mystery and several, also like Kane, proceed through a multiplicity of viewpoints and perspectives which nevertheless fail to yield certainty concerning the underlying questions.

borable. Godard's tracking shot format insists on a single per-spective and on the sufficiency of a single comprehensive sur-vey for understanding of the transparent, easy-to-understand bourgeois world. Whereas in montage and composition-in-depth, complex form works on simple material, working it up as complex also, in Godard simple form works on simple ma-terial. The tracking shot and single-plane construction suggest an infinitely thin, absolutely flat bourgeois substance that can-not be elaborated but only surveyed. Finally, the single camera range represents not only a refusal to participate in bourgeois space, through forward camera movement, intercutting camera ranges, etc., it also has to do with the maintenance of critical perspective. Given that the film's subject is the historical bourgeoisie, Godard keeps his subject before him at all times. He refuses to pick and choose within the bourgeois world or to prefer any part of it to any other—even for a moment—because that involves partial eclipse of the whole. The nature of the bourgeois totality and the project of criticizing it require that it never be lost from view, or broken up into parts and aspects, but always be kept before the viewer as single and whole. Obviously the long-shot range is the range of the total-ity and the tracking shot the instrument of its critical survey. For this reason also Godard does not allow the close-up and medium-close ranges to be filled, for a face or figure huge in the foreground literally obstructs the whole and distracts at-tention from it in an emotional and intellectual sense also. Flatness in *Weekend*, in its various senses, is in fact the result of a formal totality that refuses to relinquish total perspective on the socio-historical totality that is its subject.

1970

WALTER BENJAMIN
THE WORK OF ART
IN THE AGE OF
MECHANICAL
REPRODUCTION

*"Our fine arts were developed, their types and uses were estab-
lished, in times very different from the present, by men whose
power of action upon things was insignificant in comparison with
ours. But the amazing growth of our techniques, the adaptability
and precision they have attained, the ideas and habits they are
creating, make it a certainty that profound changes are impending
in the ancient craft of the Beautiful. In all the arts there is a physical component which can no longer be considered or treated as it
used to be, which cannot remain unaffected by our modern knowledge and power. For the last twenty years neither matter nor space
nor time has been what it was from time immemorial. We must
expect great innovations to transform the entire technique of the
arts, thereby affecting artistic invention itself and perhaps even
bringing about an amazing change in our very notion of art."*
—Paul Valéry, PIÈCES SUR L'ART,
"La Conquète de l'ubiquité," Paris.

PREFACE

When Marx undertook his critique of the capitalistic mode of
production, this mode was in its infancy. Marx directed his efforts
in such a way as to give them prognostic value. He went back to
the basic conditions underlying capitalistic production and through
his presentation showed what could be expected of capitalism in

the future. The result was that one could expect it not only to exploit the proletariat with increasing intensity, but ultimately to create conditions which would make it possible to abolish capitalism itself.

The transformation of the superstructure, which takes place far more slowly than that of the substructure, has taken more than half a century to manifest in all areas of culture the change in the conditions of production. Only today can it be indicated what form this has taken. Certain prognostic requirements should be met by these statements. However, theses about the art of the proletariat after its assumption of power or about the art of a classless society would have less bearing on these demands than theses about the developmental tendencies of art under present conditions of production. Their dialectic is no less noticeable in the superstructure than in the economy. It would therefore be wrong to underestimate the value of such theses as a weapon. They brush aside a number of outmoded concepts, such as creativity and genius, eternal value and mystery — concepts whose uncontrolled (and at present almost uncontrollable) application would lead to a processing of data in the Fascist sense. The concepts which are introduced into the theory of art in what follows differ from the more familiar terms in that they are completely useless for the purposes of Fascism. They are, on the other hand, useful for the formulation of revolutionary demands in the politics of art.

I

In principle a work of art has always been reproducible. Manmade artifacts could always be imitated by men. Replicas were made by pupils in practice of their craft, by masters for diffusing their works, and, finally, by third parties in the pursuit of gain. Mechanical reproduction of a work of art, however, represents something new. Historically, it advanced intermittently and in leaps at long intervals, but with accelerated intensity. The Greeks knew only two procedures of technically reproducing works of art: founding and stamping. Bronzes, terra cottas, and coins were the only art works which they could produce in quantity. All others were unique and could not be mechanically reproduced. With the woodcut graphic art became mechanically reproducible for the first time, long before script became reproducible by print. The enormous changes which printing, the mechanical reproduction of writing, has brought about in literature are a familiar story. However, within the phenomenon which we are here examining from the perspective of world history, print is merely a special, though particularly important, case. During the Middle Ages engraving and etching were added to the woodcut; at the beginning of the nineteenth century lithography made its appearance.

With lithography the technique of reproduction reached an essentially new stage. This much more direct process was distinguished by the tracing of the design on a stone rather than its incision on a block of wood or its etching on a copperplate and permitted graphic art for the first time to put its products on the market, not only in large numbers as hitherto, but also in daily changing forms. Lithography enabled graphic art to illustrate everyday life, and it began to keep pace with printing. But only a few decades after its invention, lithography was surpassed by photography. For the first time in the process of pictorial reproduction, photography freed the hand of the most important artistic functions which henceforth devolved only upon the eye looking into a lens. Since the eye perceives more swiftly than the hand can draw, the process of pictorial reproduction was accelerated so enormously that it could keep pace with speech. A film operator shooting a scene in the studio captures the images at the speed of an actor's speech. Just as lithography virtually implied the illustrated newspaper, so did photography foreshadow the sound film. The technical reproduction of sound was tackled at the end of the last century. These convergent endeavors made predictable a situation which Paul Valéry pointed up in this sentence: "Just as water, gas, and electricity are brought into our houses from far off to satisfy our needs in response to a minimal effort, so we shall be supplied with visual or auditory images, which will appear and disappear at a simple movement of the hand, hardly more than a sign." Around 1900 technical reproduction had reached a standard that not only permitted it to reproduce all transmitted works of art and thus to cause the most profound change in their impact upon the public; it also had captured a place of its own among the artistic processes. For the study of this standard nothing is more revealing than the nature of the repercussions that these two different manifestations —the reproduction of works of art and the art of the film—have had on art in its traditional form.

850

THE WORK OF ART

Even the most perfect reproduction of a work of art is lacking in one element: its presence in time and space, its unique existence at the place where it happens to be. This unique existence of the work of art determined the history to which it was subject throughout the time of its existence. This includes the changes which it may have suffered in physical condition over the years as well as the various changes in its ownership. The traces of the first can be revealed only by chemical or physical analyses which it is impossible to perform on a reproduction; changes of ownership are subject to a tradition which must be traced from the situation of the original.

The presence of the original is the prerequisite to the concept of authenticity. Chemical analyses of the patina of a bronze can help to establish this, as does the proof that a given manuscript of the Middle Ages stems from an archive of the fifteenth century. The whole sphere of authenticity is outside technical—and, of course, not only technical—reproducibility. Confronted with its manual reproduction, which was usually branded as a forgery, the original preserved all its authority; not so *vis à vis* technical reproduction. The reason is twofold. First, process reproduction is more independent of the original than manual reproduction. For example, in photography, process reproduction can bring out those aspects of the original that are unattainable to the naked eye yet accessible to the lens, which is adjustable and chooses its angle at will. And photographic reproduction, with the aid of certain processes, such as enlargement or slow motion, can capture images which escape natural vision. Secondly, technical reproduction can put the copy of the original into situations which would be out of reach for the original itself. Above all, it enables the original to meet the beholder halfway, be it in the form of a photograph or a phonograph record. The cathedral leaves its locale to be received in the studio of a lover of art; the choral production, performed in an auditorium or in the open air, resounds in the drawing room.

The situations into which the product of mechanical reproduction can be brought may not touch the actual work of art, yet the quality of its presence is always depreciated. This holds not only for the art work but also, for instance, for a landscape which passes in review before the spectator in a movie. In the case of the art object, a most sensitive nucleus—namely, its authenticity—is interfered with whereas no natural object is vulnerable on that score. The authenticity of a thing is the essence of all that is transmissible from its beginning, ranging from its substantive duration to its testimony to the history which it has experienced. Since the historical testimony rests on the authenticity, the former, too, is jeopardized by reproduction when substantive duration ceases to matter. And what is really jeopardized when the historical testimony is affected is the authority of the object.

One might subsume the eliminated element in the term "aura" and go on to say: that which withers in the age of mechanical reproduction is the aura of the work of art. This is a symptomatic process whose significance points beyond the realm of art. One might generalize by saying: the technique of reproduction detaches the reproduced object from the domain of tradition. By making many reproductions it substitutes a plurality of copies for a unique existence. And in permitting the reproduction to meet the beholder or listener in his own particular situation, it reactivates the object reproduced. These two processes lead to a tremendous shattering of tradition which is the obverse of the contemporary crisis and renewal of mankind. Both processes are intimately connected with the contemporary mass movements. Their most powerful agent is the film. Its social significance, particularly in its most positive form, is inconceivable without its destructive, cathartic aspect, that is, the liquidation of the traditional value of the cultural heritage. This phenomenon is most palpable in the great historical films. It extends to ever new positions. In 1927 Abel Gance exclaimed enthusiastically: "Shakespeare, Rembrandt, Beethoven will make films . . . all legends, all mythologies and all myths, all founders of religion, and the very religions . . . await their exposed resurrection, and the heroes crowd each other at the gate." Presumably without intending it, he issued an invitation to a far-reaching liquidation.

III

During long periods of history, the mode of human sense perception changes with humanity's entire mode of existence. The manner in which human sense perception is organized, the medium in which it is accomplished, is determined not only by nature but by historical circumstances as well. The fifth century, with its great shifts of population, saw the birth of the late Roman art industry and the Vienna Genesis, and there developed not only an art different from that of antiquity but also a new kind of perception. The scholars of the Viennese school, Riegl and Wickhoff, who resisted the weight of classical tradition under which these later art forms had been buried, were the first to draw conclusions from them concerning the organization of perception at the time. However far-reaching their insight, these scholars limited themselves to showing the significant, formal hallmark which characterized perception in late Roman times. They did not attempt—and, perhaps, saw no way—to show the social transformations expressed by these changes of perception. The conditions for an analogous insight are more favorable in the present. And if changes in the medium of contemporary perception can be comprehended as decay of the aura, it is possible to show its social causes.

The concept of aura which was proposed above with reference to historical objects may usefully be illustrated with reference to the aura of natural ones. We define the aura of the latter as the unique phenomenon of a distance, however close it may be. If, while resting on a summer afternoon, you follow with your eyes a mountain range on the horizon or a branch which casts its shadow over you, you experience the aura of those mountains, of that branch. This image makes it easy to comprehend the social bases of the contemporary decay of the aura. It rests on two circumstances, both of which are related to the increasing significance of the masses in contemporary life. Namely, the desire of contemporary masses to bring things "closer" spatially and humanly, which is just as ardent as their bent toward overcoming the uniqueness of every reality by accepting its reproduction. Every day the urge grows stronger to get hold of an object at very close range by way of its likeness, its reproduction. Unmistakably, reproduction as offered by picture magazines and newsreels differs from the image seen by the unarmed eye. Uniqueness and permanence are as closely linked in the latter as are transitoriness and reproducibility in the former. To pry an object from its shell, to destroy its aura, is the mark of a perception whose "sense of the universal equality of things" has increased to such a degree that it extracts it even from a unique object by means of reproduction. Thus is manifested in the field of perception what in the theoretical sphere is noticeable in the increasing importance of statistics. The adjustment of reality to the masses and of the masses to reality is a process of unlimited scope, as much for thinking as for perception.

IV

The uniqueness of a work of art is inseparable from its being imbedded in the fabric of tradition. This tradition itself is thoroughly alive and extremely changeable. An ancient statue of Venus, for example, stood in a different traditional context with the Greeks, who made it an object of veneration, than with the clerics of the Middle Ages, who viewed it as an ominous idol. Both of them, however, were equally confronted with its uniqueness, that is, its aura. Originally the contextual integration of art in tradition found its expression in the cult. We know that the earliest art works originated in the service of a ritual—first the magical, then the religious kind. It is significant that the existence of the work of art with reference to its aura is never entirely separated from its ritual function. In other words, the unique value of the "authentic" work of art has its basis in ritual, the location of its original use value. This ritualistic basis, however remote, is still recognizable as secularized ritual even in the most profane forms of the cult of beauty. The secular cult of beauty, developed during the Renaissance and prevailing for three centuries, clearly showed that ritualistic basis in its decline and the first deep crisis which befell it. With the advent of the first truly revolutionary means of reproduction, photography, simultaneously with the rise of socialism, art sensed the approaching crisis which has become evident a century later. At the time, art reacted with the doctrine of *l'art pour l'art*, that is, with a theology of art. This gave rise to what might be called a negative theology in the form of the idea of "pure" art, which not only denied any social function of art but also any categorizing by subject matter. (In poetry, Mallarmé was the first to take this position.)

An analysis of art in the age of mechanical reproduction must do justice to these relationships, for they lead us to an all-important insight: for the first time in world history, mechanical reproduction emancipates the work of art from its parasitical dependence on ritual. To an ever greater degree the work of art reproduced becomes the work of art designed for reproducibility. From a photo-

854

graphic negative, for example, one can make any number of prints; to ask for the "authentic" print makes no sense. But the instant the criterion of authenticity ceases to be applicable to artistic production, the total function of art is reversed. Instead of being based on ritual, it begins to be based on another practice—politics.

V

Works of art are received and valued on different planes. Two polar types stand out: with one, the accent is on the cult value; with the other, on the exhibition value of the work. Artistic production begins with ceremonial objects destined to serve in a cult. One may assume that what mattered was their existence, not their being on view. The elk portrayed by the man of the Stone Age on the walls of his cave was an instrument of magic. He did expose it to his fellow men, but in the main it was meant for the spirits. Today the cult value would seem to demand that the work of art remain hidden. Certain statues of gods are accessible only to the priest in the cella; certain Madonnas remain covered nearly all year round; certain sculptures on medieval cathedrals are invisible to the spectator on ground level. With the emancipation of the various art practices from ritual go increasing opportunities for the exhibition of their products. It is easier to exhibit a portrait bust that can be sent here and there than to exhibit the statue of a divinity that has its fixed place in the interior of a temple. The same holds for the painting as against the mosaic or fresco that preceded it. And even though the public presentability of a mass originally may have been just as great as that of a symphony, the latter originated at the moment when its public presentability promised to surpass that of the mass.

With the different methods of technical reproduction of a work of art, its fitness for exhibition increased to such an extent that the quantitative shift between its two poles turned into a qualitative transformation of its nature. This is comparable to the situation of the work of art in prehistoric times when, by the absolute emphasis on its cult value, it was, first and foremost, an instrument of magic. Only later did it come to be recognized as a work of art. In the same way today, by the absolute emphasis on its exhibition value the work of art becomes a creation with entirely new functions, among which the one we are conscious of, the artistic function, later may be recognized as incidental. This much is certain: today photography and the film are the most serviceable exemplifications of this new function.

VI

In photography, exhibition value begins to displace cult value all along the line. But cult value does not give way without resistance. It retires into an ultimate retrenchment: the human countenance. It is no accident that the portrait was the focal point of early photography. The cult of remembrance of loved ones, absent or dead, offers a last refuge for the cult value of the picture. For the last time the aura emanates from the early photographs in the fleeting expression of a human face. This is what constitutes their melancholy, incomparable beauty. But as man withdraws from the photographic image, the exhibition value for the first time shows its superiority to the ritual value. To have pinpointed this new stage constitutes the incomparable significance of Atget, who, around 1900, took photographs of deserted Paris streets. It has quite justly been said of him that he photographed them like scenes of crime. The scene of a crime, too, is deserted; it is photographed for the purpose of establishing evidence. With Atget, photographs become standard evidence for historical occurrences, and acquire a hidden political significance. They demand a specific kind of approach; free-floating contemplation is not appropriate to them. They stir the viewer; he feels challenged by them in a new way. At the same time picture magazines begin to put up signposts for him, right ones or wrong ones, no matter. For the first time, captions have become obligatory. And it is clear that they have an altogether different character than the title of a painting. The directives which the captions give to those looking at pictures in illustrated magazines soon become even more explicit and more imperative in the film where the meaning of each single picture appears to be prescribed by the sequence of all preceding ones.

VII

The nineteenth-century dispute as to the artistic value of painting versus photography today seems devious and confused. This does not diminish its importance, however; if anything, it underlines it. The dispute was in fact the symptom of a historical transformation the universal impact of which was not realized by either

856

of the rivals. When the age of mechanical reproduction separated
art from its basis in cult, the semblance of its autonomy disappeared forever. The resulting change in the function of art transcended the perspective of the century; for a long time it even
escaped that of the twentieth century, which experienced the development of the film.

Earlier much futile thought had been devoted to the question of
whether photography is an art. The primary question—whether
the very invention of photography had not transformed the entire
nature of art—was not raised. Soon the film theoreticians asked the
same ill-considered question with regard to the film. But the difficulties which photography caused traditional aesthetics were
mere child's play as compared to those raised by the film. Whence
the insensitive and forced character of early theories of the film.
Abel Gance, for instance, compares the film with hieroglyphs:
"Here, by a remarkable regression, we have come back to the level
of expression of the Egyptians. . . . Pictorial language has not yet
matured because our eyes have not yet adjusted to it. There is as
yet insufficient respect for, insufficient cult of, what it expresses."
Or, in the words of Séverin-Mars: "What art has been granted a
dream more poetical and more real at the same time! Approached in
this fashion the film might represent an incomparable means of
expression. Only the most high-minded persons, in the most perfect and mysterious moments of their lives, should be allowed to
enter its ambience." Alexandre Arnoux concludes his fantasy about
the silent film with the question: "Do not all the bold descriptions
we have given amount to the definition of prayer?" It is instructive
to note how their desire to class the film among the "arts" forces
these theoreticians to read ritual elements into it—with a striking
lack of discretion. Yet when these speculations were published,
films like *L'Opinion publique* and *The Gold Rush* had already appeared. This, however, did not keep Abel Gance from adducing
hieroglyphs for purposes of comparison, nor Séverin-Mars from
speaking of the film as one might speak of paintings by Fra Ange-
lico. Characteristically, even today ultrareactionary authors give
the film a similar contextual significance—if not an outright sacred
one, then at least a supernatural one. Commenting on Max Reinhardt's film version of *A Midsummer Night's Dream*, Werfel states
that undoubtedly it was the sterile copying of the exterior world
with its streets, interiors, railroad stations, restaurants, motor-

cars, and beaches which until now had obstructed the elevation of the film to the realm of art. "The film has not yet realized its true meaning, its real possibilities . . . these consist in its unique faculty to express by natural means and with incomparable persuasiveness all that is fairylike, marvelous, supernatural."

VIII

The artistic performance of a stage actor is definitely presented to the public by the actor in person; that of the screen actor, however, is presented by a camera, with a twofold consequence. The camera that presents the performance of the film actor to the public need not respect the performance as an integral whole. Guided by the cameraman, the camera continually changes its position with respect to the performance. The sequence of positional views which the editor composes from the material supplied him constitutes the completed film. It comprises certain factors of movement which are in reality those of the camera, not to mention special camera angles, close-ups, etc. Hence, the performance of the actor is subjected to a series of optical tests. This is the first consequence of the fact that the actor's performance is presented by means of a camera. Also, the film actor lacks the opportunity of the stage actor to adjust to the audience during his performance, since he does not present his performance to the audience in person. This permits the audience to take the position of a critic, without experiencing any personal contact with the actor. The audience's identification with the actor is really an identification with the camera. Consequently the audience takes the position of the camera; its approach is that of testing. This is not the approach to which cult values may be exposed.

IX

For the film, what matters primarily is that the actor represents himself to the public before the camera, rather than representing someone else. One of the first to sense the actor's metamorphosis by this form of testing was Pirandello. Though his remarks on the subject in his novel *Si Gira* were limited to the negative aspects of the question and to the silent film only, this hardly impairs their validity. For in this respect, the sound film did not change anything essential. What matters is that the part is acted not for an audience but for a mechanical contrivance—in the case of the sound film, for two of them. "The film actor," wrote Pirandello, "feels as if in exile—exiled not only from the stage but also from himself. With a vague sense of discomfort he feels inexplicable emptiness: his body loses its corporeality, it evaporates, it is deprived of reality, life, voice, and the noises caused by his moving about, in order to be changed into a mute image, flickering an instant on the screen, then vanishing into silence. . . . The projector will play with his shadow before the public, and he himself must be content to play before the camera." This situation might also be characterized as follows: for the first time—and this is the effect of the film—man has to operate with his whole living person, yet forgoing its aura. For aura is tied to his presence; there can be no replica of it. The aura which, on the stage, emanates from Macbeth, cannot be separated for the spectators from that of the actor. However, the singularity of the shot in the studio is that the camera is substituted for the public. Consequently, the aura that envelops the actor vanishes, and with it the aura of the figure he portrays.

It is not surprising that it should be a dramatist such as Pirandello who, in characterizing the film, inadvertently touches on the very crisis in which we see the theater. Any thorough study proves that there is indeed no greater contrast than that of the stage play to a work of art that is completely subject to or, like the film, founded in, mechanical reproduction. Experts have long recognized that in the film "the greatest effects are almost always obtained by 'acting' as little as possible. . . ." In 1932 Rudolf Arnheim saw "the latest trend . . . in treating the actor as a stage prop chosen for its characteristics and . . . inserted at the proper place." With this idea something else is closely connected. The stage actor identifies himself with the character of his role. The film actor very often is denied this opportunity. His creation is by no means all of a piece; it is composed of many separate performances. Besides certain fortuitous considerations, such as cost of studio, availability of fellow players, décor, etc., there are elementary necessities of equipment that split the actor's work into a series of mountable episodes. In particular, lighting and its installation require the presentation of an event that, on the screen, unfolds as a rapid and unified scene, in a sequence of separate shootings which may take hours at the studio; not to mention more obvious montage. Thus a jump from the window can be shot in the studio as a jump from a scaffold, and the ensuing flight, if need be, can be shot weeks later when outdoor scenes are taken. Far more paradoxical cases can easily be construed. Let us assume that an actor is supposed to be startled by a knock at the door. If his reaction is not satisfactory, the director can resort to an expedient: when the actor happens to be at the studio again he has a shot fired behind him without his being forewarned of it. The frightened reaction can be shot now and be cut into the screen version. Nothing more strikingly shows that art has left the realm of the "beautiful semblance" which, so far, had been taken to be the only sphere where art could thrive.

x

The feeling of strangeness that overcomes the actor before the camera, as Pirandello describes it, is basically of the same kind as the estrangement felt before one's own image in the mirror. But now the reflected image has become separable, transportable. And where is it transported? Before the public. Never for a moment does the screen actor cease to be conscious of this fact. While facing the camera he knows that ultimately he will face the public, the consumers who constitute the market. This market, where he offers not only his labor but also his whole self, his heart and soul, is beyond his reach. During the shooting he has as little contact with it as any article made in a factory. This may contribute to that oppression, that new anxiety which, according to Pirandello, grips the actor before the camera. The film responds to the shriveling of the aura with an artificial build-up of the "personality" outside the studio. The cult of the movie star, fostered by the money of the film industry, preserves not the unique aura of the person but the "spell of the personality," the phony spell of a commodity. So long as the movie-makers' capital sets the fashion, as a rule no other revolutionary merit can be accredited to today's film than the promotion of a revolutionary criticism of traditional concepts of art. We do not deny that in some cases today's films can also promote revolutionary criticism of social conditions, even of the distribution of property. However, our present study is no more specifically concerned with this than is the film production of Western Europe.

It is inherent in the technique of the film as well as that of sports that everybody who witnesses its accomplishments is somewhat of an expert. This is obvious to anyone listening to a group of newspaper boys leaning on their bicycles and discussing the outcome of a bicycle race. It is not for nothing that newspaper publishers arrange races for their delivery boys. These arouse great interest among the participants, for the victor has an opportunity to rise from delivery boy to professional racer. Similarly, the newsreel offers everyone the opportunity to rise from passer-by to movie extra. In this way any man might even find himself part of a work of art, as witness Vertoff's *Three Songs About Lenin* or Ivens' *Borinage*. Any man today can lay claim to being filmed. This claim can best be elucidated by a comparative look at the historical situation of contemporary literature.

For centuries a small number of writers were confronted by many thousands of readers. This changed toward the end of the last century. With the increasing extension of the press, which kept placing new political, religious, scientific, professional, and local organs before the readers, an increasing number of readers became writers—at first, occasional ones. It began with the daily press opening to its readers space for "letters to the editor." And today there is hardly a gainfully employed European who could not, in principle, find an opportunity to publish somewhere or other comments on his work, grievances, documentary reports, or that sort of thing. Thus, the distinction between author and public is about to lose its basic character. The difference becomes merely functional; it may vary from case to case. At any moment the reader is ready to turn into a writer. As expert, which he had to become willy-nilly in an extremely specialized work process, even if only in some minor respect, the reader gains access to authorship. In the Soviet Union work itself is given a voice. To present it verbally is part of a man's ability to perform the work. Literary license is now founded on polytechnic rather than specialized training and thus becomes common property.

All this can easily be applied to the film, where transitions that in literature took centuries have come about in a decade. In cinematic practice, particularly in Russia, this change-over has partially become established reality. Some of the players whom we meet in Russian films are not actors in our sense but people who portray *themselves*—and primarily in their own work process. In Western Europe the capitalistic exploitation of the film denies consideration to modern man's legitimate claim to being reproduced. Under these circumstances the film industry is trying hard to spur the interest of the masses through illusion-promoting spectacles and dubious speculations.

XI

The shooting of a film, especially of a sound film, affords a spectacle unimaginable anywhere at any time before this. It presents a process in which it is impossible to assign to a spectator a viewpoint which would exclude from the actual scene such extraneous accessories as camera equipment, lighting machinery, staff assistants, etc. — unless his eye were on a line parallel with the lens. This circumstance, more than any other, renders superficial and insignificant any possible similarity between a scene in the studio and one on the stage. In the theater one is well aware of the place from which the play cannot immediately be detected as illusionary. There is no such place for the movie scene that is being shot. Its illusionary nature is that of the second degree, the result of cutting. That is to say, in the studio the mechanical equipment has penetrated so deeply into reality that its pure aspect freed from the foreign substance of equipment is the result of a special procedure, namely, the shooting by the specially adjusted camera and the mounting of the shot together with other similar ones. The equipment-free aspect of reality here has become the height of artifice; the sight of immediate reality has become an orchid in the land of technology.

Even more revealing is the comparison of these circumstances, which differ so much from those of the theater, with the situation in painting. Here the question is: How does the cameraman compare with the painter? To answer this we take recourse to an analogy with a surgical operation. The surgeon represents the polar opposite of the magician. The magician heals a sick person by the laying on of hands; the surgeon cuts into the patient's body. The magician maintains the natural distance between the patient and himself; though he reduces it very slightly by the laying on of hands, he greatly increases it by virtue of his authority. The surgeon does exactly the reverse; he greatly diminishes the distance between himself and the patient by penetrating into the patient's body, and increases it but little by the caution with which his hand moves among the organs. In short, in contrast to the magician — who is still hidden in the medical practitioner — the surgeon at the decisive moment abstains from facing the patient man to man; rather, it is through the operation that he penetrates into him.

Magician and surgeon compare to painter and cameraman. The painter maintains in his work a natural distance from reality, the cameraman penetrates deeply into its web. There is a tremendous difference between the pictures they obtain. That of the painter is a total one, that of the cameraman consists of multiple fragments which are assembled under a new law. Thus, for contemporary man the representation of reality by the film is incomparably more significant than that of the painter, since it offers, precisely because of the thoroughgoing permeation of reality with mechanical equipment, an aspect of reality which is free of all equipment. And that is what one is entitled to ask from a work of art.

XII

Mechanical reproduction of art changes the reaction of the masses toward art. The reactionary attitude toward a Picasso painting changes into the progressive reaction toward a Chaplin movie. The progressive reaction is characterized by the direct, intimate fusion of visual and emotional enjoyment with the orientation of the expert. Such fusion is of great social significance. The greater the decrease in the social significance of an art form, the sharper the distinction between criticism and enjoyment by the public. The conventional is uncritically enjoyed, and the truly new is criticized with aversion. With regard to the screen, the critical and the receptive attitudes of the public coincide. The decisive reason for this is that individual reactions are predetermined by the mass audience response they are about to produce, and this is nowhere more pronounced than in the film. The moment these responses become manifest they control each other. Again, the comparison with painting is fruitful. A painting has always had an excellent chance to be viewed by one person or by a few. The simultaneous contemplation of paintings by a large public, such as developed in the nineteenth century, is an early symptom of the crisis of painting, a crisis which was by no means occasioned exclusively by photography but rather in a relatively independent manner by the appeal of art works to the masses.

Painting simply is in no position to present an object for simultaneous collective experience, as it was possible for architecture at all times, for the epic poem in the past, and for the movie today. Although this circumstance in itself should not lead one to conclusions about the social role of painting, it does constitute a serious threat as soon as painting, under special conditions and, as it were, against its nature, is confronted directly by the masses. In the churches and monasteries of the Middle Ages and at the princely courts up to the end of the eighteenth century, a collective reception of paintings did not occur simultaneously, but by graduated and hierarchized mediation. The change that has come about is an expression of the particular conflict in which painting was implicated by the mechanical reproducibility of paintings. Although paintings began to be publicly exhibited in galleries and salons, there was no way for the masses to organize and control themselves in their reception. Thus the same public which responds in a progressive manner toward a grotesque film is bound to respond in a reactionary manner to surrealism.

XIII

The characteristics of the film lie not only in the manner in which man presents himself to mechanical equipment but also in the manner in which, by means of this apparatus, man can represent his environment. A glance at occupational psychology illustrates the testing capacity of the equipment. Psychoanalysis illustrates it in a different perspective. The film has enriched our field of perception with methods which can be illustrated by those of Freudian theory. Fifty years ago, a slip of the tongue passed more or less unnoticed. Only exceptionally may such a slip have revealed dimensions of depth in a conversation which had seemed to be taking its course on the surface. Since the *Psychopathology of Everyday Life* things have changed. This book isolated and made analyzable things which had heretofore floated along unnoticed in the broad stream of perception. For the entire spectrum of optical, and now also acoustical, perception the film has brought about a similar deepening of apperception. It is only an obverse of this fact that behavior items shown in a movie can be analyzed much more precisely and from more points of view than those presented on paintings or on the stage. As compared with painting, filmed behavior lends itself more readily to analysis because of its incomparably more precise statements of the situation. In comparison with the stage scene, the filmed behavior item lends itself more readily to analysis because it can be isolated more easily. This circumstance derives its chief importance from its tendency to promote the mutual penetration of art and science. Actually, of a screened behavior item which is neatly brought out in a certain situation, like a muscle of a body, it is difficult to say which is more fascinating, its artistic value or

864

its value for science. To demonstrate the identity of the artistic and scientific uses of photography which heretofore usually were separated will be one of the revolutionary functions of the film.

By close-ups of the things around us, by focusing on hidden details of familiar objects, by exploring common place milieus under the ingenious guidance of the camera, the film, on the one hand, extends our comprehension of the necessities which rule our lives; on the other hand, it manages to assure us of an immense and unexpected field of action. Our taverns and our metropolitan streets, our offices and furnished rooms, our railroad stations and our factories appeared to have us locked up hopelessly. Then came the film and burst this prison-world asunder by the dynamite of the tenth of a second, so that now, in the midst of its far-flung ruins and debris, we calmly and adventurously go traveling. With the close-up, space expands; with slow motion, movement is extended. The enlargement of a snapshot does not simply render more precise what in any case was visible, though unclear: it reveals entirely new structural formations of the subject. So, too, slow motion not only presents familiar qualities of movement but reveals in them entirely unknown ones "which, far from looking like retarded rapid movements, give the effect of singularly gliding, floating, supernatural motions." Evidently a different nature opens itself to the camera than opens to the naked eye—if only because an unconsciously penetrated space is substituted for a space consciously explored by man. Even if one has a general knowledge of the way people walk, one knows nothing of a person's posture during the fractional second of a stride. The act of reaching for a lighter or a spoon is familiar routine, yet we hardly know what really goes on between hand and metal, not to mention how this fluctuates with our moods. Here the camera intervenes with the resources of its lowerings and liftings, its interruptions and isolations, its extensions and accelerations, its enlargements and reductions. The camera introduces us to unconscious optics as does psychoanalysis to unconscious impulses.

XIV

One of the foremost tasks of art has always been the creation of a demand which could be fully satisfied only later. The history of every art form shows critical epochs in which a certain art form aspires to effects which could be fully obtained only with a changed

technical standard, that is to say, in a new art form. The extrava-
gances and crudities of art which thus appear, particularly in the
so-called decadent epochs, actually arise from the nucleus of its
richest historical energies. In recent years, such barbarisms were
abundant in Dadaism. It is only now that its impulse becomes discernible: Dadaism attempted to create by pictorial—and literary—
means the effects which the public today seeks in the film.

Every fundamentally new, pioneering creation of demands will
carry beyond its goal. Dadaism did so to the extent that it sacrificed
the market values which are so characteristic of the film in favor
of higher ambitions—though of course it was not conscious of such
intentions as here described. The Dadaists attached much less importance to the sales value of their work than to its uselessness for
contemplative immersion. The studied degradation of their material
was not the least of their means to achieve this uselessness. Their
poems are "word salad" containing obscenities and every imaginable waste product of language. The same is true of their paintings,
on which they mounted buttons and tickets. What they intended
and achieved was a relentless destruction of the aura of their creations, which they branded as reproductions with the very means
of production. Before a painting of Arp's or a poem by August
Stramm it is impossible to take time for contemplation and evaluation as one would before a canvas of Derain's or a poem by Rilke.
In the decline of middle-class society, contemplation became a
school for asocial behavior; it was countered by distraction as a
variant of social conduct. Dadaistic activities actually assured a
rather vehement distraction by making works of art the center of
scandal. One requirement was foremost: to outrage the public.

From an alluring appearance or persuasive structure of sound the
work of art of the Dadaists became an instrument of ballistics. It
hit the spectator like a bullet, it happened to him, thus acquiring
a tactile quality. It promoted a demand for the film, the distracting
element of which is also primarily tactile, being based on changes
of place and focus which periodically assail the spectator. Let us
compare the screen on which a film unfolds with the canvas of a
painting. The painting invites the spectator to contemplation; before it the spectator can abandon himself to his associations. Before
the movie frame he cannot do so. No sooner has his eye grasped a
scene than it is already changed. It cannot be arrested. Duhamel,
who detests the film and knows nothing of its significance, though

something of its structure, notes this circumstance as follows: "I can no longer think what I want to think. My thoughts have been replaced by moving images." The spectator's process of association in view of these images is indeed interrupted by their constant, sudden change. This constitutes the shock effect of the film, which, like all shocks, should be cushioned by heightened presence of mind. By means of its technical structure, the film has taken the physical shock effect out of the wrappers in which Dadaism had, as it were, kept it inside the moral shock effect.

XV

The mass is a matrix from which all traditional behavior toward works of art issues today in a new form. Quantity has been transmuted into quality. The greatly increased mass of participants has produced a change in the mode of participation. The fact that the new mode of participation first appeared in a disreputable form must not confuse the spectator. Yet some people have launched spirited attacks against precisely this superficial aspect. Among these, Duhamel has expressed himself in the most radical manner. What he objects to most is the kind of participation which the movie elicits from the masses. Duhamel calls the movie "a pastime for helots, a diversion for uneducated, wretched, worn-out creatures who are consumed by their worries . . . , a spectacle which requires no concentration and presupposes no intelligence . . . , which kindles no light in the heart and awakens no hope other than the ridiculous one of someday becoming a 'star' in Los Angeles." Clearly, this is at bottom the same ancient lament that the masses seek distraction whereas art demands concentration from the spectator. That is a commonplace. The question remains whether it provides a platform for the analysis of the film. A closer look is needed here. Distraction and concentration form polar opposites which may be stated as follows: A man who concentrates before a work of art is absorbed by it. He enters into this work of art the way legend tells of the Chinese painter when he viewed his finished painting. In contrast, the distracted mass absorbs the work of art. This is most obvious with regard to buildings. Architecture has always represented the prototype of a work of art the reception of which is consummated by a collectivity in a state of distraction. The laws of its reception are most instructive.

Buildings have been man's companions since primeval times.

Many art forms have developed and perished. Tragedy begins with the Greeks, is extinguished with them, and after centuries its "rules" only are revived. The epic poem, which had its origin in the youth of nations, expires in Europe at the end of the Renaissance. Panel painting is a creation of the Middle Ages, and nothing guarantees its uninterrupted existence. But the human need for shelter is lasting. Architecture has never been idle. Its history is more ancient than that of any other art, and its claim to being a living force has significance in every attempt to comprehend the relationship of the masses to art. Buildings are appropriated in a twofold manner: by use and by perception—or rather, by touch and sight. Such appropriation cannot be understood in terms of the attentive concentration of a tourist before a famous building. On the tactile side there is no counterpart to contemplation on the optical side. Tactile appropriation is accomplished not so much by attention as by habit. As regards architecture, habit determines to a large extent even optical reception. The latter, too, occurs much less through rapt attention than by noticing the object in incidental fashion. This mode of appropriation, developed with reference to architecture, in certain circumstances acquires canonical value. For the tasks which face the human apparatus of perception at the turning points of history cannot be solved by optical means, that is, by contemplation, alone. They are mastered gradually by habit, under the guidance of tactile appropriation.

The distracted person, too, can form habits. More, the ability to master certain tasks in a state of distraction proves that their solution has become a matter of habit. Distraction as provided by art presents a covert control of the extent to which new tasks have become soluble by apperception. Since, moreover, individuals are tempted to avoid such tasks, art will tackle the most difficult and most important ones where it is able to mobilize the masses. Today it does so in the film. Reception in a state of distraction, which is increasing noticeably in all fields of art and is symptomatic of profound changes in apperception, finds in the film its true means of exercise. The film with its shock effect meets this mode of reception halfway. The film makes the cult value recede into the background not only by putting the public in the position of the critic, but also by the fact that at the movies this position requires no attention. The public is an examiner, but an absent-minded one.

868

EPILOGUE

The growing proletarianization of modern man and the increasing formation of masses are two aspects of the same process. Fascism attempts to organize the newly created proletarian masses without affecting the property structure which the masses strive to eliminate. Fascism sees its salvation in giving these masses not their right, but instead a chance to express themselves. The masses have a right to change property relations; Fascism seeks to give them an expression while preserving property. The logical result of Fascism is the introduction of aesthetics into political life. The violation of the masses, whom Fascism, with its *Führer* cult, forces to their knees, has its counterpart in the violation of an apparatus which is pressed into the production of ritual values.

All efforts to render politics aesthetic culminate in one thing: war. War and war only can set a goal for mass movements on the largest scale while respecting the traditional property system. This is the political formula for the situation. The technological formula may be stated as follows: Only war makes it possible to mobilize all of today's technical resources while maintaining the property system. It goes without saying that the Fascist apotheosis of war does not employ such arguments. Still, Marinetti says in his manifesto on the Ethiopian colonial war: "For twenty-seven years we Futurists have rebelled against the branding of war as antiaesthetic .... Accordingly we state: ... War is beautiful because it establishes man's dominion over the subjugated machinery by means of gas masks, terrifying megaphones, flame throwers, and small tanks. War is beautiful because it initiates the dreamt-of metalization of the human body. War is beautiful because it enriches a flowering meadow with the fiery orchids of machine guns. War is beautiful because it combines the gunfire, the cannonades, the cease-fire, the scents, and the stench of putrefaction into a symphony. War is beautiful because it creates new architecture, like that of the big tanks, the geometrical formation flights, the smoke spirals from burning villages, and many others. ... Poets and artists of Futurism! ... remember these principles of an aesthetics of war so that your struggle for a new literature and a new graphic art ... may be illumined by them!"

This manifesto has the virtue of clarity. Its formulations deserve to be accepted by dialecticians. To the latter, the aesthetics of today's war appears as follows: If the natural utilization of productive forces is impeded by the property system, the increase in technical devices, in speed, and in the sources of energy will press for an unnatural utilization, and this is found in war. The destructiveness of war furnishes proof that society has not been mature enough to incorporate technology as its organ, that technology has not been sufficiently developed to cope with the elemental forces of society. The horrible features of imperialistic warfare are attributable to the discrepancy between the tremendous means of production and their inadequate utilization in the process of production—in other words, to unemployment and the lack of markets. Imperialistic war is a rebellion of technology which collects, in the form of "human material," the claims to which society has denied its natural material. Instead of draining rivers, society directs a human stream into a bed of trenches; instead of dropping seeds from airplanes, it drops incendiary bombs over cities; and through gas warfare the aura is abolished in a new way.

"*Fiat ars—pereat mundus,*" says Fascism, and, as Marinetti admits, expects war to supply the artistic gratification of a sense perception that has been changed by technology. This is evidently the consummation of "*l'art pour l'art.*" Mankind, which in Homer's time was an object of contemplation for the Olympian gods, now is one for itself. Its self-alienation has reached such a degree that it can experience its own destruction as an aesthetic pleasure of the first order. This is the situation of politics which Fascism is rendering aesthetic. Communism responds by politicizing art.

1935

BIBLIOGRAPHY

Affron, Charles. *Star Acting*. New York: Dutton, 1977.
Agee, James. *Agee on Film: Reviews and Comments*. Boston: Beacon Press, n.d.
Agel, Henri. *Le Cinéma et la sacré*. Paris: Éditions du Cerf, 1961.
———. *Poetique du cinéma*. N.p.: Éditions du Signe, 1973.
Andrew, J. Dudley. *The Major Film Theories*. New York: Oxford University Press, 1976.
———. *André Bazin*. New York: Oxford University Press, 1978.
Arnheim, Rudolf. *Art and Visual Perception*. Berkeley and Los Angeles: University of California Press, 1954.
———. *Film as Art*. Berkeley and Los Angeles: University of California Press, 1966.
Ayfre, Amédée. *Cinéma et mystère*. Paris: Éditions du Cerf, 1969.
———. *Le Cinéma et sa vérité*. Paris: Éditions du Cerf, 1964.
———. *Conversion aux images?* Paris: Éditions du Cerf, 1964.
Balázs, Béla. *Theory of the Film: Character and Growth of a New Art*. New York: Dover Publications, 1970.
Barnouw, Eric. *Documentary: A History of Non-Fiction Film*. New York: Oxford University Press, 1974.
Barr, Charles. "CinemaScope: Before and After." *Film Quarterly* XVI, No. 4, Summer 1963.
Barsam, Richard Meran. *Nonfiction Film: A Critical History*. New York: Dutton, 1972.
———. *Nonfiction Film: Theory and Criticism*. New York: Dutton, 1975.
Barthes, Roland. *Elements of Semiology*. Translated by Annette Laversy and Colin Smith. New York: Hill and Wang, 1967.
———. *Mythologies*. Selected and edited by Annette Laversy. New York: Hill and Wang, 1972.

BIBLIOGRAPHY

Battcock, Gregory, ed. *The New American Cinema*. New York: Dutton, 1967.

Bazin, André. *What is Cinema?* Volume I. Berkeley and Los Angeles: University of California Press, 1971.

———. *What is Cinema?* Volume II. Berkeley and Los Angeles: University of California Press, 1971.

Benjamin, Walter. *Illuminations*. Edited and with an introduction by Hannah Arendt. New York: Harcourt Brace, 1968.

Bergman, Andrew. *We're in the Money*. New York: Harper Collophon, 1972.

Bergson, Henri. Laughter, in *Comedy*. Edited by Wylie Sypher. Garden City, New York: Doubleday Anchor, 1956.

Bluestone, George. *Novels into Film*. Berkeley and Los Angeles: University of California Press, 1966.

Bobker, Lee R. *Elements of Film*. New York: Harcourt Brace, 1969.

Brakhage, Stan. "Metaphors on Vision." *Film Culture*, No. 30, Fall 1963.

Braudy, Leo. *The World in a Frame*. Garden City, N.Y.: Anchor Press, 1976.

Burch, Noël. *Theory of Film Practice*. Translated by Helen R. Lane and with an Introduction by Annette Michelson. New York: Praeger, 1973.

Cavell, Stanley. *The World Viewed: Reflections on the Ontology of Film*. New York: Viking, 1971.

Cawelti, John. *The Six-Gun Mystique*. Bowling Green, Ohio: Bowling Green Popular Press, n.d.

Cocteau, Jean. *Cocteau on the Film*. Translated by Vera Triall. New York: Roy Publishers.

Cohen-Séat, Gilbert. *Essai sur les principes d'une philosophie du cinéma*. Paris: Presses Universitaires de France, 1958.

———. *Problemes du cinéma et de l'information visuelle*. Paris: Presses Universitaires de France, 1961.

Corliss, Richard. *Talking Pictures: Screenwriters in the American Cinema*. New York: The Overlook Press, 1974.

Doesburg, Theo van. "Film as Pure Form." *Form* (Cambridge), No. 1, Summer 1966.

Durgnat, Raymond. *Films and Feelings*. Cambridge, Mass.: The M.I.T. Press, 1967.

Earle, William. "Revolt Against Realism in the Films." *The Journal of Aesthetics and Art Criticism* XXVII, No. 2, Winter 1968.

Eco, Umberto. *A Theory of Semiotics*. Bloomington, Ind.: Indiana University Press, 1976.

Eisenstein, Sergei M. *Film Form*. Edited and translated by Jay Leyda. New York: Harcourt Brace, n.d.

872

————. *The Film Sense.* Edited and translated by Jay Leyda. New York: Harcourt Brace, n.d.

Faure, Élie. *The Art of Cineplastics.* Boston: Four Seas Company, 1923.

Fenin, George N. and William K. Everson. *The Western.* New York: Grossman, 1973.

Ferguson, Otis. *The Film Criticism of Otis Ferguson.* Edited and with a preface by Robert Wilson. Foreword by Andrew Sarris. Philadelphia: Temple University Press, 1971.

Film Comment. "Hollywood Screenwriters" (Special Issue). VI, No. 4, Winter 1970–71.

Film Comment. "The Men with the Movie Cameras" (Special Issue). June 1972.

Fredericksen, Donald L. *The Aesthetic of Isolation in Film Theory: Hugo Munsterberg.* New York: Arno Press, 1977.

Gessner, Robert. *The Moving Image: A Guide to Cinematic Literacy.* New York: Dutton, 1968.

Gouhier, Henri. *L'essence du théâtre.* Paris: Plon, 1948.

————. *Le théâtre et l'existence.* Paris: Auber, 1952.

Grierson, John. *Grierson on Documentary.* Edited by Forsyth Hardy. New York: Harcourt Brace, 1947.

Harrington, John. *The Rhetoric of Film.* New York: Holt, Rinehart, and Winston, 1973.

Haskell, Molly. *From Reverence to Rape: The Treatment of Women in the Movies.* New York: Holt, Rinehart, and Winston, 1974.

Hauser, Arnold. *The Social History of Art.* Four volumes. New York: Knopf, n.d.

Hjelmslev, Louis. *Essais linguistiques.* Copenhague: Nordisk Sprog-og kulturforlag, 1959.

————. *Prolegomena to a Theory of Language.* Bloomington, Ind.: Indiana University Publications in Anthropology and Linguistics, 1953.

Huss, Roy, and Norman Silverstein. *The Film Experience: Elements of Motion Picture Art.* New York: Harper and Row, 1968.

Jacobs, Lewis. *The Rise of the American Film: A Critical History.* New York: Teacher's College Press, 1967.

Jowett, Garth. *Film: The Democratic Art.* Boston: Little, Brown, 1976.

Kael, Pauline. *I Lost It at the Movies.* Boston: Little, Brown, 1965.

Kauffmann, Stanley. "Notes on Theater-and-Film." *Performance* I, No. 4, October, 1972.

———— with B. Henstell. *American Film Criticism.* New York: Liveright, 1972.

Kelman, Ken. The Reality of New Cinema, in *The New American Cinema.* Edited by Battcock. New York: Dutton, 1967.

Kitses, Jim. *Horizons West*. Bloomington, Ind. and London: Indiana University Press, 1970.

Kozarski, Richard. *Hollywood Directors, 1914–1940*. New York: Oxford University Press, 1976.

Kracauer, Siegfried. *From Caligari to Hitler*. New York: Noonday, 1959.

———. *Theory of Film: The Redemption of Physical Reality*. London, Oxford, New York: Oxford University Press, 1960.

Langer, Susanne K. *Feeling and Form*. New York: Scribner's, 1953.

Lawder, Standish D. *The Cubist Cinema*. New York: New York University Press, 1975.

Lawson, John Howard. *Film: The Creative Process*. New York: Hill and Wang, 1964.

Lebovici, Serge. "Psychoanalyse et cinéma." *Revue internationale de filmologie* II, No. 5.

Lessing, Gotthold Ephraim. *Laocoon: An Essay Upon the Limits of Painting and Poetry*. New York: Noonday, n.d.

Lévi-Strauss, Claude. Structural Analysis in Linguistics and in Anthropology, in *Structural Anthropology*. New York: Basic Books, 1963.

Lindgren, Ernest. *The Art of the Film*. Revised edition. London: Allen and Unwin, 1963.

Lindsay, Vachel. *The Art of the Moving Picture*. Revised edition. New York: Macmillan, 1922.

Lotman, Jurij. *Semiotics of the Cinema*. Translated by Mark E. Suino. Ann Arbor: University of Michigan Press, 1976.

Macbean, James Roy. *Film and Revolution*. Bloomington, Ind.: University of Indiana Press, 1975.

MacCann, Richard Dyer. *Film: A Montage of Theories*. New York: Dutton, 1966.

Manvell, Roger. *Film*. London: Penguin Books, 1946.

———. *Shakespeare and the Film*. New York: Praeger, 1971.

Marcel, Gabriel. "Possibilités et limites de l'art cinématographique." *Revue internationale de filmologie* V, Nos. 18–19.

Marinetti, Filippo T. *Selected Writings*. Translated by Arthur A. Coppotelli and R. W. Flint. New York: Noonday, 1972.

Martin, Marcel. *La langage cinématographique*. Paris: Éditions du Cerf, 1955.

Martinet, André. *Elements of General Linguistics*. Translated by Elisabeth Palmer. London: Faber and Faber, 1960.

Mast, Gerald. *The Comic Mind: Comedy and the Movies*. New York: Bobbs-Merrill, 1973.

———. *Film/Cinema/Movie: A Theory of Experience*. New York: Harper and Row, 1977.

Merleau-Ponty, Maurice. The Film and the New Psychology, in *Sense and Non-sense*. Translated by Hubert L. and Patricia A. Dreyfus. Evanston, Ill.: Northwestern University Press, 1964.

Metz, Christian. *Film Language: A Semiotics of the Cinema.* Translated by Michael Taylor. New York: Oxford University Press, 1974.

———. *Language and Cinema.* Translated by Donna Jean Umiker-Seboek. The Hague: Mouton, 1974.

Meyerhold, Vsevolod. *Meyerhold on Theater.* Edited by Edward Braun. New York: Hill and Wang, 1969.

Mitry, Jean. *Esthétique et psychologie du cinéma.* Two Volumes. Paris: Éditions Universitaires, 1963–65.

Moholy-Nagy, László. *Vision in Motion.* Chicago: University of Chicago, 1947.

Montagu, Ivor. *Film World.* Baltimore: Penguin, 1964.

Morin, Edgar. *Le Cinéma ou l'homme imaginaire.* Paris: Éditions de Minuit, 1956.

———. *The Stars.* Translated by Richard Howard. New York: Grove Press, 1960.

Münsterberg, Hugo. *The Film: A Psychological Study.* New York: Dover, 1969.

Nichols, Bill, ed. *Movies and Methods.* Berkeley and Los Angeles: University of California Press, 1976.

Nicoll, Allardyce. *Film and Theatre.* New York: Thomas Y. Crowell, 1937.

Olson, Elder. *The Theory of Comedy.* Bloomington, Ind., and London: Indiana University Press, 1968.

Orwell, George. Boys' Weeklies, in *Collection of Essays.* New York: Doubleday, 1954.

Panofsky, Erwin. "Style and Medium in the Motion Pictures." *Critique* I, No. 3, January–February 1947.

Perkins, V. F. *Film as Film: Understanding and Judging Movies.* Baltimore, Penguin, 1972.

Powdermaker, Hortense. *Hollywood, the Dream Factory.* Boston: Little Brown, 1960.

Pudovkin, Vsevolod I. *Film Technique and Film Acting.* Edited and translated by Ivor Montagu. New York: Grove Press, 1960.

Quarterly Review of Film Studies. "Interdisciplinary Approaches to Film Study" (Special Issue). I, No. 2, Summer 1976.

———. "Film and Semiotics" (Special issue). II, No. 1, Winter 1977.

Reisz, Karel. *The Technique of Film Editing.* New York: Hastings House, 1968.

Renan, Sheldon. *An Introduction to the American Underground Film.* New York: Dutton, 1967.

875

Richter, Hans. "The Film as an Original Art Form." *Film Culture*, I, No. 1, January 1955.

Rotha, Paul, Road Sinclair, and Richard Griffith. *Documentary Film*. London: Faber and Faber, 1966.

Sadoul, Georges. *Histoire générale du cinéma*. Five Volumes. Paris: Éditions Denoël, 1946–54.

Sarris, Andrew. *The American Cinema: Directors and Directions 1929–1968*. New York: Dutton, 1969.

————. Notes on the *Auteur* Theory in 1962, in *Film Culture Reader*. Edited by Sitney. New York: Praeger, 1970.

————. "Notes on the *Auteur* Theory in 1970." *Film Comment* VI, No. 3, Fall 1970.

————. "Film Criticism in the Seventies." *Film Comment* XIV, No. 1, January 1978.

de Saussure, Ferdinand. *Course in General Linguistics*. Translated by Wade Baskin, New York: McGraw-Hill, 1966.

Schnitzer, Luda and Jean, and Marcel Martin, eds. *Cinema in Revolution: The Heroic Age of the Soviet Film*. New York: Hill and Wang, 1973.

Seldes, Gilbert. *The Great Audience*. New York: Viking, 1950.

————. *The Movies Come From America*. New York: Scribner's, 1937.

————. *The Public Arts*. New York: Simon and Schuster, 1956.

Sitney, P. Adams, ed. *Film Culture Reader*. New York: Praeger, 1970.

————. *Visionary Film: The American Avant-Garde*. New York: Oxford University Press, 1974.

Sklar, Robert. *Movie-Made America*. New York: Random House, 1975.

Sontag, Susan. *Against Interpretation*. New York: Farrar, Straus & Giroux, 1966.

————. *Styles of Radical Will*. New York: Farrar, Straus & Giroux, 1969.

————. *On Photography*. New York: Farrar, Straus & Giroux, 1977.

Spottiswode, Raymond. *A Grammar of the Film*. Berkeley and Los Angeles: University of California Press, 1950.

Stephenson, Ralph, and J. R. Debrix. *The Cinema as Art*. Baltimore: Penguin, 1965.

Tudor, Andrew. *Theories of Film*. New York: Viking, 1973.

Tyler, Parker. *The Hollywood Hallucination*. New York: Simon and Schuster, 1970.

————. *Magic and Myth of the Movies*. New York: Simon and Schuster, 1970.

————. *Sex Psyche Etcetera in the Film*. Baltimore: Penguin, 1971.

Vorkapich, Slavko. "Toward True Cinema." *Film Culture*, No. 19, March 1959.

BIBLIOGRAPHY

Warshow, Robert. *The Immediate Experience.* New York: Doubleday Anchor, 1964.
Wolfenstein, Martha, and Nathan Leites. *Movies, a Psychological Study.* Glencoe: The Free Press, 1950.
Wollen, Peter. *Signs and Meaning in the Cinema.* New and enlarged. Bloomington, Ind., and London: Indiana University Press, 1972.
Wood, Michael. *America at the Movies.* New York: Basic Books, 1975.
Youngblood, Gene. *Expanded Cinema.* New York: Dutton, 1970.